11,12,13,14

PERSONAL LAW

Business Law Textbooks from John Wiley and Sons

Atteberry, Pearson, and Litka: REAL ESTATE LAW, 3rd

Cataldo, Kempin, Stockton, and Weber: INTRODUCTION TO LAW AND THE LEGAL PROCESS, 3rd

Delaney and Gleim: CPA REVIEW: AUDITING

Delaney and Gleim: CPA REVIEW: BUSINESS LAW

Delaney and Gleim: CPA REVIEW: THEORY AND PRACTICE

Dunfee and Gibson: LEGAL ASPECTS OF GOVERNMENT REGULATION OF BUSINESS, 3rd

Dunfee, Gibson, Lamber, and McCarty: MODERN BUSINESS LAW: INTRODUCTION TO THE LEGAL ENVIRONMENT OF BUSINESS

Dunfee and Gibson: AN INTRODUCTION TO CONTRACTS, 2nd

Erickson, Dunfee, and Gibson: ANTITRUST AND TRADE REGULATION: CASES AND MATERIALS

Gleim and Delaney: CPA EXAMINATION REVIEW: VOLUME I OUTLINES AND STUDY GUIDE

Gleim and Delaney: CPA EXAMINATION REVIEW: VOLUME II PROBLEMS AND SOLUTIONS

Griffith: LEGAL ENVIRONMENT OF BUSINESS

Henszey and Friedman: REAL ESTATE LAW, 2nd

Inman: THE REGULATORY ENVIRONMENT OF BUSINESS, GOVERNMENT REGULATIONS

Litka and Inman: LEGAL ENVIRONMENT OF BUSINESS, PUBLIC AND PRIVATE LAWS, 3rd

Litka and Jennings: BUSINESS LAW, 3rd

Walder: PASS THIS BAR

Wolfe and Naffziger: THE LAW OF AMERICAN BUSINESS ORGANIZATIONS, AN ENVIRONMENTAL APPROACH

PERSONAL LAW

ROBERT D. ROTHENBERG

STEVEN J. BLUMENKRANTZ
State University of New York, Oneonta

John Wiley & Sons
New York   Chichester   Brisbane   Toronto   Singapore

To Werner, who helped me find my values,
and to Sarah, who helps me live them
To Carole and Katie—the two women in my life

Cover Photo: Mary M. Harrington

ISBN 0-471-09639-3   83-19773

Printed in the United States of America

10 9 8 7 6 5 4 3 2 1

ABOUT THE AUTHORS

Robert D. Rothenberg is an assistant professor of Business and Accounting at the State University of New York at Oneonta. He received a Bachelor of Business Administration from the City University of New York and a Juris Doctorate from New York University. Professor Rothenberg is a Certified Public Accountant and a practicing attorney. He teaches Introductory and Advanced Accounting courses as well as courses in Law, Business, and Real Estate. He is admitted to practice before the U.S. Supreme Court as well as New York State Courts and is a member of the New York State Bar Association, the American Institute of Certified Public Accountants, and the New York State Society of Certified Public Accountants.

Steven J. Blumenkrantz is an assistant professor of Business and Accounting at the State University of New York at Oneonta. He received his Bachelor of Science in Accounting from the State University of New York at Buffalo and his Juris Doctorate from Brooklyn Law School. Professor Blumenkrantz is a Certified Public Accountant and a practicing attorney. He teaches Introductory and Advanced Accounting courses as well as courses in Law, Business, and Real Estate. He is admitted to practice before the U.S. Supreme Court as well as New York State Courts and is a member of the New York State Bar Association, the American Institute of Certified Public Accountants, and the Otsego County Bar Association.

PREFACE

In teaching various law and accounting courses we realized that our students desired practical legal information so we designed a course to provide this material. The course was called "Personal Law" and its reception was overwhelmingly positive. In reviewing the market for a textbook suitable for such a course, we discovered that there was nothing available offering legal information relevant to the everyday lives of lay people. This observation precipitated the writing of this text.

During our work on this book we continued to teach a personal law course. Various chapters from the manuscript were reproduced and distributed to the class each semester. The manuscript was changed based on our teaching experience and student comments. Over a number of semesters all of the chapters in the text were tested in this manner.

The practice of law today includes the knowledge of various forms, which are used in this text. In addition, we integrated relevant and interesting cases to illustrate how particular fact patterns might be decided by courts. It is our conviction that after reading this text students will be reasonably familiar with various aspects of law. We caution students to remember the adage: A little knowledge is a dangerous thing. This textbook is not to be used as a substitute for the knowledge and expertise of an attorney. Its purpose is to ensure that individuals have sufficient legal information to discuss details of their legal problems intelligently with professional legal counsel.

We have designed this text to provide flexibility in course presentation. Any cases cited in the text are briefed in the teacher's manual and can be integrated in the course to give greater depth. The teacher's manual also suggests various methods and approaches to teaching the course. The growth of this text is directly attributable to the questions and suggestions of our students and colleagues.

Our thanks to all those students whose inquiries over the years initiated the writing of this book. We would also like to extend special thanks to the following: Sheri Herring, Kate Moon, Arabella Meadows-Rogers, Jean Coons, Charlize Fazio, Barbara Lifgren, Sue Lapine, Donna Lambros, and Sheila Reynolds who contributed to the typing and proofreading of this manuscript. Will Bookhout gave us the use of his law library. The National Bank and Trust Company of Norwich and DeMulder Realty, Inc., provided various forms. Thomas Potter provided expertise in the area of taxes; and Dave Muehl gave us helpful insurance information. The State University of New York, College at Oneonta and the Albany Law School provided support and library services.

Numerous reviewers offered suggestions and corrections: Jay Ashman, University of Vermont; Eloise Rippie, Iowa State University; Penny Mercurio, California State University, Northridge; William H. Parks III, Orange Coast College; Frederick Kempin, Wharton School, University of Pennsylvania; Darlene Alioto, City College of San Francisco; Maryanne Donnelly, LeMoyne College; and Douglas Anderson, Marion Technical College.

Despite all this help, any errors or omissions are our responsibility.

We would also like to thank Lucille Sutton, our editor, for all her assistance, and extend kudos to our families for their unswerving support.

RDR
SJB

CONTENTS

PART ONE

THE LEGAL SYSTEM

The legal system encompasses a broad area that includes laws, creation of laws, places where laws are upheld, and the people who participate in the process.

Chapter 1 discusses creation of laws, including the U.S. Constitution, the legislature, and administrative agencies, as well as the federal and state court systems.

Chapters 2, 3, and 4 discuss the types of laws that we categorize as criminal, tort, and contracts.

CHAPTER 1

The Legal Environment

INTRODUCTION

Nature and Sources of the Law

Law has been defined in many different ways. Some definitions refer to rules and sanctions; others, to the outcome of particular cases; others, to right and wrong; and still others, to impacts on social behavior. We define law as a system of resolving disputes, guiding behavior, and providing sanctions.

The primary purpose of law and a legal system is to provide a resolution to any given issue. Disagreements are wasteful both to individuals and to society. Time spent in argument over who owns a piece of property could be more productively spent in planting a garden or in other pursuits. Hostility builds when an issue is unresolved (although sometimes also when it is), and a system of law mitigates these problems. Resolution of disputes on an individual basis would resolve these problems. However, a good legal system should do more.

In a society, stability, as well as knowledge of the consequences of an act, becomes important. A person making a decision needs to know what will happen because of the decision and what else to do if the result should be different. Therefore, a good legal system should provide a large measure of consistency. If a given fact pattern has been decided, others in the society can plan how to structure their activities provided the same fact pattern, if litigated a second time, would produce the same results. The courts' commitment to consistency is called the doctrine of stare decisis. Stare decisis is the term used for a rule of law, that once a legal principle has been established by a number of judicial decisions, it becomes binding and should be followed. This rule is designed to foster judicial efficiency (by preventing repetitive trials of the same issues) and to provide a needed element of stability in the law. The doctrine allows an attorney to plan a course of action with knowledge of the legal consequences thereof.

As a general rule, stare decisis will require a decision to be followed even where the court would have decided the case otherwise if there had not been any precedent. It is not, however, an absolute rule. The doctrine will not be followed in cases where the rule laid down in the prior case is wrong. The doctrine may be ignored in some cases where the facts warrant a departure from precedent.

Another characteristic of some legal systems is flexibility. Different persons disagree about the extent to which this is a desirable characteristic; however, our system includes a degree of flexibility. This may come into conflict with the consistency principle. In an agrarian society, population density is low, and property rights interfere with the freedom of movement of individuals. Property rights then become secondary to a person's right to be safe and free from harm. As a society produces greater technological innovations, a flexible legal system evaluates these. Thus, a court may have to deal with electronic eavesdropping devices, computer fraud, and so on.

Law is sometimes confused with morality or justice. These are not the same. Morality generally is a high standard of conduct. It is also subjective to a degree. A legal system should try to promote a high standard of conduct, but not necessarily as high as some moral standards. Justice generally evokes an image of fairness to both parties. A good legal system strives for justice, but recognizes that resolution of conflicts is of paramount priority. In some instances, justice is possibly unattainable. For example, the issue of abortion has equities on both sides. To allow abortions is to value a woman's right to control her body more than a fetus's right to survive. To prohibit abortions is to make the reverse choice. Neither choice is "fair" to the interests of the other party. From a societal viewpoint, however, a choice must be made so that pregnant women know what they may do. A third approach is to view this as a strictly moral issue and leave it to the discretion of the women involved. A court in such a case would refuse to deal with the problem.

Our legal system developed from the English system. Both our system and the English system can be divided into two major categories: the common law and statutory law. Common law consists of principles developed in judicial decisions by reason, justice, conscience, and the needs of the times. Specific rules of common law may change as the times require, but the basic underlying concepts remain. Thus, the common law may from time to time establish new rights when necessary. (For example, the development of sophisticated eavesdropping devices made it necessary for the courts to expand the doctrines of privacy.)

The term *common law* is also sometimes used in contrast to the civil law. In this sense, common law refers to the law of England as opposed to the laws of France or Spain. Most states have adopted the common law. In a few states, where the Spanish or French influence was great, some of the civil law concepts still apply (e.g., Louisiana and the Southwestern states).

Statutory law refers to the rules and principles that have been set forth by legislatures in written statements known as statutes. These may deal with the same or different topics as may be covered under the common law. In the event of conflict, statutes will override the common law unless the statute is found to be unconstitutional.

The early system of English law consisted of a number of courts that dealt only with certain types of issues. A person who had a grievance that could not be properly resolved in the "law" courts could petition the king to do what was fair in that situation. These petitions became known as proceedings in equity or in chancery. Courts of equity are more concerned with the administration of justice than are courts of law. Their primary function is to provide a remedy for an injured party where the courts of law are unable to do so. For example, if a buyer enters into a contract to buy a house from a seller and the seller later refuses to deliver ownership of the house, a court of law may punish the seller for breaking the contract; a court of equity may force the seller to transfer the house to the buyer.

The process of bringing a case in a court of law was made very difficult by the imposition of complex procedural rules. (For example, trespass is an action for interference with another's property rights. There are many different types of trespass. A party who was sued for the wrong type could have the action dismissed on that basis. If the process were sufficiently lengthy, the party suing might lose the ability to sue on the proper action because the party's time period expired.) Our legal system began with a dual court system: law courts and equity courts and had a complex system of procedural rules. Today, however, in most states the dual systems have been merged into a single court that may grant either legal or equitable relief. Procedural rules have been simplified to the point where an aggrieved party need only state (and prove) the facts in order to recover. It is no longer necessary to identify the claim by the precise legal terminology.

Jurisdictions

There are 51 separate court systems in the United States. Each of the 50 states has its own court system, and the federal government also has one. This section will cover the federal court system and the basics of a typical state court system.

Federal courts (Exhibit 1–1) have jurisdiction over federal matters. Federal matters include rights established under federal statutes in areas such as patents, copyright, admiralty, antitrust laws, and so forth. Federal courts also interpret the Constitution and U.S. treaties with Indians or other countries. The federal courts cannot review state court proceedings except in cases in which the state laws or state court decisions are in violation of the Constitution of the United States. The federal courts have concurrent (overlapping) jurisdiction with the state courts in areas where federal statutes create private claims (e.g., the Taft-Hartley Act authorizing an employee to sue an employer, the Securities Act giving rights to defrauded investors, and the Civil Rights Act). In addition, the federal courts have jurisdiction in cases based on diversity of citizenship (where an individual from one state is suing an individual from another state) even when there is a state question involved.

State courts (Exhibit 1–2) have jurisdiction over state matters. This includes questions involving state statutes and also the entire body of law dealing with property rights, contracts, and torts (negligence, etc.). Frequently, where there is concurrent jurisdiction, the state courts will deal with the issue first. Most of the topics

EXHIBIT 1-1
Federal Court System

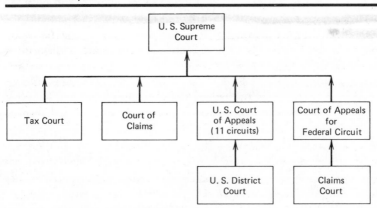

EXHIBIT 1-2
State Court System

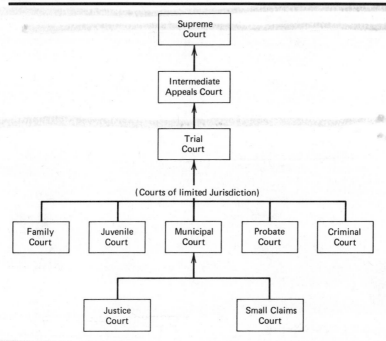

covered in this book are within the jurisdiction of the state courts. If a court has the ability to hear a matter, it is said to have subject matter jurisdiction. A court's subject matter jurisdiction may also depend on the amount of the controversy. Many courts cannot hear a case unless the amount of money involved is within certain dollar limits. For example, the federal courts do not have jurisdiction in cases regarding diversity of citizenship unless the amount of the controversy is over $10,000. Other courts cannot hear cases involving more than a specified amount (e.g., small claims courts).

A court must also acquire jurisdiction over a particular controversy. This is usually accomplished by acquiring personal jurisdiction over the defendant. Personal jurisdiction may be acquired if the defendant is present within the territorial confines of the particular court. In some cases, jurisdiction over a particular case may be acquired if certain property is within the territorial limits of the court's authority. For example, a court may resolve an issue of ownership of a piece of real estate located in its area even if both parties live outside its area (called in rem jurisdiction). Some states have personal jurisdiction over the defendants when their activities have taken place within the borders of the particular state even though neither the defendants nor their property is in the state (so-called long arm statutes). However, federal courts have jurisdiction over all persons within the boundaries of the United States.

Let's assume a court has jurisdiction; even so, it should not hear an action unless it also is the appropriate venue. Venue designates the county or city in which a court with jurisdiction may hear a case. A court has proper venue if an injury has occurred within the geographic area or neighborhood of the court. Venue has a relationship to convenience of the litigants. Decisions as to the propriety of venue are within the discretion of the court and may be waived by consent of the litigants.

Trial versus Appellate Courts

All court systems are divided into courts of original jurisdiction and appellate courts. Courts of original jurisdiction are courts in which trials are conducted. Appellate courts provide a forum for the review of trial court decisions.

The federal courts of original jurisdiction include 94 district courts. These are located geographically throughout the country. In addition to the U.S. district courts, the federal system includes specialized courts of original jurisdiction. These include the customs court, which was created in 1926 to hear appeals from decisions made by customs collection personnel; the court of appeals for the federal circuit, which will hear appeals from the customs court; the claims court, which is the court specializing in claims against the United States; and lastly the tax court, which has concurrent jurisdiction with the federal district court in cases concerning the Internal Revenue Service.

In addition to courts of original jurisdiction, the federal court system has courts of appellate jurisdiction. The United States is divided into 11 geographic areas called circuits (Exhibit 1–3). Each area has a federal circuit court of appeals, which hears appeals from the U.S. district courts in that circuit. It also hears appeals from decisions of certain federal agencies.

The highest court in the federal system is the Supreme Court of the United States. This court is composed of nine justices. It is the court that may make final decisions with respect to questions involving the U.S. Constitution and the U.S. federal statutes, regulations, and treaties. The Supreme Court of the United States may also hear appeals from state courts in cases involving a federal question.

The U.S. Supreme Court often has discretion whether or not to review a particular decision. A writ of certiorari, which is a formal request to review, must be obtained in order to have an appeal heard by the U.S. Supreme Court. The Supreme Court must hear certain cases without a writ of certiorari: cases in which the United States is a party; cases where a lower court holds a federal act unconstitutional; cases where a suit is brought to enforce the Sherman Antitrust Act, the Interstate Commerce Act, or the Federal Communications Act; cases where the federal district court issues an injunction against an order of the Interstate Commerce Commission; cases where a state court holds a federal statute invalid; and cases where a court holds a state statute valid against the appealing party's contention that the statute violates the federal constitution.

The Supreme Court has original jurisdiction over controversies between two or more states and proceedings against ambassadors, councils, public ministers or for-

EXHIBIT 1–3
Circuit Map of the U.S. Courts of Appeals

Puerto Rico	1 circuit
Virgin Islands	3 circuit
Alaska	9 circuit
Guam	9 circuit
Hawaii	9 circuit

eign nations, and the like. This original jurisdiction is concurrent with the federal district court's jurisdiction. (Suit can be started in either court.)

All states have lower courts that have criminal as well as civil jurisdiction. These courts have various titles, such as justice of the peace courts, criminal courts, city courts, or small claims courts. They have jurisdiction over minor criminal matters, such as misdemeanors, traffic violations, disturbances of the peace, and violations of zoning ordinances. These courts are also where a criminal is arraigned, as discussed in Chapter 2. The civil jurisdiction of these lower courts usually has dollar limitations ($1000–$2000). These lower courts are not considered courts of record, and if an appeal is taken, the case must be tried all over again. A lawyer is not necessary to represent an individual in justice courts or small claims courts, and this is of great benefit to individuals who wish to proceed on their own without the expense of counsel.

The next step in the state court system consists of local trial courts of general jurisdiction. These courts have jurisdiction over all civil and criminal proceedings; there may be one court for both, or one for each. They are usually distributed throughout the state in each county. These courts are known by such names as district courts, circuit courts, and superior courts. Some have limitations as to the monetary value of a case to be tried. Many states have several tiers of local trial courts depending on the density of population.

Many states have probate courts or surrogate's courts. These are set up to handle the estates of deceased persons. Probate means to prove a will, and procedures in these courts are discussed in Chapter 12. States that do not have separate probate courts will serve the same function in local courts of general jurisdiction. A few states have separate courts of equity or chancery, but the general rule is that the local court of general jurisdiction will hear cases with respect to equitable relief.

The majority of our states have one appellate court called the supreme court. New York calls its appellate court the Court of Appeals, and Massachusett's highest court is called the Supreme Judicial Court. Generally, appeals courts do not have original jurisdiction and will hear cases from the lower courts to review the law involved. Some states have intermediate appellate courts. These courts are used to relieve the highest court of some of its work load. They do not have original jurisdiction. Some states have a system of regional appellate courts. These regions are usually called districts or circuits, and each one would have its own appellate court. This is a geographic designation, and it is set up procedurally to enable decisions to be reviewed from the lower level local courts in the geographic area.

The doctrine of stare decisis (let the decision stand) was referred to earlier as a method of improving consistency. The doctrine, however, has limitations. A decision by a higher court is binding on a lower court, but not vice versa. A decision is only binding within the jurisdiction (e.g., each state or federal circuit or district); federal decisions do not control the state or vice versa with the exception of certain federal Supreme Court cases. Decisions that are not controlling may be used as indicative of trends and may persuade a court's decision.

THE CONSTITUTION

The Constitution of the United States in Article 6 says that this Constitution "shall be the supreme law of the land" (Article 6, Section 2). Regardless of which state you are from, the basic rights granted to all citizens by the U.S. Constitution apply to you. State constitutions also have provisions that parallel the basic rights outlined by the Constitution of the United States. There is an interrelationship between the state and federal constitutions that ensures protection of every individual citizen regardless of his or her state of residence. This section will discuss the Constitution of the United States and will deal in detail with those sections that are important to individuals.

First Amendment

"Congress shall make no law respecting an establishment of religion, or prohibiting the free exercise thereof; or abridging the freedom of speech, or of the press; or the right of the people peaceably to assemble, and to petition the government for a redress of grievances."

This amendment establishes several basic rights: freedom to worship as one pleases, freedom to communicate to others, and freedom to gather together and complain. Each of these is important in practice as well as in theory. Freedom of religion prevents state persecution of nonaccepted religions. Conflicts between Catholic and Protestant or Moslem and Christian, such as exist in other countries, probably could not arise in the United States. The state must remain neutral. The freedoms of speech and press protect all citizens in their conversations and attempts to inform others. Thus, the publicity surrounding the Watergate break-in was able to occur only because the government recognized a free press. The right of divergent political factions to be heard only exists where the government recognizes free speech. A citizen's right to march to Washington, to protest government farm policies, or to demonstrate for a nuclear freeze are protected under the third clause of the First Amendment. Without such freedom, many of these protesters would be in jail.

A citizen's rights, however, are not absolute. Thus, a parent may not endanger a child's life by refusing medical care on the grounds of religious beliefs. Freedom of speech and press carry with them an obligation of responsibility. Defamation laws allow a person to recover for some spoken or printed slurs. A person may not make statements that create a danger to others (Schenck v. United States, 249 U.S. 47, [S. Ct. 1919]). One's right of assembly may be curtailed where it creates the possibility that innocent bystanders will be hurt in a demonstration (note that the First Amendment refers to peaceful assembly). The courts have to balance the rights of one individual against another or against the rights of society generally. In July 1982, the U.S. Supreme Court held that "kiddie porn" was not protected by the First Amendment because the state's interest in the welfare of children was paramount (N.Y. v. Ferber, 102 S. Ct. 3348 [S. Ct. 1982]).

In addition, the First Amendment applies to students. The freedom a student obtains may also be limited. School authorities have the right to establish reasonable regulations governing student publications, activities, and the like because of the unique nature of schools. The school authorities may be able to tell a student or a student group writing a newspaper that they cannot publish certain things. Although this seems to be an infringement on the rights to freedom of speech and press, courts have allowed the school authorities to establish reasonable regulations because of the role these officials have in the development and education of young people.

First Amendment freedoms may frequently clash with the school regulations, and the courts will have to balance the interest of the parties. In Des Moines, Iowa, several students wanted to protest against the war in Vietnam. The school authorities made a rule that any student wearing an armband would be asked to remove it; upon refusal, the student would be suspended. Several junior and senior high school students, with knowledge of the ruling, wore armbands and were suspended. They argued that the rule violated their First Amendment right of free speech. The U.S. Supreme Court held in favor of the students. The Court held that the wearing of symbols could not be prevented unless such conduct materially interfered with the requirements of proper discipline in the school's operations. The Court noted that there was no evidence that the work of the school or any classes were interrupted (Tinker v. Des Moines Independent Community School District, 393 U.S. 503 [S. Ct. 1969]).

Fourth Amendment

"The right of the people to be secure in their persons, houses, papers, and effects, against unreasonable searches and seizures, shall not be violated and no warrants shall be issued, but upon probable cause, supported by oath or affirmation, and particularly describing the place to be searched, and the person or things to be seized."

This amendment establishes the principle commonly known as the right to privacy. This right will vary depending on the place, circumstances, and activity involved. For example, an individual is usually permitted to possess pornographic materials at home for private use, and the issuance of a search warrant specifying such material would be unconstitutional. If the same person opens a theater to show pornographic movies to the public, that person and the theater may be subject to a legal search and criminal prosecution. The use of controlled substances (dangerous drugs) is prohibited both in public and in private. Therefore, a warrant would be valid regardless of the nature of the premises to be searched.

Students also are protected under the Fourth Amendment right to privacy from unreasonable searches in school. Though a public school teacher is responsible for the discipline and security of the student body, the Fourth Amendment of the Constitution prohibits random, causeless, and unnecessary searches. If a search is made without benefit of a warrant, there must be probable cause. The courts will consider the student's age and school record, as well as the seriousness of the particular problem in determining whether probable cause existed.

Students' lockers have not been afforded the same Fourth Amendment protection as a student's person. A student's locker, in most instances, is still under the control of the school authorities (as they have retained either a master key or the combination). The student has possession of the locker as against other students, but school authorities may search such lockers either themselves or through the police without meeting the constitutional requirement for probable cause. (See also Chapter 2.)

Fifth, Sixth, Eighth, and Fourteenth Amendments

Fifth Amendment: *No person shall be held to answer for a capital, or otherwise infamous crime unless on a presentment of indictment of a Grand Jury, except in cases arising in the land or naval forces or in the militia when in actual service in time of war or public danger; nor shall any person be subject to the same offense to be twice put in jeopardy of life or limb; nor shall be compelled in any criminal case to be a witness against himself, nor be deprived of life, liberty or property, without due process of law; nor shall private property be taken for public use, without just compensation.*

Sixth Amendment: *In all criminal prosecutions, the accused shall enjoy the right to a speedy public trial, by an impartial jury of the state and district wherein the crime shall have been committed, which district shall have been previously ascertained by law, and to be informed of the nature and cause of the accusation; to be confronted with the witnesses against him; to have compulsory process for obtaining witnesses in his favor, and have the assistance of counsel for his defense.*

Eighth Amendment: *Excessive bail shall not be required, nor excessive fines imposed, nor cruel and unusual punishments inflicted.*

Fourteenth Amendment: *Section 1. All persons born or naturalized in the United States, and subject to the jurisdiction thereof, are citizens of the United States and of the State wherein they reside. No state shall make or enforce any law which shall abridge the privileges or immunities of citizens of the United States; nor shall any state deprive any person of life, liberty, or property, without due process of law; nor deny to any person within its jurisdiction the equal protection of the laws.*

These amendments are collectively referred to as the due process clauses. Statutes that define crimes must give fair notice to people of ordinary intelligence that actions they may be contemplating are forbidden. Persons charged with felonies or misdemeanors have right to counsel, and they must be advised that a lawyer will be appointed by the Court if they cannot afford one. (This right to counsel does not apply with respect to traffic infractions.)

The due process amendments also protect students. In an administrative proceeding for suspension, a student (if the student is under age of consent, the parent or guardian) must be given a fair hearing upon reasonable notice. The student may be represented by counsel and may question witnesses brought against him or her.

The equal protection clause in the Fourteenth Amendment is applicable to actions of the state as well as to private discrimination. This clause does not totally prohibit distinctions from being made between different classes of people. If there *was* a rational basis for making a differentiation and if the differentiation is not arbitrary, then equal protection has not been denied. An example of this fact is state juvenile offender provisions that allow for youngsters under a certain age to be treated more leniently for crimes and offenses that they have committed.

Young people may be treated differently from adults because they are still maturing and have yet to assume full adult responsibilities and attitudes. Each state sets its own age requirement for an individual to be treated as a adult (see Chapter 2, Exhibit 2–4). These requirements are applied to purchasing of alcoholic beverages and entering into a contract, as well as driving and getting married. Each state also has its own statutory requirements with respect to criminal conduct or youthful or juvenile offenders. Federal labor law places restrictions on employing minors, especially in areas where dangerous machinery or explosives may be involved. State statutes also regulate the employment of minors and indicate at what age a minor may undertake a particular job assignment.

The Fourteenth Amendment's equal protection clause is applicable in many areas. In the area of education the courts have applied the equal protection clause to prevent the denial of admission of students to public schools because of race or sex (Brown v. Board of Education of Topeka, 347 U.S. 483 [S. Ct. 1954]). This amendment also has been used to eliminate racial imbalance in many public schools.

The Fourteenth Amendment has been the basis for the affirmative action programs that have recently appeared in publicly funded universities. These programs have enabled minorities to obtain preferences in admission as well as for positions of employment. The case of Regents of the University of California v. Bakke, 438 U.S. 265 [S. Ct. 1978]) has indicated that schools using affirmative action programs for student admission must exercise care to avoid reverse discrimination against white students (the use of quotas was held discriminatory). We have, again, an example of the delicate balance in the Constitution.

In the area of sex descrimination, courts have been using the equal protection amendment to broaden women's rights in keeping pace with the social attitudes of the times. For example, courts have made it illegal to distinguish between men and women in advertising for help wanted as well as requiring that worker's compensation be awarded to both men and women on the same basis.

THE LEGISLATIVE PROCESS

The process by which a law is created is complex. A proposed statute, called a bill, is introduced in either the House of Representatives or Senate. (Each has jurisdiction under the Constitution, to initiate certain types of bills.) The bill is referred to the appropriate committee for consideration. A committee report is prepared, including amendments, and so on. The bill is then presented to the entire house for consideration. There may be amendments or debates or both, after which a vote is taken and the bill passes or dies. Following passage in one legislative chamber, the other house considers the bill. If the second house changes the bill, it goes to a joint committee to iron out any amendments. When both houses have passed the bill, it goes to the President for signature. If the President disapproves, it is returned to the Congress, which may override his veto.

A bill that becomes law may be challenged in court. The Constitution is silent with respect to the judicial power to review legislative enactments. In 1803, the Supreme Court in Marbury v. Madison, 5 U.S. 137 (S. Ct. 1803) held a federal statute to be unconstitutional, and the doctrine of judicial review was firmly established.

There are certain requirements that a statute should fulfill if it is to be held constitutional. The statutory provisions must be reasonably clear and definite. This requires that a reasonable person reading the statute should be able to determine what is expected. Though there is a presumption in favor of statutes, occasionally one will be held improper (Day v. Armstrong, 362, P.2d 137 [Wyo. 1967]). A statute may also be held unconstitutional if its provisions are unreasonable in what they try to do. For example, a statute designed to protect the community's health and welfare required filing a map if any piece of land was divided into more than four parcels. The court found the statute unclear in failing to define the term *parcel* and held the law unconstitutional (State v. Rutkowski, 379 N.Y.S. 2d 279 [N.Y. 1975]).

ADMINISTRATIVE PROCEDURES

There are many federal administative agencies that have the power to monitor or regulate behavior or do both in many areas. These agencies include, among others, the Internal Revenue Service, the Federal Communications Commission, the Securities and Exchange Commission and the National Labor Relations Board. Many of their decisions are in the nature of educated opinions, and although these agencies are not courts, their rulings and decisions may have the force of law in cases where no appeal is taken. In some cases, Congress has specifically authorized the agencies to promulgate rules that will have the same effect as if they had been made by Congress.

An example of the power of a government agency is shown in Title 19, U.S.C., §§482, 1581(f) and 1582, which provide that the U.S. Customs Service is able to search vehicles and persons. The search may include the trunk of the vehicle and a body search of the individual. This would normally be contrary to the U.S. Constitution, but when people cross into the United States, they subject themselves to such a search. The customs officials may seize any contraband and the automobile and may arrest the person. They may use all necessary force to accomplish this. The statute in question may circumvent constitutional protections for two reasons:

(1) individuals have voluntarily subjected themselves to such provisions by coming into the United States from a foreign country and (2) citizens surrender their constitutional rights when leaving the country.

MISCELLANEOUS TOPICS

Small Claims Courts

In addition to the elaborate court system outlined in the previous sections, all states have small claims courts, which provide for litigation of cases involving relatively small amounts of money. The costs involved to the plaintiff in the small claims court are nominal, usually less than $5. The procedure is very simple. An individual who has a claim goes to the clerk of the court (city court or local justice court) and fills out a simple application, paying the application fee. The court then notifies the defendant that he or she must appear on a particular date.

Unlike most legal actions, small claims proceedings are conducted informally and usually quite soon after the plaintiff fills out the papers. The proceedings are held in front of a qualified judge or arbitrator (usually, if arbitration is used, no appeal is allowed). The plaintiff and defendant and all witnesses are usually sworn in, and the trial is conducted according to the rules of substantive law.

The term substantive refers to the body of rules that creates and prescribes rights. Substantive law refers to rules with respect to contracts, criminal law, and so on. Substantive law may be contrasted with procedural law, which regulates the legal process. Procedural law establishes the method by which a trial may be commenced, sets forth rules for admitting evidence, and the like. The technical procedures used in most court cases are not utilized in the small claims court. In some jurisdictions, such as California, neither party may be represented by an attorney; in other jurisdictions, attorneys are allowed. After the individual tells his or her side of the story and brings witnesses to tell their views, the defendant then tells his or her side of the story. The judge then makes the decision as to who should win.

Juries and Jury Selection

Juries are vital to our system of law. All citizens of the United States between the ages of 21 and 70 who are in possession of reasonable faculties and are in reasonably good health might one day be called to serve upon a jury unless they qualify for one of the exemptions stated under federal or state laws. Exemptions usually cover convicted felons, members of organizations advocating the violent overthrow of the government, and certain professionals (doctors, lawyers, priests, police officers, fire-fighters, and members of the military).

Since 1971, 85 of 95 federal district courts have gradually begun using juries of 6 to 8 members (instead of the usual 12) to hear civil cases. Thirty-eight states have adopted similar reductions in size for some civil cases; and 34, for some criminal cases. All federal jury verdicts must be by unanimous vote. Twenty-nine states allow less-than-unanimous vote in certain civil cases, and 5 states allow nonunanimity in criminal cases.

In a civil action, the jury's role is to determine whether the plaintiff or defendant wins and, if damages are to be awarded, how much the winner should receive. In criminal proceedings, the jury is the trier of fact, and the Constitution provides that there will be a jury in all criminal prosecutions. (A defendant may be able to waive this right in some cases.)

There are two types of juries that you might be selected for—the petit jury or the grand jury. The petit jury is the jury that determines the guilt or innocence in a criminal action or determines the facts and damages in a civil action. The grand jury functions only in criminal proceedings. Before an individual may be tried for a felony in front of a petit jury, his peers must hear evidence to determine whether he should or should not be indicted. This hearing is heard by the grand jury (see Chapter 2). Grand juries are supposed to protect citizens against intimidating prosecutions.

The states differ in how they go about compiling a list of prospective jurors. Some states get the names from voter registration lists, tax assessment rolls, or even driver's license applications. The compilation of lists is usually done by a commissioner of jurors on a county-by-county basis. The commissioner determines the competency and qualification of each individual. When jurors are needed, the commissioner will contact individuals from the list and order them to appear. The prospective jurors must meet qualifications set by the various states. For example, most states require jurors to be citizens, between 21 and 70 years old, and in good physical and mental health. Once the commissioner calls a person for jury duty, that person must wait to be questioned by the judge and the lawyers. This waiting period may take several days, depending on the particular state, county, or city in which the trials are held.

After the waiting period, the prospective juror will be summoned to the court room for questioning. The questioning is called voir dire. The purpose of a voir dire is to allow the lawyers to eliminate potential jurors who have already received information or formed opinions about the case. Such persons, as well as those who have indicated bias or relationship to the parties will be disqualified for cause. In addition, the lawyers are each allowed to dismiss a limited number of jurors without cause (preemptory challenge). It is common for the jury selection process to take longer than the trial itself in many cases.

Suppose you are chosen for jury duty. You will receive a daily pay, which can be as much as $45 a day and as little as $1. During the trial, you must listen to the evidence presented. Some trials may go on for many weeks; you must listen to the evidence and determine who is telling the truth and who isn't. At the end of the trial, you and the other jurors return to the jury room to deliberate, argue, and discuss, until such time as you can all reach a verdict. Prior to your retiring to the jury room, the judge will give you directions as to the rules of law and other matters that might effect your decision.

A jury pool is supposed to be a representative cross section of the community. In fact, this is not always the case and has led to charges that have reversed many verdicts on constitutional grounds. If the trial on which you are a juror is of a sensitive nature and covered by the press, when you are not in the court, you may be locked in a hotel or motel room (sequestered) and be forbidden to have television or telephone and be constantly watched by police officers. One particular trial held in Chicago, that of the so-called Pontiac 10 prisoners, took nearly eight months, during which the jurors were locked up for the whole time. (Jury selection for this trial took five months.)

Letting jurors take notes is forbidden in some states and frowned on in others. The reason is that taking notes intimidates those who do not take notes and encourages jurors to give their notes undue weight as evidence. The jurors are allowed to view all the evidence presented as well as the transcripts of the trial while they are making their deliberations.

Selecting a Lawyer

One of the major purposes of this text is to prepare the student for discussions with an attorney, if the need arises, on various topics that may arise in the student's lifetime. It is imperative that students not only possess information about court structure, legislative process, and substantive rules, but also that they understand the roles that the lawyer plays in society. It is in the best interest of students to follow the path of preventive law. This means that students should try to avoid unfavorable consequences of their daily actions. Therefore, consultation with a lawyer would be appropriate prior to involving oneself in leases and contracts, as well as in some of the other aspects of every day life.

Lawyers can act not only as advocates, but also as counselors. They also may be useful in drafting documents such as contracts and deeds. In selecting a lawyer, one should be aware that all lawyers have a common basic training. Law school curriculums give a lawyer a basic understanding of different elements of substantive as well as procedural law. No lawyer is an expert in all facets of the law, whether it be substantive or procedural. Whereas a general practitioner can usually handle routine matters dealing with negotiation, advocacy, or counseling, it may be advantageous for the consumer in some cases to find a specialist. Specialists usually cost more per hour but because of their experience can resolve an issue more quickly or more accurately or both.

Finding such a specialist or even a good general practioner is not always easy. Lawyers are not always permitted to solicit clients, and it is up to the individual to contact an attorney. It is imperative that this contact be made early in one's career so that if problems do arise, one can feel comfortable about having a counselor who seems compatible with one's personality. Attorneys should be able to make time to sit down and discuss the relationship. They should also be candid with details of their areas of expertise and education as well as their limitations. When talking with an attorney, the consumer should fully disclose any and all relevant facts. This text will provide a general understanding of the law to help the consumer eliminate possible irrelevant questions and focus on the important points.

Once an individual has established a rapport with an attorney, it will be easier to call the attorney and acquire information prior to embarking on a particular course of action.

Suppose you have found an attorney to your liking. Information that you communicate to your attorney will be subject to the attorney-client privilege. This means it may not be revealed by the attorney without your consent. There are several requirements that must be met in order to invoke the privilege. First, you must be a client of the attorney or communicate the information while trying to hire the attorney. Second, the person hearing the communication must be an attorney acting as an attorney. Third, the information must be communicated outside the presence of others and must be for the purpose of obtaining legal aid and not for the purpose of committing a crime. Fourth, the privilege must be claimed and must not be waived.

This privilege is based on the fundamental principle that an individual is entitled to the benefit of legal counsel and should be placed in a position of trust with the lawyer. Clients should be able to give their attorney information relevant to preparing a case without concern that the information will be used against them—now or later. Even so, the privilege is not absolute. An attorney is an officer of the court and, in that capacity, has certain obligations to society. If you are ever in a position of giving information to an attorney, it might be a good idea to ask what types of information the attorney feels he or she would have to reveal to the court.

QUESTIONS

1 Willie Francis was convicted of murder in Louisiana and sentenced to be electrocuted. He was prepared for the electrocution and placed in the chair. The shock that he received was not sufficient to cause his death. The failure was blamed on the mechanical difficulty with respect to the electric chair. Francis was returned to prison, and another date was set for his execution. Discuss the implications of the state's conduct in the context of the prohibition against cruel and unusual punishment in the Eighth Amendment.

2 Gamble went to see a prison doctor after a bale of cotton fell on him. The doctor prescribed painkillers and rest. Gamble rested for a week and then was ordered back to work. He refused to work and was brought before a disciplinary committee. He was given additional medicine and sent back to work. He refused again and was brought before the committee. A medical assistant working for the prison testified to the committee that Gamble was in perfect health. The committee then placed Gamble in solitary confinement. Subsequent examinations showed that Gamble had been in poor health. Does the government have an obligation to provide medical care for those in prison? Is the deliberate indifference to medical needs of prisoners a violation of the Eighth Amendment?

3   Robinson was convicted of narcotic violations on the basis of testimony by two Los Angeles police officers, who observed scar tissue and discoloration on the inside of Robinson's right arm, as well as numerous needle marks on his left arm. The California statute made it a crime for a person either to use narcotics or be addicted to the use of narcotics. Robinson was found guilty of being addicted to narcotics. Discuss the possible reasons for holding the statute unconstitutional.

4   Robert Garrow was being tried for murder. Garrow had admitted killing three students, but only one of the bodies had been found. He had given his attorneys a detailed description of the crime and a map of the area where he had dumped the bodies. The attorneys found the other bodies and took pictures, but they told no one of their discovery. Does the attorney-client privilege protect this information? Discuss.

5   Thomas Johnson was arrested on January 7, 1972, and indicted for murder. He was arraigned on February 18 and pleaded not guilty. It took 18 months before he was tried, and he was imprisoned for the entire time. The reason the trial took so long was that there was a shortage of trial lawyers in the prosecutor's office. When the trial was scheduled, the defendant pleaded guilty to manslaughter because an important defense witness could no longer be located. Is the defendant's lengthy incarceration contrary to the provisions in the Constitution for a speedy trial? Discuss.

6   Schenck and his codefendant Baer were convicted of having willfully conspired to print and circulate literature to men who were drafted. The material in question extorted the individuals to resist the draft and to assert their rights, stating that the draft was a violation of a person's rights, was a wrong against humanity, and was in the interests only of ''Wall Street's chosen few.'' The defendants argued that their right to make such statements was protected under the First Amendment. Decision for whom? Discuss.

7   Police received information from a reliable informant that an individual was selling narcotics out of the trunk of an automobile parked at 439 Ridge Street. The police drove to the area in question, saw the described vehicle, noted that the driver matched the description given by the informant, and stopped the car. While they searched the driver (Ross), they discovered a bullet on the car's front seat. They then searched the interior of the car and found a pistol in the glove compartment. The defendant was arrested and handcuffed, and the trunk of the car was searched, disclosing a brown paper bag that was found to contain narcotics. A subsequent search further disclosed a zippered red leather pouch, which contained a quantity of money. At no time was a warrant obtained. Were the searches constitutionally proper? Discuss.

8   A woman was convicted of killing her husband with a baseball bat. She brought an action complaining that she had been denied due process of law because she had been tried by an all-male jury. The practice at the time in the state was to include in the jury pool only those women who volunteered for jury selection (approximately one fifth of 1 percent of the jury pool). Was Mrs. Hoyt denied due process of law? Discuss.

9   The population of Lafayette Parish was 21 percent black. Jury questionnaires that were returned indicated a response rate for blacks of slightly less than 14 percent. The jury pool for the defendant consisted of only 5 percent black jurors, none of whom was found suitable for the jury. The defendant argued that he was subjected to discrimination and denied due process because he was not given a jury based on his peers. Decisions for whom? Discuss.

10 Kenneth Clark, a minor, was admitted to a hospital with burns on 40 percent of his body. The hospital indicated that the child's blood condition was deteriorating and that it might become necessary at any time to administer blood transfusions. The child's parents refused to authorize such transfusions because the religious sect to which they belonged forbade it. May the court order the administration of blood transfusions over the objections of the parents? Decision for whom? Discuss.

CHAPTER 2

Criminal Law

SUBSTANTIVE CRIMINAL LAW

Criminal law is the area of law composed of wrongs against society, as opposed to civil law, which encompasses wrongs against individuals. All acts for which penal sanctions (either imprisonment or fine) may be imposed are defined as offenses. Offenses are further categorized as criminal or petty, depending on their severity. Crimes (criminal offenses) are acts or omissions by an individual that the law considers to be serious. Petty offenses are considered to be less serious and have lighter penalties. The classification is not the same in all states; therefore, we will outline the areas according to federal codes (see Exhibit 2–1).

Categories of Crimes

Crimes are divided into three categories: treason, felonies, and misdemeanors. Treason is defined in the United States Constitution as levying war against the United States; adhering or giving aid and comfort to its enemies (Article 3, §3). A felony is defined as an offense for which extensive imprisonment or death is designated as a penalty. For example: the federal code defines a felony as an offense for which imprisonment of more than one year may be imposed (18 U.S.C.A. §1) whereas other jurisdictions indicate that offenses punishable by death or imprisonment in state or federal prison are felonies (e.g., Michigan, Colorado, Arizona, Alabama, Iowa. Felonies are the gravest crimes in our society. Some states divide felonies into categories or classes (e.g., class A to class E with class A being the most severe), depending on the length or place of imprisonment.

Misdemeanors are crimes for which imprisonment is also a penalty, but the term of imprisonment is less than that for a felony (e.g., federal law less than one year); or the place of imprisonment is other than federal or state prison (county jail and the like).

Conviction for commission of any crime, whether a felony or a misdemeanor, will give the individual convicted a criminal record.

Noncriminal or petty offenses have two categories: violations and traffic infractions. A violation is defined as conduct that will be offensive to society and that requires a term of imprisonment not exceeding the minimum term imposed for the lowest class of misdemeanors (e.g., six months, U.S.C.A.§ 1). These offenses include failure to pay license fees, creating a public nuisance, and so on. Traffic infractions are governed by each separate jurisdiction and are generally violations of laws or regulations with respect to traffic. There are some traffic infractions that are specifically declared to be felonies or misdemeanors, and these items (e.g., driving while intoxicated, reckless driving) would be treated under those categories.

Elements of Crimes

Most crimes require the commission of an act (e.g., homicide, burglary, rape). Thoughts or ideas are usually not the subject matter of criminal sanctions. In some

EXHIBIT 2-1
Classification of Offenses

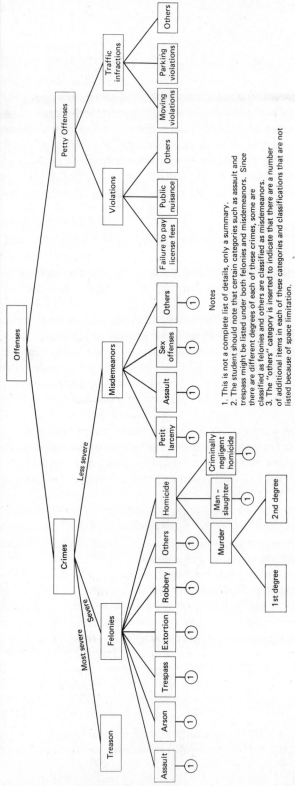

Notes

1. This is not a complete list of details, only a summary.
2. The student should note that certain categories such as assault and trespass might be listed under both felonies and misdemeanors. Since there are different degrees of each of these crimes, some are classified as felonies and others are classified as misdemeanors.
3. The "others" category is inserted to indicate that there are a number of additional items in each of these categories and classifications that are not listed because of space limitation.

cases, the omission of an act may also result in a crime. This would be true where a person has a legal duty to perform an act. For example, a police officer sees a friend driving down the wrong side of a street and fails to take any action (although he or she could have), and several blocks later the driver hits and kills a pedestrian. The police officer may be liable for a criminal act. He or she had a duty, was aware of it, and had the ability and opportunity to perform this duty, but didn't. The average citizen in a similar situation has no duty to act and would not be guilty of a crime.

Another important element of crimes is intent. Intent may be manifested in several different ways. Some crimes require intent to commit the criminal act. For example, murder is generally defined as the willful deliberate killing of an individual; the intent present is to kill the victim. Manslaughter is defined as killing a person while intending only to do harm. The intent in this case is intent to commit a wrongful act (to do another harm) although clearly not to kill. A third concept is exemplified by criminally negligent homicide. This requires no intent to do wrong, but merely a reckless disregard for the safety of others. Drivers who are drunk may not intend to do harm, but probably don't care about the consequences of their driving. The law will hold such individuals criminally liable for the consequences of their acts. Certain crimes are considered so heinous that the law requires no intent at all. These are specified by statute and are sometimes referred to as strict liability crimes. For example, laws regulating the possession of narcotics usually do not refer to the possessor's intent. Persons who pick up the wrong suitcase in an airport may find themselves in ''possession'' of narcotics and could be convicted.

Crimes are often classified by the object of the offense; crimes can be against a person, against property, or against society. Some of these are listed and discussed as follows. These classifications may vary from state to state.

Crimes against the Person

Assault and Battery An assault is an intentional, unlawful attempt by one individual to do physical injury to another individual. For example, attempting to hit, kick, or trip or pointing a gun at someone would be considered assault. Words cannot amount to an assault, no matter how threatening. Some states require that the perpetrator of an assault actually have the ability to do harm. A battery is the infliction of violence on another person without permission. An assault can occur without battery. Numerous states indicate that a battery must include an assault.

Reckless Endangerment Reckless endangerment is a crime defined as the reckless engaging in conduct that creates a substantial risk of serious physical injury or a grave risk of death to another while evidencing a depraved indifference to human life. An example of this type of crime would be shooting into a crowd without causing an injury. If injury or death takes place, there would be a battery or homicide.

Homicides Homicides are crimes that cause the death of a person. In some states, killing a fetus after a certain number of weeks is also considered homicide (in New

York State, a 24-week-old fetus). Homicide can be broken into three categories, depending on the intent of the perpetrator.

Murder is the most severe type of homicide. Murder is the willful, deliberate, intentional, malicious premeditated killing of a person; the reckless killing of a person; or the killing of a person in the course of committing another serious felony (felony-murder). For example, a robber is holding up a bank. In the course of the robbery, the robber's revolver accidentally discharges and kills a bank employee, a bystander, or a police officer. Even though there was no intent to kill, the robber is subject to conviction under the felony-murder rule.

Manslaughter is defined either as killing a person without malice while intending to cause serious physical injury to that person or another or as killing a person intentionally while under the influence of extreme emotional disturbance. For example, in a case where a wife stabbed and killed her husband in a jealous rage, the court found her guilty of manslaughter because the killing occurred ''without malice in the sudden heat of passion'' (United States v. Chandler, 393 F.2d 920 [4th Cir. 1968]). Manslaughter in some jurisdictions includes the reckless causing of the death of another person or aiding another person to commit suicide.

The last category of homicide is criminally negligent homicide. This is causing the death of another individual when the perpetrator acts with criminal negligence. Criminal negligence is defined as a failure to perceive a substantial and unjustifiable risk that death will occur from one's actions. For example, an individual was engaged in a ''drag race'' on a large city street. Each racer had passengers in his vehicle. One of the racing vehicles was struck by a truck, and the passenger was killed. The driver of the other vehicle was charged with criminally negligent homicide and was convicted (State v. Petersen, 522 P.2d 912 [Or. 1974]).

Sex Offenses   Each state has different crimes that are defined under the broad category of sex offenses. These crimes cover sexual activity involving either force or compulsion or cover acts with a person who is under age (in federal law, 16 years) or incapable of consent by reason of being physically helpless or mentally incapacitated or defective. Offenses range from sexual misconduct (including deviate sexual intercourse with an animal or a dead body) to rape or sodomy or both as well as sexual exploitation of children.

Sexual abuse is also a crime and entails the touching of the sexual or other intimate parts of a person for the purpose of gratifying the perpetrator's sexual desires. The categories of sexual offenses depend on the age of the complainant, whether or not there was consent, and the degree and type of compulsion used (see Table 2–1).

Crimes against Property

Criminal Trespass   Criminal trespass includes situations where an individual knowingly enters or remains unlawfully on any premises. The severity of the crime depends on the type of premises violated and the intention of the trespasser. If the trespasser is in possession of explosives or a deadly weapon, the seri-

TABLE 2-1
Ages of Consent

Age	State
12	Delaware — I Hate U. of Delaware
13	New Mexico
14	Georgia, Iowa, Kentucky, Maine, Pennsylvania, Utah
15	Vermont
16	Alabama, Alaska, Arkansas, Colorado, Connecticut, District of Columbia, Hawaii, Illinois, Indiana, Kansas, Maryland, Michigan, Minnesota, Missouri, Montana, Nebraska, Nevada, New Hampshire, New Jersey, North Carolina, Ohio, Rhode Island, South Carolina, South Dakota, Virginia, West Virginia
17	Louisiana, New York, Texas
18	Arizona, California, Florida, Idaho, Massachusetts, Mississippi, North Dakota, Oklahoma, Oregon, Tennessee, Washington, Wisconsin, Wyoming

ousness increases. For example, a protester who takes over public buildings (e.g., a college campus building) or who refuses to leave when ordered to do so may be found guilty of criminal trespass.

Burglary In cases where there is forcible entry of a building and an intent to commit another crime, the offense is termed burglary. Burglary can have several categories. These depend on whether the building was entered at night, the burglar was armed, a human being was present, physical injury was caused to anybody, or anybody was threatened. Where there is forcible entry without the intent to commit another crime, the offense is usually called breaking and entering. In some jurisdictions, this is considered a subcategory of burglary.

Arson Arson covers the damaging of a building or structure by fire, and the degrees of this crime depend on whether the fire was the result of reckless or intentional conduct. The most serious type of arson occurs when an individual intentionally sets a building on fire, another person is present in the building, and the perpetrator knows, or should have known, that it was reasonably possible that someone else might be injured.

Larceny The taking of property without the owner's consent, with the intent of permanently depriving the owner of its use, is larceny. The defendant in a case had hired the plaintiff, a carpenter, to make certain repairs. When the defendant was unhappy with the plaintiff's work, he ordered the plaintiff to leave. The plaintiff took his tools with him and in the process accidentally carried off several tools that were owned by the defendant. The defendant requested that the plaintiff return the tools, but the plaintiff never received the message. When the tools were not returned, the defendant filed a complaint with the police, who arrested the plaintiff and charged him with larceny. The plaintiff subsequently filed an action against the defendant for malicious prosecution. In the malicious prosecution case, the court held that, because the plaintiff had taken the tools by mistake, he lacked the criminal intent required for an action of larceny. The plaintiff was awarded a judgment for malicious prosecution. The appellate court found that it was proper for the jury to find a lack of probable cause for the arrest of the plaintiff and could also find that the defendant acted on the basis of malice toward the plaintiff (Roy v. Connor, 247 A.2d 21 [N.H. 1969]). There are two categories of larceny: petty larceny and grand larceny. The distinction between the two has to do with the dollar value of the property intentionally taken (e.g., in federal law, $100; in California, $200).

Unauthorized Use of a Vehicle   The unauthorized use of a vehicle with the intent of returning it when one is finished (joyriding) is another crime against property.

Robbery   The forcible stealing of property from an individual or from the immediate presence of an individual by the use of, or threatened use of, physical force is robbery. There are several degrees of robbery. These depend on the extent of the injuries that were threatened and whether a deadly weapon was used in the threat. For example, a thief breaks into your garage and steals your car while you are sleeping. The thief has committed burglary (the breaking in with the intent to steal) and larceny (the taking away of the car). If you catch the thief in the act and he or she holds a gun on you while taking the car, then the thief has committed burglary and robbery.

Offenses against Society

Dangerous Drug Offenses   Dangerous drug offenses include possession, manufacture, transport, cultivation, sale, or use of certain types of controlled substances such as marijuana, heroin, and cocaine.

Tables 2–2 and 2–3 illustrate the penalties that may be imposed under New York State statutes for the possession and sale of narcotics (Table 2–2) and marijuana (Table 2–3).

Disorderly Conduct   Disorderly conduct is committed when a person, intending to cause public inconvenience, annoyance, or alarm, engages in violent behavior; uses abusive or obscene language or gestures; disturbs a lawful assembly of persons; obstructs traffic; knowingly places a false fire alarm or bomb threat; and so on.

Public Intoxication   Public intoxication is committed when an intoxicated person creates a disturbance in a public or private place or business. Walking down the street in an inebriated condition may be sufficient to be guilty of this offense.

Harassment   Harassment is committed if a person, with intent to harass or alarm, subjects another to offensive physical contact; publicly insults this person in a man-

TABLE 2-2
New York State Narcotic Penalties

Classification	Possession	Sale	Sentence
Class A			
A-1	4 oz. and over	2 oz. and over	Min. 15 yrs. to life
A-11			
First offenders	2 oz.–4 oz.	½ oz.–2 oz.	Min. 3 yrs. to life Max. 8⅓ yrs. to life
Second offenders	2 oz.–4 oz.	½ oz.–2 oz.	Min. 6 yrs. to life Max. 12½ yrs. to life
Class B			
First offenders	½ oz.–2 oz.	Up to ½ oz.	Min. 1 to 3 yrs. Max. 8⅓ to 25 yrs.
Second offenders	½ oz.–2 oz.	Up to ½ oz.	Min. 4½ yrs. to 25 yrs.

Source: American Bar Association Manual.

ner likely to provoke a violent response; communicates anonymously by telephone or mail; and so on. For example, a person who places an obscene phone call with the intent to harm is guilty of this offense.

Prostitution Prostitution takes place whenever a person engages in or offers sexual activity for a fee.

Defenses to Criminal Liability

The primary defense to criminal liability is innocence. A defendant may offer proof that he or she was somewhere else when the crime was committed (alibi). In addition, the defendant may show that the period of time within which the people may bring their action (statute of limitations) has expired. This time limit applies to all crimes except murder and must be asserted by the defendant when answering the complaint (see section on criminal process).

A defendant may also present evidence of circumstances that may mitigate his or her guilt or sentence. These are generally referred to as defenses and are discussed in the criminal process section of this chapter.

TABLE 2-3
New York State Marijuana Penalties

Classification	Possession	Sale	Penalty
Violation	Up to 25 grams[a] (second offense) (third offense)		Up to $100 fine Up to $200 fine Up to $250 fine or 15 days in jail or both
Class B Misdemeanor	Over 25 grams or any public use or display	Gift up to 2 grams or 1 cigarette	Up to 3 months in jail or $500 or $500 fine
Class A Misdemeanor	Over 2 ounces	Up to 25 grams	Up to 1 year in jail or $1000 fine
Class E Felony	Over 8 ounces	Over 25 grams	Up to 4 years in prison
Class D Felony	Over 16 ounces	Over 4 oz. or any amount to a minor	Up to 7 years in prison
Class C Felony	Over 10 pounds	Over 16 ounces	Up to 15 years in prison

Source: American Bar Association Manual.
[a]The quantity of 25 grams equals about seven eighths of an ounce.

CRIMINAL PROCESS

Introduction

A criminal action is commenced by filing an accusatory instrument against a defendant in a criminal court or by an arrest (Exhibit 2–2). The form of an accusatory instrument and the procedure for filing depend on the jurisdiction in which the criminal action is commenced. The accusatory instrument may be termed an information, a simplified information, a prosecutor's information, a misdemeanor complaint, or a felony complaint. Regardless of its title, it is a sworn written complaint against the defendant.

In the case of a felony, the Fifth Amendment to the Constitution of the United States indicates that an individual can only be prosecuted on the basis of an indictment (Exhibit 2–3). An indictment is a written accusation by a grand jury charging the defendant with the commission of a felony. The grand jury indictment is an indication that evidence has been heard by a jury of the defendant's peers, consisting of from 15 to 23 members, and the indictment must spell out a legally sufficient (prima facie) case against the defendant. There must be reasonable cause by the grand jury to believe that the defendant committed the offense charged.

Function of Grand Jury

A grand jury is usually impaneled by a court of original jurisdiction for the purpose of hearing the evidence concerning the offense charged. All types of information can be presented to the grand jury in its deliberations, including evidence not admissible in a normal criminal trial (e.g., hearsay, fruits of illegal searches). The prosecutor presents the facts and is adviser to the grand jury. The grand jury may not receive advice from any other source. The grand jury proceedings are closed, and witnesses before the grand jury must give the testimony that the grand jury requests. (A refusal to testify may result in the imposition of criminal sanctions.) A witness who gives evidence to the grand jury receives immunity unless he or she has waived such immunity. In some states, an attorney may appear with a witness inside the grand jury room if the witness waives his or her immunity, but generally no attorney is allowed.

If the grand jury determines that the evidence before it establishes that a person has committed an offense other than a felony, the grand jury can direct the district attorney to file a prosecutor's information, alleging a misdemeanor, with the local criminal court.

Summons and Arrest Warrant

The next step in the criminal process (after preparation of an accusatory instrument for a misdemeanor or handing down an indictment for a felony) is for a criminal court to issue a summons or arrest warrant. A summons directs the defendant to appear before the court at a specified time to hear the charges of the particular offense. An arrest warrant is an order to the police and others to bring the defendant in for the court appearance. The preliminary court appearance is called an arraignment (discussed after arrest and related procedures).

Criminal proceedings can also be initiated by an arrest. After the arrest, a complaint is prepared, and the defendant is brought before a judge for arraignment. If the charges are for a felony, the case will be referred to the grand jury. If the charges are for a misdemeanor, a trial will be scheduled. In either case, the defendant will be held in jail or released on bail until the trial date or until the grand jury finishes its deliberation.

Arrest

An arrest entails the restraint of a person or taking a person into custody. An arrest can take place pursuant to a warrant of arrest or without a warrant. An arrest pur-

EXHIBIT 2-2
Criminal Trial Procedure

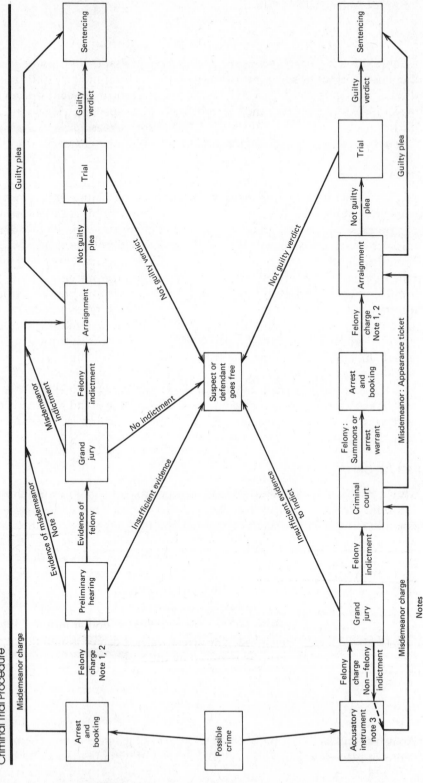

Notes

1. Misdemeanor or felony complaint is prepared, as appropriate.
2. Defendant will be jailed, released on bail, released on his or her own recognizance, or released in custody of another until preliminary hearing.
3. These can take the form of: a. Information
                               b. Simplified information
                               c. Prosecutor's information
                               d. Complaint

EXHIBIT 2-3
Indictment

COURT

COUNTY OF

The People of the State of

-against-   INDICTMENT
                                                  No.

Defendant

THE GRAND JURY OF THE COUNTY OF   , by this indictment, accuse the
defendant of the crime of BURGLARY IN THE THIRD DEGREE committed as follows:

The defendant, in the County of   , on or about   , did knowingly
enter and remain unlawfully in a building of   in the Village of   , State
of   , with intent to commit the crime of larceny therein.

AS AND FOR A SECOND COUNT, THE GRAND JURY AFORESAID, by this
indictment, further accuse the defendant of the crime of GRAND LARCENY IN THE
SECOND DEGREE committed as follows:

The defendant, in the County of   , on or about   did steal from
                  , certain property having an aggregate value in excess of $1500.00, to wit:
Electric drills, a jigsaw, staple guns, cassette player, a chain saw, a quantity of pocket knives,
electric sander, a quantity of socket sets, a quantity of metric sockets, a quantity of
combination wrenches, a quantity of metric combination wrenches, a quantity of pliers, a
quantity of gloves, one calculator, two flashlights, and U.S. money.

/S/ _____   /S/ _____

---

suant to a warrant is made by a police officer, federal marshal, county sheriff, or
other law enforcement officer. This warrant (see Exhibit 2-4) is issued by a magistrate, a justice of the peace, a judge, or any other judical officer, and must be addressed to the police officer making the arrest or to another individual to whom the
job has been legally delegated. The arrest warrant can be issued only under a finding of "reasonable cause" as required by the Fourth and Fourteenth Amendments
of the U.S. Constitution.

An arrest may be made on any day of the week and at any hour of the day or
night; moreover, the officer must normally inform the defendant that he or she is
arresting pursuant to the issuance of a warrant. The officer must also indicate to the
defendant what offense is charged. The Supreme Court has indicated that police
officers, when making arrests, must inform suspects of their rights to remain silent,

EXHIBIT 2–4
Arrest Warrant

WARRANT OF ARREST
(CPL Sec. 120.10)

Oneonta City Court, City of Oneonta;
County of Otsego, New York

In the Name of the People of the State of New York,

TO ANY MEMBER OF THE ONEONTA CITY POLICE:

An ACCUSATORY INSTRUMENT having been filed with this court charging the offense(s) of___Petit Larceny___

contrary to __Section 155.25 of the New York State Penal Law__ has (have) been

committed and designating __Olga G. Doe__ as the

defendant who committed it.

YOU ARE, THEREFORE, COMMANDED TO FORTHWITH ARREST SAID DEFENDANT, and to bring him before this court for the purpose of arraignment on such accusatory instrument.

This warrant issued on this __31st__ day

of__February__ , 19_50_

at Oneonta City Court
Oneonta, New York

BAIL: $100.00

*A duplicate copy of the accusatory instrument
 is attached hereto

_____
Oneonta City Judge

*Delete if not attached

_____

their rights to counsel, and the fact that any statement the defendants make may be held against them. Failure to inform a defendant will preclude admission of any confession obtained as the result of interrogation when the "*Miranda* warnings" are not given. Officers may enter premises to effect an arrest if they reasonably believe the defendant to be present. Officers must give notice of their authority prior to such entry. An exception will be made if an officer reasonably believes that giving such notice will result in the defendant's attempting to escape, endangering the life or safety of the officer or another person, or destruction of or damage to evidence material to the case. In the event that an arrest is made illegally, either because of a faulty warrant or unreasonable procedures, the arrested individual may have a defense to a subsequent criminal trial or a case for malicious prosecution or false arrest or all these. (These latter items will be discussed in the chapter on civil wrongs or torts.)

An individual may be arrested by a police officer without a warrant when the officer reasonably believes that the individual committed an offense in the officer's presence or committed a crime whether that crime was committed in the officer's presence or not. In the latter case, the officer must have probable cause to believe that the person has committed a crime. Reasonable or probable cause means that the state of facts would lead a person of ordinary caution or prudence to believe that the person committed a crime or offense. For example, a postmaster received a ''suspicious'' package. He contacted a U.S. customs agent, who then contacted the sheriff. They opened the package, which contained 65 grams of morphine. The package was rewrapped and picked up by Bolton. As she left the post office with the package, the sheriff arrested her. He did not have a warrant. The court held that the officer could act where he believed the suspect to be guilty based on facts and circumstances within his own knowledge or on information given by reliable and credible, third persons, provided there were no offsetting facts. The information supplied by the customs agent and the possession of the package by Bolton constituted reasonable cause for a belief that Bolton had committed or was committing a crime (Kuhr v. District Court of Elizabeth Judicial District in and for Hill County, 268 P. 501 [Mont. 1928]).

In effecting an arrest, a police officer (including a sheriff, a marshal, or the FBI) may use force to prevent the arrested person from escaping custody. This force may not be deadly and must be reasonable in respect to the circumstances of the arrest. The police officer may use deadly force (a force capable of causing death or serious physical injury) when the officer believes that the person is committing or attempting to commit a felony involving the use of or threatened use of physical force. Police officers will be charged with criminal negligence when they do not exercise a reasonable degree of care. For example, if an officer shoots an innocent bystander or if an officer shoots at a prisoner who is escaping into a crowd of individuals, the officer will be liable for such actions.

A private citizen may also arrest a person when the citizen believes that person has committed a felony or when that person commits an offense in the citizen's presence. Some states require that the person be reasonably suspect of committing a felony (providing a felony has actually been committed) whereas other states require that the felony be committed in the presence of the citizen making the arrest. A citizen making an arrest must normally advise the person being arrested of the reasons for the arrest and must make an attempt to deliver the arrested person to the custody of the appropriate police officer without any unnecessary delay.

A private citizen may use physical force to arrest a person who has committed an offense and may use deadly physical force to arrest a person who has committed murder, manslaughter, robbery, forcible rape, or any crime of a violent nature. Peace officers and private citizens may use deadly physical force to defend themselves or third persons from what they reasonably believe to be the use of deadly physical force. This rule may apply to a person in control of a building when this person reasonably believes another individual is committing or attempting to commit a burglary.

Searches

In addition to the powers given to the police and peace officers to make arrests, either pursuant to or without a warrant, a police officer may "stop and frisk" a suspect when that police officer reasonably believes the individual has committed or is about to commit a felony. (See Terry v. Ohio, 392 U.S. 1 [S. Ct. 1968]; also United States v. Robinson, 414 U.S. 218, [S. Ct. 1973].) The officer may demand the name and address of the suspect as well as an explanation of the suspect's conduct. If the officers reasonably suspect that they are in danger of physical injury, they may frisk the person for a deadly weapon. Any evidence found in a reasonable frisk may be used at the trial. If the search goes beyond what is reasonable, the evidence will be excluded from trial.

EXHIBIT 2-5
Search Warrant, 2 pages

Application for Search Warrant
(Sec. 690.35 C.P.L.)

Local Criminal _____ Court, _____ City _____ of _____ Oneonta, N.Y., _____ County of _____ Otsego

I, _____, a police officer of the State of New York, to wit, a(n) _____ of the Oneonta Police Department at Oneonta, N.Y., do hereby state that there is reasonable cause to believe that property of a kind or character described in Section 690.10 of the Criminal Procedure Law may be found in or upon a designated or described place, vehicle, or person.

THE FACTS SUPPORTING MY STATEMENT ABOVE and the request for special authority set out below (on my personal knowledge) (on information and belief) and the sources of my information and belief are:

A.   CHARACTER OF PROPERTY AS STOLEN, UNLAWFULLY POSSESSED, USED TO COMMIT OFFENSE, AS EVIDENCE, ETC. (Sec. 690.10 C.P.L.)

_____
_____
_____

B.   THE PROPERTY IS: (describe fully)

_____
_____
_____

C.   DESIGNATION OR DESCRIPTION OF PLACE, VEHICLE OR PERSON TO BE SEARCHED: (include specific address, where applicable)

_____
_____
_____

In addition to searches and stop-and-frisk rules, police officers' powers include searches of premises and vehicles. These searches, except under certain circumstances, must be made with a warrant issued according to the rules set out by the particular state and limited by the Fourth Amendment requirement of reasonableness.

A search warrant (Exhibit 2–5) is usually issued by a local criminal court under a written, verified application. The application must show that there is reasonable cause to believe that property, either stolen, unlawfully possessed, or possessed to commit or conceal a crime, may be found in the designated dwelling or vehicle or upon the individual person.

All aspects of a search must be reasonable. Unless the warrant authorizes searches to be conducted at any time of day or night, they must be made during reasonable hours. Police officers must generally give notice to the person being searched or the occupant of the place or vehicle being searched unless the warrant specifically authorizes entry without notice ("no knock"). A police officer may use

EXHIBIT 2–5, cont.

D.   SOURCE OF INFORMATION AND BASIS OF BELIEF: (if not of personal knowledge)

_____

_____

_____

I THEREFORE REQUEST THAT THE COURT ISSUE A SEARCH WARRANT DIRECTING THE SEARCH at of _____ FOR _____ AND THE SEIZURE THEREOF.

I FURTHER REQUEST THAT SUCH WARRANT BE MADE EXECUTABLE AT ANY TIME OF THE DAY OR NIGHT BASED ON THE FOLLOWING FACTS:_____

_____

_____

I FURTHER REQUEST THAT SUCH WARRANT AUTHORIZE THE EXECUTING POLICE OFFICER TO ENTER PREMISES TO BE SEARCHED WITHOUT GIVING NOTICE OF HIS AUTHORITY OR PURPOSE BASED ON THE FOLLOWING FACTS:_____

_____

_____

_____

_____
                                        (signature of member)

Subscribed and sworn to before me this
_____ day of _____ 19____

_____
              (signature)

_____
                (title)

EXHIBIT 2-5, cont.

_____ Court, _____ of _____

TO: ANY MEMBER OF THE CITY OF ONEONTA, N.Y., POLICE DEPARTMENT: _____

YOU ARE HEREBY DIRECTED TO SEARCH _____

_____

_____

_____

FOR THE FOLLOWING PROPERTY: _____

_____

_____

_____

_____

_____

_____

_____

_____

_____

_____

_____

AND IF ANY SUCH PROPERTY IS FOUND, you are hereby directed to seize the same and, without unnecessary delay, return it to this Court together with this warrant and a written inventory of such property subscribed and sworn by you.

YOU ARE DIRECTED TO EXECUTE THIS WARRANT: BETWEEN THE HOURS OF 6:00 A.M. AND 9:00 P.M., AT ANY TIME OF THE DAY OR NIGHT.

YOU ARE AUTHORIZED, IN THE EXECUTION OF THIS WARRANT, TO ENTER THE PREMISES TO BE SEARCHED WITHOUT GIVING NOTICE OF YOUR AUTHORITY AND PURPOSE.

This search warrant issued this _____ day of _____ 19 _____

_____
(Signature of Judge)

_____
(Title)

physical force in implementing a search, but the officer may not use deadly force except in self-defense or in defense of a third person.

A search may be made under certain situations without a warrant. These situations include the previously discussed frisks by officers in protecting themselves from concealed weapons or in searches that are incidental to a lawful arrest. When an item is in the police officer's plain view or when it has been abandoned, it may be seized without a search warrant. In circumstances where obtaining a warrant would be impractical, it need not be obtained (e.g., a blood test taken on the highway for a charge of driving while intoxicated, Schmerber v. California, 384 U.S. 757 [S. Ct. 1966]). If an individual consents to a search, the property seized under such a search is also admissible unless the individual has been deceived (Bumper v. North Carolina, 391 U.S. 543 [S. Ct. 1968]).

Booking

After being arrested, an individual must be booked. Booking is an informal procedure at the police station consisting of the preparation of a ''card'' or a ''sheet'' showing the name of the accused, the crime, the time of the crime, and the time of booking. Booking includes fingerprinting and photographing of the accused. After booking, the accused must be brought before the court without unnecessary delay for preliminary examination or to be arraigned. If delay is unreasonable, the accused's attorney may get a writ of habeas corpus, which will release the accused.

Preliminary Hearing

A preliminary hearing or examination is held before a judge or magistrate to ascertain whether there are reasonable grounds for believing a crime has been committed (Webb v. Commonwealth, 129 S.E. 2d 22 [Va. 1969]) and if there is ''probable cause'' that the accused committed the crime. This hearing is not necessary if the grand jury has already indicted the individual. The equal protection and due process clauses of the U.S. Constitution do not require a preliminary hearing (Lem Woon v. Oregon, 229 U.S. 586 [S. Ct. 1913]). The main purpose of such a hearing is to prevent the incarceration of innocent persons for a long time prior to trial by having a judge or magistrate review the information available as soon as possible. An accused may waive the right to preliminary examination by pleading guilty to the charges.

Arraignment

At the arraignment, the defendant appears before the court, which informs him or her of the charges by reading the indictment or the information. The court must also advise the defendant of his or her right to counsel, and the court will adjourn to allow the defendant to obtain counsel. Defendants must be able to communicate with counsel as well as inform a relative or friend of their circumstances free of charge by letter or telephone. In cases where an individual is unable to afford counsel, the court must appoint counsel. If defendants wish to proceed without counsel, the court may either permit them to do so or require that they have counsel. If defendants proceed without counsel, they do not waive their right to counsel at a future point in the proceedings.

At the arraignment, the charges may be dismissed by the judge for any reason within the judge's jurisdiction, including insufficient evidence. If the charges are not dismissed, the defendant is asked to enter a plea of guilty or not guilty. In some states and also in federal court, a plea of nolo contendere may be entered. This plea means "I do not wish to contend." A defendant who pleads nolo contendere agrees to allow the court to sentence him or her as though he or she had pleaded guilty. It is not an admission of guilt and, therefore, cannot be used against the defendant in a civil action. If a plea of guilty or nolo contendere is entered, the judge may immediately sentence the defendant or may postpone sentencing in order to review the defendant's records. In some states, if the crime has a death penalty or a life imprisonment penalty, a guilty plea may not be entered; the defendant must plead not guilty. Silence when the defendant is required to enter a plea will be interpreted as a plea of not guilty.

If the defendant pleads not guilty, a trial will be scheduled. The court may either release the defendant on his or her own recognizance, fix bail, or commit the defendant to the sheriff for future appearance. The court may also grant an adjournment in contemplation of dismissal, in which case the defendant is released in his or her own recognizance, but the court may resume the proceedings within six months (e.g., if the defendant commits a second offense).

Plea Bargaining

Many cases never go to court because of a procedure called plea bargaining. Plea bargaining is the process whereby the defendant agrees to plead guilty if the prosecutor agrees to charge him or her with a lesser offense. The agreement is made between the defendant's attorney and the district attorney and must be approved by the judge. Many district attorneys approve of plea bargaining as it saves the public money and time that would otherwise have to be spent on a trial.

The reduction of a charge by one degree may not change the sentence in many cases because the minimum penalty for the greater charge may be the same as the maximum penalty for the lesser charge. By plea bargaining the defendant is assured at worst of the maximum penalty for the lesser charge as opposed to gambling on being convicted of a greater charge and having a greater penalty imposed. Plea bargaining may compensate for errors of judgment by arresting officers who charge a defendant with a crime that is too severe.

Trial

The next step in criminal procedure is a trial. The trial is the proceeding during which the people must prove the defendant's guilt beyond a reasonable doubt.

The trial is the place where the defendant has the constitutional right to confront his or her accusers. The trial can either be by judge or by judge and jury. The right to jury trial is protected by the Fifth Amendment of the Constitution. The defendant has this right to jury trial when charged with a serious crime, but this right can be waived (Duncan v. Louisiana, 391 U.S. 145 [S. Ct. 1969]; Aldwin v. New York, 399 U.S. 66 [S. Ct. 1970]). A jury usually consists of 12 persons, but a lesser number is allowable (Williams v. Florida, 399 U.S. 78 [S. Ct. 1970]; six jurors held to be all right).

During the trial, the Constitution is the guide for protecting the defendant's rights. The due process amendments (IV, V, VI, VIII, XIV) give the defendant the right to a fair trial. Examples of violations of this right are the following: a defendant is required to go to trial in prison clothes (Estelle v. Williams, 425 U.S. 501 [S. Ct. 1976]), or a defendant is tried by a mayor who is responsible for the village finances, which come substantially from fines (Ward v. Monroeville, 409 U.S. 57 [S. Ct. 1972]). A defendant is also entitled to a speedy trial as defined in the Sixth and Fourteenth Amendments of the Constitution. This trial must be public as well. If the trial is not speedy or not public, the defendant is entitled to be be released (Barker v. Wingo, 407 U.S. 514 [S. Ct. 1972] and Strunk v. United States, 412 U.S. 434 [S. Ct. 1972]).

The Fifth Amendment protects the defendant against self-incrimination. This right excuses defendants from taking the stand and testifying when they do not wish to. It does not prevent the admission of blood tests (Schmerberg v. California, 384 U.S. 757 [S. Ct. 1966]); breathalyzer readings (State v. Wardlaw, 107 So. 2d 179 [Fla. 1958]); fingerprints (Cutton v. Murphy, 412 U.S. 291 [S. Ct. 1973]); voice recordings (United States v. Dionisio, 410 U.S. 1, [S. Ct. 1973]); handwriting samples (United States v. Mara, 410 U.S. 19 [S. Ct. 1973]); or information obtained in a lineup (Neil v. Diggers, 409 U.S. 188 [S. Ct. 1972]). The right against self-incrimination does prevent the use of a stomach pump to supply evidence (Rochin v. California, 342 U.S. 165 [S. Ct. 1952]). With respect to the Fifth Amendment right to remain silent, the courts have held that no unfavorable inference may be drawn from the failure of defendants to testify in their own behalf (Doyle v. Ohio, 426 U.S. 610 [S. Ct. 1976]; United States v. Hale, 422 U.S. 171 [S. Ct. 1975]; Griffin v. California, 380 U.S. 356 [S. Ct. 1972] and Anderson v. Nelson, 390 U.S. 523 [S. Ct. 1968]). The defendant also has the right to be present at his or her own trial (Seale v. Hoffman, 306 Fed. S. 330 [N.D. Ill. 1969]). Another right that is protected is the defendant's right to have any information favorable to the accused in the prosecutor's possession admitted to court.

During the trial, evidence must be presented by the people to tip the scales of justice against the defendant beyond a reasonable doubt to warrant a verdict of guilty. The jury (or judge) must listen to this evidence as it is presented and make a decision as to the guilt or innocence of the defendant. In most states, the jury verdict must be unanimous (Johnson v. Louisiana, 406 U.S. 356 [S. Ct. 1972]; Apodaca v. Oregon, 406 U.S. 404 [S. Ct. 1972]—unanimity not necessary).

A trial proceeds according to a set of rules that are defined in each state's code of criminal procedure. There is also a federal code of criminal procedure for crimes against the United States. Criminal procedure is similar to civil procedure outlined in Chapter 3. One set of procedural rules that is extremely important is the rules of evidence. For example, the exclusionary rule indicates that certain items shall be excluded from the trial. These exclusions will include fruits from an illegal search as well as evidence gained by exploiting illegal evidence from the illegal search. This has been termed the "fruit of poisonous tree doctrine" (Nerclone v. United States, 308 U.S. 1 [S. Ct. 1939]; Silverthorne Lumber Company v. United States, 251 U.S. 385 [S. Ct. 1920]); Wang Son v. United States, 371 U.S. 471 [S. Ct. 1963]).

In addition to the exclusionary rule, the hearsay evidence rule is also applicable. This rule states that information is not admissible at the trial from third parties who were not present at the event. For example, a police officer who hears an individual make a statement about a defendant's guilt may not testify as to that statement. The individual who made the statement must testify.

The rules of evidence also protect the defendant from confessions that were given either through coercion or involuntarily. In making a determination as to whether or not a confession is admissible, the courts must consider the totality of the circumstances (Escobedo v. Illinois, 378 U.S. 478 [S. Ct. 1964]; Miranda v. Arizona, 384 U.S. 436, [S. Ct. 1966]).

After the people have presented their case, the defendant may present evidence to instill reasonable doubt as to his or her guilt in the minds of the jury or judge. The triers of fact are not to infer that a defendant committed a criminal act because the defendant was brought to trial (State v. Rivers, 287 N.W. 790 [Minn. 1939]).

If the evidence shows that the defendant is guilty beyond a reasonable doubt, the defendant may wish to introduce evidence with respect to certain defenses that may mitigate the sentence or lead to a verdict of not guilty. These defenses include duress, renunciation, entrapment, justification, infancy, incapacity, insanity, and intoxication. Persons who act under a mistake of fact or law cannot use such a mistake as a defense unless they can show that they did not have the state of mind required by law for an intentional crime or that the statute governing the crime allows such a mistake as a defense. "Ignorance of the law is no excuse."

The defense of justification may sometimes be applicable. For example, where the conduct of defendants was necessary to avoid imminent public or private injury and where the injury or imminent injury was not created by the fault of the defendants, or when defendants used physical force because they reasonably believed it was necessary to defend themselves or a third person against imminent or unlawful force by the other person, these items can be introduced by the defendant in justification of illegal conduct such as assault, battery or even homicide.

If a defendant can show that he or she was coerced into committing a crime by use of physical force or the threat of use of physical force, the defense of duress may be available. In addition, if defendants can show that they changed their minds about committing the crime charged and that they made a substantial effort to prevent the crime from being committed, the defense of renunciation may be available.

The defense of entrapment can be used if the defendant can show that a public servant induced the defendant to participate in the illegal activity, that he or she was not disposed to commit the crime beforehand, and that the public servant induced or encouraged the defendant to do something that she or he would not have done beforehand.

Another defense could be insanity. If the defendant lacks the capacity to understand the proceedings against him or her or to assist in his or her defense, insanity may be pleaded. In addition, if the defendant was insane at the time he or she committed the crime, he or she will not be criminally punished.

Although intoxication is not normally a defense to a criminal charge, it can be used if it shows an element of the crime charged was missing (such as intent). Deliberate intoxication, giving the defendant the courage or nerve to commit the crime, will not be available as a defense.

A defendant may use infancy as a defense, and each state has a different age below which an individual will not be criminally responsible for his or her conduct (see Table 2–4). Each state has its own juvenile and youthful offender statutes that will define the ages and punishment for wrongs against society perpetrated by a minor.

When a defendant has finished providing his or her evidence, the judge will give the case to the jury. The jury will be required to reach a verdict of guilty or not guilty. In the event that the jury cannot come up with a verdict, there is a so-called hung jury; in such case, a new trial is set. After the jury makes its decision, either side has the ability to appeal to the judge to set aside the verdict.

The next step in the process is for a judgment to be rendered by the judge, who will then either approve the jury's verdict or, in some instances, change the jury's verdict. If the final judgment is that the defendant is guilty, the next step in the process is sentencing. The sentencing procedure and sentences for various crimes are defined by each state as well as by federal laws. Felonies are generally punishable by indeterminate sentences of imprisonment. The sentence usually has a maximum

TABLE 2–4
Age below Which Individual Will Not Be Criminally Responsible

Age	State
16	Connecticut, New York[a] North Carolina, Vermont
17	Colorado, Georgia, Louisiana, Massachusetts, Michigan, Missouri, South Carolina, Texas
18	Alabama, Alaska, Arizona, Arkansas, California, Delaware, District of Columbia, Florida, Hawaii, Idaho, Indiana, Iowa, Kansas, Kentucky, Maine, Maryland, Minnesota, Mississippi, Montana, Nebraska, Nevada, New Hampshire, New Jersey, New Mexico, North Dakota, Ohio, Oregon, Pennsylvania, Rhode Island
19	South Dakota, Tennessee, Utah, Virginia, Washington, West Virginia, Wisconsin, Wyoming
17 male 18 female	Illinois
16 male 18 female	Oklahoma

[a]New York has a provision for treating heinous crimes of juveniles as adult crimes.

as well as a minimum period that must be served (i.e., the specific number of years will be determined by the judge or jury). These sentences are usually determined by category of offense. (For example, the federal crime of second degree murder carries a sentence of life imprisonment as a maximum and any term of years as a minimum.)

Sentencing

If an individual is imprisoned for an indeterminate term, he or she forfeits any public office, and his or her civil rights are suspended. In many jurisdictions, a person imprisoned for life is deemed to be civilly dead, in which case the individual's spouse may remarry. Many states allow harsher sentences for certain violent felony offenses as well as for persistent violent felony offenders. When more than one sentence is imposed on the same person (for more than one offense), the sentences can run either concurrently or consecutively. Concurrent sentences run together, and the time served will be the longest of the sentences imposed. Consecutive sentences are served one after the other so that the combined total of sentences would be the total time served.

Persons who are sentenced to an indeterminate term of prison are committed to the custody of the state's correction department. The minimum sentence must be served before the individual can be allowed release under a parole program. Parole is a conditional release under supervision and may be granted as a matter of discretion by the particular state's parole board. Minor crimes, including misdemeanors as well as traffic violations and infractions, are punishable according to the separate schemes outlined by the various states' laws.

In addition to imprisonment, sentencing could include probation, conditional discharge, or unconditional discharge or a combination. Probation is a situation in which the criminal offender remains in the community under the supervision of a probation officer during the period of probation. The criminal offender is considered to be in the custody of the court, and the court can specify the conditions that the criminal offender must comply with during the period of probation. The court can modify or enlarge the condition at any time it wishes. The periods of probation are set by the various state statutes, and a probation can be revoked and the offender can be sent back to prison if the conditions of the probation are breached.

Conditional discharge allows the offender to be released without the supervision of a probation officer. That individual is subject to certain conditions imposed by the court, and the court can modify those conditions whenever it wishes. If the conditions of the conditional discharge are breached (e.g., by commission of another offense), the sentence may be revoked, and the offender may be imprisoned. An unconditional discharge is a release without supervision of the probation officer and with no conditions attached. It is a final judgment of conviction and gives rise to a criminal record. It has no term, and it cannot be revoked or modified.

Sentencing may also include fines, but these are imposed only in areas of misdemeanors and violations. Felonies do not have fines imposed as sentences (except in some jurisdictions in cases where a felon gained money or property through the commission of a crime). Fines may be imposed in conjunction with sentences of conditional discharge or probation or both. Finally, if either side is not happy with the verdict, he or she may appeal. The appeal process is similar to that discussed under civil practice, in Chapter 3.

QUESTIONS

1 Two men were arrested when a police officer found a loaded gun underneath a rug in the rear of an automobile in which they were sitting. The occupants of the automobile said they knew nothing about the gun. The defendants were charged with a violation of the penal law that said, ''The presence in an automobile, other than a public omnibus, of a pistol . . . shall be presumptive evidence of its illegal possession by all the persons found in such automobile at the time such weapon . . . is found.'' May a penal statute properly eliminate the element of intent? Discuss the constitutionality of such a statute.

2 Four union men planned to beat Albert. They armed themselves with deadly weapons and proceeded to beat and stab him, as a result of which Albert died. Testimony in the case indicated that the four individuals only intended to beat Albert and not kill him. What crimes were committed? Discuss.

3 The defendant was driving his vehicle on the west side of a highway and tried to pass a truck. He crossed to the east side of the highway, left the pavement, and hit and killed Mr. Frizell, who was standing at his mailbox. The defendant continued to drive for several miles and was arrested two hours later. Evidence was introduced to show that he might have been intoxicated or just upset and unnerved. Discuss the rules with respect to manslaughter and criminally negligent homicide, and make a decision as to what crime the individual should be convicted of.

4 Defendants were officers and employees of a construction company. During the construction process, children got into the habit of playing in the construction site. A number of complaints had been made to the police, who chased the children away from the area. The school principal had also warned the children repeatedly that they should stay away from the construction site. There is no state statute, local law, or ordinance that required any further steps on the part of the construction company. The contract with the state also did not require any further action on the part of the contractor. During the construction process an embankment was built. The embankment was undisturbed for a period of time in excess of 24 hours. The evidence indicated that approximately 10 children began digging tunnels in the embankment after having been repeatedly chased away by the police. The evidence also indicated that several children were on top of the embankment jumping and kicking gravel down on the children situated below. The embankment caved in and buried several of the children. Are the defendants guilty of any criminal wrong with respect to the deaths of the children? Discuss.

5 The defendant and his brother, who was armed with a pistol, entered a cabin. After entering the cabin, they bound the occupant and demanded the combination to a safe in another building. The victim told the intruders the combination to the safe. The defendant contends that he should not be charged with burglary since his intent was to commit a larceny in another building, which was 100 yards from the building he was in. What crimes have been committed? Discuss.

6 The defendant attempted to open the doors of a retail store that had just closed for the evening. He was wearing rubber gloves and was in possession of a loaded pistol and a mask. The store owner contacted the police, who arrested the defendant before any actual break-in occurred. Has burglary or attempted burglary been committed? Discuss.

7 The defendant bored three holes with a 2-inch auger through the walls of a granary into a mass of wheat stored there. The weight of the grain forced several bushels of wheat out through the holes, and the defendant took the wheat and sold it. Is this considered an entry into the granary sufficient to allow a charge of burglary? Discuss.

8 The defendant was sent by his employer to Calhoun's house to collect money. When Calhoun did not pay the money, an argument started, and the defendant put his hand into his pocket, drew out a knife, and remarked that he was going to cut Calhoun's throat. The evidence shows the defendant never got closer than 7 to 10 feet to Calhoun. The defendant contends that he did not have the present ability to inflict an injury with the knife necessary for an assault. Should the defendant be convicted of an assault? Discuss.

9 The defendant drove up to a parked car to find the complainant, Lemsecks, asleep in the car. The defendant wakened him and demanded some alcohol that Lemsecks had in the car. The defendant said he ''was an officer, and if he (Lemsecks) would give him $100, he would turn him loose.'' Lemsecks only had $60, which he gave to the defendant. Did a robbery take place? Discuss.

10 The defendant Jones was walking with Kehl. Kehl was drunk and fell down. When Jones and several others went to lift him up, Jones put his hands in Kehl's pocket, took Kehl's wallet out, and shoved it in his own pocket. Kehl said, ''You have my pocketbook''; Jones called Kehl a liar and hit him. What crime was committed? Discuss.

11 The defendant fraudulently obtained bank withdrawal slips from Mrs. Rockwell without her knowledge or consent and had her sign them. He then used these withdrawal slips to obtain money from her bank account. Is this larceny? Discuss.

12 The defendants took $1500 over a period of several months from the New York City Subway System by falsifying records. Their contention is that they are only guilty of petty larceny since each of their thefts was only $.05, well below the $100 statutory figure for grand larceny. Is this a grand larceny or a petty larceny? Discuss.

13 A police officer experienced in the enforcement of narcotics laws knew the defendant, Rudy Chin, was a user of narcotics. An informant told the officer that Chin was the connection for another person. Acting on this information, the officer proceeded to a hotel room where Chin lived. Looking from the light well through a window into the room, the officer observed the defendant in the room. On a dresser table the officer saw two small white packets wrapped in bundle shape and an object that was covered with tissue paper. The officer formed the opinion that the two white packets were probably bundles of heroin. He then told Chin he was under arrest, instructed him to open the door, and not to touch anything on the dresser. The defendant complied. The defendant was handcuffed, and the two white packets, which later were analyzed to contain heroin, and the paper-covered object, which wa a hypodermic needle, were seized. Was this search legal? Discuss.

14 A police officer had been receiving information that the defendant and her male companion were involved in the sale of narcotics. One hour prior to the arrest of the defendant and her male companion, the officer received information from a confidential informant that the defendant was in possession of a quantity of narcotics either on her person or in her bedroom. The officer went to the defendant's home without a search warrant, arrested the defendant, and, while searching the premises, found heroin in the defendant's bedroom. Was the search lawful? Discuss.

15 Nicholson was a police officer who on several occasions had given money to Garcia. On each of such occasions, Garcia would take the money, disappear for anywhere from 10 minutes to one-half hour, and return with some marijuana cigarettes, which he would deliver to Nicholson. Officer Shoemaker would observe Garcia leaving Nicholson's presence and driving his car into Adame's driveway. Someone would then leave Adame's house, go to the driver's side of Garcia's car, spend several minutes there, and then the car would leave. On the most recent occasion, Garcia returned to Nicholson's presence on foot. Nicholson gave a signal, and two other police officers arrested Adame and Ingle in Garcia's car. The first searched Adame, who had in his possession numerous marijuana cigarettes. They then searched Ingle, who had in his possession $20 of marked bills (which had previously been given by officer Nicholson to Garcia for the purpose of effecting a purchase of marijuana, and the keys to Ingle's apartment. With the consent of Ingle's wife, the police officer searched the apartment and found a considerable quantity of marijuana. Both Adame and Ingle were found to have fluorescent powder on their hands identical to powder that had been placed on the marked bills that had been given to Garcia for the purchase of marijuana. Traces of powder were also found on Ingle's wallet.

Adame was convicted of possession of narcotics and certain other charges and appealed, and his appeal affirmed the position of the lower court. Ingle was convicted of similar crimes and is appealing on the basis that the search was illegal with respect to him because it was not based on reasonable or probable cause and that therefore the evidence produced was inadmissible. He further contended that the only reason he was searched was because he was in the presence of a known or suspected dealer of drugs and that the police had no other basis for searching him. What decision should be reached on his appeal? Discuss.

CHAPTER 3

Torts

INTRODUCTION

Torts are wrongful acts committed by one individual against another or his or her property. Torts include such acts as assault, battery, libel, slander, trespass, conversion, malicious prosecution, negligence, fraud, deceit, and the like. A tort (civil wrong) must be distinguished from a crime (criminal wrong) and a breach of contract. Crimes are wrongs against society as discussed in Chapter 2. Contracts are discussed in Chapter 4. In order to distinguish between a lawsuit for tort and one for crimes, one should look at the identity of the party bringing the suit (plaintiff). If the government is prosecuting, it is generally a criminal suit. If an individual is the plaintiff, it is a tort or a contract action.

Torts are breaches of duty. There are duties placed on each and every one of us by society. We have a legal duty not to cause personal injury, property damage, or damage to another individual's reputation. A tort is distinguished from a breach of contract in that the duty owed on a tort is involuntary and defined by law whereas the duty owed under a contract is voluntary and defined by the parties entering into the agreement.

Breach of contract, tort, and criminal liability could all stem from the same fact pattern. For example, a used car is purchased under contract from a used-car dealer. Several months after the car is purchased, the police seize the automobile, claiming that the vehicle indentification numbers are not correct and were taken from another vehicle. There are three courses of action available to the buyer. One is to swear out a complaint against the used-car dealer according to criminal procedure. This would begin a criminal action as discussed in Chapter 2. The second is to sue the used-car salesperson for breach of the contractual warranty of title (see Chapter 5). Third, a suit can be brought in a tort action for fraud and misrepresentation. Any of the remedies available may be selected. The contract and tort claims could be tried in a single action in the same civil court. The criminal action would have to be tried separately.

No matter which type of tort has been perpetrated and no matter how great the injury or damage, there can be no recovery unless certain facts are established. The preponderance of the evidence must favor the plaintiff. This proposition is exemplified conceptually by the blindfolded woman holding the scales of justice. "A preponderance of the evidence" means that the plaintiff must put at least enough evidence on the scale to move the scales slightly in his or her favor. The burden of proof in a civil case is distinguished from a criminal case, in which the evidence must prove guilt beyond a reasonable doubt. Proof beyond a reasonable doubt requires a severe imbalance in those scales.

There are three categories of torts. The first category includes negligence or acts that result from negligence. The second category consists of the intentional torts such as assault and battery, false imprisonment, malicious prosecution, defamation of character, libel, and slander. The third category is strict liability, consisting of statutory torts in which negligence or intention is not necessary.

NEGLIGENCE

In order to prove negligence, the plaintiff must prove that the defendant did something wrong or failed to do something the law required him or her to do for the protection of the public or the plaintiff. This is called either active or passive negligence. The standards that are used to determine whether an individual acted improperly are the standards of conduct that a reasonable person would use under the same circumstances. This is referred to as the "reasonable man" doctrine. In the absence of negligence, the courts will dismiss the case.

The civil courts in the United States are crowded with cases brought by individuals as a result of the negligent actions of others. It is likely that an individual will at some time be directly or indirectly involved in an automobile accident. This involvement might be as a result of either the individual's own negligence or the negligence of somebody else. No matter how great the damage sustained in an accident, there can be no civil court recovery unless the plaintiff can prove that the defendant was negligent.

Proximate Cause—Contributory Negligence

In addition to negligence, the plaintiff must show that the damage or injury resulted from the defendant's activities or actions. This is called proximate cause. In the absence of negligence, proximate cause, and injury (damages), the plaintiff will not be able to succeed in his or her action. If the plaintiff has been contributorially negligent (meaning that the plaintiff is wholly or partially at fault because the plaintiff did not use reasonable care in the exercise of his or her legal duty either for his or her own protection or for the protection of someone else), the plaintiff will not be able to succeed in litigation. For example, in the case of Cierpisz v. Singleton, 230 A.2d 629 (Md. 1967), an action was brought by a passenger to recover damages against the driver for injuries sustained in a vehicular accident. The court instructed the jury that if they found the passenger failed to use an available seat belt and found that her injuries were due to this failure, she could not recover damages.

As of 1981, 32 states have changed the all-or-nothing rule with respect to contributory negligence. These jurisdictions are called comparative negligence states. In these jurisdictions, plaintiffs who are contributorially negligent may recover from parties who were negligent. The amount of recovery will be proportionately reduced according to the amount of damages the jury or the judge determines was the fault of the plaintiff's own negligence. For example, if the plaintiff is hit by the defendant in a head-on auto collision in the plaintiff's lane, the fact that the plaintiff's injuries might have been aggravated by the plaintiff's excessive speed or failure to wear a seat belt will reduce the plaintiff's recovery. The trier of fact will have to decide how much of the plaintiff's injury was due to his or her own negligence.

Burden of Proof

The burden of proof in any civil litigation, with few exceptions, will rest on the plaintiff. This means that it is up to the party claiming negligence to come forward in a court of law with the proof. If the plaintiff fails to introduce this evidence, the court can dismiss the plaintiff's claim. In most accident cases, the question involved is one of facts and circumstances. A person is expected to act in a manner consistent with the behavior of a reasonable person under similar circumstances. An individual is expected to ''know the qualities and habits of human beings and animals and the qualities, characteristics, and capacities of things and forces in so far as they are matters of common knowledge at the time and in the community'' (restatement of Torts Second §290). Failure to act in a reasonable manner is considered negligence. An individual is required to know whether or not his or her automobile is mechanically sound as well as the fact that a worn tire could cause an accident. In addition, every individual is presumed to know the law, both legislative enactments and common law.

We will elaborate on the elements of negligence by discussing automobile accidents, accidents on public streets, and accidents in buildings. Each of these areas will indicate the standard of care an individual is required to give as well as the legal duty that an individual owes.

Automobile Negligence

Automobile negligence can be broken down into three categories: the negligence of the owner, the negligence of the driver, and the negligence of the passenger.

Like any other driver, the owner of an automobile is responsible for his or her negligence while driving. The owner is also liable for maintenance of the automobile. In the event that the automobile is not mechanically sound and an accident results from the mechanical failure, the owner could be held liable. Suppose that you lend your vehicle to a friend, and the vehicle has bald tires. If your friend is involved in an automobile accident because bald tires caused the car to skid, you, the owner, could be held liable for damages arising from the accident. There may be circumstances under which the owner of a vehicle will be liable either by statute or under common law for damages arising out of an accident in which he or she is not negligent (e.g., master-servant rules, strict liability statutes).

Drivers of automobiles are liable for their negligent acts. The driver must operate the automobile using reasonable prudence. There are certain factual scenarios that give rise to prima facie liability against the driver. These include cases in which a driver is speeding or loses control of the automobile owing to distractions, fright, or sickness. If a driver leaves the vehicle improperly parked on a hill and it careens down the hill causing an accident or if a driver hits the rear of another vehicle or ignores restrictions on his or her driving license (such as wearing glasses), the driver will also be subject to prima facie liability. A prima facie case arises when the facts proved by the plaintiff will be sufficient to hold the defendant liable unless contradicted and overcome by evidence submitted by the defendant.

Last Clear Chance. Drivers may also be liable under the doctrine of ''last clear chance'' if they could have avoided an accident despite the fact that the victim created the danger. This proposition requires the jury to decide who had the last clear chance to avoid the accident. In the landmark case in England (Davies v. Mann, 152 Eng. Rep. 588, Ex. 1842), the plaintiff left an ass tied on the highway, and the defendant hit the ass with a vehicle. The defendant was found to be liable even though the plaintiff was negligent in leaving his ass on the highway because the jury determined that the defendant could have avoided hitting the ass.

There are five requirements for an individual to be held liable under the "last clear chance" doctrine. These requirements are as follows: (1) The plaintiff was negligent. (2) As a result of the plaintiff's negligence, the plaintiff is in a position of danger from which he or she cannot possibly escape. (3) The defendant is aware of the plaintiff's dangerous position. (4) The defendant has a clear chance to avoid injury by exercising ordinary care but fails to do so. (5) The plaintiff is injured. If all of these elements are present in an accident, the doctrine of "last clear chance" applies, and the defendant will be liable.

Comparative Negligence   Some states have done away with the last clear chance doctrine. These states apply the doctrine of comparative negligence. This doctrine allows a jury to weigh the actions of both the plaintiff and the defendant and to determine what portion of an accident has been caused by the negligence of each. For example, the plaintiff was driving an automobile on the wrong side of the road. The defendant was driving a truck without clearance lights. The court found both parties negligent (even though the defendant's negligence was slight) and held that the jury should determine what percentage of the responsibility for the accident should rest with the defendant truck driver (McGuiggan v. Hiller Bros., 245 N.W. 97 [Wis. 1932]).

Assumption of Risk   Since a passenger is not in control of an automobile, there is ordinarily no question with regard to negligence or contributory negligence on behalf of the passenger. Because of this fact, a passenger in a two-car collision may sue both drivers. In a situation where the passenger decides to sue both drivers, each may be found liable for a portion of the passenger's injuries. If a passenger gets into an automobile knowing that the vehicle is defective (brakes, lights, tires, and so on), or that the driver is intoxicated or where the passenger condones the driver's excessive speed, the passenger may be unable to recover from the driver. This is termed assumption of risk. The assumption can be either expressed or implied and will prevail in most situations. Some courts find it against public policy to allow a driver of a vehicle to remain without liability and award damages to a passenger notwithstanding the latter's assumption of risk.

A passenger might fail to collect fully for injuries sustained by the driver's negligence if the passenger failed to make use of seat belts and the jury determines that because of this the passenger did not exercise reasonable care in the avoidance or mitigation of his or her injuries. In an action brought by the passenger to recover for those injuries, the courts may deny recovery for damages that would not have occurred if a seat belt had been worn.

A pedestrian who is involved in an automobile accident may be able to shift the burden of proof to the driver with respect to the driver's negligence. When pedestrians are hit by an automobile, they need only prove that they were hit by the car, and the defendant must then prove lack of negligence. This is contrary to normal procedure in civil litigation where the plaintiff must prove the case by a preponderance of the evidence. If a pedestrian is negligent (crossing against traffic lights, jaywalking, or entering the street from between or behind parked automobiles), the burden of proof will not shift to the defendant, and the plaintiff will have to prove that the defendant was negligent.

Role of the Spectator It is important to understand the circumstances under which you could be held liable for negligence. It is also important to be aware of what you should do if involved in an automobile accident, either as the cause, as a victim, or as a witness. The first thing to do is to attend to all persons who may be injured or who are in danger of becoming injured. One should never move a seriously injured person unless that person is in a position of danger. Some states have "good Samaritan" laws that would relieve doctors and nurses, as well as rescue squad volunteers with emergency medical qualifications, from being held liable while moving an injured person. For example, New York has a statute that provides that if a licensed physician or surgeon voluntarily aids an injured person without expectation of compensation at the scene of the accident, such a doctor will not be liable for damages resulting by reason of his or her act or omission in providing first aid unless grossly negligent. Unless the state where the accident occurs has a "good Samaritan" law, any individuals who move an injured person at the scene of an accident could be held liable if they have worsened the position of the injured person.

The next thing to do is call the police. If anyone has been injured, an ambulance should be summoned. Do not move the automobiles involved in the accident until the police arrive. It is important that the police observe the exact scene of the accident in order to make a determination and report as to the liability of the parties. Photographs of the automobiles and the accident scene might be helpful at a later point in proving liability.

Role of the Driver Drivers involved in automobile accidents should immediately exchange the following information. (1) Names and addresses of drivers and owners of automobiles, drivers' license numbers, the type and make of the automobiles, and the names of insurance companies should be given. (2) All witnesses including police, should be interviewed to obtain their names, addresses, and telephone numbers for future reference. (3) The time and place of the accident should be noted as well as the weather and road conditions. Although all this information may be included in police reports, it is a good idea to duplicate the information because police reports must be gotten from the police agency and could be lost or inaccurate. Some witnesses may not be willing or able to wait for a police interview, and thus your notes may be the only record. Most states have requirements with respect to notification of insurance companies and motor vehicle bureaus or police departments. All states require reports of accidents involving injury, death, or property damage in excess of specified amounts (usually $50 to $500). These reports must be filed fairly soon after the accident. Some states require immediate notification; most require filing within 5 to 15 days.

Insurance   Automobile insurance usually is obtainable for such perils as bodily injury, property damage, collision, and uninsured or underinsured motorists. Some states have "no fault" insurance (Arkansas, Colorado, Connecticut, Delaware, Florida, Georgia, Hawaii, Kansas, Maryland, Massachusetts, Michigan, Minnesota, Nevada, New Jersey, New York, North Dakota, Oregon, Pennsylvania, South Carolina, South Dakota, Texas, Utah, and Virginia). Although each state's "no fault" insurance has different provisions and different requirements, no fault auto insurance limits (but does not eliminate) the right of individuals involved in an automobile accident to bring a personal injury action for damages. The objectives of no fault insurance are to make sure that every injured person is eligible for insurance payments regardless of fault. Usually, the injured person's insurance company is the company that will pay the claim for medical expenses or lost earnings.

Accidents on Public Streets

Negligence is a breach of a duty that the wrongdoer owes to the plaintiff. The same rules that apply to negligence and liability in an automobile accident also apply to accidents on a public street. These rules include the doctrine of last clear chance, assumption of risk, comparative negligence, contributory negligence, and such. A pedestrian has the right to assume that a thoroughfare is free and unobstructed. Pedestrians may be considered contributorially negligent if they fail to observe the condition of the thoroughfare.

It is up to the owner of a street to maintain it in a reasonably safe condition. Failure to do so will render an owner liable to pedestrians or drivers who are injured owing to the condition of the street. In some jurisdictions, the individuals who own houses also own the street in front of their home. In other jurisdictions, the streets belong to the municipality. If an individual destroys, defaces, or obstructs a public street, that individual will be liable for the resulting damage.

A municipality is subject to the same general rules of negligence as a private owner. (However, the statutes of limitations with respect to negligence actions brought against municipalities are usually very short; e.g., New York State requires one to file a notice of action within 90 days.) Some municipalities require that notice of defective condition must have been given to the municipality and that it must have had an opportunity to repair the defect before it can be held liable. This notice could be either actual or constructive. For example, if the municipality inspectors or a private citizen has reported damage or if an individual has reported an accident because of a damaged roadway, there would be actual notice. Constructive notice occurs after a sufficient amount of time if the roadways or walkways are used by municipal employees even though a formal report is not filed. Under the doctrine of constructive notice, the law will hold the municipality liable as if actual notice were given.

Accidents in Buildings and Stores

An owner of a building owes a duty to all individuals to exercise a standard of care in maintaining the building that a reasonably prudent person in a similar situation would exercise. Reasonable care is based on foresight, not on hindsight. The mere fact that an accident occurs on a person's premises does not create a cause of action. If you are involved in an accident in a building or store, check whether the owner used reasonable care in complying with the building maintenance and health codes that exist in the state or municipality in which the building or store is located.

The owner of a building does not completely insure the safety of all persons entering the building. The duty of care that the owner owes depends on the status of the injured party, that is, invitee, licensee, or trespasser. Traditionally, an owner of a building owes invitees (those whose presence is desired) a duty to exercise reasonable care for their safety while they are on the premises. In most jurisdictions, a mere licensee (one whose presence is merely tolerated) is entitled to a lesser degree of care. The distinction between an invitee and a licensee is that a licensee is there for his or her own purposes whereas an invitee is there at the request of the property owner and for the benefit of the property owner. For example, an employee who returned after work to his employer's building to obtain forgotten items of personal property was held to be a licensee at that time (Grassmann v. Fromm, 56 N.E.2d 114 [N.Y. 1944]).

A property owner owes the least degree of care to a trespasser (one who enters onto or remains on another's property without legal right). Individuals who enter a building as invitees or licensees may change their status to that of trespassers by leaving the part of the premises into which they have been expressly permitted. For example, if you go into a department store and decide to wander around in the area marked ''Employees Only,'' you have changed your status from that of invitee to trespasser. The department store owner would owe you a lesser degree of care in the maintenance of the inventory room than he or she would in the maintenance of the store itself. The owner of a building owes no greater duty to trespassers than to avoid injuring them by willful, wanton, or intentional conduct or by maintaining a trap or pitfall on the premises. Some courts in this country have disregarded the traditional distinctions between invitee and licensee and have substituted the broad test of reasonable care under the circumstances.

Anyone involved in an accident in a building or store should check to see whether the owner used reasonable care in maintaining the building. Local health or building codes may be useful in determining the duty of care that store owners owe the public.

Accidents in Private Dwellings

In cases of injury occurring in private dwellings (as in public buildings), the liability of the owner depends on the status of the person injured. A social guest will generally be considered a licensee, and the host would be responsible only for actions of affirmative negligence or injuries caused by reckless, wanton, or willful misconduct. Some states provide that the duty owed to a social guest is greater than that owed to a licensee. The duty owed to an invitee is that of ordinary care to keep the premises in substantially safe condition. The requirements vary with the circumstances of each case.

A homeowner has a duty to warn invitees and licensees of dangerous conditions of which they are not aware. For example, a guest was judged entitled to recover for injury resulting from colliding with a sliding glass door because his host failed to warn him of the danger involved (Simon v. Rizek, 296 F. Supp. 602 [D. Okla. 1969]).

The rules with respect to invitees and licensees extend to the outside of the premises. A homeowner has a duty in eliminating or guarding against hazards in the front yard and in walkways that may imperil an invitee. For example, an owner of the premises is responsible for maintaining his or her lawn in reasonably good condition. The owner will not be liable for small holes in the lawn in which invitees might hurt themselves if the owner does not have notice of such a defect. The owner will be free from liability as to licensees and trespassers if those individuals are hurt by obstructions or depressions in the front yard or lawn if the owner maintains suitable approaches to his or her house that do not require guests to walk on the lawn. If guests customarily do walk across the lawn, the owner may be liable for injuries caused by not filling in depressions or leaving obstructions on the lawn (Hackney v. Klintworth, 153 N.W.2d 852 [Neb. 1967]).

An owner of private premises is not generally liable to adults who drown or are injured in natural or artificial bodies of water maintained on his or her land provided that these bodies of water are free from concealed dangers or hidden traps. A partially filled swimming pool may be considered a trap and may give rise to liability (Reynolds v. Willson, 331 P.2d 48 [Cal. 1958]). The owner of the swimming pool or body of water has no duty to ascertain whether or not a child wishing to use such a pool can swim before admitting the child to the pool. In Mullen v. Russworm, 90 S.W.2d 530 (Tenn. 1936), the court stated '' . . . that if the owner of a swimming pool was to be held negligent an ordinary city boy could never learn to swim.'' Owners may be held negligent if they failed to place a guardrail along a sidewalk provided for the use of invitees where that sidewalk runs alongside a pond or a pool.

Some states apply the attractive nuisance doctrine to swimming pools. An owner who maintains a condition (swimming pool) on his premises that is dangerous or can be reasonably expected to attract children owes a duty to exercise reasonable care to protect them against the dangers of the attraction.

In some states there are zoning ordinances that require that swimming pools be fenced. An owner of a pool who does not comply with the ordinance can be held liable for negligence. To determine the possible liability resulting from death or injury in their swimming pools property owners must review the case law and zoning ordinances in their localities.

OTHER TORTS

Intentional Torts

Intentional torts include assault, battery, trespass, false imprisonment, and conversion. An intentional tort is a wrong committed by one individual against another or his or her property resulting from an intentional act. There need be no hostility or desire to do harm for a tort to be intentional, only the desire to accomplish a particular action.

Assault and Battery   Assault and battery are related torts that may also be crimes (although under different names). A person is entitled to be free from fear of a harmful or offensive contact. Interference with this freedom is an assault. Actual contact is not necessary. There is no such thing as negligent assault. In order for an individual to be held liable for assault, that individual must have intended the act that interfered with the plaintiff. Battery is the actual physical contact and is contrasted with assault, which is merely causing an individual to be placed in fear of physical harm.

False Imprisonment or False Arrest   False imprisonment or false arrest occurs when one individual restrains another individual. There must be no way of escape left for the plaintiff. If there is a means of escape left open that is not an unreasonable means, then there is no false imprisonment (Davis & Allcott Co. v. Boozer, 110 So. 28 [Ala. 1926]). The imprisonment need not be for any length of time, and there is no necessity that damage result. Therefore, a brief detainment of the plaintiff will be sufficient for an action of false imprisonment. Preventing individuals from doing something they have a legal right to do is false imprisonment (Amos v. Prom, Inc., 115 F. Supp. 127 [D. Iowa 1953]).

Trespass   Another intentional tort is trespass. It entails the unauthorized entry upon another's property. There does not have to be intent to violate another's property rights. The intent is setting foot on the property. In cases of trespass, the cause of action accrues when the invasion occurs (National Copper Co. v. Minnesota Mining Co., 23 N.W. 781 [Minn. 1885]). For an individual to bring an action for trespass, that individual must have exclusive possession of the property. Trespass may also be committed by an individual remaining on another individual's property after the former's right to do so has terminated.

Conversion   The unjustified acquisition or possession of another's personal property without permission is called conversion. Included in the area of conversion is the removal of a chattel from its location or the transfer of its possession to an innocent third party. Failure to deliver property to the rightful owner also qualifies as conversion. Destruction, alteration, and use of an individual's property without authorization are all acts of conversion.

There are some torts that may be committed either negligently or intentionally. These include nuisance, deceit, defamation, and so on.

Nuisance   Nuisance is a tort that entails an invasion, by the defendant, of the plaintiff's interest in property. Nuisance may result from the defendant's malicious desire to do harm to the plaintiff or his or her negligent conduct (Miles v. A. Arena & Co., 73 P.2d 1260 [Cal. 1937]). A nuisance can be either private (affecting one individual) or public (affecting the general public). Private nuisance has been found to include disturbance of the use of an individual's property by unpleasant odors, loud noises, smoke, excessive light, and the like. Public nuisance includes interference with public health, safety, and morals as well as the public peace and comfort.

Deceit   Deceit is a tort that can be classified as intentional (fraud) or negligent (misrepresentation). Fraud is a false representation where the defendant *knowingly* misleads the plaintiff. Misrepresentation is a representation that is false, but the defendant honestly believes it to be true. It is an actionable tort because the defendant did not exercise reasonable care in ascertaining the facts. In order to hold the defendant liable for deceit, the plaintiff must have relied on the facts represented by the defendant, and such reliance must have been reasonable and justifiable. In addition, the plaintiff must have suffered damages. In the case of fraud, the misrepresentation must be coupled with an intent to mislead and damages are also necessary.

Defamation   Defamation is composed of libel and slander. A statement that holds the plaintiff up to hatred, contempt, or ridicule or causes him or her to be shunned or avoided is considered to be defamation (Kimmerly v. New York Evening Journal, 186 N.E. 217 [N.Y. 1933]). When statements cause the reputation of an individual to be diminished and those statements are in writing, the tort is called libel. When statements are oral, it is called slander. In order to have defamation, communication to a third party is essential. Words of abuse indicating that the defendant dislikes the plaintiff are in and of themselves not actionable as defamation. Defamation requires specific charges against an individual. In the event the statements made are proved to be true, there is no defamation.

Strict Liability

Strict liability is another category of tort. Under strict liability a defendant can be held liable for wrongs committed even when the defendant is "without fault." There is no necessity to prove either intent or negligence for torts that are included in the category of strict liability. Strict liability arises from conduct that is legal but that causes damages. For example, as a general rule, keeping cows, horses, chickens, and the like in a rural area is not illegal. Owners of those animals will be held strictly liable for damages caused by the animals' trespassing (McKee v. Trisler, 143 N.E. 69 [Ill. 1924]; Pegg v. Gray 82 S.E.2d 757 [N.C. 1954]). Domesticated dogs and cats are not included under this doctrine unless an animal has a propensity to do wrong (Perkins v. Drury, 258 P.2d 379 [N.M. 1953]).

Another area in which strict liability will be imposed is one in which a defendant damages another individual by doing something that is not illegal but that is normally dangerous and inappropriate in light of the character of the surroundings in which it is done (Euclid v. Amber Reality Company, 272 U.S. 365 [S. Ct. 1926]). Use of a "dangerous instrumentality"—such as explosives, flammable liquids, dangerous chemicals, dust and noxious gases—which causes injury to a third party will usually subject the user to liability under the doctrine of strict liability.

Strict liability has been expanded by state and federal statutes. When a dangerous situation such as a fire set during the dry season exists (Seckerson v. Sinclair, 140 N.W. 239 [N.D. 1913]), state statutes have made the individual responsible for the fire strictly liable for the consequences. Strict liability also applies to certain products.

In the landmark case, MacPherson v. Buick Motor Co., 217 N.Y. 382 (N.Y. 1916), the defendant sold an automobile to a retail dealer, who resold the auto to the plaintiff. While the plaintiff was driving the automobile, a defective wood spoke crumbled, and the vehicle suddenly collapsed. The wheel incorporating the wood spoke was bought from another company. There was no claim by the plaintiff that the defendant knew of the defective spoke and willfully concealed it. The court found that Buick could have found the defects by a reasonable inspection that did not take place.

In cases where strict liability is applicable, the defendant acts "at his peril" (Exner v. Sherman Power Construction Company, 54 F.2d 510 [2d Cir. 1931]). The defendant becomes an insurer against the consequences of his or her conduct even though he or she has taken every possible precaution to prevent harm and is not at fault.

CIVIL LITIGATION

Is Litigation Warranted?

Not every tort leads to litigation. First you should seek a voluntary settlement. If this fails, then you can decide whether or not to litigate. In making this decision, you need to know whether there is substantive law that protects you, what remedies are available, and what the costs involved will be. The substantive law was discussed in the first section of this chapter; remedies and costs are discussed here.

There are three forms of remedies the law recognizes: monetary damages, injunctive relief, and specific performance. Monetary damages are the most prevalent form of civil remedy available. These damages are given not only for specific amounts of money you may have lost as the result of a wrong that has been committed, but also for pain and suffering, loss of wages, punitive damages, and so on. In a suit for monetary damages, either party has the right to trial by jury.

The second remedy that may be available to you in a civil suit is an injunction. An injunction is an order by the court prohibiting the defendant from doing something or commanding the defendant to do something. In an action for injunction, no right to jury trial exists. For example, where an individual had a right of way to cross a specific piece of property and another individual (without legal proceedings and with knowledge that the road is used as a right of way) forcibly closed it, the first party was entitled to a mandatory injunction requiring removal of the barricade (Deisenroth v. Dodge, 111 N.E.2d 575 [Ill. 1953]).

The third form of remedy is specific performance. The court orders the defendant to do a specific act. This remedy is available only in contract actions. The remedy is usually not available unless the particular item that you are suing for is unusual. As an example, Mr. Jones has a contract with Mr. Smith to purchase his house. Mr. Smith refuses to perform according to the agreement. Mr. Jones may bring an action for specific performance, asking the court to direct Mr. Smith to execute a deed according to his agreement. If the contract was one for 500 dozen eggs, Mr. Jones would only be able to sue for monetary damages, that is, the difference between the contract and the cost to replace the eggs. The distinction between the two is that in the first instance the land is a unique parcel, and therefore specific performance would be allowed whereas in the second instance it is possible to purchase eggs from many different suppliers, and therefore monetary damages would be the appropriate remedy. Specific performance would also be a remedy in purchases of rare antiques or any other unique or unusual item. In an action for specific performance, there is no right to jury trial.

Once you have determined the type of remedy that may be available to you, you must review the costs involved in litigation. There are two areas of costs. The first includes witness fees, filing fees, court costs, process-serving fees, and various disbursements.

The second area is attorney's fees. There are several common methods by which an attorney is compensated. The fixed fee (whether you win or lose) and the contingent fee (the attorney is compensated only if there is a recovery) are the two most common. Contingency fees run anywhere from an amount equal to 10 percent to one third of your recovery or more (see Exhibit 3–1). It is possible to combine the two methods resulting in a retainer coupled with a contingency agreement. Another method of compensation is the hourly rate. These rates vary from attorney to attorney and can range from nominal amounts to hundreds of dollars per hour. The fixed hourly rate is utilized in complicated cases where many hours of research and litigation are necessary.

Many states have statutory regulations with respect to amounts of fees that can be charged in a civil action. It is advisable to check with the local bar association or the court or county clerk in the jurisdiction in which you litigate to determine if there are any statutory limits to fees. If limits exist, an attorney would have to get permission from the court to charge more. In determining the amount of financial

EXHIBIT 3-1
Contingent Fee Agreement and Retainer

  Client employs attorney to render all necessary legal services in the _____ Court of _____, State of _____, in defending an action now pending in the court entitled "_____ v. _____." For services rendered, client agrees to pay attorney the sum of _____ dollars ($_____) cash as a retainer fee and an additional sum of _____ dollars ($_____), contingent on the successful defense of the action. If the action results in a judgment for plaintiff and against defendant in a sum less than _____ dollars ($_____), it will constitute a successful defense, but in such event, the amount of the contingent fee shall be reduced at the rate of _____ dollars ($_____) for every _____ dollars ($_____), or major fraction thereof, by which the amount of the judgment is so reduced.

  If the action terminates in a settlement out of court without trial, the amount of additional compensation to attorney shall be _____ percent (___%) of what it would have been under this contract had judgment been rendered against defendant in the amount settled for.

  In case of an appeal, client shall pay attorney _____ dollars ($_____) for services rendered on such appeal.

---

gain that can be expected from litigation, an individual must decide the dollar value of the judgment and subtract from that estimated recovery the attorney's fees and court costs. The plaintiff's time spent and wages lost should also be considered.

  Now that the amount of possible future financial gain has been determined, the decision as to whether or not the lawsuit is worth pursuing is easier to make. A lawsuit is usually a last resort. An attorney and client should attempt to settle out of court. In considering whether or not a settlement is possible, the defendant should be examined to see if he or she can afford the amount of damages that may be warranted. Many individuals have insurance policies such as homeowners or business insurance that will provide coverage for monetary damages resulting from commission of a tort by the defendant. Some defendants have the financial assets available to compensate you even if they are uninsured.

  The client should be aware of the time costs involved in litigation as well as the probability of a successful suit. There are many calendar delays and procedural tactics that can be used in order to procrastinate. There are defenses that may be spurious or factual that can cause the outcome of the case to change from what the plaintiff may expect. A simple lawsuit could take from 5 to 10 hours of an attorney's time. At $50 per hour, a plaintiff could anticipate total fees of from $250 to $500. All of these items should be weighed in determining a reasonable settlement.

Civil Law Suit Procedure

Pretrial A lawsuit is a request of the court to determine the rights and obligations of two or more parties (Exhibit 3-2). The lawsuit may be commenced by serving a summons (Exhibit 3-3) upon the defendant. The summons serves to notify the de-

EXHIBIT 3-2
Civil Trial Procedure

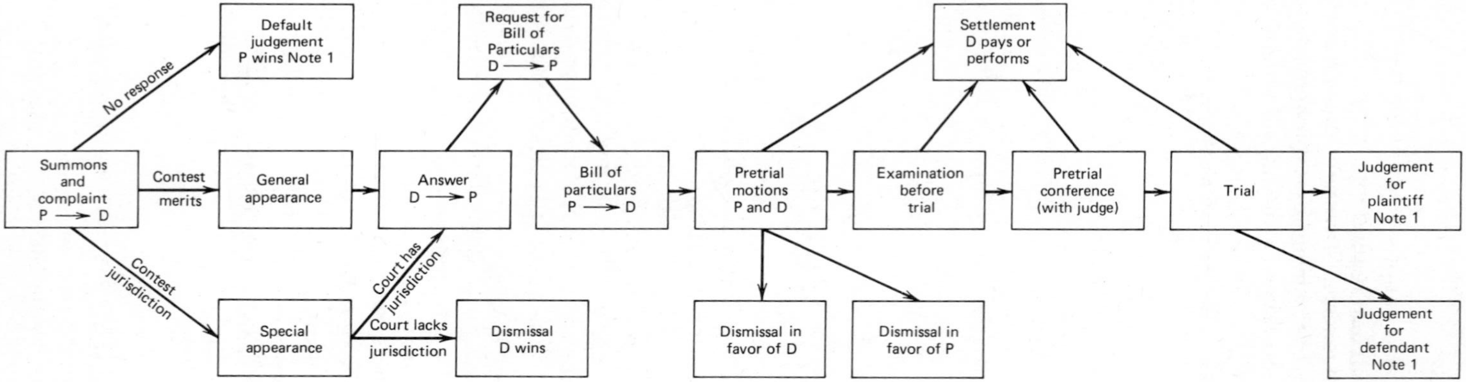

fendant of the suit. The typical summons contains the name of the court, the names of the parties (both the plaintiff and defendant), as well as the name and address of the plaintiff's attorney. There is also a statement that indicates the amount of time the defendant has to answer. In the event that the defendant fails to appear or answer, a default judgment can be taken. A default judgment is a declaration that the plaintiff is the winner. The time that is allowed for a defendant to respond is different from state to state. Federal rules, as well as those of some states, allow 20 days as the maximum.

Before a summons can be issued against the defendant, a determination must be made as to whether or not the particular court that is being used has jurisdiction over the defendant. In many cases, both the plaintiff and defendant live or do business in the same county where the lawsuit arises. This will enable the plaintiff to bring an action in his or her local court and serve the defendant locally. In cases

EXHIBIT 3-3
Summons

State of _____   Court, County of _____

                                                              Plaintiff

    -against-

                                                              Defendant
_____

The People of the State of _____ to _____ (name of defendant), greeting:
    You are hereby directed and required to _____
(serve on plaintiff's attorney or file with the clerk of this court) a written responsive pleading to the complaint in this action, a copy of which is annexed hereto and served on you, within _____ days after personal service of the summons and complaint on you within the State of _____ or within _____ days after service is complete if summons and complaint are not personally delivered to you within the State of _____.
    You are notified that unless you _____
(serve or file a written responsive pleading within the above-specified time), plaintiff will take judgment against you by default for the relief demanded in said complaint.
    The basis of the above-designated venue is _____
(specify, such as: plaintiff's residence at _____
[street address] in the City of _____, County of _____,
State of _____).
Dated _____, 19____.
                      or, if required by statute
    Given under my hand and seal of the _____ Court, County of _____, State of _____, this _____ day of _____, 19____.
(seal, if required)

                                                              (Signature)

where the defendant lives in another county or state, the plaintiff may sue the defendant in the defendant's home state. There are certain situations in which a plaintiff could bring the action in the plaintiff's state. For example, if the amount of money in the lawsuit is $10,000 or greater and the defendant lives in a separate state from the plaintiff, the federal district court may be the appropriate place to proceed.

A summons is usually issued by the court clerk at the request of either the plaintiff or the plaintiff's attorney. This is true in both the federal courts and in many of the state courts. Service is effected by a federal or state marshal or other designated person. Some states allow the plaintiff's attorney to issue a summons without going through either the courts or the court clerk. In these jurisdictions anyone over the age of majority who is not a party to the action can serve the summons.

The usual way that a summons is served is through the personal delivery of the summons on the defendant (see Affidavit of Personal Service, Exhibit 3–4). There are also alternative methods of service that may be allowed. These include serving the defendant at his or her home by giving the summons to a person of suitable age and discretion who is found to reside at the home. If you refuse to accept a summons and the process server leaves it on the premises, you have been effectively served (Neilsen v. Braland, 119 N.W.2d 737 [Minn. 1963]). Some states allow service to be effected by mail. Defendants who are in the military service are afforded special treatment since their primary obligation is to the United States, and they may not be able to be present at a trial if called to duty. Once a summons has been served, all future papers in the action may be served by mail on either the defendant or the defendant's attorney in cases where an attorney is designated.

In addition to serving the summons, a complaint is also sent to the defendant either with the summons or shortly thereafter. The complaint sets forth the substance of the plaintiff's grievance. A typical complaint is shown in Exhibit 3–5. It contains a number of allegations and starts off with the plaintiff's basis for jurisdiction over the defendant. The complaint concludes with what is known as a prayer for relief. This statement may be a request for monetary damages, specific performance, injunctive relief, or any additional or alternative relief that might be justified.

Once the defendant has been served, he or she has several alternatives. The defendant may ignore the summons, in which case there is a default, and the plaintiff can enter a default judgment. In the case where the plaintiff claims a definite sum or a sum that can be made definite by mere computation, all that is necessary is for the plaintiff to deliver the default judgment to the county clerk. In a case where the amount of money cannot be determined as a certain amount, the plaintiff must apply for a judgment to the judge of the court.

The second alternative that the defendant has is to appear in the action. An appearance requires a formal notice to the court and the plaintiff that the defendant will be represented by an attorney or *pro se* (by himself). There are two types of appearances: a general appearance and a special appearance. The special appearance is notification that the defendant's counsel will appear to argue that the court lacks

EXHIBIT 3-4
Affidavit of Personal Service of Summons

State of _____   Court, County of _____

                                                          Plaintiff

                              -against-

                                                          Defendant

_____

                    Affidavit of Personal Service of Summons

State of New York:
                    ss.:
County of   :   _____

being duly sworn, deposes and says that he served the summons in the above-entitled
action upon the following named defendant at the following place and time, viz:

NAME   STREET, CITY, AND STATE   TIME AND DATE

by delivering to and leaving with defendant, personally, a true copy thereof, and deponent
further says that he knew the person so served to be the same person mentioned and
described in the said summons as defendant therein and that, at the times of making such
service, deponent was over eighteen years of age and not a party to this action. That he
asked defendant whether defendant was in the military service of the United States
government, in any capacity whatever, and defendant replied he was not. Defendant was
clad in ordinary civilian clothes and wore no military uniform of any kind.

Deponent further states that he describes the person actually served as follows:

Sex	Skin Color	Hair Color	Age (approx.)	Height (approx.)	Weight (approx.)
( ) Male	( ) Black	( ) Light	( )	( )	( )
( ) Female	( ) White	( ) Med.			
	( )	( ) Dark			
		( )			

Other Identifying Features:

                                        _____
                                        (Print Name below Signature)

Sworn to before me, this _____,
day of _____, 19____.

_____
Notary Public—Commissioner of Deeds

EXHIBIT 3-5
Complaint

STATE OF _____

_____ COURT : COUNTY OF _____

....

_____, an infant under the age of
fourteen (14) years by _____ and
_____ parents and natural guardians,

_____

Plaintiffs

vs

_____

_____

Defendants

....

COMPLAINT

Index No.

Plaintiffs by their attorney Steven Blumenkrantz, alleges:

1. Upon information and belief at all times hereinafter mentioned defendant, _____, is a New York State Corporation with offices at _____, New York.

2. Upon information and belief at all times hereinafter mentioned, the defendant, _____, was and still is the owner of a certain _____ automobile bearing New York State registration Number _____ for the year 19____.

3. At all times hereinafter mentioned, the infant plaintiff was a passenger in a _____ automobile owned and operated by her father, _____, bearing New York State registration Number _____ for the year 19____.

4. At all times hereinafter mentioned, State Route ____ in the County of _____ and State of New York was and still is a public highway commonly used by the residents of the County of _____ and others.

5. Upon information and belief, on or about the ____ day of _____, 19____, the Defendant, _____, loaned their said automobile to one _____ and

jurisdiction either substantive or personal (see Chapter 1 on courts regarding jurisdiction). A general appearance waives the defendant's right to object to the court's jurisdiction in the future and requires the defendant to argue the merits of the case (see Exhibit 3–6). Once an appearance has been made by the defendant's attorney the correspondence that takes place in the future is only between the two attorneys.

If an appearance is made before the plaintiff has served a complaint, the defendant's attorney in his or her appearance will request the complaint to be served. In a case where the complaint has already been served, the defendant's attorney will serve an answer. The answer can contain admissions, denials, affirmative defenses, or counterclaims with respect to the plaintiff's complaint (see Exhibit 3–7). A denial of a particular paragraph in the complaint creates an issue. If the plaintiff

EXHIBIT 3-5, cont.

gave to said person full permission to use the said automobile in any way or manner he saw fit and generally to exercise the right of ownership over said automobile.

6. Upon information and belief, on or about the ____ day of _____, 19____, at about ____ o'clock in the afternoon, the Defendant Corporation's automobile was being operated by Defendant _____ with the consent and permission of Defendant Corporation.

7. On the said ____ day of _____, 19____, Plaintiff's father was legally and lawfully operating his said automobile in a southerly direction on the said State Route ____ in a careful and prudent manner, when the said automobile of the Defendant Corporation operated by Defendant _____ with the consent and permission of Defendant Corporation, was being operated in a northerly direction on the said State Route ____. The said _____ so negligently and carelessly operated the said automobile of the Defendant Corporation that it struck and collided with the automobile of the Plaintiff's father, causing the injuries to the infant plaintiff hereinafter alleged.

8. The said accident and the injuries sustained by the infant plaintiff resulted solely and wholly from the negligence of the Defendant Corporation and of the person or persons operating said automobile with the Defendant's consent and permission and without any negligence on the part of the Plaintiffs contributing thereto.

9. The infant plaintiff suffered a "serious injury" within the meaning of Section 671, Subdivision 4, of the Insurance Law.

10. That as a result of said accident, the infant plaintiff received personal injuries, including pain and suffering, some of which are permanent and has been damaged in the amount of $_____.

WHEREFORE, Plaintiff _____, an infant, by _____ and _____, her parents and natural guardians, demand judgment against the Defendants _____ in the sum of $_____.

Steven Blumenkrantz
Attorney at Law

fails to prove the material allegation that the defendant denies, then it is likely that the plaintiff's case will be lost.

Even though the plaintiff proved all the facts normally necessary to support a judgment, an affirmative defense may deprive the plaintiff of the right to recover. A defendant must allege the affirmative defense in his or her answer in order to take advantage of the defense. In an action against a driver of an automobile by a pedestrian, if the pedestrian was negligent in walking across the street at a point other than the intersection, the defendant driver would have to allege the plaintiff's negligence in order to take advantage of the defense.

A counterclaim is an allegation of fact that the defendant might have asserted in a complaint of his or her own if a suit had been brought by the defendant in the first instance. The counterclaim can include demands for relief that are greater

EXHIBIT 3-6
Notice of General Appearance

STATE OF
COUNTY OF   COURT

                                            Plaintiff

        -against-

                                            Defendant

To _____, Attorney for plaintiff:
    You are hereby notified that the undersigned have been retained by and appear for _____, the defendant in the above-entitled action, and demand that copies of all papers subsequent to the summons and complaint be served upon us at our office at _____.
    Dated: _____, 19____.

                                               Attorneys for defendant

than, equal to, or less than the amount that is demanded in the complaint. It is possible that each party can succeed in his or her claim. Some states require strict separation of affirmative defenses and counterclaims. In the event that an individual pleads a counterclaim that should have been an affirmative defense, courts in these jurisdictions will deny recovery. Other jurisdictions, including federal courts, allow for flexibility in pleading.

    In addition to the answer that is submitted by the defendant, he or she may also demand, in some jurisdictions, a bill of particulars. A bill of particulars is a document that elaborates on the plaintiff's complaint, spelling out dates, times, places, and so on (see Exhibit 3–8).

    The issue has been joined when the summons and complaint and the answer have been served on the parties. After the issue is joined, there are various procedures that can be followed by either the plaintiff or the defendants. These procedures are initiated by motions. One motion that can be made by the defendant is a motion to strike the complaint or a portion of the complaint for vagueness and ambiguity. This motion can either be used as a delaying or harassment tactic or can in fact be used by the defendant when the complaint is vague or ambiguous (Al Tidmore v. Mills, 32 So.2d 769 [Ala. 1947]; Van Rogen v. Osborn, 309 P.2d 630 [Kan. 1957]).

    Another motion that can be used by the defendant is to dismiss for failure to allege a cause of action or for failure to state a claim upon which relief can be granted. In these motions the defendant is arguing that the plaintiff should not be allowed his or her day in court because even if all of the facts that the plaintiff al-

EXHIBIT 3-7
Answer

STATE OF NEW YORK
_____ COURT   COUNTY OF _____
. . . .

_____, an infant under the age of
fourteen (14) years by _____ and
_____, parents and natural guardians,
_____

                                                                    Plaintiffs,

        vs.

_____
_____

                                                                    Defendants.
. . . .

The defendants answering plaintiff's complaint herein, through
_____, their attorneys:

    1.   Admit the allegations contained in paragraphs numbered ''1,'' ''4,'' ''5,'' and
''6.''

    2.   Deny sufficient knowledge or information to form a belief as to the allegations
contained in paragraphs numbered ''3'' and ''9'' and therefore deny the same.

    3.   Deny the allegations contained in paragraphs numbered ''2,'' ''7,'' ''8,'' and
''10.''

                    AS AND FOR A SEPARATE AND AFFIRMATIVE
                    DEFENSE, THE DEFENDANTS ALLEGE:

    4.   On information and belief, the plaintiff's father's own culpable conduct and
negligence caused or contributed to the injuries and damages alleged to have been sustained
and, therefore, recovery should be denied or diminished by the extent of said culpability or
negligence.

    WHEREFORE, defendants demand judgment dismissing the plaintiff's complaint,
together with the costs and disbursements of this action; in the alternative, defendants
demand judgment against the plaintiff's father, for such sum of monies as may be recovered
against these defendants by the plaintiff, _____, an infant, under the age of
fourteen (14) years by _____ and _____, parents and natural guardians,
or in the alternative, in the event that there is a factual finding that the defendants and
plaintiff's father were responsible, that a further factual finding be made apportioning the
responsibility between the defendants and the plaintiff's father, and that the defendants
have judgment against the plaintiff's father, for a sum that represents the apportioned
percentage of responsibility of the plaintiff's father, together with the costs and
disbursements of this action.

                                            _____
                                            Attorneys for Defendants
                                            Office and P.O. Address

EXHIBIT 3-8
Bill of Particulars

STATE OF NEW YORK
_____ COURT : COUNTY OF _____
. . . .

_____, an infant under the age of
fourteen (14) years by _____ and
_____ parents and natural guardians,

_____
                                            Plaintiffs

         vs

_____

_____

                                    Defendants
. . . .

Plaintiffs by their attorney Steven Blumenkrantz, Esq. as and for their _____ Bill of
Particulars, respectfully set forth and allege as follows.

    1. The accident occurred on _____, 19____ at approximately ____ P.M.
about ____ miles North of the Village of _____, New York, on New York State
Route ____.

    2. The defendants and their agents, servants and/or employees were negligent in the
control, operation and management of its automobile, driving at speeds imprudent for
conditions, failure to use proper care to avoid an accident, failing to drive in the proper lane,
driving in a reckless and wanton manner and in other ways being negligent.

    3. Dates of birth:
        Father—_____, 19____;
        Mother—_____, 19____;
        Plaintiff—_____, 19____.

    4. Injuries suffered by infant plaintiff _____ include facial injuries, back of
head injuries, pelvic region injuries and emotional trauma. All injuries may leave permanent
damage. Infant plaintiff _____ has been treated by the following physicians:
        Dr. _____, Surgeon, _____ County General Hospital
        Dr. _____, Pediatrician, _____ Hospital, one time;
        Dr. _____, Ophthalmologist, one time;
        Dr. _____, two times;
        Dr. _____, Plastic Surgeon, one time.

    5. Infant plaintiff _____ was confined to _____ County General
Hospital from _____, 19____ until _____, 19____; she was confined to
bed at home for four days, and she was confined at home exclusive of bed confinement for
two days.

    6. Infant plaintiff _____ attended _____ Elementary School,
_____, New York. She was absent from school for six and one-half days by reason
of her injuries.

    7. Plaintiff suffered significant disfigurement.

Dated:

TO: _____,
    Attorneys for Defendants

_____

_____

STEVEN BLUMENKRANTZ
Attorney for Plaintiffs

_____

leges in his or her complaint are true, there is no basis in law to find in the plaintiff's favor (State v. Spencer, 29 A.2d 398 [N.J. 1942]). Under this type of a motion, the plaintiff is generally allowed time to amend his or her complaint. In the event that the motion is overruled, the defendant is not injured in any manner in proceeding with his or her own case.

An additional motion that can be made is for summary judgment. This motion is made by either party. It is granted only in the case where the court believes that there is no genuine or substantial issue of fact. The judge can dispose of the case with a ruling on the applicable law because the facts are clear and there is no reason to go to trial. (Fellheimer v. Wess, 45 N.E.2d 89 [Ill. 1942]).

Another preliminary proceeding that is used to facilitate the exchange of information prior to the trial is the examination before trial or pretrial examination, commonly called E.B.T. The courts favor out-of-court settlements rather than trials. E.B.T.'s encourage settlements by giving each party a chance to discuss what evidence the other party will use at the trial. In order to have an E.B.T., one must usually show that the particular information that is sought is material and necessary and cannot be readily obtained except by examination. An E.B.T. takes place at the request of either party and is an examination of the other or of both parties. It is not a court proceeding, but minutes are taken by a stenographer, and these can be used in the trial to attempt to discredit statements made at the trial. In addition to E.B.T.'s, physical examinations may also be required of the plaintiff in cases where physical injuries are being claimed. Physical examinations requested by the defendant are made by the defendant's doctor.

In cases where a suit is brought on contractual grounds, a party may use discovery proceedings to inspect and examine the defendant's books and papers in order to determine whether material in the possession of either party is relevant to the case.

Just prior to the trial, a pretrial conference is usually held. This conference includes a judge as well as the attorneys for the plaintiff and the defendant. The pretrial conference is used to simplify and eliminate issues, to obtain admissions of fact, to limit expert witnesses, to procure admissions that will avoid unnecessary proof, and so forth. Anything that is reasonable in expediting the case can be discussed at the pretrial conference, including waiving one's right to trial by jury. There is a great likelihood that a settlement can be made at a pretrial conference.

The Trial   After all preliminary proceedings and examinations have taken place, a case is placed on the court calendar as being ready for trial. Depending on the court congestion in the jurisdiction of litigation, it may take several weeks, months, or even years for the trial to commence after being marked ready.

Jury selection   A litigant can chose between a jury trial or a trial by judge or referee. The United States Constitution in the Seventh Amendment indicates that ''in suits at common law where the value in controversy shall exceed Twenty Dollars the right for trial by jury shall be preserved.'' Most state constitutions have a similar provision to allow trial by jury in civil matters. Federal as well as state rules provide that a litigant waives the right to jury trial unless a demand for jury trial is made. The trial procedure is similar in either a judge or jury trial.

As each juror is chosen from the jury list, the attorneys from both sides as well as the judge may question the jurors. This is called a voir dire examination. This examination is set up to determine whether a juror is qualified or not. Either attorney or the judge may excuse any juror who is not acceptable because he or she is prejudiced to the case or related to one of the parties or attorneys in the case. In addition, jurors can be excused if they have knowledge of the facts. These are termed challenges for cause, and if the judge feels the reason is adequate, the juror will be excused, and a new prospective juror will be selected from the panel. In addition to unlimited challenges for cause, each attorney has a limited number of preemptory challenges. This allows the attorney to excuse any juror without giving a reason.

In a trial by jury, the jury must determine the facts of the case. The judge has the duty of administering the oath to the jurors, running the proceeding with respect to the civil court rules on admission of evidence and so on and charging the jury (informing them of the law). In a trial without jury, the judge is also the trier of fact.

Evidence After the jury is chosen, the trial proceeds with opening arguments from each side. The opening arguments consist of a brief summary of the facts that each side expects to prove as well as the issues involved and the nature of the action. In some jurisdictions, the defendant's attorney may reserve the opening statement until the plaintiff's case is completed.

The next step is the presentation of the evidence. The individual having the ''burden of proof'' with respect to the principal issue presents his or her case first. The presentation consists of oral as well as documentary proof. Each witness is examined by the attorney that calls the witness. This is called direct examination. After the direct examination, the opposing attorney has an opportunity to examine the witness. This is called cross-examination. After cross-examination the first attorney has a right for additional examination, called redirect examination.

There are strict rules with respect to the admission of evidence. Those witnesses who may be needed for the oral part of the testimony can be compelled to come to court by a subpoena. Documents and documentary proof can be brought into court by means of a subpoena duces tecum (under penalty you shall bring with you). Failure to appear by either subpoena is punishable by contempt of court. A witness must take an oath or, in cases of a religious objection, an affirmation before testifying.

In the examination of a witness, certain rules of evidence must be adhered to. An attorney may not ask a leading question, that is, a question that suggests the answer (e.g., ''Were you in San Francisco on June 6?'' is leading, as opposed to ''Where were you on June 6?''). This rule is true for direct examinations only. In addition, a party who is presenting a case is not required to offer evidence of facts that have been previously admitted in either the pleadings or in any of the pretrial conferences. A person is not required to offer evidence to prove facts that are so well known that a court may take "judicial notice" of them (e.g., there are 365 days in a year, the earth is round, and so on). Generally, either party or anyone else may be brought in to testify, but only evidence that is relevant may be admitted.

　　In addition to direct evidence, circumstantial evidence is also admissible. Oral or written evidence of what some person said or wrote outside the court is not admissible for the purpose of establishing the truth of what was said or written. This type of third party evidence is termed hearsay evidence. For example, if John told Mary that he was in San Francisco on June 6, and Mary told you, your testimony would be hearsay and not admissible. Mary's would not be hearsay and would be admissible. An exception to the "hearsay evidence rule" is in a case where someone is in imminent fear of death. In such a case, a witness may testify as to what the deceased person has said while under such fear of immediate death. Courts look for proof from primary evidence or original documents. Rules of evidence will not allow secondary evidence (i.e., photocopies or carbon copies) to be admitted.

　　In addition to the rules of admission of evidence, there are also certain situations where testimony can be prevented. Such items come under the category of privilege. For example, the Fifth Amendment provides that a person shall not be compelled to testify against himself or herself. This amendment has been interpreted to mean that a person in a civil suit will not be required to give information that would tend to establish that that person might be guilty of a crime (i.e., anything tending to subject him or her to a fine or imprisonment or forfeiture or confiscation of land or a penalty). In addition, a spouse can not be compelled to testify as to confidential communications with the other spouse during the marriage relationship. Privilege extends to attorneys and clients, to clergymen and penitents, to physicians and patients, and in some states even to accountants and their clients.

　　It is up to each attorney to point out to the judge when a particular rule of evidence is being broken by the adversary. This is usually done by making an objection to the judge, who in turn will rule as to whether the objection is valid (sustain the objection) or invalid (overrule the objection). A judge may also stop the questioning of a witness or prohibit evidence without a specific objection from one of the attorneys. Failure to sustain or overrule a particular objection could lead to reversal of the outcome of a case on appeal.

Verdict　After the evidence has been presented by the plaintiff, the plaintiff's lawyer will "rest." At this time the defendant's attorney may move for a directed verdict. This motion is a request to the judge to dismiss for failure to make out a prima facie case (i.e., to decide whether the plaintiff's evidence, if uncontested, is sufficient to support a judgment for the plaintiff). The judge is requested to make this decision, and in a case where a jury has been impaneled, the judge is requested to decide whether the jury has a function. If a reasonable jury could not find for the plaintiff on the plaintiff's own evidence, this would be grounds for a motion for a directed verdict to be approved.

　　In a case where a defendant has moved for a directed verdict and the plaintiff realizes that in fact a case has not been made, the plaintiff may move for a voluntary nonsuit. This motion will allow the plaintiff to start the action over again. In a case where a defendant's motion for a directed verdict is approved, the case ends, and plaintiff may not begin a new action.

The next step in the lawsuit is for the defendant to bring forward his or her case, using the same rules of evidence that governed the plaintiff. After the defendant's last witness is examined, the defendant will rest his or her case, at which time the plaintiff's attorney may move for a directed verdict. If this motion is denied, the plaintiff may then introduce evidence in rebuttal of the defendant's evidence. If the plaintiff rebuts the defendant, the defendant may also introduce evidence to rebut the plaintiff. This process will continue until both parties rest.

When both parties have rested their case, summations or closing arguments are made. In summation, either attorney may comment only on the evidence introduced and not on facts that were not part of the record of the trial. The plaintiff's attorney closes first. Some jurisdictions limit the time in which a closing argument can be made.

After the closing arguments, the judge ''charges'' the jury. This means that the judge instructs the jury about the law of the case. The judge will point out the issues, will review the evidence, and will explain to the jury how he or she wishes the evidence to be weighed as a matter of law. The jury will decide the questions of fact and fix the amount of damages. The judge will determine the law.

In deciding the case, the jury will have to decide that the evidence presented by the party having the burden of proof must be more convincing and more creditable than that introduced by the opposing party (''by a preponderance of the evidence''). The jury will make these deliberations in a closed room and will come forward after deliberating with a ''verdict.'' A verdict, in most states, must be unanimous. In a federal court, parties may enter into a stipulation (a written agreement) that the verdict of a majority will be sufficient. In the event that the jury cannot reach its verdict, there is a ''hung jury,'' and a new trial before a new jury will be necessary. There are two types of verdicts that may be rendered: a general verdict, which is a simple finding that either the plaintiff or the defendant is liable, or a special verdict, which requires that the jury find answers to specific questions posed by the judge.

After the verdict is rendered, there are two motions that can be made by the parties. First is a motion for ''a judgment notwithstanding the verdict,'' and the second motion is ''a motion for a new trial.'' A motion for a judgment notwithstanding the verdict is a request to the judge to review the evidence and grant the losing party a judgment because the judge feels that a reasonable jury could not have decided against the moving party. This motion is similar to a directed verdict, but is granted after the trial. If the trial judge is in error in granting this motion, a successful appeal will not require a new trial as opposed to the case of a directed verdict.

''A motion for a new trial'' will be granted when new evidence is discovered, there are errors by the court, or the verdict is against the weight of the evidence.

In the event that none of the preceeding motions is granted, a judgment will be entered. The judgment usually awards costs to the successful party. Costs usually do not include expenses such as attorney's fees. Costs are usually amounts fixed by statute and are minimal when compared to the actual cost of litigation.

The Appeal   The losing party, who wants to have an appellate court review his or her case to determine whether it has been properly decided must take an appeal. All states as well as the United States provide appellate courts. The party taking the appeal is called the appellant, and the opposing party is called the appellee.

The first step in taking an appeal is to file a notice of appeal with the clerk of the trial court and to serve a notice on the appellee. The time for filing is usually limited by statute. The appellant should also obtain an order from the court to stay execution of the judgment. This will eliminate the need to pay the damages granted by the lower court until the appeal is heard. If the appellant is successful, he or she will not have to pay damages. An appellant may also be required to post security, which may be either cash or a bond from a surety company (New York State requires $20 per thousand). Security covers possible costs and disbursements that may be awarded should the appellant lose. In some jurisdictions, a second bond must also be provided to cover the lower court judgment that was stayed.

The next step in an appeal is to prepare the record on appeal. This is done by a stenographer, who transcribes the minutes of the lower court trial. These minutes are used to inform the appellate court of the proceedings in the lower court. The transcripts include the testimony of the witnesses, the exhibits offered in evidence, motions, objections, jury instructions, and charges to the jury. In addition to the record, both parties' attorneys file briefs with the appellate court clerk. A brief is a legal position paper that outlines the litigant's position on appeal. The appellant's brief will outline the legal arguments as to why the lower court should be reversed. The appellee's brief will argue why the trial court is correct.

Appellate courts are composed of three, five, seven, or nine justices who review the briefs and the lower court record. They will also listen to the attorneys' oral arguments that highlight the important points in the brief. No witnesses are heard at the oral arguments. In some instances, an attorney or attorneys may not argue the case orally but may just submit their briefs and the lower court record for a filing. This is generally not a good idea as appellate judges may not be able to wade through the lengthy material to find those items that the oral argument would underscore.

Grounds for an appeal must be on the law. Courts hearing an appeal generally do not have authority to make independent findings of fact. During a lawsuit there are many rulings that are made. Each and every one is an area for possible appellate review. An appellate court will only consider questions of law when the appellant made a timely and sufficient objection during the trial. Such objections might come about with respect to the admissibility of evidence or with respect to errors by the trial court, jury selection process, and such. The appellate court can either dismiss or affirm the lower court decision, reverse the lower court decision, or modify the judgment of the lower court. In addition, the appellate court could order a new trial (remand) or direct the trial court to enter a particular judgment. The scope of the court's review includes the whole trial court record. The appellate court decides by a majority of the judges sitting.

The expenses for an appeal are usually exorbitant. They include the cost of posting bonds, paying the stenographer for the transcript of the minutes, attorney's fees for preparation of briefs and reply briefs, as well as printing of the minutes and pleadings and providing copies of everything for each member of the appellate court. Decisions on whether to appeal must weigh not only the legal factors but also the financial factors.

QUESTIONS

1 Mrs. D had rented the upstairs of a two-family house from Mrs. P for several years. Mrs. D parked her automobile in the garage and proceeded to walk down the driveway. There were snow and ice covering a hole in the driveway. The hole had been there for more than a year. Mrs. D attempted to go around the hole and slipped on the ice; her heel struck the hole and she fell, fracturing her ankle. Question: Is Mrs. P liable as the owner of property for damages to her tenant, Mrs. D? Discuss.

2 Mr. L was driving home from a fishing trip sometime after dark. He failed to see a stalled truck trailer belonging to Ashland Oil Co., which was parked on the side of the road without running lights. The truck had had mechanical problems approximately 3 hours before Mr. L came by. Mr L swerved his car to the left, across the center line of traffic, and collided with another vehicle. Mr L was instantly killed. Question: Is the defendant, Ashland Oil, liable? Discuss.

3 Mr. C was threatened by Mr. O. The threats indicated that if Mr. C did not leave the premises, Mr. O would strike Mr. C with great force and violence; would hit, beat and strike him; and would commit immediate bodily harm. As a result of these statements, Mr. C suffered great emotional distress. Question: What torts, if any, were committed? Discuss.

4 Mrs. Chapman was injured at 11:30 P.M. while riding in a car with her husband, who was driving at approximately 15 miles an hour. Their automobile hit a pile of gravel in the road, which was unguarded and unlighted. The pile of gravel had been placed there by the defendant, who was hired to pave the particular roadway. Mrs. Chapman was severly injured. Evidence at the trial indicated that her husband was drunk at the time of the accident. Question: Can Mrs. Chapman recover from the defendant? Discuss.

5 Jerry Houck drove into a gas station, followed by his brother, David, who stopped from 3 to 5 feet behind Jerry's car. The gas station attendant (plaintiff) began filling Jerry's automobile. David got out of his vehicle, leaving the engine running at the request of his passengers, because of the bitter cold. He did not set the parking brake. David's two-year-old son attempted to climb from the rear seat into the front seat, and in doing so he accidentally put the car in gear. The car moved forward and struck the plaintiff before the other passengers in the car could hit the brake or put the transmission back into park. Plaintiff sued Jerry, David, and the passengers in David's car. Discuss the negligence of the various parties, and decide whether the plaintiff should receive damages for his back injuries.

6 The plaintiff, Bernice Stannard, sues to recover for injuries sustained when she fell in attempting to exit from the rear seat of a Datsun automobile at night. Her contention is that the defendant driver was negligent in not turning on the lights of the automobile and that she caught her foot in the safety belt and tripped. She also contends that the defendant should have warned her of the safety belt's presence or should have removed the safety belt from her path. The plaintiff also sued Nissan Motor Co., alleging negligence in the design and manufacture of the seat belt as well as breach of express and implied warranties of safety, merchantability, and fitness for a particular purpose. Discuss the doctrine of contributory negligence and comparative negligence as they might apply to this case.

7 Melanie, a 14-year-old, was at her cousin's house, swimming in the swimming pool. Between the pool patio and the house was a sliding glass door. During the day, Melanie went in and out between the patio and the family room without having to open the glass door. That evening Melanie came from upstairs to answer a telephone call, the lights in the family room were turned off, and the patio was well lighted. As Melanie stepped to reach the phone on the patio, she smashed the glass door, which had been closed during the early evening, shattering the glass and causing injuries to herself. She sues the homeowner for recovery of damages. Is the homeowner liable? Discuss.

8 A six-year-old boy wandered onto the defendant's property and accidentally drowned as a result of falling into the defendant's swimming pool. The pool was 200 feet from the public street and was adjacent to a private path leading across the defendant's property, running from one street to another. Children had frequently used the private path in going to and from school and for purposes of play. The defendant knew that the path was used by the children. The water in the pool was 7 feet deep. The guardrail around the pool was inadequate in height and design and had an opening in it that had no gate. The sides of the pool were slippery. Is the landowner liable for the death? Discuss.

9 The defendant maintained a swimming pool on his premises. The pool was surrounded by a block fence, which was 6 feet in height and had several wooden gates. The city in which he lived required that private swimming pools be fenced and that gates be equipped with self-closing and self-locking devices. The defendant's gates did not contain a self-closing device. A three-year-old child wandered onto the premises because his mother failed to watch him properly. The child fell in the pool and drowned. Question: Would the mother's failure to watch the child properly prevent her from recovering damages? Was the defendant liable? Discuss.

10 A three-year-old child was injured when his neighbor's workman left weeds burning. The defendant was not home. The three-year-old infant came onto the property and played around the remains of the fire, igniting a stick by poking it in the hot ashes. His clothing caught fire, and he was severely burned. Was the property owner liable for the damages? Discuss.

11 A plaintiff testified that when she left a restaurant through a revolving door, she was struck in the back by the door when an unidentified man coming through the door at the same time pushed the door. The plaintiff said that she was propelled with such force that she lost her footing and fell down a step to the sidewalk. It is the plaintiff's contention that the revolving door exit was dangerous because the door spun very rapidly. There was no evidence presented of any defect in the structure or in the condition of the door. There was no evidence that it failed in any respect to comply with the standards of such doors. Is the owner of the premises liable? Discuss.

12 The plaintiff was driving down the road when the defendant suddenly slowed down and stopped without warning. The plaintiff hit the defendant, and the bumpers of the automobiles interlocked. The plaintiff got out of his vehicle, disengaging the bumpers, and was standing between the two automobiles when his automobile was hit from behind, causing him injuries. Was the defendant liable for these personal injuries? Discuss.

13 A 17-year-old plaintiff was riding with several friends in the defendant's vehicle. They had played hooky from school and had started riding around at 11:00 A.M., making several stops to purchase and consume liquor. The plaintiff sustained injuries when the defendant lost control of his vehicle as they were passing a truck at the speed of 60 to 65 miles per hour. Was the defendant driver liable for the plaintiff passenger's injuries? Discuss.

14 The plaintiff was standing on a railroad platform of the defendant's railroad. A train stopped at the station, and two men ran forward to catch it. One of the men was carrying a package. In trying to board the train, which was starting to move, the package was dislodged and fell upon the rails. The package contained fire works, and when it hit the rails, it exploded. The shock of the explosion dislodged some scales that were hanging at the other end of the platform, and they hit the plaintiff, causing injuries for which she sues. Is the defendant railroad liable for damages? Discuss. (The answer may require outside research.)

15 Mrs. Crabtree entered a food store about 4:00 P.M. to buy some catfood. While walking down one of the aisles, she slipped and fell. She sat up and found a bottle cap 18 inches from her right foot. Mrs. Crabtree testified that she did not know what she slipped on when she fell. All she knows is that she slipped and, after she fell, there was the bottle cap. The store had a Pepsi machine that had a bottle-cap holder and that was full. The Pepsi machine was in a highly traveled area of the store. Was the store liable for injuries to Mrs. Crabtree? Discuss.

CHAPTER 4

General Principles of Contract Law

INTRODUCTION

Almost everybody has been or will be involved in a contractual agreement. Contracts are common in transactions such as purchasing or renting a home or an apartment, creating a business, or purchasing consumer goods, such as automobiles, appliances, and clothing. Therefore, it is important to understand what obligations and rights are imposed upon a party to a contract and also to understand how a contract is formed. The purpose of this chapter is to present the legal principles that apply to contracts. Subsequent chapters will deal with various types of contractual commitments in greater detail.

DEFINITION AND CLASSIFICATION OF CONTRACTS

A contract has been defined as "an agreement between two or more persons consisting of a promise or mutual promises which the law will enforce or the performance of which the law in some way recognizes as a duty" (Simpson, *On Contracts*, 2d ed.). A contract has also been defined as "a promise or a set of promises for the breach of which the law gives a remedy, or the performance of which the law in some way recognizes as a duty" (Restatement [Second] of Contracts §1 [1973]).

The essence of a contract is mutuality. A contract requires an agreement between two or more persons. It is impossible for one person to make a contract or for two persons to contract if they have not agreed on the terms of the contract. A common expression of the requirement of mutuality is that there must be a "meeting of the minds." This generally recognizes that parties to a contract must come to some understanding that has similar, if not identical, implications in their minds. Take the following example. If you agree to sell and I agree to purchase a piece of property described as a lot at 15 Gilbert Street, it appears as though there is a meeting of the minds. If, however, there are two streets with the same name and I believe I am purchasing a lot on one street, and you believe you are selling a lot on the other street, we have not reached a mutual agreement; there has been no meeting of the minds and there is no contract (Raffles v. Wichelhaus, 2 H. & C. 906 [Ex. 1864]).

Another essential element of a contract is the idea of a bargained for exchange. A gratuitous promise is usually not enforceable as a contract. For example, if I promise to give you $500 and you say you'll take it, a contract is not formed. A gratuitous promise does not create a meeting of the minds but merely shows an intention on my part to do something that I may or may not follow through on. (See section entitled "Consideration.")

Formal and informal is one classification for contracts. A formal contract is one that is binding because of the form of the contract. Formal contracts include contracts under seal, negotiable instruments, and such. Informal contracts are those that the law considers enforceable because of the substance of the transaction rather than because of the form in which the promises are made. Most of the contracts you will encounter will be informal contracts, and our discussion will be confined to that topic.

Express and implied is another classification for contracts. Express contracts are formed where the agreement of the parties is in oral or written form. If I promise to buy your car and you promise to sell it and we agree to price, terms, and the like, this is an expressed promise. If the agreement of the parties and its terms are inferred from their actions, the contract is said to be implied or implied in fact. If I enter a taxi and ask the driver to take me to a certain location, there is an implied promise on my part to pay for the trip.

A quasi contract, sometimes referred to as a quasi contractual relationship, is not a contract. A quasi contract is created in situations where the law considers it unjust to leave an individual without a remedy and treats the parties "as if" they had made a contract. For example, persons under a certain age (minors) are not able to make contracts. However, the law does not want such persons to be unable to obtain necessaries such as food, clothing, and shelter. Therefore, the law will treat a minor's agreement to pay for necessaries "as if" it were a contract. A very important difference between a contract and a quasi contract is that the other party will only be entitled to recover the reasonable value (quantum meruit) of goods and services rendered to the minor even if this differs from the agreed upon price.

Courts also use the doctrine of quasi contract to prevent a party from unjustly benefiting at another's expense. For example, you come to my house and start to mow my lawn. I see you but make no effort to stop you. When you are done, you ask for payment, and I refuse. Courts will apply the doctrine of quasi contract to prevent my "unjust enrichment." I will have to pay you the value of the service rendered.

Unilateral and bilateral is another classification of contracts. A unilateral contract is a contract in which a promise of one party is exchanged for performance by the other party. If I promise to pay you $500 to paint my house, this is a request to enter into a unilateral contract. If you then paint my house, you create a unilateral contract. A bilateral contract is one in which each party makes a promise to the other. If I promise to pay you $500 in exchange for your promise to paint my house no later than September 30, 1982, we have created a bilateral contract.

Executed and executory is still another classification of contracts. An executed contract is one in which all parties have performed their obligation under the contract. An executory contract is one in which the performances have not been completed. For example, if I promise to pay you $500 and you promise to paint my house, there is a bilateral contract. At this time the contract is executory because neither of us has performed. When you are done painting and I have paid you, the contract is referred to as executed.

Voidable, unenforceable, valid, and void are other types of contracts. A contract that is voidable is one in which one of the parties has a right to elect to avoid or disaffirm his or her obligation. Unless the election is made, the law will enforce the contractual obligation. If the election is made too late, it will be ineffective. An example of a voidable contract is one entered into by a minor. (See section on capacity.) An unenforceable contract exists when the law can not enforce its provisions. A party to an unenforceable contract does not have the right to disaffirm the contract. The court lacks the power to compel performance or provide a remedy for the party's refusal to perform as required. An example of an unenforceable contract is an oral contract that is required under the statute of frauds to be in writing. (See the section on statute of frauds and parol evidence.) A valid contract is one which is neither voidable nor unenforceable.

Some courts also refer to *void contract*. This is a contradiction in terms. If an agreement is void, it cannot be a contract. A void agreement (a preferable term) is a nullity from its inception. An example of a void agreement is an agreement to rob a bank. (See the section on illegality.)

Offer

Generally, in order for a contract to be formed, one party must make an offer to the other. The party making the offer is called the offeror; the party receiving the offer is called the offeree. A statement that purports to be an offer must be definite and certain and must show the intent to make an offer. A statement by an individual to another like ''I would like to sell you my car for $100. Do you wish to purchase it?'' is a definite and certain offer showing intent. A statement like ''I am thinking about selling my car for $100'' is not an offer because it lacks certainty as to the offeror's intent to sell.

The *intent* of the offeror to make an offer is of primary importance. Though it is impossible to know what is happening in the mind of an individual, one can look to circumstances surrounding the transaction to determine the intent of the offeror. Courts use an objective standard to determine intent. If a reasonable person would interpret the statements and circumstances to create an offer, it will be interpreted as such even where the offeror had not intended to make an offer. For example, a store publishes the following statement in a newspaper: ''Saturday 9:00 A.M. sharp—Three Brand-New Fur Coats Worth up to $100—First Come First Served—$1 Each.'' This type of statement can be considered an offer in which the first three individuals who tender $1.00 each have accepted the offer and are entitled to receive their $100 fur coats (Lefkowitz v. Great Minneapolis Surplus Store, Inc., 86 N.W.2d 698 [Minn. 1957]).

In O'Keefe v. Lee Calan Imports, Inc., 262 N.E.2d 758 (Ill. 1970), the defendant advertised a 1964 automobile for sale in a local newspaper. The defendant had instructed the newspaper to advertise the cost of the automobile at $1795. The newspaper erroneously advertised the price at $1095. The plaintiff examined the automobile at the defendant's store and indicated that he wished to make the purchase for $1095, the advertised price, and the defendant refused to sell the car for that price. The court held that the advertisement in the newspaper was an invitation to the public to make an offer rather than an offer. By statute in many jurisdictions, newspaper advertisements are considered to be offers rather than invitations to make an offer.

Communication is a second important element of an offer. The communication need not be in words, but the offeree must be aware of the offer. A person who is not aware of the offer cannot accept it. If I lose my watch and put an advertisement in the newspaper offering a $50 reward to anyone who finds it, the advertisement would be an offer. If you find my watch and return it after reading my advertisement, I am obligated to pay you the $50 reward since you have accepted the offer. If, however, you find my watch and return it to me and later discover my offer, I am under no obligation since the act that you performed was not pursuant to my offer.

Termination of an offer occurs with the occurrence of one of several events: acceptance by the offeree, revocation by the offeror (statement that offeror is no longer willing to perform), rejection by the offeree (statement that offeree is not willing to act as requested), death or insanity of the offeror or offeree, subsequent illegality of the subject matter of the offer, destruction or prior sale of the subject matter, expiration of the time stated in the offer, or expiration of a reasonable period of time. It is difficult to determine in any given situation what a reasonable time period is. If the offeror is of the opinion that the offer has lapsed and the offeree is of the opinion that it has not and accepts the offer, it may be necessary to go to litigation in order to resolve this issue.

A *special offer* refers to an option, which is an offer that by agreement will be held open for a specific period of time. For example, you offer to sell me a piece of property for $10,000. In order to decide whether I wish to purchase the property, I will need a week to evaluate several factors. During that time I don't want anyone else to purchase the property, and so I request that you not sell the property to anyone else during that week. If you agree to this request, you have granted me an option.

When an auctioneer ''offers'' merchandise at an auction, it is not legally considered to be an offer. It is considered under law to be an invitation to people at the auction to make an offer to the auctioneer. The auctioneer has the right to accept any offer or to reject all offers. When the auctioneer signifies the sale of the merchandise by knocking it down with his hammer, that act is an acceptance of the most recent offer. If an auction is specifically stated to be *without reserve*, the auctioneer must sell the goods at the highest bid and, therefore, cannot reject all of the bids. In all other cases, an auction is *with reserve*, and the auctioneer does not have to accept any bid.

Acceptance

An acceptance is an overt act by the offeree, indicating a positive, unequivocal intention of agreeing to the terms of the offer. An acceptance generally must be communicated to the offeror. In the case of a bilateral contract, the acceptance is in the form of a promise by the offeree to do what was requested by the offeror. In the case of a unilateral contract, the acceptance constitutes the performance by the offeree of the act requested by the offeror. An acceptance can only be made by the offeree. If I make an offer to A, offering to sell him my car for $500 and if the offer is also seen by B, only A can accept the offer. B was not an intended offeree and, therefore, is not in a position to accept the offer. If B approaches me and says he is willing to purchase my car for $500, his purported acceptance constitutes an offer, which I may then accept or reject. Silence generally will not constitute an acceptance. Terms in an offer to the effect that "if I do not hear from you, I assume you have accepted my offer" will be disregarded by the courts unless it can be shown that the parties have had a prior course of dealing that would render such conduct acceptable.

The nature of acceptance is strictly defined. An acceptance must conform to the terms of the offer. If I offer to sell you my car for $500 and you say you will purchase it for $450, you have not accepted. By changing the terms of my offer, you have rejected it and have made a counteroffer that I may accept or reject. Once you make a counteroffer, my offer is terminated, and if I refuse to accept your offer, you can no longer accept mine. If you agree to pay the $500 (after the $450 is rejected), this will be an offer from you. I am free to accept or reject it. An acceptance that makes only minor changes will not be considered a rejection. The specific determination of whether a change is a major or minor one is a matter of fact that has to be determined in each situation. An acceptance that adds terms may operate either as an acceptance or a rejection. If the additional terms are major, the acceptance will operate as a rejection of the original offer and become a counteroffer. If the new terms are minor in comparison with the rest of the contract, then the acceptance will be effective.

The acceptance of an offer must be unequivocal. It must be clear to the offeror that the offeree's statement is an acceptance. The determination of whether a particular expression is in fact an acceptance of an offer or not is an issue of fact that is to be determined by a jury and that will vary depending on the circumstances of each individual case.

Communication of acceptance takes various forms. An acceptance creates a contract. In order for an acceptance to take place, it must be communicated to the offeror. If I offer to sell you my car and you type a letter accepting my offer and never send it to me, you have not communicated your acceptance, and no contract takes place. An acceptance may be communicated to the offeror in any of a number of ways. The most desirable medium to communicate an acceptance to an offeror is the same that was used by the offeror to communicate the offer to the offeree. An acceptance, if communicated in the same manner as the offer, is effective when the acceptance is placed into the channels of communication. Thus, if I send you a letter with an offer and you mail me an acceptance, the acceptance becomes effective at the instant that it is mailed. Even if I fail to receive the acceptance, communication will be deemed to have taken place. If, however, the acceptance is communicated by a different means of communications, it is not effective until received by the offeror. Thus, if I telegraph an offer and you accept by mail, the acceptance is not effective until I receive it. Had you responded by telegraph, it would have been effective upon delivery to the telegrapher's office.

In the case of an offer for a unilateral contract, the form of acceptance must be the performance requested by the offeror. If I offer you $500 if you will paint my house, your promise to paint my house, even if under oath, is not effective as an acceptance. You must actually paint my house. If I request that an acceptance be communicated in a particular fashion or by a particular time, failure to utilize the method of communication or failure to reach me by the specified time, in most cases, will cause the offer to terminate, and there will be no contract.

Ambiguities present problems. An offer that is ambiguous cannot create a contract. The classic case is Raffles v. Wichelhaus, 2 H.&C. 906 (Ex. 1864).This is an English case in which merchandise was offered to be sold and delivered on the ship *Peerless* from Bombay. There were two ships by the name of *Peerless*, both of which left Bombay, but one of them arrived at the port of delivery in September; and the other, in December. The seller had intended to ship on a certain date on one of these; the buyer accepted, thinking that the shipment was to be made on the other. The court held there was no contract. It held the offer sufficiently vague or ambiguous so that there could have been no meeting of the minds.

Another situation that creates problems is where there is a typographical error in the buyer's acceptance of the seller's offer. If I offer to sell you gold at $425 per ounce and the offer is communicated through the error of the telegraph company at $425 per pound, the offer cannot be accepted. In such a case, the courts have ruled that a reasonable buyer should be aware of the error and could not possibly expect to make a contract at that price. A more difficult question arises where the offering price is erroneously transmitted as $420 per ounce. In such a case, where a reasonable person could have believed that the actual stated price was the correct price, it will be held that a contract has resulted. Any damages resulting from the error in transmission are the responsibility of the telegraph company.

Consideration

If there has been an offer and an acceptance, a contract is normally created. A promise that is unsupported by consideration, however, even if accepted, does not create a contract. If I promise to pay you $500 and you say that you accept my promise, a contract does not result. There is no reason why I should pay you this money, and though I may fulfill my gratuitous promise, it will not be enforced by law. Consideration is giving something that has value to another party (benefit) or giving up something that has value to oneself (detriment). For a contract to exist, consideration must go both ways. For example, if you found my lost dog and I offered you $500, after the fact, the offer would not be binding because it lacks consideration, but the statement ''if you find my dog, I will give you $500'' is a binding offer. If you find the dog, I would have to pay. In the first example, there is nothing bargained for. Your appearance on my front porch with my dog was not an exchange that was contemplated by either of us. In the second example, I am making an offer with the intent of inducing you to do something you are not legally bound to do, that is, look for my dog; therefore, consideration is present.

Suppose I promise to pay you $500 if you agree to stop smoking for a year. My promise to pay you $500 is both a detriment to me, the promisor, and a benefit to you, the promisee. It is, therefore, consideration from me to you. Courts recognize that there is a detriment to the promisors if they agree to do something they are not otherwise obligated to do or agree to refrain from doing something which they have a right to do. Since you have the choice whether or not to smoke, your agreement to refrain from doing so for a year will constitute a legal detriment to you. It is, therefore, adequate consideration to support my promise, and there is a contract. Contrast this with the example where I promise to pay you $500 and you accept. I, as promisor, have suffered a detriment, and you, as promisee, have had a benefit. However, your acceptance causes you no detriment, nor does it give me any benefit. Because there is no detriment to you and no benefit to me, there is no consideration flowing from you to me, and, therefore, all we have is a one-sided promise that cannot constitute a contract (see Exhibit 4–1).

Legal and economic consideration is a factor. The law will not consider the economic sufficiency of consideration. It is not of concern whether the items given up by each of the parties to the contract are equal in value so long as a person gets what was bargained for and it is of some value in the eyes of the law. The courts will not inquire whether it is of any monetary value or whether its value is in any way proportionate to the promise given in return. This is particularly true where the parties have been able to bargain freely for the required exchange. The essence of legal consideration is that each party has bargained for an exchange that they consider of sufficient value to do what they have promised.

Legally inadequate consideration has these aspects. Consideration can be a promise to do something or a promise not to do something. It can be an act, or it can be

EXHIBIT 4-1
Flow of Consideration

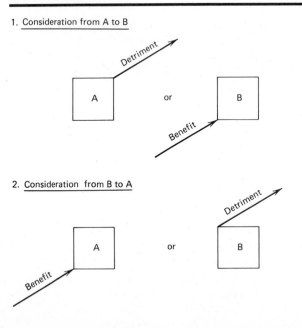

1. Consideration from A to B

2. Consideration from B to A

the forbearance from doing an act. If a person promises not to do something that he or she has no right to do in the first place, it is not consideration. For example, you steal my car. I agree not to prosecute (criminal case) if you pay for the car. This is not consideration. The decision to prosecute is the right of the district attorney, not of private individuals. My agreement not to file a complaint with the police is also not consideration. The law imposes a duty on citizens to file complaints. I may not use a societal obligation for my personal benefit.

Consideration is also not present where a person does something that he or she is already legally obligated to do. An individual who is an officer of the law has an obligation to arrest criminals. If a reward is offered for the arrest of a criminal and an officer of the law makes such an arrest, that officer is not entitled to the reward.

Assume that I owe you $10,000 payable today and I fail to pay you. If you come to me tomorrow and say that you will accept $9,500 in exchange for what I owe you, my payment is not consideration for your promise to forgive the other $500 of the debt. The reason is that I am already under an obligation to pay you the full $10,000. If, however, you come to me a day before the payment is due and make the same arrangement, there is consideration because I am not obligated to make the payment early. The fact that receiving the money one day early may not be worth the $500 reduction is not relevant.

A promise that is so indefinite and uncertain that it cannot be enforced cannot be consideration. Such promises are often referred to as illusory because they appear enforceable when, in fact, they are not. A promise to purchase ''such coal as I may *wish* to order from you'' is illusory. The offeror or buyer is free to purchase as much or as little as he or she may wish. Therefore, the promise lacks certainty or definiteness (Wickham and Burton Coal Co. v. Farmers Lumber Co., 179 N.W. 417 [Iowa 1920]). This type of promise should be contrasted with a promise made to purchase ''all such coal as I may *need* during the forthcoming year.'' In the latter case, need is a definable concept. Even though it is not clear ahead of time how much coal the particular business person may need, it is implied that all such needs will be purchased from the other party to the contract as opposed to any other person. Therefore, there is a restriction in the second example that was not present in the first (Liema Locomotive Co. v. National Steel Co., 155 F.77 [Ohio 1907]; Brightwater Co. v. Monadnock Mills, 161 F.2d 869 [Mass. 1947]). An executory contract that allows a promisor to cancel at any time is illusory (Farmers Handy Wagon Co. v. Newcomb, 159 N.W. 152 [Mich. 1916]; Fawcett v. Fawcett, 132 S.E. 796 [N.C. 1926]; Gurfein v. Werbelovsky 118 A. 32 [Conn. 1922]).

Where a promise is made to do something as a result of moral obligations, many courts take the position that there is no legal consideration. If I take care of an elderly relative for many years without compensation, some courts feel that I do so because of the moral obligation. If my elderly relative promises to leave me money in his or her will and fails to do so, these courts will not allow me to enforce that promise. Other courts take the point of view that since a person has no legal compulsion to care for another, the promise to leave money to that individual is made with the intent of inducing the person to continue to care for the invalid. In these cases, the courts argue there is a bargained-for exchange and, therefore, a contract does exist.

Unforeseen obstacles occur. If a party to a contract encounters unforeseen obstacles in completing the contract and goes to the other party, explains the situation, and indicates that the fee will have to be higher, there is a diversity of opinion as to whether the new promise is binding. If I am already obligated to a certain degree of performance and you agree in exchange for the same degree of performance to pay me a higher sum of money, I have not given any consideration to you because I am not obligated to do anything that I wasn't originally obligated to do. Therefore, since I have not given consideration, many courts argue that the second promise is not binding. Other courts find that the parties have agreed to terminate their rights and obligations under the existing contract and have entered into a brand-new contract, where one party's standard of performance was the same as under the old contract, but the other party's has been increased. An alternative approach, which avoids this problem, is to renegotiate the deal and have one party agree to do something different from what was originally agreed. This change in performance will be sufficient consideration for the receipt of the additional sums of money under the new contract.

Estoppel is another issue to consider. Certain gratuitous promises will be enforced without consideration. For example, I promise to employ you. In reliance on my promise, you quit your job. I then refuse to hire you, claiming you gave no consideration for my promise. Courts take the position that where you have reasonably relied on my promise, have acted to your detriment, and I could have foreseen your actions, it would be unfair to allow you to suffer because of something that I had started (Hunter v. Hayes, 533 P.2d [Colo. 1975]). The courts will prevent me (estop me) from denying the validity of my promise. This is called promissory estoppel. Charitable pledges are sometimes enforced under the doctrine of promissory estoppel (Mt. Sinai Hospital v. Jordan, 290 So.2d 484 [Fla. 1974]; Timko v. Oral Roberts, 215 N.W.2d 750 [Mich. 1974]).

Deceit, Duress, and Mistake

Deceit has several subcategories. Where two parties have exchanged what appears to be consideration and entered into what appears to be a contract, there are several defenses that may be raised that will cause the contract to be voidable by one of the parties. The first of these defenses is fraud. Fraud is defined as an intentional misrepresentation of a material fact made for the purpose of inducing another person to rely upon that fact to do something that would not otherwise have been done. Fraud is a subcategory of deceit. Misrepresentation, a second act that allows a party to a contract to disaffirm the contract, is essentially the same as fraud except that a misrepresentation need not have been made intentionally. Misrepresentation is also a subcategory of deceit. If any material fact is improperly represented (i.e., stated to be true when it is not), the party to whom the misstatement has been given has the right to disaffirm the contract without penalty. The fact that the statement was intentionally or unintentionally made to deceive the party in question is not relevant. Degree of intent merely changes the nature of the offense but does not change the remedy.

For example, in Miller v. Plains Insurance Company, 409 S.W.2d 770 (Mo. 1966), Mrs. Miller was riding in a vehicle driven by Gayles. The automobile was in an accident, and both Miller and Gayles were killed. There was an insurance policy issued by the defendant providing for protection against uninsured motorists. Mr. Miller filed a claim against the insurance company to recover the amount of the policy because of the loss of his wife. The defendant argued that Gayles, in applying for the insurance policy, had made untrue representations that she had never been involved in an automobile accident or arrested for moving violations within the preceding three years. The insurance company also proved that their practice at the time this policy was issued was to refuse to insure any person who had been involved in an accident in the preceding five years or had been arrested for any moving violation within the preceding three years.

The court held that Miller could not recover on the insurance policy. The court pointed out that a material misrepresentation of fact makes a transaction voidable against the person who makes the misrepresentation and also against anyone who stands in that person's shoes.

Puffing is another aspect to consider. Not every statement that is untrue constitutes deceit. It is important that there be a misstatement of a material fact. An opinion or comments such as are generally recognized as salespersons *puffing* are not statements of fact and, therefore, would not constitute an act of deceit. Furthermore, if a particular fact is misrepresented but it is not material (i.e., knowledge of the true state of facts would not have caused a person to change his or her conduct), then disaffirmance of the contract would not be allowed. It is also essential for the defense of deceit to prevail that the plaintiff (the person to whom the statement has been made) have relied on the statement of the defendant and not on some independent source.

For example, in Vokes v. Arthur Murray Inc., 212 So.2d 906 (Fla. 1968), the plaintiff was a 51-year-old widow who had a desire to become an accomplished dancer. She signed up for an introductory course of lessons for $14.50. Over a period of 16 months, she was sold 14 different dance courses aggregating more than 2000 hours lessons at a cost in excess of $31,000. During the period during which she was purchasing these courses, employees of the dance studio told her that she had grace and poise, that she was rapidly improving and developing her dancing skill, and that additional lessons would make her a beautiful dancer, capable of dancing with the most accomplished dancers. It appeared that, in fact, she had little, if any, dancing ability and had difficulty in hearing the beat of the music she was dancing to. Plaintiff brought an action against the defendant franchisor, as well as the particular school involved, alleging that she was induced by fraud to sign the contract and that it was, therefore, voidable. The defendants responded by arguing that they had made, at most, statements of opinion; to the extent that their opinions were not truthful, they came under the category of puffing, and a reasonable person would not have paid attention to those statements and would not have been influenced by them.

The court held that the defendant had exceeded the limits of puffing. Statements of opinion generally are not misrepresentations of an actionable nature, nor are items that come under the category of *trade puffing*. However, they identified certain situations in which a statement of opinion might in fact be actionable: where there is a fiduciary relationship between the parties, where the person making the representation has employed some artifice or trick, or where the parties do not deal at arm's length. They noted that, in this particular situation, the party making the representation was a party who had some degree of superior knowledge, being in the business of training people how to become dancers.

It is also necessary, in order to maintain an action for deceit, that plaintiff's reliance on the statement of the defendant has been reasonable. If the plaintiff should have known better than to listen to the defendant or should have been sufficiently aware of circumstances to know that it was necessary to get an independent opinion, then the plaintiff will be considered to have contributed to the deceit and will not be allowed to maintain an action.

Duress and undue influence comprise a second category of acts that allows one party to a contract to disaffirm the contract. Duress is any action that causes individuals to do something that they would not otherwise have done or to refrain from doing something that they would otherwise have done. Duress formerly concentrated primarily on threats to do physical violence, but in modern times it has expanded to recognize mental and psychological duress as well as, in some cases, economic duress. If a person enters a contract under duress, the contract is voidable by that person. For example, in Laemmar v. J. Walter Thompson Company, 435 F.2d 680 (Ill. 1970), the plaintiff, Laemmar, was an employee of the defendant, J. Walter Thompson Company. The plaintiff had purchased a number of shares of the defendant company's stock for the benefit of his children. The stock was purchased subject to an option on the part of the defendant to repurchase the stock from the plaintiff if the plaintiff left his employment with the company for any reason. In late 1964 or early 1965, various officers of the defendant approached the plaintiff, requesting that he sell the stock back to the defendant. The plaintiff refused to do this and was threatened that if he did not do so, he would be discharged. Because of this threat, the plaintiff finally agreed to sell his stock to the defendant and executed a contract doing so. Several years later the plaintiff advised the defendant of his intention to rescind the contract of sale and offered to refund to the defendant the amount of money that the plaintiff had received. The defendant refused to return the stock, and the plaintiff sued the defendant.

The federal circuit court held that a threat of discharge from one's employment may constitute economic duress that would make a contract voidable. The defendant argued that the company was entitled to terminate the plaintiff's employment and would have been able to get the stock back in that manner. The court addressed this stating, "The question thus becomes whether a threat to pursue an action to which one is legally entitled may constitute duress under Illinois law if made as an inducement to execute an agreement. We conclude that it may." The court held that pressure generated by noncriminal acts of a party may constitute duress where their clear effect was to undermine the other party's ability to refuse to execute a specific agreement.

Not every case of economic hardship will be the basis of duress. Courts will not usually prevent an individual from taking advantage of another's hardship unless the first individual was instrumental in creating the hardship.

Undue influence is taking advantage of a difference in the bargaining capacity of parties that results from a special position that is occupied by one of the parties. Undue influence does not exist where a good businessperson and a poor business-person get together and negotiate a contract favorable to the good businessperson. Undue influence exists where there is a special obligation on the part of the stronger party to protect the interests of the weaker party. This obligation is referred to under law as a fiduciary obligation. It exists in relationships such as attorney-client, doctor-patient, executor-beneficiary (under a will), and trustee-beneficiary (in a trust arrangement). Where a person who is in a fiduciary capacity takes advantage of the beneficiary of that relationship, the person who has been taken advantage of has the right to disaffirm the contract that has been made.

Mistake and ambiguity form the last category of transactions that effect the validity of a contract. Mistakes come in several different kinds, some of which make the contract voidable. A mistake is different from ignorance or the exercise of poor judgment. If you purchase a piece of property with knowledge of the fact that it has thousands of dollars worth of marketable timber on it and I, the seller, am unaware of this fact, this is a situation of ignorance or poor judgment; there has been no mistake. You have merely exercised good business judgment to purchase something at a price at which you can make a profit.

Where a contract is ambiguous (i.e., susceptible to two different interpretations), the courts will generally consider that there is no contract. This was the case in *Raffles* v. *Wichelhaus* cited earlier. If both parties to a contract enter the contract in a mistaken belief that a certain material fact exists (described under law as a mutual mistake of material fact), the contract is voidable by either of the parties. Where only one of the parties is mistaken as to a material fact, the contract will only be voidable if the other party is aware of the first party's mistake and takes advantage of that mistake. If one party is mistaken as to a specific fact and the other party, unaware of the first party's error, enters into a contract in good faith, the contract is not voidable by either of the parties. An exception to this rule occurred in the case of Reed's Photomart v. Monarch Marking System Company, 475 S.W.2d 356 (Tex. 1971). In this case, the plaintiff sued the defendant for the purchase price of 4 million small gum labels, which were allegedly ordered by defendant. The defendant had been doing business with the plaintiff for almost 20 years. In their prior dealings the defendant had never ordered anywhere close to even a million labels but generally ordered several different styles in quantities of several thousand each. The shipping instructions on Reed's order was parcel post. The salesperson from Monarch changed this from parcel post to BestWay. A truckload of labels arrived, and Reed refused to accept them.

The court held that even in a case of unilateral mistake, there may be grounds for relief where the party who does not make the mistake has reason to know of the error. The salesperson indicated in his testimony that he knew it was virtually impossible to ship 4 million labels by parcel post, that previously he had never taken an order this large from any one customer, and his largest order (which was only 1 million labels) was shipped over a period of several months. The court also pointed out that Monarch had an existing policy of checking orders received before filling them if there were any discrepancy or reason to be concerned. The court felt on this basis that Monarch should have known that this order was in error and, therefore, should not be able to profit from shipment of a far greater number of labels than Reed would ever be able to use.

Capacity

Despite the presence of an offer and an acceptance, freely given by both parties, and consideration, the law recognizes that contracts entered into by certain persons shall be voidable by those persons. The two major categories of persons who lack *capacity* to enter into a contract are infants and persons who have a degree of mental limitation because of insanity or drunkenness. A contract entered into by a person who lacks contractual capacity because of one of the preceding reasons will be voidable by the person who lacks the capacity. It is not voidable by the other party under any circumstances. The minor or mentally incompetent party generally must elect to disaffirm the contract, and that election must be made in a timely manner.

A *minor* who enters into a contract has the right to disaffirm that contract any time prior to attainment of majority and for a reasonable length of time thereafter. The major exception to the minor's right to disaffirm is contracts for necessaries. A necessary is an item that is personal to the individual and essential for his or her existence or general welfare or both. Items such as food, shelter, clothing, and medical care are usually classified as necessaries. Other items may, in fact, be necessaries depending upon the individual's station in life. It has been clearly established that things that are necessaries for one person may not be necessaries for another. Because of the obligation of a man to support his wife and children, their food, clothing, shelter, and medical and educational needs have been held to be necessaries. Because of the fact that necessaries must be personal to the individual, items acquired for a minor to engage in business have generally been held not to be necessaries even where the business is the minor's primary source of income (Wallace v. LeRoy, 50 S.E.243 [W. Va. 1905]; Larosa v. Nichols, 103 A. 390 [N.J. 1918]; Covault v. Nevitt, 146 N.W. 1115 [Wis. 1914]). If a minor enters into a contract to purchase necessaries and disaffirms the contract, he or she can be held liable for the reasonable value of the goods or services received. This is a quasi-contractual liability arising out of a contract implied by law. It is not based on the contract that was entered into by the minor.

When a minor disaffirms a contract, the rule has traditionally been that the minor must return any benefits received under the contract to the extent that he or she still has them. If the minor has consumed the consideration received, destroyed it, or in any other way parted with it, the courts generally have not required the minor to repay its value. The reason for this is that to require return of the consideration would be to create a substantial bar to the minor's ability to disaffirm the contract. This is undesirable because a minor's right to disaffirm is deemed an important aspect in protecting minors from unscrupulous dealers in the marketplace. There is an increasing trend of decisions requiring minors who no longer have the consideration to make restitution for the value of the consideration received.

In cases where a minor has misrepresented his or her age and entered into a contract, courts will generally require the minor to return the consideration received. In cases where the consideration has been dissipated, more courts now require the minor to make restitution for the fair value of the consideration received. Other courts, reluctant to hold a minor liable on a contractual basis, have refused to require the minor to return the consideration to the contract but have allowed the other party to the contract to maintain an action under tort principles for deceit (see Chapter 3). The measure of damages generally is equivalent to the value of the consideration received by the minor.

In order to disaffirm a contract, a minor in most cases has to make an election and must notify the other party of that election. If, after attaining age of majority, the individual acts in a manner consistent with the contractual obiligation, he or she will lose his or her right to disaffirm the contract. This is referred to as an act of ratification. Ratification can only take place after attaining the age of majority. When a contract is made between a minor and an adult, only the minor has the right to disaffirm the contract. The adult is and will at all times be required to perform according to the terms of the contract.

Other infirmities exist in contract law. Contracts entered into by persons who are insane are voidable by the insane person. Disaffirmance of the contract needs to be made by the insane person during periods of lucidity or if he or she never regains lucidity by a committee or guardian appointed to act on his or her behalf. As in the case of minors, an exception is made for contracts for necessaries entered into by insane persons. The other party to the contract cannot disaffirm at any time for any reason. A contract made by an insane person can also be ratified by that individual during a period of lucidity. Insanity is generally defined as a state of mind such that the individual lacked the capacity to comprehend the business involved. A person who has been adjudicated in a court of law to be insane is incapable of entering into any contract at any time. An agreement made by such other party will be considered void from the moment it was entered into. A contract that is void is not effective and the noninsane person also has no obligation to perform.

Persons who are drunk are subject to the same rules as minors and persons who are insane. The fact that drunkenness is a self-induced state will not prevent a person from disaffirming a contract entered into while under the influence of alcohol if he or she could not understand the impact of the contract. Though there probably has been little litigation on the matter to date, one can also extend this doctrine to include persons under the influence of narcotics. Acts of disaffirmance (or acts of ratification or both) would have to be made during periods when the individual is no longer affected by the alcohol or drugs. Consideration received would have to be returned if it were available. It is probable that most courts today would require an individual receiving consideration and dissipating it before disaffirming the contract to make restitution.

Illegality

A contract is not binding if made for an illegal purpose even when there is mutual assent, parties are competent, and there has been exchange of consideraton. A contract made for an illegal purpose in many cases cannot be referred to as a contract because it is considered void. Such attempts at contracts should be referred to as illegal agreements. Illegal agreements can be broken into four basic categories: those that are violations of substantive law, those which are violative of specific statutory provisions, those that are contrary to public policy, and those which are ''unconscionable.''

An agreement to commit an act that is prohibited by law even where the agreement itself is not the subject of a specific statute, is an illegal bargain, and is generally considered void. An example of such would be an agreement to rob a bank, commit a murder, or do some other criminal act.

Violations of statutes, the second category, includes bargains that are specifically dealt with by statute. Statutes are of two major types: those that prohibit certain contracts, making them either void, voidable, or unenforceable, and those that are regulatory in nature. An example of a statute making a particular type of bargain illegal is one that prohibits gambling contracts or usurious contracts or prohibits parties from engaging in business on certain days of the week. A contract entered into in violation of such a statute is declared to be void, voidable, or unenforceable by the statute. These will differ from state to state, and no general statement can be made with respect to the appropriate remedy by law.

The second type of statutes comprises regulatory statutes. The purpose of a regulatory statute is to establish certain standards to which the community must conform. Statutes requiring doctors, lawyers, and other professionals to be licensed are generally considered to protect the general public by maintaining the quality of such services at a uniformly high level. A party contracting to render such services in violation of the regulatory requirements (i.e., a person who is not licensed to perform such services under the law) will not be able to enforce such a contract (Ronaldson v. Moss Watkins Inc., 127 So. 467 [La. 1930]).

There are also regulatory statutes that are primarily revenue-raising statutes. A violation of a revenue-raising statute generally will not allow a party to the contract to disaffirm the contract. Revenue-raising statutes can usually be identified as such in that their requirements are strictly financial. If a statute has educational or performance standards required as well as a fee, such statutes are not purely revenue-raising statutes. If, however, anybody can obtain a license by merely paying a specific sum, the statute is primarily revenue-raising, and failure to obtain a license does not render a contract unenforceable.

Plaintiff Wilson was a licensed architect in the state of Hawaii. HIs license lapsed because he failed to pay a $15 renewal fee. Subsequently, he rendered services for the defendant in the amount of almost $34,000. The defendant refused to pay for said services solely on the basis that plaintiff was not licensed and, therefore, the contract entered into was void.

The court examined the rationale behind illegal agreements and found that not all contracts that are illegal are necessarily void. It is necessary to determine the degree of offense, the degree of public harm, and the moral quality of the conduct of the parties. Bargains that do not involve serious moral turpitude perhaps should be enforceable, particularly in cases where the statute in question sets out a specific penalty for the illegality in question. The statute involved here set forth a $500 fine and up to a year imprisonment for practicing architecture without a license. The appellate court held that the renewal requirements under this particular statute were primarily revenue-raising and were not for the purpose of protecting the public from fraud, incompetence, or poor quality. Such a statute will not require an additional penalty, and contracts made in violation of this statute should nonetheless be enforced (Wilson v. Kealakekua Ranch Ltd., 551 P.2d 525 [Hawaii 1976]).

Violations of public policy involve the third category of agreements that are sometimes not enforced by courts, that is, agreements that are contrary to public policy. The transactions covered by such agreements are not in and of themselves crimes, nor do they necessarily violate any statutes. They simply are offensive to what society recognizes as acceptable standards of conduct or morality. For example, public policy encourages people to get married. A contract that would have the effect of discouraging an individual from getting married would be contrary to public policy and would not be enforceable in a court of law.

Another example occurs in the area of free trade. Public policy encourages free enterprise and free trade. Contracts in derogation of a person's right to engage in free trade are contrary to public policy. Such contracts would be unenforceable. Under certain circumstances, it is necessary for an individual to enter into a contract curtailing his or her ability to conduct business when such contract is ancillary to a second contract. Thus, if I sell a business and, as part of the sale of the business, enter into a contract not to compete with the buyer of the business, this will be enforceable. My contract not to compete is clearly in restraint of trade but will be enforced because it is ancillary to the contract for the sale of my business. However, if the limitation upon my competition is unreasonable (e.g., excessive time or geographical area), my contract not to compete will be in restraint of trade, contrary to public policy, and not enforced.

Unconscionability is a fourth category of ''illegal'' agreements that has been created under the Uniform Commercial Code (U.C.C.). The term used for those contracts is unconscionable. Courts will not enforce contracts that are unconscionable. Though codified under the Uniform Commercial Code, this is a principle that has previously existed under the law of equity as well. Unconscionability requires no specific facts or circumstances but generally will arise in a situation where one party takes advantage of another party in a manner that is considered to be unfair or commercially unreasonable. If a court finds a contract or provision of a contract to be unconscionable, it has the choice of refusing to enforce any part of the contract, enforcing the contract without the unconscionable portion, or limiting the application of the unconscionable clause in such a way as to avoid unconscionable results. Where there is a question of unconscionability, both parties should have the opportunity to present the facts and evidence indicating whether the claim of unconscionability is or is not valid (Vlases v. Montgomery Ward, 377 F.2d 846, [3d. Cir. 1967]; Central Budget Corp. v. Sanchez, 279 N.Y.2d 391 [N.Y. 1967]).

Statute of Frauds and Parol Evidence Rule

Generally, a contract does not have to be in writing in order to be binding. Most oral contracts are perfectly legal, enforceable, and valid. A difficulty that exists with respect to oral contracts is establishing their content if and when litigation may be required. Because of the fact that there is no written document, testimony concerning the contents of a contract will be dependent upon the statement of the opposing parties. In cases where there are witnesses, they may be hard to find or to bring to court. Therefore, even though most oral contracts are legally acceptable, it is a good proposition that no contract should be entered into unless its terms are reduced to writing.

The Statute of Frauds is another aspect of contracts to consider. Certain contracts are required to be in writing by various state statutes that collectively are referred to as statutes of frauds. There are several categories of items that are covered almost uniformly by statutes of frauds. These are contracts for the sale of an interest in real estate; contracts that by their terms cannot be completed in less than a year; contracts for the sale of goods in excess of $500; and contracts to answer for the obligations of another person. There are also several other items that are highly technical and will not be discussed in this text. Contracts that are prepared orally and are required under the statute of frauds to be in writing are not enforceable against either of the parties. If both parties choose to perform, there generally is no problem. If one party chooses not to perform, the court cannot compel performance.

In order to satisfy the statute of frauds, there must be a written memorandum indicating the existence of the contract. It is not necessary that the terms of the contract be spelled out. It is only necessary for the writing to show that a contract exists. Oral testimony will be allowed to indicate what the terms of the contract were. The statute of frauds also requires that the party who is to be held liable must have signed the memo. A written memorandum need not constitute a single document; it may consist of letters back and forth between the parties or notations on several different pieces of paper. In some states a written contract is required, and there a series of memoranda would not be sufficient to satisfy the statute of frauds.

Contracts to answer for the debt of another must be in writing. This statement by a father to a car dealer, ''I will pay this obligation if my daughter doesn't,'' would be considered unenforceable unless it were in writing. The exception to this rule is termed the main purpose doctrine or leading object rule. In situations where the object of the promissor is to obtain a benefit that he or she did not previously enjoy, the contract is not covered by the statute of frauds and need not be in writing. Such a contract is deemed to be a primary contract by the promissor rather than a contract of guarantee. For example, the defendant prepared and supervised the printing of 25,000 art catalogs for a private school. The defendant told the plaintiff that payment of the printing costs would be made within 10 days and that if the school (of which the defendant was chairperson and held 100 percent of the voting stock) did not pay, the defendant would pay the full amount. Upon nonpayment by the school, the plaintiff printer sued. The defendant pleaded the statute of frauds as a defense (i.e., the contract was to answer for the debt of the school, was not in writing, and was therefore unenforceable). The court held that since the defendant was being directly benefited because of his position as chairperson of the board and principal stockholder, his statement to pay for the debt of another would be enforceable even though it was not in writing (Stewart Studio Inc., v. National School of Heavy Equipment, Inc., 214 S.E.2d 192 [N.C. 1975]).

Contracts that are not able to be performed within one year must be in writing. The test the courts use is whether or not performance is possible within the one-year period. In a case where an individual is hired for two years, it would appear that the contract would take longer than one year to complete. The courts have ruled that the contract need not be in writing because the employee may not live for more than a year (Co-op Dairy, Inc. v. Dean, 435 P.2d 470 [Ariz. 1968]). In a situation where a farmer agrees to sell a food distributor corn each year for three years at $2.00 a bushel, there must be a written contract in order for the parties to enforce the contract since by its terms it cannot be performed within a year.

The parol evidence rule states that oral evidence of dealings before or at the time of the contract cannot be used to change the language of a written contract. This rule is a rule of evidence, and though it does not allow additions to the contract, it will allow oral evidence to be used to help interpret the terminology of a contract. Oral evidence is also permissible to show clerical or typographical errors, lack of contractual capacity, or to prove various defenses to a contract (fraud, duress, and such). Oral evidence is also admissible to prove conditions precedent to (prior to) a contract. If a contract is not to take place until an event occurs, oral evidence will be allowed to indicate (1) that a contract was conditioned to an event and (2) that the condition has either been met or not.

In a case where a plaintiff filed a suit to recover the price of installation of an awning in front of the defendant's store, oral evidence was allowed to show that the store owner needed to obtain the landlord's permission for the installation of the awning and, therefore, the landlord's permission was a condition precedent to the contract (Washington Tent and Awning Co. v. 818 Ranch, Inc., 248 A.2d 126 [D.C. 1968]).

Oral evidence is also admissible to prove agreements to modify or rescind a contract based on a future event or a condition subsequent. Other exceptions to the parole evidence rule occur in cases where individuals have had prior dealings, trade custom or usage indicates that contracts are normally oral in nature, the contracts are partially written and partially oral, or goods have already been received.

Assignments

An assignment is a transfer of the rights of one party to a contract to another party. An assignor is the individual assigning the right and an assignee is the individual to whom the right is assigned. A contract is composed of two elements: obligations and rights. Obligations are those duties that are imposed on an individual by the contract whereas rights are those benefits that the individual receives under the terms of the contract. As a general rule, an individual may transfer or assign rights acquired in a contract. These rights may include property and services as well as present or future rights to receive money. Many legislatures and courts have determined that it is against public policy to prohibit an assignment of rights. Whereas a contract may have a clause that indicates that the rights may not be assigned without the second party's approval, that approval may not be unreasonably withheld. Assignments can take the form of wage assignments and gift assignments. In the case of a gift assignment, delivery of the property is necessary to make the gift irrevocable. As a general rule, the obligations of a contract may not be assigned without the consent of the other party. These obligations include personal service contracts, contracts to marry, and the like.

In an assignment, the assignee acquires only the rights that the assignor has in the contract. The assignee gets to stand in the shoes of the assignor. He or she acquires no new rights. Contracts that are personal in nature cannot be assigned because the right of the third party would have to change as in the case of an artist. The other party (third party) to the contract continues to maintain the same position that he or she previously held. Defenses of the assignor with respect to fraud, duress, and so on continue to be valid. The third party continues to maintain rights against both the assignor and the assignee unless he or she releases the assignor. In the case where an assignment is made of moneys due, an assignee will lose the right to receive this money if the third party, the debtor, pays the assignor before having notice of the assignment (General Factors, Inc. v. Beck, 409 P.2d 40 [Ariz. 1965]). Partial assignments are allowed.

In making an assignment, the assignor makes certain implied warranties. The assignor warrants that he or she will do nothing to defeat the assignment and also that all the rights that he or she is assigning exist, and any writing evidencing the assignor's right is genuine.

Third Party Beneficiary Contracts

A contract entered into between two individuals specifying that a third individual is to receive certain rights is called a third party beneficiary contract (Lawrence v. Fox, 20 N.Y. 268 [N.Y. 1859]). There are three types of third party beneficiary contracts:

creditor beneficiary, donee beneficiary, and incidental beneficiary. These contracts are distinguished by two features. The first is the beneficiary's relationship to the promisor, and the second is the beneficiary's rights with respect to the contract. In a creditor beneficiary contract, the promisor owes the beneficiary a duty, making the beneficiary a creditor of the promisor. When the promisor makes a contract naming the creditor as beneficiary, the creditor beneficiary acquires rights against both parties.

For example, A owes C, its creditor, $100. A is termed the debtor. A promises B to perform certain services for B in return for $100, the $100 to be paid directly to C. A is the promisor, B is the promisee, and C is a third party creditor beneficiary. If not paid, C may sue either A on the original obligation or B on the third party beneficiary contract.

In a donee beneficiary contract, there is an intent by the promisor to make a gift to the third party. The donee beneficiary has rights against the promisee but not against the promisor. For example, A promises to perform certain work for B if B will pay $100 to D. D is a friend of A, and A wishes to bestow a birthday present on him. D is a donee beneficiary. D has no rights against the original promisor A because there is no obligation to provide a gift, but D does have rights against B, the promisee in the amount of $100 (assuming A did the work for B).

In an incidental beneficiary contract there is no direct intent to bestow a benefit on the third party, and therefore the third party derives no rights against either the promisee or the promisor of the original contract. As an example, E is patiently waiting for a new interstate highway to open so he can get to work faster. The state has a contract with the X construction company to build the highway. E is an incidental beneficiary of this contract. He has no right to sue either party if there is a construction delay.

In an action by a donee or creditor beneficiary, the promisee may assert any defense that he or she has or may have. Such defenses were covered in the previous section and include fraud, duress, and so on.

Discharges and Remedies

A *discharge* of contract is anything that will cause a binding promise to cease to be binding. Discharge may result from performance, prevention of performance, breach of contract or disaffirmance, release, discharge of a joint debtor, mutual recision, renunciation, accord and satisfaction, novation, material alteration, and merger. In addition, certain laws, or changes of laws, such as subsequent illegality or bankruptcy or both will also cause a contract to be discharged.

Performance means the completion of all one's duties under the contract. If someone prevents you from completing your duties under a contract, that is called prevention of performance and will also discharge a contract. If someone fails to perform under the terms of the contract, there is a breach of contract.

One party to a contract may relinquish the right to compel the other party's performance under the contract; if this is done, there is a release. When a release is executed by both parties, there is no further obligation under the contract. But if you release an individual who is jointly liable on a contract (a joint debtor), then you have also released the other individual (other joint debtor). When each party releases the other, it is sometimes called mutual recision. A renunciation occurs when one or both parties state that they are no longer going to abide by the contract.

An accord and satisfaction consists of a new contract called an accord. The accord will state that the old contract has been satisfied. This means that a new contract changes the existing contract and satisfies all its requirements. A novation is also a new contract and differs from an accord and satisfaction in that in a novation one of the parties to the new contract was not a party to the old contract. In an accord and satisfaction, the parties are the same in both contracts. The term *merger* is sometimes used to describe what happens in an accord and satisfaction or a novation.

If an individual materially alters a contract by fraud or otherwise or if the terms of the contract become illegal after the contract has been entered into, there is a discharge of contract.

Declaration of bankruptcy, (discussed in Chapter 6), causes the bankruptcy court to declare that some of a bankrupt's contractual obligations are no longer binding.

Remedies are alternatives the individual who has been harmed has when a contract has been discharged because of a wrongful act. These alternatives are called remedies and include monetary damages, which can be liquidated, compensatory, or punitive. Damages are computed by taking into consideration what the individual, who is not guilty of the breach, has lost from the other individual's actions. These damages can include lost wages, and such; the damages are computed as actual dollars lost.

Liquidated damages are specific amounts set forth in the contract. Compensatory damages are awarded to compensate for losses that are not presently definable in terms of exact dollars. They are estimates of possible future dollar losses. Punitive damages are those monetary awards imposed by the courts to punish the party who has breached the contract. Punitive damages are awarded in situations where the defendant has breached the contract with wanton disregard for the rights of the other individuals involved. In determining the amount of monetary damages, courts require a plaintiff to attempt to limit his or her losses (mitigate the damages). Courts will not allow a plaintiff to recover for losses that could have been prevented had the plaintiff acted in a reasonable manner. For example, if a plaintiff landlord contracted with a defendant tenant to rent an apartment and the tenant breaches the contract, the landlord must make a reasonable attempt to mitigate his or her damages by trying to rerent the apartment.

Another remedy that may be available is specific performance. Specific performance is a mandate by the court ordering the defendant to perform under the terms of the original agreement. This remedy is appropriate when a specific, unique, and unusual property exists, such as real estate or rare antiques. When monetary compensation would be inadequate or inappropriate, courts will allow specific performance. An injuction is a form of specific performance used by the courts to restrict an individual from doing something that legally should not be done. For example, a professional singer is engaged to sing at a specific theater. The singer subsequently is engaged to sing at another theater during the same time period. The first theater owner cannot compel specific performance but could obtain an injunction prohibiting appearance at the second theater.

QUESTIONS

1. The plaintiff, Womack, was engaged in gambling in Saline County, Arkansas. The defendant was a judge of the Circuit Court of Saline County. The plaintiff during a period of time paid the defendant in excess of $1600 in order that the defendant would prevent the plaintiff from being prosecuted or punished for engaging in gambling. The plaintiff then sued the defendant, asking for return of the $1600 bribe on the grounds that the contract made with the defendant was void and unlawful. Decision for whom? Discuss.

2. Defendant Rogers was nineteen years old, emancipated, and married, and his wife was expecting a child. The defendant quit school and decided to go to work. He went to the office of the plaintiff employment agency and signed an agreement to pay a specified fee in the event that the plaintiff was instrumental in finding him a job. The plaintiff found the defendant a job the defendant accepted. The plaintiff sued the defendant to recover the commission, which the defendant refused to pay. The defendant argued that he had entered into the contract while a minor and, therefore, was not liable to the plaintiff for the amount of the employment fee. Decision for whom? Discuss.

3. The defendant's father was admitted to a hospital at which the plaintiff was a physician. The defendant's father was in need of medical attention, and the question arose as to payment of the bills. The defendant made statements to this effect: "Go right ahead, and give him whatever is necessary to save his life, and I will pay for it"; "we want you to do everything you can to save his life, and we don't want you to spare any expense because whatever he needs, Doctor, you go ahead and get it, and I will pay you." Services were rendered in the amount of $3000, and the defendant refused to pay the bulk of this amount. The defendant's argument is that the services were rendered for the benefit of his father and therefore his promises constitute gratuitous promises and under the statute of frauds are required to be in writing. Decision for whom? Discuss.

4. Corcoran received a copy of a proposed contract, which specified that if it were not signed by him and returned to the school district on or before a specified date, the board had the right to withdraw the offer. The superintendent of the school called his attention to this provision in the employment contract, and Corcoran informed the superintendent that he was considering employment elsewhere. The contract was not returned until two days after the required date, and the school board indicated they would not rehire Corcoran. Corcoran brought an action on the grounds that he had accepted the contract and was, therefore, entitled to the job. The school district defends on the basis that the requirement within the contract for an acceptance date was an integral part of the contract and, since it had not been met, there was no acceptance. Decision for whom? Discuss.

5. Rollins was a convict who was involved in a prison riot, capturing a guard, and holding him hostage. An official of the prison, fearing for the safety of the prison guard, agreed

to meet the demands of the prisoners, including a promise for immunity from all prosecution resulting from the incident at the prison. Subsequently, the attorney general brought an action to prosecute Rollins, and he contended that such prosecution was precluded by the agreement made with the prison official. Decision for whom? Discuss.

6 The defendant, Burgess, signed a document that ostensibly granted the plaintiff university a 60-day option to purchase the defendant's home. The agreement stipulated that the defendant had received the sum of ''$1.00 and other valuable consideration.'' It was conceded at the trial that neither the dollar nor any other consideration was ever paid or tendered to the defendant. The plaintiff subsequently gave defendant written notice of its intent to exercise the option. The defendant rejected the plaintiff's tender of the purchase price. The plaintiff sued the defendant for specific performance. The defendant's argument is that the agreement is void for lack of consideration even though there was a recitation of consideration received. The defendant argues that such a recitation is not binding if the consideration, in fact, has not been received. Decision for whom? Discuss.

7 The defendent, Brimmel, was the owner of property. He entered into a contract with Semro for him to act as a general contractor to construct a home for Brimmel. Semro acquired fill from the plaintiff, Gebhardt, and had it delivered to the property. Brimmel testified that he had been advised by Semro that there would have to be some fill brought onto the property but that he understood that the cost of the fill was included in the cost of the general contract agreement. Brimmel was further assured by the general contractor at the time of completion of the house that all bills were paid and the property was free and clear of any claims. Gabhardt (plaintiff) tried to collect payment for the fill from Semro but was unsuccessful. Subsequently, he brought an action against Brimmel, demanding payment for the fill. The basis for the suit was that in the absence of Brimmel's payment to Gebhardt, Brimmel would be unjustly enriched by the value of the fill. Judgment for whom? Discuss.

8 The defendant acquired an automobile from the plaintiff by financing the bulk of the purchase price. The defendant represented that she was an adult but was only a minor. She gave possession of the vehicle to another individual, who delivered it to a third individual, and, at the time of the trial, it was not available to either the plaintiff or the defendant. The plaintiff sued the defendant for the purchase price of the automobile. The defendant argued that at the time she purchased the vehicle she was a minor, had not ratified the contract since that time, had disaffirmed the contract, and therefore was not obligated for the purchase price. Decision for whom? Discuss.

9 Glover's daughter was dating an individual who was wanted for a crime. The police visited Mrs. Glover, who told them that her daughter and her boyfriend had left the area. The police requested information as to friends and relatives that the daughter might be visiting, and Glover told them of several individuals. The police subsequently found both Glover's daughter and the individual they wanted at one of these addresses, arrested the individual, and brought him back for trial. He was convicted. Unknown to Glover, at the time all this took place, the defendant had published an advertisement in the newspaper offering a reward of $500 ''to the person or persons furnishing information resulting in the apprehension and conviction of the persons guilty of the murder of. . . .'' The individual arrested as a result of the information that Glover gave the police, in fact, was the individual responsible for the above crime. Glover instituted this suit to recover the $500 reward from the defendant. Decision for whom? Discuss.

10 The plaintiff worked for the defendant. They entered into an agreement "to share the profit" from the sales of houses being built by the defendant in addition to the payment of a salary to the plaintiff. After several years, the plaintiff had not been paid any share of profits (he believed the defendant had earned at least $200,000). The plaintiff brought an action claiming that he was entitled to at least 10 percent of the profits in exchange for services he has rendered. Decision for whom and why?

11 The plaintiff was a worker working in the defendant's place of business. He was engaged in dropping a cement block from the second floor of a building to the first floor when he saw that the defendant was beneath the place where the item would be dropped. In order to avoid hitting the defendant, the plaintiff fell through from the second floor to the first floor holding onto the block to divert it from the defendant. The defendant was not injured, but the plaintiff was. As a result of the plaintiff's actions, the defendant agreed to maintain the plaintiff for the rest of the plaintiff's life and to pay him an amount of money sufficient that he would be able to survive. Payments continued until the death of the defendant and were discontinued by the defendant's estate. The plaintiff sued the estate to have the payments continued until his death. The issue presented was whether there was consideration for the promise of the defendant to the plaintiff. Decision for whom? Discuss.

12 Loral Corporation was awarded a contract by the U.S. Navy for the production of radar units. There was a schedule of deliveries and a liquidated damages clause for failure to meet those deliveries. There were 40 separate components needed to produce the radar sets and Austin was awarded a subcontract for 23 of these units. Loral subsequently obtained a second contract and solicited bids again. Austin indicated that unless they were given the contract on all 40 units, they would refuse to deliver the parts that they were awarded on the first contract. In addition, they indicated that they would not make any deliveries unless they were given substantial increases in the prices that they were awarded under the first contract. Loral refused to consent to this, and Austin stopped delivery. After contacting a number of other suppliers and being unable to find the needed parts within the requisite time period, Loral finally accepted Austin's demands. Upon completion of the contracts, Loral sued Austin, claiming damages in the amount of approximately $22,000. They argued that the terms of the new contract that they had entered into were voidable on grounds of economic duress. Decision for whom? Discuss.

13 The plaintiff corporation was a collection agency. The defendant entered into a six-year employment contract with the plaintiff and agreed that for a period of two years after termination of the contract he would not go into competition with the plaintiff. The reason was that the plaintiff, in the process of training, would give the defendant certain trade secrets and information that he did not wish the defendant to utilize in a competing business. Later, the defendant terminated his employment and after one month organized a collection agency located approximately 200 feet from the plaintiff's business. He also acquired a number of accounts that previously had been serviced by the plaintiff. The agreement entered into between the plaintiff and defendant stipulated that, in the event of a breach of the covenant of noncompetition, there were damages to be awarded to the plaintiff in a liquidated amount of $5,000. The trial court found in favor of the plaintiff. The defendant appeals on the grounds that the covenant was not reasonable and that the liquidated damage provision constituted a penalty and therefore was void. Decision for whom? Discuss.

PART TWO

SALES AND PERSONAL PROPERTY—CONSUMER LAW

Consumer law is a body of law that encompasses state and federal laws providing protection for individuals in the marketplace. Chapter 5 includes the statutory enactments in the Uniform Commercial Code, as well as federal agencies and law set up to protect the consumer from breach of warranty, deceptive advertising practices, and so forth.

Consumer protection encompasses sales by mail, door-to-door, or in stores. Chapter 6 discusses credit buying and debtors' rights as well as individuals' rights in banking transactions. Chapter 7 discusses an individual's personal property rights as they relate to various matters such as money, renting a car, or having one repaired.

CHAPTER 5

Sales

UNIFORM COMMERCIAL CODE (U.C.C.)

The Uniform Commercial Code (U.C.C.) is an act that has been adopted in whole or in part in all 50 states. It deals with commercial transactions and modifies the common and statutory law of personal property and contracts. The code's purpose is to achieve uniformity of the laws of commerce ("the sale of and payment for goods") throughout the states. The code includes nine parts called articles, including Sales (Article 2); Commercial Paper (Article 3); Bank Deposits and Collections (Article 4); and Warehouse Receipts, Bills of Lading, and Other Documents of Title (Article 7). These articles deal with all phases of commercial transactions, from the contract of sale and payment (including credit) to the transfer or storage of the goods.

Offer and Acceptance

There are many sections in the code that apply to the consumer. For example, the Uniform Commercial Code in the article devoted to sales indicates that an offer to make a contract may be accepted in any manner and by any means that seem to be reasonable unless the offeror has made it clear that he or she requires a particular form of acceptance. This modifies the common law rules of contracts outlined in Chapter 4 requiring that mailed offers be accepted by mail, and so on. Offers to buy goods for prompt shipment may be accepted by a prompt promise to ship or by the prompt shipment of goods (conforming or nonconforming). A shipment of nonconforming goods does not constitute an acceptance if the seller notifies the buyer that the shipment is offered only as an accommodation to the buyer.

The U.C.C. also allows contracts to be formed even though one or more of the terms are left open. In the event that the time of formation of the contract cannot be determined, the parties have intended to make a contract, and there is a reasonably certain basis for giving the remedy, the courts will hold the parties to the least that they have bargained for.

The code changes the common law rules with respect to firm offers. Under common law an offer could be terminated at the option of the offeror unless the offeree had paid for the option. The U.C.C. indicates that an offer by a merchant to sell goods in a signed writing that states that the offer will be held open is not revocable for up to three months, even if consideration is lacking.

Usage of Trade

In dealing with acceptance, the Uniform Commercial Code allows for acceptance to include nonconforming goods as well as additional terms if the additional terms are not material and are not objected to by the offerer. The code goes on to explain that the course of performance, usage of trade, and course of dealings will also be used in determining the meaning of agreements. For example, a contract calls for the delivery of 10 cords of firewood. If it is normal to deliver the wood unstacked (in a pile), the customer cannot insist on stacking as a prerequisite for acceptance unless this is specifically agreed to as part of the contract. (Usage of trade is sometimes also called custom and usage.)

If stacking were normal practice and the first several cords were delivered unstacked without objection by the buyer, the buyer may not now be able to insist on stacking (course of performance). If in prior years this buyer had not insisted on stacking and had dealt with this seller, the buyer could not insist on stacking after making the contract (course of dealing).

Unconscionability

The U.C.C. indicates that if a contract or clause is "unconscionable" at the time it was made, a court may refuse to enforce the contract or the clause. *Unconscionable* means "against public policy or so one-sided as to be shockingly unfair, harsh, unjust, or outrageous. This section of the code has been utilized to help customers in many cases. For instance, in one case the court held that a disclaimer of warranties did not limit the plaintiff from obtaining recourse against the seller of a new car when the seller delivered a car with substantial mileage. In addition, this section of the code was used by Bekkevold v. Potts, 216 N.W. 790 (Minn. 1927), where the court refused to allow warranty of fitness imposed by law to be negated by a clause excluding all warranties made by the seller.

Other Departures from Common Law

Other sections of the code that change common law and protect consumers give a buyer the right to inspect goods prior to delivery. If an item does not conform to the contract or breaches implied or express warranties, a buyer can accept any part of the shipment or reject the entire shipment. A rejection must be made within a reasonable time after the goods have been delivered. Buyers must notify a seller of their rejection within a reasonable time after they discover the defect or breach of contract. After rejection, the buyer cannot exercise any ownership rights over the goods; the buyer must hold the goods for the seller. If an item is rejected and it is perishable, the buyer may hold the goods and charge the seller for the reasonable cost of protecting the goods from spoiling.

In the event that a contract has been breached by the seller, the Uniform Commercial Code provides a buyer with remedies for the breach. If a seller does not deliver goods, the buyer may make a good faith, timely, reasonable purchase of similar goods from another seller. The buyer is then entitled to recover the difference in the market price at the time of the breach and the original contract price. This remedy is called cover. If the buyer is unable to recover and the goods are specifically identified at the time of the contract, the buyer may be entitled to replevin. Replevin is a remedy entitling the buyer to get the goods.

If the buyer accepts goods that do not conform to the contract, he or she may notify the seller that the goods do not conform and may recover damages. The measure of damages is equal to the difference, at the time and place of acceptance, between the value of the goods accepted and the value they would have had if they had conformed to the contract. A buyer may also be able to recover consequential damages or, if the goods are unique, specific performance.

Buyers, on notifying the seller of their intention, may deduct all or part of damages resulting from a breach of contract from any part of the price still remaining to be paid under the contract.

For sellers to avail themselves of any of these remedies, the sellers must bring an action on the contract for sale within four (4) years after the cause of action has accrued. The cause of action accrues when the breach occurs regardless of the aggrieved party's lack of knowledge of the breach. A breach of warranty occurs when tender of delivery is made unless there is an explicit extension of the warranty.

Auctions

The Uniform Commercial Code also provides rules for sales by auction. A sale by auction is complete when the auctioneer announces that sale by the fall of the hammer. If a bid is coming at the time that the hammer is falling, it is up to the auctioneer to make a determination as to whether or not the bidding should be reopened. The two methods in which auction sales take place are those ''with reserve,'' which is the normal procedure, and those ''without reserve.'' When an auction is ''with reserve,'' the auctioneer may withdraw the goods at any time until he or she announces completion of the sale by the fall of the hammer. In an action ''without reserve,'' after the auctioneer calls for bids, the article cannot be withdrawn unless no bid is made. In either type of auction, bidders may retract their bids until the auctioneer announces completion of the sale. A bidder's retraction of a bid does not revive any previous bid. An owner of goods is able to bid at an auction unless prohibited by contract or statute.

WARRANTIES

Warranties are promises by sellers or manufacturers to stand behind their products. There are several types of warranties: written, which includes full and limited warranties; spoken; and implied. Both Federal and State laws have provisions with respect to warranties.

Under state law, implied warranties are outlined in the Uniform Commercial Code, Article 2. This article protects the buyer against defects in title and merchantability. The buyer of goods is given a warranty, in the absence of an express statement to the contrary, that title to the goods that are being transferred to him or her is ''rightful'' and that the goods are delivered free from ''security interest or liens.'' What this means to you is that if the appliance or automobile you bought was stolen or subject to a lien, you will have an action against the individual who sold the items for any damages you may incur as a result of the breach of warranty. This rule is operational so long as the seller is not outside the jurisdiction of the courts.

Merchantability—Fitness for Particular Purpose

The warranty of merchantability is the seller's promise that the product is fit for the ordinary use of that product. For example, if you went to a restaurant and ordered fish, it would be fit for human consumption and would not contain any foreign material. This warranty extends to all goods sold by a merchant unless there are variations by agreement.

If you go into a clothing store and the salesperson tells you that the raincoat you're buying is waterproof or the label indicates that the raincoat is waterproof, the warranty of fitness for a particular use will cover any damages that may occur to you because of the severe drenching you get in a spring shower. Such damages may include illness or destruction of clothing that you might be wearing underneath the raincoat.

The code goes on to require further that if you rely on the seller's skill, judgment, or advice to furnish you with suitable goods for a particular purpose, those goods must be fit for that purpose. The seller will be liable for damages if the goods are not suitable for that purpose.

There is a distinction between merchantability and fitness for a particular purpose. The latter envisions a specific use by the buyer that is peculiar to the nature of his or her business. Merchantability envisions the ordinary purpose for which goods are used and applies to the uses that are customarily made of the goods. For example, shoes used for the purpose of walking upon ordinary ground would be covered under warrant of merchantability and should not wear out after several miles. If the seller knows or should know that a particular pair is going to be used to climb mountains, the warranty of fitness for a particular purpose would be applicable.

The implied warranties of fitness for a particular purpose and merchantability can be excluded or modified only by a specific disclaimer of the warranty. With respect to the implied warranty of merchantability, the disclaimer must mention merchantability and must be conspicuous if the contract is in writing. With respect to the implied warranty of fitness for a particular purpose, the exclusion can be in general language. If the contract is in writing, the exclusion must be conspicuous.

Exclusion of Implied Warranties

All implied warranties may be excluded by expressions in the contract such as ''as is,'' ''with all faults,'' or other language that, under common usage, would bring a buyer's attention to the fact that these warranties are excluded. In cases where a buyer examines a sample or model or refuses to examine goods before entering into the contract, the warranty regarding defects to which an examination would have enlightened the buyer is waived. It is not sufficient that the goods are available for inspection in order to cause the transaction to be within the scope of this waiver. The seller must demand that the buyer examine the goods fully. If the offer to examine the goods is accompanied by words from the seller that they are merchantable or that they have specific attributes and the buyer indicates clearly that he or she is relying on the seller's words rather than on the examination, then the express warranty will prevail.

Express Warranties

The U.C.C. also deals with express warranties. The contract of sale need not have a written clause indicating "warranty." The code says that a seller has warranted an item expressly if any of the following take place: (1) any affirmation of fact or promise made by the seller to the buyer relating to the goods; (2) any description of the goods that is made part of the basis of the bargain; (3) any sample or model that is made a part of the bargain. In the event that any of the three items is present in your discussions and final bargain with the seller, this will be a valuable tool to you in getting repaid for damages that you have incurred as a result of a product that did not work according to the expectations you had. (For an example of an express warranty, see statements in Exhibit 5–1).

A word of caution. The code does not allow for restitution when the seller has only been giving you his or her opinion with respect to the goods. You must be careful with respect to "puffing" and other types of sales practices that are fair game. The proposition "let the buyer beware" is often still in effect.

It is important for the consumer also to be aware that the U.C.C. warranties only apply if the seller is a merchant (one who regularly trades in goods) with respect to the goods sold (Conald v. City National Bank, 329 So. 2d 92 [Ala. 1972]).

The code also provides that users of a product, other than the purchaser, are also protected by expressed and implied warranties. The category of users may include individuals in the immediate family or household, as well as guests who might use a particular product. Some states extend the protection to all individuals who may use the product.

Magnuson-Moss Warranty Act

The Magnuson-Moss Warranty Act is a federal statute that applies to warranties of consumer products costing more than $15. The act does not require that all goods be warrantied, but it does require that warranties may be available for consumers to see before they buy. This federal act requires that all warranties be in writing and use ordinary language. The warranties must be easy to read and understand. Every term and condition must be clearly spelled out. Fine print is not allowed.

If a company gives a "full warranty," then it must repair or replace a defective product for free, including removal and reinstallation when necessary. The law also requires that a product will be repaired within a reasonable time after you have told

EXHIBIT 5-1
Full Warranty

WE WANT YOU TO BE A HAPPY SATISFIED CUSTOMER

IF YOU NEED SERVICE OR ASSISTANCE, WE SUGGEST YOU FOLLOW THESE 4 STEPS.

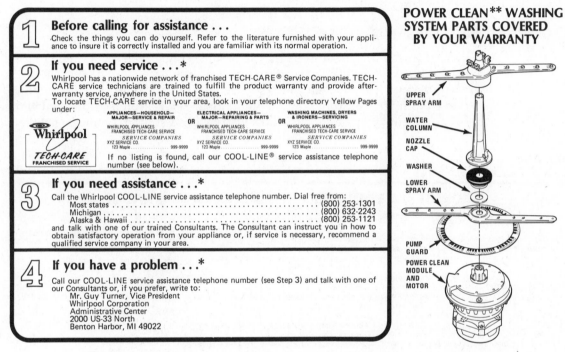

1 **Before calling for assistance . . .**
Check the things you can do yourself. Refer to the literature furnished with your appliance to insure it is correctly installed and you are familiar with its normal operation.

2 **If you need service . . .***
Whirlpool has a nationwide network of franchised TECH-CARE® Service Companies. TECH-CARE service technicians are trained to fulfill the product warranty and provide after-warranty service, anywhere in the United States.
To locate TECH-CARE service in your area, look in your telephone directory Yellow Pages under:

APPLIANCES—HOUSEHOLD—MAJOR—SERVICE & REPAIR	ELECTRICAL APPLIANCES—MAJOR—REPAIRING & PARTS	WASHING MACHINES, DRYERS & IRONERS—SERVICING
WHIRLPOOL APPLIANCES FRANCHISED TECH-CARE SERVICE *SERVICE COMPANIES* XYZ SERVICE CO. 123 Maple 999-9999	WHIRLPOOL APPLIANCES FRANCHISED TECH-CARE SERVICE *SERVICE COMPANIES* XYZ SERVICE CO. 123 Maple 999-9999	WHIRLPOOL APPLIANCES FRANCHISED TECH-CARE SERVICE *SERVICE COMPANIES* XYZ SERVICE CO. 123 Maple 999-9999

Whirlpool TECH-CARE FRANCHISED SERVICE

If no listing is found, call our COOL-LINE® service assistance telephone number (see below).

3 **If you need assistance . . .***
Call the Whirlpool COOL-LINE service assistance telephone number. Dial free from:
Most states . . . . (800) 253-1301
Michigan . . . . (800) 632-2243
Alaska & Hawaii . . . . (800) 253-1121
and talk with one of our trained Consultants. The Consultant can instruct you in how to obtain satisfactory operation from your appliance or, if service is necessary, recommend a qualified service company in your area.

4 **If you have a problem . . .***
Call our COOL-LINE service assistance telephone number (see Step 3) and talk with one of our Consultants or, if you prefer, write to:
Mr. Guy Turner, Vice President
Whirlpool Corporation
Administrative Center
2000 US-33 North
Benton Harbor, MI 49022

POWER CLEAN WASHING SYSTEM PARTS COVERED BY YOUR WARRANTY**

UPPER SPRAY ARM
WATER COLUMN
NOZZLE CAP
WASHER
LOWER SPRAY ARM
PUMP GUARD
POWER CLEAN MODULE AND MOTOR

*If you must call or write, please provide: model number, serial number, date of purchase, and a complete description of the problem. This information is needed in order to better respond to your request for assistance.

** Tmk.

the company about the problem and that you will not have to do anything unreasonable to get the warranty service (e.g., drive to another state). A full warranty is good for anyone who owns the product during the warranty period. If the product has not been repaired after a reasonable number of tries, you can get a replacement or a refund (Lemon provision). You do not have to return a warranty card for a product with a full warranty, but a company may give you a registration card and suggest that it be returned. This return is voluntary. A full warranty cannot disclaim, deny, or limit the implied warranties such as merchantability or fitness for particular purpose.

The Magnuson-Moss Warranty Act defines limited warranty as a warranty that gives the consumer less than the full warranty protections. For example, any warranty that requires the consumer to pay for labor, reinstallation, and the like, or that requires the consumer to bring a heavy product back to the store would be considered a limited warranty. A product can have more than one written warranty; for example, an automobile may have a full warranty on engine and transmission and a limited warranty against rust, tire damage, and the like. (See Exhibit 5–2 for an example of limited warranty.)

Oral Warranties

Statements made by salespersons that are not in writing such as ''We will fix anything that breaks,'' are legally considered to be warranties with the same effect as a written warranty. The problem with a spoken warranty is that it is difficult to prove, so it is important to get your warranty in writing. Service contracts are sometimes called extended warranties or additional warranties. A service contract is not really

EXHIBIT 5-2
Limited Warranty

ORIGINAL EQUIPMENT TIRES LIMITED WARRANTY

WHAT IS COVERED

Each tire supplied as original equipment on your new Nissan/Datsun vehicle is warranted by one of the warrantors* listed at the end of this warranty.

This warranty does not cover ''Foldable Spare'', ''Space Saver Spare'' or The Goodyear Tire & Rubber Company's tires. These are covered by separate warranties. Other exceptions are listed below under the caption ''WHAT IS NOT COVERED.''

This warranty covers defects in materials or workmanship that cause your tire to become unserviceable.

WHAT THE WARRANTOR WILL DO AND FOR HOW LONG

The warrantor will replace any tire without charge if tires become unserviceable during the first 25% of original tread depth for steel belted radial tires, during the first 50% of original tread depth for temporary spare tire or during the first 10% of original tread depth for other tires. Mounting and balancing are included.

If a tire becomes unserviceable after the tread depth stated above, the warrantor will provide a replacement tire at a reduced price, charging you for the amount of tread depth actually used. This is called ''treadwear proration.'' Free mounting and balancing are not provided.

This warranty ends when the tread has worn down to the tread wear indicators molded into the tire.

WHAT IS NOT COVERED

This warranty does not cover:
- Damage, failure or premature wear due to:
  Road hazard (for example, nails, glass, etc.)
  Accident, theft or fire
  Oil or chemical action
  Use of tire chains
  Off-road use, including use in racing or other competitive events.
  Misuse
  Misalignment, improper inflation, wheel imbalance or overloading
  Defects in your vehicle covered by your vehicle warranty
  Temporary spare tire used over 50 MPH (80 km/h)
- Repairable punctures
- Tires worn down to the tread wear indicators molded into the tire.
- INCIDENTAL OR CONSEQUENTIAL DAMAGES SUCH AS LOSS OF USE OF THE TIRE OR VEHICLE ON WHICH IT IS USED, INCONVENIENCE OR COMMERCIAL LOSS. Some states do not allow the exclusion or limitation of incidental or consequential damages, so the above limitation or exclusion may not apply to you.

WHAT YOU MUST DO

- In order to obtain warranty service, you must deliver the unserviceable tire to an authorized Nissan/Datsun dealer or to an authorized dealer of the warrantor in the United States or Canada. Their names and addresses are listed in telephone directories.

- If ''treadwear proration'' applies, you must pay for the amount of tread depth actually used on the unserviceable tire when you receive your new tire. You must also pay for taxes, mounting, balancing, and any additional services which are not covered by this warranty.

OTHER WARRANTY TERMS AND STATE LAW RIGHTS

- ANY IMPLIED WARRANTY OF MERCHANTABILITY AND FITNESS FOR A PARTICULAR PURPOSE SHALL BE LIMITED TO THE DURATION OF THIS WRITTEN WARRANTY. Some states do not allow limitations on how long an implied warranty lasts, so the above limitations may not apply to you. This warranty gives you specific legal rights, and you may also have other rights which vary from state to state.
- The tire warrantors do not authorize any person to create for them any other warranty, obligation or liability in connection with this vehicle.

*THE WARRANTORS

- The warrantor of Bridgestone Tires is Bridgestone Tire Company of America, Inc., 2000 West 190th Street, Torrance, California 90504.
- The warrantor of Toyo Tires is Toyo Tire (U.S.A.) Corporation, 3136 East Victoria Street, Compton, California 90221.
- The warrantor of Yokohama Tires is Yokohama Tire Corporation, 1530 Church Road, Montebello, California 90640.
- The warrantor of Dunlop original equipment tires is Dunlop Japan Limited. However, Dunlop Tire and Rubber Corporation, Buffalo, New York 14240, will, through their dealer organization honor all tires warranted by Dunlop Japan Limited in the U.S.A.

a warranty. Warranties come free with the product, and you must pay extra for a service contract. If you are offered a service contract on a product, it is important for you to review the written warranties and think about the implied warranties; then read the service contact and see if it offers additional protection. In many cases, the service contract may not be necessary because you are already protected by warranty, either expressed or implied.

Breach of Warranty

When a warranty is breached, a consumer's normal recourse is to sue for both actual and consequential damages. An award of actual damages requires that the company must fix or replace the defective product. An award of consequential damages requires that the company must pay for any damage that the failure of their product caused. For example, when you purchase a new refrigerator and the

EXHIBIT 5-2, cont.

CONSUMER ASSISTANCE

Your complete satisfaction with your vehicle is of primary concern to your Nissan/Datsun dealer and NISSAN. Your Nissan/Datsun dealer is always available to assist you with all your automobile service requirements.

If a problem arises that you feel has not been handled satisfactorily through normal channels, please take the following steps:

STEP 1. Discuss the problem with your Nissan/ Datsun dealership management first.

If you feel something more should be done, and the dealer is unable to resolve the matter satisfactorily, follow step 2.

STEP 2. Contact the Consumer Relations Department at the Nissan/Datsun regional office listed under the caption "NISSAN/DATSUN OFFICES." The Consumer Relations Department will ask for the following information:
● Your name, address and telephone number
● Vehicle identification number
● Date of purchase
● Odometer reading
● Your Nissan/Datsun dealer's name
● Nature of problem

If after completion of step 2 further assistance is still required move to step 3.

STEP 3. Write to the address below.

> Consumer Relations Department
> National Service Department
> Nissan Motor Corporation in U.S.A.
> P.O. Box 191, Gardena, CA 90247

PLEASE

May we reiterate that ultimately your questions will most likely be resolved at your dealership, utilizing his facilities, equipment and technical personnel. So HELP US TO SERVE YOU! —USE the three STEPS in sequential order 1, 2, and 3.

refrigerator fails to operate while it is loaded with food, the actual damages that the company will have to pay for would be the repair or replacement of the refrigerator. In addition, the company would have to pay consequential damages for the loss due to spoilage of the food in the refrigerator. A seller can avoid paying for consequential damages by having the warranty specifically exclude these types of damages.

In the event that you do have a warranty problem, it is important to have your sales slip, your warranty, and the date you purchased the product. Some warranties are for a limited time and only cover original purchasers. If a warranty extends to subsequent purchasers, the subsequent purchaser must obtain this information from the original purchaser. In addition, it is important that you follow any warranty maintenance that is required by the company and that you use the product according to the manufacturer's instructions.

If the product breaks, the first step you should take is to read the product instructions and warranty to make sure that you are covered. The next step is to contact the right person in the right company, describe the problem, and specify exactly what relief you want, that is, repair, refund, replacement, or consequential damages. Make sure that all correspondence is by certified mail, and keep all copies. If the company does not resolve your problem, the next step would be to contact the local consumer protection office and complaint center or a national trade group (AUTO CAP) or a federal agency (FTC) or both. If none of the above avenues is satisfactory, a lawsuit as discussed in Chapter 3 might be contemplated. If the product was manufactured after July 4, 1975, you can sue the company under the Magnuson-Moss Warranty Act. If the product was manufactured prior to that date, state laws with respect to warranties as discussed under the Uniform Commercial Code should protect you.

SHOPPING BY MAIL

The Federal Trade Commission (FTC) has a rule that gives you rights when you order by mail. This rule provides that you must receive the merchandise when the seller says you will. If merchandise is not delivered within this time period, you can cancel your order and get your money back. The seller must ship the merchandise to you no later than 30 days after your order is received unless a longer period is specified. This rule supplements the U.C.C. rule (§ 2-206) defining acceptance.

A seller must notify a consumer if the promised delivery date cannot be met. The seller must also tell the consumer what the new shipping date will be and give the consumer the option either to cancel the order and receive full refund or to agree to the new shipping date. The seller must also provide the consumer with a free way to answer, such as a stamped envelope or a postage paid postcard. If you do not answer, it means you agree to the shipping delay. If you cancel a prepaid order under the terms of the Federal Trade Commission rule, the seller must mail you a refund within seven business days. If the sale was a credit sale, the seller must adjust your account within one billing cycle (30 days). This mail order rule does not apply to photofinishing, magazine subscriptions and other serial deliveries (monthly, weekly), mail order seeds and growing plants, C.O.D. orders, or credit orders where the buyer's account is not charged prior to shipment of the merchandise.

Whenever you order anything through the mail, it is important to protect yourself. You should read the product description and make sure the product offered is what you really want. Do not rely on pictures. If possible, investigate the advertisers' claims. Find out what the merchandise return policy is, keep a copy of your order blank, make a note of the merchant's name and address and the date you sent in your order, and hold on to your canceled check and charge account records. If you have any problems at a later date, the preceding advice and information may be useful to you in resolving these problems. In addition, if your purchase is by credit card, you have certain rights applicable to all users of credit cards (see Chapter 6).

In addition to the mail order rule, the Federal Trade Commission also has a rule that allows for only two kinds of merchandise to be mailed to you without your prior consent. These items include free samples and merchandise mailed by a charitable organization for contributions. It is illegal for the sender to pressure you to return unordered merchandise or to send you a bill for these items. This same rule applies to unordered charitable merchandise. To make sure that you are on firm legal grounds, you should write to the sender and ask for proof that you placed your order. It is possible that either you forgot about an order that you placed or a friend might have placed the order for you at your request; if it is really unordered, you are entitled to keep it at no cost.

If you have a complaint against a mail order company, either for nondelivery, misleading advertising, or damages caused by poor wrapping, the first thing you should do is to write directly to the company. If they do not resolve the problem, you can call the local or state consumer protection office or Better Business Bureau or your local postmaster. In addition, you might wish to contact the magazine or newspaper publisher where you saw the advertisement. Publishers often try to resolve problems between their readers and their advertisers.

DECEPTIVE ADVERTISING PRACTICES

Federal Law

Federal guidelines protect consumers against many deceptive advertising practices. One of those practices is called "bait and switch." Bait and switch occurs where merchandise is advertised at an exceptionally low price. When you go to the store to purchase the merchandise advertised, you find that it is either not available or, that the salesperson, who is trained at "bait and switch" selling, tries to steer you away from the item by indicating its inferior quality and the like. The salesperson directs your attention to another item that costs more but is supposed to be well worth the extra dollars. The salesperson then tries to talk you into taking the better item at a higher price. Bait and switch is an illegal way to sell products. If you are a victim of bait and switch, complain. You can protect yourself and other consumers as well. The first place to complain is to the merchant. If the salesperson you talk to is of no help, go to his or her superior. If necessary, contact the owner or the president or the chairman of the board. You should keep copies of sales slips, claim checks, letters, contracts, newspaper ads, and so on, and don't release them; they may be necessary as evidence if you decide to present your case to a court.

Try to protect yourself against bait and switch. Plan ahead before going to the store, and take your time while in the store. Don't be rushed or high-pressured into buying something you hadn't planned to buy. If you want the low-priced bait, insist on the merchant's responsibility to sell it to you. The FTC has rules that indicate that stores ought to have advertised specials readily available at the advertised price during the advertised sale period. If a branch store will not have the advertised item, that store must be clearly listed in the ad. General statements such as "available at most of our stores" are not good enough to satisfy the FTC rule. If the merchant still insists that the goods are not available, ask the merchant for a rain check, and have him or her write down on the rain check the date you can come back and pick up the sale item and the sale price you will pay for it.

State Law

In addition to the federal regulations with respect to advertising practices, states also have protective statutes. For example, the California Business Professional Code, § 17500 and § 3369 of the California Civil Code, indicates that a misleading picture in an advertisement is illegal. The law protects consumers by prohibiting unfair business practices and misleading advertisements. The California law also provides that an advertiser can't notify you that you have won a prize if you must purchase any goods or services to receive it. The California law also requires advertisers to be able to prove advertising claims that are supposedly based on fact. However, general terms or "puffing" statements, such as "low, low prices," do not have to be proved. California statutes also indicate that an ad that is absolutely true but misleading is also illegal. The test for whether an ad is misleading is what the average reasonable person would assume to be true from reading the ad. For example, an advertisement read, "Special Sale—Firestone Convoy Tubes 50% off regular first-line tube list price." The natural tendency that a reader would have in looking at this advertisement would be to believe that the convoy tubes were first-line tubes and were to be specially sold at 50 percent off regular list price. In fact, the convoy tubes were third-line tubes, and the advertisement, though literally true, was held to be deceptive and misleading (People v. Wahl, 100 P. 2d 550 [Cal. 1942]).

Case Law

In addition to the federal and state standards set by statute, case law holds advertisers liable to persons who have suffered product-caused injuries when the product was purchased because of the advertiser's promises. Cases have held that an advertiser's promise constituted a warranty. Actions have been successful for breach of warranty if there was proof that the advertised product was in fact other than advertised.

Here is an example. Rogers purchased a Toni home permanent set labeled ''Very Gentle.'' She followed the directions placed on the package by the manufacturer (the defendant), and her mother gave her a permanent wave. The ingredients in the product were harmful and caused her hair to ''assume a cottonlike texture and become gummy . . . her hair refused to dry; and . . . when the curlers furnished by defendant were attempted to be removed, her hair fell off to within one inch of her scalp.'' The court found the defendant liable under the express warranty of their advertising. Where a manufacturer of a product in its advertising makes representation as to the quality and merit of his or her product, aims it directly at the ultimate consumer, urges the consumer to purchase the product from a retailer, and the consumer does so with reliance on the advertisement and suffers harm in using the product, then the consumer may maintain an action for damages against the manufacturer on the basis of express warranty (Rogers v. Toni Home Permanent Co., 147 N.E. 2d 612 [Ohio 1958]).

In Rachlin v. Libby-Owens-Ford Glass Company, 96 F.2d 597 (2d Cir. 1938), the defendant's advertisement for safety glass stated that it was better than ordinary glass. Plaintiff was injured when the safety glass broke and sued for breach of the express warranty of the advertisement. The court denied recovery, holding that the advertisement did not warrant that plaintiff would be safe from all injury, only that safety glass was a better product.

A consumer who is trying to recover for breach of express warranty must prove that the particular advertisement constitutes an express warranty and not merely a description of the product or ''puffing.'' The consumer may not need to prove that the advertising statements were relied on. In Pritchard v. Liggett & Myers Tobacco Company, 295 F.2d 292 (3d Cir. 1965), the court refused to allow the defendant to disclaim its liability on the grounds of lack of reliance. The court held the warranty to be an integral part of the sale.

A consumer who is injured by a breach of an advertiser's duty must show that the statements contained in the advertisement were actually a breach of a duty owed toward the consuming public. Of course, if the dealer can show that the words were only ''puffing'' or sales talk, no liability will be found.

A manufacturer or seller of a product can also be liable for fraud if he uses deceptive advertising. The plaintiff must be injured by the product advertised and be able to prove that the statements were not merely sales talk or puffing. In order to prove fraud, the plaintiff must show not only a misstatement of facts, but also an intent to defraud. In other words, the manufacturer or seller must have had knowledge of the untruth and must have been connected in some way with the advertisement. This may be difficult for the consumer to prove. (The elements of fraud include a fact that was misrepresented with intent to defraud and reliance by the plaintiff and damage. Exaggerated statements as to the value and quality of a product are usually not actionable.)

Some courts have held that the U.C.C. provisions for implied warranty (§ 2-314) could be applicable to hold an advertiser liable when the product does not meet the specifications of the advertisement. For example, in Coca-Cola Bottling Co. v. Enas, 164 S.W. 2d 828 (Tex. 1942), the plaintiff Enas drank a portion of the contents of a bottle of Coca-Cola that contained a decomposed body of a spider. He indicated that he had observed a peculiarity in the taste and color of the beverage and that, upon investigation, found the body of the spider adhering to the inside of the bottle near the bottom. Shortly after drinking the beverage, he became violently ill. He brought action against Coca-Cola for the damages incurred. The court found that there was an implied warranty on the part of the defendant that the bottle contained a pure and wholesome beverage, free from poisonous or deleterious substances.

Some courts have held advertisers liable for negligence when they sold a product that was not up to the standards advertised. For example, in Bryer v. Rath Packing Co., 156 A.2d 442 (Md. 1959), the defendant advertised ''ready to serve'' boned chicken. The court found the defendant liable for negligence when a bone was found in a chow mein dish that was prepared using the defendant's chicken. The court indicated that the defendant had to exercise such a degree of care as would enable a user to rely on the advertisement with reasonable safety (all bones had been removed).

PURCHASING AN AUTOMOBILE

The purchase of a new automobile is usually the second largest purchase that a consumer may make, the first being the purchase of a home. It is important for consumers to be conscious of the many federal laws that protect them in purchasing a new vehicle. It is also important that consumers educate themselves as to the type of car to buy, where to buy, and so on. The first place for consumers to start in order to educate themselves about the automobile industry is a consumer magazine. Automobiles should be compared for such things as roominess, gas mileage, and repair records, as well as performance and style.

Federal laws require manufacturers to make information available to consumers regarding automobiles. This information can be found in the dealers' showroom. The information can also be found in the glove box of the vehicle or the owner's manual. The information includes the tire reserve load (which is a measure of excess tire load-carrying capacity), the braking performance (which tells the stopping distance of the vehicle at specific speeds and load conditions), and the accelerating and passing ability (which should indicate the low and high speed times).

In addition to studying statistical comparisons, you should also road test various automobiles. The road tests should be done on the type of roads you normally travel, both in town and on the highway. If you are going to be carrying heavy tools or equipment, you should weight the vehicle down for the road test; you should also consider the weight and space requirement of other members of the family or persons with whom you form a car pool.

In deciding where to purchase a car, you may find the lowest price not always your best bet. You should consider both service and convenience in purchasing your vehicle. If a dealer is 100 miles from your home, even though the price of the auto may be several hundred dollars cheaper, consider the fact that you may have to drive a great distance for a minor part or repair. You should check with friends, relatives, and acquaintances with respect to the dealer's reliability and service. You should also call the county or city consumer protection agency or the local Better Business Bureau to determine whether a large number of complaints have been lodged against any particular dealer. Another factor worth considering would be "loan car" arrangements. Some dealers provide free loaner cars while servicing your car; others do not.

Safety Standards

The National Highway Traffic Safety Administration issues federal motor vehicle safety standards. These standards are basic requirements for cars manufactured in the United States for performance of certain components systems and equipment critical to the occupant's safety. All people who drive cars are not the same. The size and shape of a particular vehicle, though it may meet federal safety standards, may not meet your requirements. Do not buy an automobile on a salesperson's oral promise that needed adjustments will be made. You should emphasize the fact that these adjustments must be made to your satisfaction before you sign and finally accept the automobile. Remember to check the fuel economy rating of the car that you are interested in. The MPG (miles per gallon) ratings of new model cars are published each year by the U.S. Department of Energy and the U.S. Environmental Protection Agency in a gas mileage guide.

It is also a good idea to look over the owner's manual for the car you are considering. Pay attention to special features or special equipment you may become dissatisfied with later. For example, many cars now come equipped with a spare tire that is designed to conserve limited trunk space. A review of the owner's manual before buying the car would eliminate surprise when you find a spare tire that is not similar to the other tires on the vehicle.

In addition to all of the research and review previously discussed, comparisons of the warranties should also be made. The federal government provides special provisions for warranties under the Magnuson-Moss Warranty Act. Even though federal law defines ''full and limited warranties,'' these can differ in the number of months or miles that are covered. Be careful of extended warranties at additional cost. These items are really service contracts that give you extra protection for an extra fee. Make sure you understand the various stipulations of such extended warranties. Some of them require that you use a certain brand of oil when you have your car serviced; others require that the service be done at a specific location.

Contract

After you have done all the research, test-driven different makes and models, and checked a dealer price and reputation, you will have to sign a contract for the purchase of your new car. This contract is governed by the rules set out in Chapter 4. It is important that you read and understand the contract before you sign it. Make sure it includes all essential terms, including price, model, color, and options. A typical auto purchase contract can be found in Exhibit 5–3.

From the moment you take possession of your new car until the time the warranty expires, the required warranty service of the vehicle is the joint responsibility of the dealer and the manufacturer. In order to fully protect yourself under your warranty and under the contract law that applies to purchase of an automobile, you must follow the following procedure. First, you should make sure the car you are buying is exactly what you ordered. The window sticker will list every accessory, and, according to federal law, the window sticker must remain with the car until it is delivered to you. You should check the receipted bill of sale against the window sticker and the car to see if there are any differences. If there are differences, they should be tracked down immediately. Insist on a correction of the problem before you sign anything. For your future protection, the car and the window sticker and the bill of sale must all match. You should keep both the window sticker and the bill of sale in order to have an exact record of what you paid for and what the dealer accepted payment for.

Delivery

The next thing you should do is to make sure that the dealer preparation is completed by the dealer. Your bill of sale notation that dealer prep has been done and paid for or, if there is no charge, a notation on the bill of sale ''dealer preparation completed, no charge'' is your proof that any problems that should have been remedied by the dealer are clearly the dealer's responsibility if they crop up a few days later (e.g., loss of engine oil for failure to tighten loose nuts).

You should inspect the car inside and out and road test it before you sign for it. It may pay to drive it through a car wash to see if it leaks. While you are road testing the vehicle, check the odometer. The federal odometer law is intended to protect car buyers from deceptive practices of concealing a car's true mileage by disconnecting or turning back the odometer. You should not buy any car without a functioning

EXHIBIT 5-3
Automobile Purchase Contract

VEHICLE CASH PURCHASE AGREEMENT

 LANDMARK DATSUN, INC.
331 CHESTNUT STREET
ONEONTA, N. Y. 13820
(607) 432-0201

THIS AGREEMENT IS NOT BINDING UNLESS SIGNED BY THE SELLER AND THE BUYER.

BUYER Robert Rothenberg	SALESMAN Jim Garcia	
STREET Box #350-A	HOME PHONE 539-8318	BUS. PHONE
CITY Treadwell	STATE New York	ZIP 13753

THE TRANSACTION

I ORDER AND AGREE TO PURCHASE FROM YOU, ON THE TERMS CONTAINED ON BOTH SIDES OF THIS AGREEMENT, THE FOLLOWING VEHICLE:
(READ OTHER SIDE)

THE VEHICLE

YEAR 1983	☐ NEW	☐ USED	☐ DEMONSTRATOR	MAKE Nissan	MODEL Sentra	SERIES
TYPE	COLOR Blue	TOP	TRIM	V.I.N. JNIPB12S3DU028516		
TO BE DELIVERED ON OR ABOUT 2-14-83 12:00 NOON			MILEAGE	STOCK NO. (IF RESERVED) #234		

THE PRICE

VEHICLE PRICE	(+) $	BASE	$5184 00
TRANSPORTATION (IF NOT INCLUDED IN VEHICLE PRICE)	(+)	PDM PKG.	199 00
FACTORY INSTALLED EQUIPMENT	(+)	SNOW TIRES	30 00
		RT. SIDE MIRROR	51 00
		AM-FM STEREO	204 00
		MUD FLAPS	31 00
		RUSTY JONES PKG.	385 00
		FLOOR HEATER	59 00
		SHOP MANUAL	22 00
			6165 00
		DEALER INSTALLED EQUIPMENT AND SERVICES (+)	
		TOTAL $	6165 00

THE TRADE-IN

	DESCRIPTION OF TRADE				LESS TRADE-IN CREDIT (–) (BUYER SEE 1 AND 6(b) ON BACK)	1531 00
YEAR 1978	MILEAGE 78000	MAKE DATSUN	COLOR BLUE	MODEL B210		
PLATE NO.	EXP. DATE	V.I.N.			CASH PRICE $ 4634 00	
TRADE-IN IS CLEAR OF ALL LIENS EXCEPT:			AMOUNT OWED $			

TAXES AND OTHER FEES

IF YOU AGREE TO ASSIST ME IN OBTAINING FINANCING FOR ANY PART OF THE PURCHASE PRICE, THIS ORDER SHALL NOT BE BINDING UPON YOU OR ME UNTIL ALL OF THE CREDIT TERMS ARE PRESENTED TO ME IN ACCORDANCE WITH REGULATION "Z" (TRUTH-IN-LENDING) AND ARE ACCEPTED BY ME. IF I DO NOT ACCEPT THE CREDIT TERMS WHEN PRESENTED, I MAY CANCEL THIS ORDER AND MY DEPOSIT WILL BE REFUNDED.	SALES TAX % (+)	185 36
	DEALER'S FEE FOR OBTAINING REGISTRATION AND/OR CERTIFICATE OF TITLE (FEE MAY NOT EXCEED TEN DOLLARS) (+)	5 00
	REGISTRATION FEE (ESTIMATE) (+)	
	INSPECTION FEE (+)	
	OTHER—ITEMIZE GAS (+)	10 00
	TOTAL CASH PRICE DELIVERED $	4834 36
	LESS CASH DEPOSIT SUBMITTED WITH ORDER (–)	34 36
	PLUS BALANCE OWING ON TRADE-IN (+)	
	CASH DUE ON DELIVERY $	4800 00

I have read the terms on the back of this agreement and have received a completed copy of this agreement.

BUYER'S SIGNATURE Robert R. Rothenberg	DATE 2/12/83
CO-BUYER'S SIGNATURE	DATE
SELLER APPROVED BY	DATE 3/12/83

SEE OTHER SIDE FOR ADDITIONAL TERMS

IMAGE BUSINESS FORMS INC.   FORM NYS C6-3N REV. 4/82

EXHIBIT 5-3, cont.

ADDITIONAL TERMS OF AGREEMENT

"I", "me", and "my" refer to the Buyer and Co-Buyer. "You" and "your" refer to the Seller.

I agree this order is subject to the following terms:

1. Trade-in Credit May Change. If I do not deliver the trade-in vehicle to you when this Agreement is signed, I agree, that at the time the trade-in vehicle is delivered to you, should the value of my trade-in be materially diminished as a result of physical damage, alteration or deterioration in mechanical condition other than normal wear and tear, YOU HAVE THE RIGHT TO REAPPRAISE THE VEHICLE. AS A RESULT OF SUCH REAPPRAISAL, I UNDERSTAND THAT THE TRADE-IN ALLOWANCE ON MY VEHICLE MAY BE REDUCED AND THAT THIS WILL IN TURN INCREASE THE NET PRICE WHICH I WILL HAVE TO PAY FOR THE VEHICLE IF I DECIDE TO PURCHASE THE VEHICLE. If the trade-in credit is reduced and I am not satisfied, I understand that I can cancel this agreement IF the purchased vehicle has not been registered in my name or delivered to me or you have not accepted delivery of the trade-in vehicle.

2. Trade-In; Buyer's Obligations. At the time I deliver the trade-in vehicle to you, I promise to sign a Bill of Sale and a mileage certification statement and give you satisfactory proof that I own the vehicle. I warrant (guarantee) (a) that there are no liens on the trade-in vehicle and that I owe no one any money for the vehicle or repairs to the vehicle, except as may be shown on the face of this agreement; (b) that the trade-in vehicle does not have a welded or bent chassis and that the motor block and cylinder heads are not cracked, welded or repaired; and (c) that the vehicle has not been flood damaged or declared a total loss for insurance purposes; and (d) that emission control devices have not been altered and/or removed, and nothing has been removed from the trade, including all seat belts, that was originally seen. The engine and/or transmission has not been tampered with to pass your inspection.

3. Buyer's Refusal to Purchase. Unless this agreement is non-binding because you are arranging credit for me, I understand that the cash deposit I have given to you can be retained, in accordance with your refund policy, to offset your damages if I refuse to complete my purchase. I also understand that I may be responsible for any other damages which you may incur as a result of my failure to perform my obligations under the terms of this agreement.

4. Delays in Delivery. I understand that you shall not be liable for delays caused by the manufacturer, accidents, sureties, fires or other causes beyond your control. Provided you promptly place my order with the manufacturer and the manufacturer refuses to accept the order or fails to deliver the vehicle after accepting the order, upon your prompt notification and refund of my deposit, I will not hold you liable and this agreement shall be cancelled.

5. Disclaimer of Warranties. I UNDERSTAND THAT YOU EXPRESSLY DISCLAIM ALL WARRANTIES, EXPRESS OR IMPLIED, IN-CLUDING ANY IMPLIED WARRANTY OF MERCHANTABILITY OR FITNESS FOR A PARTICULAR PURPOSE, AND THAT YOU NEITHER ASSUME NOR AUTHORIZE ANY OTHER PERSON TO ASSUME FOR YOU ANY LIABILITY IN CONNECTION WITH THE SALE OF THE VEHICLE, except as otherwise provided in writing by YOU in an attachment to this Agreement or in a document delivered to ME when the vehicle is delivered.

Limitation on Implied Warranties. Some States do not allow either (1) Limitations on how long an implied warranty lasts or (2) the exclusion or limitation of incidental or consequential damages, so these limitations may not apply.

6. Price Changes.

(a) THE TOTAL CASH PRICE DELIVERED LESS THE TRADE-IN ALLOWANCE SHOWN ON THE FRONT OF THIS AGREEMENT IS THE FINAL CONTRACT PRICE TO WHICH YOU AND I HAVE AGREED, AND, IF THE VEHICLE IS A NEW MOTOR VEHICLE, NO ADDITIONAL FEE OR CHARGE WILL BE IMPOSED OR COLLECTED DUE TO CHANGES IN THE MANUFACTURER'S LIST PRICE, OR CHANGES IN THE COST OF FREIGHT OR SERVICES PROVIDED BY YOU.

(b) A REDUCTION IN THE VALUE OF THE TRADE-IN MAY RESULT IN AN INCREASE IN THE CASH PRICE DELIVERED I WILL HAVE TO PAY AS PROVIDED IN PARAGRAPH 1 OF THIS AGREEMENT.

(c) IF THE BALANCE I OWE ON MY TRADE-IN AT THE TIME OF DELIVERY OF THE TRADE-IN TO YOU IS DIFFERENT THAN THE AMOUNT I HAVE TOLD YOU AND WHICH AMOUNT IS SHOWN ON THE FRONT OF THIS AGREEMENT, THEN THE CASH PRICE DELIVERED OF THE VEHICLE I AM PURCHASING SHALL CHANGE ACCORDINGLY.

(d) IF THE REGISTRATION FEE VARIES FROM THE AMOUNT YOU HAVE ESTIMATED ON THE FRONT OF THIS AGREEMENT, THEN THE CASH PRICE DELIVERED SHALL CHANGE ACCORDINGLY.

(e) I AGREE THAT I WILL PAY THE FINAL CASH PRICE DELIVERED AS SHOWN ON THE FRONT OF THIS AGREEMENT. IF THERE HAVE BEEN ANY CHANGES IN THE TOTAL CASH PRICE DELIVERED FOR REASONS STATED IN THIS PARAGRAPH 6 THEN I WILL PAY THE CASH PRICE DELIVERED AS CHANGED BY ANY SUCH ADJUSTMENT MY PAYMENT WILL BE EITHER IN CASH, BANK, OR CERTIFIED CHECK AT THE TIME OF DELIVERY OF THE VEHICLE I HAVE PURCHASED.

7. Change of Design. I understand that the manufacturer has the right to change the design of the vehicle, its chassis, accessories or any parts at any time without notice to YOU or ME. In the event of such a change by the manufacturer, YOU shall have no duty to ME except to deliver the vehicle as made by the manufacturer.

8. No Other Agreements. There are no understandings or agreements between you and me other than those set forth in this Agreement and attachments to this Agreement, if there are any such attachments.

9. New York Law Applies. You and I agree that this Agreement is governed by New York State Law odometer. Make sure that you receive an odometer disclosure statement (Exhibit 5–4) as required by the federal law, and compare the mileage on the odometer with that on the statement. The disclosure statement must contain information as to the odometer reading at the time of the transfer; the date of transfer; the seller's name, address, and signature; the make, body type, year, and model; vehicle ID number; and a statement certifying that the seller is complying with the Motor Vehicle Information and Cost Savings Act of 1972 and is aware of his or her civil liability under its provisions. The odometer law prohibits disconnecting or resetting the odometer, operating a vehicle with a nonfunctioning odometer with intent to defraud, advertising, selling, using or installing a device that causes an odometer to register incorrectly, or knowingly falsifying the written odometer statement.

Problems

In the event that you have a problem with your automobile, you should immediately pursue your rights under the warranty. You should insist on an itemized receipt for everything done to your car whether under warranty or not. This will prevent dealers from billing the manufacturer and not fixing the vehicle under warranty. These receipts should be kept as long as you own the car. Be persistent about solving warranty problems. Your prime objective is to reach the end of the warranty period with a car free of problems. Owners often complain of many breakdowns through the warranty period only to discover that the root of the problem was a major repair that had to be done at their cost after the warranty had expired. If persistence and patience don't work, a complaint to the manufacturer is in order. The first letter should go to the zone or district representative. If necessary, the next letter should go to the customers' relations office. Don't forget to keep all copies of letters that you send.

If appeals to the manufacturer don't work, a local complaint organization, county or city consumer protection agency, or a local volunteer consumer organization such as AUTOCAP (Automotive Consumer Action Program), might be of assistance. AUTOCAPs are complaint-handling groups that have been organized by state or local automobile dealer associations. They are set up to settle disputes by using panels that have both consumer members and industry members. You can locate your state or local AUTOCAP by inquiring at a local automobile dealership. If your complaint involves the safety of your automobile, you should contact the National Highway Traffic Safety Administration. If all of the above remedies do not work, you may have to consider legal action.

FEDERAL CONSUMER PROTECTION AGENCIES

The Federal Trade Commission

The Federal Trade Commission (FTC) (see Exhibit 5-5) is charged with the prevention of certain unfair or deceptive acts or practices. The FTC has jurisdiction over

EXHIBIT 5-4
Odometer Mileage Statement

Robert D. Rothenberg   #4259
CUSTOMER'S NAME   STOCK NO.

ODOMETER MILEAGE STATEMENT

(Federal regulations require you to state the odometer mileage upon transfer of ownership. An inaccurate or untruthful statement may make you liable for damages to your transferee, for attorney fees, and for civil or criminal penalties, pursuant to sections 409, 412, and 413 of the Motor Vehicle Information and Cost Savings Act of 1972 (Pub. L. 92-513, as amended by Pub. L. 94-364).

I, ___Landmark Datsun, Inc._____ state that the odometer
SELLER OR TRANSFEROR'S NAME (PRINT)

on the vehicle described below now reads __36.7__ miles/kilometers.
(Check one box only)

☒ I hereby certify that to the best of my knowledge the odometer reading as stated above reflects the actual mileage of the vehicle described below.

☐ I hereby certify that to the best of my knowledge the odometer reading reflects the amount of mileage in excess of designed mechanical odometer limit of 99,999 miles/kilometers of the vehicle described below.

☐ I hereby certify that to the best of my knowledge the odometer reading as stated above is NOT the actual mileage of vehicle described below, and should not be relied upon.

MAKE	MODEL	BODY TYPE
Datsun	Sentra	2 dr

VEHICLE IDENTIFICATION NUMBER	YEAR
JN1PB12S2DU-022516	1983

(Check one box only)

☒ I hereby certify that the odometer of said vehicle was not altered, set back, or disconnected while in my possession, and I have no knowledge of anyone else doing so.

☐ I hereby certify that the odometer was altered for repair or replacement purposes while in my possession, and that the mileage registered on the repaired or replacement odometer is identical to that before such service.

☐ I hereby certify that the odometer was altered for repair or replacement purposes while in my possession, and that the repaired or replacement odometer was incapable of registering the same mileage, that it was reset to zero, and that the mileage on the original odometer or the odometer before repair was_____ miles/kilometers.

331 Chestnut Street, Oneotna, New York 13820
(SELLER OR TRANSFEROR'S ADDRESS)   CITY   STATE   ZIP

X _____   2-15-83
(SELLER OR TRANSFEROR'S SIGNATURE)   DATE OF THIS STATEMENT

Robert D. Rothenberg
BUYER OR TRANSFEREE'S NAME

Box 350A Delhi, New York1 3753
BUYER OR TRANSFEREE'S ADDRESS   CITY   STATE   ZIP

Receipt of a copy of this statement is hereby acknowledged X _____
BUYER OR TRANSFEREE'S SIGNATURE

FORM ODOM-103-N (2-78)   THE REYNOLDS & REYNOLDS CO., CELINA, OHIO

EXHIBIT 5-5
Federal Trade Commission

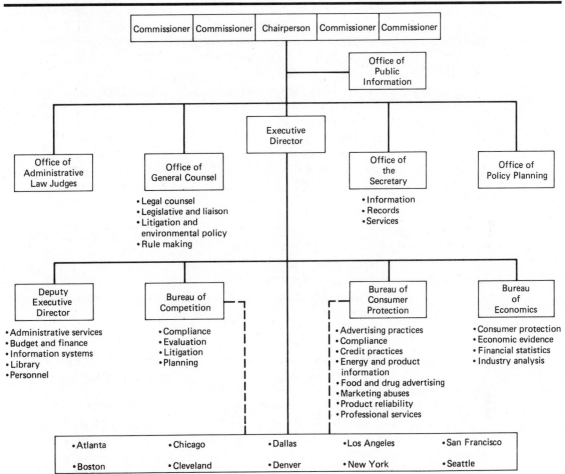

advertising of nonprescription items covered by the Food, Drug, and Cosmetic Act. In addition, the FTC administers the Wool Product Labeling Act (1939), the Fur Products Labeling Act (1951), the Textile Fiber Products Identification Act (1958)—these acts made labeling of clothing by percentage of fiber contents mandatory—the Fair Packaging and Labeling Act, the Truth in Lending Act, the Fair Credit Reporting Act, the Magnuson-Moss Warranty Act, and the Fair Credit Billing Act.

FTC enforcement procedures center on the "cease and desist order." This order begins with an informal complaint, which can originate from a consumer, a competitor, or any government agency, including the FTC. If the complaint gives the FTC reason to believe that unfair or deceptive practices contrary to the public interest are being perpetrated, the FTC may decide to pursue the matter further. The cease and desist order may be granted after an investigation by the FTC and a presentation of the facts in the case to an administrative law judge. The administrative law judge can recommend dismissal of the complaint or can order that the company cease and desist its practice. Either the FTC or the company that is being complained against can appeal the judge's decision to the commissioners of the FTC. After the FTC commissioners make their final decision, a company has 60 days to appeal to the U.S. court of appeals.

Companies that fail to adhere to the cease and desist order can be charged $10,000 per violation per day. The FTC also has power to obtain temporary injunctions to prevent false advertising of foods, drugs, and cosmetics. In addition, the FTC under the Magnuson-Moss Warranty Act is allowed to bring a civil suit in the U.S. district court against anyone who knowingly violates a rule concerning deceptive acts and practices. Although the FTC appears to have greater powers in helping the consumer deal with his or her problems, it must be pointed out that the commission works very slowly. It may take as long as five years for a final determination in any particular matter.

An example of how the Federal Trade Commission works can be found in the case of Speigel, Inc. v. The FTC, 411 F.2d 481 (7th Cir. 1969). Speigel Inc., published various advertisements, an example of which follows: "Dollar sale. Fruit of the loom quilts, price of one quilt $8.98, two at $9.98." In small print "save $7.98 when you buy two of these quality brand quilts." The FTC found 51 such advertisements involving seven different items. Words such as "regular" price, "special purchase," "now sale price," "amazing offer," "once in a lifetime chance," and "now one of the greatest offers we've made" were used in the various ads. The FTC found that in all cases the items mentioned for sale were never sold singly.

The FTC issued the following order: "It is ordered that the respondent Speigel, Inc. . . . in connection with offering for sale . . . bedspreads, quilts, blankets, or any other product in commerce . . . do forthwith cease and desist from: (1) representing, directly or by implication, that any price is respondent's former or usual price for said products when such amount is in excess of the actual, bonafide price at which respondent offered or sold the said products to the public for a reasonable, substantial period of time in a recent, regular course of business; (2) representing, directly or by implication, through the device of a $1 sale, or in any other manner, that a stated number of units of respondent's merchandise may be purchased for the price of one or more units, plus $1, or any other amount, when the price of unit or units required to be purchased is in excess of the actual, bona fide price at which respondent offered or sold the said merchandise to the public for a reasonable substantial period of time in a recent, regular course of business; and (3) misrepresenting in any manner the savings available to purchasers of respondent's merchandise."

This cease and desist order was issued because Speigel had breached the FTC's rulings that advertising that gives a fictitious price or fictitious claim of savings constitutes a material influence on the consumer's decision to purchase and is deceptive. Speigel did not operate any retail stores allowing the consumer to inspect the items prior to purchasing, and the advertisement alone had possibly deceived consumers.

Speigel brought a suit for a review of the cease and desist order, contending that the order was too broad. The court agreed, striking Part 3. The court indicated that the order was too broad in that the last clause had no reasonable relation to the unlawful practices found. The court limited the order to the type of sale that was found to have been violated.

Consumer Product Safety Commission

The Consumer Product Safety Commission, which was set up in 1973, administers the Consumer Products Safety Act, the Federal Hazardous Substance Act, the Flammable Fabrics Act, the Poison Prevention Packaging Act, and the Refrigerator Safety Act. The objectives of the Consumer Product Safety Commission are to protect the public against unreasonable risk or injury, assist consumers in evaluating the comparative safety of consumer products, develop uniform safety standards, and promote research and investigation into the causes and prevention of product related deaths, injuries, and illnesses. Its jurisdiction does not extend to consumer products regulated by other agencies, such as food, drugs, cosmetics, tobacco products, automobiles, and so on.

The commission may set safety standards for various products that are reasonably necessary to prevent or reduce an unreasonable risk of injury associated with that product. If the commission finds that there is no product standard that will protect the public, the commission may remove the product from the market, declaring it a hazardous product, and the commission may file an action for seizure of the product in the U.S. district court. In addition, consumers or consumer groups may petition the commission to commence a proceeding for issuing, amending, or revoking their product safety rules. If the commission does make a ruling, the organization that is adversely affected has 60 days to file an objection with the U.S. district court. The commission also has the power to require manufacturers to notify purchasers that repair or replacement is necessary for a product that the commission finds hazardous. The Consumer Product Safety Commission can subject individuals to civil penalties of $2000 for each violation, with a maximum of $500,000. If a consumer sustains injury from a product that has violated the Consumer Product Safety Act, he or she can recover damages as well as the cost of the suit in a U.S. district court proceeding. The act also allows for criminal penalties for individuals who knowingly and willingly violate the act. The maximum penalty is $50,000 or one year in jail or both.

Aside from the FTC, the Consumer Product Safety Commission (and their regulatory powers and acts), the Consumer Credit Protection Act, and the Uniform Commercial Code, there are several other federal consumer protection legislation acts. These include the Food and Drug Act of 1906, which guards against unsafe and adulterated food, and the Meat Inspection Act of the same year, as well as the Food and Drug Cosmetic Act of 1938, which expands the jurisdiction of the Food and Drug Administration. The food additives legislation in 1958 prohibits the use of additives that cause cancer in people or animals. In 1966 the National Traffic Motor Vehicle Safety Act established compulsory standards for automobiles. This list is not comprehensive. Legislation is constantly changing the composition of consumer protection statutes and agencies.

CLASS ACTIONS

A class action is a suit by one individual representing all other individuals who have or may have been damaged by the action of a particular defendant. If a company causes a small amount of damages to a large group of people, it may not be economical for each "victim" to sue the company. A class action is a judicial procedure that allows any victim to sue the company for his or her damages and also for those of all the other victims in a single suit.

Most states except for California have framed class action laws in such a manner as to prevent meaningful litigation by restricting the procedures for bringing a class action. Federal Rules of Civil Procedure limit federal jurisdiction of class actions to cases where the amount in controversy is $10,000 or more. This $10,000 does not represent the aggregate claim, but must be met by at least one victim. There is an exception to this rule, which allows class actions to be brought under breach of warranty under the Magnuson-Moss Warranty Act if any individual claim is $25 or more, the total claims of the class amount to $50,000 or more, and the number of plaintiffs is equal to or greater than 100. (See Eisen v. Carlisle & Jacquelin, 417 U.S. 156[S. Ct. 1974] and Darr v. Yellow Cab Co., 433 P.2d 732 [Cal. 1967]).

The rules with respect to class actions eliminate federal courts as a useful source to resolve consumer complaints. We hope that in the future the procedural rules with respect to jurisdiction will be relaxed to allow federal courts to entertain many more consumer problems.

QUESTIONS

1   The plaintiff sued Purex Corporation for damages caused when a bottle of Purex bleaching solution exploded in the plaintiff's hands. Expert testimony indicated that the cause of the explosion was external pressure from the twisting of the cap combined with a defect in the bottle. There was also evidence showing that Purex is an unstable chemical solution that decomposes gradually and forms a gas, creating internal pressure. Other evidence indicated that Purex Corporation did not have an extensive inspection program at its plant. Discuss the liability of Purex for plaintiff's injuries in conjunction with warranties.

2   Helen Maize died as a result of inhaling fumes of a poisonous chemical (carbon tetrachloride), which comprised 45 percent of the cleaning fluid designated by the defendant as "SAFETY CLEAN." The cans that contained the cleaning product had advertis-

ing on them indicating that it was a highly efficient dry cleaner, in letters 5/16 inch high, followed by "for every dry-cleaning purpose" in letters 3/16 inch high, followed by "will not injure finest fabrics." A caution followed in letters ¼ inch high, followed by words in 1/8 inch type "Do not inhale fumes. Use only in a well-ventilated place." "SAFETY CLEAN" appeared on the cans in letters ranging from ½ inch to ¾ inch high. Mrs. Maize used the product to clean some rugs, was taken ill, and subsequently died. Is the defendant, Atlantic Refining Co., liable for this death? Discuss.

3   The plaintiff smoked Chesterfields for 30 years, using at least a carton a week. The jury found that smoking the Chesterfields was the cause of the plaintiff's lung cancer. The plaintiff alleges that the defendant breached warranties that were contained in advertisements published in newspapers and magazines. These advertisements featured, in bold type, such factual affirmations as follows:

"Chesterfields are best for you."
"Chesterfields are as pure as the water you drink and the food you eat."
"A good cigarette can cause no ills."
"Nose, throat, and accessory organs not adversely affected by smoking Chesterfields."

These advertisements implied that whereas other brands of cigarettes might be harmful, Chesterfields were not. The case took place prior to the current publicity given to the hazards of smoking cigarettes. The plaintiff had no knowledge of the cancer-causing effect that a cigarette has. Is the defendant liable for deceptive advertising or breach of warranty or both? Discuss.

4   The plaintiff purchased a used automobile from the defendant. The conditional sales contract provided that the sale of the car was made "in its present condition" and also that "this agreement constitutes the entire contract and no waivers and modifications shall be valid unless written upon or attached to this contract, and said car is accepted without any express or implied warranties, agreements, representations, promises, or statements unless expressly set forth in this contract at the time of purchase." In addition, there was a purchase order reading, "no salesman's verbal agreement is binding on the company; all terms and conditions of this sale are expressed in this agreement. We do not guarantee the mileage or model . . . agreed to take the above car AS IS . . ." Several days after the plaintiff picked up the automobile, the brakes locked, the car turned over, and the plaintiff and his wife were injured. The plaintiff contends that the seller, after the sale and delivery of the automobile, made statements to the effect that he would put it in good condition. Is the plaintiff entitled to recover from the defendant under express or implied warranty that the automobile was fit for the purpose for which it was sold? Discuss.

5   The plaintiff rented a golf cart from Gerardi, who had purchased the cart from the defendant. The defendant had advertised the golf cart to be safe and fit for its intended use. The plaintiff sued the defendant because of injuries sustained after falling from the golf cart. He fell because the back rest and arms of the golf cart loosened. Is the defendant liable? Discuss.

6   The personal representative of the decedent's estate brings an action on behalf of the decedent's widow for damages on the grounds that his death was caused by the negligent design of an automobile manufactured by the defendant. The Chevrolet that the defendant was driving in had an "X" frame. As a result of an accident, the left side of the decedent's car collapsed, inflicting fatal injuries. Evidence showed that the car

would not have collapsed if it had used a perimeter frame, which would have been safer. Did General Motors breach the warranty of fitness for a particular purpose in not making their automobiles with the stronger perimeter frame? Discuss.

7   A plaintiff sues Ford Motor Co. for injuries suffered when he was struck by an automobile that was a new Ford product. The plaintiff was given the keys to a new nine-passenger automobile and was told to clean the automobile and get it ready for delivery. The plaintiff unlocked the door of the automobile, which had an automatic transmission. The automobile was in neutral, and the hand brake was on. He started the automobile, put it in drive, and released the hand brake. He proceeded to the garage door when he stepped on the foot brake, stopped the car, and put the selector in neutral. He brought the hand brake up, opened the car door, got out leaving the motor running, and went to open the garage. He bent down to pick up a piece of glass, and the automobile pinned him against the garage door, seriously injuring him. His boss came out, backed the automobile away from the plaintiff, and noticed that the gear selector was still in neutral. Did Ford breach any warranties making the company liable for damages to the plaintiff? Discuss.

8   The plaintiff sues American Motors, alleging that, after delivery of his new automobile, he discovered the following defects: the cargo area was out of line, could not be opened, and continually squeaked and rattled; the trim about the door was torn; the doors were out of line and squeaked and rattled; the door handles were loose; the motor was extremely noisy; the steering gear was improperly set and creaked when turned; the transmission emitted a groaning noise; the brakes squeaked; the front seats squeaked and rocked; and loose parts inside the car fell out from time to time endangering the occupants of the car. The plaintiff made additional allegations of other numerous defects. The plaintiff also alleged that he had brought the defects to the attention of the defendant, who failed and refused to correct them. Was the defendant American Motors liable to the plaintiff? Discuss.

9   The plaintiff purchased a new Dodge manufactured by the defendant Chrysler Corporation in June. On August 2 of the same year, the automobile was wrecked, allegedly as a result of a defective tie-rod. The plaintiff sues Chrysler Corporation for injuries sustained as a result of the accident. Chrysler Corporation warranted "each new motor vehicle . . . chassis or part manufactured by it to be free from defects and material workmanship to be under normal use and service." Chrysler was obligated under this warranty to make good at its factory any part or parts thereof that shall "be returned to it with transportation charges prepaid if its examination disclosed to its satisfaction that the parts were defective." This warranty was given expressly in lieu of all other warranties express or implied, and all other obligations or liabilities on its part. In light of this warranty and its stated limitations is Chrysler Motors liable for damages? Discuss.

10 The plaintiff purchased a used automobile from the defendant. The contract of sale had the following warranty: "In case the car covered by this order is a used car, the undersigned purchaser states that he has examined it, is familiar with its condition, is buying it as a used car, as-is, and with no guaranty as to condition, model, or mileage, unless otherwise specified herein in writing. No oral representations have been made to the purchaser, and all terms of the agreement are printed or written herein . . ." In fact, the defendant told the plaintiff that he would adjust the brakes prior to the plaintiff's taking delivery. Several days later, the plaintiff, while driving at about 55 mph, was unable to

stop the car and ran off the road. He was injured, and the car wrecked. Is the defendant liable in an action brought by the plaintiff for damages? Discuss.

11 The plaintiff purchased a truck from the defendant for use in hauling logs. The truck was built in such a faulty manner as to be useless to the plaintiff. He complained to the defendants, and they made several efforts to put the truck in working condition, but were unable to do so. The plaintiff returned the truck and demanded his money be refunded. The plaintiff indicated that the defendant made statements that the truck would "do the job" for which it was purchased and that it was suited for the purpose of hauling logs. The defendant also made representations that this new truck would do a much better job than the truck previously owned by the plaintiff. The truck had a written factory warranty as follows: "Parts and labor warranted—there will be no charge for parts deemed defective by manufacturer during the first 4000 miles of operation, or during the first 90 days after delivery—whichever shall first occur. There shall be no charges for labor in replacing such defective parts during this period." Is the defendant liable? Discuss.

12 The plaintiff purchased a roll of film from the defendant, Kodak Co. The plaintiff was a commercial photographer and took the film to Alaska, where it was properly exposed. The plaintiff delivered the film to the defendant's laboratory. It was in good condition when received by the defendant for processing. During its development a substantial portion was damaged by a deposit of foreign material and ink, and the film became commercially valueless. The plaintiff sued the defendant, and the defendant cited the following warranty, which was on the box: "Film price does not include processing." "This film will be replaced if defective in manufacture, labeling, or packaging or if damaged or lost by us or any subsidiary company. Except for such replacement, the sale or subsequent handling of this film for any purpose is without warranty or other liability of any kind. Since dyes used with color films, like other dyes, may, in time, change, this film will not be replaced for, or otherwise warranted against, any change in color." The plaintiff was aware of the nature of the label's contents. Is the label effective to limit the defendant's liability for negligence in developing the film? Discuss.

13 The plaintiff purchased a used car. The odometer read 22,283 miles. Upon inspection of the driver's manual, the plaintiff discovered that the mileage reading some eight months before was also 22,283. The plaintiff claimed a violation of the Motor Vehicle and Cost Savings Act of 1972 by the defendant dealer. The defendant acquired the automobile as a trade-in on another car. The defendant's sales manager was present when the previous owner filled out the odometer mileage statement, and he took a test drive in the car. He noticed that the speedometer was working, and he testified that he had never heard of an odometer failing to work if the speedometer was working since both operate off the same cable. Is the defendant automobile dealer liable for fraud under the Motor Vehicle Cost Saving Act? Discuss.

CHAPTER 6

Credit Sales, Debtors' Rights, and Banking

CREDIT SALES

Consumer installment sales and loans are prevalent in today's society. As an educated consumer, you should be aware that the principles of law discussed in Chapters 4 and 5 apply to consumer credit contracts. In addition, there are various laws that apply to installment sales and other credit transactions. These will be discussed in Chapter 6.

In the event that you wish to buy on the installment method through a particular credit card company, the individual seller, bank financing, or any other types of financing (General Motors Acceptance Corporation, Household Finance, among others), you must establish credit. Establishing credit may be difficult if an individual has never had credit before. Credit card companies, banks, and other lenders base their decision to give credit on an individual's ability to repay and his or her past performance on previous loans (credit reports maintained by various reporting companies). If you are attempting to establish credit for the first time, borrowing a small amount of money from a bank (student loan) and repaying it can establish a track record. A local bank might be willing to approve a small loan based *only* on your ability to repay. Another method for obtaining a loan would be to provide a cosigner or guarantor.

Fair Credit Reporting Act

In the event that you are denied credit because of a bad credit report, you have the legal right under the Federal Fair Credit Reporting Act (tit. VI of the Consumer Credit Protection Act) to review the information contained in your credit report.

If you dispute information contained in your file, the consumer agency shall within a reasonable time reinvestigate the information, and if the information is found to be inaccurate or can no longer be verified, the consumer reporting agency shall promptly delete the disputed information. If the reinvestigation does not resolve the dispute, you can include in your file a brief statement setting forth the nature of the dispute. This statement should be 100 words or less. In future reports the consumer agency must include your disputed statement. The consumer reporting agency shall also furnish notification to persons who, according to your designation, have, within two years prior to the disputed information, received a report for employment purposes or, within six months prior thereto, received a consumer report for other purposes. The consumer reporting agency may impose a reasonable charge on you for making the disclosure unless your credit rating had been adversely affected by an inaccurate report. If the consumer reporting agency fails to comply with the requirements, it can be liable for actual damages as well as punitive damages.

Truth in Lending

Not only are you protected with respect to your right to a correct credit report, but you are also protected from unscrupulous lenders by the Federal Truth-in-Lending

Act, 15 U.S.C.A. tit. I, which requires that the lender disclose the total amount of interest being charged, in writing, before you sign the contract. This disclosure must include interest charges as well as any other fees. All fees and interest must be computed on a yearly basis. The Truth-in-Lending Act preamble indicates that the purpose of the act is "to assure a meaningful disclosure of credit terms so that the consumer will be able to compare more readily the various credit terms available to him and avoid the uninformed use of credit."

This standard method of computing and disclosing finance charges is called the annual percentage rate (APR). There are many different methods of computing interest such as the add on method and the discount method. The federal statute calls for the actuarial method (the interest on declining balances method). The formula for computing the actuarial or "simple or true" interest is $I = P \times R \times T$. I is the finance charge, P is the amount of credit extended, R is the rate, and T is the time that the credit is extended for. Each time an installment is paid, the first thing that is paid is the finance charges, and then the balance of the installment reduces the amount of credit outstanding. This is the same procedure discussed in Chapter 9 with respect to mortgages. (See Exhibit 9–6 for a typical loan reduction schedule.) If a lender uses any other method of computing interest, that lender must convert to the annual percentage rate to enable consumers to make comparisons between different loans.

Other fees that must be added to the term finance charge include service or carrying charges, finder's fees, loan fees, investigation fees for credit reports, and insurance fees for protecting the creditor against the debtor's default, as well as insurance premiums for credit, life, accident, or health insurance when they are written in connection with the consumer credit loan. Insurance premiums for liability insurance may also be part of the finance charges if the creditor would not extend credit without the property damage insurance. The federal statute provides criminal penalties for those who do not follow the APR reporting method. The criminal penalties include a fine of not more than $5000 or imprisonment for not more than one year or both.

Regulation Z of the Truth-in-Lending Regulations (tit. XII, pt. 226) was promulgated to assist in implementing the Truth-in-Lending Act and the Fair Credit Billing Act. Regulation Z requires disclosure of terms and costs of consumer transactions. The regulation gives consumers the right to cancel certain credit transactions when these involve a lien on the consumer's principal dwelling. It also regulates credit card practices and provides a means of fair and timely resolution of credit billing disputes. Regulation Z requires that a creditor make disclosure conspicuously, in writing, in a form that the consumer may keep. Finance charges and annual percentage rates should be more conspicious than other information. Disclosure shall be furnished before the initial transaction. The regulation also requires that the creditor provide periodic statements of the balance due on an account.

The truth-in-lending statute regulates only the disclosure of credit costs; it does not set usury limits. These limits remain the function of the states. There is no uniformity from state to state with respect to maximum rates or methods for calculating those charges. Not only do the states differ on the usury rate, but each state has different usury rates for different types of transactions.

Equal Credit Opportunity

If you feel you have been discriminated against with respect to an installment credit loan or any other type of credit, the Federal Equal Credit Opportunity Act, tit. VII of the Consumer Credit Protection Act (CCPA), states that all credit applicants must be considered on the same footing. Factors such as race, color, age, sex, marital status, religion, and receipt of public assistance may not be used to discriminate against you in any part of a credit transaction. If a creditor fails to comply, he or she will be liable to you for your damages as well as punitive damages in an amount not greater than $10,000. The costs of the action, together with reasonable attorney's fees, are also allowed. You may request the attorney general of the United States to pursue violations.

A creditor may not cancel or change terms of a credit account when marital status changes. This means that a woman's credit cannot be canceled arbitrarily when she becomes divorced or her husband dies. The Equal Credit Opportunity Act does not guarantee that anyone will get credit. The law does require that an individual be told within 30 days of applying for credit whether or not credit has been approved.

Not only does federal law protect you and your rights with respect to acquiring consumer credit, it also protects you and your credit privacy. The Right to Privacy Act requires a government agency to give an individual prior notice if it is seeking access to that individual's bank records. The notice must contain the reasons for such access and allow the individual the opportunity to challenge that access in court. Legislation is currently being considered that would limit the use of information not only for governmental agencies, but also by banks, insurance companies, and medical organizations.

Fair Credit Billing

The federal government also protects you under the Fair Credit Billing Act, tit. I CCPA, which provides that you may withhold payment on damaged or shoddy goods or poor quality services purchased with a credit card as long as you have made a real attempt to solve the problem. Purchases must be over $50 and must have been made in the same state or within 100 miles of the account mailing address.

The Federal Trade Commission has a regulation requiring a three-day "cooling off" period for door-to-door sales. This would include regular cash sales as well as installment sales. The rule requires that the salespersons (1) inform consumers of their right to cancel the contract, (2) give consumers two copies of the cancellation form, and (3) give consumers a dated receipt or contract that shows the name and the address of the seller. In the event that the consumer decides to cancel the purchase, he or she must sign and date one copy of the form and mail it to the address given for cancellation anytime before midnight of the third business day after the contract date (Exhibit 6–1). This rule applies not only to door-to-door sales at the home but also to any agreements made by a seller in other than the seller's normal place of business. This includes merchandise parties hosted in homes and sales made in rented hotel rooms. The act does not cover sales made totally by mail or phone, sales under $25, sales of real estate, sales of insurance or securities, or sales for emergency home repairs, such as fixing thawing pipes that have frozen or patching a leaky roof in a storm.

Many states have laws protecting consumer credit; for example, various states have ceilings on the maximum amount of interest that can be charged. A charge greater than the statutory ceiling would be called usurious.

Shopping for a Loan

In shopping for a loan the consumer should look for the best deal. The following questions should be asked to help you compare and evaluate different lenders' rates and services.

1 What is the annual percentage rate?
2 What is the total cost of the loan in dollar amounts?
3 How long do you have to pay off the loan?
4 What are the number, amounts, and due dates of payments?
5 What is the cost of deferring or extending the time period of the loan?
6 What is the cost of late charges for overdue payments?
7 If you pay the loan off early, are there any prepayment penalties?
8 Does the loan have to be secured; if so, what collateral is required?
9 What is the cost of credit life or other insurance that is being offered or that may be required?
10 Are there any other charges you may have to pay?
11 What are the penalties for late payments?

When you apply for credit, an application is usually required. A typical application is shown in Exhibit 6–2 entitled ''Retail Installment Credit Agreement.'' This agreement contains all the disclosure required by the federal government with respect to interest, and so on. This particular contract contains an assignment provision. The creditor may sell its right to receive your money to another. You still may exercise any defense you have for defective merchandise against the third party.

FEDERAL CONSUMER LEASING ACT

The Federal Consumer Leasing Act, tit. I of the Consumer Credit Protection Act, ch. 5, requires leasing companies to give the consumer facts about the cost and

EXHIBIT 6-1
Notice of Cancellation

NOTICE OF CANCELLATION
Date of Transaction:_____

You may cancel this transaction, without any penalty or obligation, within three business days from the above date.

If you cancel, any property traded in, any payments made by you under the contract or sale, and any negotiable instrument executed by you will be returned within 10 business days following receipt by the seller of your cancellation notice, and any security interest arising out of the transaction will be cancelled.

If you cancel, you must make available to the seller at your residence, in substantially as good condition as when received, any goods delivered to you under this contract or sale; or you may, if you wish, comply with the instructions of the seller regarding the return shipment of the goods at the seller's expense and risk.

If you do make the goods available to the seller and the seller does not pick them up within 20 days of the date of your notice of cancellation, you may retain or dispose of the goods without any further obligation. If you fail to make the goods available to the seller, or if you agree to return the goods to the seller and fail to do so, then you remain liable for performance of all obligations under the contract.

To cancel this transaction, mail or deliver a signed and dated copy of this cancellation notice, or send a telegram, to (name of seller)_____
_____ ,
at (address of seller's place of business)_____
_____ ,
not later than midnight of (date)_____ .

I hereby cancel this transaction.
Date:_____
(Your Signature)_____

---

terms of their lease contracts before the consumer agrees to lease. The consumer must get a written statement of cost, including the amount of any security deposit, the monthly payments, and the cost of any licenses, insurance, registrations, taxes, maintenance, and so on. The consumer must also get a written statement of the terms of the contract, including guarantees. This statute applies to leases of personal property for a period of time exceeding four months and for a total obligation

EXHIBIT 6-2
Retail Installment Credit Agreement

1262 NEW YORK 9/78

RETAIL INSTALLMENT CREDIT AGREEMENT (Continuous Credit Plan)

Buyer's Name		Age	No. Dependents		Soc. Sec. No.		Driver's License No.
Home Address	City	State	Zip	How Long? Yrs. Mos.		Phone or Nearby	

NOTE: (In this contract, the words I, me, mine, and my means each and all who made the purchase and signed this contract. The words you, your, and yours mean the Seller and/or Westinghouse Credit Corporation who will purchase this contract from the Seller.)

I understand that by signing this Agreement, I am applying to you for a Continuous Credit Charge Account and for a Continuous Credit Identification Card. If you accept my application for credit and sell me goods or services on credit under this Agreement, it is agreed that:

If my account with you is in good standing, I will have the right to purchase goods and services up to the limit that you establish for my account. All purchases made under the terms of this Agreement may be evidenced by an invoice, sales slip or memorandum signed by me.

I will pay to you the money that I owe you under this Agreement (plus an insurance charge, if insurance was purchased) in consecutive monthly payments as listed in the minimum monthly payment schedule on the back of this Agreement.

A payment is due by me when I receive the first monthly bill from you requesting a payment and each month thereafter until all the money that I owe you under this Agreement is paid in full. The amount of my monthly payment to you will increase as additional purchases increase the amount of money that I owe you, but the amount of the monthly payment will not decrease as the monthly payments reduce the amount of money that I owe you.

FINANCE CHARGES will be calculated on the average daily balance of money that I owe you under this Agreement. The daily balance is determined by adding to the Previous Balance of money owed, the unpaid cash price of new purchases, the amount of any insurance charges, if insurance coverage has been chosen, and any previously incurred FINANCE CHARGES, and by subtracting from the total any payments I have made and credits I have received from you. The average daily balance is then determined by dividing the total of all daily balances by the number of days in the billing period.

FINANCE CHARGES will be determined by multiplying the first **$500** of the average daily balance by a monthly periodic rate of **1.5%**, which is an **ANNUAL PERCENTAGE RATE** of 18% and by multiplying the average daily balance in excess of **$500** by a monthly periodic rate of **1%**, which is an **ANNUAL percentage rate of 12%**. A **FINANCE CHARGE of 70 cents** will be charged even if the average daily balance is less than **$46.66**.

I agree that you may change the rates, charges and other terms of this Agreement from time to time if I am given prior notice of such change and if the rates do not exceed the **FINANCE CHARGE** rate allowed by law.

I agree to make each monthly payment within 20 days of the billing date shown on the bill. If I do not make any payment when it is due, you may (without any notice to me) declare all the money that I owe you under this Agreement to be immediately due in full. In the event of such default, I will return to you my Continuous Credit Identification Card, and if you have to sue me to enforce this Agreement, I will pay court costs plus attorney's fees up to 20% of the amount of money that I owe you under the Agreement. I do not have to pay any attorney's fee to any of your salaried employees.

This Agreement will remain in full force until you or I give the other written notice of cancellation of the Agreement. If the Agreement is cancelled, the cancellation does not affect the amount of money that I owe you under the Agreement, the payment terms or the goods or services purchased, and I will pay you the money that I already owe you under the terms of this Agreement.

AT ANY TIME I MAY PAY YOU IN FULL ALL THE MONEY THAT I OWE YOU UNDER THIS AGREEMENT.

INSURANCE OPTION — The Buyer whose signature appears at the bottom of this box has received a copy of the Notice of Proposed Group Credit Insurance printed on the back of this Agreement and certifies that he has been advised of the cost of Group Credit Life and Group Credit Property Insurance as printed below, if obtained for Buyer by Seller or by Creditor.

GROUP CREDIT LIFE INSURANCE. I understand that you do not require Credit Life Insurance and whether or not I buy such insurance is not a factor in your consideration of my application for credit under this Agreement. No such insurance is provided unless I have checked the box and signed my name below.

GROUP CREDIT LIFE INSURANCE. I understand that you do not require property insurance. If property insurance is written in connection with the extention of credit under this Agreement, I may obtain the insurance through you or through any authorized insurance agent or broker of my choice. No such insurance will be provided by you unless I want to have you purchase it for me and I check the box and sign my name below.

I shall pay to you monthly the cost of any insurance that I choose to obtain through you, and until further notice, the monthly rate for Credit Life Insurance shall be not more than 6.9 cents per one hundred dollars of the amount of money that the insured Buyer owes you under this Agreement, and the monthly cost for credit property insurance shall be not more than 25.4 cents per one hundred dollars of so much of the money owed under this Agreement that is applicable to the item or items of insured property. I may cancel any insurance that I have obtained through you at any time by giving you written notice of my cancellation.

The insurance coverage purchased will remain effective until this Agreement is terminated or the insurance is otherwise cancelled.

Buyer is proposed insured unless otherwise shown below:

☐ **Credit Life Insurance**   ☐ **Credit Property Insurance**   ☐ **No Insurance Desired**

_____   BUYER _____ _____
(Please Print)   (Signature)   (Date)

EXHIBIT 6-2, cont.

NOTICE OF CANCELLATION – ALL PRIOR CONTINUOUS CREDIT PLAN AGREEMENTS BETWEEN BUYER AND SELLER WITH RESPECT TO THE ACCOUNT NUMBER SHOWN ABOVE ARE HEREBY CANCELLED.

NOTICE TO THE BUYER –   (1) DO NOT SIGN THIS CREDIT AGREEMENT BEFORE YOU READ IT OR IF IT CONTAINS ANY BLANK SPACE.
(2) YOU ARE ENTITLED TO A COMPLETELY FILLED-IN COPY OF THIS CREDIT AGREEMENT.

NOTICE: SEE REVERSE SIDE FOR OTHER IMPORTANT INFORMATION REGARDING YOUR RIGHTS TO DISPUTE BILLING ERRORS.

ACCEPTED: THE FOREGOING AGREEMENT IS HEREBY ASSIGNED UNDER THE TERMS OF THE ASSIGNMENT ON THE REVERSE SIDE.

I HAVE RECEIVED A COMPLETE SIGNED COPY OF THIS RETAIL INSTALLMENT CREDIT AGREEMENT.

Seller _____

Signature _____
                                    Buyer   (Date)

Business
Address _____
          Street   City   State

Signature _____
                                  Co-Buyer   (Date)

By _____ Date _____

THE APPLICANT, IF MARRIED, MAY APPLY FOR A SEPARATE ACCOUNT.

Previous Address		City		State		Zip		How Long?	

☐ Rent   ☐ Own Home | Amt. Payment | Name of Landlord or Mortgage Holder | Address | Phone
☐ Residence Provided

Buyer Employed by		Occupation	How Long? Yrs. Mos.	Salary $ ☐ Hr. ☐ Wk. ☐ Mo.

Employer's Address	City	State	Zip	Phone No.	Supervisor

Previous Employer	Address and Phone	How Long? Yrs. Mos.

Additional income from child support, alimony, child maintenance need not be disclosed.
Additional Income, If Any: Source: _____   Amount $ _____   Total Combined Income $ _____

Military Personnel Serial No.	Organization Post, Camp or Ship	Name and Rank of CO

Banks With:	Bank Acct. in Name of	Loan Acct. No.	Checking Acct. No.	Savings Acct. No.

If Owns Car - Make	Year Model	Financed by:	Address

NOTICE: Spouse information is required, if answer is "Yes" to either of the following questions.
1. Will Buyer rely on community property and/or spouses income as a basis for repayment of credit requested: .... Yes ☐   No ☐
2. Will Buyer rely on alimony, child support or maintenance payments from spouse for repayment of credit requested: .... Yes ☐   No ☐

Co-Buyer Name	Age	Driver's License No.	Soc. Sec. No.

Co-Buyer Employed by	Occupation	How Long? Yrs. Mos.	Salary $ ☐ Hr. ☐ Wk. ☐ Mo.

Co-Buyer Employer's Address	City	State	Zip	Phone No.	Supervisor

Names of Finance Companies, Banks & Stores Dealt With (Give Address)	Date Opened	Account Number	Items Purchased	High Credit	Payment	Balance

RELATIVES OR FRIENDS NOT LIVING WITH BUYER

Name	Address	City	State	Zip	Relationship	Phone Number

Dear Customer:

A consumer report may be requested in connection with this application for credit. Upon request, you will be informed whether or not a consumer report was so requested, and if a report was requested, of the name and the address of the consumer reporting agency that furnished the report. Subsequent consumer reports may be requested or utilized in connection with an update, renewal, or extension of the credit for which this application was made.

not to exceed $25,000. The lessor (the person who is regularly engaged in leasing under a consumer lease) is not only liable for the disclosure of costs but also must give the consumer a description of the leased property and a statement determining who is liable for damage to the property as well as a statement determining the amount of liabilities the lease imposes on the lessee at the end of the lease and whether or not there is an option to purchase the leased property. All express warranties and guarantees must be in writing.

The act also has provisions to determine the lessee's liabilities on the expiration of the lease. A lessor who deceptively advertises a consumer lease is subject to penalty. Any advertisement with respect to such a lease must advertise that it is a lease. It must include the amount of any payment required at the inception of the lease; the number, amounts, and due dates of the scheduled payments; and the total payments under the lease. It must also include information as to whether the lessee would be liable for the differential between the anticipated fair market value of the property leased and its appraised value at the termination of the lease. The advertisement should also include a statement of the amount or method of determining the amount of liability the lease imposed upon the lessee at its expiration or both as well as a statement as to whether or not there is an option to purchase the leased property and the price and the time for exercising this option. The Consumer Credit Protection Act provides for damages, both compensatory and punitive, with the punitive subject to a maximum of $1000.

THE COLLECTION OF DEBTS

Most consumers pay their debts when due. A major reason for default on most consumer debts is loss of a job. The second most common reason is illness of the chief wage earner. When a consumer does not pay for the merchandise purchased, a creditor will normally attempt to collect the debt himself or herself. This may be done by communicating with the consumer, attempting to find out the reason for nonpayment, and making arrangements for payment. If the creditor fails in this attempt, the creditor normally turns over the account to a collection specialist or ''debt collector.''

The federal government has found that there has been abundant evidence of abusive, deceptive, and unfair debt collection practices, which have contributed to personal bankruptcies, loss of jobs, and even suicide. For example: In State *ex rel.* Richardson v. Edgeworth, 214 So. 2d 579, Miss, 1968 two justices of the peace allowed, and perhaps even encouraged, the abusive use of the courts' criminal process for the sole purpose of collecting civil debts. They permitted creditors to sign criminal affidavits in blank without advising them of the criminal nature of the documents. The judges and police officers also charged excessive fees for the collection services. After several attempts at collection, accompanied by using threats of arrest, Billie Jo Richardson committed suicide. At the trial (against the justices for wrongful death), a psychiatrist testified that the criminal warrants approved by the two justices and the impending arrest by the police officers were the proximate cause of Billie Jo's death. The court found that the justices committed intentional torts. The federal government has put together a protective act under tit. VIII Debt Collection Practices, in 15 U.S.C.A. §§ 1692 et seq. The purpose of tit. VIII is "to eliminate abusive debt collection practices by debt collectors, to insure that those debt collectors who refrain from using abusive debt collection practices are not competitively disadvantaged, and to promote consistent state action to protect consumers against debt collection abuses."

Debt Collection Practices

The federal act prohibits a debt collector from communicating with any person other than the debtor with respect to the debt except if the debt collector is trying to acquire information about the consumer, such as information of the consumer's location or job. In the event that the debt collector is trying to acquire location information, the collector may not state that the consumer owes a debt. The debt collector must identify himself or herself and state that he or she is confirming or correcting information concerning the consumer. The communication can be made only once and may not be done by postcard. There may not be any language or symbol on the envelope or in the contents of the communication to indicate that the writer is the debt collector. When the debt collector is communicating with the consumer, this communication cannot be done at any unusual time or place or at any time or place that is known or should be known to the debt collector to be inconvenient. The statute indicates that convenient times for communicating with the consumer are after eight o'clock in the morning and before nine o'clock at night. If the debtor has an attorney, unless the attorney allows direct communication with the debtor, such communication is not allowed.

In addition, the act prohibits individuals from trying to collect debts from contacting consumers at their place of employment if the debt collector knows or has reason to know that the consumer's employer prohibits the consumer from receiving such communication. In the event that a consumer refuses to pay a debt or that the consumer wishes the debt collector to cease further communication with the consumer, the debt collector shall not communicate further with the consumer except to advise the consumer that the debt collector's further efforts are being terminated and to notify him or her that the debt collector is going to proceed further through litigation and so forth.

A debt collector is not allowed to harass or abuse the consumer. The threat of violence as to person or reputation or property as well as the use of obscene or profane language is strictly prohibited. Publishing a list of consumers who allegedly refuse to pay debts except to consumer reporting agencies is prohibited. Using the telephone repeatedly or continuously with the intent to annoy, abuse, or harass is also prohibited.

A debt collector may not use any false, deceptive, or misleading representation in trying to collect a debt. This means that any representation as to the debt collector's connection with the state or federal government is prohibited. Representations with respect to the fact that nonpayment of the debt will result in arrest or imprisonment are also prohibited.

A debt collector may not use unfair or unconscionable means to collect or attempt to collect any debt. These unfair practices are specifically defined in the Consumer Credit Act (§ 808) and include, but are not limited to ''(1) the collection of any amount unless such amount is expressly authorized by the agreement creating the debt or permitted by law. (2) The acceptance by a debt collector from any person of a check or other payment instrument post-dated by more than five days unless such person is notified in writing of the debt collector's intent to deposit such check or instrument not more than 10 days nor less than 3 business days prior to such deposit. (3) The solicitation by a debt collector of any postdated check or other postdated payment instrument for the purpose of threatening or instituting criminal prosecution. (4) Depositing or threatening to deposit any postdated check or other postdated payment instrument prior to the date on such check or instrument. (5) Causing charges to be made to any person for communications by concealment of the true purpose of the communication.'' In addition, the law further prohibits using any language or symbol other than the debt collector's address on any envelope when communicating with the consumer by use of the mails or by telegram, or using a postcard to communicate with the consumer.

Consumers have the right to full disclosure with respect to their debt. This is provided for in the Consumer Credit Protection Act. The disclosure shall include the amount of the debt and the name of the creditor as well as a statement providing that the consumer must notify the debt collector within 30 days if there is a dispute of the validity of the debt or any portion of the debt. If the consumer does not notify the debt collector, then the debt is assumed to be valid. If the consumer does notify the debt collector of any dispute, the debt collector must obtain verification of the debt from the creditor and mail such verification to the consumer. If the consumer notifies the debt collector within 30 days in writing that the debt or portion of the debt is in dispute, the debt collector must cease to try to collect the disputed portion of the debt until he or she obtains verification of the debt. If the consumer owes several different debts and makes payment on part of the debt obligation, the debt collector may not apply that payment to the disputed portion of the debt.

The act further limits the jurisdiction of the courts in pursuing legal recourse against the debtor. An action can only be brought in the district in which the consumer has signed the contract or in which the consumer resides unless property is pledged as security, and in that case proceedings can be brought in the court in the county in which the property is located.

Failure of a debt collector to adhere to the rules of the Consumer Credit Protection Act will cause the debt collector to be liable for any damages sustained by the consumer and for additional punitive damages not to exceed $1000. The debt collector will not be liable if in fact his or her failure to follow the act has been unintentional or has resulted from a bona fide error.

After the creditor has turned over information to the debt collector and the debt collector has made attempts to collect, the next procedure to be followed is to implement court action. This requires a filing of a summons and complaint as outlined in Chapter 3 on civil practice. In most states, a summons and complaint is in a form that allows a default judgment to be obtained from the clerk of the court without the necessity of a trial. Most attorneys have found that judgment debtors will default in the majority of these consumer actions, and the process can be handled expeditiously without the necessity of spending the time in court to prove the case. After the judgment has been obtained, whether it be a default judgment or through litigation, the procedures that are available for collection of the debt include income execution and property execution.

Garnishment

An income execution called a garnishment is limited by state law in terms of amount and procedure. Some states' legislatures have enacted statutes prohibiting wage garnishments; other states limit the amount of money that can be garnished (Exhibit 6–3). Not only do state laws provide restrictions on garnishment, but the Federal Consumer Credit Protection Act, 15 U.S.C.A. tit. III, also has certain restrictions. The federal statute provides that a garnishment may not exceed 25 percent of the weekly disposable earnings or the amount by which a debtor's disposable income for the week exceeds 30 times the federal minimum hourly wage, whichever is less. For example, if you were employed and making minimum wage, 30 hours of that work week would be exempt from garnishment whereas 10 hours would be subject to garnishment, and you would have to compare that figure with the 25 percent and take the lower number. These restrictions do not apply for debts owed to the United States or for state or federal tax debts or for orders of support. If a state has a more stringent restriction, the state's restriction will apply.

The Consumer Credit Protection Act indicates that no employer may discharge an employee by reason of the fact that his earnings have been garnished, and if somebody violates that section, that person or company is subject to a fine of not more that $1000 or imprisonment of not more than one year.

Information Subpoena

In order to assist judgment creditors in searching for assets, some states have procedures that compel the judgment debtor to disclose the nature, value, and location of his or her assets. A New York statute provides that disclosure shall be effected by serving a subpoena upon the judgment debtor, and if the judgment debtor fails to comply with the subpoena, he or she is liable for contempt of court. The subpoena could require attendance of the debtor for the taking of a deposition or an Information subpoena that has questions accompanying it. If a judgment debtor does not comply with the subpoena, he or she can be brought before the court, and if, in fact, the judgment debtor is found guilty of the contempt, he or she can be fined in an amount sufficient to indemnify the creditor, and he can be incarcerated in jail in New York for up to 90 days or until the fine is paid.

EXHIBIT 6-3
Garnishment of Wages

State	Wages Exempt from Garnishment
Alabama	Consumer debts, the greater of 80% or 50 times federal minimum hourly wage; consumer debts, 75%.
Alaska	The greater of 75% of disposable earnings or $114 per week.
Arizona	50% of earnings within 30 days preceding writ of garnishment; after writ, the greater of 75% of disposable earnings or 30% of federal minimum hourly wage.
Arkansas	$500 ($200 if unmarried) of money earned within 60 days preceding writ of garnishment or 60 days' wages, whichever is less; $25 per week after issuance of writ of garnishment.
California	The greater of 75% of disposable earnings or 30 times federal minimum hourly wage.
Colorado	The greater of 75% of disposable earnings or 30 times federal minimum hourly wage.
Connecticut	The greater of 75% of disposable earnings or 40 times federal minimum hourly wage.
Delaware	85% of earnings (except when garnishment is for debts to state).
District of Columbia	The greater of 75% of disposable earnings or 30 times federal minimum hourly wage.
Florida	The greater of 75% of disposable earnings or 30 times federal minimum hourly wage.
Georgia	The greater of 75% of disposable earnings or 30 times federal minimum hourly wage.
Hawaii	Generally, 95% of the first $100 of monthly earnings; 90% of the next $100; 80% of monthly earnings over $200.
Idaho	The greater of 75% of disposable earnings or 30 times federal minimum hourly wage.
Illinois	The greater of 85% of gross earnings or 30 times federal minimum hourly wage.
Indiana	The greater of 75% of disposable earnings or 30 times federal minimum hourly wage (resident householders may qualify for higher exemptions).
Iowa	The greater of 75% of disposable earnings or 30 times federal minimum hourly wage (no single garnishment may exceed $250 a year).
Kansas	The greater of 75% of disposable earnings or 30 times federal minimum hourly wage.

EXHIBIT 6-3, cont.

State	Wages Exempt from Garnishment
Kentucky	The greater of 75% of disposable earnings or 30 times federal minimum hourly wage.
Louisiana	The greater of 75% of disposable earnings or 30 times federal minimum hourly wage.
Maine	100%
Maryland	The greater of $120 per week or 75% of earnings; in Caroline, Kent, Queen Anne's, and Worcester counties, the greater of 75% of earnings or 30 times federal minimum hourly wage.
Massachusetts	$125 per week.
Michigan	No specific provision.
Minnesota	The greater of 75% of disposable earnings or 40 times federal minimum hourly wage (plus 100% of earnings within 30 days preceding writ of garnishment if necessary for family support).
Mississippi	75% of earnings.
Missouri	The greater of 75% of earnings or 30 times federal minimum hourly wage; 90% of earnings for resident head of household.
Montana	100% of wages earned by head of household or a person over 60 within 45 days preceding writ of garnishment; after issuance of writ of garnishment, 50% for gasoline debts incured by head of household or his family.
Nebraska	The greater of 75% of disposable earnings or 30 times federal minimum hourly wage; 85% of disposable earnings for head of household.
Nevada	The greater of 75% of disposable weekly earnings or all disposable weekly earnings in escess of 30 times federal minimum hourly wage.
New Hampshire	50 times federal minimum hourly wage earned before issuance of writ of garnishment (except in suit on a debt on a New Hampshire judgment); all wages earned after issuance of writ of garnishment.
New Jersey	$48 per week plus 90% of excess; the court may fix a larger percentage if annual income exceeds $7,500.
New Mexico	The greater of 75% of disposable earnings or 40 times federal minimum hourly wage.
New York	90% of earnings; if earnings are less than $85 per week, garnishment is not permitted.
North Carolina	100% of wages earned 60 days preceding order to satisfy judgment debt if wages are necessary for family support.

EXHIBIT 6-3, cont.

State	Wages Exempt from Garnishment
North Dakota	The greater of 75% of disposable earnings or 40 times federal minimum hourly wage.
Ohio	The greater of 75% of disposable earnings or 30 times federal minimum hourly wage, within 30 days preceding writ.
Oklahoma	Before judgment, 75% of all earnings in last 90 days and 100% of earnings for personal services; after judgment, 75% of all earnings and 100% of earnings for 90 days if necessary for family support.
Oregon	The greater of 75% of disposable earnings or 40 times federal minimum hourly wage.
Pennsylvania	100%, but no exemption is given if suit is for support or for board for 4 weeks or less.
Rhode Island	$50 per week.
South Carolina	100%.
South Dakota	No specific provision.
Tennessee	The greater of 75% of disposable earnings or 30 times federal minimum hourly wage.
Texas	100%.
Utah	The greater of 75% of disposable earnings or 40 times state minimum hourly wage.
Vermont	No specific provision.
Virginia	The greater of 75% of disposable earnings or 30 times federal minimum hourly wage.
Washington	The greater of 75% of disposable earnings or 40 times state minimum hourly wage.
West Virginia	The greater of 80% of disposable earnings or 30 times federal minimum hourly wage.
Wisconsin	The greater of 75% of disposable earnings or 30 times federal minimum hourly wage.
Wyoming	The greater of 75% of disposable earnings or 30 times federal minimum hourly wage.

Property Execution

The other alternative that a creditor has in trying to obtain moneys due from a judgment debtor is the property execution. Under a property execution, the judgment debtor's property is subject to seizure by the sheriff when the creditor notifies the sheriff of the judgment lien. When the property is seized, it is then held for sale at public auction, and the proceeds from the sale are used to pay the creditor's judgment as well as administrative costs. If there is a balance left due to the creditor, a deficiency judgment is obtained and filed for this balance.

A creditor can also obtain rights to debtor's property when the debtor signs a security agreement at the time that the credit is obtained. This agreement and security interest are authorized by art. 9 of the Uniform Commercial Code. The security interest may, in addition to covering the property that is purchased on credit, include any other property that may be in existence or may be acquired after the date that credit is given. The procedures under art. 9 include the provision for filing of the secured interest in the county in which the property is kept (Exhibit 6–4). This filing establishes various creditors' rights as against each other to a debtor's property. Under U.C.C. art. 9, the secured party has a right to take possession of the property after the default without judicial process so long as this can be accomplished without breach of the peace, and the secured party may sell, lease, or dispose of the collateral and take reasonable expenses as well as satisfy the indebtedness. If there are any additional moneys received, the secured party must give the debtor the surplus. The disposition of the sale of the collateral may be by public or private means and may be done in any way commercially accepted. Notice must be given to the debtor of the method and time of sale. The secured party can also utilize the courts to effectuate a repossession of the goods by having the court direct the marshall or sheriff to take the goods from the debtor.

Other methods used by creditors to expedite the collection of default loans include requirement for cosigners, wage assignments, and confessions of judgment. Cosigners may include a spouse, parent, or friend or relative who has a better credit rating than the debtor does. The Consumer Credit Code (§ 3.208) provides that cosigners shall be given specific notification as to their personal liability. The form of this notification is provided in Exhibit 6–5.

Confession of Judgment

A confession of judgment (Exhibit 6–6) gives the creditor the ability to enter a judgment immediately against the debtor without the requirement of going to court. This can be done without notice to the debtor and without opportunity for the debt to be challenged. The confession of judgment acts in the same manner as any other judgment in putting the creditor in a position to attach personal property and automatically attaches the real property. Some state laws allow confessions of judgment to be opened for good cause; others do not allow confessions of judgment at all.

An assignment of wages is a contract giving a creditor a percentage of the debtor's wages in the amount necessary to satisfy the debt. These assignments are

EXHIBIT 6-4
U.C.C. Financing Statement

NEW YORK STATE, PENNSYLVANIA AND TEXAS
Uniform Commercial Code — FINANCING STATEMENT — Form UCC-1

JULIUS BLUMBERG, INC. 80 EXCHANGE PL. NYC 10004 212-431-5000
IMPORTANT — Read instructions on back before filling out form

This FINANCING STATEMENT is presented to a Filing Officer for filing pursuant to the Uniform Commercial Code.	No. of Additional Sheets Presented:	Maturity Date 3. (optional):
1. Debtor(s) (Last Name First) and Address(es):	2. Secured Party(ies): Name(s) and Address(es):	4. For Filing Officer: Date, Time, No.-Filing Office

5. This Financing Statement covers the following types (or items) of property:

6. Assignee(s) of Secured Party and Address(es)

7. ☐ The described crops are growing or to be grown on: *
☐ The described goods are or are to be affixed to: *
* (Describe Real Estate Below).

☐ Proceeds —   ☐ Products of the Collateral are also covered.

8. Describe Real Estate Here:

9. Name(s) of Record Owner(s):

No. & Street	Town or City	County	Section	Block	Lot

10. This statement is filed without the debtor's signature to perfect a security interest in collateral (check appropriate box)

☐ under a security agreement signed by debtor authorizing secured party to file this statement, or
☐ already subject to a security interest in another jurisdiction when it was brought into this state, or
☐ which is proceeds of the original collateral described above in which a security interest was perfected:

By_____   By_____
Signature(s) of Debtor(s)   Signature(s) of Secured Party(ies)

(1) Filing Officer Copy — Numerical   Approved by the New York Secretary of State, the Texas Secretary of State
9/65 STANDARD FORM NEW YORK STATE FORM UCC-1   and the Secretary of the Commonwealth of Pennsylvania

commonly taken at the time the debt is obtained. The Consumer Credit Code and many state laws limit the security by providing that a consumer may not authorize confession of judgment and that a creditor may not take an assignment of earnings of the consumer in payment.

BANKRUPTCY

Bankruptcy laws, as defined by the United States Code, are designed to provide an orderly and equitable distribution of the assets of an insolvent debtor. At one time, all bankrupts were considered defrauders and criminals. They were subject to severe social and criminal sanctions that even included a degrading form of dress. It was a disgrace to be bankrupt. Today the bankruptcy laws are used for the rehabilitation of debtors, and there are various types of arrangements and reorganizations that provide for the discharge of unpaid portion of debts in order to give a debtor a new start in life.

Bankruptcy is governed by the federal government. The bankruptcy laws can be found in 11 U.S. Code and include eight subdivisions called chapters (chs. 1, 3, 5, 7, 9, 11, 13, and 15). The bankruptcy law provides for the liquidation proceedings to be commenced by either the bankrupt himself or herself (voluntarily) or by his or her creditors (involuntarily). This chapter will discuss proceedings initiated by the bankrupt under two chapters of the bankruptcy law: Chapter 7, which is called "Straight Bankruptcy," or liquidation, and Chapter 13, which is called "Wage Earners Plan," or reorganization.

Petition

Any bankruptcy proceeding is started by a petition to the U.S. district court. The petition is usually accompanied by a list of the debtor's assets and creditors, as well as the amount due to each. Filing of a petition results in an automatic stay of all proceedings, including both judicial and administrative. The automatic stay prohibits creditors from issuing process (starting a lawsuit), executions against debtor's property (foreclosures or wage garnishments, and so on), turnover of property (if the

EXHIBIT 6-5
Consumer Credit Code Notice

You agree to pay the debt identified below although you may not personally receive any property, services, or money. You may be sued for payment although the person who receives the property, services, or money is able to pay. This notice is not the contract that obligates you to pay the debt. Read the contract for the exact terms of your obligation.

IDENTIFICATION OF DEBT YOU MAY HAVE TO PAY

_____
(Name of Debtor)

_____
(Name of Creditor)

_____
(Date)

_____
(Kind of Debt)

I have received a copy of this notice.

_____
(Date)

_____
(Signed)

EXHIBIT 6-6
Affidavit for Judgment by Confession

SUPREME COURT OF THE STATE OF NEW YORK
COUNTY OF OTSEGO

_____

Plaintiff

vs.

Defendant

_____

STATE OF NEW YORK:

ss.:

COUNTY OF OTSEGO:

_____ being duly sworn, deposes and says:

1. I am the defendant above-named, and I reside at _____

_____.

2. I confess judgment, pursuant to Section 3218 of the Civil Practice Law and Rules, in favor of the plaintiff, for the sum of _____, less any payments that may hereafter be paid by me and hereby authorize plaintiff to enter judgment in the event of any default in payments.

3. This Confession of Judgment is not for the purpose of securing the plaintiff against a contingent liability and is not an installment loan within the prohibition of Section 3201 of the C.P.L.R.

_____

Sworn to before me this
_____ day of September, _____.

_____

Notary Public _____

---

sheriff has seized debtor's property under income execution or property execution, that property will not be able to be forwarded to the creditor), imposition of liens against the debtor's property, acts of harassment with respect to collection, tax court proceedings, and creditor's rights to set off (when the debtor owes the creditor money and when the creditor owes the debtor money, the right of set off allows one amount to be deducted from the other). The automatic stay is effective except with respect to criminal proceedings against the debtor, collection of alimony, maintenance of support, or proceedings by governmental units pursuant to their police or regulatory authority or for proceedings re tax deficiencies. The automatic stay will continue until the courts terminate the stay by modifying the conditions, dismissing the case, or granting or refusing a discharge.

When a debtor files a petition of bankruptcy, his or her property immediately comes under the jurisdiction of the bankruptcy court. The term that is used to define this property is an "estate." This estate includes all legal and equitable interest of the debtor at the time of the petition. In addition, the estate includes property that the debtor acquires within 180 days after the date of filing the petition. This estate is held by an interim trustee appointed by the court until the first meeting of the creditors, where a disinterested person is elected trustee. (The debtor must appear at this meeting and submit to examination under oath.) It is up to the trustee to determine how the creditors are to be paid.

Trustee

Trustees have great powers with respect to the debtor's property. They may use, sell, or lease property of the estate. The trustee may avoid a transfer that was made for the benefit of creditors on account of a prior debt while the debtor was insolvent within 90 days preceding the filing of the petition in bankruptcy. A similar right exists with respect to transfers made to friends or relatives (insiders) within one year. If the creditor receives a greater percentage of the claim than he or she would have received under the distribution made by order of the bankruptcy court, the trustee has the right to set aside the transfer and recover the amounts paid. The bankruptcy court also allows the trustee to abandon property that is burdensome or of no value to the estate. Moreover, the trustee has the ability to operate the debtor's business if it is in the best interest of the estate and liquidate the business over a limited period of time. The trustee is given great flexibility in the disposal of property in the estate if another entity has an interest such as a lien. He or she can dispose of the property through sale, abandonment, or other means that are appropriate to ensure the interests of the secured party. The trustee may also sell a debtor's property free and clear of a debtor's joint interest or of a debtor's interest as a tenant by the entirety. The trustee must show, in cases of joint interest and tenancies by the entirety, that the property cannot be partitioned and that the sale will result in a significant benefit to the trust estate and that the benefit to the estate outweighs the detriment to the nonbankrupt co-owner. In cases of the co-ownership, the co-owner will have the right of first refusal.

When the bankruptcy petition is filed, creditors are notified as to the status of the debtor, and they in turn are requested to file claims with the bankruptcy court. Claims are listed in the following order of priority:

1 Administrative expenses.
2 Involuntary bankrupt's debts incurred between filing the petition and its final disposition.
3 Employee wages and fringe benefits.
4 Money deposited for purchase, lease, or rental of property or services for personal use.
5 Taxes (including withholding, sales, and property taxes).
6 Secured creditors.
7 Unsecured creditors.

The basic job of a trustee in a Chapter 7 bankruptcy is to amass all the information with respect to the assets and liabilities of the debtor, to sell those assets, and to pay the creditors according to the priorities set out earlier. The debtor is entitled to exemptions from this sale. Exemptions are provided under both federal and state law. The Federal Bankruptcy Code entitles the debtor to 11 categories of exemptions. Each state has different exemptions. It is up to the debtor to choose between the federal or the state exemptions. Some states do not allow a choice and require the debtor to use their exemption. Exhibit 6–7 lists the 50 state exemptions.

Exemptions

The federal exemptions include the homestead exemption, which is applicable to the individual's residence and allows the individual to retain $7500 of real or personal property used as a residence. This means that if you claim bankruptcy and elect the federal exemption and your house is worth $50,000 with a mortgage of $42,500, your house will not be taken by the bankruptcy court and sold for the benefit of creditors. This exemption, like the others, is doubled if both spouses claim bankruptcy.

The second exemption includes $1200 of equity in a motor vehicle. If you own a motor vehicle worth $6000 and the finance company has a $4800 lien on that vehicle, you are entitled to keep that vehicle. Of course, in both of these situations, you must continue to pay the secured lien after bankruptcy.

The third category of federal exemptions includes personal property, household goods, furnishings, clothing, pets, and so on. There is a $200 limit for each item. Bankruptcy courts have allowed for accelerated rates of depreciation on purchased items of personal property. This means that if you purchased a stereo 10 years ago for $1000, even though the market value of that stereo may be more than the $1000 you paid, the courts will say that that property is worth less than $200 because they allow a reduction in the purchase price for each year the property is used.

The fourth category is jewelry. A debtor is allowed to retain $500 in jewelry.

The fifth category is a general exemption equal to $400 of property plus any "spillover" of the unused portion of the homestead exemption. This general exemption can be applied against any of the debtor's property that has not been exempt under one of the other federal exemptions.

The sixth category includes professional or trade materials and exempts up to $750 in professional books or implements or tools of the debtor's trade.

The seventh category is life insurance, which includes any unmatured insurance contract except for credit life insurance.

The eighth category is the loan value life insurance that is the value that an individual having insurance can borrow against the equity in that insurance policy, and this amount is up to $4000.

The ninth category includes prescribed health aids, such as hearing aids, eyeglasses, pacemakers, and so on. There is no dollar limitation on this category.

EXHIBIT 6-7
Homestead Exemption Laws

State	Protected from Creditors
Alabama	160 acres, not more than $2,000.
Alaska	160 acres outside town or 1/4 acre in town, not more than $12,000; $8,000 mobile home.
Arizona	Not more than $20,000; $10,000 mobile home.
Arkansas	160 acres outside town or 1 acre in town, not more than $2,500; 80 acres outside town or 1/4 acre in town regardless of value.
California	Not more than $40,000 for head of household or person age 65 or older; $25,000 for all others.
Colorado	Not more than $7,500.
Connecticut	Homestead not protected.
Delaware	Homestead not protected.
District of Columbia	Homestead not protected.
Florida	160 acres outside town or 1/2 acre in town.
Georgia	Not more than $5,000 combined real and personal property, or 50 acres plus 5 acres for each child under 16 outside town; not more than $200, or land in town worth $500.
Hawaii	1 acre, not more than $30,000 for head of household or person age 65 or older; $20,000 for others.
Idaho	Not more than $10,000 for head of household; $4,000 for others.
Illinois	Not more than $10,000.
Indiana	Homestead not protected.
Iowa	40 acres outside town or 1/2 acre in town.
Kansas	160 acres outside town or 1 acre in town.
Kentucky	Not more than $1,000.
Louisiana	160 acres, not more than $15,000.
Maine	Not more than $5,000.
Maryland	Homestead not protected.
Massachusetts	Not more than $40,000.
Michigan	40 acres outside town or 1 lot in town, value not over $3,500.
Minnesota	80 acres outside town or 1/2 acre in town.
Mississippi	160 acres, not more than $15,000.

EXHIBIT 6-7, cont.

State	Protected from Creditors
Missouri	Not more than $10,000.
Montana	320 acres outside town or 1/4 acre in town, not more than $20,000.
Nebraska	160 acres outside town or 2 city blocks, not more than $4,000.
Nevada	Not more than $25,000.
New Hampshire	Not more than $2,500.
New Jersey	Homestead not protected.
New Mexico	Not more than $10.000.
New York	Not more than $10,000.
North Carolina	Not more than $1,000.
North Dakota	Not more than $60,000.
Ohio	Not more than $1,000.
Oklahoma	160 acres outside town or 1 acre in town, not more than $5,000; 1/4 acre in town regardless of value.
Oregon	160 acres outside town or 1 block in town, not more than $12,000.
Pennsylvania	Homestead not protected.
Rhode Island	Homestead not protected.
South Carolina	Not more than $1,000.
South Dakota	160 acres outside town or 1 acre in town, not more than $30,000; land acquired under U.S. mining law is limited to 40 acres outside town or 1 acre in town.
Tennessee	Not more than $1,000.
Texas	200 acres outside town or lots in town, not more than $10,000.
Utah	Not more than $6,000 for head of household plus $2,000 for spouse and $800 for each additional family member.
Vermont	Not more than $5,000.
Virginia	Not more than $5,000.
Washington	Not more than $20,000.
West Virginia	Not more than $5,000.
Wisconsin	Not more than $25,000.
Wyoming	Not more than $6,000.

The tenth category includes social security, unemployment benefits, public assistance, alimony, support, pension, or other future earning benefits such as stock, bonds, or profit-sharing plans. The full amount of these benefits is excludable.

The last category of federal exemptions is bodily injury or wrongful death claims. There is no dollar limitation on this category. The court will exempt that amount reasonably necessary for the support of a debtor or a dependent.

The next step in the Chapter 7 process is the sale of the assets; after the sale, creditors will receive a pro rata share of the proceeds, and the bankrupt debtor will be discharged of all liens, debts, and obligations previously owed, except for nondischargeable debts. These include taxes, money obtained by false pretense, debts that were not listed on the bankruptcy petition, fraudulently obtained debts, alimony and support, obligations arising from willful or malicious injury (or both), government fines and penalties, educational loans, and debts owed from a previous bankruptcy case. It is up to the creditors to initiate proceedings with respect to the nondischargeability of debts involving false statements, embezzlement, larceny, or a case of willful or malicious injury.

Reaffirmation

After debts have been discharged, the bankruptcy law (§ 524 [c] and [d]) allows a debtor to reaffirm certain debts only with court approval. Such an agreement of reaffirmation must be made before the granting of discharge, and the debtor has 30 days after such effective date in which to rescind. A discharge will not be granted if the debtor has intentionally transferred, concealed, or destroyed property or records within one year prior to the filing of the petition or after the filing or if the debtor acts fraudulently with respect to the case by making false statements, and so on. If the debtor has refused to obey a lawful order of the court or has been granted a discharge within six years before the petition was filed, a discharge will not be granted.

Chapter 13

The other chapter applicable to individuals under the U.S. Bankruptcy Code is Chapter 13. Chapter 13 is considered the ''wage earner'' plan of bankruptcy. It allows debtors to reorganize their finances and continue to function without complete dissolution. Individuals who have regular income, with unsecured debts of less than $100,000, may file. In Chapter 13 all secured debts are paid completely, and all unsecured debts are paid over a period of three years (up to five with court permission) at a rate to be determined by the debtor (i.e., 30 cents on the dollar).

The procedure for Chapter 13 includes the filing of a voluntary petition, which causes an automatic stay. (There is no involuntary form of Chapter 13). The petition must include a filing fee of $60 (same for Chapter 7), together with schedules of assets and creditors and an itemized plan of how the debtor proposes to pay his or her debts. The plan includes a budget of household expenses, such as the mortgage payments, food, clothing, gasoline, and entertainment. These expenses are subtracted from the total monthly income to come up with a total proposed amount to be turned over to the court-appointed trustee for the benefit of the creditors. The petition is sent to the bankruptcy court, and a hearing (called a 341 hearing named after the section in the law) date is set. The court will then forward the papers to a trustee. The trustee will review the petition and the plan to see if the plan of payment is feasible over the three-year period. The trustee will contact the debtor or the debtor's attorney if the plan does not seem to be feasible and try to work out a feasible plan. At the 341 hearing, the debtor is sworn in and examined; questions are asked with respect to the debtor's property and the proposed plan. Creditors are allowed to be present, and they may also examine the debtor. In addition, values of collateral are decided for the secured creditors.

After the 341 hearing, a confirmation hearing is held before a federal bankruptcy judge. At the confirmation hearing, the trustee recommends confirmation of the plan if it is feasible and proposed in good faith and if all of the values of the collateral are established and if there is no objection to the confirmation of the plan from the creditors. The debtor must be sworn in and examined at the confirmation hearing. All payments under the plan are to come from payroll deductions and are to go directly to the trustee. The trustee, in turn, will pay the creditors. After the plan is completed in three years (five years if a court order is obtained), the creditor will have received what the plan has called for, and the debtor will be released from court supervision and discharged in bankruptcy.

The Chapter 13 plan is not only available for wage earners, but it is also available for individuals who are running their own businesses as sole proprietors. They can reorganize business debts as well as personal debts.

A debtor is entitled to convert from a Chapter 13 to a Chapter 7 as a matter of right at any time. This conversion can also be done on request of a party in interest (i.e., a creditor) after notice and hearing. In the event of a conversion to Chapter 7, the Chapter 13 trustee will be replaced by a Chapter 7 trustee, and the proceedings will take the same course as Chapter 7.

Under a Chapter 13 bankruptcy, unsecured creditors must receive as much as they would if a Chapter 7 bankruptcy had been filed. The priority claims listed under Chapter 7 bankruptcy for taxes, wages, and so on also receive priority in a Chapter 13 plan. All taxes less than three years old must be paid in full but over the course of the plan. With respect to the payment for unsecured creditors, most courts hold that there should be a meaningful payment to unsecured creditors. Thus a zero or very low percentage plan is not meaningful. This would be the equivalent of straight bankruptcy. It is up to each individual bankruptcy court judge to determine what is meaningful. Plans have been approved for as little as 10 cents on the dollar.

Discharge may be granted even if the debtor does not complete the plan as long as he or she has acted in good faith and the property distributed to date was greater than creditors would have gotten in a Chapter 7 (''hardship discharge'').

BANKING

Banking institutions are organized under various state and federal laws. Banking institutions include commercial banks, savings and loans associations, and savings banks.

Historically, commercial banks were oriented toward business accounts whereas savings institutions were oriented toward individuals. In recent years there has been increased pressure by both to enter markets previously reserved to the other. Today the distinction between commercial and savings institutions is rapidly disappearing. Both have become full-service financial institutions offering small- and large-scale savings accounts, trust services, pension consulting, tax counseling and return preparation, money management and investment advice, estate administration, life insurance, and so on.

Commercial banks are the largest in terms of size and number of dollars on deposit.

Savings and loan associations and savings banks are governed by the same rules as commercial banks and generally offer the same services. (Savings banks exist primarily in the northeastern states.) Credit unions are federally or state chartered organizations. They have maximum rates based on the time a deposit is held. The underlying concept of a credit union is that the individuals who form the credit union are members of the same organization, or have something in common.

The major function of a bank is to attract money from business and individuals in the form of savings by offering interest for the use of the funds. Then the bank will lend these funds for mortgages, commercial loans, and so on and charge interest to the borrower. The difference between the interest charged borrowers and the interest given to the savers is used to operate the bank and to generate profits for the owners of the bank.

There are certain state and federal laws that govern the interrelationship that consumers have with their banks. In addition to these laws, the contract a consumer enters into with the bank will also define the obligations of the parties. A consumer should always review the contract carefully before opening an account or retaining a bank to provide other services (safe deposit, checking, trust, and so on).

Here are some of the major points consumers should be aware of when they are deciding on a savings account. Savings in a commercial bank, savings and loan association, savings bank, or credit union usually are covered by federal insurance up to a maximum of $100,000. The consumer should make sure that the bank he or she is considering has this insurance and that the account he or she is opening is covered. When an individual has more than $100,000 in any account, a second account should be opened.

The consumer should also be aware that dormant accounts (accounts in which there have been no deposits or withdrawals) will be paid to the state after a certain length of time as defined by state statutes. It is advisable to make a periodic deposit or withdrawal in all accounts to prevent this. It is also advisable to check the procedures with the bank prior to opening any account.

The consumer should also be aware that banks have the option of delaying payment of a requested withdrawal from a savings account for up to 30 days. If a bank has this procedure in effect, you may create a problem for yourself if you find out about the rule after you have made a deposit.

Checks and Checking Accounts

In addition to savings account, banks also offer checking accounts. The charges on these accounts depend on many factors, including the bank's success in attracting savings. Banks may charge for checking service on a per check charge, on the activity in the account, on the average balance in the account, or on some combination of methods.

There are two types of checking accounts: regular and special. Regular accounts base their charges on the number of checks written and deposits made during the month. (If the depositor maintains a minimum monthly balance, the service may be provided free.) Special accounts base their charges on a cost per check or additional monthly service charge or both. Special checking accounts usually provide additional options that regular accounts do not. These options include items such as interest paid to the depositor on the account balance, overdraft writing privileges, and so on.

Checks are used on a regular basis in our consumer society (Exhibit 6–8). They are a lot less risky and a lot more convenient than cash for paying bills. The Uniform Commercial Code, arts. 3 and 4, governs the relationship a consumer has with

EXHIBIT 6-8
Check

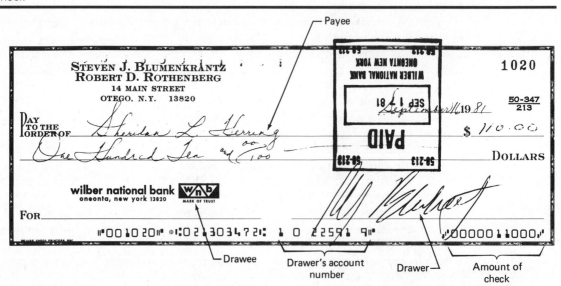

the bank as well as his or her rights with respect to checks and other negotiable instruments (promissory notes and so forth). For a check to be transferable (negotiable), it must be signed by the drawer (the person writing the check). In addition, it must contain an unconditional promise to pay a certain sum of money. It also must be payable on demand or at a definite time, and the words *to order* or *bearer* must be included on its face. Unless these criteria are met, the check that you write will not be valid. Usually, the bank you open an account with will provide you with forms for drawing checks, but a check can be prepared on other than the bank forms and be binding.

A check is an order that you (drawer), give to your bank (drawee), telling the bank to pay another individual (payee) a certain sum of money. This order is made pursuant to the contract that you have entered into with your bank. Unless your contract provides for automatic borrowing privileges (overdraft checking), the bank is only obligated to pay out funds that are on deposit in your account. (The U.C.C. allows a bank to charge the customer's account for items that were payable even though such payment would create an overdraft. An overdraft is a situation in which the individual has taken too much from his or her account and the individual would be liable to the bank for the balance due.)

An order to a bank to pay out funds that you do not have (if you are aware of the circumstances) is a violation of criminal statutes. If you "postdate" a check (date a check in the future), it may not be cashed until the date on the check. If at the time you write the check you intend to deposit the necessary funds and believe you can do so, there is generally no violation if you are subsequently unable to

EXHIBIT 6-8, cont.

Endorsements

make the deposit. If you postdate a check without the intent or ability to deposit the proceeds on time (''cover''), you are subject to criminal sanction.

Checks may be drawn to ''bearer'' and to ''order.'' A bearer check may be cashed by anyone who has possession of it. The casher need not endorse the check and in no way guarantees its payment. An order check is drawn to a specific person and can only be cashed by that person. An order instrument must be endorsed (signed) by the payee before the drawee is obligated to cash the check. The payee's endorsement also serves as a guarantee. Checks must be presented to the bank on which they are drawn in order to be cashed. (If the payee does business with a different bank, that bank may be willing to lend him or her money until the drawer's bank makes payment.)

Liabilities of Parties

The liabilities of parties to a check are as follows: The drawee is primarily liable. This means that if the bank fails to pay your check when there is money in your account, the bank will be liable to all persons who are damaged by this failure, including you. The drawer and endorser are secondarily liable in the order in which they sign. In the event you receive a check from Jones (Exhibit 6–8A), the Wilber Bank must pay you pursuant to my order. If they do not pay because I do not have the funds available (NSF), your recourse is to proceed against Jones, who would proceed against Herring, who would proceed against me for the amount of the check. If Herring and I have disappeared, you are stuck. If you receive a bearer check, the bank cannot proceed against you, and they must find Herring or me. If you endorse the bearer check (which you need not do), you accept responsibility for it and will be liable.

If you wish to restrict the transfer of a check, you may do so by endorsing the check for the specific purpose intended. For example, suppose you wish to mail a check to be deposited in your account. If you sign your name and the check is found or stolen by a third party, that party may cash the check. To prevent this, you can endorse the check ''for deposit only to account number 123456789.''

Forgery is the unauthorized signing of a person's name. When it occurs on a check or other negotiable instrument, it is ineffective to transfer funds. The bank is responsible to the drawer for payments made on forged checks if the drawer's signature is forged. On the other hand, if you sign a check and it is subsequently stolen, you are liable for the amount of the instrument.

If you endorse a forged check, you are liable. This is one reason many individuals refuse to accept checks from third parties. Know your endorser! A material alteration of a check (e.g., change in the amount) is also considered a forgery. A person perpetrating a forgery is subject to criminal sanctions.

Banks usually consider a check outstanding for longer than six months as stale, and a bank does not have to pay the customer's check, other than a certified check, if it is presented more than six months after the date. If a bank does make the payment, the bank is not liable for such a payment if it is made in good faith. Neither the death nor the incompetence of a customer revokes a bank's authority to pay on a customer's account until the bank knows of the fact of the death or the adjudication of incompetency and has a reasonable opportunity to act.

Cashier's Checks, Traveler's Checks, and Certified Checks

In addition to the check shown in Exhibit 6–8, there are other types of checks, including cashier's checks, traveler's checks, and certified checks. A cashier's check is one that the bank writes on itself. The consumer gives the bank money, and the bank draws a check payable to whomever the consumer designates. A cashier's check is often preferred by payees because the check will not be returned for insufficient funds. Traveler's checks are more readily negotiable than ordinary checks because of the nature of the issuer's service. When a person certifies a check, the bank guarantees that the funds to cover the check are in the drawer's account. The bank sets aside the cash to pay the certified check. Either the drawer or payee may ask to have a check certified. The drawer should never destroy a certified check because it could be difficult to get the funds back into his or her account. If the drawer does not use the certified check, it should be returned to the bank.

A bank may pay certified checks for 10 days after the drawer's date of death or incompetency even if the bank has knowledge of the death or incompetency. According to the U.C.C., "The tremendous number of checks handled by banks and the countrywide nature of the bank collection process require uniformity in the law of bank collections. Individual federal reserve banks process as many as one million items a day; large metropolitan banks average 300,000 a day; banks with less than $5 million on deposit handle 1000 to 2000 daily." The great number of transactions in the banking industry is the reason that there is a uniform statute dealing with interrelationships between banks and their customers as well as providing a uniform system of transfer of money. Checks and other commercial papers are used in business in the same manner that cash is. The contract that you enter into with your bank will be the superseding document, and you should read the terms of this contract in order to determine what your rights are.

Banking Process

After an item has been received by a bank, it goes through a series of processes, varying with the type of item that it is; it moves from the teller's window, branch office, or mail desk at which it is received through settlement and proving departments until it is forwarded or presented to a clearing house or another bank, if it is a transit item, or until it reaches the bookkeeping department, if the bank receiving it is the payor bank. In addition, in order that the books of the bank always remain in balance while items are moving through it, the amount of each item is included in lists or proofs of debits or credits several times as it progresses through the bank. The running of proofs, the making of debit and credit entries in subsidiary and general ledgers, and the striking of general balances for each day require a considerable amount of time. If these processes are to be completed on any particular day during normal working hours without the employment of night forces, a number of banks have found it necessary to establish a "cut off hour" to

allow time to obtain final figures to be incorporated into the bank's position for the day.''
(U.C.C. official comment, § 4107)

The U.C.C. allows the banks to have such a cutoff so long as the hour is not earlier than 2:00 P.M. If the hour is fixed, items received after the cutoff time are treated as being received the next banking day. A bank is liable to its customers for damages caused by the wrongful dishonor of an item. Dishonor is the nonpayment of an item. When an item has been dishonored through mistake, liability is limited to the actual damages that the customer may prove. These damages must be proximately caused by the dishonor. A customer may stop payment of any item payable by giving the bank a ''stop payment'' order in time to give the bank opportunity to act. Unless otherwise provided by contract, the Uniform Commercial Code indicates that an oral stop payment order is binding upon the bank for only 14 calendar days and must be confirmed in writing within that 14-day period. A written order is effective only for six months unless it is renewed in writing.

If a customer has a loss as a result of the bank's inaction on a stop-payment order, it is up to the customer to establish the facts with respect to the loss. The U.C.C. is silent as to your right to stop payment after certification of a check. This gives the bank the option of accepting or refusing such an order.

A bank customer should review his or her bank statement promptly to determine whether items were paid correctly and whether items were paid owing to an unauthorized signature or alteration. The customer must notify the bank promptly after discovery in order to hold the bank liable for any breach of its contract. If the customer fails to use reasonable care to notify the bank promptly, the bank will not be liable for unauthorized signatures or alterations if the bank also has suffered a loss. The bank will also not be held liable for future unauthorized signatures or alterations by the same wrongdoer.

Safe Deposit Boxes

Banks also provide safe deposit boxes. This is your private bank vault that only you have access to unless you die, creditors place a lien on your account, or you fail to pay the box rental. The contents of your safe deposit box are not insured against fraud or theft. You should carry insurance on the contents in order to minimize any losses. Failure to do so will necessitate a lawsuit against the bank and proof that the bank was negligent in dealing with your valuables. When you die, the state will seal your safe deposit box. It may take several days for a state tax official to release the seal. It may even be necessary in some cases to obtain a court order. This is usually done to ensure that the estate taxes are paid and that the decedent's wishes as to property that might exist can be protected.

Notes

A promissory note is similar to a check (Exhibit 6–9). A check is a mechanism for making current payment; a note is a promise to pay in the future. All the rules discussed with respect to negotiable instruments, including holder in due course and warranties of transfer and presentment, are applicable to a promissory note.

A promissory note is distinguished from a check in that a promissory note is a two-party instrument. The maker and the payee are the only parties. The maker is the party who is promising to pay; the individual who is going to receive payment is called the payee. A promissory note is a form of an "I owe you." Notice on the exhibit that there is a sum certain, payable at a definite time, without any conditions. A note may be interest-bearing or noninterest-bearing. It may require payment in full at a specified date or in installments, as in the exhibit. A note may contain clauses that allow for prepayment without penalty, acceleration under a number of conditions, granting collateral (mortgage), and so on.

CREDIT CARDS

Not only do banks provide for savings and checking accounts (as well as loans), but many banks also issue credit cards.

It is illegal for a bank to send a credit card to a consumer unless the consumer requested or applied for one. (A bank may send you substitute or renewal cards without request.) So your statement "I just happened to have this card in my wallet, and that is why I happened to run up such a large bill" is not a valid defense. If you use a credit card, you accept the terms under which it was issued and must pay the bill.

EXHIBIT 6-9
Promissory Note

FOR VALUE RECEIVED, the undersigned jointly and severally agree to pay to the order of   , the sum of $ with interest at ten (10%) percent per annum in monthly installments as follows:
$ on the   day of   , 1982, and $ on the day of each month thereafter to and including the   day of   , 1987, on which date the balance of the principal indebtedness, together with arrears of interest, if any, shall become due.

Each of the foregoing payments shall be applied first to interest at the rate above set forth, and the balance shall be applied to reduction of the principal indebtedness.

In the event that any payment due hereunder shall not be made on the due date, or within fifteen (15) days thereafter, the unpaid principal indebtedness together with arrears of interest, if any, shall, at the option of the holder, become immediately due and payable.

The balance of the principal indebtedness may be prepaid at any time without penalty or fee.

The balance of the principal indebtedness shall become immediately due and payable in the event of the death of either of the makers.

Under the U.C.C. art. 3 § 302, an individual who used a credit card or bought goods on credit and signed a promissory note could not withhold payment on his or her account if the original seller transferred the debt to a third party. This was called the "holder in due course" rule. All personal defenses, such as a defect in the product, would not be allowed against the third party (credit card issuer). For example, suppose you purchased a stereo with a credit card that is not the seller's card. The seller transferred the obligation to the bank (a third party). The stereo does not work correctly. You may not refuse to pay your debt obligations by using the fact that the stereo was defective as a defense. Today, federal and state laws cause a credit card issuer to be subject to claims or defenses that a purchaser may have against the seller. This change also applies to buyers of merchandise under installment notes when the notes are transferred to third parties.

The Uniform Consumer Credit Code provides that a credit card company issuing credit cards is subject to claims and defenses of the cardholder against the seller of the goods if the customer makes an attempt in good faith to resolve the agreement, if the credit card transaction is more than $50 and if the residence of the cardholder and the place where the sale took place are within 100 miles of each other. This provision, which has been adopted in some states, provides that the bank will be able to police sellers in its local area to determine which ones have shady sales practices. They may refuse to do business with those companies and thereby protect the consumer. In addition, the consumer will have rights to go after the individuals who have purchased the consumers' finance contracts. These rights could include the deferral of payments until the defects are corrected.

If you have a problem with an item purchased on credit, the first thing you should do is contact the merchant and give him or her the chance to correct the problem; if you have no success in resolving the problem, you should then notify the bank that holds the credit card agreement.

If your credit card is lost or stolen, the first thing you should do is to contact the issuer immediately. In many cases, you will not be liable for charges made if the issuer is notified before the thief uses the card. If the thief does use the card before it is reported, you would most likely be liable only for a maximum of $50. The limitation is applied under federal law as long as the consumer is not negligent in handling the notification to the issuer or in lending his or her card to a third party. It is a good idea for the consumer to keep an up-to-date list of the credit card accounts and numbers along with the telephone number of each company that issued a card. A copy of this list should be kept in various places.

The provisions of the General Truth-in-Lending Act regarding errors in your account also apply to credit cards. State and federal laws spell out only part of the legal obligations between the consumer and the credit card issuer. Additional rights and duties of the parties can be found in the contract between the consumer and the bank (Exhibit 6–10). All credit card agreements must include information regarding the APR. The agreement must also include the federal regulations outlined earlier. The cardholder's agreement also provides information about your liabilities if you fail to pay in the required amount on time. A consumer should read his or her agreement prior to using his credit card.

ELECTRONIC FUNDS TRANSFER

A new area of banking is electronic funds transfers, which are transfers of funds other than by check. These transfers include point-of-sale transfers (when the consumer buys goods and the money is automatically transferred from the consumer's account to the store's account through an electronic terminal), automated teller machines, and transfers initiated by telephone. The federal government, realizing what the unique characteristics of such transfer systems are and that the protections offered by various state laws are inadequate, passed Title IX (15 U.S.C.A. § 1693 et seq) of the U.S. Code. This defines the rights and liabilities of the consumer as well as of the bank and any intermediary (such as the seller of goods) in electronic transfer transactions.

All terms and conditions of electronic funds transfer accounts must be disclosed at the time a consumer contracts for an electronic funds service. The disclosure must include a statement of the liabilities for electronic fund transfers, the telephone number and address of a person or office to be notified by the consumer of unauthorized transfers, and a detailed description of the type and nature of the electronic fund transfers that the consumer may initiate. The bank must also spell out the charges involved to the consumer and the consumer's right to stop payment. In addition, the bank must make available to the consumer written documentation of any transfers made. The documentation must include the amount and date of the transfer, the type of transfer, the identity of the party to whom the funds were transferred, and the location of the electronic terminal involved. The bank must also provide consumers with periodic statements of their account.

A preauthorized electronic fund transfer from a consumer's account must be authorized in writing, and a consumer may stop payment on a preauthorized transfer by notifying the bank orally or in writing at any time up to 3 business days preceding the date of the transfer. The bank may require written confirmation, as in a stop payment order for a check. This authorization must be provided within 14 days of the oral notification.

If a consumer finds that an electronic funds transfer has been made in error, the consumer must notify the bank of the nature of the error within 60 days after receipt of either documentation of the transaction or the periodic statement. The consumer can notify the bank either orally or in writing. If the consumer notifies the bank orally, the bank may require a written confirmation within 10 business days. If an error did occur, the bank must promptly correct the consumer's account. If the error did not occur, the bank must send an explanation of its findings to the consumer within 3 business days after it concludes its investigation. In no event can the investigation process take more than 10 days.

A consumer is liable for any unauthorized electronic funds transfer involving his account if his or her card is lost or stolen and he or she does not notify the bank within 2 business days after learning of the loss or theft (in extenuating circumstances, such as extended travel or hospitalization, a long period will be allowed). The liability is up to $50 for unauthorized use. If the consumer does not notify the bank within 2 days of the detection of the loss or 60 days of notification of unau-

EXHIBIT 6-10
Credit Card Loan Agreement

MINIMUM PAYMENT. Your monthly minimum payment on Purchases is figured on the total of your Purchases New Balance(s) at the end of the month. If this total exceeds $360, 1/36 of it is due. If this total is from $10 to $360, a minimum of $10 is due. If the total is less than $10, the full amount is due. If, because of unusual activity, the FINANCE CHARGE due is larger than the current minimum figured as above, only the amount of that FINANCE CHARGE is due. Of course, you must also pay in any month each amount which is past due. In addition, the annual Membership Fee will be added to your minimum payment in the months it is billed.

COLLECTION COSTS. You agree, if the entire balance is declared due, to pay our collection costs including, if we refer the case to an attorney, a reasonable attorney's fee not exceeding 20% of the amount due and payable.

You (the Buyer) may at any time pay your total Purchases indebtedness.

LOAN AGREEMENT

This part of the Agreement covers your Loans. It takes effect when you first get a Loan. A Loan is made when we post it to your Account.

MINIMUM PAYMENT. We first figure the minimum principal payment for the month. We do this by multiplying the total of your Loans principal balance(s) as of the date of your latest Loan by the fraction you chose for your repayment. For example, a $540 balance times 1/36 equals a $15 payment. If the resulting figure is less than $10, the minimum principal payment will be $10. If your unpaid principal is less than $10, it is all due.

We add to the minimum principal payment the total of the Loans FINANCE CHARGE for the month and any Late Charge you owe. Of course, you must also pay each month any amount that is past due.

COMPUTING FINANCE CHARGE: We figure the **FINANCE CHARGE** each day on each Loans principal balance for that day, including, as noted below, new Loans from the date they are posted. If you opened your Account after January 1, 1981, you have only one Loans balance. If, however, you opened your Account before January 1, 1981, there will be one principal balance for any indebtedness outstanding on Loans obtained prior to March 1, 1981, and a separate principal balance for any indebtedness outstanding on Loans obtained on or after that date. We may, to resolve questions about the date of Loans obtained close to March 1, continue for several days thereafter to post those Loans to your pre-March 1 balance.

To get a daily balance, we start with each opening principal balance for the day. We add new Loans and other debits posted and subtract payments and other credits posted that day to that balance. We then multiply each resulting daily balance by the appropriate Periodic Rate as follows:

Type of Balance	Daily Periodic Rate on Entire Balance	Corresponding **ANNUAL PERCENTAGE RATE**
A. Accounts Open Before January 1, 1981		
1. Pre-March 1, 1981, Transactions:		
— without credit life insurance	.03287%	12%
— with credit life insurance*	.03514%	12.75%
2. Transactions March 1, 1981, or later:		
— without credit life insurance	.04931%	18%
— with credit life insurance*	.05158%	18.75%
B. Accounts Opened After January 1, 1981		
All Transactions:		
— without credit life insurance	.04931%	18%
— with credit life insurance*	.05158%	18.75%

*Daily Group Credit Life Insurance Charge is .00227%.

That gives us the daily charge for each balance. Then we add up all the daily charges to get your **FINANCE CHARGE** for the month for that balance.

LATE PAYMENTS AND CHARGES. Any payment you do not make by the due date shown on your statement is late. We will charge you a Late Charge of up to $5, but not more than $.04 per $1 of the principal of the payment due, if you let a payment become a month late. Late Charges are limited to $15 per calendar year. If we collect more than that, we will credit the excess to you within 60 days.

COLLECTION COSTS. You agree, if the entire balance is declared due, to pay our actual collection costs including, if we refer the case to an attorney, a reasonable attorney's fee not exceeding 20% of the amount due and payable.

thorized transfer by statement, he or she will be liable for a maximum of $500 for unauthorized usage. If the bank finds out and can prove that the consumer has been a party to the theft, he or she will be liable for the full amount as well as criminal process.

A bank is also liable to the consumer if the bank breaches its contract with the consumer by failing to make an electronic funds transfer in accordance with the contract unless the consumer's account has insufficient funds or the funds are subject to legal process, such as a lien and so on. A bank is also liable for issuing any

EXHIBIT 6-10, cont.

Cardholder's Agreement signed for the Bank by _William H. Monroe_

Senior Vice President - Personal Credit

Dated: As of February 1, 1981

In Case of Errors or Inquiries About Your Bill

The Federal Truth in Lending Act requires prompt correction of billing mistakes.

1. If you want to preserve your rights under the Act, here's what to do if you think your bill is wrong or if you need more information about an item on your bill:
   a. Do not write on the bill or on your check. On a separate sheet of paper write (you may telephone your inquiry but doing so will not preserve your rights under this law) the following:
      i. Your name and account number.
      ii. A description of the error and an explanation (to the extent you can explain) why you believe it is an error.
         If you only need more information, explain the item you are not sure about and, if you wish, ask for evidence of the charge such as a copy of the charge slip. Do not send in your copy of a sales slip or other document unless you have a duplicate copy for your records.
      iii. The dollar amount of the suspected error.
      iv. Any other information (such as your address) which you think will help the Bank to identify you or the reason for your complaint or inquiry.
   b. Send your billing error notice to the address shown on the face of your bill listed after the words: "Direct inquiries about your account to this address."

   Mail it as soon as you can, but in any case early enough to reach the Bank within 60 days after the bill was mailed to you. If you have authorized the Bank to automatically pay from your checking or savings account any credit card bills from the Bank, you can stop or reverse payment on any amount you think is wrong by mailing your notice so the Bank receives it within 16 days after the bill was sent to you. However, you do not have to meet this 16-day deadline to get the Bank to investigate your billing error claim.

2. The Bank must acknowledge all letters pointing out possible errors within 30 days of receipt, unless the Bank is able to correct your bill during that 30 days. Within 90 days after receiving your letter, the Bank must either correct the error or explain why the Bank believes the bill was correct. Once the Bank has explained the bill, the Bank has no further obligation to you even though you still believe that there is an error, except as provided in paragraph 5 below.

3. After the Bank has been notified, neither the Bank nor an attorney nor a collection agency may send you collection letters or take other collection action with respect to the amount in dispute; but periodic state-
ments may be sent to you, and the disputed amount can be applied against your credit limit. You cannot be threatened with damage to your credit rating or sued for the amount in question, nor can the disputed amount be reported to a credit bureau or to other creditors as delinquent until the Bank has answered your inquiry. However, you remain obligated to pay the parts of your bill not in dispute.

4. If it is determined that the Bank has made a mistake on your bill, you will not have to pay any finance charges on any disputed amount. If it turns out that the Bank has not made an error, you may have to pay finance charges on the amount in dispute, and you will have to make up any missed minimum or required payments on the disputed amount. Unless you have agreed that your bill was correct, the Bank must send you a written notification of what you owe; and if it is determined that the Bank did make a mistake in billing the disputed amount, you must be given the time to pay which you normally are given to pay undisputed amounts before any more finance charges or late payment charges on the disputed amount can be charged to you.

5. If the Bank's explanation does not satisfy you and you notify the Bank **in writing** within **10** days after you receive its explanation that you still refuse to pay the disputed amount, the Bank may report you to credit bureaus and other creditors and may pursue regular collection procedures. But the Bank must also report that you think you do not owe the money, and the Bank must let you know to whom such reports were made. Once the matter has been settled between you and the Bank, the Bank must notify those to whom the Bank reported you as delinquent of the subsequent resolution.

6. If the Bank does not follow these rules, the Bank is not allowed to collect the first $50 of the disputed amount and finance charges, even if the bill turns out to be correct.

7. If you have a problem with property or services purchased with a credit card, you may have the right not to pay the remaining amount due on them, if you first try in good faith to return them or give the merchant a chance to correct the problem. There are two limitations on this right:
   a. You must have bought them in your home state or if not within your home state within 100 miles of your current mailing address; and
   b. The purchase price must have been more than $50.

   However, these limitations do not apply if the merchant is owned or operated by the Bank, or if the Bank mailed you the advertisement for the property or services.

means of access to an electronic funds transfer terminal unless it was requested or is a renewal.

No person may condition the extension of credit to a consumer on the repayment by means of a preauthorized electronic funds transfer. No person may require a consumer to establish an account for receipt of electronic funds transfer with a particular institution as a condition of employment or receipt of government benefits.

The Consumer Credit Protection Act also has provisions for civil and criminal liability for failure to comply with provisions of the act. These include civil liability of $100 to $1000 on individual cases and up to $500,000 for class actions. Criminal liability includes imprisonment of not more than one year or a fine of $5000 or both.

QUESTIONS

1 The plaintiff, Silvia, had his tax returns prepared by an accountant for more than 25 years. The accountant filled out the tax forms and prepared a check, which Silvia would sign. The accountant would then send the check and the return to the Internal Revenue Service.

One year the accountant increased Silvia's tax liability by approximately $2500 (by creating nonexistent profits from Silvia's business). The accountant prepared Silvia's check made payable to Internal Revenue Services. Silvia signed the return and the check. The accountant subsequently added the words by John J. Mahoney (the accountant's name). The payee of the check thus became ''Internal Revenue Services by John J. Mahoney.'' The accountant endorsed the check and purchased a series of checks from the defendant (drawee). The accountant used the cashier's checks to pay personal debts.

The plaintiff first became aware of this situation when the Internal Revenue Service notified him of failure to file his return or pay his taxes. At the time this event occurred, the accountant had died. The plaintiff sued the bank, claiming that the bank had honored an altered check and, therefore, the bank was liable to the plaintiff. Decision for whom? Discuss.

2 The plaintiff, S, issued a check on Tuesday. The following Monday morning he went to the bank and asked the bank to place a stop payment order on the check. He waited at the bank for approximately 25 minutes while a bank employee checked the records to see whether the instrument had previously cleared the bank. After making this check, the bank employee gave the plaintiff a printed notice confirming his request to stop payment and charged his account $5. On the previous Saturday morning the check had been cashed. At the time the bank's employee checked, the transaction had not been processed. The plaintiff sued the bank for payment of the instrument contrary to his stop payment order. Decision for whom? Discuss.

3 On October 10, the plaintiff issued a check payable to O. Five days later, after O failed to receive the check, plaintiff G issued a stop payment order to the bank. G paid O. No additional stop payment orders or renewals of stop payment were made. On November 10, 1969, more than a year after the issuance of the original check, the defendant bank, without contacting the plaintiff, paid the check in question and charged the plaintiff's account. The plaintiff seeks to recover the amount charged his account from the bank. The bank argued that the stop payment order had expired and that it paid the stale check in good faith. Decision for whom? Discuss.

4 The plaintiff was married to O. O died, and the plaintiff became the beneficiary under certain pension plans. B was the attorney who handled matters arising out of O's death. The plaintiff received a check, which B told her belonged to the estate and would have to be held for tax settlement purposes. She was told by B that the check would have to be placed into an estate account of her late husband. B wrote on the back of the check the following ''Pay to the order of Estate of O.'' The plaintiff endorsed the check, and subsequently B wrote the following: ''Estate of O—For deposit B Trustee.'' B's secretary then wrote "For deposit B Trustee." The check was collected, and the proceeds were placed in B's trust account. The bank never inquired as to whether B had power to endorse the checks for the estate. After some time, the plaintiff became suspicious and began to investigate the circumstances of this transaction and subsequently found that B had embezzled a portion of these funds. She recovered some of the funds from B and sued the bank for the remaining funds on the grounds that the bank had paid out a check on an improper endorsement. Decision for whom? Discuss.

5 S, the owner of the plaintiff corporation, testified that he prepared a bank deposit of business receipts, drove to the bank, placed the deposit in the night depository, and returned home. Several days later, not having received confirmation of the deposit, S phoned the bank and found out that the bank had no record of the deposit's ever having been made. The night depository agreement signed by S stated that the use of the night depository is at the sole risk of the depositor and that the bank will have no liability for safekeeping of any deposits. The agreement further stated that any question as to whether a deposit was made was to be determined conclusively by the report of the employee of the bank who opens the safe the next morning. The plaintiff sued the bank for misappropriation or theft of the plaintiff's money or both. Decision for whom? Discuss.

6 The plaintiff, Losner filed a petition for bankruptcy and was adjudicated a bankrupt. The defendant, a creditor of Losner, objected to the discharge. The basis of his objection was that during the 12-month period immediately preceding the filing of the petition, Losner had withdrawn money from the checking account that was used to pay several of his creditors. Is this conduct sufficient to warrant a denial of a discharge in bankruptcy? Decision for whom? Discuss.

7 The plaintiff, Fultz, issued a number of checks and endorsed them as follows: "Pay to the order of the First National Bank, Graham, Texas, For deposit only—W. B. Fultz." One of Fultz's employees, who was known by the bank to be one of Fultz's employees, cashed some of these checks at the defendant bank. Was the action of the bank proper? Discuss.

8 Sims deposited a check in her account. It normally takes 3 days for a check to clear, but owing to a bank mistake, the check was held for 10 days. During this time Sims wrote several checks that were returned to her because they were drawn against uncollected funds. She testified that she was embarrassed, humiliated, and mortified because of this and also that she was upset because she had considerable difficulty in getting the bank to correct its mistake. Sims brought an action against the bank for damages for wrongful dishonor of the checks. Decision for whom? Discuss.

9 The plaintiff, Williams, was approached by an individual, who told her that he represented a lightning rod company and that she needed a new clamp on her lightning rod. She told him that he should put the clamp on the lightning rod. He indicated to her that the fee was $1.26 and that he would need a check so that he could pay the company. He offered to fill out the check for her and did so writing a $1.26 both in numbers and letters. He wrote the numbers and letters on the right-hand side of the space provided for such entries. She signed the check, and he left. The individual then altered the check by inserting the words *Six Thousand Eight Hundred Forty* and the numbers 684 to the left of the previously entered items. The bank, after receiving the check, determined that there were sufficient funds in the account to pay it, checked for signature to the signature on the signature card at the bank, and then cashed the check. Williams sued the bank for payment of an altered instrument. Decision for whom? Discuss.

10 Portland Cement Association made a check payable to J. Y. Barnes. The money was to be deposited to an account in Denver, Colorado. Barnes endorsed the check ''J. Y. Barnes, Jack Y. Barnes, for deposit only,'' and mailed the check to the Denver Bank. The envelope containing the check was stolen by W. W went to the defendant bank and opened an account in the name of Jack Barnes. W represented that he was Jack Barnes and over a period of time either cashed checks or paid bills for virtually all of the amount of the stolen check. The real Jack Barnes sued the bank for making payments on a forged signature. Decision for whom? Discuss.

11 K talked to the plaintiff, Burchett, and convinced him to install aluminum siding on his house. K indicated that the house would be used for advertising purposes and that Burchett would receive a credit of $100 for each aluminum siding contract sold as a result of this advertising. The amount was to be applied to the amount of his debt. The plaintiff was told that by this method he would be able to receive the aluminum siding free. Burchett was given a contract to read and was lead to believe that, while he was reading the blank contract, K was filling out a copy for them to sign. They then signed the other copy without reading it. What they, in fact, signed were notes and mortgages and contracts that did not discuss the so-called credit that they were to receive. The aluminum siding was then placed on the house in a less-than-satisfactory manner. The plaintiff was then contacted by the defendant finance company, who indicated that they had purchased the notes and mortgages that the plaintiff had signed and that the plaintiff was delinquent in his first payment. The plaintiff sued defendant to have the instruments set aside. Decision for whom? Discuss.

12 The plaintiff, Mr. Boudreaux, was obligated to the defendant, Allstate Finance Corporation, on a promissory note in the amount of $185 with interest. The indebtedness was in arrears. The plaintiff was unemployed as a result of illness. The defendant called the plaintiff at the homes of neighbors because the plaintiff had no telephone. The defendant's employees called the neighbors frequently and at deliberately chosen inconvenient hours. The plaintiff was compelled to explain the delinquency in the presence of neighbors and acquaintances. On several occasions, the plaintiff's problems were discussed with neighbors whose phone the plaintiff used. The plaintiff requested that Allstate cease these practices, but they did not. Allstate even showed up at the plaintiff's home on one occasion and created a disturbance, using loud and abusive language. These conversations could be heard by the neighbors. Does plaintiff have grounds to sue defendant? Discuss.

13 Guy Hartsook issued a check to the plaintiff on December 20, 1960. Guy died on July 13, 1961. The check had not been cashed. May the check be cashed? Is the decedent liable on the debt? Discuss.

14 A wife sold the family home to her relatives. The husband and wife continued to live in the house, leasing it from the relatives. The wife used the proceeds of the sale to pay premiums on life insurance policies and to repay loans outstanding on these policies. Approximately five and one half months later, she and her husband filed voluntary petitions in bankruptcy and were adjudicated bankrupts. They had no assets other than the life insurance policies, which had a face value of $275,000. They claimed these policies as exempt property. The creditors objected to the discharge. Was the discharge proper?

15 The plaintiffs (L&M) were partners doing business in New Mexico under the name of L&M Paint and Body Shop. M had borrowed $402 from the bank, which was due. The bank charged the partnership account for $402 and reduced the balance in its account to $3.66. The bank then refused to honor nine checks drawn on the account. The total amount of these checks came to $210. Did the bank act properly? Discuss.

16 The plaintiff brought an action against the drawee bank, claiming that the bank paid checks drawn by the plaintiff without any endorsement. In addition, the plaintiff contends that the bank cashed checks where the payee's signature had been forged. The forgery was set up by a Mr. Albers, who presented fictitious payment vouchers to the plaintiff's office personnel. The office personnel then prepared checks paying for certain logs and naming various individuals as payees. Albers then forged the payee's signature and cashed the checks or deposited them in his account. When he was caught, he confessed to the forgeries and was imprisoned. Is the bank liable to the plaintiff for payment of these checks?

CHAPTER 7

Personal Property

ACQUISITION

Personal property is a movable thing, either tangible or intangible. Tangible property includes goods, commonly called chattel goods, which an individual can touch. Intangible property includes choses in action: items giving certain rights but that cannot be touched (except for the paper documenting those rights). Ownership of property is the interest that an individual has in a particular item. Acquisition of ownership can occur in many ways. One is by occupancy whereby one acquires rights to unowned property by taking possession with the intent of owning (e.g., when you catch a fish or shoot a wild animal or bird).

Property can also be acquired by gift, either inter vivos (while the individual is alive) or testamentary (when an individual dies and transfers the property by will). (See Chapters 11 and 12.) Other methods of acquiring property include accession, which is an increase in property by what it produces. For example, if you have a cow and it gives birth to a calf, you have an increase in the property by virtue of the fact that you now have two animals. Property can be acquired by confusion, which is the intermingling of certain fungible goods (goods that are of the same character, such as grain). Confusion can take place by consent, mistake, tortious conduct, or negligence. If there is a mistake or consent, the owners of the goods have an undivided interest to the extent of their contributions. For example, if you have 300 pounds of corn and add it to my 500 pounds, we each own a portion of the 800 pounds; you own 3/8, and I own 5/8. Each of us may have acquired grains of corn that formerly belonged to the other. If you have intentionally combined your corn with mine, you would forfeit your rights to the corn unless you can prove what proportion was yours. This is also true if you were negligent in combining the corn.

Found Property

Another method in which you can acquire ownership of property is if the property has been abandoned, lost, or mislaid. You're riding on a train, and you find an envelope. Inside the envelope are three crisp $100 bills. What are your rights with respect to this property? The answer to this question depends on the nature of the property you found and (in other cases) where you found it.

If the individual who had previous ownership intentionally discarded the property, it is considered abandoned, and you would have absolute rights to ownership irrespective of where it was found. (Lieber v. Mohawk Arms Inc., 314 N.Y.S.2d 510 [NY 1970]).

If property is found in a place it was not put by the owner, then it will be considered lost property. The original owner of lost property has absolute right to the property, but, you, as finder, have rights superior to everyone else and must hold the property in custody for the original owner. This is an involuntary bailment you must exercise.

If the property is located at a place where it was put by the original owner but now forgotten, then the property will be considered mislaid or misplaced property.

You, as the finder, must turn the property over to the owner of the premises where the property was found (i.e., the company that owns the train). The owner of the premises would hold the property for the original owner, and they would have superior rights to keep the property above all others except for the original owner. The reason for this is that it is presumed the owner will return to the place the property was mislaid. This is an involuntary bailment, and the owner of the premises where the property was mislaid has a duty to exercise slight care in holding the property for the rightful owner. *Slight care* is defined as that degree of care that a reasonable, prudent person would exercise with his or her own property, given the nature of that property. The finder of a roll of $100 bills might be held liable by the owner for subsequent damage to the property if the finder used the bills to kindle a fire.

The distinction between lost and mislaid property can be made by looking at the intention of the owner of the property. Ascertaining the intention of an individual who is obviously not available is difficult. In deciding the intent of the owner, the courts look at the particular place where the property was found. For example, eight $100 dollar bills found by a hotel chambermaid under a paper lining of a dresser drawer in a room she was cleaning was considered to be mislaid property since it was found in a private place where someone might reasonably have hidden it with the intention of returning to claim it. The hotel became the owner of the property and not the finder (Jackson v. Steinberg, 200 P.2d 376 [Or. 1948]). In a case where an assistant steward of a ship found money on the floor of a restroom, the courts held that the property was lost because it was found in a public place and that the finder was entitled to ownership (Kalyvakis v. The *TFF Olympia*, 181 F. Supp. 32 [1960]). In another case, a passenger on a train found a package on the seat opposite him, which had been left behind by a passenger who had left the train. The court found that the package was mislaid property belonging to the railroad company. The court said that to lose is not to place or put anything carefully and voluntarily in the place you intend and then forget it (Faulke v. New York Consolidated Railroad Company, 127 N.E. 237 [N.Y.1920]).

VOLUNTARY BAILMENTS

A bailment occurs when one individual, the bailor, delivers goods to another individual, the bailee, according to an agreement that states that the goods must be returned to the bailor. There are several different categories of bailments. There are "involuntary" bailments, which occur when an individual finds lost or mislaid property. There are "voluntary" bailments, in which a bailment is created for the benefit of either or both parties. Mutual benefit bailments are transfers of possession of property accompanied by the intent that each party will benefit from the bailment. Examples of mutual benefit bailments include the delivery of clothing to a coatcheck attendant or the cleaners, the delivery of an automobile to a parking lot attendant, and so on. There are bailments for the sole benefit of the bailee. These include borrowing your neighbor's lawn mower, auto, and so on. There are bailments for the sole benefit of the bailor, for example, having a neighbor watch your parakeet while you are on vacation.

The essential element in all bailments is delivery; if the bailor does not deliver the goods to the bailee, there is no bailment. For example, if you hang your coat on a hook in an unattended checkroom in a restaurant, the owners of the restaurant would not be liable according to the rules of bailment if your coat were stolen. They might be liable if you could prove negligence. The bailee's and bailor's rights are usually determined by the contractual bailment agreement.

In the absence of any contrary understanding between the parties, the bailee's duty is to deliver the goods to the bailor upon completion of the bailment agreement. Any failure to deliver could make the bailee liable for breach of contract or possibly for the tort of conversion. A bailee who services goods maintains a possessory lien on them. In the case of automobile and appliance repairs, you are the bailor, and the mechanic is the bailee. In the event that you do not pay for the required repairs, the mechanic may keep your goods. In the event that the bailee surrenders possession of the goods, his or her lien is terminated.

Bailments terminate when the agreed purpose is completed, when the bailment period expires, when the goods that were the object of the bailment are damaged, or when the bailee materially breaches the bailment agreement.

Each type of bailment has a legal requirement with respect to the duty of care owed by the bailee to protect the bailor's property. In an involuntary bailment, the bailee is required to exercise only "slight care" in using the property. In the case of a mutual benefit bailment, the law imposes upon the bailee the standard of care of a "reasonably careful person" who might be in the same position and under the same circumstances. It is a question of fact for a jury to decide whether the bailee has acted reasonably. In a bailment for the sole benefit of the bailee, the bailee's duty of care is considered to be "great." If a bailment is for the sole benefit of the bailor, the degree of care is termed "slight."

The consumer must remember that the posting of an "exculpatory clause" (one that purports to relieve an individual of liability for negligence) in and of itself may not be sufficient to relieve the bailee of liability. If you deliver goods to another individual with the expectation that those goods would be returned in as good or better condition, there is a bailment. Depending on the type of bailment, the bailee well may have liability regardless of statements to the contrary.

If you feel your rights have been jeopardized as a result of a bailee's obligation, it is advisable to contact your local consumer office, the Better Business Bureau, or the U.S. Office of Consumer Affairs or possibly an attorney or legal aid office.

Innkeepers and Common Carriers

There are also special bailment situations for innkeepers and common carriers. These special bailments include liability that may be termed absolute; that is, the bailee is an insurer for loss. Inkeepers include motel and hotel operators. A common carrier is a carrier that transports goods and offers its services to the general public. A private carrier carries goods or persons occasionally or serves a limited number of persons. Under common law, the liability of an innkeeper and common carrier was that of an insurer. The only exception to this liability was for goods that were lost or damaged because of acts of God, public enemies, bailor's actions or negligence, or the inherent attributes of the particular property (e.g., perishable food).

State statutes typically limit the liability that an innkeeper has for money, jewels, ornaments, bank notes, bonds, negotiable securities, and precious stones belonging to the guests that are stolen from a room providing that the innkeeper maintains a safe on the property for deposit of these valuables and that the innkeeper gives notice to the guests of the availability of the safe. The notice must be in a conspicuous public place in the office and in the public rooms of the hotel or motel. If a guest avails himself or herself of the safe, statutes limit the liability to a specific dollar amount (e.g., in New York—$500). Some states require that individuals who own and operate hotels and motels must have a license. Failure to comply with the licensing statute may cause the innkeeper to be liable for damage to guests in a greater amount than the state statute that limits liability indicates.

Other provisions in state law also limit the liability for loss of wearing apparel and other personal property within the confines of the inn. Again, a dollar amount is placed on the liability (e.g., in New York State—$500 for goods in the lobby hallways and rooms and $100 for property in storerooms, baggage rooms, and so on). There is also a requirement, as with the innkeeper's safe, that individuals must be put on notice as to the limitation of liability with respect to their personal belongings. This notice must be a public notice and must be in a conspicuous place on the premises. In most states, a common carrier is allowed to limit its liability to a shipper by contract. To effect this limitation, the carrier must show that the shipper knew of and consented to the limitation. Statutes do not limit the liability of innkeepers and common carriers when the loss incurred was caused by the negligence of the bailor or the bailor's employees.

Car Rentals

Renting a car (from a major car rental company or from a friend) creates a bailment situation. Like all other bailments, you are responsible for returning the vehicle that you rent in the same condition it was in when you borrowed it, normal wear and tear excepted.

If you do not wish to have to pay for minor damages, you should accept the collision damage waiver clause usually contained in the rental contract (Exhibit 7–1). Failure to accept collision damage insurance could cause you to be liable for damages, including scratches and small dents, which may occur in the parking lot and so forth. Car rental companies usually charge extra for this coverage, and in order for the coverage to be effective, you must make a designation on the car rental agreement.

EXHIBIT 7-1
Automobile Rental Agreement

Lessor: The Hertz Corporation

Hertz®

SARASOTA-BRADENTON AIRPORT
P.O. BOX 13085 — AIRGATE STATION
SARASOTA, FLORIDA 33578-5036

PHONE (813) 355-8848

Rental Agreement No.

38585420 6

2016

SHOW THIS NO. ON ALL CORRESPONDENCE
MINIMUM RENTAL CHARGE - ONE DAY (24 HRS)
RATES DO NOT INCLUDE REFUELING SERVICE

TO BE PAID BY

7935 965 9
IRVING LEVIN
167 DONNA LEA
WILLIAMSVILLE NY 14221

OWNING CITY LOC. NO.	TIME IN	2012 MAR 26 16:43
RIH/LIT	TIME OUT	2016 MAR 24 12:42
60 OTHER		

VEHICLE NO. 2586584
EXCHANGE VEHICLE NO.

VEHICLE LIC. NO. ZSL 261 STATE FL
VEHICLE LIC. NO. STATE

VEH. MAKE - BODY STYLE Datsun CLASS B
RETURNED TO CITY/STATE Clearwater

OWNING CITY/STATE 1398
SUB.
AREA/LOC. 2016-15

| | CREDIT CARD #1 CLUB NO. | CREDIT APP / DATE / AMT | CASH ON REF |
| HCC | V38 350/0 | No |

OTHER IDENTIFICATION: AAA-WESTERN NY, AUTO CLUB 00084
C.D.P. I.D. NO.

DRIVER'S LICENSE NO. L05800816004908721 STATE NY EXPIRES 1/2/25

HOME OR BUSINESS ADDRESS 167 Donna Lea Blvd

CITY/STATE Williamsville NY ZIP CODE 14221

VEHICLE TO BE RETURNED TO (CITY/STATE) SARASOTA LOC. NO. FL02016 DATE DUE 03/31/82

VEHICLE RENTED AT (CITY/STATE) SARASOTA, FLORIDA AREA & LOCATION NO. 2016-12

LOCAL ADDRESS

HOME/BUSINESS PHONE NO. 716-632-6767

SUM00 11

MILEAGE IN	4177
MILEAGE OUT	4018
MILES DRIVEN	159
MILES ALLOWED (If Any)	
MILES CHARGED	

| DAYS 25 | 2799 | 51 98 |
| PER EXTRA HRS. | 750 |
| WKS. 129 00 |
| MILES ® | nil |

NOTE:
Unless car is returned to renting location a drop charge may apply. If returned outside Florida, time & mileage rate will apply plus a drop charge if applicable.

SUBTOTAL

IF CUSTOMER ELECTS TO RETURN THE VEHICLE WITH LESS FUEL THAN WHEN RENTED, A REFUELING SERVICE CHARGE WILL BE MADE. Credit Card Customer authorizes Lessor to process a credit card voucher (if applicable) in Customer's name for charges and consents to the reservation of credit with the card issuer, for an amount equal to estimated charges due. Vehicle shall NOT be operated by any person except Customer and the following Authorized Operators who must be validly licensed to drive and who have Customer's prior permission: persons 21 or over who are members of Customer's immediate family and permanently reside in Customer's household; the employer, partner, executive officer, or a regular employee of Customer; additional authorized operator(s) approved by Lessor in writing.
THE VEHICLE IS RENTED UPON THE CONDITIONS SHOWN ON THIS PAGE AND THE REVERSE HEREOF. CUSTOMER REPRESENTS HE HAS READ, UNDERSTANDS AND AGREES WITH THE CONDITIONS. ALSO SEE NOTE AT LEFT.

REFUELING SERVICE
☐ .1058 PER MILE ☐ .154 PER GALLON
IN E 1/8 1/4 3/8 1/2 5/8 3/4 7/8 F
OUT E 1/8 1/4 3/8 1/2 5/8 3/4 7/8 F
See Par. 6b on Reverse Side for explanation.

DECLINES COLLISION DAMAGE WAIVER (CDW): X ACCEPTS CDW: X
BY INITIALS
Customer declines or accepts at rate shown, Lessor's CDW is Customer's responsibility for the first $600.00 of accidental vehicle damage due to collision or upset, as per Par. 4 on Reverse Side. CDW IS NOT INSURANCE.

DECLINES PERSONAL ACCIDENT INSURANCE (PAI): X ACCEPTS PAI: X
BY INITIALS, Customer declines or accepts PAI. If "Accepts", Customer accepts coverage at rate shown and acknowledges to have read the SYNOPSIS of Coverage Limits furnished by Lessor at rental.

SUBTOTAL	51 98
SERVICE CHARGE	
REFUELING SERVICE	9 22
CDW (Per Day) $5.50	11 00
SUBTOTAL	72 20
TAX 4%	2 89
PAI (Per Day) $2.25	
TOTAL CHARGES	75 09
MISC.	

X _Irving Levin_

LEVIN I SN SRQ 0043
24MAR 1220 PE 0340 07DYS CCLAS 12

RESERVATION I.D. NO.	REFERRAL SOURCE	PREPAID/TOUR
44500014700	00547912	YES ☐ NO ☒
I.T. NO.	VOUCHER NO.	RATE/PLAN NO. Evor

BK030882 0949 TR DISCOUNT QUOTED
RFS FOUR DOOR CRACec

820322 0249
Ex RA# 38356003-1

REFUND EXPLANATION - AMT. $

REFUND RECEIVED BY X

DEPOSIT $ NONE

PREPARED BY COMPUTED BY

ORB DATE | PAID BY | CASH | CHECK | DIRECT BILL | CENT. BILL | DIRECT BILL | INTL. TRAVEL BILL | GUARANTEED | LOCAL REC. CODE NO. | AUDIT-ED BY

NET DUE	75 09
LESS DEPOSIT (If Any)	
NET DUE	75 09

56 39

DO NOT PAY FROM THIS COPY
Direct all inquiries to:
THE HERTZ CORPORATION
P.O. BOX 26141
OKLAHOMA CITY, OKLA. 73126

NOTE: CHARGES SUBJECT TO FINAL AUDIT

NOTE • Customer is liable for all parking and driving violations and must remit payment directly to proper authorities • Customer must report all accidents, notify local police authorities and complete a Hertz accident report.

The bailment contract is spelled out in the rental agreement. You should read that agreement and find out not only what the maximum amount of damage is that you might be liable for, but also whether the company will provide you with certain amenities, such as 24-hour road service. The contract also spells out eligibility requirements. Many companies will not rent to individuals under 25. Other companies may rent to women who are over 18 but only to men over 21.

If you rent a vehicle that is defective, and you suffer injury because of the defect, since your contract is with the car rental agency, it is primarily liable. (It may, in turn, sue the manufacturer.)

MOVING, WAREHOUSING, AND STORAGE

The Interstate Commerce Commission (ICC) regulates interstate motor carriers of household goods. The ICC has prescribed strict rules to regulate carriers' handling of consumers' household articles. Though state laws may also regulate moving companies (particularly intrastate ones), this text will deal only with the federal rules.

Lost Goods

Whenever you move, there is a chance that some of your goods may be damaged or lost. You, the shipper, must be aware of the mover's (carrier's) responsibility for your goods while they are in his or her custody. The federal government requires that a mover must insure your goods up to a value of $.60 per pound per article at no extra cost. Unless you are being reimbursed for losses by insurance, $.60 per pound per article will not be sufficient. If you are willing to ship at this low liability level, you must write ''$.60 per pound per article'' in the valuation statement found on your bill of lading and sign it (see Exhibit 7–2).

There are two methods of increasing the mover's liability for your shipment. The first is not to sign the valuation statement on the bill of lading so that the rate will automatically be set at $1.25 per pound times the weight of your shipment. If this value is also inadequate, you may enter on the bill of lading a lump sum valuation or an amount per pound that you consider adequate for your shipment. In any of these alternatives, the carrier is allowed to charge you $.50 per $100 of valuation for this higher protection. Under any valuation option, except for the $.60 per pound option, the shipper is liable for either the actual value of lost or damaged items or the specific rate per pound, whichever is lower. Actual value is the depreciated value or market value of the goods at the time of shipment.

The ICC requires that a moving company furnish to consumers a pamphlet describing the carrier's dispute settlement program and a booklet published by the Interstate Commerce Commission entitled ''Your Rights and Responsibilities When You Move.'' The ICC also has information regarding a carrier's performance that in-

EXHIBIT 7-2
Household Goods Bill of Lading

PRESS HARD - YOU ARE MAKING 8 COPIES

northAmerican VAN LINES
P.O. BOX 988
FORT WAYNE, INDIANA 46801
IN CASE OF NEED CONTACT AREA CODE (219) 429-2511

HOUSEHOLD GOODS BILL OF LADING AND FREIGHT BILL

NOT NEGOTIABLE   I.C.C. MC-107012

PLEASE REFER TO THIS NUMBER IN ▷ ALL CORRESPONDENCE

CONTRACT NBR

TARIFF	SECT.	COMMODITY	TYPE OF SHIPMENT	VEHICLE NO.	LEAD CODE	ASSIST CODE	ACTUAL PICKUP DATE

☐ NATL ACCT   ☐ C.O.D.   ☐ GOVT.

SHIPPER _____   COUNTY _____   CONSIGNEE _____   COUNTY _____
STREET ADDR. _____   STREET ADDR. _____
CITY/ST. _____ ZIP _____   CITY/ST. _____ ZIP _____
PHONE _____   FLOOR _____   NOTIFY _____ PH _____
AGREED LOADING DATE (OR PERIOD OF TIME) FROM ___ / ___ / ___ TO: ___ / ___ / ___   AGREED DELIVERY DATE (OR PERIOD OF TIME) FROM ___ / ___ / ___ TO: ___ / ___ / ___
BOOKING AGENT CODE _____   ESTIMATING AGENT CODE _____   IF SHIPPER REQUESTS NOTICE OF CHARGES ☐ OR IN THE EVENT OF DELAY IN DELIVERY, NOTIFY
DESTINATION AGENT _____ CODE _____   NAME _____
DEST. AGT. CITY/ST. _____ PH _____   ADDRESS _____ PHONE _____
AMOUNT OF ESTIMATED CHARGES $ _____   CITY/ST. _____

SHIPPER: THE TARE WEIGHT OF THE VEHICLE (INCLUDING THE SHIPMENTS ON BOARD) MUST BE ENTERED ON THIS LINE PRIOR TO ➔ LOADING YOUR SHIPMENT ON THE VEHICLE.

WEIGHT	ORIGINAL	REWEIGH
GROSS		
TARE		
NET		

RECEIVED SUBJECT TO CLASSIFICATIONS, TARIFFS, RULES AND REGULATIONS INCLUDING ALL TERMS PRINTED OR STAMPED HEREON OR ON THE REVERSE SIDE HEREOF IN EFFECT ON THE DATE OF ISSUE OF THIS BILL OF LADING

TOTAL WEIGHT	BILLABLE MILES	BILLABLE WEIGHT	RATE	CHARGES	CODE
				$	

LENGTH OF BOAT ___ Ft. (WEIGHT ADDITIVE) ➔
SAIL BOAT ___ Ft.
BOAT TRL ___ Ft.   TOTAL ➔

		RATE PER $100 VALUATION	CHARGES
X			$

VALUATION STATEMENT

VALUATION: $ _____ (Computed or Declared)

UNLESS THE SHIPPER EXPRESSLY RELEASES THE SHIPMENT TO A VALUE OF 60 CENTS PER POUND PER ARTICLE, THE CARRIER'S MAXIMUM LIABILITY FOR LOSS AND DAMAGE SHALL BE EITHER THE LUMP SUM VALUE DECLARED BY THE SHIPPER OR AN AMOUNT EQUAL TO $1.25 FOR EACH POUND OF WEIGHT IN THE SHIPMENT, WHICHEVER IS GREATER.

THE SHIPMENT WILL MOVE SUBJECT TO THE RULES AND CONDITIONS OF THE CARRIER'S TARIFF. SHIPPER HEREBY RELEASES THE ENTIRE SHIPMENT TO A VALUE NOT EXCEEDING $ _____
(TO BE COMPLETED BY PERSON SIGNING BELOW)

NOTICE: THE SHIPPER SIGNING THIS CONTRACT MUST INSERT IN THE SPACE ABOVE, IN HIS OWN HANDWRITING, EITHER HIS DECLARATION OF THE ACTUAL VALUE OF THE SHIPMENT, OR THE WORDS "60 CENTS PER POUND PER ARTICLE." OTHERWISE, THE SHIPMENT WILL BE DEEMED RELEASED TO A MAXIMUM VALUE EQUAL TO $1.25 TIMES THE WEIGHT OF THE SHIPMENT IN POUNDS.

(Shipper) _____ DATE: _____

SHIPPER'S SIGNATURE REQUESTING SPECIAL SERVICES

X _____ ◀ Expedited service ordered by shipper. Deliver on or before _____

X _____ ◀ Exclusive use of a _____ cu. ft. vehicle ordered. (Min. 1400 cu. ft.)

BILLING INSTRUCTIONS: Charges payable in cash, certified check, traveler's check, or bank check (per tariff) made payable to North American Van Lines at _____

☐ ORIGIN   ☐ BEFORE DELIVERY   OR   ☐ CARRIER SHALL BILL

IF SHIPMENT MOVING FREIGHT CHARGES COLLECT, SHIPPER MAY REQUEST DELIVERY UPON PAYMENT OF $ _____ (ESTIMATED CHARGES PLUS 10%).
IF CREDIT EXTENDED ON BASIS OF SHIPPER'S HIS EMPLOYER'S OR OTHER PROMISE TO PAY PART OR ALL CHARGES, SHIPPER ACKNOWLEDGES HE REMAINS PRIMARILY LIABLE FOR PAYMENT.

ON EMPLOYER PAID MOVES, AMOUNT TO BE COLLECTED FROM CUSTOMER AT DESTINATION FOR CHARGES NOT AUTHORIZED BY EMPLOYER ➔ $ _____

APU INVOICE - CARRIER USE ONLY
WAS APU PERFORMED? ☐ YES ☐ NO   APU CONT'L NO _____
DRIVER SIGNATURE X _____ DATE _____

1.	TOTAL **ALL** CHARGES PER FORM #65 (COPY MUST BE ATTACHED)	➔	CHARGES $	CODE
2.	TOTAL **ALL** CHARGES PER FORM #65 (COPY MUST BE ATTACHED)	➔	CHARGES $	CODE
3.	TOTAL **ALL** CHARGES PER FORM #65 (COPY MUST BE ATTACHED)	➔	CHARGES $	CODE
4.	TOTAL **ALL** CHARGES PER FORM #65 (COPY MUST BE ATTACHED)	➔	CHARGES $	CODE

STORAGE IN TRANSIT (S.I.T.)

WAS THERE PARTIAL DELIVERY AT S.I.T.? ☐ YES ☐ NO
S.I.T. LOCATION (WAREHOUSE) _____ COUNTY: _____
CITY _____ ST _____ ZIP _____
ACTUAL IN/OUT STORAGE DATE: FROM: ___ / ___ / ___ TO: ___ / ___ / ___
STORAGE WEIGHT _____ PICKUP/DELIVERY MILES _____
STORAGE RATE _____ PICKUP/DELIVERY RATE _____
HANDLING RATE _____ PICKUP/DELIVERY SCHEDULE _____

STORAGE CHARGE ➔ $ _____ CODE _____
HANDLING CHARGE ➔ $ _____ CODE _____
PICKUP/DELIVERY CHARGE ➔ $ _____ CODE _____
ADDITIONAL VAL. CHG (10% OF STORAGE) ➔ $ _____ TOTAL ➔ $ _____ S.I.T. CHGS.

S.I.T. AT ☐ ORIG. ☐ DEST   S.I.T. CONT'L NO. _____
WAS BULKY ARTICLES PLACED IN S.I.T. ☐ YES ☐ NO
STORED: ☐ INSIDE ☐ OUTSIDE OF WAREHOUSE

GRAND TOTAL CHARGES $ _____ ◀ SUBJECT TO AUDIT BY CARRIER

PREPAID AT ORIGIN $ _____ ◀ NOTE: ALL COLLECTION DATA MUST BE RECORDED ON FORM #125

PAID AT DEST. $ _____

BAL DUE ➔ $ _____ (C.O.D.) ◀ SUBJECT TO AUDIT BY CARRIER

HAULER NAME	HAULER CODE	WEIGHT	SET OFF A.T. CODE	VAN TO VAN	CITY	STATE
1st				☐ VAN TO VAN		
2nd				☐ VAN TO VAN		
3rd				☐ VAN TO VAN		
4th				☐ VAN TO VAN		

CARRIER AGREES TO TRANSPORT THE GOODS AND EFFECTS TENDERED BY THE SHIPPER SUBJECT TO THE PRECEDING TERMS AND CONDITIONS. Carrier provided or assured that shipper or his representative previously received required I.C.C. information material, including I.C.C. booklet form BOP 103, the Public Advisory #4 Booklet, and the carrier's current performance report.

Carrier or Authorized Agent X _____

This B/L Rated By _____ (CODE)
ACTUAL DELIVERY DATE _____

X _____
SHIPPER OR CONSIGNEE

DELIVERY ACKNOWLEDGMENT: The above services were rendered and the property described has been received, in apparent good condition except as noted on the shipping documents.

NO. 389976

ANY MOTOR CARRIER, OR OTHER PERSON, OR ANY OFFICER, AGENT, EMPLOYEE, OR REPRESENTATIVE THEREOF, WHO SHALL KNOWINGLY AND WILLFULLY NEGLECT OR FAIL TO MAKE FULL, TRUE, AND CORRECT ENTRIES OR WHO SHALL KNOWINGLY AND WILLFULLY FALSIFY, DESTROY, MUTILATE, OR ALTER THIS RECEIPT OR BILL OF LADING, SHALL BE SUBJECT TO A PENALTY OF $5,000 FOR EACH SUCH OFFENSE (SEC. 222; 49 U.S.C. 322)

ORIGINAL If charges are C.O.D., record collection, and give this copy to shipper. Otherwise mail this copy to Ft. Wayne.

FORM NO. 15

cludes such items as the number of days required to settle claims, the percentage of claims settled during a calendar year, the percentage of shipments delivered late, the percentage of shipments on which a claim was filed, and so on. This information can be obtained upon request from the ICC.

Charges

Charges for shipping vary from shipper to shipper. The exact cost of your move cannot be determined until your household goods are weighed after they are loaded into the truck. If you ask, the carrier will furnish you with rates and a method of estimating weights. In addition, the mover is required to give you a written estimate (Exhibit 7–3) of what your shipment will weigh and the probable cost of your move. These estimates may be binding or not binding upon the mover. The mover is allowed to charge you for providing a binding estimate. Binding estimates must clearly describe the shipment and all services provided. You cannot be required to pay more than the amount of the estimate. To be binding, the estimate must be in writing and signed, and you must receive a copy before you move. A copy must also be attached to the bill of lading. A mover is not permitted to charge for giving a nonbinding estimate. The ICC guidelines also require that a tariff showing the rates and charges of each company be filed with the ICC; no interstate mover may charge you more or less than the ICC tariff rates that are on file.

For consumers to protect themselves, they should go to the scale with the truck after the truck has been loaded to make sure there are no additional persons or items on board the truck. Vehicles must be weighed by a certified weight master or on a certified scale. Usually, the moving van is weighed before loading your shipment and after loading your shipment. The weight of your shipment is determined by the difference between the two numbers. The ICC requires that if you request such information, a shipper must notify you in advance of the location of the scale that that is going to be used to weigh your shipment. Movers must allow you to observe the weighing. The truck must be weighed with full fuel tanks, and the driver and all equipment (dollies, handtrucks, and so on). In the event that no fuel is available at the weighing station, the truck may be weighed, but may not add fuel until after your furniture is loaded and it has been weighed again. The carrier may not charge you for weighing. The shipper must furnish you with two copies of the weight tickets; one will show the weight of the vehicle before loading (tare weight), and the other will show the weight of the vehicle after loading. The carrier is forbidden by ICC regulations to make any additions to or alterations of the weight ticket. Exhibit 7–4 shows a typical weight tickets. In addition, the bill of lading is required to show the preloading weight of the vehicle. The consumer should check the weight certificates and the bill of lading to make sure that the weights are consistent.

The ICC has provisions that allow consumers to request a reweighing of the vehicle at its destination. The consumer may observe this reweighing. The ICC requires that the lower of the two shipment weights be used in determining your

EXHIBIT 7-3
Estimate Cost Sheet

northAmerican VAN LINES

ESTIMATED COST OF SERVICES
NORTH AMERICAN VAN LINES, INC.
P.O. BOX 988 FORT WAYNE, INDIANA 46801 DATE _____ 19 _____

NAME OF CARRIER _____

ADDRESS OF CARRIER _____

NAME OF SHIPPER _____ ADDRESS _____ PHONE _____

SHIPMENT MOVING FROM _____ TO _____

SHIPPER'S DESTINATION CONTACT _____ PHONE _____

PACKING DATE OR PERIOD OF TIME REQUESTED _____

LOADING DATE OR PERIOD OF TIME REQUESTED _____

DELIVERY DATE OR PERIOD OF TIME REQUESTED _____

IMPORTANT NOTICE. This estimate covers only the articles and services listed. It is not a guarantee that the actual charges will not exceed the amount of the estimate. Common carriers are required by law to collect transportation and other incidental charges computed on the basis of rates shown in their lawfully published tariffs, regardless of prior rate quotations or estimates made by the forwarder or its agents. Exact charges for loading, transporting, and unloading are based upon the weight of the goods transported, and such charges may not be determined prior to the time the goods are loaded on the van and weighed. Charges for additional services will be added to the transportation charges.

ESTIMATED COST OF SERVICES (Based on Tariff _____ MF-I.C.C. NO. _____) **ESTIMATED CHARGES**

Transportation: Est. wt. _____ lbs.; _____ mi, @ $ _____ per 100 lbs. $ _____

Valuation Charge: { for liability on part of carrier in excess of that assumed when its lowest rates are charged }
(Tariff Item 190-
WST Item 785)

On Transportation: $ _____ @ 50¢ per $100, or fraction thereof

On Storage-in-Transit @ _____ ¢ per cwt. (10% of monthly storage rate)

ADDITIONAL TRANSPORTATION CHARGES: (Explain) for each 30 days or fraction thereof
✝ (Tariff Item 170)

PICKUP OR DELIVERY FOR STORAGE IN TRANSIT
✝ (Tariff Section 7) _____ lbs.; @ _____ ¢ per 100 lbs.

STORAGE IN TRANSIT AT _____ lbs.; @ _____ ¢ per 100 lbs. (for each 30 days or fraction thereof)
✝ (Tariff Item 185)

WAREHOUSE HANDLING _____ lbs.; @ _____ ¢ per 100 lbs. (one time charge)
✝ (Tariff Item 185)

EXTRA PICKUP OR DELIVERY AT _____
✝ (Tariff Item 115)

SPECIAL SERVICING OF APPLIANCES _____
✝ (Tariff Item 195)

PIANO OR ORGAN CARRY _____
✝ (Tariff Item 135)

HOISTING OR LOWERING HEAVY ARTICLES _____
✝ (Tariff Rule 34, Item 120) (Explain)

CONTAINERS (see below) _____
✝ (Tariff Item 104 or 105)

PACKING (see below) _____
✝ (Tariff Item 104 or 105)

UNPACKING (see below) _____
✝ (Tariff Item 104 or 105)

LABOR _____ man/men for _____ hrs; @ _____
✝ (Tariff Item 120) (Per man per hour)

OTHER SERVICES _____
(Explain)

ESTIMATOR: You must include the tariff reference for all services entered on this line.

TOTAL ESTIMATED COST: $ _____

TOTAL ESTIMATED CHARGES $ _____

I HEREBY ACKNOWLEDGE that I have received from (check one)

_____ the carrier supplying this estimate

_____ a carrier supplying another estimate

_____ other source

Summary Of Information for Shippers of Household Goods, Form BOp 103 Prospective shipper also acknowledges receipt of I.C.C. booklet, Public Advisory #4 and North American's Past Annual Performance Report.

X _____
Shipper or His Representative

If the total tariff charges for the listed articles and services exceed this estimate by more than ten percent, then, upon your request, the carrier must relinquish possession of your shipment upon delivery in advance of the payment of the total amount of tariff charges shown on the bill of lading or freight bill. You are still obligated to pay the balance of the total charges within 15 days.

Maximum amount to be paid on delivery of your C.O.D. shipment in cash, certified check, traveler's check, or bank check (per tariff) is

(TOTAL ESTIMATED COST PLUS 10%) $ _____

ESTIMATED COST OF CONTAINERS, AND PACKING AND UNPACKING SERVICES

	CONTAINERS			PACKING			UNPACKING		
	ESTIMATED NUMBER	PER EACH	TOTAL	ESTIMATED NUMBER	PER EACH	TOTAL	ESTIMATED NUMBER	PER EACH	TOTAL
DRUM, DISH-PACK, BARRELS ETC. ___									
CARTONS, LESS THAN 3 Cu. Ft. ___									
3 Cu. Ft. ___									
4½ Cu. Ft. ___									
6 Cu. Ft. ___									
6½ Cu. Ft. ___									
WARDROBE CARTON NOT LESS THAN 10 Cu. Ft. ___									
CRIB MATTRESS CARTON ___									
MATTRESS CARTON TWIN SIZE ___ (NOT EXCEEDING 39" X 75")									
MATTRESS CARTON REGULAR SIZE ___ (NOT EXCEEDING 54" X 75")									
MATTRESS CARTON KING SIZE ___ (EXCEEDING 54" X 75")									
MATTRESS CARTON (39" X 80") ___									
MATTRESS COVER ___									
CORRUGATED CONTAINERS (Specially designed for mirrors, paintings, glass or marble tops, and similar fragile articles) ___									
___ CRATES-SHOW TOTAL CU. FT. CHARGEABLE ___ (WHEN CU. FT. RATE APPLIES)									
CRATES WHEN MINIMUM RATE APPLIES (Mirror Cartons) ___									
	ESTIMATED CONTAINER	COSTS $		ESTIMATED PACKING	COSTS $		ESTIMATED UNPACKING	COSTS $	

REMARKS

NOTICE: It is mandatory that the total cubic footage shown on the table of measurements be multiplied by not less than 7 to determine the total estimated weight. Articles not to be shipped should be indicated by a "check mark" in the column provided on the table of measurements.

If the prospective shipper has not previously been furnished with the Summary of Information For Shippers of Household Goods, form number BOp 103, the Public Advisory #4, and the North American's Past Annual Performance as required by the Interstate Commerce Commission, he should be furnished these documents at this time.

(TABLE OF MEASUREMENTS ON REVERSE SIDE)

FORM 11 REV. 5-77

ESTIMATING AGENT _____ CODE _____

ADDRESS _____ PHONE _____

Signature and Title of Estimator _____

Estimator's Code Number _____

transportation costs. The average shipment of household goods will weigh about 40 pounds per item. (Each box is considered a single item.)

Payment

Once you have received an estimate of the cost of your move, there are several methods for payment. One method is to request credit from the shipper. The Federal Equal Credit Opportunity Act, discussed in the previous chapter, prohibits discrimination against credit applicants on the basis of race, color, religion, national origin, sex, marital status, or age. If you get a nonbinding estimate and the total actual charges do not exceed the estimate plus 10 percent, you must pay the actual charges prior to the unloading of your goods. However, if the total actual charge exceeds the estimate by more than 10 percent, the mover is required, on request, to deliver your goods upon payment of the estimated charges plus an additional 10 percent, and you have 30 days, after date of delivery, in which to pay the balance.

Storage

If you cannot move directly from your present address to your new address, you must store your goods. If you want the mover to continue to be responsible for your goods while they are in storage, you should request that the goods be held on a "storage in transit" basis. A mover may hold goods for 180 days as "storage in transit." After 180 days, the responsibility for your goods shifts to the warehouse operator.

If your goods are held by a local warehouse, then the mover's liability ceases when the local storage contract starts. A warehouse operator's liability is usually

EXHIBIT 7-4
Weight Tickets

Weighed on Standard Scales	LEGAL WEIGHTS Pounds per Bushel
No._____19____	Alfalfa 60
	Barley.............48
	Bran..............20
Load of_____	Beans 60
	Carrots 50
From_____	Clover Seed.......60
	Corn, on cob......70
To_____	Corn, shelled......56
	Flax Seed.........56
Gross_____ *lbs.*	Hemp Seed........44
	Millet Seed........50
Driver on_____ Tare_____ *lbs.*	Oats..............32
	Onions 57
Driver off_____ Net_____ *lbs.*	Peas..............60
	Potatoes, Irish......60
Fee_____ Net_____ *bush.*	Quinces 48
	Rye...............56
_____ Weigher	Timothy Seed...... 45
★	Wheat 60

less than that of a mover, and the consumer should make sure to get appropriate insurance. In the event your goods are held in a ''storage in transit'' position and are to be converted to a permanent storage basis, the mover must notify you of the changeover at least 10 days prior to the change. Notification must include the date of the change and the fact that you have 9 months from that date to file a claim with the mover and that the liability of the mover is replaced by the liability of the warehouse operator.

Pickup

Movers are required to transport shipments with reasonable promptness. This means that performance of transportation dates on the order of service and bill of lading must be followed. If the mover is unable to make pickup and delivery on the dates specified, the mover must promptly notify you by telephone, telegraph, or in person, at his or her expense, of the date on which the pickup can be made.

When the movers arrive to pick up your goods, they will take an inventory of all the articles that you are shipping. They will make notations as to the condition of your goods. Since the moving company is required to deliver your goods in the same condition and quantity as they were picked up, this inventory becomes your receipt and the basis of a subsequent claim for damages. At the top of the inventory there will be certain code letters used by the carrier to show preexisting damage of particular items. You should make sure that a proper description of the condition of your furniture is entered on the inventory. Before signing the inventory, make a note of any item, the description of which you disagree with. This note should be made directly on the inventory, and you should keep a copy.

Delivery

The most important date in your move is the delivery date. It is imperative that you or an agent be present. Do not sign any delivery papers, receipts, or inventory until you have inspected your goods. If there is damage or loss, you should make notations as to the loss or damage that has occurred. Failure to do this will make it difficult at a later date to present evidence that damage was done during the move. Though it may not be possible to check every item and every carton, you should open cartons that appear to be damaged or that you know contain valuable or fragile items. You should also check the number of cartons to make sure that none are missing. If you find damage done, after the driver has left, leave the damaged items in the original carton and contact the shipper immediately. The longer you wait to report damage, or loss, the less likely that the carrier will pay a claim.

Claims

If your goods are damaged or missing, you must file a written claim with the mover for recovery. You have up to 9 months after your move to file such a claim, but it is advisable to file the claim as soon as possible as it may be more difficult to process or to prove loss many months after the fact. If you fail to file a claim within 120 days after delivery and later bring a lawsuit, you may not be able to recover attorney's fees even if you win the suit. ICC carriers are required to provide you with claim forms on request. The completed form should be mailed to the shipper, along with any estimates or appraisals of value and a copy of the bill of lading or inventory, noting that the goods were either missing or damaged. (Shippers will usually not process a claim unless all charges have been paid. Don't forget to keep copies of all items for your files.)

In making your claim, you should be prepared to justify the value you have placed on the lost or damaged goods. Sales slips, local mail order house catalogs, or any estimate from a store can be used to obtain proof of value. The ICC requires every mover receiving a written claim for loss or damage to acknowledge the claim in writing within 30 days after receipt. In addition, the mover is required either to pay, decline, or make a firm compromise settlement in writing within 120 days after receipt of the claim. In the event that the movers are unable to do so, they are required to notify the customer every 30 days thereafter in writing of the status of the claim and the reasons for the delay in settling. If the claim is not resolved under the ICC rules, you may have to go to court to obtain a resolution. If the mover participates in a dispute resolution program, you may submit the claim to arbitration. This procedure may be less expensive and more convenient. Movers who do participate in this program are required to advise the shipper of all details before they accept shipment.

Movers are required to designate an agent for the service of legal process in every state in which they operate. Thus, if legal action is necessary, appropriate court papers may be filed on the designated agent in the state in which you live. There is no necessity to go out of state. (A list of agents can be obtained from the director, Bureau of Operations, ICC, 12 Constitution Avenue, N.W., Washington, D.C. 20423.)

Movers are also required to notify the ICC of their insurance carrier. This will make sure that payment of any claims for which the insurer may be liable is at least backed up by a reputable insurance carrier. Normally, the mover's insurance company will take the same position as the mover, as their liability is the same, but you can get information from the ICC as to the insurance carrier and go directly to the carrier.

AUTO REPAIRS

Automobile repairs are the number one consumer problem. Your rights in the auto repair process depend on which state you live in. Less than half of the states have laws governing auto repair practices. The states that do have auto repair statutes include Alaska, California, Colorado, Connecticut, Florida, Hawaii, Maryland, Massachusetts, Michigan, Montana, Nevada, New Hampshire, New Jersey, New York, Ohio, Oregon, Rhode Island (auto body shops only), Texas, Utah, Washington, Washington, D.C., and Wisconsin. The central element of the state laws is disclosure to enable the consumer to understand what repairs are needed, how much the repairs will cost, when the repairs will be finished, and what guarantees accompany the work. Some states even extend auto repair regulations to cover deceptive practices and shoddy repair work.

Typical state provisions require written estimates for work that costs over $25 or $50. The estimate must include a description of the vehicle's problem, a description of the repair work to be performed, and an estimate of all charges for this work, as well as time and date for completion of the work. If the repair is going to exceed 10 percent of the initial estimate, the consumer must be informed and asked to OK the additional charges, usually in writing. In California, a repair shop can get telephone authorization when an individual brings a vehicle to the repair shop prior to its opening and a written estimate is prepared and reviewed with the consumer, and the circumstances of the verbal authorization are noted.

States with laws requiring written estimates generally permit a shop to charge a reasonable fee for making such estimates, but require that the fee be disclosed. The shop must also disclose the nature, extent, and duration of any warranty on the work.

State disclosure statutes also provide that automotive shops must return replaced parts to the consumer unless these parts are covered under a warranty agreement that requires that they be returned to the manufacturer or unless the parts are so large that returning them is impractical. In addition, consumers must be given an invoice noting all repair work done and stating whether new, rebuilt, or reconditioned parts were used. This bill must also identify the mechanic who did the work. Shops must keep copies of these invoices for a specified period of time.

Most states have "mechanic's lien laws." These laws indicate that a repair shop is entitled to keep your car if you refuse to pay the bill no matter how outrageous that bill may be. In some of the states that require written estimates and authorization for repairs, the mechanic's lien law is waived if the shop does not comply with the estimate and authorization rule.

States' laws also require shops to post signs notifying customers of their rights to a written estimate, a written copy of any guarantee, return of replacement parts, and a detailed invoice. Some states also require that the shops post a notice of where complaints can be filed. State regulations also prohibit shops from making false promises to get the consumer to authorize repairs, allowing consumers to sign blank documents relating to any repairs, charging for any work not performed, performing unnecessary repairs, or misrepresenting the cost of authorized repairs.

Several states—California, Connecticut, Hawaii, Michigan, New York, and Washington, D.C. (Rhode Island auto body shops only)—have laws requiring repair facilities to register with the state government.

Michigan, Hawaii, and the District of Columbia carry auto repair legislation one step further by requiring mechanics to pass a certification test for the type of repair work they usually perform. The fees paid for such registration are used to finance and enforce the repair shop disclosure laws.

In addition to the state regulations, the American Automobile Association (A.A.A.) has attempted to take some of the risk out of repair shops by identifying those that provide quality repair in selected areas. Under the A.A.A. program, those shops that are designated as A.A.A. approved have agreed to provide A.A.A. members with written estimates, make available all parts that have been replaced, guarantee repair work for 90 days or 4000 miles, and abide by the A.A.A. decision in any dispute between the customers and the repair shop.

There are certain things consumers can do to protect themselves from disreputable repair facilities. When choosing a facility, consumers should consider the reputation of the facility and the qualifications of the mechanics. (Have they been licensed or certified?) In addition, some of the things that should be looked at are how long the shop has been at its present location and whether it appears to be well equipped, clean, and organized. In addition, the consumer should check the costs to see if they are competitive, and even in states that do not provide statutory disclosure, the consumer should see if the shop will give a written estimate and advise of additional costs. The consumer should also see if the shop will guarantee its work in writing.

QUESTIONS

1   The plaintiff went into the defendant's clothing store to purchase a vest. The clerk was busy with another customer and directed the plaintiff to a table on which vests were piled. The plaintiff selected a vest and took off his coat and vest to try on the new vest. The plaintiff laid his coat and vest on a table with the knowledge that nobody was watching him. The table was about six feet from where the plaintiff stood. The plaintiff's watch, chain, and cigar cutter were stolen from the plaintiff's clothing. Was there a bailment? If so, what type? Discuss the liability of the defendant.

2   John Wiley was the owner of a truck that was being driven by his employee Siegfried. The driver stopped at the defendant Johnson's diner and parked his truck in an open area about 75 feet from the gas pumps. He shut the motor off, put the truck in gear, set the hand brake, and went into the diner to wash up and eat. He expected that while he was inside eating, the truck would be moved to the fuel pump by the service station attendant and the tank filled, as it had been on previous occasions. The truck was driven to the pump. The truck rolled back and pulled the hose from the pump spraying fuel all over the truck. The fuel ignited and caused damage to the truck. Was there a bailment? Is so, what type? Discuss the liability of the defendant.

3   The plaintiff went into the defendant's restaurant for dinner. She gave her coat to the coatroom attendant. The attendant told her there were no more checks, but that since she knew the plaintiff, she would accept the coat without giving her a check. When the plaintiff finished eating and was ready to leave, she went to the checkroom. The attendant was unable to find the plaintiff's Persian lamb coat. The checkroom was small and open to the restaurant except for a half-gate across the doorway. Was there a bailment? If so, what type? Discuss the liability of the defendant.

4   The plaintiff, Mr. Wood, an English schoolteacher from Liverpool, came to the United States as a passenger on one of the defendant's steamers. One of his trunks, which had been delivered to the defendant in England, had never been found. Included in the trunk was clothing worth $100 and the only copy of a manuscript that Wood had writ-

ten. Wood claims $5000 for his loss. The steamship company ticket, the so-called passenger contract, contained many provisions covering three and a half pages. On the back was a "Notice to passengers," followed by seven paragraphs containing various provisions. One provision stated, "Neither the steamship owner nor the passage broker agent is in any case liable for loss of or injury to or delay in delivery of luggage or personal effects to the passenger beyond the amount of $15 unless the value in excess of the sum be declared at or before the issue of the contract ticket. . . ." The ticket was not signed by the passenger, nor was his attention called to the preceding notice. Is the steamship company liable for the $5000? Discuss.

5 The plaintiff left a mink coat with the defendant for storage and repair in the spring of 1958. The plaintiff received and signed a storage receipt and contract that contained a clause limiting the defendant's liability to $300. The plaintiff could have had additional insurance by paying a storage charge equal to 2 percent of whatever valuation she chose to place on the coat. The plaintiff failed to do so. The coat was never returned to the plaintiff in the fall when she came to claim it. Is the storage company liable for more than $300? Discuss.

6 The plaintiff brought his car to the defendant's parking garage and was given a numbered ticket that had the name and location of the garage on the front. On the reverse there appeared the following: "Notice—Parking Service Company, Inc., assumes no duty to the holder . . . to watch out for or guard against loss or damage to the vehicle or the contents thereof or accessories thereon, through fire, or theft." The plaintiff never looked at the back of the ticket, paid for the privilege of parking the automobile on the parking lot, and went about his business. When he returned, the automobile had been stolen. Is the parking lot liable to the plaintiff for the loss of the vehicle? Discuss.

7 The plaintiff brought his goods to Bekins Van and Storage Co. for storage. When he retrieved the goods, he found them to be water-damaged. In the contract with Bekins, signed by the plaintiff, there was the following declaration: "depositor hereby declares the value of all said goods to be not in excess of $.10 per pound per article, unless a higher value is declared by him in writing in which event higher charges shall apply." The bill of lading provided "the liability of this company for any piece, package or contents is limited to $.10 per pound per article unless a higher valuation is declared in writing and so noted hereon, in which case rates based on such higher valuation will be assessed." The water damage was caused by one of the sprinkler system pipes directly above the location where the goods were stored. None of the warehouse personnel had checked to see whether there were any water leaks before the goods were placed under the pipes. Can Bekins limit liability pursuant to the clause in the bill of lading and the contract? Discuss.

8 The plaintiff rented a power lawn mower from the defendant in order to mow his lawn. The mower was equipped with a safety device designed to tip the mower when the handle was pulled down so as to shield and protect the operator from the rotating cutting blades. The safety device was defective. The plaintiff, while operating the mower, slipped and fell, and his foot was seriously injured by the revolving blades. The plaintiff had signed a rental agreement that indicated that he would assume all liability arising out of the use of the power lawn mower. Was the defendant rental store liable for the damages? Discuss.

9 The plaintiff, one of the first American soldiers to occupy Germany, found some of Hitler's personal belongings, took them, and brought them back to the United States.

Twenty years later the belongings were stolen and subsequently sold to the defendant, who purchased them in good faith. The plaintiff sued to recover the property. The defendant alleges that the plaintiff never obtained good and legal title to the belongings. The defendant asserts that the German government is the true owner of the goods, and the plaintiff therefore cannot maintain the action. Decision for whom? Discuss.

10 The plaintiff found $100 within the safe deposit box vault maintained by the defendant, Dollar Savings Bank of N.Y. The vault was in the basement in an area of the bank that is walled off from other parts of the bank and is used exclusively for safe deposit boxes. In order to be eligible to rent a safe deposit box, the renter must have a savings account in the bank. Access to the restricted area is limited to box renters or officers and employees of the bank. The plaintiff contends that the property is lost, and therefore he is entitled to it. Decision for whom? Discuss.

11 The plaintiffs went to a banquet at the defendant's hotel. Near the entrance to the dining room was a rack on which guests left their hats while eating meals. The plaintiffs left the restaurant at about 10:00, and came back one hour later, intending to get their hats. The restaurant was locked. The next morning, when leaving the hotel, plaintiffs asked for their hats. The defendant was unable to produce them. No actual negligence by the defendant was proved at the trial. Is the defendant hotel liable? Discuss.

12 The plaintiff went into the defendant's hotel to rent a room. The plaintiff had turned the custody of his automobile over to a garage attendant employed by the defendant. The attendant drove his automobile into the defendant's garage to park it. When the plaintiff went to leave, his car was nowhere to be found. Is the innkeeper liable for loss of the automobile? Discuss.

PART THREE

REAL PROPERTY OWNERSHIP

The largest purchase an average consumer will make during a lifetime is the purchase of a home. Part III will discuss real property ownership and will lead you, the student, through many of the aspects of a home purchase, from securing the property to receiving the key at the closing. At this critical time in your financial life, it is absolutely essential that you as consumer have some knowledge about the intricacies of the legal process. This will enable you to communicate intelligently with your attorney on points where your knowledge may be limited and also to know where those points are (i.e., you may be a structural engineer and be able to carry the ball through procuring the property but may well need a surveyor or attorney or both by the time you get around to accepting the deed).

Real property includes land and everything that is attached to the land. This includes buildings such as houses, barns, garages, and so on, as well as trees, shrubs, plants, and crops. All other items of property are categorized as personal property. If personal property is incorporated into real property, either by being attached to the land in a permanent manner or by being attached to a building that is already permanently affixed to the land, it becomes categorized as real property. Such items of personal property are called fixtures.

The distinction between real property and personal property can be important for several reasons. First, it can make a difference in determining who is entitled to receive the property upon the death of the current owner. Second, it can be important in determining the method to be used to transfer ownership of property from one individual to another. Third, different jurisdictions impose taxes on real property or personal property or both; the determination of the amount of tax will depend on the nature of the property. Finally, different types of property can be used as collateral for debts in different fashions. Both real and personal property can be used to secure a debt, but the type of instrument executed to perfect the security interest is different for each type of property.

CHAPTER 8

Securing the Property

INTRODUCTION

There is a question that must be asked at the outset of this chapter to enable you to follow the format. Who are you? The buyer or the seller? From the seller's point of view, we must explore the relationship with a real estate broker. We must also review the various aspects of securing the property up to and including the signing of the contract. The buyer will be making some of the same decisions with respect to a real estate broker and the contract. The buyer will have the additional problem of taking title (e.g., joint tenancy, tenancy in common, tenants by the entirety). Decisions will have to be made by him or her as to how he or she wishes to take title. The buyer will also have to decide whether the title is even marketable, giving him rights to the property that are good as to all the world, including Native American land claims.

LISTING THE PROPERTY

The Buyer

An individual who is contemplating the purchase of a home must also decide whether to use the services of a real estate broker. A buyer who is able to locate the property on his or her own may save money on the purchase since the purchase price of a home purchased through a broker usually includes the commission. A real estate broker can be useful in providing expertise and guidance to a prospective buyer who is unfamiliar with the properties in a particular area. The broker may provide necessary information with respect to shopping areas, schools, and so on. Selecting properties to review may be done in the realtor's office, eliminating many hours of looking and miles of unnecessary driving. Not every home is advertised in the newspaper; therefore, a realtor may be the only person with information about a particular property, especially one that is offered through an exclusive listing. A real estate broker can also provide information with respect to financing as well as assistance in preparing the necessary loan application forms. In addition, the realtor can help prepare a purchase offer and act as a negotiator between the buyer and seller.

The Seller

A seller will have to decide whether to list the property with a real estate broker or sell it directly. There are advantages to selling a piece of property yourself. The primary advantage is that you can often save all or part of the commission you would otherwise have to pay the broker. Another advantage is that some buyers don't like to deal with brokers, and you may get customers you might not otherwise get. In addition, since you know your home, you may be able to show it to better advantage than a stranger could. You may also be better able to negotiate a deal.

The disadvantages are that a seller who wishes to sell his or her property directly will have to advertise and show the property, screen potential buyers, and be prepared to discuss financing, and so on. If a seller does not wish assistance from a real estate broker, he or she can usually get help from family members. Friends may also know of prospects looking for homes in the area in which the seller is located.

Brokers can be of help not only in advertising and selling, but also in establishing the asking price for the property, finding qualified buyers, and locating sources of mortgage money for buyers. Reducing the parade of curious strangers tromping through your home may be well worth the brokerage fee. These fees vary by location but are generally from 6 to 10 percent of the selling price of the property.

Legal Implications of Listing

The broker is an agent of the party who first employs him or her, normally the seller (Herb Tillman Co. v. Sissel, 348 S.W. 2d 819 [Mo. 1961]). The rules of law regarding principal and agent control all the interrelationships of the parties (Zwick v. United Farm Agency Inc., 556 P.2d 508 [Wyo. 1976]). The seller is liable for information the broker is authorized to convey to the buyer and may be liable for certain representations the broker makes even though not expressly authorized. As a salesperson, the broker is allowed to do some "puffing" (excessive praising of the property), however, he or she must accurately and completely represent the state of the property.

In Bennett v. Judson, 21 N.Y. 238 (1860), the seller (principal) hired the broker (agent) to sell certain property located in Indiana and Illinois. The broker made certain false representations as to the location of the property and its suitability for agricultural purposes. These representations were made based on thirdhand information (the broker had never seen the property) and were made without the seller's knowledge. The broker believed the representations to be true. The court held the seller liable for the representations of the broker, stating that the seller "cannot enjoy the fruits of the bargain without adopting all the instrumentalities employed by the agent in bringing it to a consummation." The court further pointed out that the principal may, on learning of the fraudulent act, rescind the contract and make restitution; but if the principal retains the benefits of the dealing, he or she must accept the consequences thereof.

The real estate broker is the seller's agent, and there is an inherent responsibility for absolute good faith and honesty of each to the other. In Lent-Agnew Realty Company, Inc. v. Trebert, 20 N.Y.S. 598 (N.Y. 1925), the realty company (the broker-agent) misrepresented certain facts concerning rentals to its principal, Trebert, who wished to purchase the building. Trebert had agreed to pay the broker a commission even if he failed to purchase the building. Upon discovery of the misrepresentations, Trebert refused to consummate the purchase of the building, and the realty company sued him for its commission. Trebert argued that he was not required to pay a commission because of the misrepresentations made by the realty company. The realty company defended on the grounds that the misrepresentations were not made intentionally and that the rule of "caveat emptor" (let the buyer beware) is applicable in this type of a deal.

The court held that the rule of caveat emptor "has no application in dealings between a principal and his agent, . . . for theirs was a relation based upon the utmost confidence and good faith." Accordingly, the court held that even though the misrepresentation of the agency may have been unintentional, and no proof was ever demonstrated that the agent had knowledge of the falseness of the representation, the plaintiff was not entitled to the commission.

Types of Listings

Assuming that you decide to list the property with a broker, you will be required to enter into a listing agreement (Exhibit 8–1). The listing agreement requires certain information regarding the property in order to provide information for the broker and prospective buyers about the major features of the property. In giving a listing, remember that the broker is not familiar with the property and should be told all relevant factors. The broker may ask for one of three types of listings: exclusive right to sell, exclusive agency, or open listing. The major difference between the listings is with respect to the seller's liability for the broker's commission.

Exclusive Right to Sell and Exclusive Agency

An exclusive right to sell appoints the broker in question as the sole party authorized to sell the property. When the property is sold, the broker is entitled to payment irrespective of who actually brings about the sale. If you enter into an exclusive right to sell agreement with one broker, you may sell the property yourself or sell it through another broker. However, you may end up paying twice if a second broker sells the property and will be obligated to the first broker even if you sell the property directly.

In Gaillard Realty Company, Inc. v. Roger's Wire Works, Inc., 213 N.Y.S. 616 (N.Y. 1926), the defendant owned a piece of property located in the state of New Jersey. The defendant hired the plaintiff to sell the property and entered into an agreement with the plaintiff stating that the plaintiff was the exclusive agent for the sale of the property. The agreement further stated that all inquiries concerning the property were to be referred to the agent. The plaintiff entered into negotiation with a number of companies. Prior to the termination of the agreement, the defendant independently sold the property to a party that it obtained directly, and the plaintiff sued for the commission. The defendant's position was that it was not required to pay a commission because the contract was an exclusive agency contract and not an exclusive right to sell contract.

The court held that even though the contract stated that the agent was hired as the exclusive agent, the additional statement that all inquiries concerning the property were to be referred to the broker was sufficient to make the contract an exclusive right to sell agreement. The court then cited considerable authority to the effect that "the general rule is that where an exclusive right of sale is given a broker, the principal cannot make a sale himself without becoming liable for the commis-

TABLE 8-1

Monthly Interest Factors

DeMulder-Realty Inc.

PROPERTY LISTING AGREEMENT

 **Better Homes** and Gardens®

85 Main Street	14 Main Street, Box 86	27 Main Street	2 Dietz Street	55 N. Main Street
Sidney, New York 13838	Otego, New York 13825	Franklin, New York 13775	Oneonta, New York 13820	Bainbridge, New York 13733
Telephone (607) 563-3541	Telephone (607) 988-6868	Telephone (607) 829-6000	Telephone (607) 432-2773	Telephone (607) 967-7356

 MLS
REALTOR

(Circle Office Listing Is Secured From)

Between _____ Owner(s) and
DeMulder Realty Inc., Licensed Real Estate Brokers

The undersigned, Owner(s) hereby employ the said DeMulder Realty Inc. as broker and agent for the purpose of selling or exchanging the real property of the owner(s) described as follows:

Owner				Phone				Date		Lister
Mail Address				Rooms	BR	Baths	Price	**Remarks**		
				Gal. or C.F.	Cost/Yr.		Supplier			
Lot Size	Heat									
Type	Septic			Sewer		Drywell				
Construction	Water		Depth		Plumbing					
Age	Electric				Roof					
Style	Hotwater				Gal. Type		Rented/Owned			
	General Condition			Key		Possession				
Rooms	1st Floor	2nd Floor		3rd Floor		(floor covering) C T W				
Liv.						Woodstove				
Din.						Screens/Storms				
Kitchen						Insulation				
Bath						Fireplace				
Bedroom						Porches				
Bedroom						Closets				
Bedroom						Garage				
Bedroom						Driveway			**Directions**		
Laundry						Outbuildings				
Family Rm						Fire No.				
Basement Foundation		Dry		Floor		Full/Partial				
School District				Tenant						
Terms:				Assessment $		Mortgagee				
	Appliances Included			Water/Sewer $						
Stove	Refrig.		Land	$						
Freezer	Dishwasher		School	$						
Washer	Dryer		Village	$						
Garbage Disp.			Total Taxes	$						

DeMulder-Realty Inc.
Better Homes and Gardens®

THIS INFORMATION, THOUGH BELIEVED ACCURATE, IS NOT GUARANTEED.

NAME   *ADDRESS OF PROPERTY FOR SALE*   *PRICE*

The Owner(s) agree(s) that, upon the sale or exchange of said property to a purchaser obtained through the efforts of said DeMulder Realty, Inc., or its authorized representatives, he will pay to said DeMulder Realty, Inc., a brokerage commission of   % of the total selling price, or $ minimum, whichever is larger.

☐ **EXCLUSIVE RIGHT TO SELL:** SOLE AND EXCLUSIVE RIGHT TO SELL PROPERTY.

☐ **EXCLUSIVE AGENCY:** OWNERS RIGHT TO SELL THE PROPERTY HIMSELF.

☐ **OPEN LISTING:** OWNERS RIGHT TO LIST HIS PROPERTY WITH OTHER BROKERS OR TO SELL PROPERTY HIMSELF.

check one

EXCLUSIVE LISTING EXPIRES _____ MIDNIGHT.

We (I) have read the above agreement and understand the contents thereof, and the above information is true and correct to the best knowledge of the parties whose signatures appear below.

Accepted: DeMulder Realty, Inc.

_____ Owner(s) (LS)

By: _____ Date _____
        (Authorized Representative)

_____ (LS)

I/WE grant permission to place DeMulder sign on property.
☐ Yes   ☐ No

N O T E :   If, within a period of six months after the listing has been terminated, the undersigned sells his property to purchasers who were shown the property by DeMulder Realty, Inc. prior to termination of listing, the full commission shall be due and payable.

sions.'' The court further pointed out that ''if the broker is merely the sole agent, the principal may make a sale himself without the broker's aid if such sale is made in good faith and to some purchaser not procured by the broker.''

If you wish to obtain the services of a broker and still retain the right to sell your property directly, an exclusive agency listing is appropriate. This listing will allow you to sell the property yourself without paying a commission; however, the broker is the only other person authorized to sell on your behalf (Gaillard Realty Company, Inc. v. Roger's Wire Works, Inc., *supra*).

In an exclusive right to sell and an exclusive agency, the seller enters into a contract with the broker to allow the broker to sell the property. The broker relies on this promise and invests time and money in finding a buyer for the property. If the property is sold by another broker (or someone else), the first broker's opportunity is taken away, and the time and money invested are lost. This would be unfair to the broker, and thus legal principles allow him to recover. If the broker has presented a buyer, the commission has been earned and must be paid. If the broker has been deprived of the opportunity to present a buyer, some courts will award the broker damages for breach of the contract rather than payment of a commission.

The general rule with respect to exclusive right to sell and exclusive agency contracts is that the broker cannot recover commissions as such unless his or her work has been completed (Freberg v. Calderwood, 552 P.2d 545 [Or. 1976]). The restrictive nature of the exclusive right to sell and the exclusive agency agreement makes it imperative (in many states legally mandated) that a time limit be placed on this type of a listing. In the absence of such limits, the agreement remains operative for a ''reasonable time.'' This term is subject to judicial interpretation, and should you wish to sell the property yourself three to six months after entering into the agency, the broker could insist on receiving a commission, possibly leading to an expensive law suit.

It is a matter for the jury to determine whether a broker's employment agreement has been terminated and, if it has not been terminated, whether the transaction made some time after the date of the contract was, in fact, within a reasonable time period from the date the agreement was originally entered into. The determination of what is a reasonable period of time will be made by the trier of fact in each case.

Open Listing

The most common form of listing is the open listing whereby the real estate broker is appointed as a nonexclusive agent, allowing the seller to list the property with other brokers or to sell it directly. The open listing allows the seller greater flexibility in that it usually may be terminated at will, and only the broker who sells the property is entitled to receive a commission.

While providing greater flexibility and broader exposure for the seller, the open listing may stifle brokers' attempts to sell the property. The fact that the property is listed with many brokers in the area may lessen the broker's sales effort for fear that someone else will sell the property first after he or she has spent considerable time and effort in showing it. A broker will usually invest more time and money to promote exclusive listings than the open type.

Multiple Listing Service

Multiple listing services (M.L.S.) provide a method for listing one's home with several realtors at one time (see Exhibit 8–2 for sample M.L.S. listing agreement). These services provide greater exposure for one's property and also provide buyers access to many more properties through M.L.S. participant-real estate brokers. Generally, each locality has its own M.L.S., which is coordinated through a central office. A seller who desires to list his property through M.L.S. would do so with a participating real estate broker. The broker would then get all of the particulars with respect to the property as in any other listing. The listing information is distributed to all the M.L.S. participant brokers. In the event of a sale through M.L.S., the listing broker and the selling broker would share in the commission on a contractually agreed basis.

Duties and Obligations of the Parties

The broker, even though an agent of the seller, has no obligation to sell the property. However, if the broker chooses to sell the property, he or she is obligated to use due care and skill. The broker may not misrepresent the property or in any other way act against the seller's interest. A broker may not act as agent for both buyer and seller without first disclosing this fact to the parties and obtaining approval from each.

The seller has an obligation to allow the broker to perform his or her duty without interference. Thus, the seller will have to allow the broker access to the property at reasonable times. The seller is also obligated to inform the broker of all relevant details with respect to the property. If a seller is approached directly by an individual who has previously dealt through a broker, the seller may be liable for the broker's commission even when he or she negotiates a deal with the buyer directly.

Generally, the determination as to whether the seller will be liable to the broker will depend upon whether the negotiations between the seller and the third party have been entered into in good faith. In the event that the buyer and seller agree to negotiate directly in order solely to avoid the imposition of a brokerage commission, the broker will probably recover. In the event, however, that the broker fails to negotiate a transaction and the buyer and seller are able to do so directly, the broker will not be entitled to the commission (except in the case of an exclusive right to sell agreement). It is the obligation of the broker to procure a buyer ready, willing, and able to accept the terms offered by the seller. The seller may not arbitrarily or capriciously terminate the broker's authority without incurring liability.

The primary obligation of the broker is to find a buyer who is ready, willing, and able to purchase the property on the terms specified in the listing agreement (Delaney v. Russell, 166 N.E. 623 [Mass. 1929]). When the broker has performed

EXHIBIT 8-2
Multiple Listing Agreement

EXCLUSIVE RIGHT TO SELL CONTRACT

REALTOR®

ADDRESS	CITY TOWN		RMS	BEDROOMS	BATHS	PRICE

DIRECTIONS		CALL TO SHOW	

TYPE		AGE	
CONSTRUCTION		HEAT	COST
LOT SIZE		SEWER	
ASSESSMENT		ROOF	
TAXES LOCAL SCHOOL		GARAGE	
TAX SEWER / WATER		WATER	

OWNER	MAIL ADDRESS	PHONE

ASSUMABLE 1st MORTGAGE	INT. RATE	MONTHLY PAYMENT	NAME OF MORTGAGEE	TYPE

ROOMS	1st FLOOR (SIZE)	2nd FLOOR (SIZE)	3rd FLOOR (SIZE)	POSSESSION	
LIVING				SCREENS	
DINING				STORM DOORS	
KITCHEN				INSULATION	
BATHS (½ or full)				BASEMENT	
BEDROOM				FOUNDATION	
BEDROOM				DISPOSAL	
BEDROOM				DISHWASHER	
BEDROOM				FIREPLACE	
BEDROOM				GAS	
DEN				ELECTRIC	
NUMBER CLOSETS				HOT WATER	
PORCHES				SCHOOL DISTRICT	
CARPETING				BUS LINE	
FAMILY ROOM				INCOME IF 2 FAMILY OR MORE	
				EXPENSES IF 2 FAMILY OR MORE	

PF	PFD	BC–S	A	N	HEALTH C.

RANGE	REMARKS	MLS NO.
WASHER		
DRYER		INCL. DATES
REFRIGERATOR		
DISHWASHER		

This agreement, made this ....day of ...., 19...... by and between ....
.... owner, address.. and
.............:................................, REALTOR.

That in consideration of your agreement to use your best efforts to sell the property described in this agreement at the price of $......, or at such price as we may subsequently agree upon, in consideration of your agreement to submit this listing for dissemination through the Multiple Listing Service of Otsego-Delaware, I/we hereby appoint you as exclusive agent and grant to you the sole and exclusive right to sell, lease or exchange this property and agree to refer to you all inquires about, or offers, for the property.

I/we agree that whenever, during the term of this agreement the property shall have been sold, leased or exchanged or, a customer procured, ready, willing and able to buy, lease or exchange property on the terms authorized by me/us, I/we will pay to you a commission of.... %of the gross sale price with a commission fee division ..../............. or, in the case of a lease or exchange of said property, the

selling broker   listing broker

commission which is customary and prevailing in the area served by the Otsego-Delaware Multiple Listing Service, whether the transaction shall be affected by you, me/us or any other person or corporation. I/we understand that you as the **REALTOR®** or salesman in this agreement are a member of the Otsego-Delaware Multiple Listing Service and that this listing will be referred to all members of the Otsego-Delaware Multiple Listing Service and its members may act as sub agents in procuring or attempting to procure a purchaser in accordance with this agreement and in the event a sale or exchange shall be made, all of the terms of this agreement shall apply to such transaction. I/we understand that if for some valid reason I/we must take the above described property off the market during the term of this agreement and subsequently the above described property is sold within.... or within the original terms of the contract whichever is longer, you the **REALTOR®** shall be entitled to full commission.

If, within...... after this agreement has terminated, the said property is sold or exchanged by me or a non-multiple listing broker to a person with whom any **REALTOR®** member has negotiated or whose name has been given by any **REALTOR®** member of the Otsego-Delaware Multiple Listing Service to the owner during the term of this agreement, you will be entitled to full commission. This contract shall remain in effect for a period of.... months from.......,19....to.......,19.... I/we hereby grant you permission to place a For Sale sign on the described property.

I/we agree to furnish a satisfactory abstract of title, deed and all other necessary papers at my/our own expense and to cooperate with the **REALTOR®** to bring about a sale or exchange.

The above information is true and correct to the best knowledge of the parties whose signatures appear below.

FIRM'S NAME	OWNER

FIRM'S ADDRESS	OWNER

by ...., **REALTOR®**
WITNESS   salesman

OWNER'S ADDRESS

To be signed in triplicate.

this service by securing a signed purchase offer, the commission has been earned, and no further performance will be required. If the buyer later refuses to complete the transaction, the broker is still entitled to compensation unless the buyer's failure is due to inability to meet a contingency previously set forth in the purchase offer. If the seller refuses to accept a purchase offer that is consistent with the listing agreement, the broker is entitled to collect the commission.

A real estate broker earns his or her commission when he or she produces a buyer willing and able to purchase on the terms prescribed by the seller. If the buyer assents to all of the terms that the seller has prescribed to the broker, "the broker cannot be deprived of his commission by the vendor's capricious or obstinate insistence upon additional and unreasonable provisions to be inserted in the contract of purchase. In such a case, the broker has done all that the vendor employed him to do . . ." (Davidson v. Stosky, 95 N.E. 753 [N.Y. 1911]).

The rights and obligations of the parties can usually be changed by the terms of the listing agreement. For example, the M.L.S. agreement at Exhibit 8–2 provides that if the property is sold by a nonauthorized person, the M.L.S. broker will be entitled to a full commission. Without such a clause, the M.L.S. broker might have to prove actual damages to recover.

FINANCING THE PROPERTY

Introduction

When a buyer does not have enough available funds for a cash transaction, the buyer must borrow a portion of the purchase price. Typical sources for funds are banks, savings and loan associations, credit unions, the seller, private lenders, or various government lenders such as VA (Veterans Administration), FmHA (Farm Home Administration), FHA (Federal Housing Authority), and so on.

Most institutional lenders will lend from 60 percent to 80 percent of the appraisal value or the purchase price of the property, whichever is less. (Some government programs will lend up to 100 percent of the purchase price, including attorneys' fees and certain disbursements.) The remainder of the purchase price will come from your assets or an additional loan (second mortgage).

It is also important to evaluate your ability to make payments. The amount of the payment will be the same each month and will depend upon the amount borrowed, the interest rate, and the number of years over which the loan is to be repaid. Some typical "monthly factors" appear in Table 8–1.

To determine your monthly payment, multiply the factor times the number of dollars borrowed. For example, a loan of $30,000 at 10 percent for 25 years would require monthly payments approximating $272.64, computed by multiplying $30,000 by .009088.

There are various measures of how large a mortgage payment an individual can afford. A useful rule of thumb is 25 percent of family take-home pay. This has

TABLE 8-1
Monthly Interest Factors

Term of Loan	Interest Rate						
	9%	10%	11%	12%	13%	14%	15%
10 years	.012668	.013215	.013775	.014347	.014931	.015527	.016134
15 years	.010143	.010746	.011366	.012002	.012653	.013318	.013996
20 years	.008998	.009650	.010322	.011011	.011716	.012435	.013168
25 years	.008392	.009087	.009801	.010532	.011278	.012038	.012808
30 years	.008047	.008776	.009523	.010286	.011062	.011849	.012645

recently been increased to 33 to 37 percent of take-home pay. Remember that there are other costs involved in owning a home. It would be prudent before buying a home to prepare a budget, listing estimated income and expenses.

Sources of Financing

A primary source of financing is the seller of the property. A seller who is purchasing a new home may not be able to lend you any of the purchase price. Sometimes, however, the seller may have already purchased a new home, may not need the money, and may welcome the opportunity to earn a higher rate of interest than is normally available through savings accounts. If the seller lends the buyer a portion of the purchase price, the seller may sometimes take advantage of the "installment method" of reporting a gain on the sale of the home for income tax purposes (Internal Revenue Code § 453).

If the seller cannot or will not finance the buyer's purchase, the next alternative is a bank, savings and loan association, or credit union. Generally, a loan application and interview will be required (see Exhibit 8–3). The information obtained is used by the loan officers or a loan committee to evaluate the borrower's ability to repay. A loan application requires substantial personal and financial data. A banker, real estate salesperson, or accountant could provide assistance in the preparation of this form. If the first lending institution refuses to grant a loan, you should submit another application to a second institution. Frequently, a rejection is based on the lender's lack of funds rather than the borrower's financial status. If the lender approves the loan, a commitment letter will be issued (Exhibit 8–4), stating the amount and terms of the loan. Once the commitment letter is received, the attorneys can prepare the papers for closing.

The early 1980s saw mortgage rates soar. Commercial lenders refused to lend except at very high rates, which buyers refused to (or could not) pay. As a result buyers, sellers, and their brokers and lawyers came up with numerous "creative financing" techniques. Buyers no longer shop for homes; they shop for financing. As many as 75 percent of all real estate transactions today involve creative financing as opposed to 10 to 15 percent in the late 1970s. There are a multitude of variations of creative financing, limited in nature only by the imaginations of the parties.

EXHIBIT 8-3
Residential Loan Application

NATIONAL BANK & TRUST COMPANY OF NORWICH

RESIDENTIAL LOAN APPLICATION

MORTGAGE APPLIED FOR	☐ Conventional ☐ FHA ☐ VA	Amount $	Interest Rate %	No. of Months	Monthly Payment Principal & Interest $	Escrow/Impounds (to be collected monthly) ☐ Taxes ☐ Hazard Ins. ☐ Mtg. Ins.

Prepayment Option

SUBJECT PROPERTY

Property Street Address	City	County	State	Zip	No. Units

Legal Description (Attach description if necessary)				Year Built

Purpose of Loan: ☐ Purchase ☐ Construction-Permanent ☐ Construction ☐ Refinance ☐ Other (Explain)

Complete this line if Construction-Permanent or Construction Loan	Lot Value Data	Original Cost	Present Value (a)	Cost of Imps. (b)	Total (a + b)	ENTER TOTAL AS PURCHASE PRICE IN DETAILS OF ☐ PURCHASE.
Year Acquired		$	$	$	$	

Complete this line if a Refinance Loan   Purpose of Refinance   Describe Improvements [ ] made [ ] to be made

Year Acquired	Original Cost	Amt. Existing Liens				Cost: $
	$	$				

Title Will Be Held In What Name(s)   Manner In Which Title Will Be Held

Source of Down Payment and Settlement Charges

This application is designed to be completed by the borrower(s) with the lender's assistance. The Co-Borrower Section and all other Co-Borrower questions must be completed and the appropriate box(es) checked if ☐ another person will be jointly obligated with the Borrower on the loan, or ☐ the Borrower is relying on income from alimony, child support or separate maintenance or on the income or assets of another person as a basis for repayment of the loan, or ☐ the Borrower is married and resides, or the property is located, in a community property state.

BORROWER				CO-BORROWER			
Name		Age	School Yrs	Name		Age	School Yrs
Present Address No. Years ___ ☐ Own ☐ Rent				Present Address No. Years ___ ☐ Own ☐ Rent			
Street				Street			
City/State/Zip				City/State/Zip			
Former address if less than 2 years at present address				Former address if less than 2 years at present address			
Street				Street			
City/State/Zip				City/State/Zip			
Years at former address ☐ Own ☐ Rent				Years at former address ☐ Own ☐ Rent			
Marital Status ☐ Married ☐ Separated ☐ Unmarried (incl. single, divorced, widowed)	DEPENDENTS OTHER THAN LISTED BY CO-BORROWER NO. AGES			Marital Status ☐ Married ☐ Separated ☐ Unmarried (incl. single, divorced, widowed)	DEPENDENTS OTHER THAN LISTED BY BORROWER NO. AGES		
Name and Address of Employer	Years employed in this line of work or profession? ___ years Years on this job ___ ☐ Self Employed*			Name and Address of Employer	Years employed in this line of work or profession? ___ years Years on this job ___ ☐ Self Employed*		
Position/Title	Type of Business			Position/Title	Type of Business		
Social Security Number***	Home Phone	Business Phone		Social Security Number***	Home Phone	Business Phone	

GROSS MONTHLY INCOME				MONTHLY HOUSING EXPENSE**			DETAILS OF PURCHASE	
Item	Borrower	Co-Borrower	Total		PRESENT	PROPOSED	Do Not Complete If Refinance	
Base Empl. Income	$	$	$	Rent	$		a. Purchase Price	$
Overtime				First Mortgage (P&I)		$	b. Total Closing Costs (Est.)	
Bonuses				Other Financing (P&I)			c. Prepaid Escrows (Est.)	
Commissions				Hazard Insurance			d. Total (a + b + c)	$
Dividends/Interest				Real Estate Taxes			e. Amount This Mortgage	( )
Net Rental Income				Mortgage Insurance			f. Other Financing	( )
Other† (Before completing, see notice under Describe Other Income below.)				Homeowner Assn. Dues			g. Other Equity	( )
				Other:			h. Amount of Cash Deposit	( )
				Total Monthly Pmt.	$	$	i. Closing Costs Paid by Seller	( )
				Utilities			j. Cash Reqd. For Closing (Est.)	$
Total	$	$	$	Total	$	$		

DESCRIBE OTHER INCOME		
☐ B—Borrower C—Co-Borrower	NOTICE:† Alimony, child support, or separate maintenance income need not be revealed if the Borrower or Co-Borrower does not choose to have it considered as a basis for repaying this loan.	Monthly Amount $

IF EMPLOYED IN CURRENT POSITION FOR LESS THAN TWO YEARS COMPLETE THE FOLLOWING						
B/C	Previous Employer/School	City/State	Type of Business	Position/Title	Dates From/To	Monthly Income
						$

THESE QUESTIONS APPLY TO BOTH BORROWER AND CO-BORROWER

If a "yes" answer is given to a question in this column, explain on an attached sheet.	Borrower Yes or No	Co-Borrower Yes or No	If applicable, explain Other Financing or Other Equity (provide addendum if more space is needed).
Have you any outstanding judgments? In the last 7 years, have you been declared bankrupt?			
Have you had property foreclosed upon or given title or deed in lieu thereof?			
Are you a co-maker or endorser on a note?			
Are you a party in a law suit?			
Are you obligated to pay alimony, child support, or separate maintenance?			
Is any part of the down payment borrowed?			

*FHLMC/FNMA require business credit report, signed Federal Income Tax returns for last two years, and, if available, audited Profit and Loss Statements plus balance sheet for same period.
**All Present Monthly Housing Expenses of Borrower and Co-Borrower should be listed on a combined basis.
***Neither FHLMC nor FNMA requires this information.

FHLMC 65 Rev. 8/78   FNMA 1003 Rev. 8/78

EXHIBIT 8-3, cont.

NATIONAL BANK & TRUST COMPANY OF NORWICH

RESIDENTIAL LOAN APPLICATION

MORTGAGE APPLIED FOR ☐	☐ Conventional ☐ FHA ☐ VA	Amount $	Interest Rate %	No. of Months	Monthly Payment Principal & Interest $	Escrow/Impounds (to be collected monthly) ☐ Taxes ☐ Hazard Ins. ☐ Mtg. Ins. ☐

Prepayment Option

SUBJECT PROPERTY

Property Street Address	City	County	State	Zip	No. Units

Legal Description (Attach description if necessary)	Year Built

Purpose of Loan: ☐ Purchase ☐ Construction-Permanent ☐ Construction ☐ Refinance ☐ Other (Explain)

Complete this line if Construction-Permanent or Construction Loan ☐	Lot Value Data	Original Cost	Present Value (a)	Cost of Imps. (b)	Total (a + b)	ENTER TOTAL AS PURCHASE PRICE IN DETAILS OF PURCHASE.
	Year Acquired	$	$	$	$	

Complete this line if a Refinance Loan

Year Acquired	Original Cost	Amt. Existing Liens	Purpose of Refinance	Describe Improvements [ ] made [ ] to be made
$	$	$		Cost: $

Title Will Be Held In What Name(s)	Manner In Which Title Will Be Held

Source of Down Payment and Settlement Charges

This application is designed to be completed by the borrower(s) with the lender's assistance. The Co-Borrower Section and all other Co-Borrower questions must be completed and the appropriate box(es) checked if ☐ another person will be jointly obligated with the Borrower on the loan, or ☐ the Borrower is relying on income from alimony, child support or separate maintenance or on the income or assets of another person as a basis for repayment of the loan, or ☐ the Borrower is married and resides, or the property is located, in a community property state.

BORROWER				CO-BORROWER			
Name		Age	School Yrs	Name		Age	School Yrs
Present Address No. Years ___ ☐ Own ☐ Rent				Present Address No. Years ___ ☐ Own ☐ Rent			
Street				Street			
City/State/Zip				City/State/Zip			
Former address if less than 2 years at present address				Former address if less than 2 years at present address			
Street				Street			
City/State/Zip				City/State/Zip			
Years at former address ☐ Own ☐ Rent				Years at former address ☐ Own ☐ Rent			
Marital Status ☐ Married ☐ Separated ☐ Unmarried (incl. single, divorced, widowed)	DEPENDENTS OTHER THAN LISTED BY CO-BORROWER NO. AGES			Marital Status ☐ Married ☐ Separated ☐ Unmarried (incl. single, divorced, widowed)	DEPENDENTS OTHER THAN LISTED BY BORROWER NO. AGES		
Name and Address of Employer		Years employed in this line of work or profession? ___ years Years on this job ___ ☐ Self Employed*		Name and Address of Employer		Years employed in this line of work or profession? ___ years Years on this job ___ ☐ Self Employed*	
Position/Title	Type of Business			Position/Title	Type of Business		
Social Security Number***	Home Phone	Business Phone		Social Security Number***	Home Phone	Business Phone	

GROSS MONTHLY INCOME				MONTHLY HOUSING EXPENSE**			DETAILS OF PURCHASE	
Item	Borrower	Co-Borrower	Total		PRESENT	PROPOSED	Do Not Complete If Refinance	
Base Empl. Income	$	$	$	Rent	$		a. Purchase Price	$
Overtime				First Mortgage (P&I)		$	b. Total Closing Costs (Est.)	
Bonuses				Other Financing (P&I)			c. Prepaid Escrows (Est.)	
Commissions				Hazard Insurance			d. Total (a + b + c)	$
Dividends/Interest				Real Estate Taxes			e. Amount This Mortgage	( )
Net Rental Income				Mortgage Insurance			f. Other Financing	( )
Other† (Before completing, see notice under Describe Other Income below.)				Homeowner Assn. Dues			g. Other Equity	( )
				Other:			h. Amount of Cash Deposit	( )
				Total Monthly Pmt.	$	$	i. Closing Costs Paid by Seller	( )
				Utilities			j. Cash Reqd. For Closing (Est.)	$
Total	$	$	$	Total	$	$		

DESCRIBE OTHER INCOME

▷ B—Borrower C—Co-Borrower

NOTICE:† Alimony, child support, or separate maintenance income need not be revealed if the Borrower or Co-Borrower does not choose to have it considered as a basis for repaying this loan.

	Monthly Amount
	$

IF EMPLOYED IN CURRENT POSITION FOR LESS THAN TWO YEARS COMPLETE THE FOLLOWING

B/C	Previous Employer/School	City/State	Type of Business	Position/Title	Dates From/To	Monthly Income
						$

THESE QUESTIONS APPLY TO BOTH BORROWER AND CO-BORROWER

If a "yes" answer is given to a question in this column, explain on an attached sheet.	Borrower Yes or No	Co-Borrower Yes or No	If applicable, explain Other Financing or Other Equity (provide addendum if more space is needed).
Have you any outstanding judgments? In the last 7 years, have you been declared bankrupt?			
Have you had property foreclosed upon or given title or deed in lieu thereof?			
Are you a co-maker or endorser on a note?			
Are you a party in a law suit?			
Are you obligated to pay alimony, child support, or separate maintenance?			
Is any part of the down payment borrowed?			

*FHLMC/FNMA require business credit report, signed Federal Income Tax returns for last two years, and, if available, audited Profit and Loss Statements plus balance sheet for same period.
**All Present Monthly Housing Expenses of Borrower and Co-Borrower should be listed on a combined basis.
***Neither FHLMC nor FNMA requires this information.

EXHIBIT 8-3, cont.

7. **EXISTING CONDITIONS:**
Seller to convey good and marketable title by _____, Deed with the appropriate N.Y.S. transfer tax, subject to easements and restrictions of record, and a 40 year Title Abstract continued to date, and may use part of the purchase money to pay existing encumbrances. Should the property be damaged by fire or other casualty before the passing of title, the Buyer has the option to withdraw and receive his deposit.

8. **ADJUSTMENTS:**
Interests, rents, fuel, taxes and insurance to be adjusted as of the date of transfer of title.

9. **PROPERTY INCLUDED IN SALE OF PREMISES:**
Plumbing, heating, lighting fixtures, built-in bathroom and kitchen cabinets, built-in kitchen appliances, venetian blinds, shades, storm windows and screens, storm and screen doors, awnings, pumps, shrubbery and television aerials, if now in or on said premises are represented to be owned by the Seller, free from all liens and encumbrances, and are included in the sale price together with the following items: _____

_____

10. **CONDITION OF PREMISES:**
The Purchaser has inspected the buildings standing on the premises and the personal property included in this sale and is thoroughly acquainted with their condition and agrees to take title "as is" and in their present condition and subject to reasonable use, wear, and natural deterioration between the date thereof and the transfer of title.

11. **REAL ESTATE BROKER:**
The parties agree that _____ brought about this sale and the Seller agrees to pay a professional fee as per listing agreement.

12. **DEPOSITS:**
It is agreed that the Broker shall hold any and all deposits made by the Purchaser in an escrow account until date of transfer of title, date of proper cancellation of this contract, or by written mutual consent of the parties, whichever shall first occur.

13. **TRANSFER OF TITLE:**
Deed to be delivered on or about ____ _____ at the office of

_____

14. **POSSESSION:**
Possession to be as of the date of transfer of title.

15. **ENTIRE AGREEMENT:**
This contract contains all agreements of the parties thereto. There are no promises, agreements, terms, conditions, warranties, representations or statements other than contained herein. This agreement shall apply to and bind the heirs, legal representatives, successors and assigns of the respective parties.

This agreement is made as of the _____ date of _____ 19 _____ .

PURCHASER _____   SELLER_____

PURCHASER _____   SELLER_____

Purchaser's Address   Seller's Address

_____   _____

Phone No. _____   Phone No. _____

EXHIBIT 8-4
Mortgage Loan Commitment Letter

XYZ BANK
Main Street
Oneonta, N.Y.

Robert & Sarah Rothenberg
217 Gilbert Street
Sidney, New York 13838

Dear Mr. and Mrs. Rothenberg:

MORTGAGE LOAN CONDITIONS AND TERMS

We are pleased to advise you that our Real Estate Mortgage Committee has approved your mortgage loan application to purchase property owned by Steven and Carole Blumenkrantz. The loan is in the amount of $38,900 and is payable $388.37 per month for 20 years, which includes interest at the rate of 10.5 percent per annum. This loan will be secured by a first mortgage with no intervening liens and with marketable title on real estate property located at 39 Circle Lane, Oneonta, N.Y.

LATE PAYMENT FEE, NONASSUMPTION CLAUSE, AND PREPAYMENT PRIVILEGE

The mortgage will contain a penalty of 2 percent per monthly payment if the mortgage payment is not made within 15 days of the due date. We also reserve the right to ask for payment in full of the mortgage if the property is sold. You will have the right to prepay any part of the mortgage at any time without penalty.

TRUTH-IN-LENDING (REGULATION Z) NOTIFICATION

Current regulations require that you be notified of the approximate costs of the transaction. This information is contained in the enclosed disclosure statement.

INSTRUCTIONS FOR CLOSING LOAN

Please forward to your attorney the abstract of title, recent land and school tax receipts, and any maps or surveys or other items pertaining to the real estate. We will forward our instructions to him to be used in connection with the mortgage. At such time as the legal work has been completed, a closing time may be arranged by the attorney. *Please bring your current fire insurance policy with you to the closing.* An endorsement must be obtained showing The XYZ Bank of Oneonta as first mortgagee. The amount should be at least equal to the amount of the mortgage.

ACCEPTANCE OF LOAN COMMITMENT

If the above conditions are agreeable, please indicate your acceptance by signing and returning a copy of this letter to us.

THE MORTGAGE LOAN COMMITMENT

This commitment to close the loan, which is nonassignable, will expire if the loan is not closed within 90 days or your acceptance is not received within 15 days of this letter. Our

EXHIBIT 8-4, cont.

obligation to make this loan will terminate if either of these conditions is not met without a written extension from us. An extension may be made at our option. If requested, the extension may be granted with the interest rate changed to reflect the prevailing rate at the time the request for the extension is made. Please let us know if there are any other questions regarding this transaction.

Sincerely,

David R. Banker
Vice-President

ACCEPTANCE OF THE XYZ BANK OF
ONEONTA MORTGAGE COMMITMENT

RECEIPT OF DISCLOSURE STATEMENT

I/we acknowledge receipt of a completed copy of the attached DISCLOSURE STATEMENT before signing the ACCEPTANCE below:

Date_____, 19 _____   _____
                                                    Signature of Borrower

                                                    _____
                                                    Signature of Borrower

ACCEPTANCE OF MORTGAGE LOAN COMMITMENT

I/we accept the mortgage loan commitment as outlined in the letter dated _____ , which is incorporated in this acceptance form. I/we acknowledge that I/we have received and familiarized ourselves with the contents of the enclosed mortgage loan commitment letter. I/we also agree to authorize the XYZ Bank of Oneonta, New York, to issue mortgage loan closing instructions for the loan stated above to my/our attorney for preparation of the necessary legal documents and agree to assume the financial responsibility to pay my/our attorney for the work done. My/our attorney representing me/us in this mortgage loan is _____.

Date_____, 19 _____   _____
                                                    Signature of Borrower

                                                    _____
                                                    Signature of Borrower

WPC/dgl
Enclosures

Many such variations are oriented toward reducing the buyer's initial payments (either down payment or mortgage payment or both). However, the net result is often to increase the buyer's burden somewhere down the road. It is imperative, when dealing with creative financing techniques, that the buyer understand all short-term and long-term implications of the loan agreement.

TYPES OF OWNERSHIP

It is important for the buyer to understand types of tenancies in order to be able to make intelligent decisions as to how to acquire title. Signatures on a purchase offer or contract agreement or both, together with the wording of the agreement, may dictate the manner in which the deed will be transferred, and this may make a difference in the disposition of the property on the death of one of the owners. There are several common methods of holding title that will be discussed in this chapter: tenancy in severalty, joint tenancy, tenancy by the entirety, and tenancy in common and community property.

Tenancy in Severalty

Tenancy in severalty is the sole ownership of property by a single individual (or entity). A sole owner of property has the greatest degree of flexibility in its use since no other individual has to be consulted as to its disposition. Upon the death of an owner in severalty, the property passes to the heirs (by will or intestacy). In the case of married persons who own property in severalty, state laws may grant their spouses certain interests in their property (dower, courtesy, community property).

Joint Tenancy

Joint tenancy, with right of survivorship, is the ownership of property in equal interests by two or more persons (including a husband and wife), where, upon the death of any one of them, the survivor or survivors acquire the decedent's interest in the property. Joint tenancies are recognized in all states except Louisiana, Ohio, and Oregon. If purchasers take title to property as joint tenants, each has the right to the use of the entire property. Each tenant has a right to enjoy the whole, using it fully without detriment to the other owners (Wisel v. Terhune, 204 P.2d 286 [Okla. 1949]). If joint tenancy is desired, the deed must reflect that fact with the following words: "to X and Y as joint tenants, with right to survivorship and not as tenants in common."

A joint tenancy must be created under four specific conditions. First, there must be "unity of time." Each joint tenant must acquire ownership at the same moment. The second condition is "unity of title." Joint tenants must acquire their interests from the same source. Some states allow a present owner of property to transfer title to himself or herself and another in order to create a joint tenancy. Other states do not allow such transfers. The third condition is "unity of interest."

This requires that each co-owner own an equal percentage interest and also that the nature of each interest be the same. The fourth condition is "unity of possession." This requires that each owner of the property have the unlimited use of the entire property. Joint owners cannot agree that one shall own the land and the other the house. Such an agreement would defeat a joint ownership.

Tenancy by the Entirety

Tenancy by the entirety is a method of ownership available only to married couples. It is recognized in the following states: Alaska, Arkansas, Delaware, District of Columbia, Florida, Hawaii, Indiana, Kentucky, Maryland, Massachusetts, Michigan, Mississippi, Missouri, New Jersey, New York, North Carolina, Ohio, Oklahoma, Oregon, Pennsylvania, Rhode Island, Tennessee, Utah, Vermont, Virginia, West Virginia, and Wyoming. The property owned by tenants by the entirety is considered to be owned by the legal entity created by the marriage contract. The rights of the various tenants are similar to that of joint tenancy. The right of survivorship exists, and the parties are entitled to use of the property as a whole. The major difference is that a joint tenant can convey his or her interest to a third party; a tenant by the entirety cannot. The intent of the parties to hold the property as tenants by the entirety must be clear, and the wording in the deed should be "to A and B, husband and wife, as tenants by the entirety with right of survivorship." A tenancy by the entirety requires the same four conditions as a joint tenancy plus a fifth condition. The parties must be husband and wife when they acquire their interests in the property.

Tenancy in Common

Tenancy in common is a form of ownership of real property by two or more persons in equal or unequal interests, where each holds a "severable interest." Tenancies in common are recognized by all states except Louisiana. Upon the death of any tenant in common, the estate of the deceased owner should acquire the title to the deceased's former interest in the property (Woodward v. Congdon, 83 A. 433, [R.I. 1912]). There is no right of survivorship; however, the parties take possession and have the same rights to enjoyment as in the other tenancies. Any tenancy that does not specifically show intent as to the type of ownership will be construed as a tenancy in common except if the parties are married, in which case, it would be construed as a tenancy by the entirety in states that recognize such a tenancy. For creating a tenancy in common, the only condition that is required is "unity of possession."

Community Property

Community property is a form of property ownership (applicable to both real and personal property), that dates back to French and Spanish civil law (as opposed to English common law), and it is recognized today in only a few states: Arizona, California, Idaho, Louisiana, New Mexico, Nevada, Texas, Washington, and (to some degree) Oklahoma. Minor differences will exist from state to state.

In community property states, the law generally recognizes two kinds of property: separate and community. Generally, separate property is created prior to the marriage, and community property is created after the marriage. If property is acquired after marriage as the result of the toil, talent, thrift, energy, industry, or other productive faculty of either spouse and irrespective of who takes title or in what manner (i.e., joint tenancy, tenancy in common), the property is community property. Community property is held for the benefit of both spouses irrespective of the titleholder, and irrespective of the source of the funds.

Upon the death of one spouse, the community property is divided into two portions: the decedent's and the survivor's. The survivor's share becomes his or her separate property. The decedent's share passes to his or her heirs. This may be governed by will or by laws of intestacy. (See Chapters 11 and 12.)

PURCHASE OFFERS AND BINDER AGREEMENTS

Once a buyer has been found who is ready, willing, and able to purchase the property, it is customary to enter into a binder agreement (Exhibit 8–5). The laws of most states require that agreements concerning the transfer of real property be in writing in order to be enforceable (e.g., N.Y. General Obligations Law § 5–703, Statute of Frauds). In the absence of a written agreement, either the buyer or seller may withdraw from the transaction any time prior to closing without further obligation. Once a written agreement has been entered into, a party who wishes to withdraw (breach the contract) may suffer a penalty! It is extremely important to specify all relevant terms in the binder agreement as changes may only be made with the consent of both parties. The binder agreement, in many cases, is the only written agreement entered into and should be reviewed with an attorney before execution.

A typical binder agreement is in the form of an offer and an acceptance. The law of contracts governs these agreements. The buyer (also known as the offeror), by signing the binder, offers to purchase the property, specifying certain terms and conditions; the seller (also known as the offeree) may either accept or reject the offer. An offer remains open until it is terminated by (1) passage of time, (2) rejection, (3) revocation, or (4) acceptance.

Termination

An offer terminates upon a stated date or event or upon the passage of a reasonable time period. A well-drafted offer will state that it terminates upon a certain date. This prevents the offer from being accepted long after the buyer has changed his or her mind about buying.

A rejection is the offeree's indication that he or she is unwilling to perform according to the terms specified in the offer. When a buyer offers to purchase the property on the terms stated in the listing agreement, it is reasonable to assume

EXHIBIT 8-5
Binder Agreement

REALTOR

STANDARD FORM

CONTRACT FOR THE PURCHASE AND SALE OF REAL ESTATE

OTSEGO-DELAWARE BOARD OF REALTORS, INC.

THIS IS A LEGALLY BINDING CONTRACT: IF NOT UNDERSTOOD, WE RECOMMEND CONSULTING AN ATTORNEY BEFORE SIGNING.

1. **AGREEMENT:**

   The undersigned Seller agrees to sell and the undersigned Purchaser agrees to purchase the premises including all buildings and improvements thereon under all terms and conditions stated herein.

2. **PROPERTY DESCRIPTION OF THE PREMISES:**

   The property being sold and purchased is _____

   _____

   _____

3. **PURCHASE PRICE:**

   The full purchase price is to be paid as follows:

   Deposit on signing this agreement . . . . $_____

   Additional deposit on _____ or upon acceptance by Seller . . . . $_____

   In cash or certified check upon the transfer of title . . . . $_____

   By Purchaser assuming and agreeing to pay a mortgage, now a recorded lien on the premises upon which there is an unpaid estimated principal amount of . . . . $_____

   Total . . . . $_____

   Deposit check accepted subject to collection.

4. **MORTGAGE CONTINGENCY:**

   This agreement is contingent upon Purchaser obtaining a mortgage loan of $ _____ . Purchaser agrees to use diligent efforts to obtain said approval. This contingency shall be deemed waived unless Purchaser shall notify _____ by certified or registered mail, return receipt requested, no later than _____, together with written proof of his inability to obtain said approval. If the Purchaser so notifies, then this agreement shall be deemed cancelled, null and void and all deposits made hereunder shall be returned to Purchaser.

5. **FHA OR VA MORTGAGE:**

   If the Purchaser applies for an FHA Insured Mortgage or a VA Guaranteed Mortgage, it is expressly agreed that, notwithstanding any other provisions of this contract, the Purchaser shall not be obligated to complete the purchase of the property described herein or to incur any penalty for forfeiture of earnest money deposits or otherwise unless the Seller has delivered to the Purchaser a written statement issued by the Federal Housing Commissioner or the Veterans' Administration setting forth the appraised value of the property (excluding closing costs) of not less than $_____ which statement the Seller hereby agrees to deliver to the Purchaser promptly after such appraised value statement is made available to the Seller. The Purchaser shall, however have the privilege and option of proceeding with the consummation of the contract without regard to the amount of the appraised valuation made by the Federal Housing Commissioner or the Veterans' Administration. Furthermore, the FHA appraised valuation is arrived at to determine the maximum mortgage the Department of Housing and Urban Development will insure. HUD does not warrant the value or the condition of the property. The Purchaser should satisfy himself/herself that the price and the condition of the property are acceptable.

6. **OTHER CONTINGENCIES:**

   a. _____

   _____

   b. _____

   _____

   c. _____

   _____

that the seller will accept. However, acceptance is not assured. The seller may elect to reject the offer, and the buyer has no recourse. (The broker may insist on a commission and will probably be able to collect it.) (See Westhill Exports, Limited v. Pope, 191 N.E. 2d 447, [N.Y. 1963]). Until there is a written acceptance of his offer, the buyer has no rights in or to the property. A seller's indication of willingness to perform in a manner different from that specified in the offer is a rejection of the offer and is considered to be a counteroffer. The seller is saying to the buyer, ''I do not accept your terms but will sell if you agree to the following terms.'' The seller has now become the offeror; and the buyer, the offeree.

A revocation occurs where the buyer (offeror) withdraws the offer before the seller (offeree) accepts it. Any offer, whether it meets the terms of the listing agreement or not, can be revoked provided the seller has not accepted it. Submission of the offer to the broker does not affect this right because the broker, although he or she is the agent of the seller, is generally not authorized to accept offers. If the broker is so authorized and has, in fact, accepted the offer, it is too late for the buyer to revoke.

Contents of Purchase Offer

An acceptance also terminates an offer. The offer and acceptance merge to form the binder agreement. In order to have a valid binder agreement, certain terms must be specified: price, identity of the property, and the identity of the buyer and seller.

The binder agreement, as shown in Exhibit 8–5, identifies the property. The description will often be just a street address or road name and approximate acreage. The legal description of the property, which will appear on the deed, will be supplied later.

The binder also states the purchase price, the method of payment, the broker who brought about the agreement (who is entitled to the commission), and the name of each party's attorney. Frequently, property other than land and buildings will be transferred from the seller to the buyer. These items should also be set forth in the binder. Certain items such as hot water heaters, furnaces, built-in appliances, sinks, and so on start as personal property but may become real property when they are attached to the house structure. Permanent flora (e.g., trees, bushes, bulbs) are also generally considered to be fixtures. The status of other items may be more questionable. It is imperative to list all items of personal property that are being sold with a house. This may include carpets (including the wall-to-wall variety), appliances, and lighting fixtures as well as items of furniture that are clearly personal property. Failure to list these items may lead to disputes and ultimately a lawsuit. If an item is not listed, it is generally not included.

Conditions

A binder agreement should list any conditions that may have to be fulfilled before the agreement becomes operative. The most common such condition is the method of financing. In some cases, the seller will be holding the mortgage. The binder should state the mortgage terms (interest rate, term, monthly payment, and so on). Where financing is to be secured from a third party, either a lending institution or privately, the binder should state that the offer is conditioned upon obtaining financing and should further state the amount, rate, and term of payment required. In periods of rapidly changing interest rates, fluctuations of ½ to 1 percent or more may occur within a two-week period.

Example: If a condition states that the offer is subject to financing of $38,900.00 at 10.5 percent over 20 years and the lending institution insists on an 11 percent rate or a 15-year period, the condition has not been met, and the purchase offer is not effective. Both parties are thereby released from the agreement without any further liability, and the offeror will be entitled to the return of any deposit.

Many offers for purchase of residences are contingent upon the buyer's selling a present residence within a particular time period. If the buyer cannot sell an existing home, the condition is not met, and the parties are no longer bound. Buyers may also be concerned about the structural adequacy of the premises or its suitability for certain uses (such as the operation of a professional business from a home). In such cases, the purchase offer should be conditioned upon reports from surveyors, engineers, termite inspectors, and so on, or upon obtaining clearance from the village or city officials regarding the intended use.

In the event that a husband and wife are purchasing property and both sign, the offer will often continue to be effective upon the death of either (many purchase offers have clauses stating that the agreement is binding upon heirs, executors, administrators, and assigns). If a buyer wishes to avoid this, the purchase offer must state that it is conditioned upon both parties' being alive at the date of closing.

Possession

Binders also specify when the buyer is to receive possession from the seller. This should be as close to the date of closing as possible. Occasionally, the buyer may wish to move some of his other property into the premises earlier than closing, or the seller may wish to remain on the premises for a short period after closing. This raises such questions as whether the owner should receive rent, who will be liable for any damage that may occur, who is responsible for insurance premiums, and so on. Frequently, such an overlap of possession will take place, but its duration should be kept to a minimum.

Down Payment

A buyer will generally make a small down payment ($50 to $500) when the purchase offer is rendered, which may be increased to 10 percent of the purchase price upon the signing of a formal contract. This deposit is held in escrow by an escrow agent, usually the realtor or the attorney for either party. Moneys held in escrow belong to the person who deposited them, but cannot be released by the escrow agent except for specified purposes (i.e., payment to seller at closing). If the purchase offer has stipulations, such as prior sale of the buyer's home or approval of financing, which are not met, the escrow deposit must be returned to the buyer. If the closing fails to take place, the escrow agent will not pay the money to either party until both have agreed on its disposition. In the event that the seller does not accept the buyer's offer, the money in escrow is refunded to the buyer.

Closing

The binder offer specifies the date on which closing (the legal transfer of title from seller to buyer) is to take place and where. In the case of a cash or seller-financed transaction, this usually takes place at the office of the seller's attorney; in the case of an institutionally financed transaction, this will usually be at the office of the lending institution.

There is generally a time period between entering into a binder agreement or a formal contract and closing. This period allows the various parties time to prepare for the closing. The seller's attorney needs to prepare a deed, bring the title up to date, and so on. The buyer's attorney needs time to obtain financing, prepare necessary bonds and mortgages, and review the title submitted by the seller's attorney. Thirty days is considered an adequate period for these transactions to take place, but this may vary.

The specified closing date is usually not a critical factor. Frequently, parties will anticipate a given closing date and for any of a number of reasons will be unable to meet that date. Postponements that are ''reasonable'' in duration and frequency can usually be obtained. If it is extremely important to either party to close on a specified date, a clause must be inserted in the purchase offer stating that ''time is of the essence.'' In the presence of such a clause, failure to complete the closing as scheduled terminates the contract. If the buyer is responsible for the failure to perform he or she will lose the deposit and may be liable for further damages. If the seller fails to perform, the buyer may have the option of being reimbursed for his or her costs or insisting on specific performance of the contract. In the event that the seller fails to perform, it is also possible that the broker may be entitled to a commission.

Parties' Signatures

All binders should be signed by both the buyers and sellers. It is not necessary to have a witness sign the agreement in order for the signatures to be effective. A signature by a husband or wife will not bind the other party if both have an ownership interest.

Examples: Several different situations could occur: assume in each case that Mr. and Mrs. B are potential buyers and Mr. and Mrs. S are the owners of the house:

A. Mr. B. only signs the purchase offer, and Mr. and Mrs. S both sign the acceptance. The purchase offer is binding only upon Mr. B and the sellers. Mrs. B, who has not signed the binder, is not liable. If Mr. B dies, his surviving spouse is not liable.

B. One or both buyers sign, and only Mr. S signs. Assuming the sellers own the property as husband and wife (tenants by the entirety), the contract is not binding upon the sellers and, therefore, there is no transaction.

C. Assuming that the purchase offer at Paragraph 1 states Mr. and Mrs. B agree to purchase the seller's property . . ., only Mr. B signs the agreement, and both sellers sign. The agreement is not binding since it is clearly intended that both husband and wife are to be buyers, and only one has signed the purchase offer.

Additional clauses may appear on a purchase offer to the effect that the agreement is binding on the parties, their heirs, executors, administrators, and assigns. This clause would require the parties to perform even if one or more of the buyers or sellers dies or if the buyers transfer their rights to a different buyer. If the heirs are bound, this might change several of the situations outlined earlier (for example, if only Mr. B signed a purchase offer and Mrs. B refused to sign, only Mr. B would be liable. If Mr. B dies before closing, Mrs. B would be obligated to purchase the property if she is Mr. B's heir under state law).

Assignment

The right of a buyer to assign a contract must be carefully considered before being granted by a seller. In most cases, the seller or seller's agent does a preliminary credit check on the buyer. If the buyer were free to substitute a new buyer, the seller would have no knowledge as to that party's financial responsibility. If a lending institution is involved, the seller may not object. However, if the seller is going to hold the mortgage, it is imperative that the new buyer meet with the approval of the seller.

PURCHASE CONTRACTS

Many homes are bought and sold without the benefit of a formal contract, with reliance only on the binder agreement. A binder agreement is usually limited with respect to the items covered, and, therefore, it is advisable to have a contract drawn, and it is essential if there are any additional items in the sale, aside from the land and the structures attached (e.g., going business, farm animals). If there are conditions as to the terms of closing, (time, place, and the like) or conditions as to types of personal property to be included in the sale, a contract is also advisable. In urban areas, a formal contract is generally used. A typical contract is shown in Exhibit 8–6.

Additional clauses could be added to the standard contract in a rider. These additional clauses should include all representations made by either the purchaser or

EXHIBIT 8-6
Contract of Purchase

Standard N.Y.B.T.U. Form 8041 • 4-76-70M — Contract of Sale

CONSULT YOUR LAWYER BEFORE SIGNING THIS INSTRUMENT—THIS INSTRUMENT SHOULD BE USED BY LAWYERS ONLY.

NOTE: FIRE LOSSES. This form of contract contains no express provision as to risk of loss by fire or other casualty before delivery of the deed. Unless express provision is made, the provisions of Section 5-1311 of the General Obligations Law will apply. This section also places risk of loss upon purchaser if title or possession is transferred prior to closing.

THIS AGREEMENT, made the   day of   , nineteen hundred and
BETWEEN

hereinafter described as the seller, and

hereinafter described as the purchaser,

WITNESSETH, that the seller agrees to sell and convey, and the purchaser agrees to purchase, all that certain plot, piece or parcel of land, with the buildings and improvements thereon erected, situate, lying and being in the

the seller during negotiations that were relied upon by either of the parties. Such items would include financing and condition of premises (termite inspection, premises tended, rooms swept, and so on). In addition, those items of personalty that would not be included because of lack of space in the standard clause of the contract should be included in the rider. No item should be left out of a contract that was agreed to by all the parties. Failure to include a particular representation will most likely bar an action for recovery or for damages pursuant to the statute of frauds or the parol evidence rule or both.

EXHIBIT 8-6, cont.

1. This sale includes all right, title and interest, if any, of the seller in and to any land lying in the bed of any street, road or avenue opened or proposed, in front of or adjoining said premises, to the center line thereof, and all right, title and interest of the seller in and to any award made or to be made in lieu thereof and in and to any unpaid award for damage to said premises by reason of change of grade of any street; and the seller will execute and deliver to the purchaser, on closing of title, or thereafter, on demand, all proper instruments for the conveyance of such title and the assignment and collection of any such award.

EXHIBIT 8-6, cont.

2. The price is

Dollars, payable as follows:

Dollars,

on the signing of this contract, by check subject to collection, the receipt of which is hereby acknowledged;

Dollars,

in cash or good certified check to the order of the seller on the delivery of the deed as hereinafter provided;

Dollars,

by taking title subject to a   mortgage now a lien on said premises in that amount, bearing interest at the rate of   per cent per annum, the principal being due and payable

Dollars,

by the purchaser or assigns executing, acknowledging and delivering to the seller a bond or, at the option of the seller, a note secured by a purchase money   mortgage on the above premises, in that amount, payable

together with interest at the rate of   per cent per annum payable

3. Any bond or note and mortgage to be given hereunder shall be drawn on the standard forms of New York Board of Title Underwriters for mortgages of like lien; and shall be drawn by the attorney for the seller at the expense of the purchaser, who shall also pay the mortgage recording tax and recording fees.

4. If such purchase money mortgage is to be a subordinate mortgage on the premises it shall provide that it shall be subject and subordinate to the lien   of the existing   mortgage   of $, any extensions thereof and to any mortgage   or consolidated mortgage   which may be placed on the premises in lieu thereof, and to any extensions thereof provided (a) that the interest rate thereof shall not be greater than   per cent per annum and (b) that, if the principal amount thereof shall exceed the amount of principal owing and unpaid on said existing mortgage   at the time of placing such new mortgage or consolidated mortgage, the excess be paid to the holder of such purchase money mortgage in reduction of the principal thereof. Such purchase money mortgage shall also provide that such payment to the holder thereof shall not alter or affect the regular installments, if any, of principal payable thereunder and shall further provide that the holder thereof will, on demand and without charge therefor, execute, acknowledge and deliver any agreement or agreements further to effectuate such subordination.

EXHIBIT 8-6, cont.

5. If there be a mortgage on the premises the seller agrees to deliver to the purchaser at the time of delivery of the deed a proper certificate executed and acknowledged by the holder of such mortgage and in form for recording, certifying as to the amount of the unpaid principal and interest thereon, date of maturity thereof and rate of interest thereon, and the seller shall pay the fees for recording such certificate. Should the mortgagee be a bank or other institution as defined in Section 274-a, Real Property Law, the mortgagee may, in lieu of the said certificate, furnish a letter signed by a duly authorized officer, or employee, or agent, containing the information required to be set forth in said certificate. Seller represents that such mortgage will not be in default at or as a result of the delivery of the deed hereunder and that neither said mortgage, nor any modification thereof contains any provision to accelerate payment, or to change any of the other terms or provisions thereof by reason of the delivery of the deed hereunder.

6. Said premises are sold and are to be conveyed subject to:

   a. Zoning regulations and ordinances of the city, town or village in which the premises lie which are not violated by existing structures.

   b. Consents by the seller or any former owner of premises for the erection of any structure or structures on, under or above any street or streets on which said premises may abut.

   c. Encroachments of stoops, areas, cellar steps, trim and cornices, if any, upon any street or highway.

7. All notes or notices of violations of law or municipal ordinances, orders or requirements noted in or issued by the Departments of Housing and Buildings, Fire, Labor, Health, or other State or Municipal Department having jurisdiction, against or affecting the premises at the date hereof, shall be complied with by the seller and the premises shall be conveyed free of the same, and this provision of this contract shall survive delivery of the deed hereunder. The seller shall furnish the purchaser with an authorization to make the necessary searches therefor.

Omit Clause 8 if the property is not in the City of New York.

8. All obligations affecting the premises incurred under the Emergency Repairs provisions of the Administrative Code of the City of New York (Sections 564-18.0, etc.) prior to the delivery of the deed shall be paid and discharged by the seller upon the delivery of the deed. This provision shall survive the delivery of the deed.

Clause 9 is usually omitted if the property is not in the City of New York.

9. If, at the time of the delivery of the deed, the premises or any part thereof shall be or shall have been affected by an assessment or assessments which are or may become payable in annual installments, of which the first installment is then a charge or lien, or has been paid, then for the purposes of this contract all the unpaid installments of any such assessment, including those which are to become due and payable after the delivery of the deed, shall be deemed to be due and payable and to be liens upon the premises affected thereby and shall be paid and discharged by the seller, upon the delivery of the deed.

10. The following are to be apportioned:

(a) Rents as and when collected. (b) Interest on mortgages. (c) Premiums on existing transferable insurance policies or renewals of those expiring prior to the closing. (d) Taxes and sewer rents, if any, on the basis of the fiscal year for which assessed. (e) Water charges on the basis of the calendar year. (f) Fuel, if any.

EXHIBIT 8-6, cont.

11. If the closing of the title shall occur before the tax rate is fixed, the apportionment of taxes shall be upon the basis of the tax rate for the next preceding year applied to the latest assessed valuation.

12. If there be a water meter on the premises, the seller shall furnish a reading to a date not more than thirty days prior to the time herein set for closing title, and the unfixed meter charge and the unfixed sewer rent, if any, based thereon for the intervening time shall be apportioned on the basis of such last reading.

13. The deed shall be the usual

deed in proper statutory short form for record and shall be duly executed and acknowledged so as to convey to the purchaser the fee simple of the said premises, free of all encumbrances, except as herein stated, and shall contain the covenant required by subdivision 5 of Section 13 of the Lien Law.

If the seller is a corporation, it will deliver to the purchaser at the time of the delivery of the deed hereunder a resolution of its Board of Directors authorizing the sale and delivery of the deed, and a certificate by the Secretary or Assistant Secretary of the corporation certifying such resolution and setting forth facts showing that the conveyance is in conformity with the requirements of Section 909 of the Business Corporation Law. The deed in such case shall contain a recital sufficient to establish compliance with said section,

14. At the closing of the title the seller shall deliver to the purchaser a certified check to the order of the recording officer of the county in which the deed is to be recorded for the amount of the documentary stamps to be affixed thereto in accordance with Article 31 of the Tax Law, and a certified check to the order of the appropriate officer for any other tax payable by reason of the delivery of the deed, and a return, if any be required, duly signed and sworn to by the seller; and the purchaser also agrees to sign and swear to the return and to cause the check and the return to be delivered to the appropriate officer promptly after the closing of title.

Omit Clause 15 if the property is not in the City of New York.

15. In addition, the seller shall at the same time deliver to the purchaser a certified check to the order of the Finance Administrator for the amount of the Real Property Transfer Tax imposed by Title II of Chapter 46 of the Administrative Code of the City of New York and will also deliver to the purchaser the return required by the said statute and the regulations issued pursuant to the authority thereof, duly signed and sworn to by the seller; the purchaser agrees to sign and swear to the return and to cause the check and the return to be delivered to the City Register promptly after the closing of the title.

16. The seller shall give and the purchaser shall accept a title such as

, a Member of the New York Board of Title Underwriters, will be willing to approve and insure.

17. All sums paid on account of this contract, and the reasonable expenses of the examination of the title to said premises and of the survey, if any, made in connection therewith are hereby made liens on said premises, but such liens shall not continue after default by the purchaser under this contract.

18. All fixtures and articles of personal property attached or appurtenant to or used in connection with said premises are represented to be owned by the seller, free from all liens and encumbrances except as herein stated, and are included in this sale; without limiting the generality of the foregoing, such fixtures and articles of personal property include plumbing, heating, lighting and cooking fixtures, air conditioning fixtures and units, ranges, refrigerators, radio and television aerials, bathroom and kitchen cabinets, mantels, door mirrors, venetian blinds, shades, screens, awnings, storm windows, window boxes, storm doors, mail boxes, weather vanes, flagpoles, pumps, shrubbery and outdoor statuary.

19. The amount of any unpaid taxes, assessments, water charges and sewer rents which the seller is obligated to pay and discharge, with the interest and penalties thereon to a date not less than two business days after the date of closing title, may at the option of the seller be allowed to the purchaser out of the balance of the purchase price, provided official bills therefor with interest and penalties thereon figured to said date are furnished by the seller at the closing.

EXHIBIT 8-6, cont.

20. If at the date of closing there may be any other liens or encumbrances which the seller is obligated to pay and discharge, the seller may use any portion of the balance of the purchase price to satisfy the same, provided the seller shall simultaneously either deliver to the purchaser at the closing of title instruments in recordable form and sufficient to satisfy such liens and encumbrances of record together with the cost of recording or filing said instruments; or, provided that the seller has made arrangements with the title company employed by the purchaser in advance of closing, seller will deposit with said company sufficient monies, acceptable to and required by it to insure obtaining and the recording of such satisfactions and the issuance of title insurance to the purchaser either free of any such liens and encumbrances, or with insurance against enforcement of same out of the insured premises. The purchaser, if request is made within a reasonable time prior to the date of closing of title, agrees to provide at the closing separate certified checks as requested, aggregating the amount of the balance of the purchase price, to facilitate the satisfaction of any such liens or encumbrances. The existence of any such taxes or other liens and encumbrances shall not be deemed objections to title if the seller shall comply with the foregoing requirements.

21. If a search of the title discloses judgments, bankruptcies or other returns against other persons having names the same as or similar to that of the seller, the seller will on request deliver to the purchaser an affidavit showing that such judgments, bankruptcies or other returns are not against the seller.

22. In the event that the seller is unable to convey title in accordance with the terms of this contract, the sole liability of the seller will be to refund to the purchaser the amount paid on account of the purchase price and to pay the net cost of examining the title, which cost is not to exceed the charges fixed by the New York Board of Title Underwriters, and the net cost of any survey made in connection therewith incurred by the purchaser, and upon such refund and payment being made this contract shall be considered canceled.

23. The deed shall be delivered upon the receipt of said payments at the office of

at   o'clock on   19

24. The parties agree that   is the broker who brought about this sale and the seller agrees to pay any commission earned thereby.

25. It is understood and agreed that all understandings and agreements heretofore had between the parties hereto are merged in this contract, which alone fully and completely expresses their agreement, and that the same is entered into after full investigation, neither party relying upon any statement or representation, not embodied in this contract, made by the other. The purchaser has inspected the buildings standing on said premises and is thoroughly acquainted with their condition and agrees to take title "as is" and in their present condition and subject to reasonable use, wear, tear, and natural deterioration between the date thereof and the closing of title.

26. This agreement may not be changed or terminated orally. The stipulations aforesaid are to apply to and bind the heirs, executors, administrators, successors and assigns of the respective parties.

27. If two or more persons constitute either the seller or the purchaser, the word "seller" or the word "purchaser" shall be construed as if it read "sellers" or "purchasers" whenever the sense of this agreement so requires.

IN WITNESS WHEREOF, this agreement has been duly executed by the parties hereto.

In presence of:

EXHIBIT 8-6, cont.

STATE OF NEW YORK, COUNTY OF   **ss:**

On the   day of   19   , before me
personally came

to me known to be the individual   described in and who executed
the foregoing instrument, and acknowledged that
     executed the same.

STATE OF NEW YORK, COUNTY OF   **ss:**

On the   day of   19   , before me
personally came

to me known, who, being by me duly sworn, did depose and say
that   he resides at No.

that   he is the
of

     , the corporation described
in and which executed the foregoing instrument; that   he knows
the seal of said corporation; that the seal affixed to said instrument
is such corporate seal; that it was so affixed by order of the board
of directors of said corporation, and that   he signed h   name
thereto by like order.

STATE OF NEW YORK, COUNTY OF   **ss:**

On the   day of   19   , before me
personally came

to me known to be the individual   described in and who executed
the foregoing instrument, and acknowledged that
     executed the same.

STATE OF NEW YORK, COUNTY OF   **ss:**

On the   day of   19   , before me
personally came

to me known and known to me to be a partner in
     ,

a partnership, and known to me to be the person described in and
who executed the foregoing instrument in the partnership name, and
said   duly
acknowledged that he executed the foregoing instrument for and
on behalf of said partnership.

Closing of title under the within contract is hereby adjourned to ·
o'clock, at   19   , at
as of   19   19   ; title to be closed and all adjustments to be made
Dated,

For value received, the within contract and all the right, title and interest of the purchaser thereunder are hereby assigned,
transferred and set over unto
and said assignee hereby assumes all obligations of the purchaser thereunder.
Dated,   19

               _____
                     Purchaser

               _____
                  Assignee of Purchaser

Contract of Sale

Title No.

TO

PREMISES

Section
Block
Lot
County or Town
Street Numbered Address

Recorded At Request of The Title Guarantee Company

RETURN BY MAIL TO:

Zip No.

THE OBSERVANCE OF THE FOLLOWING SUGGESTIONS WILL SAVE TIME AND TROUBLE AT THE CLOSING OF THIS TITLE

The **SELLER** should bring with him all insurance policies and duplicates, receipted bills for taxes, assessments and water rates, and any leases, deeds or agreements affecting the property.

When there is a water meter on the premises, he should order it read, and bring bills therefor to the closing.

If there are mortgages on the property, he should promptly arrange to obtain the evidence required under Paragraph 5 of this contract.

He should furnish to the purchaser a full list of tenants, giving the names, rent paid by each, and date to which the rent has been paid.

The **PURCHASER** should be prepared with cash or certified check drawn to the order of the seller. The check may be certified for an approximate amount and cash may be provided for the balance of the settlement.

CLOSING PROCEDURES

Purpose

Many weeks or even months may pass from signing the binder until the closing, where the actual transfer of ownership takes place. At the closing, payment is made for the property, together with adjustments of various items such as utilities, rents, taxes, insurance, and the like. The seller gives the keys (constructive possession) to the buyer, together with final instructions on the various idiosyncrasies of the particular premises, that is, sticking doors, garage door openers, and so on. Warranties on major appliances are also transferred when appropriate.

Roles of the Parties

Present at a typical home closing are the seller (husband or wife or both), the buyer (husband or wife or both), the attorneys representing the parties (it is advisable to have separate legal counsel representing buyer and seller), the real estate person or other representative if the sale was brought about by a real estate agent, the title insurance company representative if title insurance has been applied for, and representatives from the lending institution if an institutional mortgage is being provided or discharged or both. Each party present has a particular role that will be discussed separately.

The seller (grantor) will sign a formal written document called a "deed." The deed is a written instrument transferring ownership of a specific parcel of property. It contains the legal description of the property, as well as the names and addresses of grantor and grantee and other information. The seller's attorney will have previously prepared the deed for the seller's signature and will provide explanations as to the nature of other papers the seller may have to execute. The seller's attorney will also have reviewed either the abstract of title or the title insurance policy. The seller's attorney may also provide the acknowledgments necessary for recording of the deed. At the closing or within a few days, he or she may provide a closing statement or report to the seller.

The buyer will be responsible for paying the seller and executing all papers requested by the lender. The buyer is also responsible for securing fire and liability insurance on the premises. The buyer's attorney will have prepared the appropriate loan papers (note and mortgage) for the purchaser's signature. He or she may acknowledge the signatures necessary for recording. In closings where an abstract of title is provided, the buyer's attorney will have reviewed it to determine if the title is marketable. Where assurances of title are given by an insurance policy, the buyer's attorney should have reviewed the policy, paying specific attention to the exception sheet.

The lending institution will have the proceeds of the loan available, together with federal truth-in-lending papers, which must be signed by both buyer and seller. A copy of these documents is included (Exhibit 8–7). The attorney for the

EXHIBIT 8-7

Settlement Statement

HUD-1 Rev. 5/76		Form Approved OMB NO. 63-R-1501

A.			B. TYPE OF LOAN	

U. S. DEPARTMENT OF HOUSING AND URBAN DEVELOPMENT

SETTLEMENT STATEMENT

B. TYPE OF LOAN
1. ☐ FHA   2. ☐ FmHA   3. ☐ CONV. UNINS.
4. ☐ VA   5. ☐ CONV. INS.
6. File Number: 7. Loan Number:
8. Mortgage Insurance Case Number:

C. NOTE: *This form is furnished to give you a statement of actual settlement costs. Amounts paid to and by the settlement agent are shown. Items marked "(p.o.c.)" were paid outside the closing; they are shown here for informational purposes and are not included in the totals.*

D. NAME OF BORROWER:	E. NAME OF SELLER:	F. NAME OF LENDER:

G. PROPERTY LOCATION:	H. SETTLEMENT AGENT:	I. SETTLEMENT DATE:
	PLACE OF SETTLEMENT:	

J. SUMMARY OF BORROWER'S TRANSACTION		K. SUMMARY OF SELLER'S TRANSACTION	
100. GROSS AMOUNT DUE FROM BORROWER:		**400. GROSS AMOUNT DUE TO SELLER:**	
101. Contract sales price		401. Contract sales price	
102. Personal property		402. Personal property	
103. Settlement charges to borrower *(line 1400)*		403.	
104.		404.	
105.		405.	
Adjustments for items paid by seller in advance		*Adjustments for items paid by seller in advance*	
106. City / town taxes to		406. City / town taxes to	
107. County taxes to		407. County taxes to	
108. Assessments to		408. Assessments to	
109.		409.	
110.		410.	
111.		411.	
112.		412.	
120. GROSS AMOUNT DUE FROM BORROWER		**420. GROSS AMOUNT DUE TO SELLER**	
200. AMOUNTS PAID BY OR IN BEHALF OF BORROWER:		**500. REDUCTIONS IN AMOUNT DUE TO SELLER:**	
201. Deposit or earnest money		501. Excess deposit *(see instructions)*	
202. Principal amount of new loan(s)		502. Settlement charges to seller *(line 1400)*	
203. Existing loan(s) taken subject to		503. Existing loan(s) taken subject to	
204.		504. Payoff of first mortgage loan	
205.		505. Payoff of second mortgage loan	
206.		506.	
207.		507.	
208.		508.	
209.		509.	
Adjustments for items unpaid by seller		*Adjustments for items unpaid by seller*	
210. City / town taxes to		510. City / town taxes to	
211. County taxes to		511. County taxes to	
212. Assessments to		512. Assessments to	
213.		513.	
214.		514.	
215.		515.	
216.		516.	
217.		517.	
218.		518.	
219.		519.	
220. TOTAL PAID BY / FOR BORROWER		**520. TOTAL REDUCTION AMOUNT DUE SELLER**	
300. CASH AT SETTLEMENT FROM / TO BORROWER		**600. CASH AT SETTLEMENT TO / FROM SELLER**	
301. Gross amount due from borrower *(line 120)*		601. Gross amount due to seller *(line 420)*	
302. Less amounts paid by / for borrower *(line 220)*	( )	602. Less reductions in amount due seller *(line 520)*	( )
303. CASH (☐ FROM) (☐ TO) BORROWER		**603. CASH (☐ TO) (☐ FROM) SELLER**	

RECEIVED COMPLETED COPIES PAGES 1 & 2 BORROWER'S TRANSACTION   RECEIVED COMPLETED COPIES PAGES 1 & 2 SELLER'S TRANSACTION

SIGNATURE   SIGNATURE   DE LAND SERVICE-ALLEGAN, MICH   RES - 16

EXHIBIT 8-7, cont.

— 2 —

HUD-1 Rev. 5/76

L. SETTLEMENT CHARGES		LOAN NUMBER	
700. *TOTAL SALES/BROKER'S COMMISSION based on price* $ @ %=		PAID FROM BORROWER'S FUNDS AT SETTLEMENT	PAID FROM SELLER'S FUNDS AT SETTLEMENT
Division of Commission (line 700) as follows:			
701. $ to			
702. $ to			
703. Commission paid at Settlement			
704.			
800. ITEMS PAYABLE IN CONNECTION WITH LOAN			
801. Loan Origination Fee %			
802. Loan Discount %			
803. Appraisal Fee to			
804. Credit Report to			
805. Lender's Inspection fee			
806. Mortgage Insurance Application Fee to			
807. Assumption Fee			
808.			
809.			
810.			
811.			
900. ITEMS REQUIRED BY LENDER TO BE PAID IN ADVANCE			
901. Interest from to @ $ /day			
902. Mortgage Insurance Premium for months to			
903. Hazard Insurance Premium for years to			
904. years to			
905.			
1000. RESERVES DEPOSITED WITH LENDER			
1001. Hazard insurance months @ $ per month			
1002. Mortgage insurance months @ $ per month			
1003. City property taxes months @ $ per month			
1004. County property taxes months @ $ per month			
1005. Annual assessments months @ $ per month			
1006. months @ $ per month			
1007. months @ $ per month			
1008. months @ $ per month			
1100. TITLE CHARGES			
1101. Settlement or closing fee to			
1102. Abstract or title search to			
1103. Title examination to			
1104. Title insurance binder to			
1105. Document preparation to			
1106. Notary fees to			
1107. Attorney's fees to			
(includes above items numbers; *)*			
1108. Title insurance to			
(includes above items numbers; *)*			
1109. Lender's coverage $			
1110. Owner's coverage $			
1111.			
1112.			
1113.			
1200. GOVERNMENT RECORDING AND TRANSFER CHARGES			
1201. Recording fees: Deed $; Mortgage $; Releases $			
1202. City / county tax / stamps: Deed $; Mortgage $			
1203. State tax / stamps: Deed $; Mortgage $			
1204.			
1205.			
1300. ADDITIONAL SETTLEMENT CHARGES			
1301. Survey to			
1302. Pest inspection to			
1303.			
1304.			
1305.			
1400. **TOTAL SETTLEMENT CHARGES** *(enter on lines 103, Section J and 502, Section K)*			

lending institution will also review the deed, note, and mortgage to be certain that all have been properly signed and acknowledged, that the descriptions are identical, and so forth.

If a title insurance is to be obtained, the insurance company will have a representative (the closer) present. The closer will have reviewed the title. The closer will also review the documents to be recorded and clear up any exceptions that may exist (prior mortgages and such). The closer may phone an agent at the county clerk's office for a current search and will then issue a policy covering the buyer and the lender. The closer may take the mortgage and deed and other recordable instruments, together with filing fees, and have them recorded.

QUESTIONS

1 A real estate broker obtained an "open" listing for the sale of a residence from Forshee. Several months later the real estate agent showed the property to Mr. and Mrs. Bell and discussed the price and loan balance with them. The Bells indicated interest in buying the property but did not make an offer. The Bells contacted the defendant two days after they saw the house, and within six days they had moved in. The real estate broker brought an action against Forshee for his commission pursuant to the contractual agreement. Is the homeowner liable for the commission even though the broker did not put the buyer and seller in communication with each other? Discuss.

2 The plaintiffs, Mr. and Mrs. Bealey, purchased property from Mr. and Mrs. Kuida. The Kuidas were represented by J. W. Carter, a real estate broker, who, before the purchase agreement was signed, represented that the property could be used for construction of an apartment house. The plaintiffs never saw the warranty deed, which contained restrictions against the use of the property for an apartment house. The purchase contract (binder) indicated that the seller would deliver a warranty deed. The plaintiffs contend that the property was not free and clear of all encumbrances and that the seller should refund their money because of the fraud and misrepresentation of the real estate agent. Question: Will the plaintiffs recover? Discuss.

3 The plaintiff real estate broker sued Mr. and Mrs. Johnson and Joseph Iarussi for a commission allegedly earned in a real estate transaction. The Johnsons had entered into a written agreement with Iarussi to sell him their property. There was no question at the trial as to the fact that Dobbs brought the parties together and that he was instrumental in having them sign the contract of sale. Title did not pass because Iarussi was unable to obtain financing from the bank. Question: Was the plaintiff entitled to a commission? Discuss.

4 The plaintiff real estate broker sued the defendants for a broker's commission for services rendered in the sale of residential property. The defendants were builders and listed two properties with the plaintiff for sale. Reverend Schumann approached the real estate broker for a place to rent. The real estate broker gave the reverend the addresses of two properties she had for rent and, in addition, told him of the two properties belonging to the defendant, which she had for sale. The reverend viewed the defendants' property from the outside, went in to the office, and inquired whether the dwelling could be rented. The defendants said no. The reverend then asked how much the sale price for the property was, and a contract was entered into. Was the real estate broker entitled to a commission? Discuss.

5   Wilmore owned a piece of land and periodically rented parcels of the property to various persons, who built bungalows on them. These bungalows typically were placed on cinder blocks on top of the ground. Water and electricity was made available in such a manner that the bungalows could be removed from the property. Removal of the bungalows from the property would cause no major damage to the bungalows or the property. Wilmore sold his land to Sigrol. The contract of sale did not mention the bungalows. Upon learning of the sale, Valcich removed several of the bungalows that he owned. Sigrol brought an action to enjoin their removal, claiming that they had become part of the real estate and, therefore, were sold to him by Wilmore. Decision for whom? Discuss.

6   The owners of a motel decided that it was in need of renovation. Accordingly, they purchased a large quantity of bedspreads, curtain rods, and draperies from Sears Roebuck and Company. They failed to pay the bill amounting to almost $8000. The supplier of the items in question sought to establish a lien against the motel on the grounds that the items sold had become fixtures. Which of the items just listed are, in fact, fixtures? Discuss.

7   The defendants operated airplanes at various times over portions of land belonging to the plaintiff for the purpose of cloud seeding (artificially causing rain). The plaintiffs brought an action to stop the defendants on the theory that they were trespassing in the plaintiffs' air space. Will the plaintiffs prevail? Discuss.

8   Mrs. Quincy hired two real estate brokers to sell a large parcel of land in subdivided parcels. Her agreement with the brokers indicated that the brokers would pay all the expenses of getting the property ready to sell. No time limit was indicated in the contract. After the real estate brokers performed their part of the agreement and found buyers for several lots, Mrs. Quincy terminated the agreement for no apparent reason. Can she do this? Discuss.

9   C wanted to sell his farm for $60,000. He signed open listing agreements with realtors A and B. A found a potential purchaser who offered $60,000. The offer was accepted by C. Later the same day B produced a potential purchaser who offered $63,000 for the property. C accepted that offer and sold the farm to the second purchaser. Does C owe a commission to A? Discuss.

10   C listed his property with a real estate broker. The listing was an exclusive right to sell agreement and provided for a 6 percent commission rate. C sold the property to S for $120,000. The real estate broker had placed For Sale signs on the property and had advertised the property at a total cost of $73. The real estate broker had never told S about the property. Is C liable to the real estate broker for damages? If so, for how much?

11   P entered into an exclusive agency agreement with F, a real estate broker. F advertised the property, discussed the sale with many buyers, and had a key to the house. When F left town for one week and returned, she found out that P had sold the property to her relative for $10,000. Is the real estate broker entitled to her commission? Discuss.

CHAPTER 9

Real Property Documents and Other Topics

REAL PROPERTY DOCUMENTS

Deeds

All deeds indicate the day, month, and year in which the seller (grantor) conveys to the buyer (grantee) the property in question. All deeds spell the "legal" description of the property and contain the signature or signatures of the grantor or grantors and an acknowledgment by a notary. The standard deed is normally referred to as a "bargain and sale" deed. A bargain and sale deed may have representations, warranties or covenants (such as covenant against grantor's acts, which specifies that the grantor has not committed any acts to impair the title in any manner).

A bargain and sale deed that includes no warranties is called a "quitclaim deed." This deed provides the least protection for the buyer because the seller only conveys such interests as he or she may have. A seller's lack of representations as to the extent of his or her interests will require the buyer to rely heavily on his or her attorney's review of the title papers.

The typical warranties are these: seisin and good right to convey, quiet enjoyment, freedom from encumbrances, further assurance, title, and the fact that the grantor is not encumbered. Seisin means that the grantor lawfully owns the property and possesses the property and has authority to convey title. Quiet enjoyment means that the grantee can use the property without being disturbed by the grantor or any other person who might claim to have better title to the property. Freedom from encumbrances assures the grantee that there are no judgments, liens, charges, tax assessments, and so forth on the property. Further assurance provides that the grantor will sign or obtain any other documents that may be needed to guarantee title. Warranty of title provides the grantee with the grantor's assurance that the grantor will defend the title in the future against anyone claiming a better right to the property. The warranty that the grantor has not encumbered the property assures the grantee that the grantor has not committed any acts that would encumber the property, but does not make such warranty as to acts of prior owners.

A deed giving the warranty of *quiet enjoyment* is called a "warranty deed." This deed is the best guarantee that a purchaser can get from a seller. The grantor, by making a warranty of quiet enjoyment, indicates that he or she has title to the real estate that is good against all third persons. The grantor also warrants that there are no liens or encumbrances against the property, and if there is any breach of these warranties, in whole or part, the grantor will compensate the grantee for any losses incurred.

Note that these warranties do not mean that the grantor owns the property or that there are no defects in the title. (This is the reason for title insurance or title abstract or both.) No warranties will be implied in a deed if they are not specifically stated within the deed. In the absence of warranties, the grantee takes the property at the risk and expense of clearing any possible defects in title.

Legal Description of Property   In any purchase of real estate, a clear chain of title and a sufficient legal description to the property are essential to the purchaser. The chain of title establishes the buyer's ownership of the property; the legal description establishes boundaries.

A deed description must be adequate, or the conveyance will fail even though the description may have been sufficient to bind an individual to a sales contract. Courts often will not permit omissions or clarifications to the written deed to be added at a later date. Legal descriptions are generally of two types: those using particular bounding markers or physical features of the land (or both) to describe the bounds of the parcel and those that relate to a survey. An example of the first type of deed description is shown in Exhibit 9–1.

In rural areas, where large tracts of land exist, the descriptions are not as formalized, and the "land monument" method is usually found as the method of legal description. It is important to walk the boundaries of the property to be acquired, using the proposed deed as a map or guide. Any apparent infringement on the boundaries by neighbors, utilities, and so on could indicate future problems and should be carefully researched. Discussions with future neighbors might be useful in clarifying descriptions or boundaries or both. Remember, the courts will strictly interpret the description found in your deed. If there is any doubt as to what you are purchasing, it might be advisable to have a survey prepared.

A survey is a calculation of the boundaries of a particular parcel by measurement of distance and direction. The preliminary phase of a survey entails research at the county clerk's office as to the current description of the property and of adjoining parcels. The actual process of the field survey is as follows: a starting point is determined, usually where the property meets a *landmark* or other surveyed parcel. A permanent corner marker is placed at this point (usually an iron pin or cement marker). A direction is sighted (e.g., due north, north 30 degrees east) using a transit, and the number of feet are measured along the line in the proper direction. At a change of direction, a marker is placed, and the new direction is sighted and measured. This process continues until the point of origin is reached. An example of a legal description developed from a survey appears in the deed in Exhibit 9–2.

In urban areas, most property development has been done with surveys, and deed descriptions reflect that fact. In the purchase of an urban parcel, it is advisable to get a copy of the survey and locate the boundary markers prior to closing; any discrepancies should be clarified.

Roads Transfers of property generally include the right of ownership to the middle of any road, subject to the obvious easement in favor of the state, municipality, or other individuals to use the road. This is understood as a legal proposition, and it is not mentioned in the binder agreement. The practical importance in owning one half of a road occurs when the state undertakes a modification of the existing easement, entitling the property owner to receive compensation for any taking of property or damages or both.

EXHIBIT 9-1
Deed

Standard N.Y.B.T.U. Form 8003 • 7-73-15M— Warranty Deed With Full Covenants – Individual or Corporation (Single Sheet)

CONSULT YOUR LAWYER BEFORE SIGNING THIS INSTRUMENT—THIS INSTRUMENT SHOULD BE USED BY LAWYERS ONLY.

THIS INDENTURE, made the   29th   day of April   , nineteen hundred and seventy-eight
BETWEEN

                                    and   , his wife, both
            residing at R.D. #1, Otego, New York,

party of the first part, and

                                    and   , his wife, both
            residing in the Town of Otego, New York as tenants by the
            entirety,

party of the second part,

WITNESSETH, that the party of the first part, in consideration of ten dollars and other valuable consideration paid by the party of the second part, does hereby grant and release unto the party of the second part, the heirs or successors and assigns of the party of the second part forever,

ALL that certain plot, piece or parcel of land, with the buildings and improvements thereon erected, situate, lying and being in the   Town of Otego, County of Otsego, State of New York beginning at a point on the easterly edge of the Wheaton Creek Road where it intersects with the southerly edge of a driveway, as it exists in 1978, said driveway is located near the northerly edge of the lands owned by Howard R. Butler and Esther M. Butler, and runs in an easterly direction; thence traversing in a southerly direction along the easterly edge of the aforementioned Wheaton Creek Road, a distance of 488' $\pm$ to an old stone wall; thence in an easterly direction along the old stone wall as it twists and turns, a distance of 454' $\pm$ to a point where the stone wall intersects the driveway hereinabove mentioned; thence in a westerly direction along the southerly edge of said driveway, as it twists and turns, a distance of 565' $\pm$ to the point and place of beginning, containing TWO (2) acres of land, more or less.

Also herein conveyed is any right, title or interest which the grantors may possess along the 488" road frontage of the premises herein conveyed from the middle of Wheaton Creek Road to the easterly edge of said road.

Further included herein are perpetual spring rights to two (2) springs located on the lands of the grantors to the north of the premises herein conveyed together with the rights of ingress and egress for the purpose of maintaining said spring and placing any water lines to the lands of the grantees and maintaining said lines in operable condition. Said spring rights shall be used by the grantees herein for residential purposes only.

Excepting and reserving therefrom any and all easements and conveyances of any other nature to any federal, state or municipal government, any of their agencies of any public utilities corporation for any public purpose whatsoever. TOGETHER with all right, title and interest, if any, of the party of the first part in and to any streets and roads abutting the above described premises to the center lines thereof; TOGETHER with the appurtenances and all the estate and rights of the party of the first part in and to said premises; TO HAVE AND TO HOLD the premises herein granted unto the party of the second part, the heirs or successors and assigns of the party of the second part forever.

AND the party of the first part, in compliance with Section 13 of the Lien Law, covenants that the party of the first part will receive the consideration for this conveyance and will hold the right to receive such consideration as a trust fund to be applied first for the purpose of paying the cost of the improvement and will apply the same first to the payment of the cost of the improvement before using any part of the total of the same for any other purpose.

AND the party of the first part covenants as follows: that said party of the first part is seized of the said premises in fee simple, and has good right to convey the same; that the party of the second part shall quietly enjoy the said premises; that the said premises are free from incumbrances, except as aforesaid; that the party of the first part will execute or procure any further necessary assurance of the title to said premises; and that said party of the first part will forever warrant the title to said premises.

The word "party" shall be construed as if it read "parties" whenever the sense of this indenture so requires.

IN WITNESS WHEREOF, the party of the first part has duly executed this deed the day and year first above written.

IN PRESENCE OF:

EXHIBIT 9-1, cont.

STATE OF NEW YORK, COUNTY OF   ss:

On the   day of   19   , before me
personally came

to me known to be the individual   described in and who
executed the foregoing instrument, and acknowledged that
executed the same.

STATE OF NEW YORK, COUNTY OF   ss:

On the   day of   19   , before me
personally came

to me known to be the individual   described in and who
executed the foregoing instrument, and acknowledged that
executed the same.

STATE OF NEW YORK, COUNTY OF   ss:

On the   day of   19   , before me
personally came
to me known, who, being by me duly sworn, did depose and
say that   he resides at No.
                                                         ;
that   he is the
of
                              , the corporation described
in and which executed the foregoing instrument; that   he
knows the seal of said corporation; that the seal affixed
to said instrument is such corporate seal; that it was so
affixed by order of the board of directors of said corporation, and that   he signed h   name thereto by like order.

STATE OF NEW YORK, COUNTY OF   ss:

On the   day of   19   , before me
personally came
the subscribing witness to the foregoing instrument, with
whom I am personally acquainted, who, being by me duly
sworn, did depose and say that   he resides at No.
                                                         ;
that   he knows

                              to be the individual
described in and who executed the foregoing instrument;
that   he, said subscribing witness, was present and saw
                execute the same; and that   he, said witness,
at the same time subscribed h   name as witness thereto.

𝔚arranty 𝔇eed
WITH FULL COVENANTS

TITLE NO.

TO

SECTION

BLOCK

LOT

COUNTY OR TOWN

Recorded At Request of The Title Guarantee Company
RETURN BY MAIL TO:

Zip No.

STANDARD FORM OF NEW YORK BOARD OF TITLE UNDERWRITERS
Distributed by
**TITLE GUARANTEE-
NEW YORK**
A TICOR COMPANY

RESERVE THIS SPACE FOR USE OF RECORDING OFFICE

EXHIBIT 9-2
Survey Deed Description

Standard N.Y.B.T.U. Form 8002* 9-76-70M – Bargain and Sale Deed, with Covenant against Grantor's Acts. Individual or Corporation. (single sheet)

CONSULT YOUR LAWYER BEFORE SIGNING THIS INSTRUMENT—THIS INSTRUMENT SHOULD BE USED BY LAWYERS ONLY.

THIS INDENTURE, made the 1st **day of** December , nineteen hundred and seventy-eight
BETWEEN

        and   , residing at   Avenue,
Roslyn Harbor, New York

party of the first part, and

        and   , his wife, both residing at
Boulevard, Elmont, New York

party of the second part,

WITNESSETH, that the party of the first part, in consideration of Ten Dollars and other valuable consideration paid by the party of the second part, does hereby grant and release unto the party of the second part, the heirs or successors and assigns of the party of the second part forever,

ALL that certain plot, piece or parcel of land, with the buildings and improvements thereon erected, situate, lying and being in the Incorporated Village of Roslyn Harbor, Town of North Hempstead, County of Nassau and State of New York, known and designated as and by the Lot #12, in Block 74, on a certain map entitled, "Map of Roslyn Harbor Estates, Section 3, and amending a portion of Roslyn Harbor Estates, Section 1, wholly within the limits of the Incorporated Village of Roslyn Harbor, Town of North Hempstead, Nassau County, New York, surveyed March 16, 1950 by J.J. Bohn, Licensed Land Surveyor", and filed in the Office of the Clerk of the County of Nassau on May 12, 1950, as Map #4951 which said lot is bounded and described, according to said map, as follows:

BEGINNING at a point on the southerly side of Dogwood Avenue, distant 704.44 feet easterly and northeasterly from the extreme easterly end of the arc of a curve connecting the southerly side of Dogwood Avenue with the easterly side of Motts Cove Road; running thence NORTH 70 degrees 25 minutes 57 seconds east along the southerly side of Dogwood Avenue, 88.09 feet; running thence NORTH 59 degrees 50 minutes 22 seconds east and still along the southerly side of Dogwood Avenue, 31.91 feet; running thence SOUTH 40 degrees 23 minutes 44 seconds east, 350.38 feet; running thence SOUTH 64 degrees 00 minutes 36 seconds west. 154 feet; running thence NORTH 34 degrees 36 minutes 04 seconds West 350.85 feet to the southerly side of Dogwood Avenue, the point or place of beginning.

SAID PREMISES being known as and by   Avenue, Roslyn Harbor, New York.

The grantors herein are the same persons as the grantees in deed dated March 29, 1968, recorded April 4, 1968, in Liber 7809, page 425.

TOGETHER with all right, title and interest, if any, of the party of the first part in and to any streets and roads abutting the above described premises to the center lines thereof; TOGETHER with the appurtenances and all the estate and rights of the party of the first part in and to said premises; TO HAVE AND TO HOLD the premises herein granted unto the party of the second part, the heirs or successors and assigns of the party of the second part forever.

AND the party of the first part covenants that the party of the first part has not done or suffered anything whereby the said premises have been encumbered in any way whatever, except as aforesaid.
AND the party of the first part, in compliance with Section 13 of the Lien Law, covenants that the party of the first part will receive the consideration for this conveyance and will hold the right to receive such consideration as a trust fund to be applied first for the purpose of paying the cost of the improvement and will apply the same first to the payment of the cost of the improvement before using any part of the total of the same for any other purpose.
The word "party" shall be construed as if it read "parties" whenever the sense of this indenture so requires.

IN WITNESS WHEREOF, the party of the first part has duly executed this deed the day and year first above written.

IN PRESENCE OF:

EXHIBIT 9-2, cont.

STATE OF NEW YORK, COUNTY OF ss:	STATE OF NEW YORK, COUNTY OF ss:
On the 1st day of December 19 78 , before me personally came	On the day of 19 , before me personally came
to me known to be the individual described in and who executed the foregoing instrument, and acknowledged that executed the same.	to me known to be the individual described in and who executed the foregoing instrument, and acknowledged that executed the same.
_____ Notary Public	

STATE OF NEW YORK, COUNTY OF ss:	STATE OF NEW YORK, COUNTY OF ss:
On the day of 19 , before me personally came to me known, who, being by me duly sworn, did depose and say that he resides at No. ;	On the day of 19 , before me personally came the subscribing witness to the foregoing instrument, with whom I am personally acquainted, who, being by me duly sworn, did depose and say that he resides at No. ;
that he is the of , the corporation described in and which executed the foregoing instrument; that he knows the seal of said corporation; that the seal affixed to said instrument is such corporate seal; that it was so affixed by order of the board of directors of said corporation, and that he signed h name thereto by like order.	that he knows to be the individual described in and who executed the foregoing instrument; that he, said subscribing witness, was present and saw execute the same; and that he, said witness, at the same time subscribed h name as witness thereto.

Bargain and Sale Deed
WITH COVENANT AGAINST GRANTOR'S ACTS

TITLE NO. _____

SECTION

BLOCK

LOT

COUNTY OR TOWN

TO

Recorded At Request of The Title Guarantee Company

RETURN BY MAIL TO:

STANDARD FORM OF NEW YORK BOARD OF TITLE UNDERWRITERS

Distributed by

TITLE GUARANTEE-NEW YORK

A TICOR COMPANY

STEVEN J. BLUMENKRANTZ, ESQ.
MAIN STREET
OTEGO, NEW YORK 13825

Zip No.

RESERVE THIS SPACE FOR USE OF RECORDING OFFICE

Restrictions   Property is often sold subject to various restrictions. These include the following:

- Zoning regulations and ordinances of the city, town, or village in which the premises lie that are not violated by existing structures.
- Consents by the seller or any former owner of premises for the erection of any structure or structures on, under, or above any street on which said premises may abut.
- Encroachments of stoops, areas, cellar steps, trim, and cornices, if any, upon any street or highway.
- Covenants and restrictions that exist in the deed or other instruments of record or both, such as provisions allowing for limited building (no trailers, no buildings of more than two stores, etc., or provisions for wildlife sanctuaries, etc.).

A statement in the purchase contract or binder that the premises are subject to all facts that an accurate survey might show puts the purchaser on notice of the importance of a survey and releases the seller from possible liability with respect to statements made as to boundaries unless fraud exists. A binder agreement often leaves these areas open to custom and usage in the area in which the property is located. Some of the restrictions would appear in the title search; others would not. Discussions with neighbors and diligent research might be necessary on the part of the buyer to ascertain the extent of these items.

Note or Bond

In order to borrow money, the borrower will have to sign a note (or bond). A note is a written promise by the borrower to the lender to repay the debt, together with interest, over a stated period of time. When a husband and wife borrow money, both will have to sign the note. In some cases, other parties (a parent or sibling) may be asked to sign the note as a coborrower, comaker, or guarantor.

A mortgage note states the amount owed in numerical characters, the date the note is entered into, the borrower's name and address, the amount of the note in alphabetical characters, the interest rate per annum (per year), and the method of repayment.

The following discussion includes typical note clauses together with explanations. It is not all inclusive. The law allows a note to contain any reasonable provision that the parties may agree to.

Repayment   The method of repayment is usually a series of equal monthly payments. The initial payment is generally made one month after the closing date and is applied first to pay interest for that month on the outstanding loan balance and then to reduce the outstanding loan balance. The following month the same procedure applies with the amount of interest being computed on the now reduced loan balance. Exhibit 9–3, shows a typical loan reduction schedule. A typical payment clause for a mortgage of $38,900 for 20 years at 10.5 percent would read as follows:

Example: Three hundred eighty-eight dollars and 37 cents ($388.37) monthly; the first monthly payment of $388.37 to be due and payable on the first day of November, 1981 and a like sum of $388.37 to be due and payable on the first day of each consecutive month thereafter until the whole of the principal sum and interest is fully paid; the whole of the principal sum and interest, unless sooner paid, to be due and payable on the first day of October 2001.

Notice that the payment clause indicates a date for the last payment. Assuming a borrower agreed to pay the loan over 20 years (240 months), the last payment would usually be due 20 years after the date of the note.

A private person making a mortgage loan usually doesn't wish to wait 20 years or more for full repayment. The borrower may be unable to pay the note off in a short period of time because the monthly payments are too high. In such a situation, the parties would compromise and enter into a so-called balloon payment note. The buyer will make lower payments as though the note had been entered into for a 20- to 30-year period; however, after 5 or 10 years, the buyer will be obligated to pay the lender the remaining principal balance in a single lump sum. Usually, the buyer will refinance the loan some time prior to the date the balloon payment is due. A typical balloon payment clause would be identical to the payment clause given earlier except that the final payment is due at an earlier date.

Example: Three hundred eighty-eight dollars and 37 cents ($388.37) monthly; the first monthly payment of $388.37 to be due and payable on the first day of November 1981 and like sum of $388.37 to be due and payable on the first day of each consecutive month thereafter until the whole of the principal sum and interest, unless sooner paid, to be due and payable on the first day of October 1991.

Note that the final payment due October 1, 1991, would amount to $28,278.93. (See Exhibit 9–3, balance after 120th payment.)

An increasingly common occurrence in the late 1970s and early 1980s was the variable rate mortgage, an example of which appears below.

Example: Three hundred eighty-eight dollars and 37 cents ($388.37) on the first day of November 1981 and a like sum on the same day of each and every month

EXHIBIT 9-3
Loan Amortization Schedule

LOAN AMORTIZATION SCHEDULE FOR

INITIAL PRINCIPAL	$38,900	MONTHLY PAYMENT	$388.37
INITIAL RATE	10.500%		
TOTAL INTEREST	$54,308		

MONTH	PRINCIPAL OUTSTANDING	INTEREST	PRINCIPAL REPAYMENT
1	$38,900.00	$340.38	$47.99
2	$38,852.01	$339.96	$48.41
3	$38,803.60	$339.53	$48.84
4	$38,754.76	$339.10	$49.27
5	$38,705.49	$338.67	$49.70
6	$38,655.79	$338.24	$50.13
7	$38,605.66	$337.80	$50.57
8	$38,555.09	$337.36	$51.01
9	$38,504.08	$336.91	$51.46
10	$38,452.62	$336.46	$51.91
11	$38,400.71	$336.01	$52.36
12	$38,348.35	$335.55	$52.82
49	$36,052.23	$315.46	$72.91
50	$35,979.32	$314.82	$73.55
51	$35,905.77	$314.18	$74.19
52	$35,831.58	$313.53	$74.84
53	$35,756.74	$312.87	$75.50
54	$35,681.24	$312.21	$76.16
55	$35,605.08	$311.54	$76.83
56	$35,528.25	$310.87	$77.50
57	$35,450.75	$310.19	$78.18
58	$35,372.57	$309.51	$78.86
59	$35,293.71	$308.82	$79.55
60	$35,214.16	$308.12	$80.25
61	$35,133.91	$307.42	$80.95
62	$35,052.96	$306.71	$81.66
223	$6,441.76	$56.37	$332.00
224	$6,109.76	$53.46	$334.91
225	$5,774.85	$50.53	$337.84
226	$5,437.01	$47.57	$340.80
227	$5,096.21	$44.59	$343.78
228	$4,752.43	$41.58	$346.79
229	$4,405.64	$38.55	$349.82
230	$4,055.82	$35.49	$352.88
231	$3,702.94	$32.40	$355.97
232	$3,346.97	$29.29	$359.08
233	$2,987.89	$26.14	$362.23
234	$2,625.66	$22.97	$365.40
235	$2,260.26	$19.78	$368.59
236	$1,891.67	$16.55	$371.82
237	$1,519.85	$13.30	$375.07
238	$1,144.78	$10.02	$378.35
239	$766.43	$6.71	$381.66
240	$384.77	$3.37	$384.77

thereafter until October 1, 2001, when the entire principal indebtedness together with accrued interest shall be paid in full. From each monthly payment there shall first be deducted interest at the rate of 10.5 percent annum,* and the balance of each such payments shall be applied to reduce the principal indebtedness.

*A variable interest rate currently set at 10.5 percent and to vary with the maximum as set forth by the New York State Banking Commission for real property mortgages. Said monthly payments will be modified on the first monthly payment after the New York State Banking Commission or other appropriate agency authorizes any change in the interest rate, on real property mortgages.

During the period 1979–1981, in a period of approximately two years, mortgage note rates increased from 8½ percent to as high as 19 percent. Lending institutions are frequently paying more than 8½ percent to acquire new funds. Accordingly, they resist being locked into a fixed rate of return for 10 to 20 years or more. A variable interest rate clause allows a lender to increase the interest rate as the legal or market rate increases. This can result in (1) increased monthly payments (to pay off the loan at the same due date), (2) extending the loan term by keeping the same payment, or (3) not changing the monthly payment and requiring a balloon payment at the end of the normal payment term.

These options are illustrated by the following examples.

Example: Assume a $38,900 mortgage note at 10.5 percent for 20 years; after five years the interest rate increases to 11 percent. At that point, the note balance is $35,133.91. To pay off the loan over the remaining 15 years at the increased rate of interest, three alternatives exist:

1 The monthly payments must increase from $388.37 per month to $399.83 per month; an increase of more than $11 each month.

2 Continuing to pay $388.37 per month would pay off the balance of $35,133.91 in approximately 16 years and 2 months—an extension of more than 1 year on the original term of the note.

3 Continued payments of $388.37 per month would leave a balance of approximately $4,000 at the end of the remaining 15 years that would have to be paid at the expiration of those 15 years (balloon payment).

In 1981, the variable rate mortgage was replaced by the adjustable mortgage loan. (Variable rate mortgages may still be used by private lenders, but not by lending institutions.) The adjustable mortgage loan is a flexible loan. It has interest rates that can be adjusted by the lender from time to time. The adjustments may result in increases or decreases in the total amount of the loan (the outstanding principal loan balance), in the term of the loan (number of years in which the loan must be paid off), or in the monthly payments. It is also possible that the adjustments will affect all three. The difference between the adjustable rate mortgage and the variable rate mortgage is that, under a variable rate mortgage, the federal government sets the rates of the mortgage whereas, under the adjustable rate mortgage, the bank sets the rates. The federal regulations place no limit on the amount by which a lender may adjust payments at any one time or on the frequency of the payment adjustment. It is up to the borrower and the lender to negotiate the terms of each loan. The federal government does provide that all loans that have adjustable terms must indicate in their contract that the loan is based on an index that is readily available to borrowers and that the agreement must state specifically how the interest rate adjustment will be computed. In addition, if the index used moves down, the lender must reduce the interest rate by at least the decrease in the index. A number of banks are using the monthly national average mortgage rate index for all major lenders. This index reflects the contract interest rate on the purchase of previously occupied homes as computed by the Federal Home Loan Bank Board. This index is published monthly in the *Federal Home Loan Bank Board Journal*.

Default   There is a statement in a note that the property purchased is held as security for the loan. In the event of default on the loan, the property may be sold. (See sections on mortgages and foreclosure).

The following clause specifies what constitutes a default on the note.

Lender may declare the full amount of this note due immediately for any default. The following are defaults:

1. Failure to pay, when due, any amount payable on any of my obligations under this note.

2. Failure to do anything I am obligated to do under the mortgage. Anything that would be a default under the mortgage will also be a default under this note. This means that upon the lender's demand, I will have to pay the full amount of this debt plus any other charges that the lender is entitled to under the mortgage.

The note will often also specify that payments that are made more than 10 or 15 days after the due date are subject to a late fee, which may be a flat fee ($2 or $5) or a percentage of the monthly loan payment (1 percent or 2 percent). In the event of a default, the lender gets the right to demand that the borrower pay the full amount of the loan balance plus any other amounts due.

Prepayment   An example of a prepayment clause follows.

I can repay the entire debt in advance whenever I want, or I can repay part of the debt in multiples of $100 in advance whenever a regular monthly payment is due. There will be no extra charge for this. If I pay ahead of time, I will have to pay interest on the payment prepaid only to the date of prepayment.

This clause allows the borrower to repay the note earlier than its specified payment dates, thus saving interest. An early payment of $100 will save $.87 per month on a 10.5 percent note on the next payment date and will save more each month until maturity.

The typical mortgage note will not reduce monthly payments due to a prepayment. If a borrower wishes to make a large prepayment (several thousand dollars), it may be possible to renegotiate the monthly payment with the lender. If monthly payments are not adjusted, the mortgage note will be paid off early. Occasionally, a lender will charge a prepayment penalty, particularly when the borrower wishes to pay off the entire loan balance. Such a penalty may be 1 or 2 percent of the amount of the note.

Presentment   A presentment clause follows.

> *If the note is not paid when due, the lender does not have to notify me before the lender can enforce rights to collect all amounts due. The lender does not have to present this note, demand payment, or protest.*

The Uniform Commercial Code contains formal requirements for notification of a borrower prior to collection of a note that is in default. If these requirements are not met, parties that might be liable on a note could be partially or fully released (U.C.C. §§ 3-501 through 3-505). The clause quoted earlier waives the U.C.C. requirement of notification.

Delay/Waiver   Here is an example of a delay/waiver clause.

> *Delay or failure of the lender to take any action will not prevent lender from doing so later.*

This clause allows a lender to enforce his or her rights under the contract whenever it is desired irrespective of any prior conduct of nonenforcement. Under common law if a lender fails on several occasions to demand payment of the entire note balance where a borrower is more than 30 days past due, the borrower could argue that the lender had waived his or her right to do so for the balance of the life of the note. The clause cited earlier changes this common law rule.

Mortgage

Occasionally, a lender will advance money to a borrower on the strength of just a note. In most cases, the lender will require some security for the loan. The most common form of security is the property itself. A *mortgage* is a legal document by which the borrower pledges the property as security for the lender's loan. If the borrower fails to meet the terms of the loan, the lender has the right to *foreclose* the

"Assuming" or "Taking Subject to" Seller's Mortgage   It may be possible for a buyer to purchase a home by using financing that was previously obtained by the seller by (1) assuming the seller's note and mortgage, (2) purchasing subject to the seller's note and mortgage, (3) entering into a land contract. If the buyer assumes the seller's mortgage, the buyer, seller, and the bank agree that the buyer will pay the note that the seller has previously been paying. Usually, the seller will be released from the obligation of the note, and the property continues to serve as security (collateral) for the debt. When the buyer purchases subject to the seller's mortgage, the seller remains liable for the mortgage, and the buyer makes payments directly to the seller or seller's designee (the original bank). The property remains as security for the debt.

Example: Assume a seller previously borrowed $38,900 at 10.5 percent for 20 years (monthly payment of $388.37). After 5 years he or she sells the property to the buyer; the remaining mortgage balance is $35,133.91. The following table shows what would happen if the buyer purchases the property for $55,000:

	Assumes Mortgage	*Subject to Mortgage*
Cash paid to seller at closing	$19,866.09	$19,866.09
Buyer's monthly payments of $388.37, made to	Bank	Seller
Seller's monthly payments to bank	$ 0.00	$ 388.37
Party primarily liable on bond (note)	Buyer	Seller

A typical mortgage (see Exhibit 9–4) provides room to insert the date of the transaction, the name of the mortgagor (the person who owns or is buying the property and is giving a security interest), and the name of the mortgagee (the person who or institution that has lent the money and is acquiring the security interest).

It also provides room for insertion of the legal description of the property. Usually, the legal description is the same as the one that appears in the grantor's (seller's) deed. In the case of a purchase money mortgage (a mortgage where the borrower is simultaneously acquiring ownership of the property), the description is the same as the description in the purchaser's deed. In addition to the property, the lender may acquire an interest in additional items. These items may include buildings and improvements that are on the land, as well as any interest the borrower may have in streets, roads, and so on. Any items of personal property that become attached to the land because of their use in connection with the property (*fixtures*) will also be security for the mortgagee.

The mortgage makes it clear that household furniture shall not be considered to be fixtures. There is usually a provision that in the event any portion of the prop-

EXHIBIT 9-4
A Sample Mortgage

MORTGAGE

WORDS USED OFTEN IN THIS DOCUMENT

(A) "Mortgage." This document, which is dated .... , 19 .... , will be called the "Mortgage."

(B) "Borrower." ....
will sometimes be called "Borrower" and sometimes simply "I."

(C) "Lender." __The National Bank and Trust Company of Norwich, New York__ ....
will be called "Lender." Lender is a corporation or association which was formed and which exists under the laws of __United States of America__ .
Lender's address is __52 South Broad Street, Norwich, New York 13815__ .

(D) "Note." The note signed by Borrower and dated .... will be called the "Note." The Note shows that I owe Lender ....
.... Dollars plus interest, which I have promised to pay in monthly payments of principal and interest and to pay in full by ....

(E) "Property." The property that is described below in the section titled "Description Of The Property," will be called the "Property."

BORROWER'S TRANSFER TO LENDER OF RIGHTS IN THE PROPERTY

I mortgage, grant and convey the Property to Lender subject to the terms of this Mortgage. This means that, by signing this Mortgage, I am giving Lender those rights that are stated in this Mortgage and also those rights that the law gives to lenders who hold mortgages on real property. I am giving Lender these rights to protect Lender from possible losses that might result if I fail to:

(A) Pay all the amounts that I owe Lender as stated in the Note;

(B) Pay, with interest, any amounts that Lender spends under this Mortgage, to protect the value of the Property and Lender's rights in the Property;

(C) Pay, with interest, any other amounts that Lender lends to me as Future Advances under Paragraph 23 below; and

(D) Keep all of my other promises and agreements under this Mortgage.

DESCRIPTION OF THE PROPERTY

I give Lender rights in the Property described in (A) through (J) below:

(A) The property which is located at ....
                                                                    [Street]
.... , ... This property is in
              [City]   [State and Zip Code]
.... County in the State of New York. It has the following legal description:

NEW YORK—1 to 4 Family—9/78—**FNMA/FHLMC PLAIN LANGUAGE UNIFORM INSTRUMENT**

EXHIBIT 9-4, cont.

If this property is a condominium, the following must be completed: This property is part of a condominium project known as .... (called the "Condominium Project")
[Name of Condominium Project]
dominium Project"). This property includes my unit and all of my rights in the common elements of the Condominium Project.

If this property is in a planned unit development, the following must be completed: This property is in a development which is a planned unit development known as ....
[Name of Planned Unit Development]
.... (called the "PUD"). The PUD was created by ....
[Document Creating PUD]
.... ;

(B) All buildings and other improvements that are located on the property described in paragraph (A) of this section;

(C) All rights in other property that I have as owner of the property described in paragraph (A) of this section. These rights are known as "easements, rights and appurtenances attached to the property";

(D) All rents or royalties from the property described in paragraph (A) of this section;

(E) All mineral, oil and gas rights and profits, water, water rights and water stock that are part of the property described in paragraph (A) of this section;

(F) All rights that I have in the land which lies in the streets or roads in front of, or next to, the property described in paragraph (A) of this section;

(G) All fixtures that are now or in the future will be on the property described in paragraphs (A) and (B) of this section, and all replacements of and additions to those fixtures, except for those fixtures, replacements or additions that under the law are "consumer goods" and that I acquire more than ten days after the date of the Note. Usually, fixtures are items that are physically attached to buildings, such as hot water heaters;

(H) All of the rights and property described in paragraphs (B) through (F) of this section that I acquire in the future;

(I) All replacements of or additions to the property described in paragraphs (B) through (F) and paragraph (H) of this section; and

(J) All of the amounts that I pay to Lender under Paragraph 2 below.

BORROWER'S RIGHT TO MORTGAGE THE PROPERTY AND BORROWER'S OBLIGATION TO DEFEND OWNERSHIP OF THE PROPERTY

I promise that except for the "exceptions" listed in any title insurance policy which insures Lender's rights in the Property: (A) I lawfully own the Property; (B) I have the right to mortgage, grant and convey the Property to Lender; and (C) there are no outstanding claims or charges against the Property.

I give a general warranty of title to Lender. This means that I will be fully responsible for any losses which Lender suffers because someone other than myself has some of the rights in the Property which I promise that I have. I promise that I will defend my ownership of the Property against any claims of such rights.

UNIFORM PROMISES

I promise and I agree with Lender as follows:

1. BORROWER'S PROMISE TO PAY PRINCIPAL AND INTEREST UNDER THE NOTE AND TO FULFILL OTHER PAYMENT OBLIGATIONS

I will promptly pay to Lender when due: principal and interest under the Note; late charges and prepayment charges as stated in the Note; and principal and interest on Future Advances that I may receive under Paragraph 23 below.

2. AGREEMENTS ABOUT MONTHLY PAYMENTS FOR TAXES AND INSURANCE

(A) Borrower's Obligation to Make Monthly Payments to Lender for Taxes and Insurance
I will pay to Lender all amounts necessary to pay for taxes, assessments, ground rents (if any), and hazard insurance on the Property and mortgage insurance (if any). I will pay those amounts to Lender unless Lender tells me, in writing, that I do not have to do so, or unless the law requires otherwise. I will make those payments on the same day that my monthly payments of principal and interest are due under the Note.

The amount of each of my payments under this Paragraph 2 will be the sum of the following:
(i) One-twelfth of the estimated yearly taxes, assessments and ground rents (if any) on the Property which under the law may be superior to this Mortgage; plus
(ii) One-twelfth of the estimated yearly premium for hazard insurance covering the Property; plus
(iii) One-twelfth of the estimated yearly premium for mortgage insurance (if any).

Lender will determine from time to time my estimated yearly taxes, assessments, ground rents and insurance premiums based upon existing assessments and bills, and reasonable estimates of future assessments and bills. (Taxes, assessments, ground rents and insurance premiums will be called "taxes and insurance.") The amounts that I pay to Lender for taxes and insurance under this Paragraph 2 will be called the "Funds."

EXHIBIT 9-4, cont.

(B) Lender's Obligations Concerning Borrower's Monthly Payments for Taxes and Insurance

Lender will keep the Funds in a savings or banking institution which has its deposits or accounts insured or guaranteed by a Federal or state agency. If Lender is such an institution then Lender may hold the Funds. Except as described in this Paragraph 2, Lender will use the Funds to pay taxes and insurance. Lender will give to me, without charge, an annual accounting of the Funds. That accounting must show all additions to and deductions from the Funds and the reason for each deduction.

Lender may not charge me for holding or keeping the Funds on deposit, for using the Funds to pay taxes and insurance, for analyzing my payments of Funds, or for receiving, verifying and totalling assessments and bills. However, Lender may charge me for these services if Lender pays me interest on the Funds and if the law permits Lender to make such a charge. Lender will not be required to pay me any interest or earnings on the Funds unless either (i) Lender and I agree in writing, at the time I sign this Mortgage, that Lender will pay interest on the Funds; or (ii) the law requires Lender to pay interest on the Funds.

If Lender's estimates are too high or if taxes and insurance rates go down, the amounts that I pay under this Paragraph 2 will be too large. If this happens at a time when I am keeping all of my promises and agreements made in this Mortgage, I will have the right to have the excess amount either promptly repaid to me as a direct refund or credited to my future monthly payments of Funds. There will be excess amounts if, at any time, the sum of (a) the amount of Funds which Lender is holding or keeping on deposit, plus (b) the amount of the monthly payments of Funds which I still must pay between that time and the due dates of taxes and insurance, is greater than the amount necessary to pay the taxes and insurance when they are due.

If, when payments of taxes and insurance are due, Lender has not received enough Funds from me to make those payments, I will pay to Lender whatever additional amount is necessary to pay the taxes and insurance in full. I must pay that additional amount in one or more payments as Lender may require.

When I have paid all of the amounts due under the Note and under this Mortgage, Lender will promptly refund to me any Funds that are then being held or kept on deposit by Lender. If, under Paragraph 20 below, either Lender acquires the Property or the Property is sold, then immediately before the acquisition or sale, Lender will use any Funds which Lender is holding or has on deposit at that time to reduce the amount that I owe to Lender under the Note and under this Mortgage.

3. LENDER'S APPLICATION OF BORROWER'S PAYMENTS

Unless the law requires otherwise, Lender will apply each of my payments under the Note and under Paragraphs 1 and 2 above in the following order and for the following purposes:

(A) First, to pay the amounts then due to Lender under Paragraph 2 above;

(B) Next, to pay interest then due under the Note;

(C) Next, to pay principal then due under the Note; and

(D) Next, to pay interest and principal on any Future Advances that I may have received from Lender under Paragraph 23 below.

4. BORROWER'S OBLIGATION TO PAY CHARGES AND ASSESSMENTS AND TO SATISFY CLAIMS AGAINST THE PROPERTY

I will pay all taxes, assessments, and any other charges and fines that may be imposed on the Property and that may be superior to this Mortgage. I will also make payments due under my lease if I am a tenant on the Property and I will pay ground rents (if any) due on the Property. I will do this either by making the payments to Lender that are described in Paragraph 2 above or, if I am not required to make payments under Paragraph 2, by making payments, when they are due, directly to the persons entitled to them. (In this Mortgage, the word "person" means any person, organization, governmental authority, or other party.) If I make direct payments, then promptly after making any of those payments I will give Lender a receipt which shows that I have done so. If I make payment to Lender under Paragraph 2, I will give Lender all notices or bills that I receive for the amounts due under this Paragraph 4.

Any claim, demand or charge that is made against property because an obligation has not been fulfilled is known as a "lien." I will promptly pay or satisfy all liens against the Property that may be superior to this Mortgage. However, this Mortgage does not require me to satisfy a superior lien if: (A) I agree, in writing, to pay the obligation which gave rise to the superior lien and Lender approves the way in which I agree to pay that obligation; or (B) I, in good faith, argue or defend against the superior lien in a lawsuit so that, during the lawsuit, the superior lien may not be enforced and no part of the Property must be given up.

Condominium and PUD Assessments

If the Property includes a unit in a Condominium Project or in a PUD, I will promptly pay, when they are due, all assessments imposed by the owners association or other organization that governs the Condominium Project or PUD. That association or organization will be called the "Owners Association."

5. BORROWER'S OBLIGATION TO OBTAIN AND TO KEEP HAZARD INSURANCE ON THE PROPERTY

(A) Generally

I will obtain hazard insurance to cover all buildings and other improvements that now are or in the future will be located on the Property. The insurance must cover loss or damage caused by fire, hazards normally covered by "extended coverage" hazard insurance policies, and other hazards for which Lender requires coverage. The insurance must be in the amounts and for the periods of time required by Lender. It is possible that the insurance policy will have provisions that may limit the insurance company's obligation to pay claims if the amount of coverage is too low. Those provisions are known as "co-insurance requirements." Lender may not require me to obtain an amount of coverage that is more than the larger of the following two amounts: either (i) the amount that I owe to Lender under the Note and under this Mortgage; or (ii) the amount necessary to satisfy the co-insurance requirements.

I may choose the insurance company, but my choice is subject to Lender's approval. Lender may not refuse to approve my choice unless the refusal is reasonable. All of the insurance policies and renewals of those policies must include what is known as a "standard mortgage clause" to protect Lender. The form of all policies and the form of all renewals must be acceptable to Lender. Lender will have the right to hold the policies and renewals.

EXHIBIT 9-4, cont.

I will pay the premiums on the insurance policies either by making payments to Lender, as described in Paragraph 2 above, or by paying the insurance company directly when the premium payments are due. If Lender requires, I will promptly give Lender all receipts of paid premiums and all renewal notices that I receive.

If there is a loss or damage to the Property, I will promptly notify the insurance company and Lender. If I do not promptly prove to the insurance company that the loss or damage occurred, then Lender may do so.

The amount paid by the insurance company is called "proceeds." The proceeds will be used to repair or to restore the damaged Property unless: (a) it is not economically possible to make the repairs or restoration; or (b) the use of the proceeds for that purpose would lessen the protection given to Lender by this Mortgage; or (c) Lender and I have agreed in writing not to use the proceeds for that purpose. If the repair or restoration is not economically possible or if it would lessen Lender's protection under this Mortgage, then the proceeds will be used to reduce the amount that I owe to Lender under the Note and under this Mortgage. If any of the proceeds remain after the amount that I owe to Lender has been paid in full, the remaining proceeds will be paid to me. The use of proceeds to reduce the amount that I owe to Lender will not be a prepayment that is subject to the prepayment charge provisions, if any, under the Note.

If I abandon the Property, or if I do not answer, within 30 days, a notice from Lender stating that the insurance company has offered to settle a claim for insurance benefits, then Lender has the authority to collect the proceeds. Lender may then use the proceeds to repair or restore the Property or to reduce the amount that I owe to Lender under the Note and under this Mortgage. The 30-day period will begin on the date the notice is mailed or, if it is not mailed, on the date the notice is delivered.

If any proceeds are used to reduce the amount of principal which I owe to Lender under the Note, that use will not delay the due date or change the amount of any of my monthly payments under the Note and under Paragraphs 1 and 2 above. However, Lender and I may agree in writing to those delays or changes.

If Lender acquires the Property under Paragraph 20 below, all of my rights in the insurance policies will belong to Lender. Also, all of my rights in any proceeds which are paid because of damage that occurred before the Property is acquired by Lender or sold will belong to Lender. However, Lender's rights in those proceeds will not be greater than the amount that I owe to Lender under the Note and under this Mortgage immediately before the Property is acquired by Lender or sold.

(B) Agreements that Apply to Condominiums and PUD's
(i) If the Property includes a unit in a Condominium Project, the Owners Association may maintain a hazard insurance policy which covers the entire Condominium Project. That policy will be called the "master policy." So long as the master policy remains in effect and meets the requirements stated in this Paragraph 5: (a) my obligation to obtain and to keep hazard insurance on the Property is satisfied; (b) I will not be required to include an amount for hazard insurance premiums in my monthly payment of Funds to Lender under Paragraph 2 above; and (c) if there is a conflict, concerning the use of proceeds, between (1) the terms of this Paragraph 5, and (2) the law or the terms of the declaration, by-laws, regulations or other documents creating or governing the Condominium Project, then that law or the terms of those documents will govern the use of proceeds. I will promptly give Lender notice if the master policy is interrupted or terminated. During any time that the master policy is not in effect the terms of (a), (b) and (c) of this subparagraph 5(B)(i) will not apply.

(ii) If the Property includes a unit in a Condominium Project, it is possible that proceeds will be paid to me instead of being used to repair or to restore the Property. I give Lender my rights to those proceeds. If the Property includes a unit in a PUD, it is possible that proceeds will be paid to me instead of being used to repair or to restore the common areas or facilities of the PUD. I give Lender my rights to those proceeds. All of the proceeds described in this subparagraph 5(B)(ii) will be paid to Lender and will be used to reduce the amount that I owe to Lender under the Note and under this Mortgage. If any of those proceeds remain after the amount that I owe to Lender has been paid in full, the remaining proceeds will be paid to me. The use of proceeds to reduce the amount that I owe to Lender will not be a prepayment that is subject to the prepayment charge provisions, if any, under the Note.

6. BORROWER'S OBLIGATION TO MAINTAIN THE PROPERTY AND TO FULFILL OBLIGATIONS IN LEASE, AND AGREEMENTS ABOUT CONDOMINIUMS AND PUD'S

(A) Agreements about Maintaining the Property and Keeping Promises in Lease
I will keep the Property in good repair. I will not destroy, damage or substantially change the Property, and I will not allow the Property to deteriorate. If I do not own but am a tenant on the Property, I will fulfill my obligations under my lease.

(B) Agreements that Apply to Condominiums and PUD's
If the Property is a unit in a Condominium Project or in a PUD, I will fulfill all of my obligations under the declaration, by-laws, regulations and other documents that create or govern the Condominium Project or PUD. Also, I will not divide the Property into smaller parts that may be owned separately (known as "partition or subdivision"). I will not consent to certain actions unless I have first given Lender notice and obtained Lender's consent in writing. Those actions are:

(A) The abandonment or termination of the Condominium Project or PUD, unless, in the case of a condominium, the abandonment or termination is required by law;

(B) Any significant change to the declaration, by-laws or regulations of the Owners Association, trust agreement, articles of incorporation, or other documents that create or govern the Condominium Project or PUD, including, for example, a change in the percentage of ownership rights, held by unit owners, in the Condominium Project or in the common areas or facilities of the PUD;

(C) A decision by the Owners Association to terminate professional management and to begin self-management of the Condominium Project or PUD; and

(D) The transfer, release, creation of liens, partition or subdivision of all or part of the common areas and facilities of the PUD. (However, this provision does not apply to the transfer by the Owners Association of rights to use those common areas and facilities for utilities and other similar or related purposes.)

EXHIBIT 9-4, cont.

7. LENDER'S RIGHT TO TAKE ACTION TO PROTECT THE PROPERTY

If: (A) I do not keep my promises and agreements made in this Mortgage, or (B) someone, including me, begins a legal proceeding that may significantly affect Lender's rights in the Property (such as, for example, a legal proceeding in bankruptcy, in probate, for condemnation, or to enforce laws or regulations), then Lender may do and pay for whatever is necessary to protect the value of the Property and Lender's rights in the Property. Lender's actions under this Paragraph 7 may include, for example, appearing in court, paying reasonable attorney's fees, and entering on the Property to make repairs. Lender must give me notice before Lender may take any of these actions.

I will pay to Lender any amounts, with interest, which Lender spends under this Paragraph 7. This Mortgage will protect Lender in case I do not keep this promise to pay those amounts with interest.

I will pay those amounts to Lender when Lender sends me a notice requesting that I do so. I will also pay interest on those amounts at the same rate stated in the Note. However, if payment of interest at that rate would violate the law, I will pay interest on the amounts spent by Lender under this Paragraph 7 at the highest rate that the law allows. Interest on each amount will begin on the date that the amount is spent by Lender. However, Lender and I may agree in writing to terms of payment that are different from those in this paragraph.

Although Lender may take action under this Paragraph 7, Lender does not have to do so.

8. LENDER'S RIGHT TO INSPECT THE PROPERTY

Lender, and others authorized by Lender, may enter on and inspect the Property. They must do so in a reasonable manner and at reasonable times. Before one of those inspections is made, Lender must give me notice stating a reasonable purpose for the inspection. That purpose must be related to Lender's rights in the Property.

9. AGREEMENTS ABOUT CONDEMNATION OF THE PROPERTY

A taking of property by any governmental authority by eminent domain is known as "condemnation." I give to Lender my right: (A) to proceeds of all awards or claims for damages resulting from condemnation or other governmental taking of the Property; and (B) to proceeds from a sale of the Property that is made to avoid condemnation. All of those proceeds will be paid to Lender.

If all of the Property is taken, the proceeds will be used to reduce the amount that I owe to Lender under the Note and under this Mortgage. If any of the proceeds remain after the amount that I owe to Lender has been paid in full, the remaining proceeds will be paid to me. Unless Lender and I agree otherwise in writing, if only a part of the Property is taken, the amount that I owe to Lender will only be reduced by the amount of proceeds multiplied by the following amount: (i) the total amount that I owe to Lender under the Note and under this Mortgage immediately before the taking, divided by (ii) the fair market value of the Property immediately before the taking. The remainder of the proceeds will be paid to me. The use of proceeds to reduce the amount that I owe to Lender will not be a prepayment that is subject to the prepayment charge provisions, if any, under the Note.

If I abandon the Property, or if I do not answer, within 30 days, a notice from Lender stating that a governmental authority has offered to make a payment or to settle a claim for damages, then Lender has the authority to collect the proceeds. Lender may then use the proceeds to repair or restore the Property or to reduce the amount that I owe to Lender under the Note and under this Mortgage. The 30-day period will begin on the date the notice is mailed or, if it is not mailed, on the date the notice is delivered.

If any proceeds are used to reduce the amount of principal which I owe to Lender under the Note, that use will not delay the due date or change the amount of any of my monthly payments under the Note and under Paragraphs 1 and 2 above. However, Lender and I may agree in writing to those delays or changes.

Condemnation of Common Areas of PUD

If the Property includes a unit in a PUD, the promises and agreements in this Paragraph 9 will apply to a condemnation, or sale to avoid condemnation, of the PUD's common areas and facilities as well as of the Property.

10. CONTINUATION OF BORROWER'S OBLIGATIONS

Lender may allow a person who takes over my rights and obligations to delay or to change the amount of the monthly payments of principal and interest due under the Note or under this Mortgage. Even if Lender does this, however, that person and I will both still be fully obligated under the Note and under this Mortgage unless the conditions stated in Paragraph 19 below have been met.

Lender may allow those delays or changes for a person who takes over my rights and obligations, even if Lender is requested not to do so. Lender will not be required to bring a lawsuit against such a person for not fulfilling obligations under the Note or under this Mortgage, even if Lender is requested to do so.

11. CONTINUATION OF LENDER'S RIGHTS

Even if Lender does not exercise or enforce any right of Lender under this Mortgage or under the law, Lender will still have all of those rights and may exercise and enforce them in the future. Even if Lender obtains insurance, pays taxes, or pays other claims, charges or liens against the Property, Lender will still have the right, under Paragraph 20 below, to demand that I make Immediate Payment In Full (see Paragraph 20 for a definition of this phrase) of the amount that I owe to Lender under the Note and under this Mortgage.

12. LENDER'S ABILITY TO ENFORCE MORE THAN ONE OF LENDER'S RIGHTS

Each of Lender's rights under this Mortgage is separate. Lender may exercise and enforce one or more of those rights, as well as any of Lender's other rights under the law, one at a time or all at once.

13. OBLIGATIONS OF BORROWERS AND OF PERSONS TAKING OVER BORROWER'S RIGHTS OR OBLIGATIONS; AGREEMENTS CONCERNING CAPTIONS

Subject to the terms of Paragraph 19 below, any person who takes over my rights or obligations under this Mortgage will have all of my rights and will be obligated to keep all of my promises and agreements made in this Mortgage. Similarly, any person who takes over Lender's rights or obligations under this Mortgage will have all of Lender's rights and will be obligated to keep all of Lender's agreements made in this Mortgage.

EXHIBIT 9-4, cont.

If more than one person signs this Mortgage as Borrower, each of us is fully obligated to keep all of Borrower's promises and obligations contained in this Mortgage. Lender may enforce Lender's rights under this Mortgage against each of us individually or against all of us together. This means that any one of us may be required to pay all of the amounts owed under the Note and under this Mortgage. However, if one of us does not sign the Note, then: (A) that person is signing this Mortgage only to give that person's rights in the Property to Lender under the terms of this Mortgage; and (B) that person is not personally obligated to make payments or to act under the Note or under this Mortgage.

The captions and titles of this Mortgage are for convenience only. They may not be used to interpret or to define the terms of this Mortgage.

14. AGREEMENTS ABOUT GIVING NOTICES REQUIRED UNDER THIS MORTGAGE

Unless the law requires otherwise, any notice that must be given to me under this Mortgage will be given by delivering it or by mailing it addressed to me at the address stated in the section above titled "Description Of The Property." A notice will be delivered or mailed to me at a different address if I give Lender a notice of my different address. Any notice that must be given to Lender under this Mortgage will be given by mailing it to Lender's address stated in paragraph (C) of the section above titled "Words Used Often In This Document." A notice will be mailed to Lender at a different address if Lender gives me a notice of the different address. A notice required by this Mortgage is given when it is mailed or when it is delivered according to the requirements of this Paragraph 14.

15. AGREEMENTS ABOUT UNIFORM MORTGAGE AND LAW THAT GOVERNS THIS MORTGAGE

This is a "Uniform Mortgage." It contains "uniform promises" that are in mortgages used all over the country and also "non-uniform promises" that vary, to a limited extent, in different parts of the country.

The law that applies in the place that the Property is located will govern this Mortgage. If any term of this Mortgage or of the Note conflicts with the law, all other terms of this Mortgage and of the Note will still remain in effect if they can be given effect without the conflicting term. This means that any terms of this Mortgage and of the Note which conflict with the law can be separated from the remaining terms, and the remaining terms will still be enforced.

16. BORROWER'S COPY OF THE NOTE AND OF THIS MORTGAGE

I will be given a copy of the Note and of this Mortgage. Those copies must show that the original Note and Mortgage have been signed. I will be given those copies either when I sign the Note and this Mortgage or after this Mortgage has been recorded in the proper official records.

17. AGREEMENTS THAT APPLY TO VA LOANS

A loan that is guaranteed or insured by the United States Veterans Administration is known as a "VA loan." If the loan that I promise to pay in the Note is a VA loan, then my rights and obligations, as well as those of Lender, are governed by that law which is known as Title 38 of the United States Code and the Regulations made under that Title (called the "VA Requirements"). One or more terms of this Mortgage, or of other documents that are signed in connection with my VA loan, might conflict with the VA Requirements. For example, the prepayment terms in the Note or Paragraph 19 of this Mortgage might conflict with the VA Requirements. Lender and I agree that if there is a conflict, the conflicting terms of this Mortgage or other documents are modified or eliminated as much as is necessary to make all of the conflicting terms agree with the VA Requirements.

18. BORROWER'S OBLIGATION TO PAY MORTGAGE INSURANCE PREMIUMS

If Lender required mortgage insurance as a condition of making the loan that I promise to pay under the Note, I will pay the premiums for that mortgage insurance. I will pay the premiums until the requirement for mortgage insurance ends according to my written agreement with Lender or according to law. Lender may require me to pay the premiums in the manner described in Paragraph 2 above.

NON-UNIFORM PROMISES

I also promise and agree with Lender as follows:

19. AGREEMENTS ABOUT ASSUMPTION OF THIS MORTGAGE AND ABOUT LENDER'S RIGHTS IF BORROWER TRANSFERS THE PROPERTY WITHOUT MEETING CERTAIN CONDITIONS

If I sell or transfer all or part of the Property or any rights in the Property, any person to whom I sell or transfer the Property may take over all of my rights and obligations under this Mortgage (known as an "assumption of the Mortgage") if certain conditions are met. Those conditions are: (A) I give Lender notice of the sale or transfer; (B) Lender agrees that the person's credit is satisfactory; (C) the person agrees to pay interest on the amount owed to Lender under the Note and under this Mortgage at whatever rate Lender requires; and (D) the person signs an assumption agreement that is acceptable to Lender and that obligates the person to keep all of the promises and agreements made in the Note and in this Mortgage. If I sell or transfer the Property and each of the conditions in (A), (B), (C) and (D) of this Paragraph 19 is satisfied, Lender will release me from all of my obligations under the Note and under this Mortgage.

If I sell or transfer the Property and the conditions in (A), (B), (C) and (D) of this Paragraph 19 are not satisfied, I will still be fully obligated under the Note and under this Mortgage and Lender may require Immediate Payment In Full, as that phrase is defined in Paragraph 20 below. However, Lender will not have the right to require Immediate Payment In Full as a result of certain transfers. Those transfers are: (i) the creation of liens or other claims against the Property that are inferior to this Mortgage; (ii) a transfer of rights in household appliances, to a person who provides me with the money to buy those appliances, in order to protect that person against possible losses; (iii) a transfer of the Property to surviving co-owners, following the death of a co-owner, when the transfer is automatic according to law; (iv) leasing the Property for a term of three years or less, as long as the lease does not include an option to buy.

EXHIBIT 9-4, cont.

If Lender requires Immediate Payment In Full under this Paragraph 19, Lender will send me, in the manner described in Paragraph 14 above, a notice which states this requirement. The notice will give me at least 30 days to make the required payment. The 30-day period will begin on the date the notice is mailed or, if it is not mailed, on the date the notice is delivered. If I do not make the required payment during that period, Lender may bring a lawsuit for "foreclosure and sale" under Paragraph 20 below without giving me any further notice or demand for payment. (See Paragraph 20 for a definition of "foreclosure and sale.")

20. LENDER'S RIGHTS IF BORROWER FAILS TO KEEP PROMISES AND AGREEMENTS

If all of the conditions stated in subparagraphs (A), (B), and (C) of this Paragraph 20 are met, Lender may require that I pay immediately the entire amount then remaining unpaid under the Note and under this Mortgage. Lender may do this without making any further demand for payment. This requirement will be called "Immediate Payment In Full."

If Lender requires Immediate Payment In Full, Lender may bring a lawsuit to take away all of my remaining rights in the Property and to have the Property sold. At this sale Lender or another person may acquire the Property. This is known as "foreclosure and sale." In any lawsuit for foreclosure and sale, Lender will have the right to collect all costs allowed by law.

Lender may require Immediate Payment In Full under this Paragraph 20 only if all of the following conditions are met:

(A) I fail to keep any promise or agreement made in this Mortgage, including the promises to pay when due the amounts that I owe to Lender under the Note and under this Mortgage; and

(B) Lender sends to me, in the manner described in Paragraph 14 above, a notice that states:
- (i) The promise or agreement that I failed to keep;
- (ii) The action that I must take to correct that failure;
- (iii) A date by which I must correct the failure. That date must be at least 30 days from the date on which the notice is mailed to me, or, if it is not mailed, from the date on which it is delivered to me;
- (iv) That if I do not correct the failure by the date stated in the notice, I will be in default and Lender may require Immediate Payment In Full, and Lender or another person may acquire the Property by means of foreclosure and sale;
- (v) That I may speak with a named representative of Lender to discuss any questions which I have about the things stated in the notice;
- (vi) That if I meet the conditions stated in Paragraph 21 below, I will have the right to have any lawsuit for foreclosure and sale discontinued and to have the Note and this Mortgage remain in full effect as if Immediate Payment In Full had never been required; and
- (vii) That I have the right in any lawsuit for foreclosure and sale to argue that I did keep my promises and agreements under the Note and under this Mortgage, and to present any other defenses that I may have; and

(C) I do not correct the failure stated in the notice from Lender by the date stated in that notice.

21. BORROWER'S RIGHT TO HAVE LENDER'S LAWSUIT FOR FORECLOSURE AND SALE DISCONTINUED

Even if Lender has required Immediate Payment In Full, I may have the right to have discontinued any lawsuit brought by Lender for foreclosure and sale or for other enforcement of this Mortgage. I will have this right at any time before a judgment has been entered enforcing this Mortgage if I meet the following conditions:

(A) I pay to Lender the full amount that would have been due under this Mortgage, the Note, and any notes for Future Advances under Paragraph 23 below if Lender had not required Immediate Payment In Full; and

(B) I correct my failure to keep any of my other promises or agreements made in this Mortgage; and

(C) I pay all of Lender's reasonable expenses in enforcing this Mortgage including, for example, reasonable attorney's fees; and

(D) I do whatever Lender reasonably requires to assure that Lender's rights in the Property, Lender's rights under this Mortgage, and my obligations under the Note and under this Mortgage continue unchanged.

If I fulfill all of the conditions in this Paragraph 21, then the Note and this Mortgage will remain in full effect as if Immediate Payment In Full had never been required.

22. LENDER'S RIGHTS TO RENTAL PAYMENTS FROM THE PROPERTY AND TO TAKE POSSESSION OF THE PROPERTY

As additional protection for Lender, I give to Lender all of my rights to any rental payments from the Property. However, until Lender requires Immediate Payment In Full under Paragraphs 19 or 20 above, or until I abandon the Property, I have the right to collect and keep those rental payments as they become due. I have not given any of my rights to rental payments from the Property to anyone else, and I will not do so without Lender's consent in writing.

If Lender requires Immediate Payment In Full under Paragraphs 19 or 20 above, or if I abandon the Property, then Lender, persons authorized by Lender, or a receiver appointed by a court at Lender's request may: (A) collect the rental payments, including overdue rental payments, directly from the tenants; (B) enter on and take possession of the Property; (C) manage the Property; and (D) sign, cancel and change leases. I agree that if Lender notifies the tenants that Lender has the right to collect rental payments directly from them under this Paragraph 22, the tenants may make those rental payments to Lender without having to ask whether I have failed to keep my promises and agreements under this Mortgage.

If there is a judgment for Lender in a lawsuit for foreclosure and sale, I will pay to Lender reasonable rent from the date the judgment is entered for as long as I occupy the Property. However, this does not give me the right to occupy the Property.

EXHIBIT 9-4, cont.

All rental payments collected by Lender or by a receiver, other than the rent paid by me under this Paragraph 22, will be used first to pay the costs of collecting rental payments and of managing the Property. If any part of the rental payments remains after those costs have been paid in full, the remaining part will be used to reduce the amount that I owe to Lender under the Note and under this Mortgage. The costs of managing the Property may include the receiver's fees, reasonable attorney's fees, and the cost of any necessary bonds. Lender and the receiver will be obligated to account only for those rental payments that they actually receive.

23. AGREEMENTS ABOUT FUTURE ADVANCES

I may ask Lender to make one or more loans to me in addition to the loan that I promise to pay under the Note. Lender may, before this Mortgage is discharged, make those additional loans to me. This Mortgage will protect Lender from possible losses that might result from my failure to pay the amounts of any of those additional loans plus interest, only if the notes which contain my promises to pay those additional loans state that this Mortgage will give Lender such protection. Additional loans made by Lender that are protected by this Mortgage will be called "Future Advances." The principal amount that I owe to Lender under the Note and under all notes for Future Advances, not including the amounts spent by Lender to protect the value of the Property and Lender's rights in the Property, may not be greater than the original amount of the Note plus US $ .... (Zero - 0 -) ....

24. LENDER'S OBLIGATION TO DISCHARGE THIS MORTGAGE WHEN THE NOTE AND THIS MORTGAGE ARE PAID IN FULL

When Lender has been paid all amounts due under the Note, under this Mortgage and under any notes for Future Advances, Lender will discharge this Mortgage by delivering a certificate stating that this Mortgage has been satisfied. I will not be required to pay Lender for the discharge, but I will pay all costs of recording the discharge in the proper official records.

25. AGREEMENTS ABOUT NEW YORK LIEN LAW

I will receive all amounts lent to me by Lender subject to the trust fund provisions of Section 13 of the New York Lien Law. This means that if, on the date this Mortgage is recorded in the proper official records, construction or other work on any building or other improvement located on the Property has not been completed for at least four months, I will: (A) hold all amounts, which I receive and which I have a right to receive from Lender under the Note and as Future Advances, as a "trust fund"; and (B) use those amounts to pay for that construction or work before I use them for any other purpose. The fact that I am holding those amounts as a "trust fund" means that I have a special responsibility under the law to use the amounts in the manner described in this Paragraph 25.

By signing this Mortgage I agree to all of the above.

Witnesses:

....
                                                                     —Borrower

....
                                                                     —Borrower

State of New York, ... County ss:

On this .... day of .... , 19 ...... , before me personally came ....

.... to
me known and known to me to be the individual(s) described in and who executed the foregoing instrument, and ..he.. duly acknowledged to me that ..he.. executed the same.

....

                                     Notary Public

——————————— (Space Below This Line Reserved For Lender and Recorder) ———————————

erty is taken by a governmental unit and compensation is paid in exchange for that taking or in the event that any easements or rights of way are granted across the property, the proceeds from such transactions shall also be held as security for the lender. From a practical point of view, this would require either that any proceeds received in such a transaction be given to the lending institution or that a release be secured from the lending institution allowing the borrower to retain those proceeds for his or her personal use.

Insurance   A mortgage usually requires that the borrower (owner of the property) maintain insurance for fire and other risks and that the amount shall be an amount acceptable to the lender and that the lender shall be named in the insurance policy as a beneficiary to the extent of the lender's interest. This will require that the amount of insurance on the property be at least equal to the remaining balance of the mortgage. If a house is purchased for $52,000, with a $38,900 mortgage, the amount of fire insurance would probably be at least $38,900. A purchaser could have additional coverage and, as a matter of good sense, should insure the house for its full value. Insurance of the buildings should not be required for more than their fair market value. In addition to fire insurance, the buyer should obtain adequate liability insurance. It is advisable to review insurance coverage annually to maintain adequate protection during periods of rising property values. If the borrower fails to maintain the insurance policies, the lender may obtain insurance and will be entitled to reimbursement from the borrower.

Other Clauses   A mortgage generally requires that the owner of the property maintain the property in reasonable condition; that the property may not be sold without the consent of the lender, that no portion of the property may be sold without the lender's consent, or that the owner of the property may not change the property by decreasing or adding on to the buildings without the consent of the lender; that the borrower will pay on a current basis all taxes, assessments, water rents, sewer rents, and so forth that come due against the property. The mortgage also stipulates that the borrower must be able to show receipts for the payment of these items upon the request of the lender.

In addition, the mortgage also often states that in the event of a lawsuit affecting the property or if the lending institution's interest is challenged or if the lending institution seeks to foreclose on the property, all expenses involved in such a transaction (including the attorney's fees) shall be paid for by the borrower.

In a mortgage, the borrower further represents to the lender that the borrower is the owner of the property; that no one else has any claims against the property; that in the event someone else claims an interest in the property, the borrower will make sure that the lender has no losses or expenses because of such claims; that as the owner of the property the borrower will comply with any laws concerning the ownership and use of the property; and that in the event the borrower is in violation of any such laws, he or she will, within 90 days after notice of the violation, correct the violation.

There is also often a clause providing that in the event that the lender has to sell the property, the property may, at the lender's option, be sold as one piece or as several pieces. Frequently, a piece of property will sell for more money if it is sold in smaller pieces than if it is sold intact. It is not the obligation of the lender to sell the property under the most advantageous conditions to the borrower. The lender has the right, in the event of a default, to sell the property in the most expeditious manner for the lender. This will usually be as a single parcel.

A typical mortgage also provides that the lender or its agent may inspect the property and enter the premises at any reasonable time to determine that its security interest has not been impaired and that the requirements of the mortgage are being met. It further provides that, in the event that it is necessary to file any additional papers in order to acquire a security interest, the lender may file those papers even without the borrower's signature. Finally, there is usually a provision that the mortgage may only be changed by a written instrument signed by the various parties.

CLOSING STATEMENT AND ADJUSTMENTS

In addition to reimbursement for the purchase price, the seller may also be entitled to reimbursement for prepaid items such as insurance; city, county, village, and school taxes; fire and water assessments; unused heating fuel; and so forth. The purchaser, in turn, gets credit for payments he or she will make for items that have benefited the seller. These may include taxes and assessments and also rents paid by tenants. Down payments and the amount of seller financing are also credits to the purchaser. The balance due to the seller at closing is the purchase price plus adjustments due the seller less the credits to the purchaser.

Each party has expenses of sale that must be paid at the closing. The seller's expenses include revenue stamps, recording fees, costs of the tax search, and legal services rendered. These items are usually collected by the seller's attorney. If there is an abstract of title, the seller usually also pays for the updating of that abstract prior to closing. It is the buyer's responsibility to pay for recording the deed and mortgage and any mortgage tax imposed. The buyer may also have to pay fees to the lender for credit checks, appraisals, and so on. The buyer must also pay his or her attorney's fees and fee for the continuation of the abstract of title after closing. If there is title insurance, the cost of that insurance will be paid by the buyer. Exhibit 9–5, shows a typical closing statement in a transaction where a bank provided funds and took back a mortgage. Generally, the closing statement is prepared by the attorney for the buyer and seller for their respective clients. This statement may be useful in the preparation of an individual's tax return and in determining the basis for property at the time of a future sale.

EXHIBIT 9-5
Statement of Sale

Seller:	Steven and Carole Blumenkrantz	**Dated:**	October 1, 1981		
	No. 15 Main Street	**Buyer:**	Robert and Sarah Rothenberg		
Village:					
City or Town:	Oneonta	**County:**	Otsego	**State:**	New York

Purchase price			$52,000.00
Fuel	200 Gallons @ $99.8/Gal + 6% Tax		211.58
City taxes (adjusted)			
County taxes (adjusted)	Jan. 1 –Dec. 31	$1,200×3/12	300.00
Village taxes (adjusted)	June 1–May 30	600×7/12	350.00
School taxes (adjusted)	July 1–June 30	1,500×9/12	1,125,00
Fire taxes (adjusted)			
Total amount due seller			$53,986.58

Credits to purchaser:		
Amount paid down:	$ 500.00	
First mortgage: 10.5%×20 Years	38,900.00	
Interest: from To		
Second mortgage:		
Interest: from To		
Village taxes (assumed):		
City taxes (assumed):		
County taxes (assumed):		
Local assessment (assumed):		
School taxes (assumed):		
Water:		
Rents (prorated):		39,400.00
Balance due seller:		$14,586.58

Paid as follows:			$12,600.00
	Certified check	XYZ Bank	1,986.58
	Buyer's personal check	XYZ Bank	$14,586.58

Expenses of purchaser:		Expenses of seller:	
Recording deed	$ 7.00	Continuing search	$ 35.00
Recording mortgage	13.00	Revenue stamps, deed	57.20
Mortgage tax	291.75	Closing redate	
Escrows		Recording discharge of mortgage	4.25
Lender's fees		Recording mortgage—immediate	
Post closing search	40.00	Recording mortgage—assignment	
Title insurance		Tax and federal search	4.00
Services and disbursements	520.00	Services and disbursements	520.00
Total	$871.75	Total	$620.45

RECORDING

After the closing, the signed and acknowledged documents are sent to the clerk of the county in which the land is located for purposes of recording. This procedure gives the public *notice* of the transfer of ownership as well as of any mortgage or other encumbrances placed on the property. The importance of recording cannot be underestimated. There is a rule of law that states that any person acquiring an interest in property takes it *subject to notice* of any existing claims or rights. Recording does not affect the validity of the instrument. It protects the grantee against possible subsequent transfers of the property, which could divest him of title, by placing all persons on notice of the grantee's interest in the property.

Notice means knowledge in the legal sense, either actual (from the facts of a particular situation) or implied (i.e., which can be acquired from the facts without much difficulty). Notice also includes all items of record (county clerk, surrogate's court, and so on).

For example, an individual knows that your house has been sold to Mr. and Mrs. Jones. He or she has actual knowledge of that fact and could not get better title to your house than the Joneses by taking a deed from you even if the deed to the Joneses has not been recorded. If that same individual does not have actual knowledge of the transfer to the Joneses, he or she will still be unable to acquire a better title than the Joneses if the Joneses record the deed. Recording has given him or her implied notice of the sale to the Joneses.

All states have recording statutes that specify the requirements for recording. For example, in New York an instrument must be in recordable form. This includes designation of grantor and grantee, description of the property transferred, words of conveyance (i.e., all right title and interest, etc.), and signature of the grantor, as well as an acknowledgment before a notary public or other authorized person. There is also a requirement for a transfer tax to be paid ($4.00 per $1000 rounded upward) as well as recording fees ($1 per instrument plus $3 per page).

TITLE ASSURANCES

In light of the large outlay of capital or the large liability incurred in the purchasing of real property or both, the buyer must get more than the grantor's warranty of *quiet enjoyment*. There are two methods of assurance of quality of title used today, abstract of title and title insurance.

Abstract of Title

The abstract is the history of conveyances, relative to the premises to be transferred, showing any liens, mortgages, and/or other encumbrances. The abstract should indicate that a clear "chain of title" exists to the grantor. Note that the abstract is *only* a search of the public records; it is not an inspection of the property or a guarantee of title, legal description, or survey. After an abstract is prepared, either by an individual, an attorney, or an abstract company, it is reviewed by the buyer's attorney, who renders an opinion as to the marketability of the property (i.e., chain of title). This opinion, like the abstract, is limited and does not cover items that a survey or physical inspection of the property would show. The abstract of title becomes the property of the purchaser. In the event that there is a defect in the title that was not stated in the attorney's opinion, the purchaser and certain other persons who have reasonably relied on the opinion and abstract can proceed in litigation against the attorney for the erroneous opinion.

In the case of Glawatz v. People's Guaranty Search Co., 49 A.D. 65 (N.Y. 1900) the court held that the guaranties and warranties of either an abstract company or an attorney are contractual in nature and only amount to a guaranty to the person ordering the search, his or her heirs, devisees, and grantees.

Title Insurance

The second method of assurance a grantee can get is title insurance. In lieu of an attorney's rendering an opinion on a title, an insurance company insures the title based on their review of the public records or abstract. The amount of insurance is usually based on the purchase price and covers the purchaser in the event of title defect. The policy may also cover the mortgage holder's interest in the property. Title insurance operates in the same manner as other casualty insurance by spreading the risk of loss over a great number of insured persons. Note that title insurance does not protect against defects an accurate survey would reveal or defects that occur after title insurance has been written. Title insurance covers only the specific purchaser named in the policy and for not more than whichever is the less—the purchase price or the face value of the property.

ADVERSE POSSESSION

A problem that arises with property ownership and is not reflected on the title documents is *adverse possession*. If an individual has (1) actual, (2) exclusive, (3) open and notorious, (4) continuous possession of a parcel, (5) under a claim of right, the parcel may be claimed by that individual. This claim may prevail if the individual's possession was for the required statutory period. Most states have periods running from 10 to 20 years.

The requirement of actual possession includes two elements: intent and dominance. The adverse possessor must intend to own the land and must exercise all types of influence over the land that would indicate this intent. Casual occupancy of the land from time to time would not be sufficient. Fencing and/or making improvements or using the land for wood lot or pasture would probably indicate sufficient act of dominance with the intent to possess.

Exclusive possession requires the absence of all other persons who may have a claim. Open and notorious possession requires that the public (i.e., neighbors, authorities, and so on) would know about the adverse possessor's possession. For this condition to be met, a reasonably prudent person who inspects the land would have to be aware that the adverse possessor was there and was claiming a right. Pitching a tent in the midst of a 200-acre forest and being there for the statutory period would probably be insufficient to meet this requirement.

The adverse possessor must use the land continuously and without interruption for the term of the statute in the state in which the land is located. The use must be for the particular purpose for which the land was meant. The requirement of continuity, however, does not mean constant use, 365 days per year. For example; if the land consisted of a wood lot, the adverse possessor would have to use the lot each year for purposes of cutting wood; a summer residence would have to be used each summer. It would not be necessary to cut wood each day or to occupy the summer premises during the winter.

Claim of right requires the claimant to have reason to believe he or she has a basis in law for claiming the property. Use of property with the consent of the owner nullifies the claim of adverse possession. The adverse possessor's use must be in opposition to the interests of any true owner. The term *hostile* is often used to describe this claim. If the adverse possessor is on the premises by lease or other permission of the true owner, the adverse possession claim will fail.

Contrary to popular beliefs, payment or nonpayment of taxes is not determinative of a claimant's adverse possession. Payment might be an indication or a *piece* of evidence that could show the intent of the adverse claim.

FRAUD

After taking possession of the premises, the buyers may find certain defects existing of which they were unaware at the time of the closing. These could include such items as faulty electricity, plumbing, foundation, roof, and so on. Generally, the rule of *caveat emptor* (let the buyer beware) would control, and there would be no recourse for the buyer.

Fraud is an exception to this rule (Guy v. First Carolinas Joint Stock Land Bank of Columbia, 171 S.E. 341 [N.C. 1933]). The elements of fraud are a material misrepresentation of fact, which is reasonably relied upon by the buyers to their detriment. Misrepresentation can come about in a number of ways.

If the defects were "hidden" by the seller, the courts appear to be of the opinion that the buyer could bring a successful action to recover damages in the amount of the cost of curing the defect. Whether a defect has been hidden or not is a question of fact. For example, a seller, who, prior to sale, puts up shelving and paneling in a basement with obvious water leaks, with the intent of hiding the water marks from persons examining the property, could be liable to the buyer.

Statements made prior to sale, by the seller or his or her agents, with respect to the quality or condition of the premises, zoning, neighbors, and so on, which were not true and which were "reasonably" relied upon by the buyer, causing monetary damage, could be grounds for court relief. Sellers may also be held liable when they have a duty to speak. If questioned as to certain facts such as water leaks in the first example, a seller may be held liable for silence.

Remedies for fraud are usually left to the court on a case-by-case basis. There are several general remedies available. Allowing the party upon which the fraud has been perpetrated to avoid the contract is one. The term *voidable* is used to describe this remedy, and the party voiding the contract is no longer obligated to perform on the contract. This remedy is available only if the contract is executory.

A second remedy is rescission which provides that the injured party is placed in a position as if he or she had never entered into the contract. This remedy is available only if the contract has been completed and executed. In order to rescind, the injured party must return all benefits he or she has received from the contract.

Recent decisions have also held builder-sellers liable to a greater extent than the general public-seller. The courts have placed the builder in the position of a seller of goods, giving the buyer of a new home an *implied warranty* of merchantability. This would entitle the buyer to damages for defects such as those discussed above.

FORECLOSURE

Foreclosure is a remedy for nonpayment of the bond obligation. The lender, with the supervision and direction of the courts, causes the borrower's property to be sold, usually by the county or city marshal. The proceeds of the sale are used to pay the debts that exist against the property, including the note that the borrower signed. Any additional money that remains after the various creditors are paid will be given to the borrower. In the event that there is not enough money to satisfy the debts, a judgment may be obtainable for the deficiency against the borrower.

LAND CONTRACTS

In a period of increasing interest rates, lending institutions usually restrict the sale of property in which they have a security interest. They usually will not allow an assumption or a sale subject to a mortgage, but will require the seller to pay off the note and the buyer to execute a new note at a higher interest rate. To avoid this situation, some parties enter into a *land contract*.

A *land contract* is a long-term contract whereby the seller agrees to sell the property to a buyer, the buyer agrees to purchase the property from the seller, and both agree that buyer will make installment payments to seller and that the transfer of possession of the property is to take place immediately. Legal title will not pass until a future date. This is technically not a sale, and therefore the seller's note and mortgage will often not become due. Before using this technique, one should carefully check the seller's obligation to the bank. Some banks will demand full payment even in cases of a land contract.

The rights and obligations of the parties under a land contract are generally the same as under any other contract of sale. The terms of the contract and the intent of the parties to the contract generally control. The interpretation of land contracts and the various remedies they contain will differ from jurisdiction to jurisdiction. Generally, the rights of the seller to foreclose the contract as well as to sue for damages for breach of contract exist in all jurisdictions. The buyer's rights to *specific performance* (forcing the seller to tender the deed upon the full payment of the contract price) or damages are also available remedies.

Advantages and Disadvantages of the Land Contract

An advantage of a land contract for the buyer is the ability to take over another's financing without the formality of a loan application and sometimes also to secure a better rate of interest. An advantage to the seller is making financing more readily available in times of tight credit, when banks are reluctant to make new loans. Sometimes the seller may even make a profit on the difference in interest rates.

Example: Suppose a seller has a 10.5 percent mortgage and the rates are now 12 percent. The buyer might be able to borrow from a bank but is reluctant to pay the higher rate of interest. By entering into a land contract, the buyer may pay a negotiated rate of 11 percent, saving the buyer 1 percent and giving the seller a profit of 0.5 percent.

Land contracts are also sometimes used when the seller wishes to sell a portion of his or her property.

Example: The seller owns 10 acres, on which the lender has a mortgage. The seller wishes to sell 2 acres to the buyer. The buyer's down payment is insufficient to pay off the mortgage. By using a land contract, the seller can receive monthly payments and continue to pay the lender.

There are several disadvantages of a land contract. While the buyer may be making payments to the seller, the seller may not be paying the bank. This could result in the bank's foreclosing its mortgage. This renders the contract meaningless, as the seller no longer has the property to convey to the buyer. To avoid this, the buyer should always make his or her checks payable to the seller *and* the bank. This ensures that the bank will be paid. Problems may arise in the event that the seller dies before the land contract is fully paid and the buyer now wants a deed. There may be difficulty in obtaining a deed from the deceased seller's estate. The buyer should insist that the deed be signed at the same time as the land contract and held by an independent third party (in escrow) until the contract payments are completed.

Some attorneys use land contracts as a method of avoiding a mortgage tax. The mortgage tax in New York is 0.75 percent of the mortgage (on a $38,900 mortgage, this comes to $291.75) and is paid when the mortgage is recorded. Some attorneys advise buyers not to record the land contract in order to save this tax. This procedure subjects the buyer to the risk that the seller might convey the property to someone else. If this second conveyance (either by deed or land contract) is recorded, the first buyer loses the property (N.Y.R.P.L. § 294). (The first buyer can sue the seller for damages, but usually by this time, the seller is in Brazil.)

A typical land contract for a single- or double-family house specifies the parties to the contract, the property to be transferred, and the date the transaction is entered into, as well as the total price to be paid and the terms of such payment. It outlines the seller's responsibility to transfer the property when payments have been completed, as well as the type of deed and title assurances the buyer will be given.

The contract shifts the burden of taxes to the buyer. This logically follows the fact that the buyer is the new owner of the property. The buyer has equitable title while the seller retains legal title and usually remains on the tax rolls. Taxes are apportioned at the closing to divide the liability for the time the property is actually used by each party. (See the section on closing statement and adjustments for a more detailed discussion.)

The land contract specifies the date of possession. Since the seller retains an interest in the property, the contract calls for the purchaser to exercise due care in the use of the premises. This clause can include certain restrictions as to the demolition of buildings, walls, and so forth or the removal of natural resources without specific written permission of the seller. The seller can go to court to get an injunction against the purchaser for impairment of his or her equity in the premises.

The land contract protects the seller's equity by providing that the purchaser maintain insurance on the property in an amount equal to at least the seller's equitable interest. The seller should be specifically named in the policy and would be notified of any cancellation of the policy.

Default

Land contracts may state that in the event of default, all payments will be considered as rent. Despite such language, the courts in some jurisdictions are reluctant to follow through when a purchaser has made substantial payments. Courts have held that substantial payments on land contracts give the purchaser an equitable interest in the property that would be viewed as if the purchaser had executed a mortgage and then defaulted. A case-by-case approach is necessary to determine what the purchaser/seller's rights would be under a default.

Assignment

It is against the public policy to prohibit assignments of contractual rights. (See Chapter 4 on general principles of contract law.) A land contract can specify the necessity for notification of an assignment and require permission from the seller. This permission cannot be unreasonably withheld. Under an assignment the assignor (purchaser) can give to another (assignee) all his or her rights to the contract. This means that all the clauses (transfer of land and so on) would inure to the assignee. The original purchaser cannot be released from liability under an assignment unless the seller, in writing, accepts the assignee as fully liable and enters into a new contract with the assignee (novation).

Any number of additional clauses may be found in a land contract according to the intent of the parties. Such items as prepayment, liquidated damages, and so on may be added as the parties and their attorneys may see fit.

SECOND MORTGAGE

In some cases, the resources of the buyer when added to the funds available from lending institutions will fall short of the purchase price. The seller may lend the buyer the remainder, taking a mortgage as collateral for the loan. This mortgage is usually referred to as a *second mortgage*. Third or fourth mortgages sometimes will arise but usually only on commercial property. Mortgages other than first mortgages are also referred to as *junior mortgages*. Some first mortgages will have a clause prohibiting a second mortgage. Buyers should check with their lending institution before obtaining a second mortgage. The major difference between a first mortgage and a second mortgage is largely relevant only as related to the lender's rights at a foreclosure sale and will not be discussed here.

QUESTIONS

1 Hickman sold real property consisting of 160 acres of fruit trees and 20 acres of vineyards to Mulder. Mulder signed a promissory note, which was secured by a mortgage covering the purchased property. Mulder took possession of the property. Hickman subsequently sued Mulder, alleging waste. His complaint stated that Mulder had mismanaged the property intentionally by failing to cultivate the land, failing to irrigate the crops or fertilize the soil, failing to fumigate for insects, and failing to prune the trees. Hickman claimed that he was entitled to recover on the note because of the damage caused by Mulder's waste. Decision for whom? Discuss.

2   Brayton owned a piece of property, which she sold to Izzo. Izzo executed a mortgage in favor of Brayton with a condition that no portion of the premises be destroyed or removed without the consent of Brayton. Izzo subsequently sold the property to Pappas, who assumed the mortgage. Shortly after the purchase, Pappas demolished the building that was on the premises without obtaining Brayton's consent. Brayton instituted an action to foreclose the mortgage. Decision for whom? Discuss.

3   Standard Industries bought property from Lubin. The property was subject to a mortgage in favor of People's Savings Association. The mortgage contained a clause as follows: "If there shall be any change in ownership of the premises covered by this mortgage made without the consent of the association, the entire principal and interest accrued thereon shall become due and payable immediately at the election of the association." When Lubin sold the property to Standard Industries, he did not obtain the consent of the association. The association thereafter declared the entire mortgage note to be due and payable. Standard Industries, Inc., argued that the acceleration clause just quoted should be considered void as being contrary to public policy. Decision for whom? Discuss.

4   The defendant, through a succession of errors and negligent omissions, forgot to pay a shortage owed on his mortgage with the plaintiff. The defendant subsequently tendered the amount of the shortage, but the plaintiff refused to accept it. The plaintiff is asserting the power granted him in the acceleration clause in the note. Will the plaintiff be able to receive the total balance due on the mortgage even though the defendant is ready, willing, and able to make up the default? Discuss.

5   On November 21, 1933, Arthur signed a quit claim deed to his brother, Wallace, and his sister, Gladys. This deed was given to John Glander. In 1948, Gladys found the deed signed by Arthur on a dresser in John's house. Has Gladys acquired an interest in the property? Discuss.

6   Ivy Cook purchased a farm of 80 acres in 1922. Shortly thereafter he rebuilt the old fencing and encroached upon his neighbor's field, taking 4.69 acres. He cultivated part of the 4.69 acres, used the rest for pasture, and continued his farming operations until 1965. Since that time the property was used only as pasture. The adjoining property owner brought an action in 1975 to get back the 4.69 acres. The plaintiff contends that his deed indicates that he is the owner. Who will prevail? Discuss.

7   A deed was prepared conveying a one-half interest in a farm to Mr. Thompson, subject to a life estate in another individual. The deed was left with an attorney and was never filed. After the life tenant died, Mr. Thompson requested ownership of the property. Should the lawyer give Mr. Thompson the deed?

8   Arnold and Ross were adjoining landowners. There was a cave underneath Ross's property, the entrance to which was located on Arnold's land. Ross did not know of the existence of the cave. For a continuous period of 25 years, Arnold used the entire cave for various purposes. On a number of occasions he guided visitors through the cave in exchange for a fee. Ross learned of the existence of the cave and the use Arnold had been making of it and demanded that Arnold stop using the part of the cave underneath Ross's property. Arnold refused, claiming that he had acquired title to the cave by ad-

verse possession. Assume that the period of time for which Arnold used the property is sufficient to meet the statutory requirements for adverse possession in the state. Decision for whom? Discuss.

9 J went to his banker and asked him to prepare deeds conveying land to his grandchildren. J never gave the banker the names of the grandchildren. After J died, the banker discovered the names of the grandchildren and added their names to the deeds, which had already been signed. Are these deeds valid? Discuss.

10 There were two tracts of land, each called the "Jim Smith tract." One of these tracts was deeded to Sam and was designated in the deed as the "Jim Smith tract." The heirs of the grantor claimed that the deed was invalid because the description was defective. Are they correct? Discuss.

11 A acquired title to undeveloped land from R. It was only suitable for hunting, fishing, and recreation. E had used the land for over 20 years. E had built a hunting cabin and cleared portions of the land for hunting, fishing, and vacationing. E had also paid the property taxes for a period of 25 years. A now seeks to evict E, who claims title by adverse possession. A claims that E cannot establish adverse possession because he never fenced, posted, or lived continuously on the property. Is A correct? Discuss.

12 T acquired property and constructed a cement wall into the lake to act as a breakwater. The breakwater was partially built on land belonging to his neighbor, W. T then built a shuffleboard and planted grass and shrubs on W's property. T held the land for 20 years, at which time W sought to evict him. T claimed title to the land by adverse possession. Is T's contention correct? Discuss.

13 X conveyed a life estate in certain land to her son, S, with the remainder to T. The deed was properly executed, signed by X, and delivered to S, but it was never recorded. X died a year later, leaving S her sole heir. At a later point in time, S sold the land to P. The title records showed that the land was owned by X. P determined that S was X's sole heir and accepted the title to the property. After the sale, T, who was the occupant of the land, refused to relinquish possession to P. Who is entitled to the property? Discuss.

14 Smyth was the owner of a one-ninth interest in land. The other owners were cotenants as tenants in common. Smyth mined one-ninth of the mineral resources of the property and sold it, retaining the profits. The other tenants in common sued Smyth, seeking a division of his profits among all of them. Smyth claimed that since he took only one-ninth of the resources, the same as his ownership interest, he should not be divested of any of his profits. Decision for whom? Discuss.

CHAPTER 10

Landlord Tenant

In order to understand the area of landlord tenant law, one must know that, traditionally, a lease was considered to be an interest in real property and that the courts applied principles of real estate law to all landlord tenant transactions. This gave the landlord the upper hand, as property ownership rights of landlords were far superior to nonownership rights of tenants. Today most jurisdictions are moving away from the real estate emphasis and are considering leases to be contracts.[1] Contract law is more evenly balanced than real estate law; therefore, this trend places tenants on a more equal footing with landlords.[2]

The landlord-tenant relationship is controlled by a contractual agreement, called a *lease*. A lease can be either written or oral. (Leases for more than one year *must* be in writing; all leases *should* be in writing.) The lease states the terms under which an apartment or a house or commercial unit is rented. The tenant is called the lessee, and the landlord is called the lessor. State and local laws are used to interpret leases as well as regulate the relationship between landlords and tenants.

TYPES OF TENANCIES

If you do not sign a written lease with your landlord and have no agreement as to the length of your lease, the type of tenancy that you have is called a tenancy at will, sometimes referred to as a tenancy from period to period. In a tenancy at will, the tenant rightfully holds possession of the lease premises under arrangements other than a lease. A tenancy at will can be created by a tenant's remaining on the property with the landlord's permission after the expiration of a lease. Tenancies at will can be from month to month, week to week, semester to semester, and so on, depending upon the period for which the rent is paid.

Period-to-period tenancies are useful methods of leasing an apartment or house if you do not know the length of time that you will be staying in a particular area. This form of tenancy allows the tenant and landlord a great amount of flexibility. Either party may withdraw from the lease by giving a minimum notice of one rental period. If you wish assurance that you can stay on the premises for a specific period of time or that the landlord cannot raise the rent during that particular time period, it is advisable to enter into a lease agreement. This lease should specify the duration of the lease as well as the amount of rent that can be charged.

[1] Thirteen states (Alaska, Arizona, Florida, Hawaii, Iowa, Kansas, Kentucky, Montana, Nebraska, New Mexico, Oregon, Tennessee, and Virginia) have substantially adopted the 1972 Uniform Residential Landlord and Tenant Act (URLTA). The purpose of this act is to recognize the modern tendency of considering a lease under contract law.

[2] Under the Uniform Residential Landlord and Tenant Act, there is even a provision for leases or parts of leases to be declared ''unconscionable'' as a matter of law. This concept has been adopted from the Uniform Commercial Code and the Consumer Credit Code previously discussed (Chapters 4 and 5). If a rental agreement or part of one is highly one-sided, it may be declared null and void in states that have adopted this clause.

Oral rental agreements for more than one year are unenforceable according to the statute of frauds (see Chapter 4). Therefore, such leases should be written. The statute of frauds also requires that the contract be signed by the party to be held. This means that a lease signed only by the tenant would not be admissible in court to hold the landlord liable for its terms. The opposite is also true.

There are exceptions under which a party could be held to a lease that he or she has not signed. For example, a tenant enters into a lease for more than one year that requires an affirmative act (e.g., renovation, payment of taxes) in addition to payment of rent. The tenant does not sign the lease but performs the affirmative act. Both parties will be bound to the full term of the lease even though it is not in writing.

Another type of tenancy is called a tenancy at sufferance. In this type of tenancy, the tenant has possession of the premises without the landlord's approval although the original possession was with permission. This situation can arise when a lease expires and the landlord has given the tenant notice to leave or when the court has given the tenant an eviction notice. The tenant's liability under a tenancy at sufferance is for the reasonable rental value of the property during the time that the tenant has possession. Under this type of tenancy, the landlord can force the tenant to move by giving the tenant notice to leave and a reasonable time to remove belongings.

TYPICAL HOUSE OR APARTMENT LEASE—DISCUSSED

A lease should indicate the period of time that it is to run as well as the rent that is due. It should also spell out the landlord's and the tenant's responsibilities. A lease should indicate who pays the utilities, such as electricity, gas, and water; late penalty charges; common area fees; the type of alterations that a tenant may make; the repairs that the tenant is responsible for; the names of the persons renting the premises; whether pets are allowed; who is responsible for the maintenance of the property; and what the property includes. (Does it include the backyard, the laundry room, the basement, and so on?) The lease should also spell out whether a security deposit is required and how and when the security deposit will be returned. Any condition that the landlord and tenant agree to, as well as all promises made by the landlord or tenant, should be in writing. A tenant should fully understand the lease agreement and should not sign any agreement that contains blank spaces. Some jurisdictions now require by statute that leases as well as other legal documents be written in plain language.

Tenants Preliminary Review

It is important that the tenant read the lease carefully. It may be advisable to have an attorney review the lease to interpret the clauses. Any changes that are made in the lease that are handwritten should be dated and initialed by all parties on all copies. The tenant should make sure that he or she gets a copy of the signed lease. A tenant should be wary of leases in which the landlord is not liable for any repairs as this may cause the tenant to be responsible for major structural damage to the premises. Statements that the premises are "fine as is" should put a tenant on guard.

A tenant should carefully check the premises before moving in. This should be done with the landlord. A list of objectionable items, such as broken windows or doors, peeling paint, dirt and debris and so on, should be prepared. The tenant should make sure that all the appliances that are included in the lease are in working order. If not, these facts should also be noted on the list. A copy of this list should be given to the landlord. The landlord should give the tenant a written statement indicating when each of the objectionable conditions will be rectified.

In the event that the apartment is furnished, each item of furniture should be listed separately, including a description of its condition. A signed copy of this list should be kept by both parties and should be used when moving out to facilitate recovery of the security deposit. Documentation of items that were previously in poor condition will prevent the landlord from trying to charge the tenant for damages that were there prior to occupancy.

Improper Lease Clauses

There are certain things that a landlord and tenant may not legally agree to. A clause nullifying statutory protections given a tenant, such as the right to receive interest on a security deposit or the right to have a dwelling that is fit for human habitation, will not be upheld. Rights that cannot be bargained away are defined by state statutes. Laws in many jurisdictions allow a court to find a contract or a clause in a contract to be "unconscionable." A court may reconstruct a contract by deleting the unconscionable clause or clauses.

The fastest way an individual can resolve a particular problem is to discuss that problem calmly with the landlord and then communicate in writing, summarizing the discussion. It is advisable for a tenant to set up a file with respect to leased property and keep copies of all agreements, notices, and documents that might concern his or her rental agreement. Having documents available will help.

A lease can be relatively simple or relatively complex. Rental agreements for commercial space in shopping centers and the like can easily run to 40 or 50 pages. Residential leases are generally much simpler although there are a number of provisions that are of technical relevance that may be difficult for the lay person to comprehend immediately.

Important Lease Provisions

A lease should include the following items:

1 *The date of signing.* This is important, especially when the term is stated as one year and so on. A question may arise as to one year from when? The date also fixes the time the liability of the parties begins.

2 *The complete name of the landlord and the tenant.* It is important to make sure that the individual you are renting from is the owner of the premises or an authorized person. A check with the county clerk or tax authorities will give you the name of the person who is the owner of the property. Do not take a rental agent's word for the fact that he or she represents the landlord. Under the rules of agency, this information must come from the owner.

3 *The location of the rental unit.* This should include not only the street address but also the apartment number as well as identification of any garages, storage facilities, and so forth.

4 *The term of the lease.* This should include the date that you are entitled to possession of the premises as well as the date on which you must leave.

5 *The amount of the rent.* This should include a statement of when the rent is due and where and to whom it must be paid. Provisions should also be made in the lease as to whether and how the rent can be raised and if there are penalties with respect to late payments. In addition, a statement should be provided as to who is responsible for the utilities. In rentals where there are common areas, the landlord's and/or tenant's responsibility for the common area maintenance, utilities, and so on should also be indicated. In premises that have garages, storage areas, or washrooms, there may be extra charges for those facilities. All those charges should be indicated in the written lease.

The preceding provisions are usually spelled out in an introductory paragraph and clauses similar to the ones reproduced as follows.

TYPICAL HOUSE OR APARTMENT LEASE CLAUSES

Rental Period and Amount

An example of a lease agreement follows.

Lease Agreement

Made the   day of   , 1984; _____, (lessor), the landlord, in consideration of the agreements of _____, (lessee), the tenant, set forth below, hereby leases to lessee apartment number _____ in the apartment building located at _____, for the year commencing on the first day of September 1984.

Lessee, in consideration of said leasing, does hereby agree as follows:

To pay as rental for said apartment the sum of $2400 payable at the rate of $200 per month, in advance, commencing with the date first above mentioned. Rents and deposits on rents are not refundable.

If a lease is entered into for a period of a year, it is very common for the rent to be stated as a single figure payable in monthly installments. This would establish the right of the landlord to collect the entire amount of the full year's rental from the tenant in the event that the tenant for any reason breaches the lease. If the tenant moved out, the landlord would have an obligation to try to rent the premises to someone else, in which case any replacement rentals that the landlord would acquire would reduce the amount of rent that is owed by the tenant under the original agreement. In the case of a month-to-month lease, a landlord is only entitled to collect a single month's rent at a time, and in the event the lease is terminated, there is no large obligation on the part of the tenant. Although this is a benefit to the tenant, a corresponding detriment occurs, in that the landlord may terminate the lease at any time upon one month's notice and a tenant would then have to find another place to live. With a lease for a year, a tenant would be more secure, to the extent of the remaining term of the lease period. The URLTA provides that in the absence of an agreement, a tenant shall pay the fair rental value for the use of the property. The statute also provides that if a landlord or tenant fails to sign and/or deliver a written rental agreement and if the landlord accepts the rent, he or she will be bound to the terms of the agreement. If the tenant accepts possession, he or she will also be bound.

Rights and Duties of the Landlord

The landlord's responsibility as well as the tenant's responsibility should be spelled out in the lease. Many of these can be negotiated. A landlord cannot refuse to rent to a tenant because of the tenant's race, color, religion, age, sex, and so on. In some jurisdictions, a landlord cannot refuse to rent because the tenant has children or because the tenant has become pregnant. Many states provide laws that indicate that the tenants have a legal right to live in a place that is healthy and safe. This is called a warranty of habitability. This warranty means that the premises must be fit for human habitation. Occupants of a premises should not be subject to conditions that are dangerous, hazardous, or detrimental to their health or safety. The scope of this warranty has been interpreted differently by each state that has such warranties. It has been extended to the common areas (elevators, halls, stairs, and so on) as well as to private areas. Any breach of this warranty may result in an award to the tenant for damages. This award will be related to the actual damages sustained by the tenant owing to the breach of warranty as well as to possible punitive damages. A court may also choose to reduce the rent value of the apartment because of the conditions resulting from breach of this warranty. For example, there have been cases where the courts have determined that rent should be reduced because of lack of elevator service or heat. Agreements between the landlord and tenant waiving these rights have been determined to be unenforceable in most jurisdictions.

A possible remedy for breach of the warranty of habitability is to allow the tenant to repair the premises and deduct the cost of the repairs from the rent. Under common law this was not allowed. Many states are tending toward this ''repair and deduct'' policy. In the states that have this remedy, the usual procedure is for the tenant to notify the landlord in writing that the defect exists and that the tenant will make necessary repairs and deduct the cost of the repairs from the rent unless the landlord repairs the premises within a reasonable time. *Reasonable* is defined according to the circumstances. For normal repairs, 30 days is considered reasonable (according to URLTA, 14 days). For an emergency situation, a much shorter time may be considered unreasonable. If the tenant makes the repairs, he or she must give the landlord an accounting as to their cost.

A tenant has an alternative to rent reduction if the warranty of habitability is breached. The tenant may move out after notifying the landlord in writing (under URLTA, 30 days after receipt of notice if the defect is not cured by landlord within 14 days). After moving out, the tenant will no longer be obligated to pay rent. This is called constructive eviction, and it occurs when the landlord has deprived the tenant of use of the premises. It is distinguished from actual eviction, when the landlord goes to court to have the tenant removed. Lack of heat or utilities have been considered to be acts of constructive eviction when it is the responsibility of the landlord to provide such services.

Another remedy the tenant has when a landlord has not kept the premises habitable is to complain to local health and housing inspectors. Local codes provide standards for housing in most areas. There are usually inspectors who will inspect the premises when complaints are made, and there may be fines or warnings issued to the landlord with respect to the violations, forcing the landlord to make the necessary repairs.

In some rare cases, courts have awarded punitive damages when landlords have violated the warranty of habitability. This has occurred when the landlord has a record of continual abuse of tenants' rights. If the tenant has created the uninhabitable situation, the landlord will not be in violation of the warranty of habitability.

Landlords also have the responsibility of assuring a tenant quiet enjoyment of the premises (Colonial Apartments, Inc. v. Kurn, 163 N.W. 2d 770 [Minn. 1968]). This means that the landlord will turn over the premises to the tenant at the beginning of the lease. The landlord may only enter the premises after giving reasonable notice of his or her plan to enter and then may only enter during normal business hours. A time period of twenty-four hours has been interpreted to be reasonable notice. (Two days are required by URLTA.) Of course, the tenant can give consent and allow the landlord to enter at times other than normal business hours. In the event that the landlord violates this right to privacy and quiet enjoyment, a tenant may be able to sue the landlord for damages. A tenant may also want to contact the police in extreme cases as this may be considered to be a trespass or other criminal offense. An exception to this rule is that the landlord may enter the premises in case of emergency (to make necessary repairs) in the event that the tenant has abandoned the apartment or in the event that the landlord gets a court order to enter.

Typical lease clauses that give landlords broader rights and limits of liability follow:

A. *Lessor may enter said apartment at any time to inspect, repair, and maintain same or to show the property to any prospective buyer or loan or insurance company and, in case either party has given notice of termination of this tenancy, may show the premises to any prospective tenant.*

This first clause broadens the landlord's right under common and statutory law and allows the landlord to enter the premises at any reasonable time for any reasonable business. This clause would not give the landlord the right to harass the tenant or to invade the tenant's privacy continuously. The clause still requires that the landlord have a legitimate reason for entering the property. If a landlord wished to inspect the property every three hours, a court would find this a violation of tenant's rights to privacy notwithstanding the statement in this clause.

B. No right of storage is given by this lease, and the lessor shall not be liable for nondelivery of messages or for loss of property by fire, theft, burglary, or otherwise or for any accidental damage to person or property in and about the leased premises or building resulting from electrical wiring or water; rain, or snow that may come into or issue or flow from any part of said premises or buildings or from the pipes, plumbing, gas, or any electrical connections thereof or that may be caused by lessor's employees or any other cause whatsoever, and the lessee hereby covenants and agrees to make no claim for any such loss or damage.

This second clause, to the extent that it disclaims a landlord's liability for damage done as a result of negligence of the landlord or his or her agents, is probably unconscionable, against public policy, and not enforceable. If there are acts of God that cause damage to the tenant's property, the landlord is not liable. If there are acts of third parties (not agents of the landlord) that cause damage to the tenant's property, the landlord will also not be liable. The landlord is not responsible for giving messages to the tenant or for acting as an insurer for a tenant's personal property. The tenant should maintain his or her own insurance policy covering his or her goods because these are not normally covered under a landlord's property insurance policy.

Security Deposits

A security deposit is taken by a landlord to protect the landlord's investment. It is intended as an incentive for the tenant to adhere to the terms of the lease with respect to caring for the premises. The landlord is allowed to keep that portion of the security deposit that equals the cost of repairing damages caused by the tenant. In some states, some landlords are obligated to deposit security deposits in an interest-bearing account and may not mingle the security deposit with other funds. In states where a security deposit is required to be placed in an interest account, the landlord is entitled to a percentage of the interest for administrative expenses. Some jurisdictions also provide that in the event the landlord does deposit security in an interest-bearing account when not required to do so by statute, that interest is also payable to the tenant upon the tenant's departure. The URLTA provides that a landlord may not obtain security in excess of one month's rent.

An area for problems in the landlord-tenant relationship is the return of the security deposit. Usually, leases are vague as to when and how the deposit will be refunded. The URLTA provides that the deposit must be returned within 14 days after termination of the tenancy and demand for deposit. It is important for the tenant to make sure that the premises are in good order on vacating and that the list of defects that existed prior to tenancy, as discussed previously, should be used to support the tenant's contention that no damage was done during his or her tenancy. The tenant should have the landlord inspect the premises with the tenant before vacating. It is also important that the tenant obtain a receipt for the deposit when giving it at the beginning of the lease period. Judicial decisions in many states have held that it is improper for a tenant to apply a security deposit to the last month's rent.

If the landlord sells the rental unit, he or she must do several things to be relieved of the responsibility of the security. The landlord could return the security (less any deduction for damages that have occurred), or the landlord could turn over the deposit to the new landlord after a deduction for claims. In either case, the landlord must notify the tenant and give the tenant an itemized list of the expenses that have been deducted.

In states where there is a requirement that the security deposit be put in an interest-bearing account, the tenant's rights to this interest cannot be waived. If the tenant does not receive the security deposit back within a reasonable time after vacating the premises, the tenant may sue the landlord for the disputed amount. Some jurisdictions will allow punitive damages against landlords who have acted in bad faith in withholding security deposits.

Typical security deposit clauses read as follows:

A. To pay as a security deposit the sum of one month's rent, which shall be treated in part as a deposit for cleaning of said premises at the rate $15 per room, payable in advance. Such security deposit, less the appropriate amounts retained for cleaning will be refunded to lessor upon vacating the premises, if the premises are cleaned by the lessee to the satisfaction of the lessor or his or her agent, and if the premises are in the same condition as when rented, excepting normal wear and tear.

B. This security deposit is not an advance payment of rent and does not relieve lessee from obligations to pay rent, including the rent for the first and last month of occupancy.

C. The security deposit includes a deposit of $_____ for keys, which will be refunded when the keys are turned in. In the event the keys are not turned in, the landlord retains the right to have duplicate keys made at the tenant's expense and to deduct this amount from the security or to replace the locks if he or she deems it necessary and charge the cost of replacement to the tenant.

A security deposit will not be applied to normal wear and tear and deterioration of a unit. This is something that is required to be repaired or maintained at the expense of the landlord as one of the operating costs of running a building. The purpose of a cleaning deposit in clause A is to allow the landlord to recover for cleaning expenses incurred if the tenant fails to do an adequate job. This is an item that is not always covered by security deposits, and this clause allows the landlord to retain amounts expended for this purpose and charge them to the tenant's security. The remainder of the security less items deducted for damages would be refundable upon inspection of the premises by the lessor or his or her agent.

Many tenants utilize the security deposit as the last month's rental payment. In the event that they then leave the premises in a damaged or unclean condition, the landlord must maintain or fix the premises at his or her own expense. Many tenants subsequently will state that they were unaware of the fact that the security could not be applied to the last month's rent. Clause B spells out clearly the tenant's obligation to pay the last month's rent and would thus avoid such a situation. In the case of a month-to-month lease, this clause is relatively unlikely to appear; however, in the case of the lease for a year or a six-month period, such a clause is extremely important for the protection of the landlord.

Rights and Duties of the Tenant

The tenant must keep the premises clean and sanitary unless the landlord has agreed in writing to do so. The tenant must dispose of garbage and trash and make proper use of the plumbing and electric systems. The tenant may not permit guests to damage the property. The tenant must use the premises as a residence or according to other terms that may be specified by the lease. The tenant may make nonstructural alterations that are consistent with the use of the premises. In a determination of whether an alteration is a breach of the tenant's duties to keep the premises damage-free, the question of removability is the significant factor. If the alteration can be removed without causing any permanent serious injury to the premises, the alteration will not be considered to be damage to the premises. The tenant must make timely payment for the rent and, if required by lease, the utilities or taxes or both. The tenant is required to report all problems that may arise during the occupancy of the premises even though they may not be his or her fault. The tenant is also responsible for notifying the landlord in writing when the tenant intends to terminate his or her lease.

Typical clauses spelling out tenant duties follow:

A. The tenant may not sublet the apartment or any part thereof or keep any dog or use a waterbed or use said apartment for any unlawful or immoral purpose or play any musical instrument or radio or television set before 8:00 P.M. or after 10:00 P.M. loud enough to be heard by other tenants or violate any regulations of the board of health, village ordinances, or state laws of whatever nature. The lessee agrees that the covenants contained in this paragraph, once breached, cannot afterward be performed or cured and that, in the case of breach, unlawful detainer proceedings may be commenced at once without any notice whatsoever.

B. Said apartment and all the furniture and furnishings therein are accepted as in good condition provided, however, that if the lessee shall find any thereof not in good condi-

tion or that the inventory of the furniture set forth below is incorrect in any particular, a written statement of any objections shall be delivered to the lessor within three days after taking possession. Otherwise, it will be conclusively presumed that said inventory is correct in all particulars, and lessees agree not to permit the premises, including woodwork, floors, walls, furniture, fixtures, or furnishings contained therein, to be damaged or depreciated in any manner excepting normal wear and tear, and agree to pay for any loss, breakage, or damage thereto. The lessees specifically agree that no tacks, nails, or screws will be driven into the walls or woodwork. Lessees are also responsible for and agree to pay for any damage done by wind or rain caused by leaving windows open.

C. The lessor shall have the lien granted by law upon all baggage and other property of lessees for their rent, accommodations, and services, and the lessees hereby grant the lessor a lien upon all personal property brought into said premises. Lessor may enforce said lien as provided by law or by entering said premises and either taking possession thereof and the belongings contained therein for safekeeping or by removing said property therefrom and storing the same at the expense of the lessees. Said lien may be enforced whenever rent is due and unpaid and regardless of whether or not a 3-day notice to pay rent or quit shall have been served, and enforcement of the lien shall not operate to waive any other rights of the lessor in unlawful detainer or otherwise. If rent is still due and unpaid 30 days after the enforcement of said lien, then the lessor may sell any or all personal property taken possession of as herein provided and may apply any funds received against the unpaid rent and against any storage charges or other costs and fees, provided that any funds received in excess of the total amounts due shall be turned over to the lessees.

D. All garbage must be placed in metal or plastic cans and must be covered. Children will not be permitted to run or play in halls, entranceways or stairways or on roofs or fire escapes or in any public driveway.

E. No automatic washing machines may be installed in the apartment or outdoor radio or television aerials of any kind without the permission of the lessor or his or her agent.

Clause A defines the use of the premises so that tenants' use shall not interfere with the uses of other persons in the neighborhood, be they other tenants or owners of adjoining property. It further establishes on behalf of the tenant an obligation to utilize the premises in accordance with state and local laws and regulations. In the event of a breach of this paragraph, the tenant agrees that said breach shall be grounds for his or her ejection from the apartment and that he or she cannot, once violating this provision, make amends or cure his or her breach.

Clause B establishes the tenant's obligation to maintain the premises and requires that the tenant inspect the premises and report any problems to the landlord within three days of taking possession of the property. To the extent of any damage other than normal wear and tear, the tenant is going to be responsible for any losses incurred by the landlord.

Clause C provides the landlord with a remedy for collecting money due for back rent. This clause allows the landlord to take a tenant's personal property and sell the property to satisfy the tenant's rent obligation. This clause is not in the best interest of a tenant and should be avoided if possible. It may be unenforceable in some states for reasons of unconscionability.

Clause D attempts to define tenant's obligations for maintenance of garbage cans and also to point out to tenants that certain behavior of their children is not acceptable to the landlord or other tenants of the building. Children who play in common areas are hazards to other tenants. There are certain things that are frequently maintained in common areas that might be hazardous to children playing there. Accordingly, tenants should be advised not to allow this type of activity to occur.

Clause E is often used because of the propensity for washing machines (and automatic dishwashers) to overflow and cause water damage to the premises. It is also of concern where the electrical wiring in a house may not be strong enough to provide properly for the electrical usage of a heavy-duty machine. In such a case, a restriction against clothes dryers may also appear in the lease. The prohibition against radio and television antennae is principally because those items need to be permanently affixed to the roof of the premises and to that extent may cause some damage to the property.

Subletting

Provisions for subletting should be in the lease. In some states, a tenant who is renting a residence in a building with a certain number of residential units may have the right to sublease or assign the lease after giving the landlord written notice of his or her intention. An example is New York State, where a tenant renting a residence in a building with four or more units has the right to sublease or assign his or her lease. In jurisdictions that do not have this statutory provision, a tenant may not assign or sublease his or her apartment. Provisions must be made in the lease. An assignment is a transfer of the entire premises to a new tenant. A sublease is a transfer of less than the entire tenancy, and the original tenant has a reversionary interest. This means the original tenant has the right to come back in after the subtenant has left. Under an assignment or a sublease, the original tenant is responsible to the landlord. The only way a tenant is relieved from liability is if the landlord gives him or her a written release of lease.

The liability of multiple lessors should be spelled out. In cases where more than one individual is renting, as in a college apartment, the question as to the liability of each individual for the whole amount of rent should be addressed. An individual who rents with other individuals should be careful in terms of the liability that may be imposed by the landlord and by the lease to the total amount of rent that may be due from the one individual when the other individuals are nowhere to be found. This can also include liability for damages as well as for utilities.

Rules with respect to common areas as well as pets and guests should also be spelled out fully in the lease. Usually, a lease provides that the landlord is renting to the tenant and his or her immediate family. If the tenant is contemplating having long-term guests or pets in the apartment, it is advisable to notify the landlord of that fact and to get the permission of the landlord in the lease in writing at the outset of the contract.

A typical clause could read as follows:

To use said apartment as living quarters for the residence of said named lessees, being
2 adults and 2 children, and for no other purpose whatsoever and to pay the les-
sor the sum of $10 monthly for each person who shall occupy the apartment with
said lessee.

Many landlords want extra rent if they rent the apartment to more than a given number of individuals on the theory that the more occupants there are of a given apartment, the greater the use of that apartment. This paragraph sets up an additional fee of $10 per person for each person in excess of the agreed-upon number that occupies the premises in question.

The lease should spell out whether the apartment is to be unfurnished, partially furnished, or fully furnished and should list the items and conditions of furniture.

Termination

Provisions for terminating the lease should be made, and any renewal provisions with respect to term and rent should also be provided for in the original lease. In addition, the landlord and tenant should agree in the lease as to what the result of termination will be if the tenant leaves before the term ends. This clause could include items as to whether or not there is a penalty for leaving, whether or not the tenant will be responsible for the remaining rent, and what should be done with the security deposit, and so forth.

For example:

This tenancy may be terminated at any time by mutual consent of the parties or by ei-
ther party giving written notice to the other not less than fifteen (15) days before the
date of termination. Any provision of this lease may be changed by lessor in like manner.

It is important to note that in a lease that would cover a longer than monthly period, provisions could not be changed in the middle of a rental period. For example, if the rent were $130 per month and it were paid on the first, if the landlord gave notice to the tenant on the second that 15 days from that time the rent was increasing to $150 per month, that notice would probably not be effective. Provisions other than rent provisions probably would be modifiable by the landlord under the terms of this agreement by giving the tenant 15 days notice in writing.

If lessees should remove from said premises any furniture or baggage without the agree-
ment of the lessor, said removal shall constitute, at the option of the lessor, an abandon-
ment and surrender of the premises, and the landlord may take immediate possession
thereof and exclude lessees therefrom, removing and storing at the expense of said les-
sees all remaining property found therein.

This clause attempts to deal with the problem of a tenant who leaves the premises but leaves a substantial portion of his or her personal property behind. In such a situation, it is difficult to tell whether the tenant has abandoned the premises or intends to come back. If the landlord assumes that the tenant will return, he or she may have to bring an eviction proceeding for nonpayment of rent before he or she can remove the tenant's property. If the landlord assumes that the tenant has abandoned the premises and removes his or her property and a tenant returns, the landlord may be found guilty for civil and/or criminal trespass or other offenses. To avoid this problem, the parties agree that in the event that the tenant moves some of his or her property out of the premises, the landlord can assume that there has been an abandonment of the premises, may resume possession of the premises, and may take the tenant's property and put it into storage at the expense of the tenant.

Sale of Premises

A clause that allows the landlord to cancel the lease if he or she sells the premises is not good for the tenant as the continuity of the lease is tenuous at best. Other clauses that allow the landlord to cancel the lease at his or her discretion are one-sided and will not give the tenant the security that he is seeking. A tenant should not waive his or her right to a jury trail because juries are often more sympathetic to the problems of tenants than judges are. A tenant should also not agree to pay a landlord's attorneys fees in the event of an eviction because this is an imposition of an additional cost that courts usually do not award. A tenant should be wary of leases that refer to rules that have not yet been written or that he or she does not have a copy of. Any statements that the landlord makes or promises as to future commitments should also be in writing. Nothing should be left to the interpretation of the courts.

> *All rights given to lessor by this lease shall be cumulative and in addition to any rights given by the laws of this state, and the exercise by the lessor of any right shall not operate as a waiver of any other rights. No statement or promise of the lessor or his or her agents or employees with reference to altering the terms of this lease or with respect to any repairs or improvements of the premises and no waivers of any rights of the lessor given by this lease or law shall be binding unless specifically written and signed by lessor or his or her agent.*

This clause makes it clear that the lease is adding to but not replacing other statutory rights that may exist on the part of the landlord. It is necessary for a tenant or landlord to check local statutes to determine what rights they might have. It also points out to tenants that any representation that may have been made in the renting of the premises are not binding on the landlord unless they appear in this lease in writing.

Subsequent modifications could also be made, but again they would have to be in writing and under the terms of the lease whether in the lease or in subsequent writings, and they would also have to be signed by the landlord or his or her agent.

After the tenant has read through the lease, he or she should discuss the objectionable clauses with the landlord and try to have them removed. If there are provisions that the tenant wishes in the lease that have not been included, he or she should make sure that they are included.

Another important thing to remember is that none of the items of tenant's personal property that are on the premises will be covered by the landlord's insurance. It is essential that a tenant get renter's insurance from a reputable insurance agent in order to protect the tenant's property from fire, theft, and other perils.

Eviction

If the tenant breaks the terms of the lease by failing to pay rent, causing severe damage to the premises, becoming a nuisance, subletting the property without permission, or using the property for illegal purposes or in any other way violates the terms of the lease, the landlord may be able to evict him or her. A landlord is not permitted to terminate a lease in order to retaliate against a tenant after the tenant asserts his or her rights under the lease of if the tenant complains to the Housing Authority or Health Department about code violations on the premises (Edwards v. Habib, 397 F.2d 687 [D. Or. 1968]).

Eviction is a legal proceeding removing the tenant from the premises. A tenant cannot be forcibly removed by the landlord without a court order. A landlord may not turn off utilities or lock the tenant out, remove the doors or windows of the rented premises, or remove the tenant's belongings in an attempt to evict him or her forcibly. The landlord must go to court. Eviction proceedings may move along very quickly, and a tenant must be responsive to each step of the court proceedings, or he or she may find himself or herself without an apartment. If a tenant receives a notice of an eviction action, legal advice should be sought immediately. Many states have referral services that are available to help tenants under these circumstances. If a tenant plans to fight the eviction, he or she must file an answer within the time allowed by the statute in the particular state where the action is being brought. If the tenant does not appear in court on the date given or fails to answer with a defense, he or she automatically loses. It is important for the tenant to comply if he or she plans on keeping his or her apartment.

Once the court decides against the tenant, the court will issue a warrant that will be executed by a sheriff or marshal, giving the tenant several days to leave the house or apartment (72 hours in New York and California). If the tenant does not leave within the time allowed by the warrant, the sheriff has the authority to remove him or her and lock him or her out. This can only be done by a legal official. The landlord cannot lock a tenant out.

In an eviction proceeding, a tenant may assert any defense he or she may have against his or her landlord. A tenant's defense is termed the tenant's legal answer to the landlord's petition. If the landlord has not followed the rules of the state in which he or she is bringing the eviction action (such as serving the papers on the tenant or giving the tenant the required notice as provided in his or her lease and so on), the tenant can use these errors as defenses and demand that the court dismiss the landlord's action. If the tenant has the rent money and the landlord is evicting him or her for not having paid the rent, the tenant should offer to pay the rent to the landlord and get permission from the landlord to stay, or the rent money can be deposited in court to the judge or the clerk when the tenant appears. Even if the landlord won't accept the money and let the tenant stay, the deposit of the unpaid rent may delay the eviction.

In the event that the tenant withholds rent because of conditions of the apartment that breach the warranty of habitability, he or she should tell the judge why he or she withheld the rent. A tenant should have previously reported the conditions to the local health or housing authorities and indicate to the judge that he or she has done this as well. A tenant can make an offer to deposit rent money with the court and ask the court to use the money to order the apartment's condition to be fixed. The judge may, in his or her discretion, delay the eviction and direct the money to be given to the contractor to repair the premises. In some cases, the tenant may not be able to use the defense of breach of warranty of habitability unless he or she has notified the landlord and moved out.

> To pay all court costs and reasonable attorney's fees incurred by the lessor in enforcing by legal or otherwise any of lessor's rights under this lease or under any law of this state.

The purpose of this paragraph is to pass on to the tenant the lessor's expenses for attorney's fees in enforcing any rights that the lessor may have against the lessee under the terms of the lease or under any other statutory or common law provisions. Without such a paragraph, it might be expensive for a landlord to evict a tenant, and the tenant might have no concerns because the expenditures are primarily the landlord's. This paragraph makes a tenant responsible for the cost of eviction and, if the tenant is in the wrong, might encourage him or her to leave without a costly litigation procedure. Under the URLTA a landlord may not pass attorney's fees or other costs to the tenant.

> The acceptance by the lessor of partial payments of rent due shall not, under any circumstances, constitute a waiver of any rights of the lessor at law or under this lease or affect any notice or legal proceedings in unlawful detainer theretofore given or commenced.

This paragraph allows a landlord to proceed with an eviction even though partial rent payments have been made. To the extent that rent is due, it is all due, and partial payment should not relieve the tenant's obligations or allow the tenant to argue that an eviction proceeding should not take place. Thus, if a tenant on the first of the month pays only half a month's rent, a landlord would be entitled to bring an eviction proceeding even if the tenant were willing to pay the reminder of the rent prior to the fifteenth of the month.

> *If the lessees leave said premises unoccupied at any time while rent is due and unpaid, the lessor may, if desired, take immediate possession thereof and exclude the lessees therefrom, removing and storing at the expense of said lessees all property found contained therein.*

This provision, to the extent that it is contrary to statutory law, will be unenforceable. Its effect would be to allow the landlord to remove a tenant's goods from the premises if the tenant disappeared without having paid rent. In the absence of such a provision, a landlord might be obligated to make an extensive and expensive search for the tenant before being allowed by a court to remove the tenant's possessions.

> *Any violation of any provision of this lease by any of the lessees or any person on the premises with lessee's consent or any failure to pay rent upon the date due shall result, at the option of the lessor, in the immediate termination of this lease without notice of any kind, and the lessor may thereupon enter said premises and take and retain possession thereof and exclude lessees therefrom.*

This paragraph gives the landlord the right to retake the premises without the need for going through any formal legal proceedings. To the extent that there are statutory rules that protect the right of tenants, this clause probably would be inoperative. To the extent that no such statutory clauses exist, this clause gives a landlord a great deal of self-help remedy to retake premises in the event of a breach of any term of the lease agreement.

QUESTIONS

1 The plaintiff (tenant) brought an action against the defendant (landlord) to recover for materials furnished and labor performed by the tenant in connection with replastering and painting of rooms in her apartment. The tenant had an oral lease with the landlord that did not specify that the landlord was supposed to repair or paint the property. The plaintiff had two small children who were eating the plaster and paint that was flaking off the walls of the tenement apartment. She had complained to the landlord several times prior to undertaking the repairs herself. Question: Is the landlord responsible for reimbursing the tenant? Discuss the obligation of each party for maintenance and repairs.

2 A landlord sues a tenant for nonpayment of rent. The tenant defends on the grounds that he had leased the premises to use as an office, library, and meeting room and that noises from other tenants' printing presses prohibited him from using the premises according to his intention. The tenant contends that this is a breach of a covenant of quiet enjoyment and constructive eviction. The landlord contends that it would cost three times the tenant's annual rent to lower the noise conditions by putting in a new floor. Decision for whom? Discuss.

3 The plaintiff landlord sues the defendant tenant for 17 months' rent based on the remainder of a 3-year lease. The tenant had moved out because he could not afford the rent. The apartment was a middle-class apartment located in a middle-class neighborhood. Was the landlord under a duty to try to rerent the premises and, if so, was 17 months a reasonable or unreasonable period in which to obtain a tenant? Discuss.

4 The plaintiffs were students at the University of Wisconsin. They went to rent property owned by the defendant, and the defendant stated he would clean the property, fix it, paint it, provide necessary furnishings, and have the the house in suitable condition by the start of the school year. The tenant paid the landlord and signed the lease. The house was not in habitable condition by September 1. The house had several health code and housing violations that could not be repaired until October 1. The students vacated the premises. The landlord contends that there was no express provision in the lease that the house would be habitable by September 1 and that the general rule is that there is no implied warranty that the premises are in tenantable condition. The landlord further contends that a tenant, as a purchaser of an estate in land, is subject to the doctrine of caveat emptor. His remedy is to inspect the premises before taking them or to secure an express warranty. Who will prevail in this action? Discuss.

5 Jean Smith, the plaintiff, was raped by an individual who gained access to her apartment through the use of a pass key. Jean sued her landlord, General Apartment Company, for the damages resulting from the rape. As his defense, the landlord cites a clause in the lease, holding the landlord harmless from any claims for damages or loss sustained by the tenant. The landlord had knowledge that other rapes had occurred in his apartment complex and that the intruder involved in the other attacks had obtained entry by means of a pass key. Decision for whom? Discuss.

6 The plaintiff (landlord) sued the defendant (tenant) for 2 months' rent. The tenant's defense is that there were 14 code violations on the property including rodents, defective electrical wiring, leaking roof, inoperative toilet, unsound and unsafe ceilings, lack of window screening, absence of bathroom venting, loose and insecure front porch column, defective trap under the kitchen sink, broken eaves, improper basement drainage, and broken and defective basement steps. The tenant refused to pay rent and started looking for another apartment. It took her 2 months to find suitable rental space and the landlord is now suing for the rent for those 2 months. Is the tenant liable to the landlord for the rent? Discuss.

7 Various tenants sued their landlord for injury sustained as a result of the landlord's negligence in maintaining the common passageways. One tenant fell down an unlighted interior stairway; another fell down an exterior wooden stairway. Both of the tenants had signed leases that contained exculpatory clauses. The landlord set up the exculpatory clauses, which indicated that he was not liable for injury to tenants, families, guests, or employees as a defense. Will the tenants recover? Discuss.

8 The defendant (tenant) leased an apartment from the plaintiff (landlord), and in doing so she expressed the desire for a quiet apartment. In fact, the tenants above her were loud, noisy, and obnoxious. She requested the landlord to tell them to leave or she could not continue to rent because of the noise. The landlord told the young couple in

the above apartment that they would have to leave. The young couple did not leave, and the defendant did. The landlord sued the defendant for breach of lease and for the rent due and owing. The defendant contends that she was constructively evicted because of the unbearable noise. Decision for whom? Discuss.

9   Plaintiff B, the landlord, rented the premises to defendant H. H assigned the lease to O. The landlord approved the assignment, and the assignee took the lease under the same terms and conditions that existed for H. O defaulted on the lease, and the landlord sued O. The suit was dismissed for want of prosecution (the landlord did not proceed with due speed). The landlord then sued H, claiming that he was liable for the rental payments. Was H liable for the rent payments? Discuss.

10   Mr. and Mrs. Peterson rented a piece of business property from Mr. Platt. When the Petersons failed to pay two months' rent, Platt changed the locks on the door and refused to allow the Petersons to enter and remove their perishable goods and other personal items. Was the landlord liable for any damages? Discuss.

11   A 14-year-old girl visiting her relative Mrs. Green went to the roof of the apartment house that Mrs. Green lived in and was assisting in gathering the laundry from the line. The girl fell through a skylight that was close to the entrance to the roof. Mrs. Green's lease with the landlord indicated that she was liable only for repairs to the interior of the building. The lease made no mention of the roof and did not exempt the owner of the building from liability for roof conditions. The owner had permitted tenants to use the roof for laundry purposes, and the control of the roof remained with the owner. Is the owner liable for the injury sustained by Mrs. Green's guest when she fell through the skylight? Discuss.

12   Mrs. Putnam was injured when her shoe became caught in a hole in a driveway adjoining the parking lot leased by Grand Union from the defendant, Mr. Steigler. The hole was 10 inches in diameter and 2 inches deep, and the ground around the hole was cracked and uneven. Employees of Grand Union regularly used the driveway. The plaintiff testified that she was there two weeks prior to the accident and had observed that the area of the accident was cracked and uneven. Is either Grand Union or the landlord, Mr. Steigler, liable for the plaintiff's injuries? Discuss.

WILLS AND ESTATES

It has been said that the only certainties of life are death and taxes.

Although you cannot avoid either, there are certain plans that can be made to lessen the impact of both. Part Four will discuss the legal aspects of organizing your property and affairs in order to avoid legal problems for those who survive you.

Chapter 11 discusses a will, and Chapter 12 discusses other death-related topics such as property not covered under a will, changing a will, and legal procedures regarding an individual's property after death, including death taxes.

CHAPTER 11

Introduction to Wills

INTRODUCTION

A will is a legal document. It cannot affect the death of the maker. Many people put off making a will because they believe that doing so will somehow postpone their death. Others postpone making their wills because they cannot face the reality of their death. This is unfortunate because they may die without a will (intestate) and may thus have been deprived of the ability to determine who is to receive their property. Chapters 11 and 12 will explain the importance of making a will, describe the procedures for preparing and signing a will, and outline the process of probate and estate administration. After reading this material, you will be able to plan for your will and should be more comfortable discussing your death with your lawyer and family.

What Is a Will?

Wills can be defined as instruments executed by competent persons, in the manner prescribed by statute, whereby they make a disposition of their property to take effect on and after their death. Disposing of one's estate may involve decisions as to whether to include or exclude family members or to leave more to one family member or another. In cases where an individual has minor children, a will is useful in appointing a guardian.

A will may be used by the decedent to leave a message to loved ones or to the general public. Many individuals use a will as a vehicle for final charitable acts, bestowing both large and small amounts on existing charitable organizations or even creating new organizations (Ould v. Washington Hospital for Foundlings, 95 U.S. 303 [S. Ct. 1877]).

A will must be drawn according to the laws of the state in which the maker is domiciled at the time of signing the will. If the maker moves to another state with different requirements, his or her will may have to be revised. (Rules differ between personal property and real property.) A will does not become effective until death; therefore, it can almost always be revoked or changed. An exception occurs in the case of joint wills, whereby two persons, usually husband and wife, execute one will, which becomes effective on the first person's death.

Terminology

Before the process of preparing a will is described, an explanation of terminology is necessary.

Decedent   A decedent is a person, male or female, who died.

Testator   An individual who makes a will, is referred to as the testator, if male, and as the testatrix, if female. If the will is valid, the individual is said to have died testate. If there is no will or if the will is deemed invalid, the individual is said to have died intestate.

Executor/Administrator The person appointed by the testator to carry out the terms of his or her will is referred to as the executor, if male, and as the executrix, if female. The executor is entitled to a fee for services rendered (Exhibit 11–1). This fee is often a percentage of the estate measured on a sliding scale. As the size of the estate goes up, the percentage decreases. If a decedent dies without a will, the individual who performs the functions of the executor is appointed by the court and is referred to as the administrator, if male, and as the administratrix, if female.

Since the role of the executor is to carry out the wishes of the testator faithfully, it is important to select an executor who is sensitive to the testator's desires. Frequently, a surviving spouse will be appointed to this role because he or she was close to the decedent and would be most likely to carry out the terms of the will. This procedure may also avoid the need for payment of fees to third persons. A will should also appoint a successor executor or executrix. This is usually done by choosing someone from the remaining beneficiaries (frequently children). The successor executor will function when the original executor predeceases the testator, becomes unable to perform, or merely wishes to avoid the responsibilities of the position. Coexecutors are frequently appointed where there are several children who are the primary beneficiaries under a will and the testator does not want to show favoritism or partiality to any one of the children. The coexecutors act together to carry out the terms of the will.

Guardian The guardian is the person designated by will to take physical custody of a testator's minor children. Selection of a proper guardian is the most critical decision an individual must make. If the testator is married and the surviving spouse is a legal parent, the surviving spouse will be the guardian whether the decedent specifies a guardian in the will or not. However, if the surviving spouse is not a legal parent of the testator's children, the will must appoint a guardian.

Where there is no surviving spouse, the selection of a guardian will have to be made by the testator and frequently will be one of the testator's children. In the selection of a guardian, the only legal requirement is that the guardian be of legal age. Several other factors should be considered. A guardian should be someone likely to survive until the children's majority; otherwise, upon the death of the guardian, a new guardian will have to be appointed. It is, therefore, generally undesirable to appoint parents of the testator to be the guardians. The guardian should be someone who will care for the children as much as their deceased parent would have. The trauma of losing one's parents should not be compounded by having to live in a new home devoid of love. Close friends may sometimes make better guardians than relatives. Finally, the prospective guardian or guardians should be contacted to determine if he, she, or they are willing to serve in that capacity. Guardians may or may not be entitled to compensation. Consideration should be given to reimbursing them for out-of-pocket costs or even to providing some form of compensation in the will.

Trust A trust is created by giving property, designated "trust corpus," by one individual, the settlor, to another, the trustee. This property is held by the trustee for

EXHIBIT 11-1
Statutory Executors' Fees

Alabama	Reasonable compensation (1)
Alaska	Reasonable compensation
Arizona	Reasonable compensation
Arkansas	Sliding scale (2)
California	Sliding scale (3)
Colorado	Reasonable compensation
Connecticut	Set by court
Delaware	Reasonable compensation
District of Columbia	Set by court (5)
Florida	Reasonable compensation
Georgia	(6)
Hawaii	Reasonable compensation excluding real property
Idaho	Reasonable compensation
Illinois	Set by court
Indiana	Set by court
Iowa	Sliding scale (7)
Kansas	Reasonable compensation
Kentucky	(8)
Louisiana	(9)
Maine	Set by court (10)
Maryland	Set by court (11)
Massachusetts	Reasonable compensation (12)
Michigan	Reasonable compensation
Minnesota	Reasonable compensation
Mississippi	Set by court (14)
Missouri	Sliding scale (15)

(1) Not more than 2.5 percent of receipts and disbursements.
(2) Ten percent of first $1000; 5 percent of next $4000; 3 percent of balance.
(3) Four percent of first $15,000; 3 percent of next $85,000; 2 percent of next $900,000; 1 percent of balance.
(4) Seven percent of first $1000; 4 percent of next $9000; 3 percent of $40,000; 2 percent of balance.
(5) One to 10 percent of estate.
(6) Two and a half percent of moneys received plus 2.5 percent of cash paid out.
(7) Six percent on first $1000; 4 percent of next $4000; 2 percent of balance.
(8) Five percent of personal property and 5 percent of income received.
(9) Two and a half percent of fair market value of estate.
(10) Not more than 5 percent of fair market value of estate.
(11) Not more than 10 percent of first $20,000; 4 percent of balance; nothing for real estate.
(12) For example, 2.5 to 3 percent of first $500,000; 1 percent of balance.
(14) Not more than 7 percent fair market value of estate.
(15) Five percent on first $5000; 4 percent on $20,000; 3 percent on $75,000; 2.75 percent on $300,000; 2.5 percent on $600,000; 2 percent on balance.

EXHIBIT 11-1, cont.

Montana	Reasonable compensation (16)
Nebraska	Reasonable compensation
Nevada	Sliding scale (7)
New Hampshire	Reasonable compensation
New Jersey	(17)
New Mexico	Reasonable compensation
New York	(18)
North Carolina	Set by court clerk (19)
North Dakota	Reasonable compensation
Ohio	Sliding scale (7)
Oklahoma	Sliding scale (20)
Oregon	Sliding scale (4)
Pennsylvania	(21)
Rhode Island	Set by court
South Carolina	(22)
South Dakota	Sliding scale (20)
Tennessee	Set by court
Texas	(23)
Utah	(24)
Vermont	$4 per day
Virginia	Reasonable compensation (25)
Washington	Set by court
West Virginia	Reasonable compensation (25)
Wisconsin	2 percent
Wyoming	Sliding scale (26)

(16) Not more than 3 percent on first $40,000; 2 percent on balance.

(17) Five percent of first $100,000; balance set by court—not more than 5 percent of fair market value of estate plus 6 percent of income.

(18) Four percent of first $25,000; 3.5 percent of next $125,000; 3 percent of next $150,000; 2 percent of balance on assets received and paid out.

(19) Not more than 5 percent of amounts received and paid out.

(20) Five percent on first $1000; 4 percent on next $4000; 2.5 percent on balance.

(21) Usually, 5 percent of small estates and 3 percent of large estates on principal and income.

(22) Two and a half percent of fair market value of estate received plus 2.5 percent of assets paid out.

(23) Five percent of cash received and 5 percent of cash paid out.

(24) Not more than 5 percent on first $1000; 4 percent of next $4000; 3 percent of next $5000; 2 percent of next $40,000; 1.5 percent of next $50,000; 1 percent of balance.

(25) Usually 5 percent.

(26) Ten percent of first $1000; 5 percent of next $4000; 3 percent of next $15,000; 2 percent of balance.

the benefit of a third individual, the beneficiary, pursuant to certain instructions of the settlor as defined in the trust agreement. Trusts are often established for minor children, incompetents, children until they attain a specified age beyond majority, surviving spouses, parents, other persons, or charitable purposes.

Trustee   The person, persons, or institution responsible for conserving a beneficiary's share of a trust is called the trustee. A good trustee is one who understands and respects the financial responsibilities of his or her position. The investment philosophy of the trustee need not match that of the testator, but the trustee should not be prone to taking improper risks. For example, Mary was a very aggressive investor, prone to making highly speculative real estate investments. Her brother-in-law, Allan, was very conservative. Mary selected Allan as trustee because she knew that he would carefully invest the money that was available for her children even though his investment objectives differed from hers. A trustee has a fiduciary duty to the beneficiary.

Financial institutions are willing to serve as trustees in certain cases. There are advantages and disadvantages to appointing an institutional trustee as opposed to an individual trustee. Employees of institutional trustees frequently have greater training in managing money. Institutions survive the death of any individual and assure continuity. Institutional trustees frequently require a minimum trust corpus and inevitably charge fees. A noninstitutional trustee may be closer to the family and thus be more aware of particular needs of beneficiaries. Employees of institutions may change, and you or your beneficiaries may deal with several individuals over the course of a lifetime.

One way to overcome some of the disadvantages is to make an individual trustee and an institutional trustee cotrustees; the individual trustee would provide input as to the family's needs and desires, and the institutional trustee would provide expertise in money management, and continuity.

As in the case of guardians, trustees should be consulted as to their willingness to serve in this capacity. Trustees are entitled to fees, and this should be discussed with a prospective trustee before selection. Institutional trustees may wish to review a will before agreeing to their appointment in order to determine whether the provisions of the will are consistent with their approach to trusteeship. When appointing individual trustees, you may find it desirable to appoint a successor trustee as well in the event that the trustee is unable or unwilling to serve. (The trustee and guardian may be the same or different persons.)

Beneficiary   The person, persons, or entities who receive something under the will are referred to as beneficiaries. A beneficiary may be an adult, a minor (in which case the property left must go into a trust), or an entity (usually a charitable organization such as a church, school, and the like).

Witnesses   The persons in whose presence the will is signed are the witnesses. The number of witnesses will vary from state to state. Indiana, New Hampshire,

South Carolina, and Vermont require three witnesses; Louisiana requires a notary public plus two witnesses; all other states require two witnesses. A witness generally should be one who will be around after you die. He or she will be called upon at your death to swear to the details of the execution of your will. This would make it preferable to use young rather than old persons and stable rather than transient persons. Witnesses should be of legal age and competent. Then need not know the contents of your will, only that it is your will. Note that a beneficiary cannot also act as a witness. If your state requires two witnesses and one of them is a beneficiary, there will be a problem. The individual will have to choose between his or her status as a witness or as a beneficiary. If the individual chooses to be a witness, the will is valid, but his or her inheritance may be stricken; if the individual chooses to be a beneficiary, the will would be invalid since it has less than the number of required witnesses, and the estate may have to pass by intestacy (Walter's Estate, 33 N.E.2d 72 [N.Y. 1941]).

Devise, Legacy, Bequest *Devise, legacy, and bequest* are technical terms and are sometimes used interchangeably. They do, however, have specific meanings. A devise is a testamentary disposition of real estate, a legacy is a testamentary disposition of money, and a bequest is a testamentary disposition of any other property.

CAN YOU MAKE A WILL?

In order to make a will, you must meet certain requirements as set forth by state law. The first requirement is that you must be of legal age. State requirements as to age are as follows: Georgia—14; Louisiana—16; Alaska—19; Wyoming—21; Alabama—18 for personal property and 19 for real property; all other states—18. A second requirement is that your will manifest a clear intent to dispose of your property at your death. You need not designate the instrument as a will; you must, however, meet the statutory requirements of a will (Merrill v. Boal, 132 A. 721 [R.I. 1926]; Langfitt v. Langfitt, 151 S.E. 715 [W. Va. 1930]).

In addition, you must have knowledge of the nature and scope of your property. This does not require a precise inventory or financial statement, but would require an awareness of the degree of wealth. Another requirement is that you must know the nature and extent of your bounty. This requires an awareness of the persons who are your relatives and some appreciation of their closeness of relationship. The law does not require property to be left to the closest heirs, but will generally expect a close relative to take precedence over a distant one. If you choose to do something otherwise, it may be advisable to name the omitted parties and state that you have good reasons for leaving them out. This will reduce the likelihood of a successful will contest.

A testator must have testamentary capacity. The difficulty in defining the requirements of testamentary capacity is in applying the rule to the facts of each case. It has been stated: ''There is no rule by which it may be determined, with precision, where capacity ends and incapacity begins'' (Estate of Lacy, 431 P.2d 366 [Okla. 1967]). According to another opinion, ''It has been held over and over in this state that old age, feebleness, forgetfulness, filthy personal habits, personal eccentricities, failure to recognize old friends or relatives, physical disability, absentmindedness, and mental confusion do not furnish grounds for holding that a testator lacked testamentary capacity. . . . Mere proof of mental derangement or even of insanity in a medical sense is not sufficient to invalidate a will, but the contestant is required to go further and prove either such a complete mental degeneration as denotes other incapacity to know and understand those things which the law prescribes as essential to the making of a will, or the existence of a specific insane delusion which affected the making of the will in question'' (Ridgway's Estate, 206 P.2d 892 [Cal. 1949]).

The last requirement of competence is that a will must represent your free and uninfluenced actions. A will drawn under undue influence or duress can be successfully contested after the death of the maker if the circumstances can be proved.

PLANNING THE DISPOSITION

The steps in planning for a will are identifying your assets and identifying the ''objects of your bounty.''

Determination of Assets

A testator should prepare a list of his or her assets. Although a precise itemization is not required, each asset should be identified and approximated as to current market value. Many people, drawing up such a list, are surprised at the value of what they have accumulated. This list is also useful in forming the basis of an estate inventory, which may be required upon the death of the testator as part of the probate process. It is important not only to list assets but also to identify whether the assets are owned by the testator or are in some form of co-ownership and to show where the assets can be located. Six categories of assets are listed as follows, with some comments as to each of them. This will help you prepare a list of your assets for purposes of planning your will.

Real Property   Real property includes your home, vacation property, investment property (multiple-family dwellings), bare land, and so on. Identify the location of each parcel, the form of ownership, and the market value. (*Market value* is the property's potential current selling price less any outstanding debt [mortgages]). Values need not be based on appraisals at this time; owner estimates will be sufficient. Upon a person's death, an appraisal might be necessary for tax or probate purposes or both.

Cash and Receivables   Savings and checking accounts and certificates of deposit should be listed by bank and account number. The form of ownership should be identified. Receivables (moneys owed to you by others) should be listed at their collectible value. If your deadbeat friend owes you $500, you may wish to list it (to inform others of the debt's existence), but you should value it at zero.

Marketable Securities   Stocks, bonds, options, and the like, are marketable securities, which are publicly traded on a national or local exchange. The form of ownership should be specified. Securities should be valued at their current fair market values less any moneys owed the broker. The fair market value of publicly traded securities is reported in newspapers that have business sections such as *The New York Times*, *The Wall Street Journal*, or *Barron's*.

Business interests—If you are actively engaged in managing a business as a self-employed person, as part of a partnership, or as a shareholder in a small business corporation, your objective should be to identify the interest that you have in the business and make a reasonable estimate of its fair market value. If the business is structured in a complex manner or if there are buy-and-sell agreements that control the transfer of the business upon your death, it will probably be necessary to seek help from a professional such as a certified public accountant (CPA) or a lawyer in order to value your interest in the business.

Personal Property   Personal property includes items such as vehicles, tools, furniture, jewelry, art works, collectibles, and so on. In today's inflationary economic environment, these items may currently be worth more than what they cost when originally acquired. Silverware has substantially appreciated in value, and many homes contain valuable antiques, art works, or hobby collections, which also have considerable value. Your collection of comic books may be worth thousands of dollars but looks like junk to the rest of your family. When you list art and collectibles, it is also advisable to list a person to contact who could assist your family in a suitable appraisal and disposition of these items upon your death.

Life Insurance   Life insurance should be identified by the name of the company, the policy number, the beneficiary, the amount of death benefit, the cash surrender value, and any outstanding policy loans. It is also necessary to consider life insurance that may be provided by an employer, as well as life insurance on credit loans.

Purchasers of major items on credit, such as automobiles and houses, usually obtain a life insurance policy from the lender insuring the amount of the loan. This is sometimes referred to as *credit life insurance* or *mortgage insurance*.

Debts   Only include unsecured debts: credit card balances, charge accounts, bank loans, finance company loans, personal loans, and so forth. Secured debts (debts for which the lender has received collateral to insure his payment in the event that you default on the loan) such as mortgages or U.C.C. secured loans should have been subtracted from the asset pledged as security in computing the market value of that asset and, therefore, should not be included in this category. For example, if you have a home that is worth $100,000, on which there is a mortgage of $30,000, in preparing a list of your assets, you should list the house at $70,000 net value. (The fact that the mortgage is in existence should be specified when listing the asset.)

Determination of Your Heirs

Determining to whom you wish to leave property is usually simple. The *objects of one's bounty* are usually one's closest relatives, including spouse, children, parents, or siblings. However, the possibilities are endless as to how you might wish to distribute your assets. You may dispose of your property as you wish, to whomever you wish, subject to almost any conditions. It is not necessary that you leave property to the natural objects of your bounty, nor is it necessary to leave prop-

EXHIBIT 11-2
Right of Election

	Husband	*Wife*
Alabama	No	Yes
Alaska	Yes	Yes
Arizona	No	No
Arkansas	Yes	Yes
California	No	No
Colorado	Yes	Yes
Connecticut	Yes	Yes
Delaware	Yes	Yes
District of Columbia	Yes	Yes
Florida	Yes	Yes
Georgia	No	No
Hawaii	Yes	Yes
Idaho	Yes	Yes
Illinois	No	No
Indiana	Yes	Yes
Iowa	Yes	Yes
Kansas	Yes	Yes
Kentucky	Yes	Yes
Louisiana	No	No
Maine	Yes	Yes
Maryland	Yes	Yes
Massachusetts	Yes	Yes
Michigan	No	Yes
Minnesota	Yes	Yes
Mississippi	Yes	Yes
Missouri	Yes	Yes

erty to anybody who is even distantly related. It is perfectly legal for you to leave property to a total stranger to the exclusion of virtually all of your heirs except for a spouse.

Right of Election, Dower, Curtesy, and Homestead Exemption *not important*

Traditionally, the law has imposed several constraints upon a married person's right to dispose of property. The law in this area is complex and differs widely among the states. A surviving spouse's right of election provides that a surviving spouse is entitled to something from the decedent spouse's estate (Exhibit 11–2). This was also once referred to as the widow's share or the widow's right of election, but may apply to surviving husbands as well. The amount of the election will generally vary from one half to one third of the estate depending upon the number of children that also survive the deceased spouse.

EXHIBIT 11-2, cont.

	Husband	*Wife*
Montana	Yes	Yes
Nebraska	Yes	No
Nevada	No	No
New Hampshire	Yes	Yes
New Jersey	Yes	Yes
New Mexico	No	No
New York	Yes	Yes
North Carolina	Yes	Yes
North Dakota	Yes	Yes
Ohio	Yes	Yes
Oklahoma	Yes	Yes
Oregon	Yes	Yes
Pennsylvania	Yes	Yes
Rhode Island	Yes	Yes
South Carolina	No	Yes
South Dakota	No	No
Tennessee	Yes	Yes
Texas	No	No
Utah	No	Yes
Vermont	Yes	Yes
Virginia	Yes	Yes
Washington	No	No
West Virginia	Yes	Yes
Wisconsin	Yes	Yes
Wyoming	Yes	Yes

Many states recognize the common law right of dower, entitling a widow to a one-third life interest in her husband's real property (this even applies to property sold by the husband prior to death, if where the wife has not signed the deed). A few states give the same right to widowers; this is called *curtesy.* Some other states recognize a widow's right of homestead, which gives her a life estate in her husband's real property or a total interest in a portion of it.

Specific Bequests

Frequently, an individual wishes to leave certain assets or a given sum of money to a specific person. This can be done by will, and such an act is called a *specific bequest*. The subject of a specific bequest is often a family heirloom, a piece of jewelry, money, or other items that have sentimental value, monetary value, or both. Ownership of a sentimental asset having monetary value is frequently the center of dispute between beneficiaries of an estate. In order to resolve these disputes, it may be necessary to sell the property to a stranger for its economic value. If there is a family member who would appreciate a particular asset more than any of the other members or if it is your desire to resolve the potential dispute by designating a given member of the family to whom the property should go or if it is your desire simply to make sure that the asset remains in the family as long as possible, it may be desirable to designate one of your relatives as specific beneficiary of this property.

A parent with several children may at various times have given sums of money to some of them for various purposes. If these sums have been unequal, a well-drawn specific bequest can be used to equalize the gifts by making adjustments upon the testator's death. A specific monetary legacy is sometimes also given to offset a specific bequest of personal effects to certain family members. For example, if an individual had an antique record player worth $3,000, which she wanted to leave to her daughter, she might wish to balance this transaction by leaving her son a sum of $3,000 in cash. The remaining estate would then be divided equally between the two of them. Although the daughter received a preference in the sense that she received the family heirloom, to the extent that that heirloom had value, the son received equal value. In another case, the will of an individual who had helped several of his children purchase homes by giving them sufficient money to make the down payment provided that a comparable amount be given to the other children, after which his estate was equally divided.

Conditional Legacy

A conditional legacy is a legacy that has attached to it reasonable conditions to qualify the legatee (the person who is to receive the legacy) to receive the legacy. If the conditions are not met, the specific legacy can be given to another person (either without condition, with the same conditions, or with different conditions), or the legacy can lapse, and the amount involved will be added to the residual estate. The conditions that may be imposed upon a conditional legacy must be reasonable and may not be against public policy.

A legacy on condition that a person not marry would be deemed to be contrary to public policy, and the conditional aspect of the legacy would be stricken. The beneficiary in that instance would be entitled to receive that money irrespective of whether he or she had married. On the other hand, a legacy on the condition that a person not marry a specific individual would probably be considered within public policy. Public policy favors marriage in general but does not favor or disfavor marriage to any given individual (U.S. National Bank of Portland v. Snodgrass, 275 P.2d 860 [Ariz. 1954]).

Distributions

There are many methods of distributing assets. One such method is referred to as *per stirpes* (from the Latin, meaning "by roots"). Under per stirpes distribution, each branch of a family that has a living member will share equally in the estate. For example, in Exhibit 11–3, with W leaving $120,000 "to my children, per stirpes" (or without designation), the estate would be divided into five equal shares: S2, D2, and D3 will each receive one fifth of $120,000 or $24,000. S1's family will receive one share, and the three grandchildren (GC1, 2, and 3) would split their $24,000 share three ways and receive $8,000 each. D1's family would receive one share as well, and each of the grandchildren (GC4 and 5) would split their $24,000 share two ways, getting $12,000 each.

A second method of distribution is *per capita* (from the Latin term, meaning "by heads"). This method distributes assets equally to each surviving distributee. In Exhibit 11–3, if W left $120,000 "to my children, per capita," the three children

EXHIBIT 11-3
Intestate Inheritance

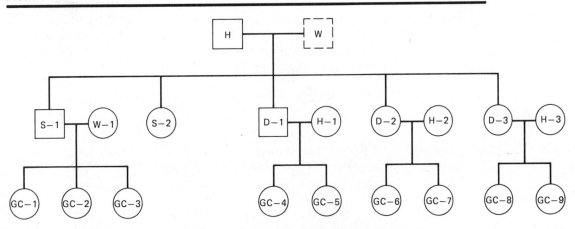

Family members who are deceased are indicated by boxes; those who are alive are indicated by circles. W has just died. She was the wife of H (previously deceased.) She is survived by S−2, D−2, and D−3. S−1 and D−1 have previously died, each leaving several grandchildren.

of the decedent (S2, D2, and D3) each would receive one third of the estate, or $40,000. The grandchildren would receive nothing.

Exhibit 11–3 illustrates just one of the problems that can be encountered in trying to plan fairly for the distribution of one's estate. A good lawyer can draft a will to make sure that your desires will be fulfilled; it is your responsibility to identify and communicate to the lawyer what your wishes are. The essential aspect in this type of planning is to consider the choices that you have available.

Exclusions

In most states, any family member may be excluded from a will except a spouse. (In Louisiana, a testator may not disinherit a child.) The testator's will should clearly show intent to exclude such a person; otherwise, there may be a question as to the testator's competence. If it can be shown that a testator forgot one or more relatives, it may be possible to declare the will invalid owing to lack of testamentary capacity. An omitted relative, such as a child, who would have inherited had the decedent died intestate, has nothing to lose by attacking the will. If one wishes to exclude a given individual, that person should be named, and it should be stated that the decedent intentionally left nothing to that individual.

One may exclude a person because of disapproval of that person and his or her behavior or because it is felt that the person does not need any additional distribution. For example, a husband was a poor individual; his wife was well-to-do. Her only sibling, with whom she was very close, was successful in business. Her will left everything to her husband and, in the event that he predeceased her, left everything to his parents and siblings. The testatrix simply felt that her husband and his family had a greater need for her assets than her family did. In such a situation, it would be advisable for the testatrix to point out in her will that she is not leaving any property to her siblings because she feels that they are adequately provided for at present and that the people to whom her estate is being left have a greater need. Without such a statement, it is possible for her family to attack the validity of the will. Even with such a statement, it is still possible for such an attack to be made, but the standards of proof and the burdens upon her family in order to sustain such an attack would be substantially greater.

MAKING YOUR WILL

In order for your will to be valid it must meet the specific statutory requirements of your state. Whereas these will vary to some extent from state to state, there are several general requirements.

Written Will   Courts will universally require either a handwritten, printed, or typed will, or some combination of all three. Approximately half the state will recognize an oral (noncupative) will but *only* if the testator is in the armed services or on his or her death bed, and so on. Oral wills not made under such limited circumstances are not valid anywhere. (Oral wills are usually only operative on personal property.) It is not important how the will is written; however, the text should be clear. Changes made by erasures, deletions, or removal of entire pages are subject to question by disgruntled heirs and should be avoided at all costs. If you use a printed will and delete a paragraph or insert a handwritten paragraph that conflicts with the printed version, the courts may have to rule on the validity of these changes and perhaps of the entire will. It is better to redo the will in its entirety (assuming the will was not prepared in an emergency situation) than to leave important questions open to litigation.

Signature   You must sign your will. Most jurisdictions will not only recognize your signature, but will also accept your mark, fingerprints, or authorization of another to sign your name or to guide your hand. Alternatives to your actual signature should be avoided whenever possible, especially since they may raise questions as to your competence.

Witnesses   All states require a will to be witnessed. Witnesses will, upon probate (proving) of the will, be required to testify as to the details surrounding the signing of the will. The witnesses must be present when you sign the will, they must sign it in your presence, and you must tell them it is your will. The witnesses need not know what is contained in your will, but they may be told if you so desire. A beneficiary to a will may not be a witness; the lawyer who prepares it usually may. Since witnesses are needed to testify on your death, they should be young persons who are not contemplating leaving the area.

Publication   This is the act whereby the testator announces to the witnesses that the document is his or her last will and testament. This is done in the written portion of the will and also verbally in the presence of the witnesses.

The procedures in executing a will are quite simple. There must be at least three persons present: you and the two witnesses. Many lawyers will secure three witnesses, so that if one of them becomes unavailable at the time of probate, there will still be two. You will read the will to determine that it meets your needs, and then the witnesses will be requested to enter the room. You will then state: "This is my last will and testament, and I would like you to witness it." You sign the will, and the witnesses sign, and it's done. Some lawyers ask testators to sign or initial each page of a will for identification purposes.

Unsigned copies are not valid wills. Frequently several copies of a will are made and retained by the testator or testatrix or given to his or her executor or left by him or her in some readily locatable place. They should *not* be executed. Never sign more than one will. If you make a new will, immediately secure the old one and destroy it. Make sure that you destroy the signed original and not just the unsigned or conformed copy (unsigned original indicating date of will and witnesses).

There is generally no need for an individual to discuss his or her estate with the beneficiaries; however, there is also no reason to avoid doing so. You may wish to advise your children of the size of the estate so that they may be prepared to deal with the responsibility of the amount of money they are going to inherit. Where the estate involved is fairly large, it may be desirable to be more open with the beneficiaries so that they may appropriately plan their estates and properly draw their wills.

SAMPLE WILL CLAUSES

The dispositive terms of a will are numerous and varied, limited only by the numbers of lawyers drafting them and the needs of the testators. To attempt to list all such provisions would be impossible, and many would vary only in minor details. We have reproduced in the following pages a number of clauses from a relatively simple will. These provisions are representative of what might be found in a ''I love you'' will or in one in which a testator leaves everything to a surviving spouse.

Recitals

An example of a recital follows.

I, Marilyn Poch, residing at 15 Gilbert Street, Fort Lee, County of Bergen and State of New Jersey, do hereby make and publish the following as and for my last will and testament and do hereby revoke all other wills, codicils, and testamentary instruments heretofore made by me.

Revocation of prior wills is of great importance where they contain provisions that may conflict with the current will. If a testatrix made a will leaving all her assets to her siblings and later prepared a will leaving everything to her nephews and nieces without destroying the first will, her siblings would have reason to attack the validity of the second will. Furthermore, the failure to destroy or revoke the first will could be argued to be evidence of the incompetence of the testatrix. Irrespective of who would win such a conflict, the costs will be substantial and will be paid for by the estate and therefore ultimately by the beneficiaries who are to receive the proceeds under the valid will.

Debts and Expenses

A statement regarding debts and payments is needed. For example:

I direct that all my just debts, funeral expenses, and administration expenses of my estate (including all inheritance and estate taxes) be paid as soon after my demise as may be practicable, and before payment of any bequests, except that the payment of any debt secured by a mortgage or pledge or real or personal property may be postponed by the executor in his or her discretion.

By law, a person's debts are considered obligations of the estate. Until a reasonable effort has been made to locate and pay all creditors, any payment by the executor to the heirs is made at his or her risk. If a distribution is made and subsequently a creditor shows up, the executor must obtain funds from the distributees to pay the creditor. If they are unable to restore such funds to the executor, the executor may be personally liable for the debts tendered.

Federal and state estate or inheritance taxes are also required to be paid before distribution of assets to the heirs. Failure to pay will be charged to the executor personally. Other administrative expenses would include the executor's fees, attorney's fees, accountant's fees, trustees' fees, funeral expenses, and other miscellaneous items.

Debts that are secured need not be paid immediately. Many of the debts involved are large, and if the asset were sold at a forced liquidation, it would bring less than its market value. Also, the heirs would often rather receive the asset subject to the debt than its net value in cash. When the estate assets are distributed to the heirs, they will be transferred subject to the debt. The creditors will not be adversely affected since the heir becomes liable on the debt. If the heir defaults, the creditor has access to the asset.

Specific Bequests

Here is an example of a specific bequest.

> *In the event she survives me, I hereby give, devise, and bequeath my wedding and engagement rings to my daughter, Elizabeth Poch, residing at R.D. No. 3, Box 22, Phoenixville, Pennsylvania.*

Specific bequests can in some cases create problems. Here is an example. John made his will at a time when he was very wealthy. He left $50,000 to his church and the rest of his estate to his family. At the time of his death, John's estate amounted to only $40,000. A specific bequest is distributed before a general bequest. In this example, John's family would get nothing, and the church would get $40,000.

Another problem that may arise from a specific bequest could come about as follows: Mary leaves her 1981 Cadillac to her nephew, Bill, and her 1981 Porsche to her niece, Janet. Two years later she sells her Cadillac and opens a savings account with the proceeds and trades her Porsche on a Jaguar. Shortly thereafter she dies. In addition to the specific bequests, her will leaves her remaining assets to the Cancer Society. The issue in this fact pattern is whether Bill or Janet will receive anything from Mary's estate. When a specific bequest of property other than money is made and the property no longer exists upon the decedent's death, the courts may trace the specific bequest to its new form, that is, money in a bank from the sale of the Cadillac, and award this to the legatee. Or the courts may take the position that had the decedent wanted the substitute property to go to the legatee, a new will would have been prepared. Was it Mary's intent to leave the savings account to Bill in lieu of the Cadillac? Would it have made any difference if the money went into her checking account or into an already existing savings account? Did Mary intend for Elizabeth to receive the Jaguar in lieu of the Porsche? These questions could have been resolved had Mary changed her will.

Many people who make specific bequests later forget them, dispose of the property, and fail to make appropriate changes to their wills. This often leads to expensive litigation, the result of which will be to reduce the estate that is available for the heirs by reason of attorney's fees and court costs.

Bequests of Remainder Interest (Residual Clause)

An example of a residual clause follows.

If he shall survive me, I give, devise, and bequeath to my husband, William Poch, absolutely and forever, all the rest, residue, and remainder of my entire estate, real, personal, and mixed.

The reason why this paragraph refers to all the rest, residue, and remainder of the estate is to make it clear that this bequest is effective after the payment of expenses, taxes, and specific bequests. A residual clause is important to make sure that all property is distributed. If one or more specific bequests fail (e.g., because the beneficiary dies), that property would pass under the residual clause.

Bequest on Prior Demise of Husband

A bequest on prior demise should be made clear.

In the event that my husband, William Poch, shall predecease me, I direct all the rest, residue, and remainder of my entire estate pass in equal portions to my children, per stirpes, and not per capita.

This residual clause will be effective if the testatrix's husband dies before the testatrix. On the prior death of any of the children, that child's share of his or her mother's estate passes to that child's children, who would be the testatrix's grandchildren.

In the event that one or more of my children shall be under age twenty-one (21) at the time such distribution is to take place, I direct that the interest of such child pass to my trustee, in trust, to hold, invest, and reinvest the same; to collect the income therefrom; and to apply so much of the income thereof to the support, education, and maintenance of such child, as my trustee shall see fit; and to accumulate, invest, and reinvest the balance of such income until such child attains the age of twenty-one (21), thereupon to pay over the unexpended principal, together with any accumulated income, to such child.

The laws in most states prohibit minors under age 18 from owning interests in real or personal property. Where a beneficiary under a will is under 18 (or any greater age selected by the testatrix), the property should be left to a trustee in trust for the benefit of such heir. In the event that the beneficiary attains the proper age before the testatrix's death and the testatrix fails to change her will, the property on her death will automatically pass directly to the beneficiary. During the time that the trust is in effect for the benefit of the child, the trustee is responsible for investing the principal of the trust and retaining as much of the income as is not required for the immediate care of the minor child. The immediate care includes primarily necessities such as food, clothing, shelter, education, and medical costs. In the event that the trust income exceeds the amounts needed for raising the child, the balance will be retained by the trustee and will be reinvested to produce more income, all of which will be turned over to the child at such time as he or she attains the appropriate age. In the event that the income from the trust is insufficient to meet the needs of the child, trusts usually will provide that a portion of the trust assets may be used to meet that child's needs. This may result in a situation where, before the minor child attains the appropriate age, all of the money that was to go to that child has been spent for the child's needs.

Definitions

Some important definitions follow.

1. *Use of the masculine gender. All reference in this my last will and testament to any individual or group by the use of a masculine term shall in no way be interpreted to exclude persons otherwise falling within the same group but who should be female.*

2. *Use of singular person. All reference in this my last will and testament in the singular person shall include plurals where the latter shall be appropriate. All references in the plural shall include the singular, where the latter shall be appropriate.*

3. *Definition of child. The term* child *shall include children not born to my husband and myself, but legally adopted by us or placed with us for adoption and adopted by my husband within one year after my death.*

These definitions are designed to prevent confusion over a will referring to persons by the wrong gender or referring to a person or group of persons in the wrong quantity. Illegitimate children, by statute, are usually entitled to inherit only from their mother. In most states, such a child cannot inherit from its father unless he acknowledges the child.

In most states, a child born after the death of its mother or father is entitled to inherit if born within nine months of the death of an intestate father. To create a similar result in the case of a will, insert a clause providing for after-born children.

Common Disaster Clause

A common disaster clause should be included. For example:

In the event that any beneficiary shall survive me, but shall die within sixty (60) days after the date of my death, then all provisions of this my last will and testament shall take effect in like manner as if such beneficiary had predeceased me.

Occasionally, both a husband and a wife die in a common disaster (automobile, plane accident, and so on). This clause enables the decedents to specify the sequence in which they will be presumed to have died. The sequence that is specified will govern even if it can be clearly set forth that the presumed sequence differs from the actual order of death. The 60-day time period referred to in the preceding clause is an arbitrary period of time and could be set at either a longer or shorter interval. The longer the interval selected, the more time it will take before an estate can be wound up and resolved because it will be necessary to wait until the expiration of that time to determine whether or not any of the ultimate beneficiaries will be presumed to have predeceased the first decedent.

A common disaster clause may affect the inheritance of family assets because a husband and wife might have separate wills with different provisions.

In Terrorem Clause

The purpose of an in terrorem clause should be clear.

> *The gifts, bequests, and devises under this my last will and testament are intended to be in lieu of any other claims of whatever nature and whether arising by statute or otherwise, by any taker hereunder, and any taker who asserts such other claim or contests this my last will and testament shall forfeit all gifts and devises to him or her hereunder. Any property forfeited hereunder shall be distributed as though the forfeiting heir had predeceased me.*

If a beneficiary under a will is dissatisfied with his or her inheritance, he or she can challenge the validity of the instrument. This clause stipulates that anyone bringing such a challenge forfeits any interest he or she inherited under the will. This threat, coupled with a bequest within a will, will make an heir think twice before challenging the validity of the will. If the heir challenges and wins, he or she will, of course, inherit more. If he or she challenges and loses, the heir will end up forfeiting the inheritance that he or she would have had had he or she not acted at all.

Appointment of Executor and Guardian

The appointment of an executor and a guardian is of paramount importance.

> *I hereby appoint my husband, William Poch, as executor. In the event that he is unable or unwilling to serve, I appoint my brother, Jason Mace, living in Sidney, New York, as successor executor. With respect to the trusts created hereunder, I appoint my sister, Lisa Ball, as trustee. In the event that she is unwilling or unable to serve in this capacity, I appoint the Second National Bank in Sidney, New York, as successor-trustee. I further direct that neither my executor nor my trustee nor my successor-executor nor my successor-trustee be required at any time to give bond or other security for the proper performance of duties. In the event that my husband, William Poch, shall not survive*

me, I appoint my sister, Lisa Ball, as guardian over any of my children who shall be under the age of eighteen (18) years. My guardian shall not be required at any time to give any bond or other security for the proper performance of duties.

An executor is considered a fiduciary, and as such he or she has a sacred duty to perform his or her tasks responsibly and to account to the estate, court, and the beneficiaries for all his or her actions. It is often desirable to name a successor-executor in the event that the executor predeceases the testator or is unable or unwilling to serve in this capacity. It may also be necessary (if there are minor or incompetent children) to appoint a guardian (to take care of the children) and a trustee (to take care of the children's money). Under some state laws, an executor is required to post a bond as security for the proper performance of his or her duties. This requires either a substantial "security deposit" or the purchase of an insurance policy (which guarantees any losses occurring owing to the malfeasance of the fiducuary). In either case, there is a burden to the estate, and the waiver appearing in the preceding clause will eliminate this burden. The waiver does not eliminate the executor's obligation to perform properly nor does it prevent a beneficiary from suing an executor who has not performed in the appropriate manner.

Discussing one's will with the proposed executor, trustee, and guardian is also very important, at least to determine their willingness to act in a fiduciary capacity. The executor is often a close family member or your lawyer, who, as part of his or her duties, will have to deal with a substantial amount of paperwork. Choosing someone who is already overburdened with personal affairs would be unfair to that person. Such a person would feel morally obligated to serve in this capacity at a time when he or she probably has more than enough things to do anyhow and possibly would end up doing a less than desirable job and possibly even subject himself or herself to suit by other members of the family who are in line for an inheritance. A trustee has an important financial obligation, and, unless the estate is large enough to warrant a professional accountant, will have to be able to keep some kind of records. Selecting someone who is comfortable with these obligations is most important, and the best way to find out whether the individual is comfortable is to talk with that person first. Even a professional trustee will, in some cases, refuse to accept responsibility for a given estate because of the nature of the trust assets, the size of the fund, or the peculiar family relationships involved. Expecting that someone who is not a professional trustee would automatically be willing to accept such a burden is again unfair.

Choosing a guardian is perhaps the most critical of the selection of fiduciaries because this is the individual who will be responsible for the day-to-day care and supervision of your children. You should ask your chosen guardians whether they would be willing to accept the responsibility of caring for the children involved. To impose such a responsibility on an individual without first asking him or her is grossly unfair, and once you have died, you can no longer change your selection. It is important for your choice to recognize the time, space, and emotional involvement that will be required in taking care of your children after you die; it is your obligation to point this out to your choice of guardians. The guardians should also be informed that if their circumstances change, they should feel free to withdraw and that if your circumstances change, you may also choose to change your selection for guardian.

Attestation Clause

An example of the attestation clause follows.

IN WITNESS WHEREOF, I have to this, my last will and testament, set my hand in and affixed my seal, having first written my name for the purpose of identification in the margin of each of the preceding pages, this _____ day of _____, 19___.

_____

Marilyn Poch (LS)

It is not necessary for a testatrix to sign each page, but doing so can eliminate questions as to possible substitutions of pages. The attestation clause is not legally required in most states but is almost universally in use by lawyers. It gives some proof that the testatrix knew what she was signing when she executed the will.

Acknowledgment

The acknowledgement concludes the will.

Signed, sealed, published, and declared by Marilyn Poch, the testatrix above named, to be her last will and testament, and in our presence, and we at her request, and in her presence, and in the presence of each other, have hereunto subscribed our names as witnesses this _____ day of _____, 19___.

_____residing at _____

_____residing at _____

_____residing at _____

The witnesses state that the testatrix signed the will in their presence and that they signed in the testatrix's presence and in the presence of each other. This is not universally required but is a good idea. In the event of an inquiry as to the testatrix's capacity at the time of signing the will, the witnesses' testimonies as to the actions of the testatrix when she signed the will may be very useful. In the event that the will is signed outside of their presence, this evidence would not be able to be submitted. The testatrix must also ask each witness to sign for the purpose of witnessing the will; however, they need not know the contents of the will.

EXHIBIT 11-4
Example of Will Recordation Statute (Vermont)

Deposit of will for safe-keeping; delivery; final disposition.

(a) A testator may deposit his will for safe-keeping in the office of the register of probate for the district in which such testator resides on the payment of a fee of $2.00 to the court. The register shall give to such testator a certificate of such deposit, shall safely keep each will so deposited and shall keep an index of the wills so deposited.

(b) Each will so deposited shall be inclosed in a sealed wrapper having inscribed thereon the name and residence of the testator, the day when and the person by whom it was deposited, and such wrapper may also have indorsed thereon the name of the person to whom the will is to be delivered after the death of the testator. Such wrapper shall not be opened until it is delivered to a person entitled to receive it or until otherwise disposed of as hereinafter provided.

(c) During the life of the testator such will shall be delivered only to him, or in accordance with his order in writing duly proved by oath of a subscribing witness, but his duly authorized legal guardian may at any time inspect and copy the will in the presence of the judge or register. After the death of the testator it shall be delivered on demand to the person named in the indorsement.

(d) If such will is not called for by the person named in the indorsement, it shall be publicly opened at a time to be appointed by the probate court as soon as may be after notice of the testator's death. If the will should be probated in a probate district other than where it has been kept, the will shall be delivered to the executor therein named or to the person whose name is indorsed on the wrapper or be filed in the office of the register of such other court as the judge of probate, in his discretion, may order.

AFTER YOU'VE MADE YOUR WILL, WHERE DO YOU PUT IT?

You should *never* execute more than one original will; you may make numerous copies, but you should sign only one original. The original should be placed in a safe location, where it will be accessible upon your death. Many people put their original wills in their safe deposit boxes; this can create problems when they die. Usually, upon an individual's death, his or her safe deposit box is sealed and can be opened only in the presence of a state tax official. A much better place to keep your original will is in the possession of your executor, your lawyer, or, if you decide to keep it yourself, in a safe place where access to it will be available upon your death. If you keep the will yourself, make sure that someone who is likely to be nearby at the time you die knows where it is.

If you leave the original will with your executor or your lawyer, you should make a copy and put it in a conspicuous place, together with instructions as to where the original can be found. The purpose for this is that upon your death, whoever makes a search of your effects should find the will fairly quickly and will know whom to contact to obtain the original and to start the probate proceeding.

If you choose to leave the original of your will with your lawyer, giving a copy to your executor is also a good idea. In addition, you may wish to give copies of the will to members of your family or to beneficiaries. This is of general importance to any beneficiary so that he or she may know what he or she is going to receive upon the death of a family member. It is of particular importance for a beneficiary who is to receive a large portion of a large estate because that beneficiary may have to plan his or her will. In the planning of one's will, it is often necessary not only to know what an individual's assets are, but also what an individual's potential for acquiring assets in the immediate future may be.

Each of the individuals who has a copy of the will ought to know where the original is located and probably ought to be aware of who the lawyer was who helped draw the will. The purpose of this again is so that the individuals in question will know whom to contact in the event of your death. In some states it is possible to record one's will prior to death (e.g., see Exhibit 11–4).

QUESTIONS

1 Barney, the deceased, wrote a letter to his lawyer by hand, in which he said the following: "What I want is that you should change my will so that [my wife] will be entitled to all that belongs to her as my wife. I am in very poor health and would like this attended to as soon as convenient. . . . I don't know what ought to be done but you do." The letter was executed in a manner consistent with the requirements of the state statute for a holographic (handwritten) will. Before the attorney could make any changes to the decedent's will, the decedent died. Was the letter testamentary in nature, or was it merely a letter authorizing the attorney to make certain changes to the will? Discuss.

2 Mr. Watkins died in 1916, leaving as his heirs four children. One of his daughters presented a document that purported to be his will. The document left the estate in five equal parts, two of which were to be given to the daughter in question; the other three were to be divided equally among the remaining children. The instrument had been executed in proper testamentary form as part of the initiation rights of the Masonic Order. The will had been executed 13 years prior to Mr. Watkins's death. Members of the Masonic Order testified that the will was a ceremonial ritual only and was not intended as a testamentary disposition. Other members testified that the purpose of this particular rite was that all Masons should die testate and should have had an opportunity to make some disposition or to reflect upon the disposition of their assets prior to their death. It was also testified by the latter group of witnesses that it was acceptable for a Mason to modify or revoke the will subsequently. Was the will valid?

3 The decedent, George M. Burt, left a will in which Harold Blair was named sole beneficiary. William Burt, the brother of the decedent, brought an action to set aside the will on the grounds that his brother lacked testamentary capacity to prepare a will. Evidence discloses that the decedent died in 1959 as a result of an automobile accident at the age of approximately 72. During 1958 he consulted with an attorney concerning the preparation of a will. Subsequent to the visit to his attorney, he made a second visit, at which he brought with him several people, including the beneficiary, Mr. Blair. In Mr. Blair's presence, the will was read to the decedent by the attorney and was signed by the decedent and properly witnessed. Facts indicated that the witness was unable to read but was able to sign his name.

The will stated that George Burt wished to leave nothing to his brother, Wilbur (whose correct name was William), because he felt that the brother was adequately provided for and that Mr. Blair had a better claim upon his (George's) generosity. Other evidence indicates that the decedent was alert, sober, and normal during the time of the execution of the will; that he listened carefully while the will was being read; and that he definitely knew what he was doing. Was the will valid? Discuss.

4 Mrs. Brown died in 1942, leaving a surviving son and several brothers and sisters. She left her son a life interest in certain real estate, and upon his death the property was to go to her brother, Clyde Emerson, and his heirs. Mrs. Brown's son brought an action to prevent the probate of the will on the grounds that the will had been influenced unduly by the brother. Evidence showed that the decedent's brother began to visit her frequently upon the onset of a terminal illness. There was evidence that the decedent had indicated a desire to deed her real property to her son prior to her death, but her brother had told her that such an act was not necessary because he didn't want her to expend the energy and concern to do so during her illness. There was also evidence to indicate that the lawyer who prepared the will was also the attorney for the decedent's brother and that the will was written without the knowledge of the plaintiff or his wife, who were physically taking care of the decedent at the time the will was written. There was also some medical testimony to the effect that it was questionable as to whether the decedent at the time of executing the will could have known what she was doing. Was the will valid? Discuss.

5 Mr. Himelfarb died, leaving an estate of approximately $1.7 million. His will provided $10,000 for each of his eight children provided they did not contest the will. The remainder of the estate was left to the Himelfarb Foundation, a nonprofit charitable foundation that had been created by the testator during his lifetime. One of Himelfarb's children brought action against the estate on the grounds that the attorney who prepared the will was not Himelfarb's regular attorney and had been initially consulted by one of the directors of the foundation, that the directors of the foundation had schemed to prevent the decedent's children from becoming members of the foundation, and that the members of the foundation subsequent to the decedent's death had entered into a number of improper business transactions. Because of this, the plaintiff argued that the will should be overturned on the grounds that it was fraudulently obtained. Decision for whom? Discuss.

6 Watson drove into a gas service station and asked the operator of the station to sign a document that he purported to be his will. He signed the will in the presence of the station operator. The station operator (Richardson), in the presence of the decedent, asked Shiver, a customer, to witness the will, and Shiver signed it in the presence of both Richardson and the decedent. Richardson then signed the will and asked another individual, Cooper, also to sign as a witness. The decedent told Cooper that this was something to make sure that the proper party received Watson's property, and Cooper said he understood that the document they were signing was Watson's will. The room in which the will was signed was only large enough for one or two persons to enter at any given point in time. While the various parties were signing the will, the decedent and one or more of the witnesses stood outside the room, looking in upon the transaction either through the doorway or a window. The statute says the a will must be executed by the testator in the presence of at least two witnesses at the same time. Was the statutory requirement complied with? Discuss.

7 Moulton prepared numerous wills during his lifetime. The heirs under several of his earlier wills filed a petition contesting the validity of his most recent will on the grounds that he lacked testamentary capacity or was unduly influenced in the execution of the will. In 1963, Moulton entered a hospital and was diagnosed as suffering from senility due to arteriosclerosis. His attorney (Hensel) prepared a draft of a will leaving the entire estate to Glessner, one of the decedent's nephews. Hensel felt that Moulton was not capable of executing the will and, therefore, would not allow the will to be finalized unless the decedent was examined by his doctors. Glessner had the decedent examined by several doctors, who indicated their opinion that decedent was not competent to make a will. Glessner then took the decedent to Higgins, another lawyer, who prepared a will, which was executed by the decedent in the presence of attorney Higgins and his secretary. Mr. Higgins was not informed and was not aware of the refusal of the attorney Hensel to prepare a will. Less than two months later, a proceeding was held declaring the decedent unable to handle his own affairs and appointing Glessner as the guardian for the decedent. Was the will valid? Discuss.

8   The testatrix had been a firm believer in spiritualism for a number of years prior to her death and frequently attended séances at her own home and elsewhere. She firmly believed that she had received communications from her deceased husband and other family members who had predeceased her. She consulted a medium before executing her will. During the séance her deceased husband had come and told her how to prepare her will. Based on the results of this séance, she went to a lawyer and had the will drawn up. Her children, who were not included in the will, brought an action to have the will set aside on the grounds that testator lacked testamentary capacity. Decision for whom? Discuss.

9   Mrs. Carpenter was 52 years old. Her husband had died 13 years earlier, and she lived alone and handled all her own business and household affairs. In 1966 she developed a disease. One of her children visited her, recognized that her mother was quite ill, and arranged to have her admitted to the hospital. The hospital room had no telephone, and Mrs. Carpenter did not have ready access to a telephone anywhere else. Several days after admission to the hospital, the daughter contacted her own attorney and asked him to come and prepare a will for Mrs. Carpenter. She told the attorney that the will was to designate her as sole beneficiary and executrix. The attorney came and spoke with Mrs. Carpenter, discussed the terms of the will to be prepared and the fact that Mrs. Carpenter's other children would be excluded from the will. After satisfying himself that this represented her wishes, he had several other individuals come in and witness the will. Mrs. Carpenter died four days later. The other children contested the execution of the will as being procured on the basis of undue influence. Decision for whom? Discuss.

10   Mr. Rinehart wrote a will leaving a portion of his estate in trust for the benefit of his daughter, to pay income to her for a period of time, and, upon the attainment of a specified age, to deliver to her the principal of the trust. He then provided that the delivery should be conditioned upon her ability to prove conclusively that she had not become a member of the Catholic faith nor ever married a man of such faith. In the event that she failed to meet the condition, she became ineligible to receive the funds, and the money was left to other individuals. The testator died. Several years after his death, his daughter married a man who was a member of the Catholic faith. She had full knowledge of the terms of her father's will. When she reached the specified age, she demanded that the trustee turn over to her the principal of the trust. Decision for whom? Discuss.

CHAPTER 12

Other Estate and Will Topics

WHAT IS NOT COVERED UNDER A WILL

Joint Property

Jointly held property confers upon its owners a right of survivorship. This means that upon the death of any of them the surviving joint owners automatically inherit the decedent's interest in the property. This is true whether the other owners would have been heirs under the decedent's will or not. A designation in a will that property that the decedent held jointly with one or more others is to be left to someone other than the surviving joint owners is totally ineffective.

A *tenancy by the entirety* is a special kind of joint ownership that relates only to married persons. A tenancy by the entirety is also unaffected by a will leaving the decedent spouse's property to a third party; it will, in fact, be automatically inherited by the surviving spouse. If you wish to own property with another person and also wish to retain control over the disposition of your property at your death, title should be taken as *tenants in common*. This is a form of ownership available to both unrelated parties and spouses. Tenancies in common generally confer the same right upon the co-owners as joint tenancies or tenancies by the entirety except that, upon the death of a tenant in common, the decedent's estate inherits the decedent's interest in the property; the surviving tenants in common receive nothing, but retain their own shares.

Life Insurance

The various kinds of life insurance will be discussed in the following pages.

Insurable Interest Life insurance, like other forms of insurance, is a gamble. The insured is betting upon the outcome of a particular transaction or the happening of a particular event, in this case, the insured's death. The insured is betting that he or she will die prematurely whereas the company is betting that the insured will survive. If the insured dies prematurely, the beneficiary receives financial compensation. If the insured lives beyond the normal life span, then the insurance company acquires additional benefits (e.g., additional premiums). Although gambling is illegal (as discussed in Chapter 4), insurance contracts are not considered gambling if the insured has an ''insurable interest.'' An *insurable interest* is defined as follows. ''Insurable interest in the matter of life and health insurance exists when the beneficiary because of relationship, either pecuniary or from ties of blood or marriage, has reason to expect some benefit from the continuance of the life of the insured'' (Nebraska Rev. Stat. §§44-102). In regard to property, ''Every interest in the property, or any relation thereto, or liability in respect thereof, of such a nature that a contemplated peril might directly damnify the insured, is an insurable interest'' (Cal. Ins. Code §280).

Life insurance comes in a number of different formats: term insurance, whole life insurance, endowment insurance, and so on.

Term Insurance   Term insurance is temporary. It can be purchased for periods of time such as 1 year, 10 years, or 20 years or until a certain age (65, 70, 100, and so on). (Flight insurance is very short-term insurance, lasting only for the duration of the flight.) Term insurance can be purchased under different premium options such as level premium term insurance or five-year renewable term insurance. With a level premium term insurance, the policy can be purchased through a specific age with equal yearly premiums. With renewable term (5-year, 10-year, and so forth), the premium is guaranteed to be the same for each term. At the end of the term, the premium will increase and be the same each year for the next term.

Term insurance can be canceled at will, and upon cancelation the benefits cease. (Term insurance generally does not pay dividends and does not build up cash surrender value.) The longer that you maintain a term insurance policy, the more expensive it becomes. Term insurance on a short-term basis is the least expensive insurance available. The net cash outlay for a term insurance policy is generally lower initially than for any other kind of policy. There are different opinions as to whether term insurance on a long-term basis is the best form of insurance or not. Decreasing term insurance is insurance whereby the amount of the payment under the policy goes down as the policy gets older. Decreasing term insurance is often provided to take care of specific needs such as a mortgage on a house.

Whole Life Insurance   An alternative to term insurance is *whole life* insurance. Whole life insurance is referred to as permanent insurance and comes in two categories: ordinary life insurance and limited payment life insurance. Under an ordinary life insurance policy, a policyholder obtains protection until the date of his or her death. There is also an obligation to make annual payments until his or her death. An ordinary life insurance policy consists of two portions: the payment that is made for the promise to pay upon your death and an additional amount that represents an investment. The insurance company basically utilizes your investment and gives you a return, building up what is known as a cash surrender value. If you purchase a whole life policy, the cash surrender value plus the dividends that you receive on the cash surrender value may be sufficient to minimize or even eliminate your future premium payments. The only way to determine whether an ordinary life insurance policy is a good investment is to compare the return under the insurance policy to the return available if you were to make alternative uses of the same amount of money.

Another form of whole life insurance is called *limited payment life* insurance. The difference between limited payment life insurance and ordinary life insurance is that the insured makes a maximum number of payments under the policy, at which point the policy is fully paid up, and the insurance remains in effect until the death of the insured. A limited payment life insurance policy requires greater cash outlays in the early years and, therefore, is most appropriate for someone who is anticipating a decline in income later on. Limited payment life insurance also consists of payments for insurance protection and investment.

Endowments and Annuities   An *endowment policy* is one for which you make periodic payments to the insurance company, and they accumulate the money and credit your account with a return on your investment. At a contractually agreed time (retirement, when your children need to go to school or college, and so forth) the insurance company will pay you the total amount that has accumulated in the policy. In the meantime, if you should die, the company contractually has committed to pay a specified amount to your estate or beneficiary, usually more than what has accumulated in the fund.

Similar to an endowment policy is an *annuity policy* whereby you pay the company a given sum of money. If you live to a certain age, the company pays periodic payments for the rest of your life. Some annuity policies will guarantee a minimum number of payments, as for 10 years, 20 years, and so on. It is also possible to purchase an annuity policy that pays to you or your spouse for life in the event that he or she should survive you. In every case, it is necessary to determine specifically with the insurance agent what kind of protection coverage you are looking for so that the terms of the insurance contract may represent your needs and or desires.

Other Life Insurance   *Group life insurance* is insurance that is written for members of a group. Because the administrative costs are less, the cost of group insurance is often cheaper than the cost of individually obtained insurance. Sometimes this insurance protection is provided automatically as part of an individual's employment package; sometimes it is available as an option that an individual can purchase. In either case, it is a form of insurance (usually term) and should not be overlooked by an individual in determining the size of his or her estate.

Another form of life insurance that many individuals carry is *creditor life insurance*. This is insurance that is purchased by some debtors to secure specific loans. It is similar to a mortgage insurance policy (decreasing term policy) except that it does not require the existence of a mortgage. Creditor life insurance is often required by banks or finance companies when making loans to consumers. In the event of the death of the consumer, the insurance company pays the creditor the amount of the debt.

In addition to the basic kinds of life insurance, there are certain additional riders that are available. *Double indemnity* is a type of insurance rider that provides additional payment in the event that you die from an accident. A *disability waiver* is a policy clause that provides that in the event that you become disabled totally and permanently, the insurance company will pay future premiums and maintain the insurance coverage. There are also policies containing riders that provide that the insured has the right at specific points in his or her lifetime to purchase additional insurance without the need of submitting to a physical examination. Therefore, if an individual becomes uninsurable at any given point in time, the insurance company will nevertheless be obligated to provide that individual with additional insurance.

Beneficiary   A life insurance policy will usually specify a particular person as the beneficiary. On your death the insurance company will be obligated by the contract (insurance policy) to pay the proceeds to this person. If you decide you would rather leave that money to someone else, you must contact the insurance company to change the beneficiary. A designation in your will naming the intended new beneficiary, even if it states that it is your intention in so doing to change the effect of the insurance policy, will not be sufficient to effect such change. Since the insurance policy is a contract between you and the company, it cannot be changed by a unilateral act of one of the parties. The insurance company is not a party to your will and is, therefore, not bound by anything you state therein. When you prepare a will, it is generally advisable to review the contents of each insurance policy you may have, including term insurance and mortgage insurance policies. Bequests you make might be affected by the designation of the beneficiary on your life insurance policy.

If you wish, you may appoint your estate as the beneficiary under all or some of your life insurance policies. This will enable you to change the beneficiaries by merely changing your will. Since your estate is the beneficiary of the insurance policy, the company remains unaware of your intentions and on your death pays your estate. The executor is then obligated to pay the appropriate amount to the proper party. This alternative may be costly to your estate because probate fees and taxes are usually based on the gross estate. (The value of life insurance passes outside the estate when a beneficiary is designated in the policy as opposed to designating the estate as beneficiary.)

Payment Options   There are several payment options available to a beneficiary when an insured person dies. One option is a lump sum payment. Under this option, the insurance company will pay the beneficiary the entire amount of the insurance policy proceeds. A second option is that the proceeds may be left with the insurance company, which pays interest at a specified rate to the beneficiary. Other options that are available combine lump sum and periodic payments until the proceeds of the insurance policy are exhausted. These can be in the form of an annuity based on the survivor's life or on a specified monthly or annual amount that is considered to be the amount that the beneficiary needs to live on. Once the beneficiary has withdrawn all the proceeds (plus any interest that the proceeds have accumulated while in the hands of the insurance company), the payments will cease. The decision in any given case as to which of these options is the best is an economic decision that should be based on the needs of the beneficiary, the alternative investments that are available to the beneficiary, and the degree of self-control that the beneficiary can exercise in managing his or her money. The party purchasing an insurance policy should make sure that all these options be available to the beneficiary upon the death of the insured unless the beneficiary is an individual who could not properly make such a decision.

Insurance policies distribute interest and dividends. Dividends represent a return of premiums previously paid. In essence, what they are giving back is your money. The dividends that you receive reduce the cost of your insurance. Interest is paid on the cash surrender value and dividends not withdrawn from the company, and it represents income to the owner of the policy.

Gifts

Inter vivos (between living persons) gifts are not included in a will. A gift is defined as a transfer of property voluntarily made without consideration. When we talk about the term *without consideration*, we include situations in which there is less than full consideration. For example, if A transfers an item to B and receives nothing in exchange, it will probably constitute a gift. If A transfers an item worth $1,000 to B and receives $300 in exchange, it will also probably be a gift. There can be difficulty in determining whether a transaction has occurred with less than adequate consideration in that it may be difficult to determine whether the items exchanged by parties are equivalent in value. Accordingly, we have to look to an additional factor, which is whether there has been an intent to make a gift. An exchange of items without the intent to make a gift will, generally speaking, not be treated as a gift.

Requirements   For a gift to be valid, several requirements exist. The donor (person who makes the gift) must be competent. There must be an intent on the part of the donor to make a gift, and this intent must exist voluntarily and without coercion or undue influence. There must be delivery. Delivery requires either an actual physical delivery or a symbolic delivery. In the case of something such as a diamond ring, delivery would be accomplished by presenting the ring from the donor to the donee (the donee is the recipient of the gift). In the case of a gift such as an automobile, actual delivery would be difficult to effectuate since nobody can lift an automobile. In such an instance, delivery is made symbolically: the donor transfers or gives the keys to the donee. The donee must accept the gift in order for the gift to be valid (the donee may refuse the gift, in which case it is invalid). The donor must give up all incidences of ownership and control over the gift and also must not receive adequate consideration for the gift.

Intent to make a gift, where there is no delivery, will not constitute a gift. By the same token, delivery of something to another person in and of itself does not constitute a gift if there was no intent. An example where an individual might deliver property without the intent to make a gift arises in the case of a bailment (see Chapter 7). In the case of a bailment, one individual gives property to another either for the benefit of the bailor or the benefit of the bailee. In either event, it is clearly understood that at some point the property is to be returned to the bailor. Since there is no intent to make a gift, there is no gift. Another example is the case of an individual who deposits money into a joint bank account. This does not constitute a gift because the individual who makes the deposit can withdraw the money at any time. There has been no delivery. There also has been no acceptance by the donee. If, however, the other joint owner of the bank account withdraws the money, at that moment, there is a gift.

A gift can be referred to as inter vivos (between living persons) or testamentary. An inter vivos gift, once made, is irrevocable. It is irrevocable because the donor has given up all incidents of ownership and control. One incident of ownership or control is the right to retain property for one's own use. When this right is given up, there is no further string attached to the donor, and, therefore, he or she cannot recover the property. A testamentary gift may be revoked by the donor's change or destruction of the will because the actual gift is not made until the donor's death.

Gifts to Minors It is frequently desirable for an individual to make a gift to a minor child. Gifts to minor children can create problems if not properly handled. Problems that can be created are questions concerning the true owner of the property (for instance, a minor is technically not allowed to own property in his or her own right until he or she attains the age of majority), as well as questions concerning the taxability of the income from the property donated. The standard approach to resolving such problems in the past has been the creation of a trust. However, since trusts are expensive to create and can be expensive to operate, most states have created a simpler method of making gifts to minors by passing what has come to be known as the Uniform Gift to Minors Act.

The Uniform Gift to Minors Act basically states that in the event that a gift is made referring specifically to the Uniform Gift to Minors Act, it will create a trust for the benefit of a minor without the requirement of a formal trust instrument. Generally, gifts under the Uniform Gift to Minors Act will be considered to be property of the minor under the supervision of the named trustee. The income from that gift will be considered to be income of the minor. The major restrictions on such gifts are that the property must be used for the benefit of the minor during his or her minority (or accumulated for his or her benefit), must be delivered to the individual upon attainment of majority, and upon the death of the minor before attaining majority must be distributed through his or her estate.

The individual who is responsible for the administration of the funds must be designated in the gift. An example of such a transfer would be writing a check to John Smith, custodian for Mary Smith, a minor, under the Michigan Uniform Gift to Minors Act. The provisions of the Uniform Gift to Minors Act in each state designate the responsibilities of the trustee or custodian of the property and the circumstances under which the property in trust may be paid directly to the minor. If you are contemplating gifts to a child or if your parents are contemplating gifts to one of your children, it is generally desirable to have a single custodian for all the gifts for the benefit of a particular child. This consolidates the administration of that child's assets.

Trusts

A trust consists of a fund of money or other valuables (corpus) left to an individual (the trustee) with instructions to use the money for the benefit of another person (the beneficiary). The person who creates the trust is referred to as the settlor. The written document that creates the terms of the trust is referred to as the trust instrument. The legal title to property that is held in trust is in the trustee. The equitable title (the right to use the property) is in the beneficiary.

Trusts can be created either during the lifetime of the settlor, in which case they are called inter vivos trusts, or upon the death of the settlor, in which case they are referred to as testamentary trusts. Trusts can be revocable (the settlor may change or terminate the trust at will) or irrevocable (the settlor has given up the right to change or terminate the trust).

Property that is placed in a trust before the death of the settlor will be transferred to the beneficiary of the trust without going through the estate probate process. Such a trust could be used to avoid probate costs or to avoid the notoriety that attends the probate of certain estates. Certain types of trusts can also be used in some cases to avoid the costs of estate taxes. Typically, revocable probate avoidance trusts do not have an impact upon estate taxes since they do not take effect until the death of the settlor and, therefore, are included in the taxable portion of his or her estate. Tax avoidance trusts, on the other hand, are irrevocable and established either during the settlor's lifetime or at his or her death. These trusts operate to avoid taxation either in the estate of the settlor or, in some cases, in the estate of one of the settlor's heirs.

Trusts are also used to protect individuals from squandering money that they might otherwise have access to. For example, assume that an individual is relatively unskilled in the use of money and that his or her parent or spouse has a substantial estate. Trust provisions can be made whereby income is paid to the beneficiary and the beneficiary may get access to some or all of the principal upon the showing of certain needs. In this manner, the financial welfare of the beneficiary may be secured.

There are also trusts, known as 10-year trusts, that can be utilized to avoid the imposition of income taxes. These require a gift of property to a trustee, who accumulates the income for the benefit of a minor child or some other person, and during the period that the trustee has the property (not less than 10 years), the income is not taxed in the settlor's income tax return.

SPECIAL KINDS OF WILLS

Joint Will

A *joint will* is a single document that is executed by both spouses. As such, it represents a contract by each. On the death of the first spouse, the survivor is unable to alter the will because of the contractual commitments made by each to the other. Each person's execution of the will is deemed to have been consideration for the other person's execution of the same provisions. Unless it is possible for both of them to consent, the contract cannot be altered. When one of the parties dies, that party cannot consent to a change, and, therefore, the survivor is locked into the terms of the joint will.

A joint will is generally undesirable since it deprives the survivor from dealing with his or her estate and with any new circumstances that may have changed as a result of the passage of time. It is also very possible that, after the death of the first individual, especially if the wills were executed when the parties were quite young, the circumstances of the survivor will have changed and the terms of the original will are no longer appropriate. The only advantage of a joint will is to clearly establish a line of descent or a specific disposition of certain property in the event of the death of one of the individuals. There are alternative methods (using a trust and an independent trustee whose judgment will not be colored by family feelings) that would be more appropriate for accomplishing the same objective. The use of a trust would not be as inflexible as the use of a joint will.

Mutual or Reciprocal Wills

Mutual or reciprocal wills are wills that are separately executed by two or more individuals (usually husband and wife) but contain the same provisions. Where the individuals both desire the same dispositions, these are the best kinds of wills to prepare. Here is an example. A husband would leave everything to his wife and, if the wife predeceases the husband, would leave everything to their children. The wife would leave everything to the husband and in the event that the husband predeceased her, would leave everything also to their children. Mutual wills do not represent contractual commitments as do joint wills. However, courts may find other circumstances, expressed or implied, that would create the same obligations between parties to an ambiguous mutual will that would exist in the case of a joint will. It would be desirable, when writing mutual wills, to express in them the fact that they may be changed at any time by the testator without the spouse's consent. It is also possible to restrict mutual wills in the same manner as joint wills by specifying in the document or in a separate document that it was the intent of the parties that the mutual wills be binding upon each of the spouses even after death of one of the spouses. Clear identification of one's intent in this area is most important.

The primary purpose of executing mutual wills is to cover situations in which parties desire the same objectives, but are aware of the possibility that in the future one of them may choose to change his or her mind. Executing mutual wills allows the surviving spouse the degree of flexibility that is not available in a joint will. Therefore, to draw up a mutual will and restrict it in the same manner as a joint will would be a foolish thing to do.

Noncupative Wills

A noncupative will is one that is not set down in writing. Oral wills are generally not valid in any state under normal circumstances. In a substantial number of states, an oral will will be recognized under certain limited circumstances, generally in instances where the maker of the will is in a situation of imminent death or peril, usually as the result of some form of military combat (Exhibit 12–1). The precise circumstances under which each state will accept a noncupative will varies greatly (some refuse to accept them under any circumstances whatsoever). In the case of a noncupative will, there must always be at least one witness present to hear the will and to offer testimony as to what the terms of the will were. You should check your state's rules regarding noncupative wills.

EXHIBIT 12-1
Validity of Noncupative Wills

Alabama	Yes (1, 2, 6)
Alaska	Yes (2)
Arizona	No
Arkansas	No
California	Yes (2)
Colorado	No
Connecticut	No
Delaware	No
District of Columbia	Yes (2)
Florida	No
Georgia	Yes (1)
Hawaii	No
Idaho	No
Illinois	No
Indiana	Yes (3)
Iowa	No
Kansas	Yes (1)
Kentucky	No
Louisiana	Yes
Maine	Yes (1, 2)
Maryland	No
Massachusetts	Yes (2)
Michigan	Yes (2, 4)
Minnesota	No
Mississippi	Yes (1)
Missouri	Yes (3)

(1) May be made by anyone during his or her last illness.
(2) May be made by soldiers or sailors.
(3) May be made by a person in imminent peril of death, who dies from that peril.
(4) May be made by anyone.

Holographic Wills

[handwritten: entirely in the handwriting of the Decedent - no witness]

[handwritten margin note: Know about the words]

A holographic will is one that is wholly written in the handwriting of the testator. A number of states recognize holographic wills. (The following states recognize holographic wills: Alaska, Arizona, Arkansas, California, Colorado, Hawaii, Idaho, Kentucky, Louisiana, Mississippi, Montana, Nebraska, Nevada, North Carolina, North Dakota, Oklahoma, Pennsylvania, South Dakota, Tennessee, Texas, Utah, Virginia, West Virginia, Wyoming. South Carolina recognizes holographic wills executed by soldiers and sailors. The remaining states and the District of Columbia do not recognize holographic wills). A handwritten will that meets all the statutory requirements regarding attestation and witnesses would be valid regardless of holographic will rules. The requirements of each of these states differ somewhat, but

EXHIBIT 12-1, cont.

Montana	No
Nebraska	No
Nevada	Yes (1)
New Hampshire	Yes (1, 2)
New Jersey	No
New Mexico	No
New York	Yes (2)
North Carolina	Yes (1)
North Dakota	No
Ohio	Yes (1)
Oklahoma	Yes (2)
Oregon	No
Pennsylvania	No
Rhode Island	Yes (2)
South Carolina	Yes (1, 7)
South Dakota	Yes (2)
Tennessee	Yes (3)
Texas	Yes (1, 2)
Utah	Yes (5)
Vermont	Yes (1, 8)
Virginia	Yes (2)
Washington	Yes (1, 2)
West Virginia	Yes (2)
Wisconsin	No
Wyoming	No

(5) May be made by one expecting to die in 24 hours.
(6) May dispose only of personal property not in excess of $500.
(7) Requires three witnesses.
(8) Requires one witness.

generally it is required that the entire document must be in the handwriting of the testator. If so much as the heading is printed, the will fails to qualify as a holographic will.

Holographic wills are generally accepted without certain formalities (attestation clauses, witnesses, and so on) that are normally required for wills, and the courts, therefore, are less inclined to accept holographic wills and will scrutinize them very carefully to make sure that they meet all of the requirements that holographic wills demand. Frequently, a lawyer, visiting a client in a hospital, will write a will in longhand for the patient to sign. This is not considered a holographic will since it is not written in the testator's handwriting. If it meets other requirements regarding witnesses and so on, it would be admissible to probate in any state.

Living Wills

A living will represents a person's statement as to the degree of medical care he or she expects or desires during severe or terminal illnesses. The living will is reproduced in Exhibit 12–2.

The law will generally respect the wishes of a competent person to refuse treatment. Even when there was clear evidence that the patient would probably die without treatment, courts have upheld a patient's right to refuse such treatment. Where there are other major factors involved (preservation of life, protection of children, and so on), the courts have sometimes refused to allow the patient to refuse treatment. However, in the case of the terminally ill, there is no hope of recovery,

EXHIBIT 12-2
A Living Will

To My Family, My Physician, My Lawyer
and All Others Whom It May Concern

Death is as much a reality as birth, growth, maturity, and old age; it is the one certainty of life. If the time comes when I can no longer take part in decisions for my own future, let this statement stand as an expression of my wishes and directions while I am still of sound mind.

If at such a time the situation should arise in which there is no reasonable expectation of my recovery from extreme physical or mental disability, I direct that I be allowed to die and not be kept alive by medications, artificial means, or "heroic measures." I do, however, ask that medication be mercifully administered to me to alleviate suffering even though this may shorten my remaining life.

This statement is made after careful consideration and is in accordance with my strong convictions and beliefs. I want the wishes and directions here expressed carried out to the extent permitted by law. Insofar as they are not legally enforceable, I hope that those to whom this will is addressed will regard themselves as morally bound by these provisions.

    1. (a) I appoint _____ to make binding decisions concerning my medical treatment.

OR

    (b) I have discussed my views as to life sustained measures with the following who understand my wishes

_____

_____

    2. Measures of artificial life support in the fact of impending death that are especially abhorrent to me are:
    (a) Electrical or mechanical resuscitation of my heart when it has stopped beating.
    (b) Nasogastric tube feedings when I am paralyzed and no longer able to swallow.
    (c) Mechanical respiration by machine when my brain can no longer sustain my own breathing.
    (d) _____

and the general feeling is that it would be impossible to demonstrate a sufficiently compelling reason whereby the state could override a patient's refusal.

Implicit in several court decisions (In the Matter of Karen Quinlan, 355 A.2d 647 [N.J. 1976] and Saikewicz, 370 N.E.2d 417 [Mass. 1977]) is the concept that in dealing with an incompetent, one should look to the intentions of that person while still competent. The best evidence of one's intentions would be an executed living will. Where the treatment offers a good chance of recovery (such as a blood transfusion), the patient's desires may be overriden; in a terminal situation, however, they would, or at least should be, respected. The legal impact of the living will is largely unclear. As of January 1979, 10 states (Arkansas, California, Idaho, Kansas, Ne-

---

EXHIBIT 12-2, cont.

---

3. If it does not jeopardize the chance of my recovery to a meaningful and sentient life or impose an undue burden on my family, I would like to live out my last days at home rather than in a hospital.

4. If any of my tissues are sound and would be of value as transplants to help other people, I freely give my permission for such donation.

5. If I have been diagnosed as pregnant, this will shall have no force or effect during the course of my pregnancy.

6. This will shall have no further force or effect _____ years after the date filled in below.

Date_____   Signed_____

We, whose names are hereto subscribed, do certify that on the _____ day of _____, 19___, _____ the testator above named, subscribes his name to this instrument in our presence and in the presence of each of us, and at the same time, in our presence and hearing, declare the same to be his wishes and directions, and requested us, and each of us, to sign our names thereto as witnesses to the execution thereof, which we hereby do in the presence of the testator and of each other on the day and date of such living will, and write opposite our names our respective places of residence.

_____residing at_____
_____residing at_____
_____residing at_____

Copies of this request have been given to _____
_____
_____

_____

vada, New Mexico, North Carolina, Oregon, Texas, and Washington) have passed legislation recognizing the validity of such a will. In most of these states, the effect of the will is to bind the physician and the hospital to the specified standards of medical care and to relieve them of any legal obligation for the death of the patient unless they are negligent. If you decide to make a living will, copies should be left with your lawyer, your physician, your hospital, and your family. It is also desirable to keep a copy of the document on your person whenever possible.

There are differences as to the circumstances under which such a will may be executed and the frequency with which the will needs to be reexecuted. A careful check of your state's requirements is necessary to determine the validity and manner of executing such a will.

Donation of Organs

Of increasing concern and interest in recent years has been the concept of donating one's body or parts thereof either to science for purposes of study and research or to various organ banks for purposes of use for transplants to other individuals. In order to leave your body for medical or scientific uses, you will find it absolutely essential to make arrangements ahead of time. An individual has two choices in this area: (1) to donate the entire body to a medical school for research or study purposes or (2) to donate certain body organs to agencies that use them for transplant purposes. As a general rule, when medical schools accept cadavers, they require that the total body be left to science intact. Thus, if you wish to make donations of organs for transplant purposes, you would not be able to leave the remainder of your body to a medical school.

It is necessary for anatomical gifts to be made quickly. Many states have adopted a Uniform Anatomical Gift Act. The procedure in California is to give each licensed driver a card that can be signed to authorize body donations. If a person is in an accident or hospitalized and has such card in his or her possession, the individuals caring for the deceased will find the card and immediately contact the appropriate agency to effectuate the gift.

An anatomical gift can also be made by including a clause to that effect in one's will. The difficulty with including it in the will is that the will may not be read for several days, and the people involved in disposing of the remains of the deceased will, therefore, be unaware of the deceased's intentions. For this reason, if you choose to put such a clause in your will, make sure that other people who are likely to be present upon your death are aware of your desires and intentions. Executors or administrators also have the power to donate the deceased's organs to various transplant banks provided that the responsible person has no knowledge of a contrary desire of the decedent.

Organs may be donated to hospitals, physicians, schools (medical schools or colleges), organ transplant facilities, or specific individuals who are involved in therapy and transplant processes. If a donation has been made prior to an individual's death, that donation may be revoked by a written, witnessed statement. There are numerous organs that are generally desired by transplant agencies; these include kidneys, eyes, bones, cartilage, ears, heart, skin, and so forth. For many of the organs in question, it is essential that they be removed within 24 hours after the death of the individual. In some cases, there are limiting factors upon the utility of the organ such as age or cause of death. A desirable approach to dealing with the problem of organ transplants would be to contact a number of the organizations that are involved in body transplants and to find out what kinds of organs are suitable for transplants and how one would go about making sure that the appropriate organs reach the appropriate organizations.

CHANGES AND REVOCATIONS—CODICILS

Because circumstances change, you should periodically review your will. It would be appropriate to change a will for any of a number of reasons. Changes in the law regarding the execution or structure of wills or intestate succession would probably warrant a change in one's will. Changes in tax laws affecting either the amount of taxation or the structure of certain tax planning devices that are utilized in a given will might also warrant the changing of a given will. The federal tax law concerning estate taxes was recently changed, and a number of attorneys at that time recommended that all their clients' wills be reviewed. In many cases, changes were warranted based on the new statutory provisions. Changes in family conditions may also warrant a review of a will with an eye toward changing it. Marriage, the birth or death of a child or spouse, divorce, separation, annulment, death of a beneficiary, marriage of a principal beneficiary, the birth of grandchildren, relocation to another state, or any other major change in one's family situation would probably be a good time to review a will. Determine with your lawyer whether it is appropriate or even necessary at that time to make a change in your will.

The manner in which you write your will may also affect the frequency with which it needs to be changed. For example, Mary's will states: ''I leave everything to my children.'' Joan's will states: ''I leave everything to my children, Fred and Lisa.'' If Mary has another child, her will need not be changed as the new child will automatically be included as a beneficiary. If Joan has a third child, he or she will not inherit unless the will is altered or unless there is a statute allowing such a child to inherit an intestate share. The death or relocation of a witness may be a reason for changing a will. Your will should probably be reviewed every three to five years or more frequently if an event affecting one of the parties to the will occurs. If it is appropriate, the will should be changed or revoked and replaced by a new one.

Most wills can be changed at any time by adding a codicil. A typical codicil appears in Exhibit 12–3. A codicil may add or delete terms to an existing will or may modify the terms of that will. A codicil must be executed with the same formalities as the original will (recitation of the fact that it is a codicil and execution by the requisite number of witnesses). In addition, all the requirements of competence of the testator must be met for purposes of a codicil just as they were for purposes of the will itself. A codicil, if properly drawn, will reaffirm all the portions of the will that

EXHIBIT 12-3
Codicil

I, Marilyn Poch, of Fort Lee, New Jersey, make this codicil to my will dated
_____, 19___:

1.   I revoke the section entitled "Specific Bequests" of that will and insert in lieu thereof the following:

Specific Bequests: In the event they survive me, I hereby give, devise, and bequeath my engagement ring to my daughter, Elizabeth Poch, residing at R.D. No. 3, Box 22, Phoenixville, Pennsylvania, and my wedding ring and silver tea set to my daughter, Charlotte Poch, residing at 15 Gilbert Street, Fort Lee, New Jersey.

*   *   *

In all other respects, I confirm and republish my will dated _____, 19___.

IN WITNESS WHEREOF, I have signed this codicil, consisting of ____ pages, this page included, and for the purpose of identification have signed my name in the margin of each preceding page this ____ day of _____, 19___.

_____
                                    Marilyn Poch (L.S.)

We certify that the above instrument was on the date thereof signed and declared by Marilyn Poch as a codicil to her will dated _____, 19___, in our presence, and that we, at her request and in her presence and in the presence of each other, have signed our names as witnesses thereto, believing Marilyn Poch to be of sound mind and memory at the time of signing.

_____Residing at_____
_____Residing at_____
_____Residing at_____

it does not delete or modify. It should also identify the will specifically and should also identify any other codicils that have previously been written and either affirm those or specifically state that those codicils are being hereby revoked. Codicils should be clear and succinct and should not become so numerous as to become unwieldy or ambiguous in interpretation. If you have made certain bequests in a will and you are now decreasing the amount of those bequests, it is certainly possible to do this by codicil. It may, however, be desirable to do this by executing a new will so that the persons whose inheritances have been reduced will not be aware of the fact that you have made a reduction. (If you have previously given a copy of your will to these beneficiaries, they have probably read it and probably will realize that you have made a change and, therefore, the preceding statement would not be applicable.)

A codicil is a formal change and cannot simply be written at the end of the will. The difference between a will and a codicil is that the codicil generally deals with only one or two clauses whereas the will contains many clauses. There is no legal limit as to the number of codicils that one may add to a will; however, at some point the structure becomes so complex that it is desirable to rewrite the entire will.

When you execute a new will, you should include a statement in it revoking the old will. In addition, to avoid any confusion or misconception, you will find it a good idea to physically destroy the original of the first will and as many copies as you can locate. The intentional destruction of a will is an act of revocation provided you destroy the original. Remember that if you destroy the first will before you execute the second and die before you are able to execute the second, you will die intestate.

INTESTACY AND STATUTORY DISTRIBUTION

The major functions of a will are to distribute one's property and to appoint a guardian over one's children; therefore, it is desirable to make a will whenever one has property or children or both. If a property owner fails to dispose of property on death, the law will specify how the property should be distributed. These statutory rules are referred to as the rules of intestate succession. An example of a typical statute can be found in Exhibit 12–4.

The effect of rules of intestate succession are dramatized by the *intestate's will* (Exhibit 12–5). Note that under the intestate's will, the decedent's spouse receives only one third of the estate if there are two or more children. (If there is only one child, the spouse receives one half; the child, the other half.) In the case of a very large estate, this may be acceptable; however, in the case of a small or moderate estate, it may place undue hardships on the surviving spouse by not giving the spouse adequate funds to survive. There are other provisions in the intestate's will that may be detrimental to the decedent's objectives.

If a decedent dies intestate, the court will appoint an administrator to make sure that the assets of the estate are distributed according to statute. The administrator is entitled to a fee for services. The court-appointed administrator may or may not be the same person the decedent would have selected.

Each state has a prescribed statutory sequence for appointment of administrators of the estate. A typical sequence is spouse, child, grandchild, parent, brother or sister, next of kin entitled to share in the estate, and public administrator. In the absence of a will, the court not only appoints an administrator, but also, in case there are minor children or incompetent beneficiaries, has to appoint a guardian and a trustee. If there is no statutory sequence for appointment of guardians and trustees, the court is free to appoint anyone to each of these positions. These positions involve a considerable degree of responsibility and compensation. The estate of an intestate decedent may be charged with expenses that could be avoided had the decedent appointed someone to these positions (if the decedent's choice had

EXHIBIT 12-4
New Hampshire Distribution upon Intestacy

Distribution upon Intestacy. The real estate and personal estate of every person deceased, not devised or bequeathed, subject to any homestead right, and liable to be sold by license from the court of probate in cases provided by law, and personalty remaining in the hands of the administrator on settlement of his account, shall descend or be distributed by decree of the probate court:

   I. If the deceased is survived by a spouse, the spouse shall receive:

      A. If there is no surviving issue or parent of the decedent, the entire intestate estate.

      B. If there is no surviving issue but the decedent is survived by a parent or parents, the first $50,000 plus one half of the balance of the intestate estate.

      C. If there are surviving issue, all of whom are issue of the surviving spouse also, the first $50,000 plus one half of the balance of the intestate estate.

      D. If there are surviving issue, one or more of whom are not issue of the surviving spouse, one half of the intestate estate.

   II. The part of the intestate estate not passing to the surviving spouse under paragraph I, or the entire intestate estate if there is no surviving spouse, passes as follows:

      A. To the issue of the decedent; if they are all of the same degree of kinship to the decedent, they take equally, but if of unequal degree, then those of more remote degree take by representation.

      B. If there is no surviving issue, to his parent or parents equally.

      C. If there is no surviving issue or parent, to the brothers and sisters and the issue of each deceased brother or sister by representation; if there is no surviving brother or sister, the issue of brothers and sisters take equally if they are all of the same degree of kinship to the decedent, but if of unequal degree, then those of more remote degree take by representation.

      D. If there is no surviving issue, parent, or issue of a parent but the decedent is survived by one or more grandparents or issue of grandparents, half of the estate passes to the paternal grandparents if both survive or to the surviving paternal grandparent or to the issue of the paternal grandparents if both are deceased, the issue taking equally if they are all of the same degree of kinship to the decedent, but if of unequal degree, those of more remote degree take by representation; and the other half passes to the maternal relatives in the same manner; but if there be no surviving grandparent or issue of grandparent on either the paternal or the maternal side, the entire estate passes to the relatives on the other side in the same manner as the half.

been willing to serve either without a fee or at a reduced fee). It has also been common in the past for courts to use appointments of guardianships, administratorships, and trusteeships as a political reward for members of the community. Having your estate depleted for the benefit of some politician is probably not your objective. The best way to avoid this happening is by drawing up a will and making the necessary appointments yourself.

   When a decedent dies intestate, the administrator and other fiduciaries may be required to post a bond. This bond acts as security for the faithful and proper performance of the fiduciary. It may be in the form of a given sum placed in escrow with the court or in the form of an insurance policy (the most common method).

EXHIBIT 12-5
The Intestate's Will

I, _____ being of sound mind, do hereby publish and declare this to be my last will and testament:

First. I give to my wife one third of all of my possessions, and I give my children the remaining two thirds of my possessions. I leave it entirely up to them to fight about who is to receive which items.

Second. In the event my wife remarries, her second husband shall receive one third of everything she possesses. In the event that my children are in need of a portion of this for their support, her second husband shall not be obligated to spend any of his share for the benefit of my children. Upon his death, her second husband shall have exclusive right to determine who is to receive his assets even to the point where he can exclude my children from receiving any of it.

Third. I hereby appoint my wife as guardian over those of my children who are minors at the time of my death. Because I do not trust her and do not know whether she can properly execute this function, I direct that she report regularly to the probate court and render an accounting of all expenditures she has with respect to the care of my children. As an additional precaution, I hereby direct my wife to post a performance bond with the court so that in the event it is determined that she has improperly exercised judgment in handling my children's money, there will be some means of redress. Furthermore, upon their attaining majority, I hereby give my children the right to demand an accounting from their mother of all her actions with respect to their money.

Fourth. Upon their attaining age 18 I hereby direct that my children have total rights to receive all moneys that have been accrued for their benefit without any consideration of whether or not they are capable of managing these funds.

Fifth. I recognize that there are certain tax laws that may be beneficial to the conservation of my estate upon my death. However, since I am no longer present, I really don't give a damn what happens to my money and therefore have made no plans for its disposition. Furthermore, I would prefer that the government get a larger share even if this is at the expense of my wife and children.

Sixth. In the event my wife predeceases me or dies while any of my children are still under age, I do not wish to appoint anyone to take care of my minor children and would rather that my relatives and my wife's relatives get together and fight over who is going to serve in this position. In the event that neither side is victorious, I direct that they shall petition the probate court to appoint an individual, who may be a total stranger to both families. It is further my intention that whoever serves in this capacity be entitled to the maximum statutory fee allowed for rendering this service.

Seventh. In the event that I have no spouse or children and all my ancestors and siblings are deceased, my estate shall go to my nephews and nieces, whom I have not seen or heard from in 20 years rather than to my good friends who have stood by me and cared for me in my time of need.

Eighth. In the event that all my relatives predecease me, my estate shall go to the state rather than to my good friends who have stood by me and cared for me in my time of need.

Ninth. I appoint my wife as the person to take care of carrying out of the provisions of this will. In the event that she is unable to do so properly and to protect the estate from her lack of ability, I direct that she be required to post a bond to guarantee her proper performance. In the event my wife predeceases me, I direct the court to appoint someone, who, in their judgment, will carry out such function properly. This person may be a total stranger and shall be entitled to the maximum fee allowed by statute.

IN WITNESS WHEREOF, I have herunto set my hand and seal this _____ day of _____, 19___.

_____L.S.

The cost of this bond can vary, but will usually amount to several hundred dollars (generally more than the cost of drawing and executing a will). The cost of the bond is a burden on the estate and may be one that a testate decedent (one who left a valid will) could have chosen to waive.

The major concern in each of the preceding examples is that the decedent lost the option to make a decision and has left that decision to the discretion of the courts.

PROBATE AND ADMINISTRATION

Probate is the legal process of filing a will with the local court, marshaling assets, paying debts and taxes, and distributing the remaining assets pursuant to the will and subject to the court's supervision and approval. In the absence of a will, the procedure is referred to as *administration*.

Costs

Probate costs consist of three items: fees imposed by the judicial system for the probating of the estate, estate or inheritance taxes imposed by the federal and state governments, and fees charged by attorneys for handling the legal procedure involved. Probate fees charged by attorneys vary from state to state and from attorney to attorney. It is not uncommon to hear estimates of 5 percent of the probate estate. Because the fees can be fairly high, many people attempt to avoid probate by transferring property during their lifetime via joint tenancies, gifts, or trusts. Many of the methods for avoiding probate fees do not save estate taxes. These taxes may be many times higher than the other probate costs. Before using any probate saving techniques, an individual should consider the respective costs of both items, as well as the potential loss of use or control over his or her assets. A properly drawn estate plan may save estate taxes that would far exceed the probate costs.

Procedures

Probate and administration rules in various states differ in terms of the specific procedures to be followed and as to the size of the estate necessary to follow particular procedures. The following procedure is typical. It is first necessary to determine the approximate size of the estate. There is a small estate procedure that applies to estates that meet statutory criteria. Where the estate exceeds the statutory criteria, the state's regular probate procedures must be followed.

Where the decedent has died without a will, it will be necessary for the heirs to petition the court to appoint an administrator. The administrator will usually be chosen from among the heirs of the estate; however, this is not absolutely required. The administrator is entitled to charge a fee for services rendered. Where there are a number of heirs and there is concern about one's obtaining more from the estate than the other, it is possible for the court to appoint all the heirs as coadministrators so that they will not only divide the estate in equal portions but will also be entitled to equal shares of whatever fees the administrator may charge. Where there is a will, the will generally designates an individual who will serve as executor. The roles of the executor and the administrator are the same, and only the terminology differs based on whether or not there is a will.

Where the will is submitted to the court (usually called probate or surrogate's court), it is generally required to submit an affidavit from each of the witnesses to the will attesting to the fact that their signatures on the will were made by them, in the presence of each other, and in the presence of the decedent and that the decedent stated to them that they were witnessing the decedent's will. Upon submission of these affidavits, unless there is objection by one or more parties, the will will be accepted as a valid instrument, and an executor will be appointed. Because wills are often witnessed years before they are probated, it can be difficult to obtain these affidavits. Witnesses often move, die, or lose contact with the testator and his or her family. Some states have statutorily provided for admitting *self-proving* wills to probate. The statute allows witnesses to execute their affidavits at the time of witnessing the will and allows these affidavits to be submitted to probate with the will. A self-proving will is similar to any other will in that it may be revoked, changed, or contested.

In addition to obtaining witnesses' affidavits, it is the executor's or administrator's duty to locate the heirs and beneficiaries of the estate. If all these parties can be found, they are asked to execute waivers of notice. As a result, the executor may be appointed, and the will may be probated, and the executor will not be obligated to inform each of the beneficiaries of the will each time there is a payment of some expense or receipt of income. In the event that all parties are not found, legal notices will have to be published as to the probate proceeding. At the probate hearing, the witnesses will establish the validity of the will, and contests will be heard. If the will is found valid, it is ordered admitted to probate, and the executor is appointed.

Once the executor has been appointed, it is customary to open an estate checking account. All receipts that are received after the date of death of the decedent are generally deposited into the estate account, and all bills are paid from this account. Where there are a husband and wife, one of whom has died, and they have maintained a joint checking account and where the surviving spouse is the sole beneficiary of the estate, it is often not necessary to open a separate account for the estate. It is generally a good idea to open an estate account not only for legal reasons but also to make the bookkeeping or accounting process for the estate a simpler one. During the time that the estate is open, it is generally a good idea to deposit all receipts that relate to the decedent in the estate account and to make all payments from that same account. If the amount of cash on hand at any given time is significant, the assets of the estate may be invested in a savings account, savings certificates, stocks and bonds, or any other suitable investment.

Marshaling Assets

The next procedure that the executor needs to go through is a process of marshaling or collecting the assets of the decedent and identifying the liabilities. This process is necessary in order to determine the amount of the estate that the decedent left for purposes of distribution to the beneficiaries, as well as for purposes of estate tax reporting. A number of attorneys like to publish advertisements in local newspapers, indicating that an individual has died and asking that any creditors of that individual come forward and make themselves known. This procedure can be helpful in identifying the creditors where there is some reason to believe that the beneficiaries are not aware of the identity and location of all possible creditors. Where the surviving beneficiaries have good knowledge as to the creditors of the decedent or where the decedent's business and personal financial transactions are such that it is unlikely that there are any hidden creditors, it is generally not necessary to publish such an advertisement. Since such publications can be rather expensive, it is desirable not to make them if it can be avoided.

At the same time that he or she is searching out creditors, the executor will be preparing a list of the assets of the decedent at the time of his or her death. In addition to making an identification of the assets, it will be necessary to value them to determine the amount that the decedent had at the time of his or her death. In the case of securities, the valuation process can be done by referring to published stock or bond prices in financial sources, such as *The Wall Street Journal*, *Barron's*, or various other reference works. In the case of real estate and collectible items, it is generally necessary to obtain an appraisal in order to get an accurate valuation.

Taxes

The state and federal governments generally have claims against the estate to the extent that there are potential taxes due. The state will often be requested to execute what is called a *release of lien*. This is necessary in the case of pieces of real property that are not owned by the decedent jointly with another person and in the cases of bank accounts exceeding certain limits ($10,000 in New York). The purpose of securing a release of lien on real estate is to enable the executor to dispose of the real estate and the buyer to take title to that property free and clear from any possible claims by the state for unpaid estate taxes. In order to obtain a release of lien, one often must file an estate tax return. If the release of real estate lien is obtained, it represents a statement by the state that it has no claims to that real property. By the same token, where there is a substantial amount of money on deposit in a bank, the bank will not release that money to the estate unless it is given a waiver. The waiver is a document executed by the state indicating that the state will not file a claim against the bank if the bank releases that money. Without such a waiver, the bank would run the risk that, in the event there were death taxes to be paid to the state and they had not been paid, the bank would be held liable for premature payment to the estate. In Iowa and Kentucky, one pays estate taxes to the federal government and inheritance taxes to the state.

An estate generally must be kept open for a minimum period (California—five months; New York—seven months). This is the time during which the various procedures of marshaling assets, determining liabilities, and complying with federal and state tax rules will take place. By statute, in the event that there is a distribution to a beneficiary under a will before the expiration of this period, the executor will be personally liable for any losses suffered by any third parties. In the case of close family relationship, (e.g., a husband, wife, and several children), this is generally not a problem. If there are premature distributions from the estate and if it should subsequently develop that there is a creditor who has not been paid, the family relationship is generally such that all the members will contribute some of their distribution back to the estate so that the creditor may be paid. However, where the estate is being distributed to distant relatives or where there is a great deal of acrimony between the various beneficiaries, it is generally advantageous and desirable for the executor to wait until the statutory period has expired before making any distributions. This would apply not only to items of great monetary value, but would probably also apply to the decedent's personal effects. Although these have minimal value as a general rule, it is possible that some of them may have certain value as antiques or collectibles, and it may at some point in the future be necessary to obtain money from beneficiaries who at that point may be unwilling to make such a distribution back to the estate. By not making any distributions to beneficiaries until expiration of the statutory period, an executor may protect himself or herself from being personally liable to unpaid creditors of the estate.

Every estate is at least potentially subject to estate taxes at the federal and possibly also at the state level. The federal government imposes taxes on all estates of all decedents. There are a number of complex rules in determining the amount of tax that needs to be paid by a particular estate. (See the section on the unified transfer tax.)

Accounting

Many states as a final procedure will require the executor to submit an accounting. The purpose of the accounting is to identify everything that the executor has received on behalf of the estate, any increments or decreases in the value of those assets between the time they were received (the date of the decedent's death) and the time they were distributed to the beneficiaries, and a narrative as to how they were distributed to which beneficiaries. An accounting is a complex piece of financial reporting, and where a state statute allows the avoidance of such a process, it is desirable to do so. Where an accounting is required, it is generally desirable to employ a professional such as an accountant or a lawyer to assist the executor in preparing such a document.

A number of estates, because of their complexity, will remain undistributed for a substantial length of time. This is often the case where a portion of the estate's assets is represented by a business that needs to be sold or disposed of in some other way before distribution can be made to all the heirs. The period during which an estate may remain open may span many years, and during that time there is a responsibility for reporting income of the estate. Where an estate remains open for any length of time, it is generally necessary to file a fiduciary income tax return (Form 1041). This return summarizes the income received by the estate and the appropriate expenses in much the same manner as an individual's income tax return would. Where the estate is completely distributed within a single tax year, it is generally not necessary to file such a return because all the income will be reported by the beneficiaries who have received it. The preparation of this return can become fairly complex. An individual should be aware of this requirement and should discuss it with his or her adviser in the event he or she is in a position involving an estate.

UNIFIED TRANSFER TAX (ESTATE AND GIFT TAX)

Historically the federal government imposed a tax on both gifts and estates. For many years the government felt it appropriate to encourage individuals to give property away prior to their death. Accordingly it imposed a two-tiered tax structure in which gifts were taxed at a lower rate than property in the hands of a decedent. Thus, if an individual held onto property until his or her death, it would be taxed at a given rate; if, however, the individual gave it away prior to death, it would be taxed at a lower rate (approximately three quarters of the rate on estates). In 1976 the government changed this system by imposing what is known as the *unified transfer tax*.

The Unified Transfer Act recognizes that property should be considered as a single unit irrespective of whether it is given away at the death of an individual or during his or her lifetime. Accordingly, the Unified Transfer Act created a single-tiered tax structure and specified that all property given away would be taxed on a unified basis. The tax is a graduated tax system. The rates for 1982 range from 18 percent to 65 percent; for 1983 from 18 percent to 60 percent; for 1984, from 18 percent to 55 percent; and for 1985 and later years, from 18 percent to 50 percent.

The Internal Revenue Code recognizes certain exemptions from taxation. Some of these exemptions apply to estate taxes; some, to gift taxes; and some, to both. A person making a gift or a testamentary transfer will be entitled to an exemption during his or her lifetime in the form of a tax credit. The *exemption equivalent* is as follows: $225,000 in 1982, $275,000 in 1983, $325,000 in 1984, $400,000 in 1985, $500,000 in 1986, and $600,000 in 1987 and thereafter. A donor may elect to utilize a portion of this exemption during his or her lifetime or to defer the use of the exemption until his or her death. In addition, a person may donate annually an amount up to $10,000 each to as many individuals as he or she wishes without incurring any tax. If a donor is married and the donor's spouse is willing to consent to the gift, this exemption can increase to $20,000 per donee per year. Under the Economic Recovery Tax Act of 1981, an individual may leave an unlimited amount of property to a spouse without paying any tax, either gift or estate.

The effect of the current federal estate tax law is that an estate can be left entirely tax-free to one's spouse, and up to $600,000 (by 1985) of property may be given to one's nonspousal heirs without the imposition of any taxes. Additional amounts can be given during the lifetime of the testator to the extent of $10,000 or $20,000 per year per donee, but excesses donated will be subject to tax at the time of the gift. If an individual is involved in an estate that exceeds the $600,000, it is advisable for that individual to consult with a professional tax adviser to determine whether there are appropriate methods for reducing or minimizing the estate taxes imposed on those assets.

Many states also impose an estate tax. In some cases, the state rules will follow the federal rules; in other cases, there will be substantial differences. A number of states in lieu of an estate tax impose inheritance taxes. These are taxes that are imposed not on the estate of the decedent, but rather on the beneficiary who inherits property from the decedent. In the case of such a tax, the amount of the tax is based upon who is inheriting the property and the amount that individual is receiving. The responsibility for paying the tax lies in the hands of the recipient of the bequest.

QUESTIONS

1 Mr. Carothers left the following document: ''This is to convey to my wife, Mrs. V. M. Carothers, during her lifetime everything that I now own or possess, including my life insurance and personal property and real estate, at my death for her to do with as she sees fit. I am doing this of my own free will and believing I am in my right mind, This fourth day of June 1938. [signature].'' Under what circumstances would this constitute a valid will?

2 Maggie Henry prepared a will in which she left her entire estate to her two children. The will had been drawn by an attorney in the City of Detroit. Six days prior to her death she sent the following letter to her attorney: ''Sometime ago I had you make my will. I wish to change it as follows:

''All of my property, estate, and holdings, to be equally divided between my son, Archie, my daughter, Myrtle, and my husband, Thomas A. Henry, each to receive one third of my entire estate, real and personal. Maggie Henry X [her cross] Bessie Yeager Signed in presence of: Mrs. Bessie Yeager, Clara M. Whiting.''

This letter was mailed to her attorney, who acknowledged its receipt. Several days later Mrs. Henry died. The husband, Thomas A. Henry, offered the letter as a codicil to the will. The trial court accepted the validity of the will but denied probate to the letter. Is the letter a valid codicil to the will? Discuss.

3 The decedent, George Thompson, wrote a letter to his niece, Katharine, in which he said, ''Katharine, I want you to know you're going to get *all* I have when I die.'' George Thompson died shortly thereafter and left surviving him a brother and several nephews and nieces, including Katharine. The instrument was presented for probate. Did the instrument constitute a will? Discuss.

4 A will was presented for probate in Rhode Island. It had been stricken through with red pencil in each and every word, including the signature. A diagonal line appeared across each clause of the instrument with the decedent's initials, the word *obliterated*, and the date. Despite the above defacements, the entire document remained legible. The Rhode Island statute concerning the revocation of wills provided as follows: ''No will shall be revoked except by another will or by some writing declaring an intention to revoke, executed in the manner in which a will is required to be executed, or by burning, tearing, or otherwise destroying the same by the testator.'' Did the action of the testator constitute a proper revocation for purposes of the statute? Discuss.

5   Grace Bradley Walters died leaving a will. The will had been prepared without the advice of an attorney and was witnessed by Weldon and Bradley. The decedent's will left all her assets to the individuals who worked for Pine Company. The witnesses to the will were employees of that company and would have been entitled to take under the terms of the will. The statute requires two witnesses to the signing of a will. It further provides that if any person shall be a subscribing witness to a will that provides for a legacy to that witness and if such will cannot be proved without the testimony of such witness, the devise to that witness shall be void. Can the subscribing witnesses, Weldon and Bradley, inherit under the terms of this will? Discuss.

6   At the time of her second marriage, Mrs. Broun's estate was substantial. Prior to this marriage, the terms of her will left her estate totally to her two daughters by her previous marriage. She subsequently prepared a new will in which she left her husband one third of her original estate. At a later point in time, she prepared a second will through her husband's attorney, leaving the substantial portion of her estate to her husband. Mrs. Broun consulted with her husband's attorney and, according to his testimony, read the entire document and, in response to his instructions, stated that she understood all the provisions of the will. Upon Mrs. Broun's death several years later, the children brought an action alleging that the will had been obtained through fraud and duress on the part of their father. The evidence further disclosed that the bulk of the estate had been inherited by Mrs. Broun from her prior husband and that she was not particularly skilled in business or finance. Decision for whom? Discuss.

7   Thomas and Sturgin were joint tenants of real property. Thomas apparently suffered a heart attack. Several of the neighbors found Thomas lying on the ground and Sturgin trying to administer first aid. One of the neighbors attempted to resuscitate Thomas but, on feeling for a pulse, was unable to find any. He endeavored to administer artificial respiration and heard a sound from the house. Upon checking in the house (after being unable to resuscitate Thomas), he found Sturgin also lying on the ground breathing shallowly. Shortly thereafter, Sturgin also stopped breathing, and neither man was able to be revived. The statute regarding joint tenancy in the state of California is as follows: ''Where there is no sufficient evidence that two joint tenants have died otherwise than simultaneously, the property so held shall be distributed one half as if one had survived and one half as if the other had survived.'' Shall the property be distributed equally between the heirs of Thomas and Sturgin? Discuss.

8   Mrs. O'Brien died survived by four children—two natural children and two adopted children. Her estate, which was valued in excess of $800,000, was left to the two natural children with a provision that the adopted children receive certain personal property. The will was drafted by her son, an attorney. The will was found to be invalid because of her son's improprieties in drafting it. It became necessary for an administrator to be appointed over the assets of estate. Mrs. O'Brien's son filed a petition to the court to have himself appointed as administrator of the estate. The bank also filed a petition to be appointed as administrator on behalf of the adopted children. The trial court found that the plaintiff had exhibited lack of care and foresight in payment of funds and management of property to the extent that he was living beyond his means. They also found that he lacked business or management ability. Who should be appointed administrator?

9 The decedent, shortly before going into the hospital for an operation from which he ultimately died, typed the following letter. ''If I should fail to pull through this operation, I want you to sell the . . . stock, which is worth about $50,000, and the bonds . . . worth about $25,000 and divide the proceeds equally among my brothers and sisters and Mamie Morrison.

''It is necessary that this arrangement be kept profoundly secret among the family.

''The above items should not be appraised with my estate as they are not a part of it.''

The decedent widow objected to probate of this item as a testamentary disposition. The proponents of the will tried to argue that since the statute accepting holographic wills refers to wills that are written, they could also include wills that were typed because it does not specify that the writing need be manual writing. Decision for whom? Discuss.

PART FIVE

FAMILY LAW

The family is the spirit of strength of the American society. The family gives stability and direction to most individuals.

Most persons are unaware of the legal implications many family interactions create. Chapter 13 discusses the creation of the family unit from a legal, as opposed to a sociological or moral, perspective. It discusses the customary foundation of the family (i.e., marriage), as well as "creative" family units, cohabitation, gay families, and communal families. The chapter also discusses additions to the family unit through birth, adoption, and foster care. Chapter 14 discusses the dissolution of the family unit through annulment and divorce as well as emancipation, abuse or neglect, and finally death.

CHAPTER 13

Creation of a Family

MARRIAGE

Introduction

Marriage, as it is commonly discussed, refers to a contractual relationship between two persons, one male and one female, arising out of the mutual promises that are recognized by law. As a contract, it is generally required that both parties must consent to its terms and have legal capacity. Marriage, because of the personal relationships of those involved, goes well beyond a normal business contract in that it creates a unique legal relationship. Marriage contracts are not revocable at the will of the parties, but only upon court order. In addition, marriage contracts are not assignable or transferable. Remedies for breach of a marriage contract differ from those for breaches of other contracts. The marriage contract is generally considered to be a permanent contract lasting for the life of the parties.

Common law held that marriage was a spiritual matter rather than a secular matter and, therefore, lay outside the jurisdiction of the secular courts. In England, in 1673, the Court of Common Pleas decided, in the case of Mary Holcroft v. Dickensen (Carter 233, 124 Eng. Rep. 933), that the marriage contract was not only a spiritual or ecclesiastical matter but was also a legal matter. In that case, the court was asked to decide whether a proposal of marriage by the defendant, which was reportedly accepted by the plaintiff, formed a binding contract. The court decided that they were not being asked to deal with the consequences of the marriage itself, but rather with the issue of a breach of the marriage contract. This, they held, was entirely a legal matter within the confines of a secular court. Following this decision there were numerous other decisions dealing with the implications of the breach of a marriage contract. Each of these cases dealt with the issue at the point at which the man (presumably) has proposed to the woman and she has accepted. At some point one of the parties indicates an unwillingness to continue to perform the act promised. The consequences of such a refusal are quite diverse.

There have been numerous cases holding that a promise to marry is binding; there have been numerous others holding that such a promise is not binding. Cases are decided on an individual basis according to the facts of each situation. Courts will generally consider why the individual in question refused to honor his or her contract. They may also consider the relative status of the individuals, their reputations within the community, their motivations for entering into the contract in the first place, and so on. The trend of current court decisions has been away from the enforcement of contracts to marry. In many states the doctrine of breach of promise to marry has been legislatively eliminated as the basis for a lawsuit.

Many individuals recovered damages for breach of the promise to marry by proving fraud rather than by suing on the basis of a contract. For example, Mr. A. promises to marry Miss B., in return for which Miss B. renders to Mr. A. sexual or other favors. Once Mr. A. receives the promised favor, he breaks his promise and refuses to go through with the marriage. Some courts will entertain an action for damages on the grounds that the promisor committed an act of fraud upon the promisee. The promisee must however prove that the promisor never intended to go through with the marriage at the time that the promise was made and that the purpose of the promise was merely to induce the consideration received.

Current practice, when two parties agree to get married, is for the male to give the female an engagement ring. If the wedding does not take place, an issue arises as to the rights of the respective parties to the ring. The general rule is that such a gift is given under the implied condition that the marriage will take place. A gift of an engagement ring is, therefore, not an absolute gift. If the contract to marry is terminated, the condition has not taken place, and the donor is entitled to the return of the ring, unless the donor has wrongfully breached the contract.

Statutory Marriage

State Regulation of Marriage Marriage is considered to be a natural right not subject to arbitrary denial or regulation and is considered to be guaranteed under the Fourteenth Amendment of the Constitution (Loving v. Virginia, 388 U.S. [S. Ct. 1966]). Marriage is, however, subject to state control and regulation with respect to its creation and termination.

States exercise their control over marriage by limiting certain types of marriages. Marriages of closely related persons have been prohibited as indecent, immoral, incestuous, and dangerous to the purity and happiness of the family and welfare of future generations. Three basic reasons why incestuous marriages are unacceptable in society are religious principles, eugenic principles (strengthening the population by prevention of inbreeding), and maintaining the sanctity of the home by preventing competition for sexual companionship between members of the same household or family. Some ''marriages'' will be declared void. This means that they will be deemed never to have been entered into. Other marriages are declared voidable. These are valid until judicially declared invalid.

Incestuous Marriage The state statutes prohibit marriages between ancestors and descendants or between siblings. Fines and imprisonment for parties to an incestuous marriage, as well as for persons who knowingly and willingly are involved in the solemnization of such a marriage, may also be imposed. Marriages between uncles and nieces or aunts and nephews are generally prohibited throughout the United States although recognized in a number of foreign countries and, therefore, possibly acceptable in the United States if entered into in a foreign country.

In a number of jurisdictions a marriage between first cousins is valid; in a number of others, specific statutory provisions prohibit such marriages. The following states allow marriages to first cousins: Alabama, Alaska, California, Colorado, Connecticut, Washington, D.C., Florida, Georgia, Hawaii, Maine, Maryland, Massachusetts, New Jersey, New Mexico, Rhode Island, South Carolina, Tennessee, Texas, Vermont, and Virginia. Parties who are more distantly related than first cousins are usually able to marry.

In a number of states, relatives of the whole blood and relatives of half blood, as well as relatives of legitimate or illegitimate birth, are considered identically in determining whether or not a marriage is incestuous. Some statutes have prohibitions against marriage to certain relatives related only by marriage (e.g., in-laws). In the case of persons who are related only by adoption, the status of their rights to marry is not clear.

Bigamous Marriages Persons who are already married cannot marry again unless their existing marital relationship is legally terminated. Divorce, annulment, or the death of the former spouse will terminate a marriage. Under many statutes a marriage will also terminate if either spouse receives a final sentence of imprisonment for life. An attempted marriage to a person whose prior marriage has not been terminated is considered void. This rule would apply even in a case where a party thought that his or her first spouse had obtained a divorce and innocently attempted to marry a second spouse. The second marriage will nonetheless be considered void. This situation occurs frequently when people who live in one state travel to another state or country solely for the purpose of obtaining a divorce. In such a situation there is often a question as to the validity of the divorce in the home state. If it has not been clearly established, a person who remarries subsequent to such an extrajurisdictional divorce falls subject to the risk that the divorce was invalid and, therefore, is still married to the first spouse.

If a husband and wife separate without obtaining a divorce and over a period of time lose contact with each other, it will be very difficult for either of them to remarry. Although there are certain statutory presumptions as to the death of a spouse whose absence has extended over a substantial period of time, under most statutes the reappearance of the spouse would render a second marriage either void or voidable.

Minimum Age State laws also set forth reasons whereby the courts may declare a marriage void. (This makes the marriage voidable.) A marriage may be declared void by a court if entered into by a party who is under the minimum legal age of consent in that state. While under Common Law this was generally 14 in the case of males and 12 in the case of females, it has been increased by statute (Exhibit 13–1). There are differences between states as to treatment of marriages between persons who are underage. Generally, if a party is under age 7, the marriage is void; if the party is older than 7 but below the legal age of consent, the marriage is voidable. A party to a marriage who is underage at the time it is entered into may ratify the relationship by continuing it after attaining the legal age.

Mental and Physical Capacity As a general rule, the marriage of a person who is of unsound mind (does not understand the consequences of the marriage contract) is either void or voidable. A party's unsoundness of mind must relate directly to the party's ability to contract a marriage. Courts have required the person to understand the special nature of a marriage contract and the duties and responsibilities that relate thereto. Thus, mere subnormal intelligence, eccentricity, or uncontrollable impulse would not be a bar to marriage. Courts have compared the capacity to

EXHIBIT 13-1
Marriage Laws

	Parental Consent Required		Parental Consent Not Required		Relatives Prohibited from Marrying, Other Than Parents, Children, Grandchildren, Grandparents, Aunts, Uncles, Nephews and Nieces
	Male	Female	Male	Female	
Alabama	14	14	18	18	Stepparent, stepchild, son-in-law, daughter-in-law
Alaska	16	16	18	18	—
Arizona	16	16	18	18	First cousin
Arkansas	17	16	21	18	First cousin
California	No provision	No provision	18	18	—
Colorado	16	16	18	18	—
Connecticut	16	16	18	18	Stepparent, stepchild
Delaware	18	16	18	18	First cousin
District of Columbia	16	16	18	18	Stepparent, stepchild, stepgrandparent, father-in-law, mother-in-law, son-in-law, daughter-in-law, spouse's grandparent or grandchild, spouse of grandparent or grandchild
Florida	16	16	18	18	—
Georgia	Under 16	Under 16	16	16	Stepparent, stepchild, stepgrandparent, stepgrandchild, father-in-law, mother-in-law, son-in-law, daughter-in-law
Hawaii	16	16	18	18	—
Idaho	16	16	18	18	First cousin
Illinois	16	16	18	18	First cousin
Indiana	17	17	18	18	First cousin
Iowa	16	16	18	18	First cousin, stepparent, stepchild, father-in-law, mother-in-law, son-in-law, daughter-in-law, spouse of grandchild
Kansas	Under 18	Under 18	18	18	First cousin
Kentucky	No provision	No provision	18	18	First cousin, first cousin once removed
Louisiana	18	16	18	18	First cousin

EXHIBIT 13-1, cont.

State					
Maine	16	16	18	18	Stepparent, stepchild, father-in-law, mother-in-law, son-in-law, daughter-in-law, spouse's grandparent or grandchild, spouse of grandparent or grandchild
Maryland	16	16	18	18	Stepparent, stepchild, father-in-law, mother-in-law, son-in-law, daughter-in-law, spouse's grandparent or grandchild, spouse of grandparent or grandchild
Massachusetts	No provision	No provision	18	18	Stepparent, stepchild, stepgrandparent, father-in-law, mother-in-law, son-in-law, daughter-in-law
Minnesota	No statutory provision	16	18	18	First cousin
Mississippi	Court order	Parental consent	17	15	First cousin, stepparent, stepchild, father-in-law, mother-in-law, son-in-law, daughter-in-law
Missouri	15	15	18	18	First cousin
Montana	16	16	18	18	First cousin
Nebraska	17	17	19	19	First cousin
Nevada	16	16	18	18	First cousin
New Hampshire	14	13	18	18	First cousin, stepparent, son-in-law, daughter-in-law
New Jersey	16	16	18	18	—
New Mexico	16	16	18	18	—
New York	16	16	18	18	—
North Carolina	16	16	18	18	Double first cousin
North Dakota	16	16	18	18	First cousin
Ohio	18	16	18	18	First cousin
Oklahoma	16	16	18	18	First cousin
Oregon	17	17	18	18	First cousin
Pennsylvania	16	16	18	18	First cousin, stepparent, stepchild, son-in-law, daughter-in-law

EXHIBIT 13-1, cont.

Rhode Island	18	16	18	18	Stepchild, father-in-law, mother-in-law, spouse's grandparent or grandchild
South Carolina	16	14	18	18	Stepparent, stepchild, father-in-law, mother-in-law, son-in-law, daughter-in-law, spouse's grandparent or grandchild, spouse of grandparent or grandchild
South Dakota	16	16	18	18	First cousin, stepparent, stepchild
Tennessee	16	16	18	18	Stepparent, stepchild, stepgrandchild, grandnephew, grandniece
Texas	14	14	18	18	—
Utah	14	14	18	18	First cousin
Vermont	16	16	18	18	—
Virginia	16	16	18	18	—
Washington	17	17	18	18	First cousin
West Virginia	18	16	18	18	First cousin, double cousin
Wisconsin	16	16	18	18	First cousin, unless female 55 years or older
Wyoming	16	16	18	18	First cousin

contract generally and have concluded that the requirements for a marriage contract may be less than for any other contract. Persons who are unable to handle their business affairs may nonetheless enter into valid marriages. It has been observed that marriage depends to a great extent on sentiment, attachment, and affection that persons with weaker as well as stronger intellects feel and that it does not depend as much as ordinary contracts on the exercise of clear reason, discernment, and sound judgment. A marriage contracted by a person who is intoxicated to the extent of being unable to understand the nature of the marriage contract and its consequences is ordinarily held to be void or voidable for lack of capacity.

Although physical health is not a requirement for a valid marriage, statutes may prohibit the marriage of persons with specific diseases or disabilities (e.g., tuberculosis, syphilis). Epilepsy is generally no longer considered to be a bar to a marriage. Sterility, which is the inability to have children, as opposed to impotence, which is the inability to have sexual intercourse, is not a disqualification of a marriage. (In some cases, the marriage of a sterile person may be declared a nullity for fraud if contrary representations were made prior to the marriage.)

Impotence is frequently held to render a marriage voidable unless the condition was known to the party not under the disability. This is true by statute in a number of states. Implicit in the marriage contract is the ability of the parties to engage in sexual intercourse. It is generally required, if there is to be a binding marriage, that such capacity exist. The concept under which a marriage is declared voidable owing to impotence is not that there was an original incapacity to contract, but rather that there has been entire and complete failure of a consideration of the marriage contract.

Consent Free consent and agreement of parties is essential to a valid marriage (Schibi v. Schibi, 69 A.2d 831 [Conn. 1949]; Hilton v. Roylance, 69 P. 660 [Utah 1902]). Without such consent, a marriage ceremony may be declared a nullity. Where participation is obtained by fraud, duress, or force, the marriage will be void or voidable owing to lack of consent. (See the section on divorce in Chapter 14.)

Miscegenation At one time a substantial number of states prohibited and punished marriages between persons of different races or at least between white persons and Negroes. These miscegenation statutes usually provided that white persons could not properly marry Negroes or persons with certain percentages of Negro blood. These statutes had frequently been held constitutional until the Supreme Court, in Loving v. Virginia, 388 U.S. 1 (S. Ct. 1966), held that they violated the Fourteenth Amendment. As a result of Loving v. Virginia, it is no longer permissible to deny a marriage license to an interracial couple who meet all other marriage requirements. It is not, however, unconstitutional for a legislature to require persons applying for a license to disclose information as to race and color for legitimate identification and statistical purposes.

Procedures for Getting Married

Procedures for getting married vary from state to state. In some states, failure to follow proper procedure will render a marriage void or voidable; in other states, it will subject the marriage partners to the possibility of criminal prosecution.

Statutory requirements include blood tests (required by all states except Maryland, Minnesota, Nevada, South Carolina, and Washington); waiting periods (from zero to seven days); obtaining a marriage license (all states); and solemnization of the marriage by an appropriate individual. (Failure to follow the prescribed procedures may make it difficult to find someone who will solemnize the marriage.)

A marriage may be solemnized by a minister or similar party; a public official such as a mayor, police justice, or city clerk; or a contract signed by both parties and witnessed by at least two witnesses and acknowledged before a judge of a court of record. State statutes do not provide any particular contractual format or ceremony for solemnization of a marriage. A typical statute requires that the parties declare in the presence of the appropriate official that they take each other as husband and wife; furthermore, there is a requirement that there be at least one witness other

than the official who is presiding. Solemnization by an unauthorized person in some states renders the marriage void (this is usually specifically stated in the statute) whereas in other states, it does not provided the married couple proceeded in good faith. After the solemnization of the marriage, it is customary for a marriage certificate to be issued that in some states is required to be registered or recorded. It is also generally required that all persons acquire a marriage license that is to be executed by the party officiating at the marriage ceremony.

Pre-nuptial Agreements

One of the concerns that some people have about getting married is the property aspects of the marriage relationship. When two parties marry, there is generally some right acquired by each spouse in and to the property of the other. Upon a subsequent dissolution of the marriage, it is possible for there to be major disagreements concerning the division of their property. It is possible for a spouse who has contributed nothing (in terms of material goods) to a given marriage to emerge from a divorce settlement with property that was entirely the other spouse's prior to the marriage. Many people endeavor to limit their future spouse's rights to their property by entering into a prenuptial agreement.

A prenuptial agreement is a property agreement made prior to the marriage. Such an agreement generally defines the property rights of each of the spouses in and to the property of the other in the event of a divorce. Such agreements may or may not be binding. It will depend upon the degree of disclosure that takes place prior to making the agreement and upon the honesty with which the parties dealt with each other in making such agreement. Even where the parties are totally open with each other, such an agreement can never deprive the state of any rights it may have to obtain support payments from one spouse when it has been supporting the other spouse. For example, Bill and Mary were married and subsequently divorced. At the time of the divorce there were no children, both parties were self-supporting, and therefore no alimony settlement was made upon the husband by the wife or vice versa. Ten years later Mary was economically destitute and applied for welfare. The social service department was able to force Bill to make payments (either directly to Mary or to them as reimbursement for payments they made to Mary) on the grounds that Bill's obligation to support Mary had never and would never totally cease. Because of the state's interest, a prenuptial agreement at best can be said to have limited validity.

Restraints on Marriage

Restraint of marriage applies to provisions in contracts, deeds, or wills that have the effect of trying to induce an individual not to marry, not to marry a specific person, or to marry only under certain specified conditions. For example, a gift in a will may state: ''to Lisa on condition she not marry'' or ''to Lisa on condition she marry someone other than a member of the Catholic faith.'' Provisions in restraint of marriage create judicial difficulties.

Traditions of English common law are heavily oriented toward property rights and the rights of persons to dispose of their property as they see fit. Therefore, traditions of common law would hold such restraints to be valid. Civil law traditions, however, place greater emphasis on a person's right to marry free from the influence of others and, therefore, have traditionally held such provisions to be void. As a result of these two conflicting approaches, the case law in this area is widely varied. Though many cases expressed the doctrine that public policy generally favors marriage and that provisions that restrain marriage are contrary to public policy, some courts qualify this position by drawing distinctions between different types of restraints upon marriage. Contracts have been held not to be violative of public policy where the restraint is not a general restraint of marriage, but rather a restraint with respect to a particular person or a particular group of persons. Thus, a provision in a will disallowing an inheritance if the party in question were to marry a member of the Catholic faith has been held to be a reasonable restraint because it does not unduly restrict the beneficiary's right to be married. (U.S. National Bank v. Snodgrass, 275 P.2d 860 [Ore. 1954]). On the other hand, a general restraint stipulating that a person not inherit property if he or she marries anyone would probably be held to be unreasonable and improper. Clauses in instruments requiring persons to get married or even to marry specified persons generally are not contrary to public policy.

Common-law Marriages

A common-law marriage is entered into by an agreement between a man and woman who have legally recognizable capacity to be married that they will be recognized as husband and wife. They do not go through the religious or civil ceremonies or obtain a license as discussed in the section on procedures for getting married in this chapter. At one time common-law marriages were widely recognized in almost every state. There were only a few in which the adoption of common-law marriages was rejected (e.g., Arkansas, Maryland, Massachusetts, Vermont, and Wyoming). Several states that have recognized common-law marriages in the past did so with considerable distaste and considered it a relationship to be tolerated but not encouraged. In recent years an increasing number of states have rejected the doctrine of common-law marriage to the point that today common-law marriages can only be entered into in Alabama, Colorado, District of Columbia, Georgia, Idaho, Iowa, Kansas, Montana, Ohio, Oklahoma, Pennsylvania, Rhode Island, South Carolina, and Texas. The importance of common-law marriage continues, however, because if valid where entered into, a common-law marriage is valid in every state in the United States. This is required under the ''full faith and credit doctrine'' of our legal system.

In order to contract a common-law marriage, the parties must have the capacity to be married. This generally requires that a person attain the minimum required age for statutory marriage. In addition to legal capacity, the parties must agree that they are husband and wife and, in most states, must hold themselves forth to the general public as husband and wife. If the relationship exists in secret only, it will not constitute a common-law marriage. Cohabitation is also generally required (the parties are expected to live or dwell together in the same place). It is important that the cohabitation be coupled with the representation of the husband-wife relationship. A male and female living together as roommates would not be considered to be married by virtue of the fact that they are cohabiting.

An example of the relevance of the doctrine of common-law marriage can be seen in the following: Dick and Jane met, fell in love, and went on an extended whirlwind tour of the country. During this time they spent several years together in several states, where they lived as husband and wife. After several years they moved to New York, where they were also recognized as husband and wife and started a business. When they split up, there was considerable property owned by the husband. The wife claimed an interest in the property on the basis of the fact that they were married. The husband alleged that they never had been married and that even though they assumed the status of husband and wife, there had never been a valid legal marriage ceremony performed in any state. The issue ultimately came down to whether the parties had ever lived in a state that recognized the validity of common-law marriage. If they had, by virtue of their holding themselves forth as husband and wife in that state while they were residents there, they would be legally married. If they had never lived in a state that recognized the validity of common-law marriage, then they would not be married, and the wife would not be entitled to any rights. (This was before the recognition of rights of persons who are simply living together.)

NONMARRIED FAMILIES

The Cohabitors

U.S. Census statistics for March of 1980 showed that there are 1.56 million households consisting of two unrelated adults of the opposite sex. This represents an increase of more than a million since the census of 1970. This figure can be contrasted with 48 million married couples. Slightly more than one quarter of these households have children living with them. Though they represent a small percentage of the total population, it is nonetheless clear that there is an increasingly large number of people who are forming family relationships without the benefit of marriage. In many cases, people choose to live without being married to pursue educational and employment opportunities. Some feel that they wish to try a family relationship without entering into any formal ties. In other cases, there may be economic advantages (owing to social security or tax rules) to living as an unmarried couple.

Cohabitation may create legal obligations. The first is the question of whether the relationship being entered into is legal. Cohabitation by parties of the opposite sex may be illegal. There are a number of states in which cohabitation constitutes an offense (usually a misdemeanor). These states are Alabama, Alaska, Arizona, Florida, Idaho, Illinois, Kansas, Massachusetts, Michigan, Mississippi, New Mexico, North Dakota, South Carolina, Virginia, West Virginia, and Wisconsin. Though these states frequently do not enforce their anticohabitation rules, it is nonetheless important to recognize that persons who cohabit in these states are exposed to criminal prosecution.

Ownership of Assets   If the relationship of cohabitation is legal in the state in which you live, the next problem likely to be encountered is the issue as to who owns which assets. For example, in Marvin v. Marvin, 557 P.2d 106 (Cal. 1976), the plaintiff, Michelle Marvin, stated that in 1964 she and the defendant, Lee Marvin, "entered into an oral agreement" that as long as "the parties lived together they would combine their efforts and earnings and share equally any and all property accumulated as a result of their efforts whether individual or combined." In addition, they had agreed to "hold themselves out to the general public as husband and wife": and that "the plaintiff further render her services as companion, housekeeper and cook to . . . defendant." The plaintiff further argued that she shortly thereafter gave up a lucrative career as an entertainer in order to devote herself full-time to the defendant in these capacities. In exchange for this, the defendant agreed to provide for all the plaintiff's financial support needs for the rest of the plaintiff's life. The plaintiff further argued that she lived with the defendant and fulfilled her obligations under this agreement and that during the time in question they amassed substantial property in the name of the defendant and that at a given point the defendant required the plaintiff to leave the household and subsequently refused to support her and also refused to give her any of the assets accumulated during the time they lived together. The plaintiff had to go to court, at great expense, to try to prove these oral promises. This type of problem can be resolved if the parties enter into a written cohabitation agreement (sometimes referred to as a living together agreement or a joint living arrangement).

Cohabitation Agreement   A cohabitation agreement is a formal agreement spelling out the rights and obligations of the parties. A well-thought-out living together agreement deals with a great many issues that the average marriage contract does not deal with. In the average marital relationship, the parties exchange vows in which they typically agree to love, honor, and cherish the other, but rarely do the parties consider the termination of the relationship or the economic realities of its continuity. A cohabitation agreement, on the other hand, deals with all these factors and forces the individuals to confront the reality they will most probably be facing.

The nature of a cohabitation agreement is basically contractual. (See chapter 4 for general contract principles.) It is an agreement by two parties that has to be supported by consideration and requires all the other elements of contract, including that it not be contrary to public policy. In *Marvin* v. *Marvin*, the court cited the preferable rule as follows: ''The fact that a man and woman live together without marriage, and engage in a sexual relationship, does not in itself invalidate the agreements between them relating to their earnings, property, or expenses. Neither is such an agreement invalid merely because the parties may have contemplated the creation or continuation of a nonmarital relationship when they entered into it. The agreements between nonmarital partners fail only to the extent that they rest upon a consideration of meretricious sexual services.'' The court continues at a later point to state the principle that ''adults who voluntarily live together and engage in sexual relations are nonetheless as competent as any other persons to contract respecting their earnings and property rights. Of course, they cannot lawfully contract to pay for the performance of sexual services, for such a contract is, in essence, an agreement for prostitution and unlawful for that reason. But they may agree to pool their earnings and to hold all property acquired during the relationship in accord with the law governing community property; conversely they may agree that each partner's earnings and the property acquired from those earnings remain the separate property of the earning partner. So long as the agreement does not rest upon illicit meretricious consideration, the parties may order their economic affairs as they choose. No policy precludes the court from enforcing such agreements.''

In the *Marvin* case the court of California, a fairly progressive court, found that contracts could be entered into between two adult spouses that, even though they included a sexual relationship, could be enforceable consistent with public policy provided that there was a basis for the relationship other than a sexual one. This is a socially evolving rule and certainly cannot be said to be the case in every state. Great care should be taken, in entering into a cohabitation agreement, to stress and focus on the portion of the relationship that is nonsexual in nature because courts in most states have rejected the validity of various claims in the nature of alimony (or what is currently referred to as *palimony*) on the grounds that the relationship between the parties is a meretricious one.

Another factor to consider is that a person who is already married and enters into cohabitation with another is committing an act of adultery (considered a crime in many states). It would be very difficult for a court not to find a contract based on such a relationship contrary to public policy.

A cohabitation agreement is protection for both parties, and if there is a genuine concern for the welfare of the cohabiting party, establishing benefits or rights of each of the parties seems to be reasonable. Exhibit 13–2 is a sample of a cohabitation agreement. A well-drawn agreement should deal with property rights, income, dissolution, children, and other pertinent topics.

Property Division   There are several options in dealing with property. With respect to property owned by the parties before they commence living together, the agreement specifies that each party shall continue to own that property separately and each party relinquishes any rights he or she may have in separate property of the other. Thus, upon termination of the relationship, each person will take away whatever property he or she had when the pair entered into the relationship. This,

EXHIBIT 13-2

Cohabitation Agreement

Agreement made and entered into the _____ day of _____, 19___, by and between _____ (here and after referred to as "A") and _____ (here and after referred to as "B") presently living in the County of _____, State of _____:

WHEREAS A and B are of legal age and fully competent to enter into this agreement, each being mature enough and possessing a sound mind sufficient to understand fully the promises and covenants made herein; and

WHEREAS the parties fully appreciate and understand the differences between their relationship and that of marriage and represent that they are not presently married to each other or anyone else; and

WHEREAS the parties wish to live together and create an agreement clearly defining, protecting, and setting forth their respective rights and obligations concerning their property, income, and their relationships with each other and their respective children; and

WHEREAS the parties have not entered into any understanding, contract, or agreement, either expressed or implied, regarding these items, or to the extent have previously entered into such agreements, such prior agreements shall terminate and this agreement shall represent their sole effective document; and

WHEREAS the parties are fully aware of the legal and practical effects of this agreement in every manner and acknowledge that it is fair and entered into without any fraud, duress, or undue influence by or upon either A or B or any other person and have carefully read and understood each and every provision hereof and each has had the opportunity to consult with an attorney of his or her choice prior to execution hereof; and

WHEREAS the parties expressly set forth and acknowledge that the consideration for this agreement is not the sexual services to be rendered by either party to the other; it is agreed in consideration of the mutual promises and agreements contained herein, as follows:

1. It is acknowledged that A and B have previously acquired property in their own names. Such property shall continue to be owned solely by the current owner and is listed on schedule 1. Each party relinquishes any right, title or interest to the other parties' property. Any income that is generated by property listed on schedule 1 shall become and remain the sole income of the individual who owns said property.

2. Any property, either real, personal, or mixed, that is acquired by either A or B through gift or inheritance during the period of this agreement shall be the sole property of the party acquiring it. The other party hereby waives any right, title, or interest to said property. Any income that shall be generated by such acquired property shall remain the sole income of the party who owns said property. Any debts that are to be paid or any claims against such property are to be paid by the party who acquires title to the property.

3. Any real or personal property that is acquired by A or B in any other manner during the term of this agreement shall be owned equally, regardless of the amount of contribution made by either party and irrespective of whether the contribution is made in money, property, or services.

4. In the event that A or B receives property as a result of a gift or an inheritance and it is impossible to determine that it was given solely to one of them, it is agreed that they will use their best efforts to reach a mutually satisfactory decision as to which of them shall be deemed sole owner of such property. If the parties are unable to reach an agreement or if the property is clearly made as a gift or inheritance to both of them, it is agreed that the property in question shall be deemed equally owned by each of them.

5. Properties acquired by either A or B out of funds that are accumulated after the commencement of the relationship shall be deemed to be mutual and equally owned property notwithstanding the fact that the property may have been acquired or may be acquired in the name of only one of the parties.

6. In the event that A or B desires to sell his or her share of a co-owned property to a third party, the following procedure shall apply:

EXHIBIT 13-2, cont.

(a) The party wishing to sell (seller) will first make a written offer to the other party (buyer), stating his or her intent to sell and giving the buyer first option to purchase the seller's interest at the fair market value.

(b) If the buyer chooses to exercise the purchase option, he or she will communicate this intent to the seller in writing within ____ days.

(c) If the buyer chooses not to exercise the option within the time period stated above, the seller will have an absolute right to convey his or her share to any third party.

7. Neither A or B shall vacate the premises where they are currently residing without giving the other party written notice 30 days prior to leaving. In the event that either party violates this clause, he or she shall be liable for damages to the other party until such time as a substitute party can be obtained or for a reasonable length of time. It is understood that the intent of the parties in entering into this agreement is to enable them to pool their economic resources for mutual benefit.

8. Subject to any other provisions herein, all income accumulated by either A or B during the period they live together shall be contributed to a joint fund, which shall be used to pay the expenses and debts of each of the parties, including household expenditures such as rent, food, utilities, clothing, and so forth. Notwithstanding the above, it is understood that income that is generated by property that is owned by A or B individually may be used by either party as he or she deems fit and need not be contributed for their joint benefit. Upon termination of the relationship, the balance of the joint funds, after payment of debts incurred during the relationship, shall be equally divided between the parties. If the amount of joint funds is insufficient to pay joint debts, each party shall be equally liable for any deficiency.

9. It is clearly understood by both A and B, notwithstanding their mutual agreement to contribute all their income to the joint care and maintenance of the family unit, that party A shall bear the primary financial burden for the maintenance of the family. The family as used in this paragraph shall include the following children who were born to B before entering into the relationship: _____. Party A agrees to provide for the maintenance and support of the household, including any children of both of them in a manner that is reasonable considering the financial situation of both parties. Party B, in return for the agreement of party A and as consideration, therefore agrees to furnish those services required by the family, none of which may be deemed to include meretricious services. The family for purposes of this clause includes the following children born to A prior to entering into this relationship. Services to be provided by party B include all necessary services, of which the following are representative but not necessarily comprehensive: bookkeeping, business planning, career counseling, child guidance, correspondence, domestic functions and errands, emotional and psychological support, financial and tax consultation, household management (including decorating, meal planning, cleaning, entertaining, shopping), record maintenance, and attendance at and scheduling of social functions.

10. Upon termination of the relationship, the parties shall divide all property and income in accordance with prior terms of this agreement. Each party specifically waives any right to income or support subsequent to the termination of the relationship.

11. In addition to the children of A and B listed at paragraph 9, A and B each have additional children who are presently residing with other parents, but who may from time to time come to vist A or B. The mutual obligations assumed by A and B herein shall extend to any and all these other children at such times as they may be visiting with the family unit. In addition, in the event that either A or B, in his or her sole discretion, shall choose to obtain custody of any other of these children, the family obligations hereunder shall automatically be extended to those other children.

12. A and B acknowledge that they have prior legal debts that arose before the execution of this agreement, such debts being listed at schedule 2. Each party agrees to continue to be solely and totally liable for said debts.

EXHIBIT 13-2, cont.

13. A and B agree that, upon the termination of their relationship, any obligations entered into on account of this agreement vis-à-vis a child of the other party will remain binding on them. This includes financial obligations as well as parental support or guidance obligations.

14. A and B hereby acknowledge that they are both parents of the following children _____, who are currently residing with them. It is understood that party A shall be primarily financially liable for support of said child and that party B shall contribute services comparable to those listed above in paragraph 9. Upon termination of their relationship, A and B agree that they shall have joint custody over these and any other children that they shall subsequently have. Joint custody as envisioned at this time shall be such that party B shall have custody of the children during the school year and party A shall have custody of the children during summers and Christmas and Easter vacations. This decision is being made because A and B both believe that joint custody will be most beneficial to the psychological and emotional well-being of their children.

15. A and B each acknowledge that they have had access to the financial information of the other party and had been fully open and disclosed all their respective assets and liabilities to the other party. Upon termination of this agreement, it is understood that each party waives any and all claims for support, alimony, or any other form of financial contribution except as has been provided to the contrary herein with respect to the children of both parties.

16. This agreement constitutes the entire agreement of the parties. To the extent that there have been any other prior or contemporary expressions or representations, promises, or agreements, they shall be deemed no longer to have any validity. This agreement may be modified only in writing executed by the parties.

17. Failure by either A or B to enforce any of the terms of this agreement shall not constitute a waiver of future performance of such term, and this agreement shall continue to be fully enforceable. In the event that any of the provisions of this agreement are found to be legally unenforceable or void, such determination shall not invalidate the entire agreement, and the agreement shall be modified so as to conform to the legal requirements. The remaining portions of the agreement shall continue to be effective.

18. This agreement shall remain valid for an indefinite period of time unless terminated. This agreement shall terminate upon written notice duly executed by both parties or in the event that they enter into a legally recognizable marriage.

IN WITNESS WHEREOF the parties have hereunto set their hands and seals this _____ day of _____ 19___.

_____

_____

STATE OF   )
) ss.:
COUNTY OF   )

On this _____ day of _____ , 19 __ , before me personally came _____ , to me known and known to me to be one of the individuals described in and who executed the foregoing instrument, and (s)he duly acknowledged to me that (s)he executed same.

_____
Notary Public

of course, requires identification of the property brought into the relationship. It is important to identify every item that has either sentimental or significant economic value.

With respect to property acquired during the relationship, it may be necessary to consider the source of the money that acquired the property. If a party to the relationship inherits property, it may be desirable for the property to be maintained as separate property. If so, it should be noted in the agreement. If property is acquired as a result of the earnings of one or both members of the relationship, then it can be decided that such property shall be considered acquired by both of them equally. An agreement may provide that parties to the relationship share the acquired assets other than equally (e.g., one third and two thirds). Such agreement should be spelled out specifically to avoid any questions later on.

Another clause that might be useful is a statement as to the length of time that one of the parties may be absent from the residence under circumstances that might result in a conclusion that he or she was not going to return, after which the party who is still at the residence may assume that the relationship has been terminated. It is important to establish this fact to enable the party who stays in the residence to take possession of the other's goods and dispose of them without being subject to a subsequent claim of trespass or theft.

When parties purchase real estate together, they should agree how to take ownership of the property (i.e., tenants in common vs. joint tenancy with rights of survivorship. For discussion of the differences, see Chapter 9). In addition to the form of ownership, there should be some consideration given to the rights of the parties upon termination of the relationship. One option is to provide that one party will sell to the other. Where parties cannot make such an agreement (i.e., where both parties wish to retain the property), the problem is much more difficult to deal with. The property would have to be sold and the proceeds distributed pursuant to court order. An agreement that one party has the right of first purchase of the property can prevent lengthy and expensive litigation. Note that the sample agreement is silent on the question of property ownership on death. This should be dealt with in a will (see Chapters 11 and 12).

Income and Expenses   Another issue that a cohabitation agreement should deal with is income and expenses. There are several options with respect to income. First is to separate income that is earned from income that is received as a result of investments. Income that is earned includes salaries, commissions, bonuses, and things of that nature. This type of income may be divided in some prearranged ratio, or it may be placed into the common pot to meet the needs of the household unit. The sample clause provides that such income is to be treated as joint funds and to be used by either party for family needs. Upon dissolution of the relationship, the balance in such a fund is to be divided equally between the parties. An alternative would be to take a given portion of money and set it aside as a joint fund with the balance to be retained by the party who earns it.

It is also appropriate to define the types of expenditures that may be made out of joint funds. In this context it should be made clear that liabilities that were accrued prior to the relationship's inception may not be paid out of the joint funds. (This assumes that assets owned prior to the formation of the relationship remain separate.) It is also possible to divide income and for each party to maintain a separate income account, paying his or her expenses out of his or her income.

The household expense and contribution paragraph is designed to designate the basis on which expenses of the household are to be maintained and entitles a party who contributes in excess of the appropriate amount to recover the other party's deficiency as appropriate.

The sample clauses presented and discussed in the agreement are by no means exclusive or comprehensive. In any given arrangement a number of other items may become important, and if there are concerns, they should be dealt with in a well-drafted, well-thought-out, and, above all, well-discussed cohabitation agreement. The execution of such an agreement will, in many cases, be highly beneficial to both parties to the relationship. The execution of such an agreement in most cases will not cause a relationship to fail although in some cases it may cause the immediate failure of a relationship that was probably doomed to fail sooner or later.

Gay Families

The creation of a gay family that is legally recognizable is extremely difficult, if not impossible. Many state statutes dealing with marriage state that it is a relationship between a man and a woman, thus making a gay marriage a legal impossibility. Other statutes, though not specifically referring to a male-female relationship in the definitional requirements, make it clear that it was contemplated that marriages consist of a male and a female partner. In addition, many religious institutions, which are legally authorized to perform marriages, do not recognize the validity of a gay marital relationship. Several churches are now becoming more liberal in their consideration and will recognize a gay marriage on an individual basis. There is also a national denomination of gay churches, known as the Metropolitan Community Church, which recognizes and will perform gay marriages.

Recognition of a gay marriage by an ecclesiastical authority does not give it legal validity at the present time. Because of the reluctance of the courts to recognize the gay family unit, it is very important for a gay unit to establish the legal consequences of their relationship in the form of a cohabitation agreement as discussed in the first part of this chapter. Though the *Marvin* v. *Marvin* case gives some support to unmarried heterosexual units in terms of their rights to acquire property from each other in the event of the dissolution of their relationship, no such precedent has been established in the area of a gay family. A cohabitation agreement for gay persons covers the same types of problems as is covered for an unmarried heterosexual family and does so in much the same manner.

The failure of a state to recognize a gay marriage means that the parties are not considered married for purposes of obtaining legal benefits that are conditional upon marriage. It also means that the parties may not enforce a normal marriage contract against each other (for items such as support or alimony) except to the extent that they have entered into an expressed provable contract providing for the same types of benefits.

The Communal Family

A communal family may be formed on the basis of religious, sociological, moral, philosophical, or other consistent values. The communal family is not a recognized legal entity; however, it may create certain rights and obligations toward other members of the family by contract in much the same way as the unmarried or gay family might do. The complexity of a cohabitation agreement for a communal family would go beyond that of an unmarried or gay family because a greater number of people are involved.

It is important to establish property rights in writing to protect parties upon dissolution of the communal family. Unlike a two-party family, which will be dissolved by the death of one party, a commune is most frequently dissolved because of the dissatisfaction of one or more members.

As values change or as people grow, there is a strong likelihood that a degree of dissatisfaction will arise and the relationship will be terminated. A communal family should approach buying property in much the same way as for forming a business partnership. The rights and responsibilities of each of the families, including their rights upon dissolution, should be clearly spelled out and outlined by the agreement.

A much more difficult problem to deal with is the issue of child custody with respect to a communal family. It should be made clear who the legal parents of the children of the communal family are, and every step should be taken by the legal parents to provide that, in the event of their death, the remaining communal parents are the ones who will acquire custody of the children if that is their intention. If such a provision is not stipulated by an agreement (possibly in the form of a will), it is very possible for family members of the deceased parents to obtain custody of the children even over the objection of the remaining communal members. In the event of a dissolution of the communal family, any agreement to the contrary not withstanding, it is most likely that the children will end up with their biological parents. In the event that two biological parents are divided in terms of their desires—that is one wishes to remain part of the communal family and the other does not—the placement of children will probably be left to the discretion of the court. It is unlikely in such a situation that a court will feel itself bound by any agreement entered into between the biological parents of the children. They will no doubt reach a decision based on their judgment of what would be best for the children involved. The presence of a well-thought-out and well-drawn-out cohabitation agreement will nonetheless provide some influence in terms of what the parents thought would be best for the children at the time that the agreement was drawn up. Since this predates any animosity between the parties, it is possible for a court to look at such an agreement as an indication as to what the parents' good faith desire for their children might have been.

CHILDREN

Birth

The birth of a child involves numerous medical, financial, sociological, and other considerations and also includes some potential legal questions. Most people fail to consider any of the legal issues before having a child.

A person has a right to have a child any place that she wishes. This means that it is not essential for a child to be born in a hospital or other medical facility. A person is free to have the child at home if she so desires. Implicit in this right is the idea that this procedure will not endanger the safety, life, or welfare of the child. A court may compel a different procedure if it feels the child's welfare could be in danger. The court's obligation is primarily to consider the welfare of the child.

Home Birth An increasing number of women are giving birth in home environments. These births are usually accompanied by services rendered by a midwife. It is important if you wish to have a child at home to establish with the midwife the procedures for birth much as you would with a physician or a hospital. You should be aware of what medical facilities the midwife will provide and which facilities you should be providing. You should also determine what facilities the midwife has to provide for emergency problems that may arise. You should consider the option of securing the services of a doctor if nothing else but on a standby basis, so that if something goes wrong, a professional with perhaps greater competency may be contacted. (Some physicians are unwilling to do this.) Remember also that if the parties involved in assisting you with your birth are negligent, you may have a right to sue them. If there is a question of negligence, you should discuss this immediately with a legal adviser and with the parties involved. It is most desirable to contact a legal professional first so that your rights will be protected to the ultimate degree. Again it may be desirable to have somebody close to you make an initial contact with a lawyer before you get out of the hospital and, whenever possible, before any evidence of what happened in the delivery room has been lost or destroyed.

Hospital Birth Before commencing with a birth procedure in a hospital, the parent or parents should be aware of the hospital procedures and what rights they have vis-à-vis the hospital. People have the right to know what medical procedures will be followed and also what will happen in the event that there is a medical emergency. In this regard, the parent or parents should make some provisions as to who may make a decision with respect to the safety or welfare of the parent and or the child in the event that an emergency arises. It is also important that the mother recognize what rights she has in terms of keeping the baby with her after it is born and also what rights she has to information concerning the baby's medical condition at and immediately after the time of birth. A father also has rights and should establish with the hospital what information and what accessibility he will have with respect to both child and mother. Many hospitals today will permit a father to be present at the birth of the child, but some hospitals will not. This again is a matter that should be determined ahead of time so that a parent is not surprised by a statement of hospital policy contrary to what the parent was expecting. Most hospitals subscribe to what is known as the patient's "bill of rights" (a copy appears in Exhibit 13–3). You should review these rights with your doctor and with the hospital staff to make sure you understand them and that the hospital considers them binding. If you feel that your rights in the hospital are being violated, you should notify the hospital immediately of this fact and, if at all possible, should communicate with somebody who is not physically debilitated at the time who will be willing and able to fight for your interests at that moment. You also should have a conversation with your physician ahead of time dealing with what possible problems can arise, what he or she proposes to do about them, and what rights you may have in terms of making decisions. If you feel you are in a position in which you will be unable to make those decisions, you should notify the physician or the person you wish to have make those decisions on your behalf. (Usually this person is named on the admission forms.)

Father's Rights and Obligations   The father of the child should determine what rights he has to visit both the mother and the child. He should be sure that the hospital will make the proper records concerning his paternity. Where the father is not married to the mother, it is important that he be identified so that he may make decisions concerning the child's welfare when the mother is unable to do so. A recent Supreme Court decision, Stanley v. Illinois (405 U.S. 645 [S. Ct. 1972]), establishes that the father of a child has certain rights with respect to that child. Paternity acknowledgments are important because, under most laws in most states, illegitimate children do not inherit from their male parents. This may be important in many cases, even where the father has minimal assets, because children may be entitled to certain benefits under worker's compensation, social security, private retirement, or other benefit plans. In the event that the child is not acknowledged by his or her father, it will be difficult for such a child to receive benefits. The biological father of the child will also be responsible for the support of that child if paternity can be proved. For this reason, it may be important for the mother of a child born out of wedlock to identify the father and, whenever possible, for the father to agree to his paternity.

Postbirth Procedures   Another concern to resolve ahead of time with one's physician and the hospital is what procedures will take place in the event that the child is born with some physical or mental handicap. It is customary for certain tests to be performed upon the birth of a child. You should discuss these tests with your physician and the possible course of action available if one or more of them indicates a problem. You should know what to do in the event that your child has certain problems at birth. You should have a general awareness of what kinds of problems can

EXHIBIT 13-3
Patients' Bill of Rights

Patients' Rights (A)   The hospital has written policies regarding the rights of patients and procedures implementing such policies. These rights, policies, and procedures afford a patient the right to:

1. Considerate and respectful care.
2. Upon request, the name of the physician responsible for coordinating the patient's care.
3. The name and function of any person providing health care services to the patient.
4. Obtain from his or her physician complete current information concerning his or her diagnosis, treatment, and prognosis in terms the patient can be reasonably expected to understand. When it is not medically advisable to give such information to the patient, the information shall be made available to an appropriate person in his or her behalf.
5. Receive from his or her physician information necessary to give informed consent prior to the start of any procedure or treatment or both and which, except for those emergency situations not requiring an informed consent, shall include as a minimum the specific procedure or treatment or both, the medically significant risks involved, and the probable duration of incapacitation, if any. The patient shall be advised of medically significant alternatives for care or treatment, if any.
6. Refuse treatment to the extent permitted by law and to be informed of the medical consequences of his or her action.
7. Privacy to the extent consistent with providing adequate medical care to the patient. This shall not preclude discreet discussion of a patient's case or examination of a patient by appropriate health care personnel.
8. Privacy and confidentiality of all records pertaining to the patient's treatment, except as otherwise provided by law or third party payment contract.
9. A response by the hospital in a reasonable manner to the patient's request for services customarily rendered by the hospital consistent with the patient's treatment.
10. Be informed by his or her physician or delegate of the physician of the patient's continuing health care requirements following discharge and that, before transferring a patient to another facility, the hospital first informs the patient of the need for, and alternatives to, such a transfer.
11. The identity, upon request, of other health care and educational institutions that the hospital has authorized to participate in his or her treatment.
12. Refuse to participate in research and that human experimentation affecting care of treatment shall be performed only with his or her informed effective consent.
13. Examine and receive an explanation of his or her bill regardless of source of payment.
14. Know the hospital rules and regulations that apply to his or her conduct as a patient.
15. Treatment without discrimination as to race, color, religion, sex, national origin, or source of payment.

Patients' Rights (B)   A copy of the provisions of this section shall be available to each patient or patient's representatives upon admission and posted in conspicuous places within the hospital.

occur and what disposition you want made if your child is born with such a problem.

For example, in Indiana in April 1982, a child was born with Down's syndrome, a condition that causes mental retardation and physical defects. The child's parents, after discussing the problem with their doctors, decided not to have an operation designed to correct certain physical deformities in the child. The operation would not have affected the child's overall condition. The couple also decided that they did not wish to provide any artificial nourishment for the child, without which, owing to the child's physical defects, it would die. the Indiana Supreme Court in a 3-to-1 decision upheld the parents' right to make such a decision. Lawyers for the child tried to get a U.S. Supreme Court order to keep the baby alive in order to determine whether the parents had the right to enter such action but before any appropriate order could be issued, the child died. It is not clear whether the parents ultimately have the right to make this type of a decision, but if parents have feelings on an issue of this nature, they should be made clear to the doctor and the hospital as early as possible. In addition, parents should identify the hospital's and the doctor's position on such an issue. A given hospital may be reluctant to allow a child to die and may impose lifesaving measures beyond the desires of the parents on its own initiative. This may be out of philosophical differences with the parents' position or out of concern over being held legally responsible for the death of the child or owing to governmental mandate. If you find that your hospital or doctor is unwilling to back up your approach to this problem, you may wish to change your hospital or physician or both.

It is interesting to note that, in the Indiana case, several people had offered to adopt the child, an alternative that this particular couple rejected. It should be noted that many children who have physical and mental handicaps can be placed for adoption in homes that will provide these children with good care, love, and attention. Thus, a couple who is not prepared to deal with a handicapped child should be prepared to surrender that child for adoption. It is this author's opinion that such a surrender should be made as early as possible for the benefit of all parties concerned, and therefore this is an issue that one should consider prior to entering the hospital or having the child.

Abandonment   It should also be noted that abandonment of a child is not an appropriate course of action. A recent example occurred in which a young coed had a child, and because she did not want anyone to know of her identity, left the child on the church steps of a nearby village. It was her hope that the child would be found by the priest and through him placed for adoption in an appropriate home. Unknown to the mother, the priest was away, and before he returned, the child died from exposure. In this kind of a situation, the mother of the child may be subjected to criminal prosecution for a crime as serious as manslaughter or perhaps even murder. A well-informed parent who does not wish to keep a child should have made a decision concerning options available to her before having the child. These options will be discussed later in this chapter but are basically foster care or adoption, either through an agency or privately.

If you give birth in a hospital, the hospital will comply with any appropriate statutes vis-à-vis preparations and submission of a birth certificate, and so on. When you give birth at home, you are required to prepare the appropriate papers yourself. You should check with the midwife assisting the delivery to make sure that each of you knows who is going to take care of the appropriate paperwork.

Artificial Insemination   An additional related topic lies in the area of artificial insemination. Artificial insemination is generally acceptable in most states, but not in all. Some states require that both husband and wife consent to the artificial insemination process. Where state statutes are complied with, a child born as the result of artificial insemination will be considered to be a naturally conceived child of the husband and the wife. Where artificial insemination takes place without the proper consent required by state law, issues can arise as to whether the father, if he was unwilling to allow the insemination, will be considered to be the legal father of the child.

Abortion   Another right that a parent should be aware of is that the mother has the right under the Supreme Court decision handed down in Roe v. Wade (410 U.S. 113 [S. Ct. 1973]) to have an abortion. This decision usually is required to be made during the first three months of pregnancy and may be made by the mother without the consent of any other person. Some states will allow abortion during the second trimester of pregnancy but may require special procedures to be followed. At this time no states allow abortions during the last trimester of pregnancy because of the dangers to both mother and child.

Adoption

Adoption is a legal proceeding by which the relationship of a parent and a child is established between persons who are not related by nature. As a result of the decree of adoption, the child for all intents and purposes becomes the child of the adoptive parent or parents. There is a distinction between the legal act of adopting a child and legitimation of a child. Under legitimation, the child is recognized as the natural child of his or her father, acquiring a legal status enabling him or her to inherit from the father. By adoption, a child acquires only those rights allowed under the adoption statute. The distinction between these two processes is relevant in dealing with the ability of the child to inherit through the father.

Although adoption has been practiced for many centuries, including in ancient Greece and Rome, there is no common law right of adoption under English common law. Accordingly, all the rights and obligations and circumstances of the adoption concept are of statutory origin and nature. A legal adoption cannot be effected by a mere declaration or contract without judicial approval.

State Control over Adoption The theory of most adoption statutes is that the adoption proceedings are based on the consent of the biological parents (or the person having custody of the child), and usually the statutes prescribe from whom consent must be received, the manner of giving the consent, and the circumstances under which consent may be set aside. If the biological parent has custody of the child at the time of the adoption proceedings, practically all statutes require that the consent of the parent be obtained or that such parent be given notice of the proceedings before he or she may be deprived of the parental rights to custody. In most cases, lack of a biological parent's consent defeats an adoption unless the parents have deserted the child or in some other way been guilty of misconduct, such as abuse. It is improper to enter into a contract to sell a child; however, consent of the biological parents will not be considered void merely because they have received money from the prospective adoptive parent for payment of hospital and medical expenses in connection with birth and care of the child.

The determination of who is eligible to adopt someone else is set forth by state statute. Most statutes provide that adoptions may be instituted by, or on behalf of, an adult who is a resident of the state in which the proceeding is being brought. In some cases, there are requirements that the adopting parent be of a specified age, a certain number of years older than the person being adopted, or of the same religion as the child to be adopted. (Most states allow single parent as well as family adoptions.)

State statutes also specify who may be adopted. Many statutes are designed to allow only for the adoption of minors. However, the mere use of the term *child* does not mean that only a minor can be adopted. In many states, the use of the term *child* has been held to include adults. In some states, statutes specifically provide that adults are eligible to be adopted.

Some adoption statutes require a separate examination of the parties, including the child, by the judge before the entry of the decree. The object is to protect those whose consent is essential to the adoption and to enable the court to ascertain whether consent was freely given. Many statutes require an investigation of the home of the adoptive parent to be conducted by duly licensed child placement agencies. In some cases, investigations are also made to determine whether the child is a proper subject for adoption.

Private Adoption Adoption can take one of two forms: private adoption or agency adoption. Private adoption occurs when a child is placed directly with the adoptive parents by the biological parent (or an individual who has guardianship or custody of the child). Private adoptions frequently take place in situations where a new parent is adopting a child (e.g., where a stepparent is adopting after the death or divorce of the second biological parent). Private adoption also takes place in cases where the biological parents of the child do not wish to become involved with an agency in placing out their child. Many biological parents wish to see the children placed in their permanent homes as quickly as possible or may wish to meet the adoptive parents or both. Agencies usually proceed relatively slowly and do not allow biological parents to meet adoptive parents.

Most states allow private placements provided that there is no financial gain to either of the parties involved. In most states an intermediary such as a minister, lawyer, or physician may charge a fee based on reasonable rates for the time spent in performing legitimate services. It is generally considered illegal for an intermediary to collect a fee for the mere transfer of the child or the mere notification to an adoptive couple of the location of a child.

When the biological parents surrender possession of the child to the adoptive parents, they also must surrender legal custody. This is usually accomplished by signing a surrender of the child in a court of law. Signing such a surrender outside of court may require that the surrender be inoperative for a given period of time. If the surrender is executed in front of a judge, it is effective immediately.

If the biological father of the child is unknown and, therefore, unable to consent in these procedures, a statement by the biological mother that the father of the child is unknown will be required. Where the father of the child is known, he must consent to these procedures (Stanley v. Illinois, 405 U.S. 645 [S. Ct. 1972]).

Agency Adoption   When adoption is through an adoption agency, the procedure is slightly different because the agency takes temporary custody of the child before the child is given to the adoptive parent. The advantage of dealing with an agency is that the agency can contact other agencies and groups with children. The disadvantages of dealing with an agency are that most agency placements are accompanied by a great deal of formal procedure and children are generally acquired at an older age. In addition, there is no direct contact between adoptive parent and biological parent. Because there is presently a large excess of willing adoptive parents over the number of children that are available for placement, it is not unusual for a couple to wait several years in order to obtain a child through an agency.

Once a child has been obtained from an agency, he or she will be placed in the home of the adoptive parents on a provisional basis. This is frequently pursuant to a preadoptive hearing. At this hearing, the court rules that the child may be placed in the adoptive home and that the agency will continue to monitor the progress of the child and the adoptive parents. At the end of a statutory period of time, generally six months to one year, an adoption proceeding may be brought. If there have been no negative developments, the adoption will be finalized. At that point in time, the child becomes a permanent member of the adoptive family, and the rights of the agency terminate.

Court Approval   The welfare of a child is the most important consideration in proceedings involving his or her adoption. The court is charged with the duty of protecting the child and the child's interests and has authority to make rules to accomplish that end. The court usually considers the normal ties of love and loyalty created by blood relationships and the conduct of the biological parent who shows a willingness to reassume the parental responsibilities previously neglected. Factors such as the age differential between the prospective adoptive parents and the child or the racial or religious background of the parents and the children are all items that may be considered by the courts.

In most cases when a child reaches a statutory minimum age (usually 10 to 14 years), the child's consent is needed for the adoption to take place. There are also many states that prescribe that a child of a certain age should be given some choice in determining whether or not the adoption should take place. In such cases, the courts are not bound by the child's wishes but may consider them in making their determination.

Birth Certificate　　Once there has been an adoption, most states require the birth certificate of the adoptive child to be changed, substituting the name and other information about the adoptive parents in place of the same information for the biological parents. Many states require that the original birth certificate and all court records pertaining to the adoption be sealed so that they are unavailable to inspection. At the present time, such records can become available only upon court order if required for medical reasons pertaining to the child. Increasing pressure is being brought by adopted children and biological parents to make such records available through an intermediary third party in the event that both the adoptive child and the biological parent agree and wish to make contact with each other. It is unclear at this time what rights, if any, the adoptive parents would have to oppose such contact.

Adoption statutes contemplate a complete severance of the child's relationship with his or her biological parents. A decree of adoption normally terminates all legal relations between the adopted child and his or her biological parents or former legal guardian. However, in some states a child may by statute retain the right to inherit from his or her biological parents. The general and usual effect of a decree of adoption is to confer a legal status of parent and child upon the adopting parents and the adoptive child as a matter of law, with all the legal consequences, obligations, and incidents arising out of that status. The termination of the relationship between the child and his or her biological parents is considered to be permanent and continuous for life. The adoptive parents are as much entitled to the custody of their adopted child as biological parents are to their natural children. The rights of the adoptive parents are of the same nature and scope as those of the biological parents and subject to the same restrictions as that of biological parents.

Foster Care

Foster care is generally a temporary arrangement whereby one family has physical custody and care of the child of another family. Foster care originally was created to provide for the care of children when their parents were temporarily unable to care for them. For example, Mr. and Mrs. A are married. Mr. A works and Mrs. A cares for the children and the household. Mr. A's occupation requires him to be out of the house frequently (e.g., he's a traveling salesperson). Mrs. A dies. Under such circumstances, it may become necessary for Mr. A to obtain a foster home for his children until such time as he can provide a more permanent arrangement. He may go to a social welfare agency in his state and request that they take custody of the children on a temporary basis. They will turn the children over to a foster family until Mr. A can make some other more suitable arrangement.

The responsibilities of a foster parent are generally described by contract or statute or both. The foster parent generally is paid a stipend from the state to provide for the needs of the child. The foster parent also generally has temporary custodial responsibility. He or she may provide for medical care for the children, enroll them in school, and so forth. The biological parents of the children have rights to see them and to visit on a regular basis. Generally, after a short period of time, the biological parents' situation improves, and they can resume control over the children. If the foster care arrangement continues for a certain length of time, without any indication of interest by the biological parents in resuming custody of the child, the supervising agency may bring a judicial procedure to have the child declared eligible for adoption. If such a declaration is made, the foster parents usually have a preference in applying for the adoption of the child. Even though the arrangement is intended as temporary, many foster parents care for children for many years, and in some cases the foster child comes to regard his foster parents as ''real'' parents.

QUESTIONS

1   Plaintiff Graham Parks, age 17, and defendant, Bertha Parks, age 20, lived in North Carolina but were married in Virginia. Under laws of the State of Virginia, the plaintiff was under legal age whereas the defendant was within legal age. Under North Carolina law, any persons of age 16 may be married. The parties were living in North Carolina and went to Virginia only for purposes of getting married. They returned to North Carolina, where they periodically cohabited together. Were the parties married? Was the marriage they entered into voidable? Discuss.

2   Sally Cooper and Daniel Owens left their respective homes one day for parts unknown. Upon their return, they announced that they were married. Several years later they left Florida and moved to Delaware, where Daniel Owens rented a house and represented Sally as his wife. Delaware does not recognize common law marriage. Owens was subsequently drafted and served in the army, at which time Sally collected benefits from his pay as his wife. On several occasions, money was borrowed, and mortgages were signed by both Daniel Owens and Sally Owens. Approximately 25 years later, Daniel Owens married Rose Philips. About a year after this marriage, Sally Cooper died, and her daughter brought an action against Daniel Owens to recover the cost of the funeral on the grounds that Sally and Daniel had been married. Discuss the question of whether or not a valid marriage existed between Sally and Daniel.

3   A state statute required that, where parties get married, if one of the parties has previously been divorced, a certified copy of the divorce decree or certificate of divorce be filed at the time of the new marriage. Failure to do so renders a marriage void from the time it is declared so by a court of competent jurisdiction at the instance of the innocent

party. Mrs. Saunders (defendant) was married to Mr. H. The marriage was terminated by a divorce. Prior to the effectiveness of the divorce, the defendant also married Mr. A, who died four years later. Four years after the death of Mr. A, the defendant married Mr. Saunders. She indicated her prior marriage to Mr. A and his subsequent death but failed to indicate her prior marriage to Mr. H, which had been terminated by divorce. The parties (Mr. and Mrs. Saunders) lived together for eight years. During at least four or five of those years, Mr. Saunders knew of Mrs. Saunders's status as a divorcée. The parties separated, and Mr. Saunders brought an action for an annulment on the grounds that there had been a violation of the statute by Mrs. Saunders at the time of their marriage. Decision for whom? Discuss.

4   Husband and wife were married. Numerous attempts to have sexual intercourse proved ineffective because of the inability of the wife's organ to allow penetration to even the slightest degree. On one occasion, the husband used force in his attempt to penetrate, resulting in ejaculation against the vulva causing a pregnancy. During the trial the evidence showed that husband and wife on several occasions consulted with physicians and psychiatrists with respect to the wife's difficulty. All these attempts failed in that the wife continued to be unable to have sexual intercourse with her husband. At one point when she became pregnant she was physically examined, and it was found that her hymen was intact. The pregnancy was spontaneously aborted, and it became necessary in order to perform a D & C for the physician to remove the hymen surgically. After additional consultation with a psychiatrist, the husband brought an action to have the marriage declared void or voidable, on the grounds that his wife was impotent. Decision for whom? Discuss.

5   Gikas and Nicholis were engaged to be married, and Nicholis broke the engagement. Gikas requested return of the ring as well as other gifts that he had made. She refused, and an action was brought by him to recover the property in question. Decision for whom? Discuss.

6   The defendant, McNab, became casually acquainted with the plaintiff, Morris. He saw her for several years, during which time he told her that his wife had died after a serious illness. The plaintiff and the defendant became engaged and subsequently married. Upon return from their honeymoon, the defendant began spending time away from the plaintiff. The plaintiff subsequently found out that the defendant was married and that the times that he was spending away from the plaintiff were spent with his first wife. The defendant was arrested for bigamy, pleaded guilty, and received a suspended prison sentence. During the time that the plaintiff and the defendant were "married," she advanced money to him. This action was brought by her to recover such moneys on the grounds that they had been obtained by false and fraudulent representations as to their use. The state in which the action was brought had a statute that abolished the right to recover damages for breach of contract to marriage. The defendant's defense was that this action was an action for breach of contract to marry and, therefore, was precluded under the terms of the New Jersey statute. Decision for whom? Discuss.

7   Fannie Dunn married W, who lived with her for four days and then deserted her. She then married Ernest. W, four years prior to living with Fannie, was married to M, who subsequently died. Thereafter, W married A, who abandoned him, and thereafter he allegedly married Fannie Dunn. Were Fannie Dunn and Ernest Dunn husband and wife? Discuss.

8 The plaintiff became emotionally upset upon learning that she was pregnant and that there was no possibility of assistance from the father of the child. She conferred with an attorney representing the defendants concerning giving the child to them for adoption. Shortly after the birth of her child, the plaintiff went to the office of the attorney, who explained the adoption forms to her, and then she signed them. There was no question of fraud or duress. About 20 days later, the plaintiff told a state welfare investigator that she did not want to give her child up and was withdrawing her consent. A notice to this effect was filed with the probate court (which had jurisdiction over adoption hearings), and the plaintiff, through her attorney, filed an objection to the approval of the adoption obligation. The defendants had taken the child from the hospital with the approval of the plaintiff and had cared for her up through the date of the proceeding. They were found to be suitable parents in a position to give the child a proper upbringing in a normal home atmosphere. They had paid all the expenses involved in the birth of the child. No money was paid to the plaintiff for the child. Should the adoption proceeding be allowed to take place, or should the child be returned to the mother? Discuss.

9 Carol Bair was living in the home of her mother-in-law with her child. Her husband was living elsewhere. Mrs. Maytia visited Mrs. Bair's mother-in-law, who suggested that Mrs. Maytia and her husband take the child into their home and care for him. Carol was present and made no objection to this proposition. About 3 months later, Mr. and Mrs. Bair visited the Maytias and requested the return of the child. Mr. Maytia angrily told Mr. Bair to take the baby and leave; however, he did not do so. Approximately 11 months later, an adoption proceeding was commenced by the Maytias. Since the first visit of the Bairs to the Maytias, there had been no further contact at all between them. The mother of the child signed a consent and stated that she wished to have custody of the child. Decision for whom? Discuss.

The following questions will require some knowledge of constitutional law (see Chapter 1) and may require referral to the case for meaningful discussion.

10 A state statute provided that persons who wished to be married had to obtain a license, for purposes of which they had to submit information, among other items, concerning their racial background (i.e., white, Mongolian, Negro, Malayan, or mulatto). Mr. Stokes and his prospective wife refused to fill out this particular section of the application, and the clerk refused to issue the license. The plaintiffs argued that this disclosure would inhibit or restrict their freedom of religion and liberty of conscience and would violate due process afforded them under the Fourteenth Amendment of the Constitution. In support of their contention, they cited a case holding that a statute prohibiting marriages between white persons and members of other races was unconstitutional. Is it proper for the state to request information concerning the racial background of potential spouses? Decision for whom? Discuss.

11 A statute in the State of Virginia made it a crime for a white person to marry a person of another race and vice versa. The statute also provided that persons who left the state in order to be married and then returned to the state would be considered as having violated the statute as if they had been married within the State of Virginia. Mr. Loving and Miss Jeter left Virginia, were married in the District of Columbia, and shortly thereafter returned to Virginia. A grand jury issued an indictment charging them with violating the statute to which they pleaded guilty. They were sentenced to one year in jail, which was suspended on condition that they leave the state and not return. Several years later, while residents outside Virginia, they brought an action to vacate the judgment on the grounds that the statutes in question violated the Fourteenth Amendment. Should the statute be upheld? Discuss.

12 Joan Stanley and Peter Stanley lived together for 18 years without being married; they had three children. When Joan Stanley died, the state took the children and placed them into homes with court-appointed guardians. The state statute specified that the state had the right and requirement to assume custody for children of unmarried fathers upon the death of the mother. No such requirement existed with respect to married fathers or unmarried mothers. Stanley brought this action, claiming that such a statute was unconstitutional in that it violated the equal protection clause of the Constitution (Fourteenth Amendment). Decision for whom? Discuss.

13 Olga Scarpetta, the plaintiff, was an unmarried native of Colombia. Seeking to avoid the shame of an out-of-wedlock child to herself and her family, she came to New York for the purpose of having the child. She was a well-educated woman, trained in the area of social sciences. Four days after the birth of her child, she placed it for board and care with the Spence Chapin Adoption Service. Ten days later she executed a document that surrendered the child to the agency. Seventeen days later the agency placed the child with a family for adoption. Five days later (22 days after signing the surrender document), the mother changed her mind and requested that the child be returned. Before surrendering the child, the mother had numerous conversations with representatives of the adoption agency. She had also been advised by her family in Colombia that they would support and back her if she attempted to raise her own child rather than surrendering it for adoption and that they strongly disapproved of the adoption. The persons who received custody of the child had not adopted the child at the time this procedure was brought. Decision for whom? Discuss.

14 Mr. Caban and Mrs. Mohammed lived together as husband and wife (although they were never married) and had several children. Both parties contributed economically and psychologically to the well-being of the family. Mohammed left Caban, took up residence with her husband-to-be, and took the children with her. For several months she allowed the children to visit with her mother, who lived in the same building as Mr. Caban. He was thus able to visit with the children on a weekly basis. When the defendant's mother returned to Puerto Rico, she took the children with her. Mr. Caban was able to communicate with the children through his mother and father, who also lived in Puerto Rico. At one point he went to visit them, received custody of the children for a temporary period of time, and, instead of returning them, took them with him back to New York. At this point Mrs. Mohammed filed a petition to adopt the children, and within two months Caban also filed a petition for adoption. The state statute provides that consent to an adoption will be required from the mother of a child born out of wedlock. The court found in favor of Mohammed and allowed her to adopt the children. Caban filed an appeal in the Supreme Court arguing that the state statute denied him equal protection under the Fourteenth Amendment. Decision for whom? Discuss.

15 Baker and McConnell, both adult males, made application to Nelson, the county clerk in Minnesota, for a marriage license. The clerk refused to issue the license on the ground that the plaintiffs were of the same sex. The plaintiffs brought a proceeding to require issuance of a marriage license on the grounds that the statute does not specifically exclude persons of the same sex from being married and that to do so would be a violation of their constitutional rights (specifically under the equal protection laws). Decision for whom? Discuss.

CHAPTER 14

Dissolution of the Family Unit

ANNULMENT

The term *annul* means "to declare invalid." An annulment of marriage dates back to the inception of the marriage. It is a declaration that the marriage never came into being. Where no marriage relationship was ever entered into, because the statute declares the attempted marriage void, it is unnecessary to obtain an annulment. In such a situation, an annulment may be sought to make a permanent record of the facts for future reference.

The grounds for annulment are usually set forth in state statutes, but in some states include common law grounds. Typical grounds for annulment include lack of age, preexisting marriage, incest, fraud, duress, lack of understanding, impotence, insanity, and, in some cases, drunkenness, jest or dare, venereal disease, narcotics addiction, and so on.

Fraud

A marriage may be held invalid for lack of consent if procured or induced by fraud. Fraud or misrepresentation must be of a material fact and made with the intent of inducing the other party to enter into a marriage relationship, without which representation he or she would not have so done. In determining what constitutes fraud in the relationship of a marriage contract, we must look to the age and character of the parties and the other circumstances under which the alleged fraud took place.

The representation must go to the fundamentals of the marriage relationship. Thus, where a party promises to perform marital obligations and at no time intends to go through with such promise and, in fact, does not perform such promises, such a fraudulent representation would go to the heart of the marriage contract and constitute grounds for avoidance of contract (for example, where a foreign individual enters into a marital relationship for the sole purpose of gaining admission to the United States without any intent to assume the marital obligation). A fraudulent representation of intention to have children generally would be grounds to declare a marriage void (Stegienko v. Stegienko, 295 N.W. 252 [Mich. 1940]).

As a general rule, representations as to character, wealth, or social position of a party to a marriage will not invalidate a marriage although there are cases to the contrary, where such representations are made to take advantage of persons who are young, naive, old, or of limited intelligence (Marshall v. Marshall, 300 P. 816 [Cal. 1931]). Representations as to age or religious affiliation may or may not constitute grounds for terminating a marriage depending upon the jurisdiction in which they take place. Representations concerning physical or mental abilities generally do not invalidate marriage except where there are serious diseases.

False representations as to prior chastity generally are not grounds for voiding a marriage; continued lack of chastity generally will constitute grounds. If the female falsely represents that she is pregnant, the husband generally may not have the marriage declared void; however, if she conceals the fact that she is pregnant by another and he marries her, he generally will be able to disaffirm the marriage. An act of fraud must be such as to affect the injured party's free consent to such contract (Wetstine v. Wetstine, 157 A. 418 [Conn. 1931]).

Duress

A marriage contracted under duress may also be declared void by the courts. The most common situation of alleged duress is where two parties have a premarital sexual relationship and the male is forced to marry the female in order to legitimize the baby. The general rule is that this type of a situation will not be legally recognized as duress. Marriage in order to escape prosecution for seduction or other sexual offense is not subject to disaffirmance because of duress. However, where there is a threat of personal violence and it continues until the marriage ceremony, the courts have often declared the marriage invalid for lack of consent on the part of the coerced party (Lee v. Lee, 35 S.W.2d 672 [Ark. 1928]).

The grounds for annulment must have existed at the time of the marriage rather than having arisen subsequent thereto. Thus, if a person was sane at the time of entering into a marriage, but becomes mentally incapacitated thereafter, the other party is not entitled to an annulment. If the mental incapacity existed at the time of the marriage, then an annulment may be requested. If grounds for an annulment existed at the time the marriage was entered into, the condition need not continue for the aggrieved party to be entitled to an annulment.

Defenses

The primary defense to an action of annulment is that the party requesting the annulment was aware of the grounds at the time of entering into the marriage. Such a defense generally will not apply to cases where by statute the marriage is void. It would apply only in incidents where the statutory position is that the marriage is voidable. If an individual finds that he or she has grounds for an annulment and continues cohabitation, an annulment will generally be denied on the theory of ratification or condonation (Wetstine v. Wetstine, 157 A. 418 [Conn. 1931]).

Entering into a separation agreement or suing for a divorce implies a recognition of the fact that a marriage was entered into; an annulment is a request to the court to declare that there was no marriage. These two require different positions, and it would be inconsistent to allow both types of actions.

DIVORCE

Introduction

A divorce is a judicial dissolution of marriage. Just as the bases of the marriage relationship are controlled by statute, the bases for divorce are also controlled by statute. The reason for a divorce is an act of marital misconduct as defined by statute arising after the marriage ceremony. (A divorce changes the status of the parties to that of single persons.) Recently, many state statutes have allowed divorces where neither party is at fault (''no fault'' divorces).

Public policy generally favors and encourages marriage. Public policy also generally recognizes a marriage relationship as a permanent one lasting for the lifetime of the parties. Divorce is allowed only in a situation where the state feels that the marital relationship of the parties can no longer be sustained, that is, where the relationship between the husband and the wife is no longer consistent with the marriage relationship.

Grounds for Divorce

The basis for granting a divorce is entirely within the area of legislative discretion. It is not necessary that a state recognize grounds that are recognized in other states. New York for many years had only one ground for divorce, namely, adultery, and refused to recognize grounds that existed in other states. Only when the legislature finally decided to amend its laws and institute new grounds for divorce in New York were those other offenses acceptable as the basis for a divorce action in that state. In determining whether or not grounds for divorce exist, it is appropriate to look at the law in effect in the place of domicile of the person bringing the action.

Adultery   Adultery is usually defined as sexual intercourse between a married person and someone other than his or her spouse. Most states do not recognize any distinction between the adultery of the husband or the adultery of the wife in determining the seriousness of the offense. In order to constitute adultery, the act of the offending spouse must show intent to commit such an act. Thus, where an individual believes that he or she has been divorced and, based on that belief, cohabits with another individual, this in and of itself does not constitute adultery.

Commission and Conviction of Crime   In order to obtain a divorce on the basis of commission and conviction of crime, it is necessary to prove that the other spouse has been convicted. The specific crime for which a divorce may be obtained depends upon the wording of the statute. In some states, the statute refers to a felony; in others, to infamous crimes; and in still others, crimes involving turpitude. In a determination as to whether a particular crime is grounds for divorce, it will also be necessary to look at the cases in that jurisdiction. Similar crimes have been held, under identical statutes, to be the basis for a divorce in one jurisdiction and not in another. If the crime was committed prior to the marriage, and the noncommitting party was aware of it before contracting the marriage, it may not be the basis of an action for divorce. In some states, a sentence to imprisonment for life automatically terminates a marriage without any judgment of divorce.

Cruelty   There appears to be no universal definition of cruelty, and courts will deal with each individual situation on its own merits. The terms in various state statutes include *cruelty*, *extreme cruelty*, and *cruel and inhuman treatment*, and they generally are interpreted to include similar types of offenses. Determining whether or not there is cruelty usually depends on the reaction of the victim rather than the intent of the perpetrator; thus, a spouse is charged with the responsibility to behave toward a fellow spouse in a manner consistent with that second individual's needs and desires and not merely with what would be normal in a given society. If the passions of the husband are so much out of his own control that continuance in his society is inconsistent with the personal safety of the wife, it is immaterial from what provocations such violence originated.

Where the act complained about is a single occurrence, it would be possible to argue that, in the absence of malice or malicious intent, there was only an innocent act, which by itself does not constitute cruelty. A repeated course of action, however, could not be dismissed as something other than cruelty. Some states require intent to establish a case for cruelty. In these states, no suffering is necessary—only the intent to do the act that was committed.

Cruelty may be based on physical acts, threats of physical violence, and mental cruelty. Verbal abuse constitutes a ground for divorce as cruelty only where it is accompanied by hatred, malevolence, or spite. Mental cruelty constitutes a ground for divorce provided that the misconduct impairs or threatens to impair the physical or mental health of the victim.

In determining whether cruelty exists, one should examine the intelligence, refinement, and delicacy of sentiment of the complaining party. As stated in one court, ''It is not all unlawful and barbarous acts that are made grounds of divorce. We do not divorce savages and barbarians because they act as such toward each other'' (Nye's appeal 17 A. 618 [Pa. 1889]).

There is an increasing tendency on the part of jurisdictions to recognize the validity of separating parties where their marriage clearly cannot function in a viable manner. To this extent, courts are liberalizing their interpretation of what constitutes cruelty in order to enable parties to obtain relief from an otherwise unacceptable or intolerable situation.

Duress Duress consists of force, restraint, or threats, such as to overcome one's will and bring about a marriage to which consent would not otherwise have been given. If at the time of the marriage there was an exercise of free will, even though proceeded by threats of death or grievous bodily harm, there is no basis for a divorce on the grounds of duress. In the case of the so-called shotgun marriage, courts are divided in their opinions as to whether an individual in this position is acting under duress or whether the individual has simply ''seen the light'' and is voluntarily going through with the marriage ceremony (Lee v. Lee, 3 S.W.2d 672 [Ark. 1928]; Jones v. Jones, 314 S.W.2d 448 [Tex. 1958]).

Fraud Fraud is a misrepresentation of a material fact made with the intent of inducing the other party to enter into a marriage relationship, without which representation he or she would not have done so. Fraud must relate to a matter essential to the validity of the marriage itself. Misrepresentations as to a party's age, name, and nationality are not the types of things that would generally lead to an action for divorce. If a party makes representations as to willingness to change religious affiliations and subsequently fails to honor these commitments, it may constitute fraud.

Impotence Impotence is the inability to have sexual intercourse. The consummation of a marriage is implicit in every marriage contract. Failure to do so may be grounds for divorce. Sexual intercourse as used in the statutory context implies ordinary and complete intercourse. The cause of the impotence is not relevant. Impotence that occurs after the marriage is not grounds for a divorce (T, plaintiff, v. M, falsely called T, defendant, 242 A.2d 670 [N.J. 1968]).

Sterility, the inability to have children, is not a basis for a divorce. If the sterile party has falsely represented that he or she is capable of having children, a divorce may be obtained on the grounds of fraud.

Insanity or Mental Incapacity *Insanity* is a term that is interpreted differently in different states. Some statutes refer to incurable insanity; others, to specific mental defects such as feeblemindedness, epilepsy, or chronic or recurrent insanity. Such statutes are generally strictly construed.

Desertion and Abandonment *Desertion* is a voluntary separation by the husband from the wife or the voluntary refusal to renew a suspended cohabitation without justification. *Abandonment* occurs when the wife leaves the husband. We will use the terms interchangeably. As a general rule, the spouse who unjustifiably leaves the other or refuses to resume marital cohabitation is the one guilty of desertion. However, in some jurisdictions, if one spouse through misconduct gives the other just cause for leaving, the former may be guilty of "constructive" desertion.

In order to find desertion, one must find cessation of cohabitation without cause and with willful or malicious intent to abandon. Intent to desert is extremely important as it represents an intent to terminate the marriage relationship. There are many cases in which parties may live apart without any intent to terminate the marriage relationship, and these would not constitute desertion. Where a party has to leave his or her spouse because of lack of support, medical reasons, or armed forces requirements, there is usually no intent to terminate the marriage. Any separation may ripen into desertion when the party leaving develops the intent not to return.

Desertion is required to continue for an uninterrupted period, frequently as short a period as one (1) year. If there is an offer on the part of the deserting individual to resume cohabitation or actual cohabitation resumes during the statutory period, this indicates that the intent to refrain from cohabitation no longer exists and, therefore, the desertion at that point is ended. This is true even where the other spouse refuses to resume cohabitation. If there is a period of time when the desertion is suspended and cohabitation has resumed, if the party leaves again, there is a new period of time that has to meet the statutory requirement.

Separation Separation differs from desertion in that both parties agree to live apart. Many jurisdictions specify that parties who live apart for a given length of time are entitled to a divorce. The theory of such statutory provisions generally is that if individuals have lived apart for a given period of time, it is an indication of their intent not to resume the reality of the marriage relationship. It would be better for society as a whole, as well as for the individuals involved, that they should be allowed to live separately.

It is important in reading the statutory provisions to determine whether a mere living apart is satisfactory or whether there has to be a written agreement or judicial decree of separation before the separation period actually begins to run. In New York State, for example, the statute provides that a divorce will be granted upon a separation of one (1) year pursuant to a written separation agreement or a judicial decree of separation. Parties who separate and live apart without such a written agreement are not entitled to a divorce on a basis of separation, no matter how long they have been living apart from each other.

Separation requires a physical separation of the parties with requisite intent not to resume marital relations. If there is a resumption of cohabitation or sexual intercourse, this will nullify the running of the separation period. If there is a temporary absence of one of the parties, such as to arrange for a relocation or to seek employment elsewhere, it is not a period of separation as would meet the statutory requirements. If during that temporary separation there is an intent formed to make the separation permanent, at that point the statutory period would begin. There is some conflict of authority (and it may result from differences in wordings of statutes) as to whether parties can live under the same roof and still be considered living separate and apart. In Gates v. Gates, 232 S.W. 378 (Ken. 1921), the court held that living separate and apart requires occupancy of different premises. However, other courts have held that the key is not whether parties live under separate roofs but whether they live separate lives (Boyce v. Boyce, 153 F.2d 229 [D.C. 1945]).

No-Fault Divorce   In addition to the various grounds for divorce listed above, most states today provide for so-called no-fault divorces. The traditional grounds for divorce establish one party as guilty and the other as innocent. Frequently, this will have an effect on the issues of alimony and custody. This often leads to protracted and acrimonious divorce proceedings.

In order to avoid such difficulties, all states with the exception of Illinois and South Dakota have adopted no-fault divorce in one form or another (as of August 1, 1980). Many of the no-fault statutes refer to "irretrievable breakdown" of the marriage or to the "irreconcilable differences" of the parties.

In many other states, a divorce may be obtained after a period of living apart (typically, six months to five years). Some states establish no-fault as the sole ground for divorce; other states retain traditional grounds as well as no-fault.

Alimony and Other Allowances

Although the primary objective of a divorce is to terminate the marriage relationship, divorce also affects the financial and property arrangements of the parties.

Alimony is an allowance for the support and maintenance of one of the divorced parties. It is possible for a husband to pay alimony to the wife or for a wife to pay alimony to the husband. Alimony awards are usually made payable in installments at stated intervals. Some jurisdictions, however, require that alimony be awarded as a lump sum payment.

It is not required in every case of a divorce that the court decree alimony. This is an issue that is at the discretion of the trial court, and a number of factors may be presented to justify the denial or granting of alimony. These factors include such things as the misconduct of the spouse, the financial conditions of the respective parties, and any contractual agreements that the parties have entered into regarding their support.

Alimony is broken into categories: temporary and permanent. Temporary alimony is an allowance made to the spouse during the period while the divorce action is pending. Permanent alimony begins from the declaration of divorce and continues thereafter under the terms and conditions set forth in the decree. Generally, unless there is a statutory provision to the contrary, permanent alimony will not be awarded to a wife if the husband obtains a divorce on the grounds of marital misconduct. Some states expressly prohibit awards to wives who are guilty of marital misconduct; other states will allow such an award.

Alimony is usually not based on the terms of the marriage contract, but on the legal duty of a husband to support his wife and vice versa. Once an individual accepts the obligation of supporting another, the state considers that agreement of vital concern to itself and will not allow the individual to terminate that obligation by divorce or by driving the other party to a divorce. Thus, in some states, where parties have been divorced for many years and they have agreed at their divorce that they were not to pay each other alimony, if one of them subsequently should become impoverished and should seek the aid of welfare, the former spouse can nonetheless be obligated to make payments to the now needy spouse. Alimony is not to be considered a punishment to the payor or a benefit to the payee, but rather a judgment by the state maintaining the obligation that one spouse previously accepted for support of the other.

Since alimony is a provision for subsequent needs of the spouse, it is generally not available to pay debts incurred prior to the decree of divorce. Debts that the wife incurs may be charged against her alimony. As a general rule, the death of either party or the remarriage of the payee terminates the obligation of alimony.

Some states will allow a wife to receive alimony if she has been guilty of desertion or cruelty, but not if she has been guilty of adultery. The ultimate determination as to the availability of alimony generally and the amount thereof and the circumstances under which it will be awarded are within the discretion of the court and are controlled by statutory provisions.

Statutes provide that a decree of alimony can subsequently be modified if it can be determined that the positions of the parties have changed. If there is an application for a change, the courts must consider the relative needs and obligations of the parties involved. It is not sufficient to find for a modification of alimony that one spouse's needs have increased beyond their measure at the time of the divorce. If the other spouse's needs have also increased and his or her income has not kept pace, a court has the right to refuse to grant the modification of the previous alimony award. If, however, the other spouse has substantially increased his or her earning potential without increasing his or her needs and the first spouse's needs have also increased, many courts will grant an additional sum of alimony to the first spouse.

Alimony should be distinguished from property settlements. A property settlement is a procedure that takes place when the parties to a divorce divide the property that they own and have acquired during their period of marriage together. In some cases, alimony settlements and property settlements are intertwined and made conditional upon each other; however, this is not necessary. An alimony settlement cannot be such as to deprive the state of its interest in protecting the parties.

Child support is usually considered a separate aspect of the divorce settlement procedures, and although the tax laws consider it a separate concept for legal purposes, it generally comes under the category of alimony. Since the parties have an obligation for support of the children after the marriage has been terminated, part of the provisions for one spouse's support is to take care of their obligations toward the children of the marriage. Therefore, as the needs or circumstances of the children change, a modification in the amount of the alimony provisions may be required. This is particularly true when children have educational requirements as they grow older.

Custody of Children after Divorce

Statutes generally authorize the court having jurisdiction of divorce proceedings to determine who shall have care and custody of the children of the marriage. Courts take into consideration the circumstances of each particular case and place the children in an environment that will provide them with proper care, attention, and education. The welfare of the child is the chief consideration. The financial condition of the parents is a relevant but not controlling factor. There are cases where custody has been awarded to a mother despite the fact that the father has superior financial resources. The wishes of the children who are mature enough to make and express a rational opinion may also be considered by the court.

There are several rules that courts will follow in placing children. Custody of an infant or a girl of more mature years will generally be given to the mother if she is fit and can supply a proper home. Attitudes of society generally are changing in this regard, and it could be expected that a larger percentage of courts in the future will be awarding children to male parents or to both parties under a joint custody arrangement.

Joint custody is a situation in which both parents have the legal custody of and responsibility for their child or children. They create an arrangement for sharing the responsibility of raising the children as well as physical control of their children's environment. In some cases, the child or children will spend an equal amount of time in the home of each of the parents, alternating between the two houses either weekly or monthly as is deemed appropriate by the parents and the court. This is a particularly suitable arrangement for mature parents who can deal with the involvement of the other parent in the upbringing of the child or children. It is also suitable where the physical proximity of both parents is such that transporting the child or children back and forth does not become a problem. If one parent were living in New York and the other in California, a joint custody arrangement might be difficult to work out in that the child or children might spend a great deal of time traveling back and forth between two states.

A court may grant divided or alternating custody by awarding custody to one parent for part of a year and then to the other parent for the remainder, repeating this each year. Courts have recognized that where one parent has custody for the bulk of the year (such as during the school year), the child or children will benefit from the input of the other parent even though the amount of time spent with that second parent is less. Courts feel that the presence of both a male and a female parent can be of extreme value to children as opposed to the input of only the male or only the female parent.

There are, however, a number of cases in which courts have declared their hostility toward divided or shared custody and suggest that it should be approved only under very exceptional circumstances (McLemore v. McLemore, 346 S.W.2d 722 [Ky. 1961]). Many authorities feel that this type of custody is detrimental to the child because it tends to shift the child from location to location and school to school, depriving the child of a real home and permanent friendships. (But see also Mansfield v. Mansfield, 42 N.W.2d 315 [Minn. 1950].)

A parent of a child cannot be disqualified because of his or her religious beliefs. If there is a difference in the religious backgrounds of the parents, the only consideration that the courts may deal with is whether the views of one parent are dangerous to the child's health or moral welfare (Welker v. Welker, 129 N.W.2d 134 [Wis. 1964]). If the religious beliefs of a parent threaten the welfare or the health of a child or would be such as would lead the parent to neglect the welfare of the child, it is grounds for selecting someone else as the guardian of the child (Battaglia v. Battaglia, 172 N.Y.S.2d 361 [N.Y. 1958]). Many cases have held that, all other considerations being equal, custody of children will be awarded to the innocent spouse.

There are a number of cases where courts have awarded the custody of a minor child to someone other than one of the parents (a grandparent, aunt, or uncle). Although there is a presumption that generally operates that a parent is the logical choice for custody of the child and that it is in the child's best interests to place him or her with the parent, there are a number of situations in which it can be determined that this presumption is, in fact, not valid, and in such cases the court will grant custody to a third person. Typically, in order for such custody to be awarded to a third person, that person has to request receiving custody. Furthermore, the burden of proof is generally on the third person to show that custody should not be awarded to the parent because the parent is unfit.

A contractual agreement (e.g., separation agreement) between parents as to who is to receive custody of the child will be considered by the court but is not binding upon it. If the parent selected by the contract is unfit or is not the most fit, the courts may award custody contrary to the terms of the contract if they feel it is in the best interests of the child.

The awarding of the custody of a child confers upon the guardian the right to determine all matters concerning that child's upbringing. Thus, the guardian of the child has discretion as to where the child should go to school, where the child should live, what religious training the child should receive, and so forth. In some cases, a guardian may be restricted from moving from one location to another because such a move might deny visitation rights to parents or grandparents.

In families with more than one child, courts have the authority to place children with each of the parents. Thus, if two parents have three or four children, several of them may go to one parent; and several, to the other. It is generally considered that the best interests of the children are for them to remain together. The controlling factor in many situations of this type is the distinct preference of older children to be with a particular parent who would not have been the logical choice of the court.

If custody of a minor child is awarded to one parent, a provision may be inserted in the divorce decree or the custody decree granting visitation rights to the parent who does not have custody. It is proper for the decree to provide specifically for such visitation rights because, in their absence, it is not clear what those rights are and under what circumstances the noncustodial parent can have temporary custody of the child. In order to avoid conflict between the parents subsequently—which conflict would be of extreme detriment to the child's welfare—it is desirable to incorporate visitation provisions in the decree itself.

It is also permissible for a court to deny visitation rights to a particular parent (Runsvold v. Runsvold, 143 P.2d 746 [Cal. 1943]). The determination of whether or not to give visitation rights to the noncustodial parent is a question of determining the welfare and best interests of the child. Courts must also consider the natural and inherent rights of parents. A prior history of cruelty on the part of a parent toward a child may be sufficient grounds to deny visitation rights to that particular parent. Visitation is usually restricted to reasonable periods.

EMANCIPATION

Emancipation is the doctrine that refers to the status of a child who has become independent. Typically, a child is subject to the control and supervision of his or her parents and entitled to support from his or her parents. A parent has a right to the earnings of the child and to utilize such for the parents' own needs (which would include support of the child). A child may become emancipated by performing an act on an ongoing basis that is inconsistent with being the dependent of another individual. Such actions include marriage, working and living away from home, joining military service, agreement, or court order. The process of emancipation does not render the child an adult, but rather allows the child to assume responsibility for his or her own behavior as though he or she were an adult. It also releases the parents from the primary obligation of supporting the child.

ABUSE AND NEGLECT

A parent or guardian has a responsibility to maintain the health and welfare of the child. If the parent or guardian is delinquent, the child may be removed. The parent may be subject to criminal prosecution, based on the severity of the offensive act. Abuse or neglect may be based on psychological, as well as physiological, damage.

Failure to provide medical care will be considered abuse or neglect even when based on religious principles. The state may intervene and order the medical care. If the medical care can be proved to be a necessity, the possibility of criminal prosecution exists.

DEATH

Cost of Death

Approximately 2 million people die annually in the United States. Funeral arrangements are generally made by survivors within a matter of hours. This does not leave time for comparison shopping, determination of what is most appropriate, and the like. Add to this the emotional vulnerability of the family, and one can readily see why funerals are as expensive as they are. In 1982 the average cost of a funeral was $2500 and represents the third largest purchase for most families (a house and a car being the first and second). This figure excludes the cost of vaults, flowers, burial clothes, newspaper notices, clergy honorariums, and transportation of the body from one place to another. It also excludes crematory or cemetery costs, including the plot opening, closing of the grave, monuments, or markers.

Usual standard items included in the price of the funeral are removal of the body to the funeral establishment (provided that the body is located nearby), use of the funeral home facilities, embalming and restoration, dressing the remains, the coffin, use of a hearse, various staff services, arranging for religious services, burial permits, death benefits and newspaper notices, arranging the bier of flowers, providing a guest register and acknowledgment cards, and the extension of credit in so far as the funeral bill may not be payable immediately. Where a funeral parlor advertises a complete package or a complete funeral, it is important to identify what items are included in the package. The Federal Trade Commission, on July 28, 1982, recommended that all funeral parlors be required to itemize all charges to allow customers to select those services they want and not pay for others. The Federal Trade Commission's recommendation also would require funeral parlors to give prices by phone.

In a discussion of funeral costs with an undertaker, it is desirable to obtain a detailed breakdown in writing of all the costs involved. Exhibit 14–1 is a typical form provided by a funeral establishment, showing a computation of all the aspects of the funeral together with a contract for services. Obtaining such a contract in writing is the consumer's best protection against unscrupulous funeral directors. Nobody should sign such a contract without first having time to read it and think about it. Whenever possible, it is desirable that a person who is not as emotionally upset as the immediate family go to the funeral home and attend to the negotiation of the funeral service. The ability to think clearly and carefully is of the utmost importance at the time of entering into such a contract.

California, Colorado, Florida, Minnesota, New Jersey, and New York require a written itemization of funeral charges by law. Other states may require a price disclosure but may not require that such disclosure be by individual components. In states that do not have specific requirements, it may be difficult to find a funeral director who is willing to itemize the charges. If you find this to be the case, consider the possibility that it may be in the funeral director's best interest not to provide such an itemization. This should serve as a warning, and you should consider whether this is the individual you wish to use.

Embalming

One of the services routinely sold by funeral parlors is embalming. The price of embalming is fairly substantial. It is often sold as a protective measure to prevent the spread of disease. Experts disagree as to whether embalming protects public health or not. Some people argue that embalming kills germs that may be dangerous to those who handle bodies. Other tests have shown that the embalming process, though it kills off a certain percentage of germs, generally does not kill most of them and frequently not the ones that are the most dangerous. The embalming process is often for the convenience or economic necessity of the funeral parlor. Funeral parlor workers prefer dealing with embalmed bodies because there is less odor and unpleasant physical deterioration. Refrigeration facilities are expensive and, therefore, even though they would represent an alternative to embalming, are frequently not available. An appropriate alternative to embalming is the immediate disposition of the body.

Some states will require embalming in the event that a body is not disposed of within 24 to 48 hours. Other states will require embalming if the body is to be transported by public carrier or in some cases from one community to another. Where death has occurred as a result of a communicable disease, embalming frequently is required by state law. Some states also allow refrigeration or enclosure in a tightly sealed outer container as an alternative to embalming.

Burial

Burial vaults (containers that enclose a coffin) are also generally not required by state law. Therefore, the purchase of such an item is voluntary. Some cemeteries,

IDENTIFICATION OF CHARGES

FUNERAL PURCHASE AGREEMENT

C. H. LANDERS, Inc.
21 Main Street
Sidney, New York 13838

Name _____ 19 _____
Date of death _____ Age _____
Place of death _____

Deceased is **(relation)** _____
of person arranging service.

A. Personal & Professional
   Service $ _____
B. Facilities & Equipment $ _____
C. Casket as selected $ _____
                          Funeral Price $ _____

I. Additional Merchandise $ _____
II. Cash Advanced $ _____
                               Total $ _____

III. Items Ordered Later $ _____
                               Total $ _____

TERMS: The debt represented by this agreement is due immediately after completion of the service to be rendered. However, no interest will be added, if account is paid in full by _____ (ANNUAL PERCENTAGE RATE OF 12%) may be added to the debt or any portion thereof unpaid on the last day of each month thereafter. The total annual interest charge will be _____ If this agreement is placed in the hands of an attorney for collection, I, or we, agree to pay attorney's fees of fifteen percent (15%) of all principal and interest owing or a minimum of **twenty** dollars ($20.00).

The foregoing statement has been read to me/us and I/we hereby acknowledge receipt of completed copy. I/we assume responsibility for payment along with such additional services and/or items ordered by me/us, and agree to terms of payment described above. (The liability hereby assumed is in addition to the liability imposed by law upon the estate and others, and shall not constitute a release thereof.

_____
(SIGNATURE OF PURCHASER)

_____
ADDRESS

_____
(SIGNATURE OF CO-SIGNER)

_____
ADDRESS

A. PERSONAL & PROFESSIONAL SERVICES

1. Transfer of deceased from home, hospital or other
2. Embalming
3. Preparation other than embalming
4. Personal and staff service for arrangements, supervision

TOTAL "A" $ _____

B. FACILITIES & EQUIPMENT

1. Operating room facilities
2. Funeral home facilities
3. Service car for local transfer
4. Casket coach for local burial
5. _____ passenger cars at $ _____
6. Flower car
7. Transportation outside local area:
   Casket coach to _____
   _____ passenger cars at $ _____
   to _____

TOTAL "B" $ _____

C. CASKET AS SELECTED

Type
Supplier
Material
Kind, gauge or weight of metal
Species of wood
Model or No.
Interior

We agree to provide services and merchandise as described above.

C. H. LANDERS, Inc.   BY: _____ N. Y. License # _____

REMARKS: _____

I. ADDITIONAL MERCHANDISE

a. Outside burial receptacle
b. Burial garments or clothing
c. Visitor register
d. Memorial cards
e. Acknowledgement cards
f. Prayer or holy cards
g.

TOTAL I $ _____

II. CASH ADVANCED

a. Cemetary charge
b. Clergy
c. Telephone & Telegraph
d. Death notices
e. Organist
f. Winter Vault charge
g. Flowers
h. Cemetery equipment
i. Certified transcripts
j. Hairdresser
k. Clark Livery Service (funeral coach)
l. _____

TOTAL II $ _____

III. ITEMS ORDERED LATER

a.
b.
c.

TOTAL III $ _____

EXHIBIT 14-1, cont.

C. H. LANDERS, Inc.

FUNERAL DIRECTORS   SIDNEY, NEW YORK

IDENTIFICATION OF STANDARD CHARGES

A. PERSONAL & PROFESSIONAL SERVICE

1. Transfer of deceased from home, hospital or other _____

2. Embalming _____

3. Preparation other than embalming _____

4. Personal and staff service for arrangements, supervision _____

TOTAL "A" $ _____

B. FACILITIES & EQUIPMENT

1. Operating room facility _____

2. Funeral home facilities _____

3. Auto Equipment _____

TOTAL "B" $ _____

ADDITIONAL MERCHANDISE

A. Visitor Register _____

B. Memorial Cards _____

C. Acknowledgement Cards _____

Total "1" $ _____

D. Prayer or Holy Cards _____

TOTAL (CATHOLIC) _____

TOTAL: Standard Service Charge . . . $ _____

TOTAL: Standard Service Charge (Catholic) $ _____

NOTE . . . Items of service and/or facilities which are not utilized are deducted from this standard charge. A courtesy discount on personal and professional charges may be allowed to accommodate a genuine need for financial assistance.

FUNERAL ARRANGEMENT REFERENCE CARD

however, for aesthetic reasons, require a vault to prevent the burial plot from collapsing as the body and coffin decay. If such a charge is imposed, it should be identified ahead of time, and a person may choose to utilize a different cemetery in order to avoid this additional cost.

In the purchase of a cemetery plot, it is important to identify not only the cost of the plot but also additional costs that may be imposed. For example, some cemeteries charge fees for opening and closing a grave. Others may charge for the annual care given to a grave site. Still others may charge a fee for placing a marker or monument at the grave site.

When you shop for a cemetery, it is important to determine whether the rules will allow you to erect any type of monument that you wish or whether they insist on having a certain type of grave marker. You should also determine whether the cemetery will allow you to bring your own markers and, if so, whether you can purchase markers consistent with cemetery requirements. Many cemeteries also have requirements concerning the planting of plants and flowers at the grave site. Some will allow you a complete choice. Others will have strict rules in this area. It is important to know ahead of time what you may be permitted to do so that if you have a preference, you may choose a cemetery whose rules are consistent with your desires.

Coffin cost is an extremely important aspect of any particular funeral. One may be able to save substantial amounts of money in this area. In many states, one may utilize a coffin made out of heavy cardboard. Though this is certainly not attractive, stylish, or fancy, it is certainly adequate. It is even possible to purchase plans for a do-it-yourself coffin, which can then be built by the decedent (before he dies) or by his family. At the opposite extreme, one can find coffins made out of fiberglass, plastic, metal, or the most expensive woods. The cost of such coffins becomes substantially higher, running into many hundreds and even thousands of dollars. Some undertakers will object to the deceased family's providing its own coffin. This is frequently because this is an item on which they generate a substantial amount of their profit. If you run into this situation, try another funeral parlor. It should be possible to find a funeral parlor willing to take your coffin and to make arrangements ahead of time as to the fact that they are agreeable to doing so. It is, at the least, inconvenient to do this kind of shopping once the deceased has died.

Alternative Dispositions

Alternatives to funeral and burial costs are cremation, direct cremation or direct burial (cremation or burial immediately after death without a funeral), or donation of all or part of the body to a medical school or scientific research center. Each of these alternatives requires preparation as does a funeral and should be thought out in advance. It should also be noted that a person's wishes with respect to what is to be done with his or her body upon his or her death generally are not binding upon the survivors. Most states allow a survivor to disregard a decedent's wish with the exception of donation of bodily organs.

Cremation Though all states require permits for burial, few require special permits for cremation. In some cases, a health department permit may be required. Most states require that the cause of death be set forth on the death certificate before cremation may take place. This requirement is generally imposed to prevent cremation for purposes of concealment of a crime. Most crematories will also require a written authorization from the next of kin or other person responsible for disposition of the deceased. Few states require coffins for cremation, and even in those states the regulations generally provide that a body may be placed in a "suitable casket." It is not clear whether a suitable casket requires a wooden coffin or would be satisfied by a less expensive and less well-constructed container. Most crematories require a suitable container. It is important to check ahead of time what the crematory's specific requirements are and, wherever possible, to find a crematory willing to perform services with the minimal requirements available. A number of states prohibit the requirement of a coffin for cremation purposes.

Once a body has been cremated, there are a number of options available with respect to the ashes of the decedent. One can place the remains in an urn and keep them in a building specifically designed for housing such remains (generally referred to as a columbarium). One can also have the remains buried in a cemetery or keep them in one's home or, in some cases, scatter the remains. Where the latter choice is desirable, reference to state law is important because some states prohibit scattering of the remains by air or on public waterways. (Indiana prohibits any scattering of remains.) If cremation is a desired alternative, check whether there are any state regulations requiring the services of a professional. If not, this is something that the family members may be willing to take care of themselves. Most states require that burials be handled by professionally licensed individuals, but do not require similar situations for the handling of a cremation. In many cases, the family is unwilling to transport the body themselves (or may be prohibited from doing so by law), yet in other cases the family is not only willing to but anxious to perform this last service for the deceased. Finding a crematorium that will accept the body directly from the family of the deceased may require some searching.

Direct cremation or direct burial is the process of performing a cremation or burial without the prior viewing and the full funeral process. This eliminates many of the costs that are associated with a funeral such as embalming, restoration, rental of premises, flowers, procession, and so on. Frequently, a person who is in charge of a direct cremation or direct burial will choose a lower-priced coffin than one who is having a body placed on view.

Organ Donation Another alternative to burial that may often be desirable is the donation of a body (or specific organs) to medical schools or hospitals or both. Many of these institutions are in desperate need of cadavers for research purposes. Frequently, once the organization accepts the cadaver, it will pay for the ultimate disposition of the remains. This may include burial or cremation. If it is desirable to make a gift to such an institution, it should be clearly spelled out ahead of time. It is also appropriate to contact a specific organization to make arrangements. Some of these will have an excess of cadavers and will recommend that a particular body be donated to a different organization that is in greater need. It is also desirable to check ahead of time to determine what responsibilities the institution is willing to assume. Alternative arrangements should be made if it becomes difficult to transport the deceased's body to the particular institution.

The Uniform Anatomical Gift Act has been passed in all the states in one form or another. The Uniform Anatomical Gift Act provides for donations of parts of human bodies to medical facilities, including hospitals. This act makes the wishes of the decedent in this area more important and superior to the wishes of the surviving family members. The act also provides the resolution of disputes between family survivors when they are unable to agree upon the disposition of various organs. Donations may be made for transplant purposes, therapy, research, medical education, and so on. Most states provide for uniform donor cards to be executed, which may be carried by the donor on his or her person at all times (Exhibit 14–2). The purpose of such a card is to notify any person who is present at the death of a particular individual that a transplant gift is desirable. This will avoid the necessity for reading the will, which may not take place for several days after the death. Many states provide a uniform donor card as a portion of a driver's license.

After a transplant, some medical schools will be willing to return the remains in a sealed coffin if requested to do so by the survivors. Most schools, however, prefer to cremate or bury the remains. The institution involved will almost always assume financial responsibility for the disposition of the body's remains, thus removing a burden from the family. There may be some religious barriers to such a gift, which are for each individual to deal with on his or her own.

If you desire to make a donation of organs, you should contact the organization and determine what papers they need. If the donation is not total, they may refer you to other organizations that would have an interest in other organs. In some cases, the institution receiving the organs may request consent from the next of kin after the death to avoid any possible disagreements later on. There are numerous different kinds of organs that are potentially useful in transplants. They include eyes, ears, skin, bone, tendons, bone marrow, kidneys, livers, pancreases, blood vessels, lungs, and hearts. Hormones extracted from pituitary glands are useful in treating children who suffer from dwarfism. An individual interested in an organ transplant should contact a particular agency and should then discuss the potential for other transplants as well.

There are several organizations that act as clearinghouses for transplant donors and recipients. One such organization is the Living Bank in Houston, Texas. These organizations are generally not-for-profit groups. Potential donors register with the clearinghouse. Upon their death, the family contacts the clearinghouse, which then contacts a facility close to where the death occurred, for purposes of receiving the organs.

Another alternative to conventional burial is the establishment of memorial societies. A memorial society exists for the primary purpose of reducing the cost of funerals and allowing individuals to arrange for the disposition of their bodies in the

EXHIBIT 14-2
Uniform Donor Card

UNIFORM DONOR CARD

OF_____
Print or type name of donor

In the hope that I may help others, I hereby make this anatomical gift,
if medically acceptable, to take effect upon my death. The words and
marks below indicate my desires.

I give: (a) _____ any needed organs or parts

(b) _____ only the following organs or parts

_____
Specify the organ(s) or part(s)

for the purposes of transplantation, therapy, medical research
or education;

(c) _____ my body for anatomical study if needed.

Limitations or
special wishes, if any :_____

Signed by the donor and the following two witnesses in the presence of
each other:

_____   _____
Signature of Donor   Date of Birth of Donor

_____   _____
Date Signed   City & State

_____   _____
Witness   Witness

This is a legal document under the Uniform Anatomical Gift Act or similar laws.

For further information consult your local memorial society or:

Continental Association of Funeral & Memorial Societies
1828 L Street, N.W., Washington, D.C. 20036

---

manner that they choose. Frequently, this consists of direct cremation or direct burial followed by a memorial service. Memorial societies are often affiliated with churches, senior citizen centers, unions, or civic groups; and if there is such an organization in your area, you should consider contacting it to determine what services it can offer you or your family.

Death Benefits

Survivors should find out as soon as possible what death benefits are available and should apply for them. Few, if any, such benefits are automatically paid. Benefits commonly available to any decedent are life and casualty insurance, both privately held and employer provided, social security or veterans benefits, credit union or trade union or fraternal organization benefits, and so on. If the death is employment-related, workers' compensation may apply. Certain federal agency or railroad employees may be entitled to benefits based on their length of service.

Social security provides a death benefit of $255 in cases where there is a survivor drawing benefits on the deceased's account. This payment is designed to be applied to funeral and burial costs, and to the extent that such costs are less than this, the lesser amount shall be paid. Since most funeral and burial expenses exceed this amount, social security benefits should be applied for in all cases. Where a body is donated to a medical facility, any expenses related to this, such as transportation of the body, will be covered under the $255 stipend. Claims must be submitted within two years from the date of death, and this is something that can be done very simply by contacting one's local social security office and filling out the appropriate forms. Veterans or their dependents are entitled to death benefits from the VA as well.

Any person who has served honorably in the armed forces and is receiving VA disability benefits is entitled to a $300 death benefit plus free burial in a national cemetery. The second of these privileges may not always be appropriate or available since a number of these cemeteries are full and, therefore, may not be able to accommodate additional bodies. Deceased spouses and minor children of veterans are also entitled to free burial in a national cemetery. Sometimes this is limited to certain circumstances, and if it is desired, one should check the full extent of applicability. If a veteran is buried in a private cemetery, an additional $150 of benefits will be paid by the VA to be applied to the cemetery expenses in addition to the $300 discussed earlier. Veterans who are not receiving disability payments are only entitled to $150 if buried in a private cemetery. Veterans are also entitled to headstones and the U.S. flag. Applications for VA benefits should be made within two years of the date of death of the veteran, or else the benefits may be lost.

Preparation of these claims is something that is generally handled by a funeral director, but can as easily be handled by the deceased's relatives. Where you choose to do this on your own, you should determine whether a reduction will be made in funeral charges.

As a general rule, the survivors of the decedent will need copies of a number of documents in order to prove death and file appropriate claims for benefits. The death certificate is an extremely important document to copy. Generally, insurance companies, social security offices, and the VA will require a certified copy of the death certificate. These can be ordered at the time that the death certificate is obtained, and the charge therefore is usually minimal. Several extra copies are useful to obtain. It becomes a nuisance if one finds it is necessary to obtain one later. Birth certificates of surviving spouses and minor children may be required by the social security office and the VA. Copies of the originals need not be certified. Marriage certificates also may be required to be presented for copying (or copies presented) in order to obtain social security or VA benefits. It may also be necessary to provide copies of W–2 or income tax returns for a recent year as proof of a decedent's employment record for social security. If VA benefits are being applied for, a copy of the decedent's discharge papers may be requested. Finally, a receipted bill from the funeral home should be available to present to the VA and social security administration for purposes of collecting the funeral and burial expense allowances. The social security number of the decedent is also an important piece of information for identification purposes to determine whether the decedent was eligible for benefits. In a case of insurance companies, the policy is generally required to be surrendered as a condition for payment. If the policy is not available, it is possible to obtain the benefits anyway by submitting an affidavit of a lost or destroyed policy. This latter procedure will be somewhat more time-consuming, and therefore one should try to find the original policies whenever possible.

QUESTIONS

1 Betty Jones filed a complaint against Milton Jones, alleging the crime of seduction. Milton was running for a political office and, to avoid publicity, appeared in court. After lengthy discussions, he secured a marriage license, married Betty, and the complaint for seduction was dismissed. Milton then sued for an annulment of the marriage on the grounds that it was induced by duress. Decision for whom? Discuss.

2 Ida Lee gave birth to a child without being married. She told her father that Fred Lee was the father of the child. The following day Ida's father took his rifle and drove to a gas station where Fred was employed. Ida's father, together with two other individuals walked up to Fred, rifle in hand, and told him that he had ruined his daughter, and he would have to go and give the baby a name. Fred was driven to his home to change his clothes and then to the county clerk's office, where a minister was waiting. A marriage license was obtained, and the party drove to Ida's home. Fred was in the front row, and Ida's father sat behind him with a rifle on his lap. They were married, and subsequently Fred sued for an annulment. Was there sufficient duress to cause the marriage to be annulled? Discuss.

3 A District of Columbia statute provides that "a divorce from bond of marriage" may be granted for "voluntary separation from bed and board for five consecutive years without cohabitation." A husband and wife continue to occupy the same premises for five years in separate rooms under the same roof but had no marital relations; they ate at different times; the husband paid support and tried to reconcile on several occasions. Is the wife entitled to a divorce on statutory grounds of voluntary separation? Discuss.

4 The plaintiff brings an action for divorce, alleging cruel and harsh treatment, based on the following alleged incidents: During her third pregnancy she requested her husband to stop spanking some of the children, and he turned on her and hit her in the stomach with his fist, as a result of which one of the twins whom she had been carrying died. In addition, her husband knocked her to the floor, as a result of which she was hospitalized. After an operation, her husband called the pharmacy and gave them instructions that his wife was not to have any more pills for her pain. One night while she was asleep, her husband shook her and slapped her and called her "you contemptible female.'' Her husband humiliated her in the presence of her children by bringing the children into the living room, pointing at her, and saying, ''Look at the miserable creature that is your mother.'' Her husband for long periods of time stated that his wife needed psychiatric care, charging she was crazy, neurotic, and queer and that she wished to destroy him and that she had ruined his career. Are these sufficient grounds for divorce? Discuss.

5   Nancy and Ralph McLemore had three children. The youngest child had a physical defect and had undergone surgery for correction. In a suit for divorce, the court provided that each parent should have custody of the children alternatively for a week at a time and that the father was to pay $50 per month for the support of the mother, the children, and all necessary medical expenses of the children. The children's ages were eight, five, and two. The fitness and stability of the parents and their respective homes, which are in the same town, are not in question. Are the interests of the children better served by their being in the custody of the mother rather than of the father or by being in split custody? Discuss.

6   A husband and wife entered into a property settlement agreement that provided for the transfer of real and personal property between them, for the care and custody of their minor children, and for payments to the wife over a period of time. The parties obtained a divorce, and the property settlement agreement was included in the court decree. The situation between the parties changed over a period of time as each was remarried, and the husband stopped paying on the property agreement. The court indicated that the husband should resume the payments and that, if he failed to comply with the court's order, he should be imprisoned. May the court send the husband to prison? Discuss.

7   The mother and father of two children were married. Twelve years later, the father obtained a divorce and the custody of the children based on the misconduct of the mother. The mother was given ''the right to visit said children at reasonable times and reasonable hours.'' A year after the divorce, the father asked to have the decree modified, preventing the mother from visiting the children. He alleged that the mother had come to visit the children in an intoxicated condition, which upset the children. Should the court allow a modification of the decree, providing that the mother should not be able to see the children? Discuss.

8   A husband and wife separated. Testimony indicated that the husband possessed a bad temper, was at times cruel to his children, and on occasion exhibited ruthless disregard for the life of others. He had threatened to kill his wife, and she was afraid he would shoot her. On one occasion, he came to her home, tried to force his entrance, and was found by the police to have a monkey wrench in his pocket. He struck his wife at times and accused her of illicit relations. He used vile language in the presence of the children. He called women in his neighborhood dirty names when he passed them on the street. There was also evidence that the police were called to the husband's home on numerous occasions because of disturbances created by him and that he had pulled his five-year-old son down the hallway by the ear and administered severe punishment to him in the bathroom. The trial court awarded custody to the wife and denied visitation rights to the father. The husband appealed. Decision for whom? Discuss.

9   The plaintiff brought an action for an annulment based on the alleged fraud of the defendant. The plaintiff indicated that the defendant represented to her that he was a man of means, having sufficient funds and income to provide for her support and mainte-

nance during their married life and that he would support and maintain her in the position that she was accustomed to. In fact, the defendant had no money and was in a bad financial position. The plaintiff and defendant were harassed by creditors. The plaintiff requested an annulment based on fraud. Is the plaintiff entitled to an annulment? Discuss.

10 The plaintiff husband brings an action against his wife for divorce based on the grounds of fraud. The plaintiff learned on his honeymoon that his wife was the mother of an illegitimate child. Several months later, while still cohabiting with the defendant, the plaintiff learned that the defendant had falsified her name and date of birth on the marriage certificate in order to hide the fact that she was Polish (she had told him that she was of French descent). The plaintiff also discovered that she had lied to him with respect to her illegitimate child and a settlement of a bastardy suit. The plaintiff had slept with his wife prior to their marriage and knew of her unchastity. Does the plaintiff have grounds to have the marriage dissolved based on fraud? Discuss.

11 The plaintiff husband requested a divorce based on cruelty. The facts of the case indicate that defendant became a believer in Christian Science two years after the marriage and began to practice as a ''doctor.'' Her husband was opposed to this practice and requested her to give it up. Twenty witnesses, including four physicians, testified that the plaintiff became morose, moody, and inattentive to business and was troubled occasionally by insomnia, loss of appetite, and so on. There was also testimony by the doctors that if the causes that produced this mental depression did not cease, they would seriously endanger his reason and injure his health. The defendant, in practicing Christian Science, in no way wished to harm her husband. Is the plaintiff entitled to a divorce? Discuss.

12 The plaintiff, a schoolgirl of 18, married the defendant, a man who falsely represented that he was an honorable member of the society of persons who had served in the armed forces. In fact, the man was a professional swindler whose life had largely been spent in penitentiaries and reformatories. Shortly after the marriage, he was arrested, convicted, and sentenced for crimes he had committed before the marriage. Immediately upon learning of the deception, the plaintiff brought an action to annul the marriage. Can this marriage be annulled? Discuss.

13 The plaintiff and the defendant were married. Two days later the plaintiff husband left the defendant wife and filed for an annulment. The plaintiff testified that before they were married, he had expressed a definite wish to have children and that she had concurred. After the marriage ceremony, when they arrived home, the defendant refused to have marital relations with him unless he used contraceptive devices. She gave as her reason the fact that she was afraid to have children because of a prior operation. The defendant knew she was incapable of conceiving or bearing children by reason of her operation and did not disclose this fact to her husband. Is the plaintiff entitled to an annulment? Discuss.

14 Grace Metalious executed a will with the following clause: ''I direct that no funeral services be held for me and that my body be given to Dartmouth School of Medicine, for the purpose of experimentation in the interest of medical science. If Dartmouth does not accept, then to Harvard Medical School.'' The defendants are the surviving spouse and children of the decedent. They objected to carrying out this clause after both medical schools declined to accept the body. The defendants sought to have a short simple funeral service and bury the body. The administrator of the estate brought an action requesting an order to forbid funeral services. Should the funeral services be allowed to be held? Discuss.

15   The plaintiff and the defendant met and had sexual relationships, and the defendant told the plaintiff that she was pregnant as a result of their relationship. The plaintiff and the defendant then got together and agreed that they would be married and that six weeks later the defendant would apply for an annulment of the marriage. The purpose of the ceremony was to give the unborn child a name. It was agreed that the plaintiff at no time would live with or cohabit with the defendant or assume the relationship of husband and wife after the ceremony, but intended to live separately and apart at all times. The marriage ceremony was held, and there has been no contact between the parties since then. The plaintiff has paid all of the expenses of the child's support and medical care; however, the defendant refused to bring the annulment proceeding. The plaintiff brought an action for an annulment on the grounds that the original marriage lacked the mutual consent of the parties. Decision for whom? Discuss.

16   John Perricone, child of the defendant, was admitted to a hospital described as a ''blue child,'' indicating lack of oxygen, was discovered to be the result of irregularities in the heart. The parents consented to a surgical operation although, because of their religious beliefs, they requested no use of blood transfusions. Doctors complied with this request until a point where they found it necessary to administer transfusions. At that time they requested permission for transfusions from the parents, which was denied. The hospital administrator then applied to the court to have a special guardian appointed over the child who would consent to the medical attention required. After some legal maneuvering and over the parents' objection, blood transfusions were administered. The child died. Discuss the question of whether the parents are guilty of abuse or neglect; discuss the constitutional issues presented by this case.

PART SIX

BUSINESS ENTITIES

Our objective in these last chapters is to help the student in organizing a business. The intention is not to be all-inclusive but to outline the various forms a business can take, including sole proprietorship, partnership, and corporation. After reading these chapters, the student should be able to answer such questions as: What is the best business organization for me? What are the legal implications of forming a partnership or corporation? What does a typical corporate structure look like, and how does it differ from the structure of a partnership or a sole proprietorship? In addition, the student will be aware of some of the tax consequences of starting and running a business.

CHAPTER 15

Proprietorships and Partnerships

PROPRIETORSHIPS

A proprietorship is a business enterprise that is owned and operated by one person. It may be a service business (e.g., involving accountants, plumbers, doctors, lawyers, architects), a merchandising business (retail or wholesale), or a manufacturing business. A proprietorship may hire employees, enter contracts, and generally do anything any business may do. It is the simplest and most common form of business entity.

A proprietorship has definite characteristics although it is not generally recognized as a legal entity separate and apart from the individual owner. The three major business characteristics of a proprietorship are duration, management responsibility, and fiscal rewards and responsibilities.

A proprietorship has limited duration. It is formed when the proprietor starts doing business and terminates when the proprietor decides to stop doing business or dies. If the business is continued by another proprietor, either after the death of the original proprietor or after a sale of the business, the entity that results is a new proprietorship separate from the old one. An existing proprietorship may be sold to a new proprietor, but again this creates a second proprietorship. This is true even when the name of the old proprietorship is continued.

EXHIBIT 15-1
Assumed Name Certificate—Individual

Certificate

It is hereby certified that:

1. The undersigned is transacting business at _____ (street address), City of _____, County of _____, State of New York, under the name of _____.

2. The full name of the undersigned is _____ and his or her residence address is _____, City of _____, County of _____, State of New York.

3. The undersigned is of full age, and no other person is interested as a partner, part owner, or otherwise in the business or the conduct of it.

This certificate is executed and filed pursuant to Section 130 of the General Business Law.

Dated: _____, 19_____.

(Signature)

(Acknowledgment) _____

The management responsibility for a proprietorship lies with the proprietor. He or she is solely responsible for decisions, although he or she may rely on professional advisors, such as accountants, lawyers, bankers, and so on. The profits from the proprietorship all inure to the benefit of the proprietor, as do losses. Furthermore, the risk of loss is not limited to the assets used in the business, but extends to all the proprietor's assets including those not utilized for business purposes.

A person may do business under his own or an assumed name. Many proprietorships never bother to file the papers necessary to register their business names. In order to protect an assumed name, a proprietorship should file a certificate of doing business (Exhibit 15–1). This is filed with the designated public official (e.g., county clerk in New York), and the costs are nominal. Once on record, it bars others from using the same name within the designated jurisdiction (e.g., county). Filing also identifies the owner of the business so that creditors will know who is liable for business debts. A proprietor doing business in his or her own name does not have to file a certificate of doing business because his or her own name is not an assumed name. It is the protection of the assumed name that requires the certificate to be filed. Once the proprietorship goes out of business, a certificate of discontinuance (Exhibit 15–2) should also be prepared and filed. This would then allow other proprietors in the future to do business in that county under the assumed business name of the no longer operating business.

LAW OF AGENCY

Agency Defined

A principal agency relationship arises out of a contract in which one individual (the principal) authorizes another individual (the agent) to act on the former's behalf. The contract between the principal and the agent can either be written or oral. (Written agreements are easier to prove than oral ones.)

Authority

The contract creates express or implied authority in the agent to bind the principal. *Express authority* is authority that the principal has actually consented to. For example, a principal (P) hires a real estate broker (A) to try and find a buyer for P's house for $50,000 in cash. A's express authority is to find a buyer willing and able to purchase the property for $50,000 in cash. *Implied authority* (sometimes called inferred authority) is the authority to do what is necessary to accomplish the objective of the agency. Implied authority arises as a result of custom and usage or course of dealings or in cases of emergency. For example, in the preceding example, if nothing is said to the contrary, the agent would have the implied authority to place "for sale" signs on the property if such an act were customary in the area. If it were not customary to put up such signs, but if P had previously given A the right to do so (on

EXHIBIT 15-2
Certificate of Discontinuance

Certificate

1. Pursuant to Section 130 of the General Business Law, a certificate to conduct business under the _____
(assumed or partnership) name of _____
at _____ (business address), was filed in the _____ county clerk's office on _____, 19_____
by _____ and _____. (If certificate was amended, add: The most recent amended certificate, dated _____,
19_____, was filed in the same office on _____, 19_____, by _____).

2. It is hereby certified that the filing of a certificate is no longer required for the reason that _____
(state reason, as: the partnership for which the certificate was filed was dissolved on _____, 19_____, its term as set forth in the partnership agreement having expired or set forth conditions under which business is conducted that render the filing of a certificate in the particular county unnecessary, with date such change of conditions occurred).

3. It is further certified that the undersigned constitute a majority of the surviving persons named in the _____
(original certificate or most recent amended certificate, dated _____, 19_____), as conducting business under the name of _____ at
_____. (If any of the persons named in the original or most recent amended certificate are deceased, add: _____,
named in the certificate _____ [as amended] as residing at _____, is now deceased.)

(Signature)

Dated: _____

(Acknowledgment)

_____

the sale of other houses) and if nothing is said, A would have the right to post such signs based on the prior course of dealings. If, while showing the property, A discovered a broken water pipe and P could not be reached, A would have authority (because of the emergency situation) to contract a plumber and have the pipes repaired.

If a principal makes a representation to a third person that reasonably induces the third party to believe that an agent has certain actual authority, the principal has given that agent *apparent authority* to act for him or her in that manner. An agent with apparent authority can bind the principal with the same effect as though he or she had actual authority. The extent of the principal's liability in an apparent authority situation is measured by what the third person reasonably could believe the principal's manifestation to him or her would mean. For example, a principal (P) sends a real estate broker (A) a letter instructing the broker to "take care of the house while I'm gone for several years." P later tells A that the house should be maintained but not rented and gives A the keys to enable him or her to enter the house. A shows a third party (T) the letter, negotiates a lease, and hands over the keys. P will be bound to the terms of the lease under apparent authority because his (or her) letter, coupled with A's possession of the keys, leads T to believe that A has actual authority to rent the premises.

A principal's manifestation to a third party can arise out of the principal's silence when he or she has knowledge that someone is misrepresenting himself or herself as the principal's agent and does not correct the statements. For example, P tells A that he (or she) has authority to sell P's car for $1000. A, in the presence of P, tells T that he (or she) (A) has the authority to negotiate the price. A has apparent authority to sell the car at a reasonable price. If P had told the third party that A could sell only for $1000, P could have limited A's apparent authority to the extent of the actual authority. A principal can be bound by the act of an agent after the fact if the principal consents to an agent's previous unauthorized transaction by the agent. This is called *ratification* and is applicable when an agent unauthorizedly does something on behalf of his or her principal that does not bind the principal. When the principal approves of the actions before the third party withdraws from the transactions, there is a ratification. For example, P authorizes A to sell P's car for $1500. A accepts an offer for $1300 and transfers the title to T. P, on hearing this, accepts the $1300 and pays A a commission. This is a ratification.

A principal can also be bound by application of the legal principle of estoppel. This principle applies if an individual makes a statement with respect to agency that is relied upon by a third party, who materially changes his or her position. The courts will not allow the party making the statement to deny that statement. For example, P introduces Andrew to T as his (or her) (P's) purchasing agent although there is no agency relationship. Andrew purchases goods on credit from T, alleging that they are for P. When P refuses to pay the bill, T sues him or her for payment. P's defense is that Andrew never was, in fact, his or her agent. T will recover. P may not now deny his or her prior assertions that Andrew was his or her purchasing agent, and even though no agency relationship actually exists, P will be liable. Of course, P can recover from Andrew because both of them knew at all times that Andrew was not P's purchasing agent.

Duties and Liabilities Between the Principal and the Agent

Principal's Duties   The principal has a duty to compensate his or her agent according to the terms of the contract and is liable for breach of contract if he or she does not. If an agent makes payments pursuant to his or her authority, the principal will have to reimburse him or her. In addition, the principal must indemnify the agent for expenses or losses incurred without the agent's fault while the agent was acting within the scope of his or her authority. A principal also has the duty of not interfering with the agent's performance of his or her duties.

If the agent has acted contrary to the principal's instructions or if the agent has acted for more than one principal without the consent of each, the principal has no duty to compensate the agent for services.

Agent's Duties   An agent has a fiduciary duty of loyalty to his or her principal. This duty requires an agent to perform in the best interests of the principal and includes a duty to disclose any adverse interests the agent may have as agent. The agent has a duty not to disclose confidential information that would be to the disadvantage of the principal to the third persons. The agent also has the duty to obey instructions and is liable for any loss caused to the principal because of his or her actions or inactions. An agent may not substitute his or her judgment for that of the principal and may refuse to obey an instruction to commit an illegal or immoral act. In addition, an agent has the duty to exercise reasonable care and to account to his or her principal for all money and property he or she has received on behalf of the principal. Moreover, an agent cannot make secret profits from his or her agency contract. Notice to an agent is construed as notice to his or her principal unless the third party knows or should know that the agent would not communicate the information to the principal. For example, a stock broker is an agent of the investor. If the stock broker makes recommendations to the investor to purchase certain stocks and if these recommendations are made based on information that is obtained in a normal businesslike fashion and if the stock subsequently declines in value, the agent will not be responsible, in most instances, for the losses of the investor. If, however, the stock broker makes the representations based on information that is not obtained in a businesslike fashion, but rather on the basis of a ''hot tip,'' the stock broker may be liable to the investor for any losses that were realized.

Duties and Liabilities Between the Principal and Third Persons

The duties and liabilities that a principal owes a third person depend on whether that principal is disclosed or undisclosed (i.e., whether or not the third party knows that the agent is an agent acting for a principal). When a principal is disclosed, unless the agent and the third party have contracted otherwise, the agent is not liable to the third person; only the principal is so liable.

It is up to the third person to ascertain whether or not an agency exists as well as the scope of authority of the purported agent. If an agent's express authority is limited, but the limitation is not known to the third party, it is usually not binding. If an agent's authority is written and the third person knows or should know of the writing, the third person is under a duty to examine the writing.

If a principal is undisclosed and his or her agent enters into a contract, only the third person and the agent are liable on the contract. If the principal is subsequently disclosed, the third party may elect to hold the principal liable instead of the agent. If there is a partially disclosed principal (the existence of a principal is disclosed but not his or her identity), both principal and agent are liable on the contract.

Agent's Torts   When an agent commits a tort that injures a third party, the agent is personally liable in all cases. The principal will be liable if the tort is committed in the course and in furtherance of the principal's business ("within the scope of the agency"). For example, if A makes intentionally false statements regarding P's products to induce T to purchase them, P as well as A would be liable to T for the consequences of this fraudulent statement. Both P and A are liable even though the tort committed by A was intentional and not merely negligent. This is true because the tort arose out of the business relationship between P and T. If A had gotten into an argument with T concerning the quality of P's product and in the process hit T, P as well as A would be liable because the tort arose while A was engaged in furthering the business relationship of P and T. However, if A was at T's place of business, saw a neighbor whom he or she disliked, and hit the neighbor, P would not be liable because there is no business relationship between P and the neighbor. A was acting outside the "scope of his or her agency."

Agent's Criminal Acts   A principal can also be held liable for the criminal acts of an agent. This will not occur as frequently as liability for the tortious acts of an agent, but it is a possibility. The general tests to be applied are whether the acts occurred while the agent was involved in the pursuit of the principal's business interest or whether the principal benefits from the agent's acts. Because criminal acts generally require intent, it is frequently hard to hold a principal liable if his or her agent violates the law.

Duties and Liabilities Between the Agent and Third Persons

Normally, an agent is not a party to a contract and is not liable for its terms. An agent who is a party to a contract with a third person (e.g., where there is an undisclosed principal) is liable for the contractual nonperformance whether or not his or her principal is a party. A person who expressly or impliedly represents that he or she is an agent warrants that he or she has authority to act and is liable for breach of this warranty. An agent who commits a tort either within or without the scope of his or her authority is liable to third persons for such tort regardless of whether the principal is liable for the tort. An agent is also liable to third parties for misfeasance (active misconduct) but is not liable for nonfeasance (failure to act). Once the agent begins to perform, he or she has a duty to act reasonably and, if negligent, causing harm to third persons, he or she will be liable to them.

Termination of Agency

A principal and agency relationship may be terminated by the terms of the agency contract, by mutual rescission (both parties deciding to cancel the contract), by the principal's revocation of the agency, or by the agent's renunciation of his or her agency. In order for the revocation or renunciation to be effective, it must be communicated to the third party. If the third party has knowledge of the revocation or renunciation, notification will be required. If the principal fails to give such notice to a third party, an agent could go out and make contracts in the name of the principal (even though the relationship had been terminated) and could bind the principal to those contracts. In this situation, the principal could recover from the agent, however, because between the principal and the third party, the principal will be responsible. If the third party reasonably believes the agent still represents the principal and deals with the agent in such capacity, the principal will still be bound.

The termination of an agency contract may require the terminating party to pay damages as to the other party. Breach of the obligations owed by the agent to the principal is grounds for the principal to terminate the agency relationship and may also give the principal the right to sue the agent for damages resulting from the agent's acts. Failure of the principal to meet his or her obligations to the agent would give the agent the right to terminate the relationship and also possibly to sue the principal for damages occurring to the agent.

An agency may also be terminated by operation of law, by the death or insanity of the principal or the agent, by a change of law that causes the agency to be illegal, by the bankruptcy of a principal, or by the destruction of the subject matter of the agency.

Some agencies are irrevocable. These arise if the agency is created by the principal as security in exchange for consideration given by the agent (A lends P $2000; P, as part of the same transaction, agrees that if he or she fails to repay A, A may sell his or her car for $3500 and apply the proceeds to pay the debt); or the agency is coupled with an interest in a subject matter (P owes A $2000. P transfers title to his or her car to A with instructions that A may sell the car for $3500 if P fails to repay the debt and apply the proceeds to the loan).

Throughout this discussion it has been assumed that the principal agency relationship is a business one; however, this need not be true. Though agents are generally retained for compensation, it is possible to become a gratuitous agent. For example, if you are ill and unable to leave your home and you ask a neighbor to drive to the store and bring you some groceries, the neighbor is probably your agent. If while the neighbor is in route, he or she negligently injures a pedestrian, you could become liable as the principal. Though such a claim is remote, both in terms of the likelihood of its being raised and the likelihood of its being maintained in a court action, we live in an era where people are looking for excuses to sue others, and a degree of caution would be well advised.

PARTNERSHIPS

Definitions

A *partnership* is an association of two or more persons to carry on a business as co-owners for profit. It is created by the intent of the parties as expressed in a written or oral agreement. The requirement of carrying on a business has been defined in many ways by many courts. In fact, one court has held that the term "carrying on a business" has no definite meaning (Connor v. City of University Park, 142 S.W.2d 706 [Tex. 1940]). A useful, although not necessarily comprehensive, definition of carrying on a business is "a commercial enterprise or establishment engaged in trade or industry." The nature of a business is that it be an ongoing activity rather than a single venture although there can be exceptions. A business can be differentiated from an investment (Securities and Exchange Commission v. Wickham, 12 F.Supp. 245 [D. Minn. 1935]) in that a business is active rather than passive in nature. The definition of business has also been held not to require profitability or even the prospect of profitability (Doggett v. Burnet, 65 F.2d 191 [D.C. Cir. 1933]).

Co-ownership requires that the assets of the partnership belong to the partners rather than to any one person. Where one individual owns a business and a second helps operate the business for a percentage of the profits, it is debatable whether a partnership exists. There is no co-ownership of the partnership assets.

Partnerships are governed by each state. The Uniform Partnership Act (UPA) was passed by all states except Georgia, Louisiana, and Mississippi to unify common law principles of partnership. The UPA, coupled with the rules of agency, are the general principles for partnership transaction.

Profits

It is not necessary that a business generate a profit in order to qualify as a business, but it is generally considered that intent to make a profit at some point is required. The application of these rules, however, can be unclear. Here is an example. If two persons purchase property, they are co-owners of income-producing assets. It is generally clear that this relationship does not create a partnership (Clark v. Sidway, 142 U.S. 682 [S.Ct. 1892]). Where, however, these same individuals own numerous apartment houses and derive their living from the profits generated by these ventures, it is more arguable that there is a business and that a partnership relationship, therefore, might exist. Organizations created for social purposes or other not-for-profit reasons are not considered to be partnerships because of the lack of the profit motive and the nonbusiness nature of these ventures (Wilson v. Bogert, 347 P.2d 341 [Idaho 1959]).

Sharing of profits from a business venture (as opposed to a sharing of gross receipts) is a prima facie indication of a partnership relationship; however, it is subject to refutation by demonstrating that the sharing of profits resulted from some other motive such as compensation, interest, or rental. For example, a business owner may pay a percentage of profits without creating a partnership. Where a lease requires the payment of a fixed monthly rent plus a percentage of profits or where an employee is entitled, as an element of compensation, to receive a percentage of net profits or where a loan is repaid out of a percentage of net profits, other factors will need to be looked at to determine whether the arrangement was a partnership or some other form of business relationship.

If a partnership relationship is created, it need not be specified what the profit-sharing ratios of the respective partners are. In the absence of a specific contrary agreement, the profit-sharing ratio will be deemed to be equal among all partners. In the absence of a contrary statement, losses will be deemed to be shared in the same ratios as profits.

Partnership Agreement

A partnership agreement may be very simple or very elaborate but must indicate the intent of the parties to create a partnership. There may be a mere statement as to the objectives or purposes of the partnership, or the agreement may include such statement and continue to describe the actual authority of each of the partners, their financial obligations, and so on. A well-planned partnership would include the drafting of a complete partnership agreement, defining the objectives of the partnership, the interrelationships of the partners, their financial obligations, and so on. Management responsibilities and termination provisions should also be dealt with in detail. This type of an agreement is sometimes referred to as a buy-sell agreement and also is often utilized in the formation of a corporation. A buy-sell agreement sets forth the sequence of events to be followed when a partner wishes to withdraw from a partnership. It may be part of the entire partnership agreement or may be a separate and subsequently written document. These agreements are dealt with in detail in the section analyzing typical partnership agreements and will, therefore, not be discussed any further here.

In many states, the formation of a partnership requires the filing of notification in the county in which the partnership is doing business and indicating the name of the partnership, its business location, and so forth. This document is signed by all of the partners and filed with the designated office. Failure to file this certificate may result in a fine, imprisonment, or both. A business may also be barred from using the courts to enforce contracts with third parties. A sample certificate entitled ''Certificate of Doing Business as Partners'' is shown in Exhibit 15–3. In the event of changes in the partnership such as the withdrawal of a partner or addition of a new partner, one or more subsequent certificates should be filed to give notice of these changes.

EXHIBIT 15–3
Assumed Name Certificate—Partnership

The undersigned do hereby certify that:

1. They are conducting business as partners at _____
_____, County of _____, State of _____, under the
name of _____.

2. The full names and residence addresses of the persons conducting the business, including all partners, and the ages of any such persons less than 18 years of age, are as follows:

Names	Residence Address	Age

3. No other person is interested as a partner or otherwise in the business or the conduct of it.

This certificate is executed and filed pursuant to Section 130 of the General Business Law.

Dated:

_____

_____

Mutual Agency

The most important characteristic of a partnership, from which many of the rules of partnership operation flow, is that each partner is an agent of all the other partners. This doctrine of mutual agency creates a mutual fiduciary relationship between the partners. It also means that the action of any partner (if authorized) can bind the partnership as well as the partners personally. Since each partner is an agent for the other partners, each has the full authority that any partner of the partnership would have. Even where the partners agree to divide their responsibilities for running the partnership, the agreement is not binding on third parties unless they consent, and each partner would have full authority to bind the partnership (Lindley v. Seward, 5 N.E.2d 998 [Ind. 1937]).

Closely related to the preceding concept is the idea that all partners have the right and obligation to participate in the management of partnership affairs. Because of this doctrine, each partner has authority to perform any act for the benefit of the partnership with certain exceptions. A third party dealing with a partner may assume that the partner has total authority. As discussed earlier in this chapter in the section on agency, an agent with apparent authority may bind the principal even where the agent lacks actual authority. Since a partner has theoretical responsibility for the total range of management of partnership affairs, the partner has implied authority to do anything that is appropriate. Unless the third party is aware of the specific limitations on the partner's authority, the third party may rely on the partner's implied authority, and said partner will bind the partnership. Though this has a substantial effect on the partnership itself, it also may have major impact on the partners personally because of their unlimited liability for business debts.

Although a partner has broad general authority to act on behalf of a partnership, there are a number of things a partner cannot do without the consent of other partners. In order to define the authority of partners properly, one must divide partnership businesses into two kinds: trading partnerships and nontrading partnerships. A trading partnership is one that is generally engaged in the buying and selling of a product; a nontrading partnership is one that is generally engaged in rendering services. Because a trading partnership needs large quantities of capital, authority for certain types of acts will exist with respect to a trading partnership, but not with respect to a nontrading partnership. What we are primarily concerned with is whether a partner has implied or apparent authority to conduct a particular transaction.

Partners' Authority

Partners in a trading partnership have authority to buy and sell property of the nature that is essential to the partnership business. Thus, if a partnership is engaged in the retail clothing business, any partner has the authority to buy or sell clothing. A partner would not have the authority to buy or sell hardware items because this is not an essential aspect of the clothing business. In the case of a nontrading partnership, a partner would not have authority to buy and sell property because that business is engaged primarily in rendering services.

A partner in a trading partnership has the authority to borrow money in the name of the partnership to the extent necessary in order to carry on the partnership's reasonable business activities. Where the amount exceeds the needs of the business or is clearly for a purpose beyond the scope of the business's activities, this authority would not exist. A partner in a nontrading partnership, because of its lesser need for capital, would not have authority to borrow money. A partner in either a trading or nontrading partnership has the authority to hire employees or independent contractors whose services are reasonably necessary for the furtherance of the partnership business. A necessary corollary to this would be that the partner also has authority to negotiate and establish salaries with such employees or contractors.

A partner of a trading or nontrading partnership would have the authority to pay partnership debts from partnership funds. No partner may use partnership assets to satisfy personal debts. A partner has authority to receive information or notices that are addressed to the partnership. To the extent that any partner acquires information, it will be imputed to all of the other partners except where the partner who has received the information is engaged in fraud.

No partner of a trading or nontrading partnership has authority to assign partnership property for the benefit of creditors, to dispose of the goodwill of the partnership business, or to do any other act that would make it impossible to carry on the ordinary business of the partnership. These requirements are imposed because, in the absence thereof, a partner could unilaterally take an action that would affect the continued ability of the partnership to operate. The preceding discussion is not intended to be exhaustive, but rather to illustrate certain types of functions that partners may or may not engage in without the consent of other partners.

Fiduciary Nature and Liability of Partners

As agents, partners have fiduciary obligations of agents to principals. Because of their total obligation to manage the business, partners are not entitled to compensation for services rendered even where said services are out of proportion to the partner's profit-sharing interest or the services rendered by other partners (except in winding up the business).

A proprietor is liable for all the debts of his or her business enterprise; these generally arise through his or her acts or those of his or her employees. A partner also has unlimited liability for the business debts of the partnership. Unlike a proprietorship, however, these debts can arise not only out of the acts of the partner or his or her employees, but also out of actions of other partners even where these actions are specifically unauthorized. Accordingly, one's choice of associates for operation of a partnership is most important. A partner who is an irresponsible person can not only cause the loss of the partnership assets but also losses of other partners' personal assets as well. If we apply the principles discussed in the section on agency, it can be seen that partners can be liable not only for bad business decisions of fellow partners, but also for accidental or intentional wrongful acts of their fellow partners. The combination of the mutual agency doctrine, the total responsibility of each partner for business affairs, and the unlimited liability doctrine creates a very large exposure for a partner.

Partner liability for partnership debts is called joint and several. The meaning of this is that partners are jointly responsible for the business debts as well as severally (separately and individually) liable. The practical effect of this is that, given a partnership of 10 partners, any one of the partners can be held personally liable for a deficiency in partnership assets. If the partnership, for example, owes $100,000 more than the total of its assets, each partner's share of this liability would normally be $10,000. However, a creditor has the right to obtain a judgment against any one partner for the full $100,000. This partner then has a right to proceed against each other partner and obtain $10,000 from each. If any partner is unable to pay his or her $10,000, the partner who paid the $100,000 can get an additional one ninth of that $10,000 from each of the other eight partners.

Limited Life of Partnerships

A partnership is characterized by a limited life, as is a proprietorship. A distinction must be drawn between the partnership and the business in which the partnership is engaged. It is possible for the partnership business to continue even though the partnership itself ends. When the partnership ends, the rights of the partners need to be established and satisfied according to partnership agreement. The continuation of the business venture assumes that the interests of the former partners can so be resolved. The continuation of the business would then be in the form of a new partnership. A partnership agreement could call for the continuity of the partnership without the former partner, and a new partnership would be created, consisting of the remaining partners. Some arrangement should also be present in the partnership agreement specifying as to disposition of a deceased partner's interest. This usually takes the form of a purchase by the surviving partners and a payment to the estate of the deceased partner. A well-drafted agreement specifies that this kind of a provision is mandatory and that the estate of the deceased partner has no option to remain in the partnership.

Ending a Partnership

The process of ending the partnership involves three distinct steps: dissolution, liquidation or winding up, and termination. *Dissolution* is defined as "the change in the relationship of the partners caused by any partner's ceasing to be associated with the carrying on . . . of the business." Acts of dissolution include such things as the death of a partner, the addition of a new partner, the expiration of the partnership term, statements or actions by the partners indicating their desire to end their arrangement, or the breach by a partner of his or her fiduciary obligations to other partners. The bankruptcy of a partner or the illegality of the partnership business is also generally considered an act of dissolution. The focus of the provisions of the Uniform Partnership Act is that when the group dynamics of a partnership change, the partnership is dissolved.

Dissolution is a specific event; it does not, however, automatically end the operations of the partnership. It requires that a *winding up* or *liquidation* of the partnership take place. This is a process whereby the partnership's assets are liquidated, creditors are paid, and the remaining assets are distributed to the partners. The dissolution ends the partners' relationships as mutual agents with respect to each other; however, this relationship will continue through the liquidation phase with respect to third persons. Thus, if after dissolution, partner A acquires additional merchandise, the act will bind the other partners to the seller, but they will be able to recover their share of the payments from A because the act took place after the dissolution of the partnership. It is permissible, under the terms of a partnership agreement, to substitute the creation of a new partnership under specified circumstances for the liquidation process. In such a situation, the liquidation of the assets of the old partnership takes place when they are purchased by a new partnership. The final phase of ending a partnership is the *termination*. This takes place when the partnership assets have been distributed and all the operations of the partnership have ceased. Upon the dissolution and termination of a partnership, a certificate of discontinuance of partnership should also be filed with the state. This certificate of discontinuance is similar to the one shown for proprietorships in Exhibit 15–2 except that it would show the assumed partnership name.

ANALYSIS OF A TYPICAL PARTNERSHIP AGREEMENT

A partnership agreement can be oral or written, simple or complex, informal or formal, and so on. However, for a partnership to have the greatest chance for success, it should be a well-planned and thought-out business arrangement, evidenced by a well-documented agreement. Furthermore, as a way to avoid subsequent conflict or lack of clarity, the agreement should be in writing. A partnership agreement should deal with a number of factors (enumerated as follows), but the terms may vary with the needs of the particular businesses. The terms presented in this analysis are for a typical partnership agreement, but may not satisfy the particular needs of the reader. In such an instance, obviously, the terms illustrated as follows should be altered.

A partnership agreement should initially deal with approximately 10 different items: a description of the partnership, the capital of the partnership, profits and loss distribution, payments of salaries and withdrawals, interest on capital, responsibilities of the partners, banking and bookkeeping arrangements, voluntary liquidation, retirement, and death. A sample agreement is provided in Exhibit 5–4.

Capital

A typical agreement sets up initial capital contributions and capital interests among the partners and defines the procedure for subsequent capital contributions. In the event that either partner cannot meet the needs of the partnership, the other may contribute the additional amounts needed and will receive interest to compensate him or her for his or her extra payment. A trading partnership (one that buys and sells merchandise) needs large amounts of capital, and provisions must be made for future obligations of the partners to contribute, as well as for sanctions against partners if the contributions are not forthcoming. Although a service partnership requires minimal amounts of capital, the provisions are more flexible.

An issue to be resolved in a partnership agreement is whether the failure of a partner to contribute his or her share shall be treated as an act of dissolution or shall merely allow other partners to collect interest on their additional contributions. Another very real concern is what will happen to a partnership when one of the partners fails to make a capital contribution. It may be that the partners are in a position in which they are willing to make their contributions, but cannot absorb the contributions that are required by other partners in the event that they don't make them. The failure of one or two partners in a partnership of moderate size to make the

EXHIBIT 15-4
Partnership Agreement

AGREEMENT made this   day of   , 1984 between PETER   , residing at 15 Bridge Street,   , TIMOTHY   , residing at 14 Church Street,   , TOD   , residing at R.D. 1, Box 87, and THOMAS   , residing at 275 Kaymar Drive.

1.   NAME and BUSINESS: The parties do hereby form a partnership under the name of   ENTERPRISES, to buy, own, build upon, alter, repair, rent, lease, sell, mortgage, and otherwise deal with real and personal property, of any kind or description, particularly the lands and premises situated in   Counties,   . The principal office of the business shall be at R.D. 1, Box 87,

2.   TERM: The partnership shall begin on April 30, 1984, and shall continue until terminated as herein provided.

3.   CAPITAL: The capital of the partnership shall consist initially of the following capital contributions:

PETER   —$500.00
TIMOTHY —$500.00
TOD   —$2500.00
THOMAS —$5000.00

Title to property will be taken in the name of the partners. It is anticipated that the first acquisition of real property will need extensive remodeling, renovation, and construction, and Peter   and Timothy   shall furnish the labor for this renovation at the rate of $10.00 per man-hour, which amounts shall be credited to their respective capital accounts. Said amounts shall be credited monthly at the end of the month. To the extent that any of the partners has a greater amount in his capital account than the smallest balance in any other capital account, each such partner shall receive interest on such excess capital in his account at the rate of one percent (1%) per month. Said interest shall be computed prior to the crediting of any account for additions to said account in the form of cash or labor. Cash contributions shall be credited at the end of each month. Cash withdrawals shall be debited at the beginning of each month.

It is intended that the partners shall have equal capital accounts. Once the balance of $2500.00 has been achieved in the Peter   and Timothy   account, moneys shall be paid to Thomas   , as it becomes available, to reduce the balance in his account to $2500.00. Until equality is achieved in all capital accounts, there shall be no withdrawal of profits or capital except that Thomas   may withdraw up to $2500.00 to reduce his capital balance.

If at any time or times hereafter the partners should determine that further capital is required by the partnership and that the capital of the partnership should be increased, the additional capital required shall be contributed by the partners equally. Such a decision shall require one hundred percent (100%) approval.

A separate capital account shall be maintained for each partner.

4.   PROFIT and LOSS: The net profits and net losses of the partnership shall be divided equally between the partners. A separate income account need not be maintained for each partner.

5.   SALARIES and DRAWINGS: No partner shall receive any salary for services

EXHIBIT 15-4, cont.

rendered to the partnership except as specified in paragraph 7 below. No partner may withdraw the credit balance in his capital or profit account unless all partners agree. No additional share of profits shall inure to any partner by reason of his capital account's being in excess of the capital account of any other except as to interest as stated in paragraph 3.

6.   INTEREST: Except as specified in paragraph 3 above, no interest shall be paid on the balances in any capital account.

7.   MANAGEMENT, DUTIES and RESTRICTIONS:

(a)   All bookkeeping, accounting, rent collection, and bill paying shall be done by Tod   , who shall be compensated at the rate of twenty-five dollars ($25.00) per month. Day-to-day management of the property, rental and showing of rental units, collection of security and first month's rent, and minor repairs shall be done by Timothy   , who shall be compensated at the rate of twenty-five ($25.00) per month.

(b)   The consent of all the partners shall be required with respect to major management or operational decisions, including, but not limited to, full power to sell and convey the property on such terms as they may determine, mortgaging the property, whether such mortgage lien shall be a first or second mortgage, and lending or borrowing money on behalf of the partnership.

(c)   Any partner may have other business interests and may engage in any other business or trade, profession, or employment whatsoever, on his own account, or in partnership with or as an employee of or as an officer, director, or shareholder of any other person, firm, or corporation, and he shall not be required to devote his entire time to the business of the partnership. No partner shall be obligated to devote more time and attention to the conduct of the business of the partnership than shall be required for the business of the partnership or than shall be required for the supervision of the ownership, operation, and management of the properties of the partnership.

8.   BANKING: All banking of the partnership, whether checking or savings, shall be done at The   Bank of   . All funds of the partnership shall be deposited in checking or savings accounts in said bank, in the name of the partnership, and checks may be written or funds withdrawn from savings upon the signature of any partner.

9.   BOOKS: The partnership books shall be maintained at the principal office of the partnership, and each partner shall at all times have access thereto. The fiscal year of the partnership shall be the calendar year. The books shall be closed and balanced at the end of each such fiscal year. An audit may be made as of the closing date.

10.   VOLUNTARY TERMINATION: The partnership may be dissolved at any time by agreement of the partners, in which event the partners shall proceed with reasonable promptness to sell the real and personal property owned by the partnership and to liquidate the business of the partnership. The partnership shall be dissolved also by the sale of all real property owned by the partnership. Upon dissolution, the assets of the partnership business shall be used and distributed in the following order:

(a)   to pay or provide for the payment of all partnership liabilities and liquidating expenses and obligations.

(b)   to discharge the balance of the capital accounts of the partners.

11.   RETIREMENT:

(a)   Any partner shall have the right to retire from the partnership at the end of any fiscal year. Written notice of intention to retire shall be served upon the partnership at the office of the partnership at least three months before the end of the fiscal year. The retirement of any partner shall have no effect upon the continuance of the partnership

EXHIBIT 15-4, cont.

business. The remaining partners shall have the right either to purchase the retiring partner's interest in the partnership or to terminate and liquidate the partnership business. If any remaining partner or partners elect to purchase the interest of the retiring partner, he or they shall serve notice in writing of such election upon the retiring partner at the office of the partnership within two months after receipt of his or their notice of intention to retire.

(b)   If any remaining partners elect to purchase the interest of the retiring partner in the partnership, the purchase price and method of payment shall be the same as stated in paragraph 12 with reference to the purchase of a selling partner's interest in the partnership.

(c)   If none of the remaining partners elect to purchase the interest of the retiring partner in the partnership, the partners shall proceed with reasonable promptness to sell the real and personal property owned by the partnership and to liquidate the business of the partnership. The procedure as to liquidation and distribution of the assets of the partnership business shall be the same as stated in paragraph 10 with reference to voluntary termination.

12.   SALE OF PARTNERSHIP INTEREST: In the event a partner wishes to sell his interest, the remaining partners shall have the right either to purchase said interest in the partnership or to terminate the old partnership and form a new one. No partner shall have the right to sell his interest to any person other than under paragraph 11 or 14. In the event of a sale under one of these paragraphs, the sale price shall be determined by the selling partner or his agent and the remaining partners, each choosing an appraiser of his choice to value the property. If the appraised values are within ten percent (10%) of each other, the values shall be averaged, and the selling price shall be eighty percent (80%) of that value. If the values are more than ten percent (10%) apart, the parties shall mutually choose a third appraiser, and the selling price shall be eighty percent (80%) of the average of all three prices. Notification of intent to sell must be given to the partners. They then shall have thirty (30) days in which to advise the selling partner of their joint or individual intent to purchase the property, at which time appraisers shall be selected. Should neither the partnership nor any partner choose to purchase under these conditions, the partnership shall be dissolved under the terms stated above at paragraph 10.

13.   DEATH: Upon the death of any partner, said partner's interest shall pass by will or intestate, and the beneficiaries of the estate shall acquire an interest in the partnership. In the event said beneficiaries choose not to continue in the partnership, they may offer said partnership interest to the remaining partners at a price equal to the value of the decedent's

necessary contributions may cause the entire partnership business to fail for lack of capital. When entering into a partnership arrangement, all the partners should be aware of their potential future liabilities and should be in a position in which they can meet the needs of the business as they might arise.

When partners contribute assets other than cash, the partnership agreement should describe each asset and should establish its agreed-upon value. This makes it clear that all partners have contributed appropriate amounts and that all parties have agreed to the value of noncash assets. Failure to do so might result in a disagreement at a subsequent date as to whether the partners have made their full contributions or as to the value of the assets contributed. The Internal Revenue Service (IRS) may also question the value of certain assets, and a recitation in the part-

EXHIBIT 15-4, cont.

interest, adjusted through the date of death. Payment for such interest shall be made over a two-year period with interest at twelve percent (12%). The value of the partnership interest shall be based on an appraisal by three (3) competent appraisers.

If the surviving partners do not elect to purchase the interest of the decedent in the partnership, they shall proceed with reasonable promptness to sell the real and personal property owned by the partnership and to liquidate the business of the partnership. The surviving partners and the estate of the deceased partner shall share ratably in the profits and losses of the business during the period of liquidation. No compensation shall be paid to the surviving partners for their services in liquidation. Except as herein otherwise stated, the procedure as to liquidation and distribution of the assets of the partnership shall be the same as stated in paragraph 10 with reference to voluntary termination.

14.   ARBITRATION: Any controversy or claim arising out of or relating to this contract, or the breach thereof, shall be settled by arbitration in accordance with the rules then obtaining of the American Arbitration Association, and judgment upon the award rendered may be entered in any court having jurisdiction thereof.

IN WITNESS WHEREOF the parties have signed this agreement.

_____ residing at _____

Social Security No. _____

_____ residing at _____

Social Security No. _____

_____ residing at _____

Social Security No. _____

_____ residing at _____

Social Security No. _____

nership agreement may be useful to overcome their objections. It is possible for a partner to contribute the use of an asset while retaining the ownership of that asset. Thus, if it were necessary for a partnership to have a business office and one of the partners owned an office building, that partner might contribute the use of the office building rent-free for a given period of time as part or all of his or her capital contribution.

Profit and Loss

The profit and loss sharing ratio of the partners should also be included in the agreement. This ratio may be equal or unequal, as the partners choose, but will be presumed equal where not otherwise stated. Losses, unless otherwise stipulated, will be shared in the same ratio as profits. Profits shall be computed in accordance with generally accepted accounting principles and sound income tax practice. Profits need not be divided in the capital ratios of the partners. These are two different concepts and, though often equal, need not be so. It is also not necessary for the partners' withdrawals to be equal. Thus, in a given partnership arrangement, if profits amount to $10,000, it may be that one partner withdraws $4,000 and another partner withdraws $4,500. (The remainder of $1,000 and $500 is credited to each partner's respective capital account.) Although there is no compelling reason for one partner to withdraw less profits than another, it sometimes simply works out that way. The partner who leaves capital in the partnership in excess of the amounts that others leave is not normally entitled to any compensation for the extra capital.

Salaries and Drawing

The general partnership rule is that no partner is entitled to compensation for services rendered to the partnership. Since each partner is obligated to perform services for the general welfare and benefit of the partnership, it is presumed that no compensation will be paid. This need not, however, be the case. Where the partners share the management of the business unequally, it is often specified in the partnership agreement that the partner who works harder shall receive a specified amount of compensation. If one of the partners performs a sales function, it is common to pay that person a percentage of sales as compensation. If partners receive compensation, whether in fixed amounts or as percentages of sales, it should be spelled out that these payments are to apply before any distribution of profits. For example, A and B are partners; A's capital account is $10,000, and B's is $30,000. A manages the business and receives $10,000 for services rendered. Interest is paid at 10 percent of the capital account balances. Assume that the profits are equally divided and are $24,000 in 1982 and $8,000 in 1983. Exhibit 15–5 shows the results if the profits were split equally and if they were allocated based on the preceding facts.

An agreement may specify the method of making withdrawals (e.g., monthly or annually) and indicate that they are not distributions of profits, but advance payments of anticipated profits. If the profits are sufficient to cover the withdrawals, then there is no problem; if, however, the profits are less than withdrawals, the deficiency comes out of the partners' capital account.

Management

Provisions in a partnership agreement can simply provide for equal sharing of responsibilities or a segregation of the partners into managing and silent partners. Silent partners usually agree not to be responsible for any phase of the operation of the business and also usually waive any rights to participate in the operation of the

EXHIBIT 15-5
Partnership Profits Distribution

A.   A and B split profits equally:

	Total Profits	A's Share	B's Share
1982	$24,000	$12,000	$12,000
1983	$ 8,000	$ 4,000	$ 4,000

B.   A and B allocate profits:

	Total Profits	A's Share	B's Share
1982	$24,000		
Management fee		$10,000	$ -0-
Interest on capital account		1,000	3,000
Profits split equally		5,000	5,000
	$24,000	$16,000	$ 8,000
1983	$ 8,000		
Management fee		$10,000	$ -0-
Interest on capital account		1,000	3,000
Losses split equally		(3,000)	(3,000)
	$ 8,000	$ 8,000	$ -0-

business. An agreement should provide that a partner who interferes in the functions allotted to another partner be liable for breach of the partnership agreement.

In addition to allocation of certain roles to each active partner, certain acts may be restricted to require the consent of several or all partners. Managing partners may be limited in borrowing or lending money without the unanimous consent of all of them. The managing partners may also be prohibited from placing any liens on partnership assets or buying or selling any assets other than inventory without the unanimous consent of the managing partners. Certain other acts, such as acting as a guarantor or any act that might change the identity of the members of the partnership may require consent even of the silent partners. Provisions in a partnership contract are binding between partners. Allocations of function are not binding on third parties unless the third parties have knowledge thereof.

Banking

A partnership is considered to be a business entity and will maintain a bank account in its own name. Partners will select the bank, open an account, and deposit and withdraw funds as would be the case with any normal checking account. The partnership should contain a set of books, and if there are special rules to be applied as to the bookkeeping methods, these should be spelled out in the partnership agreement. An audit is a review of the books by an independent party (usually a certified public accountant) to ascertain that the financial transactions reflected on the books completely, accurately, and fairly reflect the business's operations. If a business is fairly complex, an annual audit may be advisable. Where the business is simple or where each partner reviews and understands the books, an audit is usually not needed and will be done only when requested by one of the partners. A partnership agreement should specify whether an audit is required.

Retirement

All agreements should spell out provisions for a partner to retire. Options include the purchasing of the interest of the retiring partner or the winding up of the business and terminating of the partnership. The purchase option usually may be exercised by all the remaining partners or by any of them. When a partner retires it is customary for him or her to agree not to compete with the partnership within a radius of so many miles for a period of so many years. This is referred to as a noncompetition clause and is generally enforceable provided the time and geographical limitations are reasonable.

A partnership is a voluntary association and, therefore, can be dissolved by any partner at will. Where the partnership agreement restricts this right, a partner may still withdraw at will, but may be liable to the other partners for damages resulting from breach of the partnership agreement.

Death

The options available on the death of a partner are very similar to those upon a partner's retirement; the surviving partners may purchase the deceased partner's interest or wind up the business and terminate the partnership. Typical agreements provide that the deceased partner's interest shall be valued in a manner excluding goodwill and other similar assets. This is a ''penalty'' provision that deprives the estate of the deceased partner of a portion of the value of the business; however, if the partners agree to this, it is certainly not improper. In addition to valuing the deceased partner's interest, the typical agreement sets up a method of repayment. If the partner's interest is substantial in value, raising the cash necessary to purchase the deceased's partner's interest can be difficult. For this reason, many partnerships purchase life insurance on the lives of their partners. If a partner dies, the partnership or the remaining partners get the insurance proceeds and utilize the money to purchase the deceased partner's interest from his or her estate. Naturally, in such a case there would have to be an agreement between the partners specifying that on the death of one of them the estate of the deceased partner would be obligated to sell the deceased partner's interest for a specified consideration, often the amount of the insurance policy. Without such an agreement, the deceased partner's estate would have no obligation to sell at that price.

In the event that the surviving partners choose to liquidate (assuming there is no insurance), the remaining partners are charged with the obligation to accomplish this, to pay off partnership debts, and then to distribute the remaining assets to the partners, including the deceased partner's estate. The estate continues to share in profits after the partner's death but will not be personally liable for losses beyond the capital originally invested. When the partnership assets (including the name) are sold, all partners usually agree not to compete with the buyers within a certain geographical area for a reasonable period of time. This covenant is necessary to protect the interest of the individuals buying the partnership business. If the partners who were selling out were not willing to enter into such an agreement, the business interest could not be sold, and they could not receive any payments.

Arbitration

Many partnership agreements contain arbitration clauses. Arbitration is substantially less expensive than the litigation procedure. It is also easier to deal with because the rules of arbitration are generally simpler than the rules of courtroom procedure. Once the parties' problem has been resolved by arbitration, the conclusion reached by the arbitrator would be binding on all the parties. It would not be possible to appeal the arbitrator's decision in a court of law except by showing that the arbitrator's resolution was capricious and without regard to the facts as set forth at the hearing.

OTHER RELATIONSHIPS

Family Partnerships

A family partnership is a nonlegal term that applies to a business conducted by members of the same family: husband and wife, parent and children, and so on. This type of organization may run into problems if the agreement is not in writing. In one case, a husband and wife operated a business together and shared profits equally. They reported their respective shares on their tax returns. The state took the position that the absence of a written agreement prevented the existence of a partnership and that the wife merely helped the husband in his business. Whether this position could have been sustained by the state in a court action was irrelevent because the cost of bringing such an action was prohibitive. As a result, the family in question had to accept the state's determination that the business was exclusively that of the husband. (Although the wife was entitled to a reasonable compensation for the amount of time she put in, this was substantially less than half of the profits.) If one enters into a family partnership arrangement, it is highly advisable to reduce the agreement to writing and to deal among members of the family strictly in accordance with that agreement. If an agreement is entered into and the parties to the agreement fail to honor the terms of the agreement among themselves, the government or any other interested party will be justified in claiming that they, too, should be allowed to disregard the effect of that agreement.

Joint Ventures

A joint venture is a partnership organized for one particular business transaction rather than for an ongoing period of time. The authors' agreement to write this textbook is a joint venture because it extends to the production of this text only and is not a general agreement to write things in conjunction with each other. Had the authors agreed to write articles and textbooks, that would have been more in the nature of a partnership. The distinction between joint venture and partnership is academic, however, because the rules that apply to joint ventures are virtually identical with the rules applying to partnerships (Pederson v. Manitowac Co., 255 N.E.2d 146 [N.Y. 1969]). The only practical difference as stated earlier is with respect to the duration of the operation. Owing to their limited purposes, joint ventures tend to end sooner than partnerships. However, this need not always be the case.

Limited Partnerships

A limited partnership is a special kind of partnership that must be created under specific statutory provisions. Their use in normal business conditions is unusual; limited partnerships are primarily found in areas of tax shelters and other similar investment opportunities. A limited partnership limits the losses of the limited partners to their original capital contributions. Limited partners are not personally liable for business debts and may not actively participate in the management of the business. Every limited partnership must have at least one general partner with substantial at-risk capital. This is to protect the interests of the creditors so that they are always in a position in which there is some individual who will be personally liable beyond that individual's investment in the partnership. A limited partnership must be clearly designated as such in the title of the partnership. A limited partner may assign his or her interest to another individual; however, normal partnership rules would apply with respect to the general partners. A limited partnership may consist of one or more limited partners in conjunction with one or more general partners.

Partnerships by Estoppel

A partnership by estoppel is technically an inaccurate term because a partnership does not come into being. The term estopp means to prevent someone from making an assertion or denial. Thus, if I make a statement, a court may subsequently estopp me from denying that statement (prevent me from denying that statement). A partnership by estoppel is created when a individual represents that he or she is a partner with a second individual. If a third party hears that representation and takes action in reliance upon it, the party making the representation will subsequently be estopped from denying the validity of the representation. This is considered to be a partnership by estoppel. For example, I make the false statement that I am a partner with John Smith. It is overheard by Mary Jones. John Smith subsequently approaches Mary Jones to purchase certain items on credit. Mary is reluctant to give credit to John but remembers my statement to the effect that I was his partner. Mary would be willing to extend credit to me and, therefore, extends credit to what she believes to be the partnership of John Smith and me. John Smith subsequently fails to pay his bill. Mary then comes to me and asks me to pay on the grounds that I am a partner and, therefore, am also responsible for the debt. At this point I state that I am not John Smith's partner and am not responsible for payment. In this situation, the court would find against me on the grounds of partnership by estoppel. Because I had made the representation that I was John Smith's partner and because Mary Jones had relied upon the representation to extend credit, she will be able to recover from me as though I were a partner. As between John Smith and me, no partnership exists.

Silent or Secret Partners

Frequently, an individual wishes to be involved in a given business enterprise but does not want others to know that he or she is so involved. If the vehicle through which business is being done is a partnership, this individual would have to become a silent or secret partner. A silent or secret partner is one whose name is not used by the business and whose identity is not revealed to members of the public. A silent or secret partner is unable to enter into any agreement to bind the partnership. He or she is a partner in the sense that he or she is entitled to the appropriate share of profits and the appropriate distribution of assets on dissolution. As between the partners, a silent or secret partner may become involved in the management of the partnership business or in the decision making of the partnership business because this takes place in such a manner that the general public would not be aware of it. A silent or secret partner may become active vis-à-vis the general public at any time unless he or she has contractually agreed otherwise; however, he or she then loses his or her ''silent'' or ''secret'' status.

QUESTIONS

1 Respass and Sharp were partners in several business in Kentucky. One was operating a racing stable; the other was placing bets (''bookmaking,'' which was illegal in Kentucky). From time to time they advanced money to each other for various purposes of the businesses. Sharp had some money of Respass's, which had been given him specifically for the bookmaking operation, when he (Sharp) suddenly died. Respass brought an action for an accounting against Sharp's estate, seeking his money. Decision for whom? Discuss.

2   Eva Raines was doing business as Bates Shoe Store. She entered into an agreement with several individuals (defendants) to sell them the equipment and inventory of the store. The defendants signed notes in her favor in different amounts. Raines also obtained chattel mortgages from each of them covering the equipment and inventory of the business. The business subsequently failed, and Raines attempted to recover the assets of the business as a creditor of the business. Was she an individual creditor of each of the defendants? Was she entitled to participate in the partnership assets? Decision for whom? Discuss.

3   Arnold and Morgan were engaged in a partnership. Arnold was responsible for operation of the business; Morgan was responsible for managing the office and exercising general supervision over bookkeeping and accounting. Morgan offered to purchase Arnold's interest in the business and represented to him that certain financial statements prepared by Morgan correctly presented the net worth of the partnership. Arnold's interest, according to the financial statements, was $38,000. Based on Morgan's financial statements, he agreed to sell his interest to Morgan for $38,000. Arnold made no independent verification of the value of the partnership. When the company's accountants subsequently prepared a financial statement for purposes for filing tax returns, a copy was sent to Arnold, disclosing that his interest in the business was substantially greater than $38,000. Arnold sued Morgan to recover the differential in his equity interest and also punitive damages. Decision for whom? Discuss.

4   DiMicco was the owner of a boat that was seven years old. He applied for insurance from an insurance agency to cover the value of the boat. The insurance agency issued a binder and placed the policy with an insurance company. The insurance company had previously issued instructions to the insurance agency that a condition survey would have to be made before granting insurance on any boat more than five years old. No survey was ever made. Subsequently, the boat sank, and DiMicco recovered a judgment against both the insurance agency and the insurance company. The insurance company sued the agency on the grounds that an agent is liable to a principal for losses incurred by the principal as the result of the agent's negligence. Decision for whom? Discuss.

5   Dr. Cook owned a laboratory and practiced medicine. Dr. Stevens moved into the area and entered into an agreement with Dr. Cook. The agreement provided that Stevens would join Cook's practice as a partner, would pay the partnership for fixed assets currently used by Cook, would contribute all his working time, and would perform 50 percent of the work of the partnership. Stevens would not acquire ownership of the partnership assets. The ratios of profits were initially established at 70 percent for Cook and 30 percent for Stevens. The agreement indicated that after about three years the profits would be shared equally. The relationship between the doctors was terminated, and the issue arose as to whether the two doctors were partners. Were they partners? Discuss.

6   The plaintiff was the mortgagee of a motel in Huntsville, Alabama. The plaintiff entered into a written agreement with the operating supervisor of the defendant, Burns Detective Agency, whereby the agency agreed to patrol the motel and check for various items, including "such other irregularities as may come to their attention." The plaintiff, in a subsequent oral agreement with the operating supervisor of the detective agency, agreed that the defendant would also check the heating system to make sure that it was functioning properly. The heating system was not checked, it was not functioning properly, and the pipes froze, causing substantial damage to the property. The detective

agency claims that the employee-supervisor had no authority to enter into this kind of contract. Decision for whom? Discuss.

7   Galbreath was an employee of the defendant, Star Service & Petroleum Corporation. His job required that he travel throughout an area involving several states, and the company furnished him with an automobile for that purpose, allowing him to garage it at his home and to use it for personal purposes. Galbreath and his wife drove to church in the company car; on their way home, they were in an accident with a vehicle that was operated by Price, whose daughter was injured. Question: Will Star Service & Petroleum Company be held liable to Price for the actions of its agent Galbreath? Discuss.

8   The plaintiff, Dwyer, was a passenger on a streetcar. He paid his fee and entered the rear platform of the car. While he was on the platform smoking a cigar, the conductor approached him, demanding payment of a fare. Plaintiff replied that he had previously paid his fare. The conductor insisted that he had not, and considerable discussions arose. When the plaintiff attempted to leave the streetcar, the conductor refused to allow him to do so without payment of his fare and threatened to arrest him unless he made payment. The plaintiff refused; the conductor called a police officer and had the plaintiff arrested. At the trial the plaintiff was acquitted. The plaintiff then brought an action against the conductor's employer for false arrest. Decision for whom? Discuss.

9   Gramling and Belcher were partners in a retail drugstore. Gramling was responsible for supervision of the preparation of presciptions. Belcher was responsible for general management, purchasing, and selling. Belcher entered into a contract to purchase drugs from the plaintiff, United Drug Company. The contract required the execution of promissory notes as security for payment. The notes were signed by Belcher. Gramling refused to sign the notes. Are the notes a partnership liability? Discuss.

10 Webb, the Defendant, was a horse trainer who rented stalls and trained horses. He hired Dowd to assist him. Webb allowed Dowd to use one of his stables in exchange for services. The plaintiff, Dowd's brother, accompanied Dowd one morning to the stables. An altercation occurred between the plaintiff and the defendant, and the defendant stabbed the plaintiff in the face with a pitchfork, blinding him in one eye. The plaintiff sued the defendant and the owners of the horses in the rented stalls, alleging that there was a partnership or master servant relationship between the trainer and the owners or both. Decision for whom? Discuss.

11 The Plaintiff, Gearhart, was a patron in a bar owned by the defendants, Karl and Robert Angeloff. Another patron of the bar entered into an altercation with the defendant, Karl. Robert grabbed a gun and shot across the bar in the direction of the other customer and his brother. In the process, the plaintiff was wounded. He brought an action against both brothers on the grounds that the act was committed in the course of the partnership business. Decision for whom? Discuss.

12 Gilman entered into a contract with Peycke. The contract provided that they operate a "joint account business," equally dividing profits and losses. The business consists of shipping oranges and lemons, which Gilman was to secure, without any expense to the joint account, on consignment. Purchases over $500 could be made with the consent of Peycke. Gilman was entitled to a fee for each carload of fruit shipped, and Peycke was to supply all the money and do all the selling free of any charge to their joint account. Legitimate packing house costs were to be charged against the joint account. Gilman shipped a quantity of fruit, for which he received some funds. The funds were not uti-

lized for the purchase of the fruit but for other personal obligations of Gilman. The vendors of the fruit sued Peycke, claiming that there was a partnership. Decision for whom? Discuss.

13 Maurin was a partner with his brother in the business of purchasing and selling grains that were locally produced. The plaintiff, Maurin, went to another community and purchased larger-than-normal volumes of grain on speculation and signed on behalf of the partnership. The other partner, upon learning of the transaction, immediately repudiated the transaction and refused to honor the commitment. Was this an authorized partnership transaction? Decision for whom? Discuss.

14 The plaintiff and the defendant entered into a written agreement. The agreement provided that it was specifically not to be considered to be a partnership agreement and that the parties were entering into a joint venture to operate farmland owned by the defendant. Neither party was to mortgage or otherwise encumber jointly owned property; neither party was to purchase farm products, and so on, in a value exceeding a certain amount without the consent of the other; the defendant was to furnish the land and to make certain payments whereas the plaintiff was to operate the premises; income was to be equally divided, and operating expenses were also to be equally divided. The plaintiff hired an individual, who was injured on the premises and brought suit against both parties. The plaintiff settled the suit, and the defendant refused to contribute to the settlement. The plaintiff alleged that the defendant was obligated to make such a contribution because there was a partnership. Decision for whom? Discuss.

CHAPTER 16

Corporations

DEFINITIONS AND CHARACTERISTICS

A corporation is a legal entity; it is totally a creature of statute. Each state has corporate laws that provide procedures for the formation of this "legal being." There is a Model Business Corporation Act, which has been proposed by a conference of lawmakers, but, unlike the Uniform Commercial Code, this Model Corporation Act has not been adopted by all states. In fact, the Model Corporation Act has only been adopted by 35 jurisdictions, and many of these have not adopted the model act as a whole. (The states are Alabama, Alaska, Arkansas, Colorado, Connecticut, District of Columbia, Georgia, Illinois, Iowa, Kentucky, Louisiana, Maine, Maryland, Massachusetts, Michigan, Mississippi, Montana, Nebraska, New Jersey, New Mexico, New York, North Carolina, North Dakota, Oregon, Rhode Island, South Carolina, South Dakota, Tennessee, Texas, Utah, Vermont, Virginia, Washington, Wisconsin, and Wyoming). This section of the text uses material from the Model Corporation Act. It is advisable to check with your state's corporate division or secretary of state for specific regulations regarding corporations.

Regardless of where you reside, the mechanics of how a corporation works and what its detriments and benefits are basically are the same. You are permitted by state statute to create a "legal person" provided you follow the statutory procedures. This legal person has most of the legal rights and liabilities that you, as an individual, have. If you are contemplating a corporate form of business, you will have to deal with this "creature" at arm's length (as if it was a complete stranger). You are considered to be an employee of the corporation, even if you are the only shareholder. You are responsible for paying both employment and income taxes. (See Chapter 17.)

Why incorporate then? The major advantage of incorporating is a limitation of liability that the corporate structure provides. If a corporation is used correctly, as a tool for business, you may be able to enjoy the protection of having a legal person shelter you from personal liability with respect to your business debts. For example, suppose that you are in business and that the business is failing. It appears as if it will not be able to continue. Under a noncorporate structure, not only are the assets that you have amassed within the business attachable by the creditors, but your personal property (your house, car, and so on) is also fair game. Had a corporation been set up and operated according to law, only the business assets would be subject to the creditors' actions.

It must be cautioned that the corporation must have a separate existence and that there must not be any questions as to its separate identity. There have been cases in which the courts have decided that even when a separate corporation exists, it will be ignored. Case law has not absolutely defined what the equities in each case will be. The wording in the decisions indicates that where there is control to such a degree that the corporation has become a mere "instrumentality" having no separate mind, will, or existence of its own, the individual running the corporation will be personally liable. This concept has been termed "piercing the corporate veil" (Old Town Development Company vs. Langford, 349 N.E.2d 744 [Ind. 1976];

Krivo Industry Supply Co. vs. National Distributors and Chemical Corp., 483 F.2d 1098 [5th Cir. 1973]).

Another advantage of incorporating is the perpetual existence that a corporation provides. A corporation is set up for an indefinite period of time, unlike a proprietorship or partnership, which terminates each time there is a change of ownership. This gives a businessperson the ability to raise funds and to transfer assets without concern as to the life expectancies or whims of the various parties involved. If a corporate shareholder is dissatisfied with the business, he or she need not dissolve it, but need merely sell his or her interest (shares) to another.

Another important corporate characteristic is centralization of management. Partners traditionally have an obligation to participate in the management of the business. Corporations are usually managed by a small group of trained professionals who may or may not be shareholders.

All states require that corporations have a purpose that must be spelled out in the certificate of incorporation. The Model Corporation Act indicates that corporations may be organized for any lawful purpose except for the purposes of banking or insurance. These kinds of corporations are typically set up under separate statutes. If the corporate charter or bylaws do not limit the power of a corporation, statutes give a corporation numerous powers to carry out its stated purpose. A general corporation has powers that include the right to sue and be sued and to defend the corporate name.

A corporation can purchase or lease property. It can own, hold, improve, and deal in any way with both real and personal property. A corporation can lend and borrow money, make contracts, and incur liabilities. A corporation may conduct business in the state in which it was incorporated or in any other state subject to the registration requirements of that other state, if any. In addition, it can elect and appoint officers and agents to work on the corporation's behalf and can fix their compensation. It can also make and alter bylaws (the operational documents or procedures that control the interrelationship between the various parties who make up a corporation and the operation of its business). The corporation may set up pension plans, trusts, and so on. It can also be a partner in a partnership, joint venture, or other type of business entity. Moreover, a corporation can buy and sell shares of stock in itself and other corporations. Furthermore, a corporation has the right to have a corporate seal. This corporate seal, coupled with the authorized signature of one of the members of the corporation, will act as the corporation's signature.

The structure of a general corporation follows the same format regardless of the state it is formed in. The owners of the corporation are termed *shareholders*. There are two types of shareholders: those who own common stock and those who own preferred or special class stock. Shareholders have certain rights and liabilities according to both state law and the corporation bylaws.

The corporation also has a board of directors, who are appointed by the shareholders. The board of directors consists of individuals who have a "fiduciary" duty to the corporation to set the priorities and direction of the corporation. Corporations not only consist of shareholders and directors but also of officers. The officers of the corporation consist of the president, one or more vice-presidents as prescribed by the bylaws, a secretary, and a treasurer. Officers are elected by the board of directors. The officers are the agents for the corporation. They have the authority to perform management duties for the corporation. The guidelines for the performance of their duties are spelled out in the bylaws as well as by corporate laws of the particular state that the corporation is formed in.

A not-for-profit corporation is a special kind of corporation, which is set up to perform a certain business or nonbusiness functions. The term *not-for-profit* does not mean that the corporation cannot make a profit. Not-for-profit corporations are allowed to make a profit, but none of the shareholders or members may receive any profits or pecuniary interests from the operation of the corporation (they may be paid a salary for services rendered). Examples of not-for-profit corporations include churches, hospitals, schools, day-care centers, and so on. There are also not-for-profit corporations set up to provide recreational, social, and cultural activities for their members.

Another type of corporation recognized in most states is the cooperative corporation. This type of corporation is set up under a cooperative corporation law and is basically a not-for-profit type corporation. The cooperative corporation is not organized for the pecuniary profit or financial gain of the members. No part of its assets, income, or profits is allowed to be distributed to its members or officers except as permitted by law. The law usually permits salaries to be paid. The corporation is set up to assist its members by performing services connected with a particular area, for example, food co-ops, which provide wholesale-priced food to their membership.

As you can see, there is a large array of corporate organizations. It is suggested that you develop a proposal with respect to the type of venture that you are involved with and then sit down with your attorney and discuss the alternatives.

SHAREHOLDERS' RIGHTS AND LIABILITIES

Corporate shareholders have several rights, including the right of ownership, the right to vote, the preemptive right to share in new issues of stock, a right to inspect the books, and a right to dividends. The right to vote is the only right the shareholder has in the management of the corporation. This right allows the shareholder to elect directors, usually at the annual meeting of shareholders.

The bylaws of a typical corporation indicate the place and time of shareholders' meetings. Generally, there are two types of meetings. There is the annual meeting, which must be held once a year, and there are special meetings, which may be called by the board or by the president. There are also provisions for calling a special meeting if the majority of the board of directors or a majority of the shareholders request a meeting in writing. That request should also state the purpose of the proposed meeting. The business that is transacted at a special meeting must be confined to the purposes stated in the notice.

Corporate bylaws also include the criteria for fixing the date of record. This date is used for purposes of determining when a shareholder is entitled to dividends or notices or when a shareholder is entitled to vote at a shareholders' meeting. (A typical date that is set is usually not more than 50 and not less than 10 days before the date of any particular action or meeting.) Corporate bylaws also include provisions for notifying shareholders of meetings. A typical provision requires a written notice of each meeting other than the annual meeting. The notice should state the purpose or purposes of the meeting, the place, the date, and the hour of meeting. Notice can be given either personally or by mail. Notice of a meeting need not be given to any shareholder who signs a waiver of notice either in person or by proxy (Exhibit 16–1). A shareholder's presence at a meeting either in person or by proxy without protesting prior to the conclusion of the meeting will be considered a waiver of notice.

Provisions for the running of shareholders' meetings are also set out in the bylaws. One of the requirements is that a quorum of shareholders be present. A quorum is usually defined as holders of the majority of the shares entitled to vote. Once a quorum is present to start a meeting, it is not broken by the withdrawal of any of the shareholders. Shareholders who are present at a meeting may adjourn the meeting despite the absence of a quorum. A shareholder who is entitled to vote at a meeting may authorize another person to act for him or her. This authorization is called a *proxy*. Bylaws may include provisions that a proxy must be signed by the shareholder or that no proxy shall be valid after the expiration of a certain number of months from the date thereof unless otherwise provided in the proxy. Generally, proxies are revocable at the pleasure of the shareholder executing them.

A shareholder is qualified to vote if he or she is a shareholder of record. Each shareholder shall be entitled to one vote for every share which he or she holds in his or her name. Shareholders generally vote for directors and for other special cor-

EXHIBIT 16–1
Proxy

I, _____, do hereby constitute and appoint _____, attorney and agent for me, and in my name, place, and stead, to vote as my proxy at any stockholders' meetings to be held between the date of this proxy and _____, 19_____, unless sooner revoked, with full power to cast the number of votes that all my shares of stock in _____ (corporation) should entitle me to cast as if I were then personally present, and authorize _____ to act for me and in my name and stead as fully as I could act if I were present, giving to _____, attorney and agent, full power of substitution and revocation.

In witness whereof, I have executed this proxy on _____, 19_____.

In the presence of _____

_____
(Signature)

porate actions that may be presented to them (e.g., proposal to change capital structure or to sell all assets of the corporation). A director shall be elected by a plurality of the votes cast unless otherwise provided. A majority vote is needed for the approval of other corporate matters. In the event that shareholders cannot get together for a meeting, corporate bylaws provide a provision setting forth that an action may be taken in lieu of a meeting if the shareholders consent in writing. This consent must be signed by all the members and holders of the outstanding shares entitled to vote.

All states allow cumulative voting in the election of directors. Some states require cumulative voting for directors. Cumulative voting allows each shareholder one vote per share times the total number of directors running for election. Votes can be distributed among directors in any manner the shareholder wishes. Cumulative voting may permit minority shareholders to elect at least one person to the board of directors. For example, a corporation with 20 shareholders and a total of 60 shares outstanding is electing 5 directors. Under "straight voting" procedures, the holders of a majority of shares (31) can fill each of the five positions. Under cumulative voting, holders of 11 shares could elect one director. They would receive 55 votes, which would have to be cast for the same candidate. The remaining 245 votes (49 shares times 5 directors), if split 5 ways, would result in 49 votes for each position. The minority choice would win.

The shareholder's right to a preemptive offer of shares enables shareholders to maintain their relative position of ownership in the corporation. Each shareholder is allowed to subscribe to a percentage of new shares equal to the number of shares presently owned divided by the total number of shares outstanding.

A shareholder's right to inspect the books of the corporation must be reasonable. A shareholder is given the right to investigate the financial condition of the corporation as well as the quality of the management. A stockholder also has the right to inspect the books in order to organize shareholders in opposing the board of directors or to buy shares from other shareholders. Many cases have denied shareholders the right to inspect the books when it was deemed that their only purpose was to harass management or to satisfy their idle curiosity. The inspection of the books and records may be made by a shareholder or his or her agent. The Model Corporation Act indicates that a shareholder "shall have the right to examine, in person, or by agent or attorney, at any reasonable time or times, for any proper purpose, its relevant books and records of account, minutes, and record of shareholders and to make extracts therefrom."

Shareholders have a right to receive certificates representing their ownership in the corporation.

Corporate ownership interests have alway been freely transferable from one individual to another. Such a transfer will not affect the status of the business entity. When a shareholder in a public corporation sells his or her shares, the company is generally unaware of that fact. In a small "closely held" corporation, it may not be desirable to allow shareholders to transfer their interests. A shareholders' agreement is often entered into that, among other things, will restrict the right of transfer. Such restriction must be noted conspicuously on the face of the shares.

Shareholders are entitled to declared *dividends*, which are distributions of corporate earnings to a corporation's shareholders. The distribution is made according to the number and type of shares that the shareholder owns. The bylaws of a corporation will provide that dividends be declared in such amounts and at such times as the board may determine. The bylaws also provide that the board may set aside earnings in amounts that they deem proper to meet contingencies, for equalizing dividends from year to year, for repairing or maintaining property of the corporation, or for any other purpose that they feel is in the best interests of the corporation. The board may also abolish any of these reserves. There is no rule that a corporation must pay dividends. State statutes commonly provide that dividends may only be declared from surplus (assets in excess of liabilities). Once dividends are declared, the shareholders become creditors of the corporation and may sue the corporation to recover moneys due them. Usually, dividends are paid in money, but they could also be paid in property corporate shares. The general rule with respect to cash or property distributions is that the date of declaration determines the right to receive a dividend. This rule is subject to change by the board of directors. If a dividend is to be paid in stock, the party who owns the shares at the time of the distribution of the dividend is the one entitled to receive the stock dividend.

Shareholders are also entitled to receive the balance of corporate assets on dissolution of a corporation, after payment to all creditors.

Shareholders are usually not liable for acts of the corporation. State statutes may provide for unlimited liability for items such as wages or taxes, especially in corporations where shares are not traded publicly. In addition, a shareholder can be held liable for shares that are issued for less than par value. Future services or promissory notes or both will not be considered sufficient consideration for payment of shares. In situations where the shares have been purchased for less than par value, the creditors may be able to institute action to recover the balance due from each shareholder to the extent of the deficiency in his or her payment. Shareholders are also liable for dividends that were paid illegally. If a statute provides that dividends cannot be paid except out of surplus, a shareholder may be liable to creditors to the extent that the capital has been depleted by a payment from sources other than capital.

DIRECTORS

The business of the corporation is generally managed under the watchful eyes of the board of directors, who have a fiduciary obligation. This obligation requires that a director must serve in good faith and in a manner he or she reasonably believes to be in the best interest of the corporation. The standard of care is great and is that which an ordinary prudent person in a like position would use under similar circumstance. In the event that a director does not comply with this requirement, he or she can be held liable for damages that may be incurred by the corporation or the shareholders. In providing direction, a director can rely on officers or employees of the corporation, legal counsel, public accountants, and other outside professionals. A director may also rely on decisions of the committee of the board, upon which he or she does not serve.

The state Business Corporation Act, as well as a corporation's bylaws, provide the guidelines for the operation of the board of directors. These require minimum ages for directors of from 18 to 21 and spell out other requirements. Corporate bylaws can require directors to be shareholders. They can also limit the number of directors except when all the shares are owned by less than three shareholders. In that case statutes allow the number of directors to be less than three but not less than the number of shareholders. The shareholders usually elect directors at the annual meeting to hold office until the next annual meeting. In the event that there is a newly created directorship or a vacancy in one of the directorships, such a vacancy may be filled by a vote of the majority of the directors then in office. This is true except for vacancies occurring by reason of the removal of directors without cause. In that case, the vacancy would be filled by a vote (usually a majority) of the shareholders. Newly elected directors generally are allowed to hold office for the unexpired term of the predecessors. Directors may be removed from the board for cause by a vote of the shareholders or by the action of the board, but directors may only be removed without cause by a vote of the shareholders. A director may resign at any time, but he or she must give written notice to the board, president, or the secretary of the corporation. The director may specify when the resignation is effective. In the absence of such designation, receipt by the board or an officer will be sufficient to have the resignation take place.

The majority of the entire board of directors constitutes a quorum for the transaction of business. A vote of a majority of the directors present at a meeting shall be considered an act of the whole board so long as the quorum is present. Generally, each director has one vote regardless of the number of shares that particular director may own.

The typical bylaws also establish the place and time of board meetings. There is a provision for a regular annual meeting of the board, which is usually held immediately following the annual meeting of the shareholders. Regular meetings of the board of directors may be held without notice, but notice must be given for special meetings. A special meeting may usually be called by the president upon notice to each director personally, by mail, or by wire. There are also provisions for directors to request a meeting. Notice of a meeting need not be given to any director who submits a waiver of notice of meeting or who attends a meeting without protest. The majority of directors present may adjourn any meeting to another time and place regardless of whether or not a quorum is present. The notice of the adjournment shall be given to all directors who were absent at the time of the adjournment.

Meetings of a board of directors are generally run by the president of the corporation. A temporary chairperson may be chosen if the president is not able to preside. In planning for business of the corporation, the board may designate executive committees from among its members. These committees generally serve at the pleasure of the board. Members of the board of directors are generally not compensated for their services on the board. They can be given a fixed sum, including expenses for actual attendance at each regular and special meeting. An individual who is a director is usually not precluded from serving the corporation in another capacity such as president, treasurer, and so on and receiving compensation for this position. In a small corporation, this is frequently the case.

OFFICERS

Officers are the individuals who run the day-to-day business of the corporation. They take their direction from the board of directors. The officers include the president, one or more vice-presidents, a secretary, and a treasurer. The duties and powers of these officers are described in the bylaws. Officers are usually elected or appointed by the board of directors. They may be removed by the board with or without cause. In the event an officer cannot perform his or her duties because of death, resignation, or for other reasons, the board may elect a successor to fill the unexpired term. Two or more offices may be held simultaneously by the same individual except for president and secretary. The board of directors fixes the salary of the officers, and the board may require any officer to post a bond or give security for the faithful performance of his or her duties.

The president is the chief executive officer of the corporation. He or she will preside at all the meetings of shareholders and of the board. Moreover, he or she has the responsibility of managing the business of the corporation and seeing that all orders and resolutions of the board of directors are carried into effect.

The vice-president has all of the powers that the president has and exercises those powers during the absence or disability of the president. The board of directors may establish the requirements and the job descriptions for many different vice-presidential functions. Many corporate organizational structures include vice-presidents for marketing, for production, and so on.

The secretary is responsible for recording all votes and minutes of the directors' and shareholders' meetings. These minutes are kept in the corporate book. It is also the secretary's responsibility to give notice of all meetings to shareholders and to board members. The corporate seal is to be kept by the secretary, and it is to be affixed to any and all documents or instruments that the board of directors authorizes. The secretary may be required to prepare a certified list of the names of shareholders entitled to vote at each shareholders' meeting. This list should indicate the number of shares and the class of shares if there is more than one class. It is also the duty of the secretary to keep all the documents and records for the corporation and to do anything else the board of directors prescribes.

The treasurer is responsible for keeping custody of the corporate funds and securities. This responsibility extends to keeping a full and accurate account of receipts and disbursements in the corporate books as well as depositing and disbursing funds from the corporate bank account and providing an account of the financial position of the corporation at regular board meetings or whenever an accounting is required. The various duties of the corporate officers may be delegated to other employees, but the responsibility for these tasks cannot be delegated. For example, whereas the treasurer may appoint an accountant or internal controller to handle the functioning of the accounting, it is his or her ultimate responsibility.

The board of directors may require that any officer execute a bond or surety. These bonds are insurance policies. In the event that an officer is irresponsible or negligent in accounting for property or funds of the corporation, the bonding company will reimburse the corporation. Prior to issuing a bond, the bonding company will investigate the background of the officer to determine if the person has a criminal record as well as whether he or she is a good risk.

STOCK CERTIFICATES

The shares of stock of the corporation are representations of ownership in the corporation. The stock certificates should be numbered and recorded in the transfer ledger of the corporation as they are issued. The transfer ledger shows the name of the shareholder, the place of residence, the date when the individual became an owner, the certificate numbers issued, the number of shares issued, and, in the case of a transfer, from whom the shares were transferred. The stock transfer book also includes the amount paid for the shares, the date of the transfer of shares, and the individual to whom the shares were transferred. When stock is transferred, there is usually a transfer tax imposed by the state. A notation also is made in the stock transfer book as to the amount of tax paid. The tax is usually collected from the individual who has received the stock and must be paid to the state by the individual transferring the stock.

Corporate shares are usually signed by the president or vice-president and treasurer or secretary, and they usually bear the corporate seal. In the event that a stock certificate is lost or destroyed, the board may direct that a new certificate or certificates be issued. The individual who lost the stock or whose stock was destroyed must swear by an affidavit to the facts of the loss. The board of directors may, at its discretion, as a condition precedent to issuing replacement certificates, require that the owner of the lost or destroyed certificate post a bond to indemnify the corporation against any claim that may be made against the corporation with respect to the certificate that was alleged to have been lost or destroyed. It is the corporation's responsibility not to transfer certificates of shares without the specific authorization of the shareholder. A certificate that was presumed lost or stolen when, in fact, it was transferred to a bona fide purchaser could cause the corporation to issue and be liable for two shares when only one was actually paid for.

If an individual wishes to transfer shares, he or she may do so by endorsing the stock certificates and the statement showing authority to transfer. (See Exhibit 16–2.) The corporation will then issue a new certificate to the transferee and cancel the old certificate. A corporation is generally entitled to treat the holder of record of any share as the holder in fact and shall not be bound to recognize any equitable

EXHIBIT 16-2
Stock Certificate

claim to an interest in such share on the part of any person except as might be expressly provided by the law of the state in which the corporation is formed.

Corporate bylaws usually provide that the board of directors has the power to close the share transfer book of the corporation for a period of not more than 10 days prior to any shareholders' meeting, any date upon which shareholders shall be called upon or have a right to take action without a meeting, or any date fixed for the payment of a dividend or any other form of distribution. Only those shareholders of record at the time the transfer books are closed shall be recognized for the purpose of receiving notice, voting at such meeting, being allowed to take appropriate action, or being entitled to receive any dividend or other form of distribution.

A corporation can hire an individual or group of individuals or another corporation to maintain its corporate transfer ledger. This person or persons is called a transfer agent. Transfer agents provide this service for a fee, but the corporation is still ultimately liable for any wrongdoing with respect to its shares of stock.

Miscellaneous

Corporate bylaws establish the corporate seal as the official signature of the corporation. Generally, the seal is circular in form and bears the name of the corporation, the year of its organization, the words *corporate seal*, and the state in which it was incorporated.

Bylaws designate the fiscal year for the corporation. They also provide for changes, amendments, or repeal and so on. General provisions may include statements that the bylaws may be abandoned, repealed, or adopted by vote of the holders of the shares or by the board. In the event that the board of directors does amend, repeal, or adopt a bylaw provision, this provision may be amended by the shareholders at a later date. In the event that a bylaw that regulates the election of directors is adopted, amended, or repealed, the shareholders must be specifically notified of this change at the next meeting of the shareholders.

It is important that the corporate books be set up correctly. The yearly meetings that are required by the bylaws of the corporate directors and shareholders should always be held. These records might be necessary in dealing with government agencies such as the Internal Revenue Service or state taxing authorities. The records are also valuable in documenting the interrelationship between the individuals that are involved in operating the corporate business. Corporations set up by one incorporator and consisting of one shareholder or a small group of shareholders and directors are advised to keep their books and records current to prevent ''piercing of the corporate veil'' as discussed previously in the section on definitions and characteristics.

FILING REQUIREMENTS

Each type of corporation has its own particular filing requirements. The state in which you wish to incorporate should be contacted for an outline of those requirements. Generally, all jurisdictions require articles of incorporation to be filed (see Exhibit 16–3).

These articles of incorporation, sometimes called a corporate charter, must include the name of the corporation. There are certain restrictions with respect to the name. The Model Corporation Act indicates that the corporate name shall contain the word *corporation, company, incorporated, or limited* or an abbreviation of one of those terms. There are also restrictions that limit the corporate name from indicating that the corporation is organized for any purpose other than the one contained in its charter. A corporate name that is deceptive or deceptively similar to the name of another domestic corporation cannot be used. If you wished to set up a fast-food restaurant, you could not use the name *McDonald's.* It is generally advisable to reserve a corporate name prior to preparing the corporate charter for submission to the particular department in the state in which you desire to incorporate. This name reservation will alleviate possible typing changes that may have to be made to your corporate charter because the name is not appropriate.

In addition to the name, a corporate charter must also provide the address at which the business is going to be located as well as an address for service of process on the corporation. This allows a lawsuit against a corporation to be instituted with-

EXHIBIT 16-3
Certificate of Incorporation

ARTICLE ONE. Name. The name of this corporation is _____.
ARTICLE TWO. Purposes. The purpose for which this corporation is formed is:

    1. To engage in the business of purchasing, acquiring, owning, leasing, selling, transferring, encumbering, generally dealing in, at wholesale or retail, importing, exporting, repairing, renovating, and servicing all types of new and used automobiles, trucks, and other motor vehicles and any parts or accessories used in connection therewith; and the purchasing, acquiring, owning, selling, and generally dealing in all types of supplies used by all types of motor vehicles.

    2. To purchase, to receive by way of gift, subscribe for, invest in, and in all other ways acquire import, lease, possess, maintain, handle on consignment, own, hold for investment or otherwise use, enjoy, exercise, operate, manage, conduct, perform, make, borrow, guarantee, contract in respect of, trade and deal in, sell, exchange, let, lend, export, mortgage, pledge, deed in trust, hypothecate, encumber, transfer, assign and in all other ways dispose of, design, develop, invent, improve, equip, repair, alter, fabricate, assemble, build, construct, operate, manufacture, plant, cultivate, produce, market, and, in all other ways (whether like or unlike any of the foregoing), deal in and with property of every kind and character, real, personal, or mixed, tangible or intangible, wherever situated and however held, including, but not limited to, money, credits, choses in action, securities, stocks, bonds, warrants, script, certificates, debentures, mortgages, notes, commercial paper, and other obligations and evidences of interest in or indebtedness of any person, firm, or corporation, foreign or domestic, or of any government or subdivision or agency thereof, documents of title, and accompanying rights, and every other kind and character of personal property, real property (improved or unimproved), and the products and avails thereof, and every character of interest therein and appurtenance thereto; including, but not limited to, mineral, oil, gas and water rights, all or any part of any going business and its incidents, franchises, subsidies, charters, concessions, grants, rights, powers or privileges, granted or conferred by any government or subdivision or agency thereof, and any interest in or part of any of the foregoing, and to exercise in respect thereof all of the rights, powers, privileges, and immunities of individual owners or holders thereof.

    3. To hire and employ agents, servants, and employees and to enter into agreements of employment and collective bargaining agreements and to act as agent, contractor, trustee, factor, or otherwise, either alone or in company with others.

    4. To promote or aid in any manner, financially or otherwise, any person, firm, association, or corporation and to guarantee contracts and other obligations.

    5. To let concessions to others to do any of the things that this corporation is empowered to do and to enter into, make, perform, and carry out contracts and arrangements of every kind and character with any person, firm, association, or corporation or any government or authority or subdivision or agency thereof.

    6. To carry on any business whatsoever that this corporation may deem proper or convenient in connection with any of the foregoing purposes or otherwise or that it may deem calculated, directly or indirectly, to improve the interests of this corporation and to exercise all powers conferred by the laws of the State of _____ on corporations formed under the laws pursuant to which and under which the corporation is formed, as such laws are not in effect or may at any time hereafter be amended, and to do any and all things hereinabove set forth to the same extent and as fully as natural persons might or

EXHIBIT 16-3, cont.

could do, either alone or in connection with other persons, firms, associations, or corporations, and in any part of the world.

      The foregoing statement of purposes shall be construed as a statement of both purposes and powers, shall be liberally construed in aid of the powers of this corporation, and the powers and purposes stated in each clause shall, except where otherwise stated, be in nowise limited or restricted by any term or provision of any other clause and shall be regarded not only as independent purposes, but the purposes and powers stated shall be construed distributively as each object expressed, and the enumeration as to specific powers shall not be construed as to limit in any manner the aforesaid general powers, but are in furtherance of, and in addition to and not in limitation of, said general powers.
ARTICLE THREE. Registered Office. The address of the initial registered office of the corporation is _____, and the name of its initial registered agent at such address is _____.
ARTICLE FOUR. Directors.

      1. The number of directors constituting the initial board of directors is _____, and the names and addresses of the persons who are to serve as directors until the first annual meeting of the shareholders or until their successors are elected and qualified are:

Name	Address
_____	_____
_____	_____

      2. The number of directors of the corporation set forth in Clause (1) of this article shall constitute the authorized number of directors until changed by an amendment of this certificate of incorporation or by a bylaw duly adopted by the vote or written consent of the holders of a majority of the then outstanding shares of stock in the corporation.
ARTICLE FIVE. Incorporators. The names and addresses of the incorporators are:

Name	Address
_____	_____
_____	_____
_____	_____

ARTICLE SIX. Capitalization. The total number of shares of all classes of stock that the corporation shall have authority to issue is _____, (number) shares of common stock at _____ Dollars ($_____) par value each.
      In witness whereof, for the purpose of forming a corporation under the laws of the State of _____, we, the undersigned, have personally executed _____ (these articles or this certificate) of incorporation on this day of _____, 19_____.

(Signatures)

(Acknowledgments) _____

out requiring the plaintiff to find and serve the corporate officers. Service on the designated agent will suffice. The name or names and addresses of the incorporators must also be listed. State law determines the number of incorporators that are necessary. The incorporator or incorporators are the person or persons who prepare and file the charter. They must sign and deliver the articles of incorporation to the state. The incorporator also procures the financing.

There are several methods of financing a corporation. These methods include loans from banks or other sources and sales of stock certificates to the general public or to individuals known to the incorporator. Both state and federal regulations protect the public from sale of securities of nonexistent or worthless corporations. These laws have been called "Blue Sky" laws. State "Blue Sky" laws can apply only to intrastate transactions whereas the federal regulations apply to sales of securities in interstate commerce. The Securities Act of 1933 deals with original distributions of securities, and the Securities and Exchange Act of 1934 deals with secondary distributions of securities on the stock exchanges and over-the-counter markets. If a corporation wishes to sell shares of its stock, the Securities and Exchange Commission requires preparation of a prospectus for purchasers, setting forth certain information outlined by the 1933 Securities Act as amended. This requirement for registration and prospectus exists for all corporations that issue shares of $500,000 or more. The statute does not apply to transactions between private investors or to private offerings as defined in the statute. The 1933 act provides civil and criminal sanctions for failure to comply.

Articles of incorporation must include the purpose or purposes for which the corporation is organized. In addition to the purpose, the duration of the corporation must be stated. This duration may be perpetual. The charter must also designate the number of shares that the corporation shall have the authority to issue, including the class and the par value of each of the shares, par value being the legal value. A corporation can issue shares that have no par value. Failure to pay par value for a share of stock can obligate a purchaser of a share for less than par value to pay the difference between the purchase price and par value. This liability will occur only in cases where there are not enough assets to cover creditors' claims on the dissolution or bankruptcy of the corporation.

The articles of incorporation can also include provisions for the regulation of the internal affairs of the corporation, such as restricting the transfer of shares; generally, these types of items are left for the bylaws. Articles of incorporation can designate the number of directors constituting the initial board as well as the names and addresses of persons who are to serve as directors until the first annual meeting of shareholders.

Once the articles of incorporation are prepared, they are sent to the secretary of state or other designated authority in the state of incorporation, for filing with the appropriate filing fee. It should be noted that an individual is not legally able to act as a corporation or on behalf of a corporation that has not been formed. Therefore, one must make sure that the particular corporate documents have been submitted and filed with the state. A person who acts for a corporation that has not been formed will be held personally liable for his or her actions.

ORGANIZATION

After receipt of official approval of your corporation, you must prepare the corporate bylaws (Exhibit 16–4) and minute book and obtain a corporate seal. These are often available in the form of a ''corporate kit'' supplied by legal stationery stores. The corporate kit will contain minutes and bylaws as well as instruction for their completion. It will also include printed stock certificates as well as a stock transfer ledger and a corporate seal.

EXHIBIT 16-4
Business Corporation Bylaws

Article One
Offices

The principal office of the corporation shall be located at _____ (address), City of _____, County of _____, State of _____. The board of directors shall have the power and authority to establish and maintain branch or subordinate offices at any other locations.

Article Two
Stockholders

Section 1. Annual Meeting. The annual meeting of the stockholders shall be held on the _____ of _____ in each year, beginning with the year 19_____, at the hour of _____ o'clock ___M., for the purpose of electing directors and for the transaction of such other business as may come before the meeting. If the day fixed for the annual meeting shall be a legal holiday, such meeting shall be held on the next succeeding business day.

Section 2. Special Meetings. Special meetings of the stockholders, for any purpose or purposes, unless otherwise prescribed by statute, may be called by the president or by the board of directors and shall be called by the president at the request of the holders of not less than _____ (number) of all the outstanding shares of the corporation entitled to vote at the meeting.

Section 3. Place of Meeting. The board of directors may designate any place within the State of _____ as the place of meeting for any annual meeting or for any special meeting called by the board of directors. If no designation is made or if a special meeting is otherwise called, the place of meeting shall be the principal office of the corporation.

Section 4. Notice of Meeting. Written notice stating the place, day, and hour of the meeting, and, in case of a special meeting, the purpose or purposes for which the meeting is called shall be delivered not less than _____ days nor more than _____ days before the date of the meeting, either personally or by mail, by or at the direction of the president or the secretary or the officer or persons calling the meeting, to each shareholder of record entitled to vote at such meeting.

Section 5. Closing Transfer Books or Fixing Record Date. For the purpose of determining stockholders entitled to notice of, or to vote at, any meeting of stockholders or any adjournment thereof, or stockholders entitled to receive payment of any dividend, or to make a determination of shareholders for any other proper purpose, the board of directors

EXHIBIT 16-4, cont.

of the corporation may provide that the stock transfer books shall be closed for a stated period, but not to exceed _____ days.

　　Section 6. Quorum. A majority of the outstanding shares of the corporation entitled to vote, represented in person or by proxy, shall constitute a quorum at a meeting of stockholders. If less than a majority of such outstanding shares are represented at a meeting, a majority of the shares so represented may adjourn the meeting from time to time without further notice. At such adjourned meeting at which a quorum is present or represented, any business may be transacted that might have been transacted at the meeting as originally notified. The stockholders present at a duly organized meeting may continue to transact business until adjournment, notwithstanding the withdrawal of enough stockholders to leave less than a quorum.

　　Section 7. Proxies. At all meetings of stockholders, a stockholder may vote by proxy executed in writing by the stockholder or by his or her duly authorized attorney in fact. Such proxy shall be filed with the secretary of the corporation before or at the time of the meeting.

　　Section 8. Voting of Shares. Subject to the provisions of any applicable law or any provision of the certificate of incorporation or of these bylaws concerning cumulative voting, each outstanding share entitled to vote shall be entitled to one vote on each matter submitted to a vote at a meeting of stockholders.

Article Three
Board of Directors

　　Section 1. General Powers. The business and affairs of the corporation shall be managed by its board of directors.

　　Section 2. Number, Tenure, and Qualifications. The number of directors of the corporation shall be _____. Directors shall be elected at the annual meeting of stockholders, and the term of office of each director shall be until the next annual meeting of stockholders and the election and qualification of his or her successor. Directors need not be stockholders of the corporation.

　　Section 3. Regular Meetings. A regular meeting of the board of directors shall be held without notice other than this bylaw immediately after and at the same place as the annual meeting of stockholders. The board of directors may provide, by resolution, the time and place for holding additional regular meetings without other notice than such resolution. Additional regular meetings shall be held at the principal office of the corporation in the absence of any designation in the resolution.

　　Section 4. Special Meetings. Special meetings of the board of directors may be called by or at the request of the president or any two directors and shall be held at the principal office of the corporation or at such other place as the directors may determine.

　　Section 5. Notice. Notice of any special meeting shall be given at least _____ hours before the time fixed for the meeting, by written notice delivered personally or mailed to each director at his or her business address or by telegram. The attendance of a director at a meeting shall constitute a waiver of notice of such meeting except where a director attends a meeting for the express purpose of objecting to the transaction of any business because the meeting is not lawfully called or convened.

EXHIBIT 16-4, cont.

Section 6. Quorum. A majority of the number of directors fixed by these bylaws shall constitute a quorum for the transaction of business at any meeting of the board of directors, but if less than such majority is present at a meeting, a majority of the directors present may adjourn the meeting from time to time without further notice.

Section 7. Board Decisions. The act of the majority of the directors present at a meeting at which a quorum is present shall be the act of the board of directors.

Section 8. Vacancies. Any vacancy occurring in the board of directors may be filled by the affirmative vote of a majority of the remaining directors though less than a quorum of the board of directors. A director elected to fill a vacancy shall be elected for the unexpired term of his predecessor in office. Any directorship to be filled by reason of an increase in the number of directors shall be filled by election at an annual meeting or at a special meeting of stockholders called for that purpose.

Section 9. Compensation. By resolution of the board of directors, the directors may be paid their expenses, if any, of attendance at each meeting of the board of directors and may be paid a fixed sum for attendance at each meeting of the board of directors or a stated salary as director. No such payment shall preclude any director from serving the corporation in any other capacity and receiving compensation therefor.

Section 10. Presumption of Assent. A director of the corporation who is present at a meeting of the board of directors at which action on any corporate matter is taken shall be presumed to have assented to the action taken unless his or her dissent shall be entered in the minutes of the meeting or unless he or she shall file his written dissent to such action with the person acting as the secretary of the meeting before the adjournment thereof or shall forward such dissent by registered mail to the secretary of the corporation immediately after the adjournment of the meeting. Such right to dissent shall not apply to a director who voted in favor of such action.

Article Four
Officers

Section 1. Number. The officers of the corporation shall be president, one or more vice-presidents (the number thereof to be determined by the board of directors), a secretary, and a treasurer, each of whom shall be elected by the board of directors. Such other officers and assistant officers as may be deemed necessary may be elected or appointed by the board of directors. Any two or more offices may be held by the same person except the offices of president and secretary.

Section 2. Election and Term of Office. The officers of the corporation to be elected by the board of directors shall be elected annually at the first meeting of the board of directors held after each annual meeting of the stockholders. If the election of officers is not held at such meeting, such election shall be held as soon thereafter as is convenient. Each officer shall hold office until his or her successor has been duly elected and qualifies or until his or her death or until he or she resigns or is removed in the manner hereinafter provided.

Section 3. Removal. Any officer or agent elected or appointed by the board of directors may be removed by the board of directors whenever in its judgment the best interests of the corporation would be served thereby, but such removal shall be without prejudice to the contract rights, if any, of the person so removed.

EXHIBIT 16-4, cont.

Section 4. Vacancies. A vacancy in any office because of death, resignation, removal, disqualification, or otherwise may be filled by the board of directors for the unexpired portion of the term.

Section 5. Powers and Duties. The powers and duties of the several officers shall be as provided from time to time by resolution or other directive of the board of directors. In the absence of such provisions, the respective officers shall have the powers and shall discharge the duties customarily and usually held and performed by like officers of corporations similar in organization and business purposes to this corporation.

Section 6. Salaries. The salaries of the officers shall be fixed from time to time by the board of directors, and no officer shall be prevented from receiving such salary by reason of the fact that he or she is also a director of the corporation.

Article Five
Contracts, Loans, Checks, and Deposits

Section 1. Contracts. The board of directors may authorize any officer or officers, agent or agents, to enter into any contract or execute and deliver and instrument in the name of and on behalf of the corporation, and such authority may be general or confined to specific instances.

Section 2. Loans. No loans shall be contracted on behalf of the corporation, and no evidences of indebtedness shall be issued in its name unless authorized by a resolution of the board of directors. Such authority may be general or confined to specific instances.

Section 3. Checks, Drafts, or Orders. All checks, drafts, or other orders for the payment of money, notes, or other evidences of indebtedness issued in the name of the corporation shall be signed by such officer or officers, agent or agents of the corporation and in such manner as shall from time to time be determined by resolution of the board of directors.

Section 4. Deposits. All funds of the corporation not otherwise employed shall be deposited from time to time to the credit of the corporation in such banks, trust companies, or other depositaries as the board of directors may select.

Article Six
Certificates for Shares: Transfers

Section 1. Certificates for Shares. Certificates representing shares of the corporation shall be in such form as shall be determined by the board of directors. Such certificates shall be signed by the president or a vice-president and by the secretary or an assistant secretary. All certificates for shares shall be consecutively numbered or otherwise identified. The name and address of the person to whom the shares represented thereby are issued, with the number of shares and date of issue, shall be entered on the stock transfer books of the corporation.

Section 2. Transfer of Shares. Transfer of shares of the corporation shall be made in the manner specified in the Uniform Commercial Code. The corporation shall maintain stock transfer books, and any transfer shall be registered thereon only on request and surrender of the stock certificate representing the transferred shares, duly endorsed.

EXHIBIT 16-4, cont.

Article Seven
Fiscal Year

The fiscal year of the corporation shall begin on the _____ day of _____ of each year and end at midnight on the _____ day of _____ of the following year.

Article Eight
Dividends

The board of directors may from time to time declare, and the corporation may pay, dividends on its outstanding shares in the manner and on the terms and conditions provided by law and its certificates of incorporation.

Article Nine
Seal

The board of directors shall provide a corporate seal, which shall be circular in form and shall have inscribed thereon the name of the corporation and the state of incorporation and the words *Corporate Seal*. The seal shall be stamped or affixed to such documents as may be prescribed by law or custom or by the board of directors.

Article Ten
Waiver of Notice

Whenever any notice is required to be given to any stockholder or director of the corporation under the provisions of these bylaws or under the provisions of the certificate of incorporation or under the provisions of law, a waiver thereof in writing, signed by the person or persons entitled to such notice, whether before or after the time stated therein, shall be deemed equivalent to the giving of such notice.

Article Eleven
Amendments

These bylaws may be altered, amended, or repealed, and new bylaws may be adopted by the board of directors at any regular or special meeting of the board, provided, however, that the number of directors shall not be increased or decreased nor shall the provisions of Article Two, concerning the stockholders, be substantially altered without the prior approval of the stockholders at a regular or special meeting of the stockholders or by written consent. Changes in and additions to the bylaws by the board of directors shall be reported to the stockholders at their next regular meeting and shall be subject to the approval or disapproval of the stockholders at such meeting. If no action is then taken by the stockholders on a change in or addition to the bylaws, such change or addition shall be deemed to be fully approved and ratified by the stockholders.

An organizational meeting of the incorporators or the sole incorporator is the next step. At this meeting, a board of directors should be appointed. After the initial incorporators' meeting, the board of directors should meet and elect a chairperson and secretary. It is important that all individuals who were appointed directors be given notice of the meeting. In the absence of such a notice, each director should be required to sign a waiver of notice of meeting. At the initial board of directors' meeting, the positions of president, vice-president, secretary, and treasurer should be filled. Elections are held, and the official officers will assume their roles. The next action to be taken at a board meeting is for the seal to be approved and impressed upon the meeting minutes. The next order of business is for the directors to authorize a bank account. In most cases, a corporate bank resolution will be needed to open such an account. The corporate bank resolution will indicate that a meeting was held, at which time the corporate directors decided on the bank to be used (Exhibit 16–5).

Next on the agenda is the provision for individuals who wish to be shareholders to make proposals to the corporation with respect to the purchase of the shares of stock. Shares can be purchased for either cash or property, but, as indicated in the previous section, future interests or promises to pay are not sufficient consideration. The directors will then decide whether or not to accept the shareholders' proposal. It is important not to undercapitalize the corporation as future problems with either creditors or tax authorities may arise. At the time that the assets are delivered to the corporation, the corporation through its officers is then directed to execute and deliver the share certificate or certificates of shares to the particular shareholders.

At the first meeting of the board of directors, a decision should be made as to whether the corporation wishes to file under § 1244 of the Internal Revenue Code. This section provides that, if a corporation is liquidated at a loss, the loss that would otherwise constitute a capital loss may be treated as an ordinary loss. The losses must be sustained by individuals or partners. The individuals or partners must have been shareholders of the corporation at the time the § 1244 stock is issued, and the shareholder must be the original investor. The loss is limited to $50,000 in one taxable year. In order to qualify, a corporation may have only one class of common stock and must be a *small business corporation*, which is defined as a corporation having less than $1,000,000 in equity capital, of which not more than $500,000 is from issuance of 1244 stock.

At the first meeting of the board of directors, a decision should also be made as to whether the corporation wishes to file under § 1372 of the Internal Revenue Code for subchapter S status. A discussion of this procedure can be found in Chapter 17. In addition to electing Subchapter S status, the corporate directors might also wish to discuss a medical care reimbursement plan. Under the provisions of the Internal Revenue Code, a corporation may set up one or more medical and dental expense plans to reimburse employees for medical and dental expenses. A plan may cover one or more employees, and there may be different plans for different employees or classes of employees. The plans may cover officers and employees whether they

EXHIBIT 16-5
Corporate Resolution

Corporation Resolutions—Withdrawal of Funds, Borrowing, etc.

wilber national bank
ONEONTA, N.Y. 13820

w/n\b
MARK OF TRUST

....
(Name of Corporation)

I hereby certify to Wilber National Bank, 245 Main Street, Oneonta, N.Y. ....

that at a meeting of the Board of Directors of ....

a corporation organized under the laws of the State of ....duly called and

held at the office of said corporation, No..in the City of

....State of...on the..............day of...........................19........,

the following resolutions were duly adopted and are now in full force and effect:

Resolved,   that the funds of this corporation be deposited in Wilber National Bank,

245 Main Street, Oneonta, N. Y., ...

subject to checks made in the corporate name signed by any .... of the following officers:
(Number)

....

who are also authorized to make, collect, discount, negotiate, endorse, assign and deposit in the corporate
name, all checks, drafts, notes and other negotiable paper payable to or by this corporation, and that all checks
of the corporation signed as aforesaid, including checks drawn to cash or bearer or to the individual order
of the officer signing said checks, shall be honored and paid by said Bank/Trust Company, without further
inquiry, and charged to the corporation's account, the corporation hereby ratifying and approving all that said
Bank/Trust Company may do or cause to be done by virtue hereof.

Resolved,   that any..of the following officers of the corporation, to wit:
(Number)

are hereby authorized to borrow money and to obtain credit for this corporation from said

Wilber National Bank, 245 Main Street, Oneonta, New York ....

on such terms as may seem to them advisable and to make and deliver notes, drafts, acceptances, agreements and any other obligations of this corporation therefor in form satisfactory to said Bank/Trust Company
and as security therefor to pledge and trustee any stocks, bonds, bills receivable, bills of lading, warehouse
receipts and any other property of this corporation with full authority to endorse or guarantee the same in
the name of this corporation, to execute and deliver all instruments of assignment and transfer and to affix
the corporate seal; and also to discount any bills receivable or other negotiable paper held by this corporation with full authority to endorse same in the name of this corporation.

EXHIBIT 16-5, cont.

Resolved, that the secretary of this corporation be and he hereby is authorized to certify to said

Wilber National Bank, 245 Main Street, Oneonta, New York

the foregoing resolutions and that the provisions thereof are in conformity with the charter and by-laws of this corporation. That the foregoing powers and authority will continue until written notice of revocation has been delivered to Wilber National Bank, 245 Main Street, Oneonta, N. Y.

I further certify that there is no provision in the charter or by-laws of said corporation limiting the power of the board of directors to pass the foregoing resolutions and that the same are in conformity with the provisions of said charter and by-laws.

I further certify that the following persons are officers of this corporation in the capacities set opposite their respective names and that the signatures set opposite such names are their signatures.

NAME	OFFICER	SIGNATURE
	President	
	Vice-President	
	Vice-President	
	Treasurer	
	Secretary	
	Asst. Treasurer	
	Asst. Secretary	

In Witness Whereof, I have hereunto subscribed my signature to this certificate and affixed the seal of this corporation, this...........................day of...19.........

Seal

....
(Secretary)

NOTE:—In case the secretary or other recording officer is authorized to sign checks, notes, etc., by the above resolutions, this certificate must also be signed by a second officer of the corporation.

CREATIVE R. · M. · FORM 128

are shareholders or not as well as their dependents. Corporate contributions to the plan are deductible by the corporation and are nontaxable to employees.

Other matters that should be considered include fixing corporate salaries; execution of leases; borrowing; authority of certain officers to make contracts; indemnification of directors, officers, and employees against lawsuits; authorization of payment of attorneys' fees and disbursements; employment contracts with respect to attorneys and accountants; and so on, as well as the adoption of a fiscal year. A fiscal year is a year that ends on the last day of a month other than December 31.

After the meeting of the directors and after the shareholders' proposal has been accepted, the shareholders will have a meetings. At that meeting, the corporate secretary will read the role of the shareholders as they appear in the share record book of the corporation. It is important that all shareholders receive appropriate notice of this meeting (Exhibit 16–6). In the event that they do not receive notification pursuant to the bylaws, a waiver of notice of meeting signed by all the shareholders should be provided (Exhibit 16–7).

The next order of business is for the corporate secretary to read the minutes of the organizational meeting and the minutes of the first meeting of the board of directors. The shareholders will then note whether or not to adopt these minutes, including the election of officers and approval of the bylaws of the corporation. Future meetings of either the directors or the shareholders should be carefully recorded and kept together in the corporate minute book.

TERMINATION

Now that you have your corporation and have paid the required filing fees according to the dictates of the particular state in which you file, what do you do with it?

EXHIBIT 16-6
Notice of Special Meeting of Stockholders

_____ (name of corporation)
Called by stockholders

Notice is hereby given that pursuant to a call by stockholders holding not less than _____ percentage of the voting power of the corporation, a special meeting of the stockholders of _____,
a State of _____ corporation, will be held at _____,
City of _____, State of _____, on _____, 19_____, at _____ o'clock ___M. for the following purposes: _____.
The close of business on _____, 19_____, has been fixed as the record date for determining stockholders entitled to receive notice of and to vote at this meeting or any adjournment thereof.

_____ (If a proxy is enclosed, insert: If you do not expect to be present in person at the meeting, you are urged to date and sign the enclosed proxy and return it promptly in the enclosed envelope, which requires no postage).
Dated _____, 19_____.

_____
(signature of secretary)

EXHIBIT 16-7
Waiver of Notice of Stockholders' Meeting

We, the undersigned stockholders of _____, a State of
_____ corporation, each entitled to vote the number of
shares set opposite his or her name, do hereby waive notice of a _____
(regular or special) meeting of the stockholders of the corporation _____
(held or to be held) at _____ (address) in the City of
_____, State of _____, on _____, 19_____, at
_____ o'clock ____M. for the purpose of _____
(state general nature of business).

This waiver of notice of meeting shall be filed with the corporate records and made a
part of the minutes of the meeting.

Dated: _____, 19_____.

Stockholder	*Number of Shares*
_____	_____
_____	_____
_____	_____

Your best alternative is to use it correctly as a tool for doing business. Make sure you file all the required federal and state papers (federal employer identification number, state unemployment form, state income tax, and so on). It may be necessary to get a qualified person to assist you (e.g., certified public accountant or attorney or both).

If you find that you are unable to start or continue in the business because of one of several factors (i.e., lack of funds, your dreams of being an entrepreneur have not panned out, or inability to deal with all the forms), you then must consider termination. Procedure for termination can be found in the corporation law that exists in your state. The Model Business Corporation Act provides several alternatives to termination as follows: voluntary dissolution by the incorporators in the event that the corporation has not commenced business or issued any shares; voluntary dissolution by consent of the shareholders, which must be in writing; or voluntary dissolution by act of the corporation.

Though it may seem easy in your state to allow the corporation to come to a natural end, this may not be the best method. Termination papers should be filed. The corporation may be liable for taxes until its final dissolution. Mere abandonment may result in liability on the part of the officers or directors for unpaid taxes. Do not forget to notify all other agencies that were initially notified as to the corporate existence: federal government, Internal Revenue Service, the state, the state sales tax bureau, issuers of licenses, (liquor, garage, and so on), and also creditors. Failure to do so could cause continued corporate liability, as well as personal liability to the officers and directors.

QUESTIONS

1   The defendant was a private corporation organized for various purposes, including education. The defendant operated a group of private schools, from which it derived substantial revenues. The state tried to close one of the schools based on a statute that required that all children between the ages of 8 and 16 be sent to a public school for education purposes. The school argued that the statute interfered with the corporation's Fourteenth Amendment rights (see Chapter 1). The defendant argued that parents and children should have the right to select a school and the character and quality of education that such a school was administering. Decision for whom? Discuss.

2   The B's, E's, and K's formed a hardware company and prepared a certificate of incorporation. It was the clear intention of the parties that the corporation should be duly and legally formed, and they filed their certificate of incorporation with the county clerk of the county in which they were doing business. For no apparent reason, the certificate was not filed with the secretary of state. The Colorado statute read in part as follows: "Every corporation . . . incorporated by or under any general or special law of this state . . . shall pay to the Secretary of State for the use of the state a fee of $10 . . . the said fee shall be due and payable upon the filing of the Certificate of Incorporation . . . and no corporation . . . shall have or exercise any corporate powers or be permitted to do any business in this state until the said fee shall have been paid. . . ." The hardware business operated for approximately seven months when a suit was commenced by Thatcher against the E's personally. Was the hardware property available to E's personal creditors (what type of property was it)? Decision for whom? Discuss.

3   The plaintiff, Neese, acting as a trustee in bankruptcy of the First Trust Company, is arguing that the defendants, Brown and others, directors of XYZ Co., failed to use due care and diligence in the discharge of their duties as directors. The alleged acts of negligence by the defendants are as follows: (*a*) failure to give necessary time and attention to the affairs of the corporation; (*b*) abdication of their control by turning the operation and management of the corporation over to its president; (*c*) failure to keep informed as to the affairs, conditions, and management of the corporation; (*d*) failure to take any direct action or control over the company, its officers, and agents; (*e*) allowing large unsecured loans to be made by the company to affiliated companies that were owned and controlled by the president and that were not financially sound; (*f*) failure to examine the financial reports of the company, which would have disclosed the unsound and poor financial condition of the company; (*g*) reliance on portions of the reports read by the president rather than investigation of the reports themselves, which would have disclosed illegal diversion of the company's funds and waste of company assets. Does such conduct, if provable, constitute a cause of action against the company directors? Decision for whom? Discuss.

4   The plaintiff was severely injured in an accident involving a taxicab owned by the Seon Cab Corporation. Carlton is a stockholder in Seon as well as in a number of other corporations. Each corporation has, as its sole assets, two taxicabs registered in the corporate name, and each carries the minimum liability insurance required by law. The plaintiff argued that the multiple corporations are operated as a single entity; with regard to financing, supplies, and repairs, employees and garaging are operated in a manner inconsistent with their corporate existence and, therefore, the plaintiff requests that the court ''pierce the corporate veil'' and hold the defendant stockholder personally liable for damages that he has incurred. Decision for whom? Discuss.

5 The plaintiff, a corporation that operated a trucking business for several years, was ultimately liquidated as a result of financial difficulties. Its assets were distributed to its stockholders. The business had been operated by the defendant, president of the corporation, who used corporate funds to pay for personal obligations. Does the corporation or do the shareholders have any legal rights against the president? Discuss.

6 The defendant owned a company called Lamas Company, Inc. The corporation was engaged in the construction business. Lamas was never personally engaged in the construction business. The plaintiff was an electrical contractor who had been hired by Lamas to complete some work that was started by another contractor but never finished. The building permit showed that the Lamas Company, Inc., was the general contractor. There were signs posted on the construction site indicating that the construction was being done by the corporation. All bills were rendered by the plaintiff to the Lamas Company, Inc., and all checks paid to the plaintiff were by the Lamas Company, Inc. The plaintiff sues Lamas personally for damages, arguing that he was under the impression that he was dealing with Lamas as agent of the corporation. Decision for whom? Discuss.

7 The defendant was a corporation formed for the purpose of furnishing water to businesses in parts of Louisiana. The defendant hired McWilliams to perform services in connection with their business. McWilliams completed a good deal of the work, and he did not receive payment. He brought an action demanding that he be paid. He also requests that he have a right to examine the defendant company's books and records to determine whether there are sufficient assets to pay any judgment he may get or, if there is no money, whether there are sufficient funds available from stockholders to cover the amount of the judgment. Decision for whom? Discuss. Would your answer differ if the plaintiff were a stockholder?

8 Pillsbury Corporation purchased a number of shares of the defendant, Honeywell Corporation. The plaintiff admitted that the purpose in purchasing these shares was to attempt to get information regarding weapons manufactured by the defendant and being used in the Vietnam War. Pillsbury was opposed to the manufacture of these weapons and desired to make stockholders of the company aware of these facts. The plaintiff requested that Honeywell supply it with a current stockholders' ledger, together with other records dealing with the manufacture of weapons and ammunitions by the company. The defendant company refused. The plaintiff wished to communicate with other shareholders for the purpose of changing the members of the board of directors of the defendant in order to change its weapons policy. The business records were needed so that the plaintiff could obtain an accurate list of those stockholders. Is the plaintiff entitled to obtain access to the corporate records? Discuss.

9 Armington and Simms were partners manufacturing high-speed engines. They formed the corporation known as Armington and Simms Company. The next year they formed another company called Armington & Simms Engine Company and conveyed to that company all the assets of Armington and Simms Company. The engine company became financially strapped, and an agreement was entered into between various stockholders, creditors, and Armington & Simms individually. Control of the business was turned over to a creditor's committee, but it was found to be impossible to continue the business, and the property was sold at auction to Scott. Scott, together with other persons, formed a new corporation with the name Armington & Simms Company. Armington objected to the use of his name as part of the name of the new corporation and requested an injunction to prevent Armington & Simms Company from using the name *Armington*. Shall this action be sustained? Discuss.

10 The expenses of A corporation rose dramatically in August. Net earnings declined from $262,253 in July to $66,233 in August. Upon learning this, B, chairman of the board, and C, president, sold 56,500 shares of their stock at the market price of $28.

The public was not made aware of the decrease in earnings until October. At that time, the price of the stock decreased to $11. P, the plaintiff stockholder, brought charges against defendants B and C, stating that they owed the corporation the profits they realized on the sale of their stock prior to the release of the information in October. Decision for whom? Discuss.

11 A, an architect, began to work for B, C, and D, who were in the process of forming BCD corporation. Articles of incorporation were filed, but A was never informed of this fact. A stopped working for B, C, and D when they refused to pay him. A then brought an action against B,C, and D for services rendered. Were B, C, and D personally liable on the contract to A, or can A only bring judgment against BCD corporation?

12 A, a director and shareholder of C corporation, was informed of a board of directors' meeting to be held on September 12. He was given the notice on September 11. The purpose of the meeting was to amend the bylaws to change the number of directors from four to three. It was apparent that the other directors wanted to dispose of A. Can A argue that he was given insufficient notice if (*a*) he attends the meeting without protest or (*b*) he attends the meeting and protests?

13 A is president and sole shareholder in the C corporation. The IRS summoned A, as president, to bring to court certain specific books and records of the C corporation. A refused to bring the books, saying that to bring the books might incriminate him and that he would be a witness against himself according to the Fifth Amendment. Decision for whom? Discuss.

14 D was a stockholder and a director and treasurer of the C corporation, a cushion-drapery business. D handled accounts receivable, employee morale, and other C corporate business information. He also had access to many records of the C corporation. One day A, the office manager, informed D that he was unhappy with his employment in C corporation. D met on June 4 with A; and they, along with B, the workroom manager, and E, the top salesperson of C corporation, decided to open a competing cushion-drapery business. A, B, and E did not have employment contracts with the C Corporation. D told the others of confidential stock bonus plans from which they were excluded and of confidential profit-expense statistics of the C corporation. On June 23, they got a location for their business, contacted fabric suppliers, and secured a listing in the yellow pages. On July 10, D resigned as a director and as treasurer, effective August 10. The four opened a bank account, purchased goods and machines, and copied C corporate charts and forms. On August 11, A, B, and E ended their employment without notice to the C corporation. A, B, D, and E opened their business on August 13. List and discuss the areas where D had breached his fiduciary duty to C corporation.

CHAPTER 17

Taxation of Business Entities

A business is subject to taxation by both the federal and state governments. The purpose of this chapter is to outline a number of the major taxes (payroll, income) and other related expenses that are imposed on a business and to consider their effect on one's choice of a method of doing business.

The objective of this chapter is not to provide a detailed discussion of either federal or state tax laws. An individual who wishes to go into business should obtain more detailed information about federal and state taxes by consulting with professional advisers.

PAYROLL TAXES

Payroll taxes are imposed upon an employee's salary. Payroll taxes can be broken down into two major categories: those that are payable by the employer (social security, also known as FICA) and those that are payable by the employee (employee's share of social security, federal, state, and local withholding taxes). The employee's share of taxes is withheld by the employer at the time the employee receives his or her salary, and it is forwarded to the federal, state, or local government.

In addition to taxes, there are insurance charges based on an employer's payroll (i.e., federal unemployment insurance, state unemployment insurance, workers' compensation, and disability insurance).

Payroll taxes are imposed only on employees. Even though the owner of a proprietorship and the partners of a partnership may actively engage in the operation and management of the business, they are not considered employees for employment tax or insurance purposes. Individuals hired by a sole proprietor, partnership, or corporation (including shareholders) for compensation are considered employees for tax and insurance purposes if there is a strong degree of direction, supervision, and control exercised by the employer. If the employer does not maintain a strong degree of control over the individuals, they are classified as independent contractors, and payroll taxes and insurance charges are not imposed on the employer.

Sometimes it is difficult to determine whether an individual is an employee or an independent contractor. There are several tests used to make such a determination. One test is whether the individual works exclusively for the business in question or whether the individual also has other clients or customers. If an individual has numerous clients or customers and holds himself or herself out to render services to the general public, he or she is more likely to be considered an independent contractor (e.g., lawyer, doctor, or plumber). If the individual is paid on an hourly or a flat salaried basis and works exclusively for one employer, he or she is more likely to be considered an employee (e.g., secretary or clerk).

A second factor that is used is the degree of supervision and control the worker is under. An independent contractor generally makes his or her own decisions. He or she is assigned a task by his or her employer, and the mechanics and specifics of getting the job done is within his or her discretion. An employee, on the other hand, is subject to more supervision and control in that the employer may tell the employee not only what to do, but also how to do it.

In a partnership, moneys paid to partners are paid as drawings against profits of the partnerships and not as salary. Since a corporation is a separate legal entity from its owners or managers, it qualifies as an employer, and all people working for that entity (other than independent contractors) will be considered to be employees. In this context, officers, directors, and other workers are all considered to be employees. A shareholder of a corporation would not be an employee by virtue of the fact that he or she was a shareholder. If the shareholder is engaged in rendering services to the corporation, then that individual would be considered an employee unless the nature of the services being rendered was that of an independent contractor.

The major payroll tax expense that an employer must pay is one half of the social security tax. When an individual is hired as an employee and is quoted a salary, the employer has an obligation to pay, in addition the amount of the salary, 6.7 percent of the first $32,400 of the employee's salary (rates for 1982 to 1984; in 1985, 7.05 percent; from 1986 to 1989, 7.15 percent; from 1990 on, 7.65 percent! The wage base is only established yearly.) This amount is paid to the federal government under the Federal Insurance Contribution Act (FICA) for purposes of providing retirement, disability, or death benefits to employees or their families.

In addition to the employer's share of social security, he or she is responsible for collecting taxes that are assessed on the employee and remitting them to the government. In this case, even though the employer makes the actual payment, the money that is being paid comes out of the gross salary being earned by the employee. There are three major items that appear in this category: social security taxes to the extent that the employee has to pay it, federal withholding taxes, and state and local withholding taxes. The employee's share of the social security tax is equal to the employer's share. It is measured by the same percentage and on the same total dollar amount of salary.

Withholding Tax

The federal withholding tax is an entirely different concept. All individuals in this country are subject to income taxes on all income that they earn from any source (except for certain income earned by certain nonresidents). Individuals are assessed income taxes on an annual basis (January 1 through December 31). All income that is earned during that period may be subject to a tax that is payable by April 15 of the following year. Since the government does not wish to wait until April 15 to receive all its money, it has developed a "pay as you go" system, which, in the case of salaries, is referred to as the *withholding system*. Federal withholding tax law requires that an employee fill out Form W-4 before starting his or her employment (Exhibit 17-1). The form requires an individual to determine the number of dependents for which he or she qualifies. The greater the number of depen-

EXHIBIT 17-1
Withholding Certificate

Form **W-4**	Department of the Treasury—Internal Revenue Service
(Rev. October 1979)	**Employee's Withholding Allowance Certificate**

Print your full name ▶

Your social security number ▶

Address (including ZIP code) ▶

Marital status: ☐ Single ☐ Married ☐ Married, but withhold at higher Single rate

Note: *If married, but legally separated, or spouse is a nonresident alien, check the single block.*

1 Total number of allowances you are claiming (from line F of the worksheet on page 2) . . . .

2 Additional amount, if any, you want deducted from each pay (if your employer agrees) . . . . | $

3 I claim exemption from withholding because (see instructions and check boxes below that apply):

  a ☐ Last year I did not owe any Federal income tax and had a right to a full refund of **ALL** income tax withheld, **AND**

  b ☐ This year I do not expect to owe any Federal income tax and expect to have a right to a full refund of **ALL** income tax withheld. If both

    a and b apply, enter "EXEMPT" here . . . . ▶

  c If you entered "EXEMPT" on line 3b, are you a full-time student? . . . . ☐ Yes ☐ No

Under the penalties of perjury, I certify that I am entitled to the number of withholding allowances claimed on this certificate, or if claiming exemption from withholding, that I am entitled to claim the exempt status.

Employee's signature ▶   Date ▶   , 19

Employer's name and address (including ZIP code) **(FOR EMPLOYER'S USE ONLY)** | Employer identification number

-- Detach along this line --

▲ *Give the top part of this form to your employer; keep the lower part for your records and information* ▲

Purpose

The law requires that you complete Form W-4 so that your employer can withhold Federal income tax from your pay. Your Form W-4 will remain in effect until you change it, or, if you entered "EXEMPT" on line 3b above, until April 30 of next year. By claiming the number of withholding allowances you are entitled to, you can fit the amount of tax withheld from your wages to your estimated tax liability.

Introduction

If you got a large refund last year, you may be having too much tax withheld. If so, you may want to increase the number of your allowances by claiming any other allowances you are entitled to on line 1 of Form W-4. The kinds of allowances, and how to figure them, are explained in detail in the line-by-line instructions below.

If you owed a large amount of tax last year, you may not be having enough tax withheld. If so, you can claim fewer allowances on line 1, or ask that an additional amount be withheld on line 2, or both.

If the number of withholding allowances that you are entitled to decreases, you must file a new Form W-4 with your employer within 10 days from the date of the change.

If you qualify, you can claim exemption from withholding on line 3b of Form W-4.

The line-by-line instructions below explain how to fill in Form W-4. **Publication 505**, Tax Withholding and Estimated Tax, contains more information on withholding. You can get it from any Internal Revenue Service office.

For more information about who qualifies as your dependent, what deductions you can take, and what tax credits you qualify for, see the Form 1040 Instructions or call any Internal Revenue Service office.

Line-By-Line Instructions

Fill in the identifying information at the top of the form. If you are married and want tax withheld at the regular rate for married persons, check the "Married" box. If you are married and want tax withheld at the higher Single rate (because both you and your spouse work, for example), check the box "Married, but withhold at higher Single rate."

Line 1 of Form W-4

Total number of allowances.—Use the Worksheet on page 2 to figure all of your allowances. Each kind of allowance you may claim is explained below and is identified by the letter that corresponds to the line for that allowance on the Worksheet.

A. Personal allowances.—You can claim the following personal allowances:

● 1 for yourself,
● 1 if you are 65 or older, and
● 1 if you are blind.

If you are married and your spouse either does not work or is not claiming his or her allowances on a separate Form W-4, you may also claim the following allowances:

● 1 for your spouse,
● 1 if your spouse is 65 or older, and
● 1 if your spouse is blind.

If you are single and hold more than one job, you may not claim the same allowances with more than one employer at the same time. If you are married and both you and your spouse are employed, you may not both claim the same allowances with both of your employers at the same time.

Enter your total personal allowances on line A of the Worksheet.

Note: *To have the highest amount of tax withheld, claim "0" personal allowances on line 1.*

B. Special withholding allowance.—You can claim the special withholding allowance only if you are single and have one job or you are married, have one job, and your spouse does not work.

If you can claim the special withholding allowance, enter "1" on line B of the Worksheet.

Note: *Use the special withholding allowance only to figure your withholding tax. Do not claim it when you file your tax return.*

C. Allowances for dependents.—You may claim one allowance for each dependent you will be able to claim on your Federal income tax return. Enter on line C of the Worksheet the total number of allowances you can claim for dependents.

D. Allowances for estimated tax credits.—If you expect to be able to take the earned income credit, credit for child and dependent care expenses, credit for the elderly, or residential energy credit, these credits may lower your tax. To avoid having too much withheld, you may claim extra allowances for these tax credits on line D of the Worksheet.

To enter the proper figure on line D of the Worksheet, you will have to use the "Tax Credit Table for Figuring Your Withholding Allowances" on the top of page 2.

Note: *Do not claim allowances for your earned income credit if you are receiving advance payment of it.*

E. Allowances for estimated itemized deductions and alimony.—If you expect to itemize your deductions or pay alimony during the year (or both), you may want to claim additional withholding allowances so you will have less tax withheld.

See Schedule A (Form 1040) to find out what deductions you can take and to estimate the amount of your deductions.

Note: *If you are paying alimony but will not itemize deductions, enter your estimate of alimony payments for the year on lines E1 and E3 (enter "0" on line E2). Divide the amount on line E3 by $1,000, and enter the result on line E4 of the Worksheet. Round-off any fraction to the nearest whole number.*

Line 2 of Form W-4

Additional amount, if any, you want deducted from each pay.—If you are not having enough tax withheld from your pay, you may ask your employer to withhold more by filling in an additional amount on line 2.

Often, married couples, both of whom are working, and single persons with two or more jobs, will need to have additional tax withheld.

Estimate the amount by which you will be underwithheld and divide that amount by the number of pay periods in the year. Enter the additional amount you want withheld each pay period on line 2.

Line 3 of Form W-4

Exemption from withholding.—You can claim exemption from withholding only if last year you did not owe any Federal income tax and had a right to a refund of all income tax withheld, and this year you do not expect to owe any Federal income tax and expect to have a right to a refund of all income tax withheld.

If you qualify check boxes 3a and b, write "EXEMPT" on line 3b and answer Yes or No to the question on line 3c.

If you want to claim exemption from withholding, you must file a new Form W-4 with your employer on or before April 30 of next year. If you are not having Federal income tax withheld this year, but expect to have a tax liability next year, the law requires you to give your employer a new Form W-4 by December 1.

If you are covered by the Federal Insurance Contributions Act, your employer must withhold social security tax from your pay.

dents, the lower the amount of taxes that will be withheld from each paycheck. The reason for this is that individuals are entitled to deductions on their income taxes for each dependent that they have. The more deductions an employee claims, the less taxes the employee will have to pay and, therefore, the less withholding per pay period.

The federal government publishes withholding tables, which advise an employer how much to withhold for an individual in a specific salary bracket with a specific number of deductions. These tables are broken down by frequency of pay period and marital status. Exhibit 17–2 shows an excerpt from a typical withholding table for a single employee who is being paid on a weekly basis.

The withholding amounts that appear in these tables are based on estimates of the employee's total tax liability at the end of the year. If the employee's tax liability differs from the amount of withholdings, the employee will be able to receive a refund at the time that he or she files his or her return or will be obligated to pay the deficiency at the same time. It is possible for an employee to adjust the amount of withholdings voluntarily by claiming greater or fewer dependents than he or she is entitled to. Many people intentionally withhold excess amounts from their salaries on an ongoing basis so that they are able to obtain a refund when their return is finally filed. This is a form of *forced savings* that many people find desirable because they lack the willpower to put this money aside if it is paid directly to them. The techniques for claiming a lesser number of dependents than one is entitled to are to claim single status rather than married status or to write down a smaller number of dependents than one actually has. The W-4 provides space for an employee to have additional withholdings taken out of his or her salary on a periodic basis. This amount of additional withholdings is a dollar figure that can be specified by the employee and can be changed as the employee deems it desirable.

The W-4 allows an employee who anticipates having large amounts of itemized deductions to claim a greater number of dependents. This will reduce his or her year-end refund. An employee should be careful when claiming extra allowances because it is illegal to claim an excessive number. A taxpayer who claims an excessive number of allowances may be subject to a penalty.

The third category of taxes that the employer pays on behalf of the employee is state and local (city) withholding taxes. Most states today impose income taxes on individuals who reside within, work within, or have income from sources within that state. Most states' income tax systems are also funded on a "pay as you go" system very similar to that of the federal government. (As of July 1981, the following states did not impose a state tax on employment income: Alaska, Connecticut, Florida, Nevada, New Hampshire, South Dakota, Tennessee, Texas, Washington, and Wyoming. These states impose personal property taxes or taxes on dividends and interest, business profits, capital gains, and so on. The rates charged by state governments are lower than the federal rates. The base (the amount or types of income that are being taxed) will also differ from state to state and frequently will differ from the federal base (federal government taxes). An individual will have to file a return for the federal government and a separate return for the state.

EXHIBIT 17-2
Weekly Payroll Tax Table

SINGLE Persons — WEEKLY Payroll Period
(For Wages Paid After June 1982 and Before July 1983)

And the wages are—		And the number of withholding allowances claimed is—										
At least	But less than	0	1	2	3	4	5	6	7	8	9	10 or more
		The amount of income tax to be withheld shall be—										
$0	$27	$0	$0	$0	$0	$0	$0	$0	$0	$0	$0	$0
27	28	.10	0	0	0	0	0	0	0	0	0	0
28	29	.20	0	0	0	0	0	0	0	0	0	0
29	30	.30	0	0	0	0	0	0	0	0	0	0
30	31	.40	0	0	0	0	0	0	0	0	0	0
31	32	.50	0	0	0	0	0	0	0	0	0	0
32	33	.70	0	0	0	0	0	0	0	0	0	0
33	34	.80	0	0	0	0	0	0	0	0	0	0
34	35	.90	0	0	0	0	0	0	0	0	0	0
35	36	1.00	0	0	0	0	0	0	0	0	0	0
36	37	1.10	0	0	0	0	0	0	0	0	0	0
37	38	1.30	0	0	0	0	0	0	0	0	0	0
38	39	1.40	0	0	0	0	0	0	0	0	0	0
39	40	1.50	0	0	0	0	0	0	0	0	0	0
40	41	1.60	0	0	0	0	0	0	0	0	0	0
41	42	1.70	0	0	0	0	0	0	0	0	0	0
42	43	1.90	0	0	0	0	0	0	0	0	0	0
43	44	2.00	0	0	0	0	0	0	0	0	0	0
44	45	2.10	0	0	0	0	0	0	0	0	0	0
45	46	2.20	0	0	0	0	0	0	0	0	0	0
46	47	2.30	0	0	0	0	0	0	0	0	0	0
47	48	2.50	.20	0	0	0	0	0	0	0	0	0
48	49	2.60	.30	0	0	0	0	0	0	0	0	0
49	50	2.70	.40	0	0	0	0	0	0	0	0	0
50	51	2.80	.50	0	0	0	0	0	0	0	0	0
51	52	2.90	.60	0	0	0	0	0	0	0	0	0
52	53	3.10	.80	0	0	0	0	0	0	0	0	0
53	54	3.20	.90	0	0	0	0	0	0	0	0	0
54	55	3.30	1.00	0	0	0	0	0	0	0	0	0
55	56	3.40	1.10	0	0	0	0	0	0	0	0	0
56	57	3.50	1.20	0	0	0	0	0	0	0	0	0
57	58	3.70	1.40	0	0	0	0	0	0	0	0	0
58	59	3.80	1.50	0	0	0	0	0	0	0	0	0
59	60	3.90	1.60	0	0	0	0	0	0	0	0	0
60	62	4.10	1.80	0	0	0	0	0	0	0	0	0
62	64	4.40	2.00	0	0	0	0	0	0	0	0	0
64	66	4.70	2.30	0	0	0	0	0	0	0	0	0
66	68	5.00	2.50	.20	0	0	0	0	0	0	0	0
68	70	5.30	2.70	.40	0	0	0	0	0	0	0	0
70	72	5.70	3.00	.70	0	0	0	0	0	0	0	0
72	74	6.00	3.20	.90	0	0	0	0	0	0	0	0
74	76	6.30	3.50	1.20	0	0	0	0	0	0	0	0
76	78	6.60	3.70	1.40	0	0	0	0	0	0	0	0
78	80	6.90	3.90	1.60	0	0	0	0	0	0	0	0
80	82	7.30	4.20	1.90	0	0	0	0	0	0	0	0
82	84	7.60	4.50	2.10	0	0	0	0	0	0	0	0
84	86	7.90	4.80	2.40	0	0	0	0	0	0	0	0
86	88	8.20	5.20	2.60	.30	0	0	0	0	0	0	0
88	90	8.50	5.50	2.80	.50	0	0	0	0	0	0	0
90	92	8.90	5.80	3.10	.80	0	0	0	0	0	0	0
92	94	9.20	6.10	3.30	1.00	0	0	0	0	0	0	0
94	96	9.50	6.40	3.60	1.20	0	0	0	0	0	0	0
96	98	9.80	6.80	3.80	1.50	0	0	0	0	0	0	0
98	100	10.10	7.10	4.00	1.70	0	0	0	0	0	0	0
100	105	10.70	7.60	4.60	2.10	0	0	0	0	0	0	0
105	110	11.50	8.40	5.40	2.70	.40	0	0	0	0	0	0
110	115	12.30	9.20	6.20	3.30	1.00	0	0	0	0	0	0
115	120	13.10	10.00	7.00	3.90	1.60	0	0	0	0	0	0
120	125	13.90	10.80	7.80	4.70	2.20	0	0	0	0	0	0
125	130	14.70	11.60	8.60	5.50	2.80	.50	0	0	0	0	0
130	135	15.50	12.40	9.40	6.30	3.40	1.10	0	0	0	0	0
135	140	16.30	13.20	10.20	7.10	4.00	1.70	0	0	0	0	0
140	145	17.10	14.00	11.00	7.90	4.80	2.30	0	0	0	0	0
145	150	17.90	14.80	11.80	8.70	5.60	2.90	.60	0	0	0	0
150	160	19.10	16.00	13.00	9.90	6.80	3.80	1.50	0	0	0	0

(Continued on next page)

EXHIBIT 17-2, cont.

SINGLE Persons — WEEKLY Payroll Period
(For Wages Paid After June 1982 and Before July 1983)

And the wages are—		And the number of withholding allowances claimed is—										
At least	But less than	0	1	2	3	4	5	6	7	8	9	10 or more
		The amount of income tax to be withheld shall be—										
$160	$170	$20.70	$17.60	$14.60	$11.50	$8.40	$5.30	$2.70	$.40	$0	$0	$0
170	180	22.50	19.20	16.20	13.10	10.00	6.90	3.90	1.60	0	0	0
180	190	24.50	20.80	17.80	14.70	11.60	8.50	5.40	2.80	.50	0	0
190	200	26.50	22.60	19.40	16.30	13.20	10.10	7.00	4.00	1.70	0	0
200	210	28.50	24.60	21.00	17.90	14.80	11.70	8.60	5.60	2.90	.60	0
210	220	30.50	26.60	22.80	19.50	16.40	13.30	10.20	7.20	4.10	1.80	0
220	230	32.50	28.60	24.80	21.10	18.00	14.90	11.80	8.80	5.70	3.00	.70
230	240	34.50	30.60	26.80	22.90	19.60	16.50	13.40	10.40	7.30	4.20	1.90
240	250	36.60	32.60	28.80	24.90	21.20	18.10	15.00	12.00	8.90	5.80	3.10
250	260	39.00	34.60	30.80	26.90	23.10	19.70	16.60	13.60	10.50	7.40	4.30
260	270	41.40	36.80	32.80	28.90	25.10	21.30	18.20	15.20	12.10	9.00	5.90
270	280	43.80	39.20	34.80	30.90	27.10	23.20	19.80	16.80	13.70	10.60	7.50
280	290	46.20	41.60	37.00	32.90	29.10	25.20	21.40	18.40	15.30	12.20	9.10
290	300	48.60	44.00	39.40	34.90	31.10	27.20	23.40	20.00	16.90	13.80	10.70
300	310	51.00	46.40	41.80	37.20	33.10	29.20	25.40	21.60	18.50	15.40	12.30
310	320	53.40	48.80	44.20	39.60	35.10	31.20	27.40	23.50	20.10	17.00	13.90
320	330	55.80	51.20	46.60	42.00	37.40	33.20	29.40	25.50	21.70	18.60	15.50
330	340	58.80	53.60	49.00	44.40	39.80	35.20	31.40	27.50	23.70	20.20	17.10
340	350	61.80	56.10	51.40	46.80	42.20	37.60	33.40	29.50	25.70	21.80	18.70
350	360	64.80	59.10	53.80	49.20	44.60	40.00	35.40	31.50	27.70	23.80	20.30
360	370	67.80	62.10	56.30	51.60	47.00	42.40	37.80	33.50	29.70	25.80	22.00
370	380	70.80	65.10	59.30	54.00	49.40	44.80	40.20	35.50	31.70	27.80	24.00
380	390	73.80	68.10	62.30	56.50	51.80	47.20	42.60	37.90	33.70	29.80	26.00
390	400	76.80	71.10	65.30	59.50	54.20	49.60	45.00	40.30	35.70	31.80	28.00
400	410	79.80	74.10	68.30	62.50	56.80	52.00	47.40	42.70	38.10	33.80	30.00
410	420	82.80	77.10	71.30	65.50	59.80	54.40	49.80	45.10	40.50	35.90	32.00
420	430	85.80	80.10	74.30	68.50	62.80	57.00	52.20	47.50	42.90	38.30	34.00
430	440	88.90	83.10	77.30	71.50	65.80	60.00	54.60	49.90	45.30	40.70	36.10
440	450	92.30	86.10	80.30	74.50	68.80	63.00	57.20	52.30	47.70	43.10	38.50
450	460	95.70	89.20	83.30	77.50	71.80	66.00	60.20	54.70	50.10	45.50	40.90
460	470	99.10	92.60	86.30	80.50	74.80	69.00	63.20	57.50	52.50	47.90	43.30
470	480	102.50	96.00	89.50	83.50	77.80	72.00	66.20	60.50	54.90	50.30	45.70
480	490	105.90	99.40	92.90	86.50	80.80	75.00	69.20	63.50	57.70	52.70	48.10
490	500	109.30	102.80	96.30	89.70	83.80	78.00	72.20	66.50	60.70	55.10	50.50
500	510	112.70	106.20	99.70	93.10	86.80	81.00	75.20	69.50	63.70	57.90	52.90
510	520	116.10	109.60	103.10	96.50	90.00	84.00	78.20	72.50	66.70	60.90	55.30
520	530	119.50	113.00	106.50	99.90	93.40	87.00	81.20	75.50	69.70	63.90	58.20
530	540	123.00	116.40	109.90	103.30	96.80	90.20	84.20	78.50	72.70	66.90	61.20
540	550	126.70	119.80	113.30	106.70	100.20	93.60	87.20	81.50	75.70	69.90	64.20
550	560	130.40	123.20	116.70	110.10	103.60	97.00	90.50	84.50	78.70	72.90	67.20
560	570	134.10	126.90	120.10	113.50	107.00	100.40	93.90	87.50	81.70	75.90	70.20
570	580	137.80	130.60	123.50	116.90	110.40	103.80	97.30	90.80	84.70	78.90	73.20
580	590	141.50	134.30	127.20	120.30	113.80	107.20	100.70	94.20	87.70	81.90	76.20
590	600	145.20	138.00	130.90	123.80	117.20	110.60	104.10	97.60	91.00	84.90	79.20
600	610	148.90	141.70	134.60	127.50	120.60	114.00	107.50	101.00	94.40	87.90	82.20
610	620	152.60	145.40	138.30	131.20	124.10	117.40	110.90	104.40	97.80	91.30	85.20
620	630	156.30	149.10	142.00	134.90	127.80	120.80	114.30	107.80	101.20	94.70	88.20
630	640	160.00	152.80	145.70	138.60	131.50	124.40	117.70	111.20	104.60	98.10	91.60
640	650	163.70	156.50	149.40	142.30	135.20	128.10	121.10	114.60	108.00	101.50	95.00
650	660	167.40	160.20	153.10	146.00	138.90	131.80	124.70	118.00	111.40	104.90	98.40
660	670	171.10	163.90	156.80	149.70	142.60	135.50	128.40	121.40	114.80	108.30	101.80
670	680	174.80	167.60	160.50	153.40	146.30	139.20	132.10	124.90	118.20	111.70	105.20
680	690	178.50	171.30	164.20	157.10	150.00	142.90	135.80	128.60	121.60	115.10	108.60
690	700	182.20	175.00	167.90	160.80	153.70	146.60	139.50	132.30	125.20	118.50	112.00
700	710	185.90	178.70	171.60	164.50	157.40	150.30	143.20	136.00	128.90	121.90	115.40
710	720	189.60	182.40	175.30	168.20	161.10	154.00	146.90	139.70	132.60	125.50	118.80
720	730	193.30	186.10	179.00	171.90	164.80	157.70	150.60	143.40	136.30	129.20	122.20
730	740	197.00	189.80	182.70	175.60	168.50	161.40	154.30	147.10	140.00	132.90	125.80
		37 percent of the excess over $740 plus—										
$740 and over		198.80	191.70	184.60	177.50	170.30	163.20	156.10	149.00	141.90	134.80	127.60

The W-2 Forms

On or before January 31 of each year, an employee whose salary has been subjected to taxation must receive a W-2 form from his or her employer. This form (Exhibit 17–3) includes the employee's name, address, and social security number; the employer's name, address, and identification number; the amount of the employee's gross salary for the entire year; and the various items of tax that have been withheld. If an employer withholds money from the employee and fails to pay that money to the federal government, the employee (unless he or she was in collusion with the employer) will nonetheless receive credit on his or her return for the payment. The employer will be guilty of a felony and subject to a fine of not more than $10,000 or imprisonment for not more than five years or both (Internal Revenue Code § 7202).

The W-2 forms the basis for the employee to report his or her income from salaries or wages to the federal government, to compute the tax on his or her income, and to pay any deficiency due or receive any excess as a refund. If an employee receives money from an unexpected source that is not subject to withholding and if the employee does not change the amount of his or her withholding (W-4), the employee may be required to file a 1040 ES (Exhibit 17–4) and pay the federal government additional tax on this unexpected income. If the tax on these receipts is estimated to be $1500, then the employee should pay this amount in the form of estimated taxes to the federal government, either in periodic installments (the number of installments will be determined by the date on which the additional income is received) or by a single lump sum.

EXHIBIT 17-3
W-2 Form

1 Control number 22222

2 Employer's name, address, and ZIP code

3 Employer's identification number

4 Employer's State number

5 Stat. employee ☐ Deceased ☐ Pension plan ☐ Legal rep. ☐ 942 emp. ☐ Subtotal ☐ Correction ☐ Void ☐

6

7 Advance EIC payment

8 Employee's social security number

9 Federal income tax withheld

10 Wages, tips, other compensation

11 FICA tax withheld

12 Employee's name, address, and ZIP code

13 FICA wages

14 FICA tips

16 Employer's use

17 State income tax

18 State wages, tips, etc.

19 Name of State

20 Local income tax

21 Local wages, tips, etc.

22 Name of locality

Form **W-2 Wage and Tax Statement 1980**

Copy 1 For State, City, or Local Tax Department
Employee's and employer's copy compared. ☐

EXHIBIT 17–4
Declaration of Estimated Tax for Individuals

Form **1040-ES**	**Declaration of Estimated Tax for Individuals**	OMB No. 1545–0087
Department of the Treasury Internal Revenue Service		**1982**

Instructions

Paperwork Reduction Act Notice.— We ask for this information to carry out the Internal Revenue laws of the United States. We need it to ensure that you are complying with these laws and to allow us to figure and collect the right amount of tax. You are required to give us this information.

"Estimated tax" is the amount of tax you expect to owe for the year after subtracting the amount of tax you expect to have withheld and the amount of any credits you plan to take. You do not have to file a declaration of estimated tax if your 1982 income tax return will show (1) a tax refund or (2) a tax balance due of less than $200. For additional information, get **Publication 505,** Tax Withholding and Estimated Tax.

A. Who Must File.—The rules below are for U.S. citizens or residents and for residents of Puerto Rico, Virgin Islands, Guam, or American Samoa. If you are a nonresident alien, use Form 1040–ES (OIO). **Note:** After you file this declaration-voucher, you will receive additional declaration-vouchers to use for an amended estimate or for additional estimated tax payments.

You must make a declaration if your estimated tax is $200 or more AND:

(1) Your expected gross income for 1982 includes more than $500 in income not subject to withholding, or

(2) Your expected gross income is more than:

- $20,000 if you are single, a head of household, or qualifying widow or widower.
- $20,000 if you are married, can file a joint declaration, and your spouse has not received wages for 1982.
- $10,000 if you are married, can file a joint declaration, and both of you have received wages for 1982.
- $5,000 if you are married and cannot file a joint declaration. (No joint declaration may be made if: (1) either you or your spouse is a nonresident alien, (2) you are separated under a decree of divorce or separate maintenance, or (3) you have different tax years.)

Note: *If you must file a declaration and receive salaries and wages, you may not be having enough tax withheld during the year. To avoid making estimated tax payments, consider asking your employer to take more tax out of your earnings. To do this, file a new Form W-4, Employee's Withholding Allowance Certificate, with your employer and make sure you will not owe $200 or more in tax. You may also have tax withheld from certain pension, annuity, or sick pay payments you receive. To do so, determine the proper amount to be withheld by dividing your estimated tax by the number of pay-*ments you expect to receive during the calendar year from which tax will be withheld and file Form W–4P with the person from whom you receive payment.

B. How to Figure Your Estimated Tax.—Use the Estimated Tax Worksheet on page 2, the 1982 Tax Rate Schedules in these instructions, and your 1981 tax return as a guide for figuring your estimated tax.

Most of the items on the worksheet are self-explanatory. However, the instructions below provide additional information for filling out certain lines. The Economic Recovery Tax Act of 1981, Public Law 97–34, provides for a deduction by two-earner married couples. The act allows couples filing a joint return a deduction in computing adjusted gross income equal to a percentage of the lower earning spouse's qualified earned income. See **Publication 505,** Tax Withholding and Estimated Tax for details.

Caution: Generally, you are required to itemize your deductions if:

- you have unearned income of $1,000 or more and can be claimed as a dependent on your parent's return,
- you are married filing a separate return and your spouse itemizes deductions,
- you file Form 4563, OR
- you are a dual status alien.

For more information, see the 1981 Instructions for Form 1040. If you must itemize and line 2b of the Estimated Tax Worksheet is more than line 2a, subtract 2a from 2b. Add this amount to line 1 of the worksheet and enter the total on line 3. Disregard the instructions for line 2c and line 3 on the worksheet.

Line 7—Additional taxes.—Enter on line 7 any additional taxes from:

- Form 4970, Tax on Accumulation Distribution of Trusts,
- Form 4972, Special 10-Year Averaging Method,
- Form 5544, Multiple Recipient Special 10-Year Averaging Method, OR
- Section 72(m)(5) penalty tax.

Line 12—Self-employment tax.—If you and your spouse file a joint declaration and both have self-employment income, figure the estimated self-employment tax separately. Enter the total amount on line 12.

C. How to Use the Declaration-Voucher.—

(1) Enter your name, address, and social security number in the space provided on the declaration-voucher. If you are filing a joint declaration-voucher, your spouse's name and social security number should be included on the voucher. If you file a joint declaration-voucher and have different last names, please separate them with an "and." For example: "John Brown and Mary Smith."

(2) Enter the amount shown on line 17 of the worksheet in Block A of the declaration-voucher.

(3) Enter the amount shown on line 18 of the worksheet on line 1 of the declaration-voucher.

(4) If you paid too much tax on your 1981 Form 1040, you may have chosen to apply the overpayment to your estimated tax for 1982. If so, enter in Block B the overpayment from 1981.

You may apply all or part of the overpayment to any voucher. Enter on line 2 the amount you want to apply to the voucher you are using. Subtract line 2 from line 1 and enter the amount of the payment on line 3. If you are filing a declaration (or an amended declaration), mail it to the Internal Revenue Service even though line 3 is zero. File the remaining vouchers only when line 3 is more than zero.

(5) Sign the declaration-voucher and tear off at the perforation.

(6) Attach, but do not staple, your check or money order to the declaration-voucher. Make check or money order payable to "Internal Revenue Service." Please write your social security number and "1982 Form 1040–ES" on your check or money order.

For each later declaration-voucher, which you will receive in the mail, follow instruction (1) above, fill in lines 1, 2, and 3 of the form, attach check or money order, and mail.

D. When to File and Pay Your Estimated Tax.—The general rule is that you must file your declaration by April 15, 1982. You may either pay all of your estimated tax with the declaration or pay in four equal amounts that are due by April 15, 1982; June 15, 1982; September 15, 1982; and January 17, 1983. Exceptions to the general rule are listed below:

(1) **Other declaration dates.—**In some cases, such as a change in income, you may have to file a declaration after April 15, 1982. The filing dates are as follows:

If the requirement is met after:	Filing date is:
● April 1 and before June 2	June 15, 1982
● June 1 and before Sept. 2	Sept. 15, 1982
● September 1	Jan. 17, 1983

Pay your estimated tax in equal amounts on the required filing dates.

(2) **Your return as a declaration.—**If you file your 1982 Form 1040 by January 31, 1983, and pay the entire balance due, then you do not have to—

- file the required amended declaration due on January 17, 1983.
- file your first declaration which would be due by January 17, 1983.
- make your last payment of estimated tax.

(3) **Farmers and fishermen.—**If at least two-thirds of your gross income for 1981 or 1982 is from farming or fishing, you may do one of the following:

- File your declaration by January 17, 1983, and pay all your estimated tax.

EXHIBIT 17-4, cont.

1982 Estimated Tax Worksheet (Keep for your records—Do Not Send to Internal Revenue Service)

1 Enter amount of Adjusted Gross income you expect in 1982	**1**	
2 a If you plan to itemize deductions, enter the estimated total of your deductions. If you do not plan to itemize deductions, skip to line 2c and enter zero	**2a**	
b Enter ⎰ $3,400 if married filing a joint return (or qualifying widow(er))		
$2,300 if single (or head of household)		
⎱ $1,700 if married filing a separate return	**2b**	
c Subtract line 2b from line 2a (if zero or less, enter zero)	**2c**	
3 Subtract line 2c from line 1	**3**	
4 Exemptions (multiply $1,000 times number of personal exemptions)	**4**	
5 Subtract line 4 from line 3	**5**	
6 Tax. (Figure tax on line 5 by using Tax Rate Schedule X, Y, or Z in these instructions. DO NOT use the Tax Table or Tax Rate Schedule X, Y, or Z in the 1981 Form 1040 Instructions.)	**6**	
7 Enter any additional taxes from Instruction B	**7**	
8 Add lines 6 and 7	**8**	
9 Credits (credit for the elderly, credit for child and dependent care expenses, investment credit, residential energy credit, etc.)	**9**	
10 Subtract line 9 from line 8	**10**	
11 Tax from recomputing a prior year investment credit	**11**	
12 Estimate of 1982 self-employment income $................................; if $32,400 or more, enter $3,029.40; if less, multiply the amount by .0935 (see Instruction B for additional information)	**12**	
13 Tax on premature distributions from an IRA	**13**	
14 Add lines 10 through 13	**14**	
15 (a) Earned income credit **15a**		
(b) Estimated income tax withheld and to be withheld during 1982 . . . . . . **15b**		
(c) Credit for Federal tax on special fuels and oils (see Form 4136 or 4136–T) . . . **15c**		
16 Total (add lines 15(a), (b), and (c))	**16**	
17 Estimated tax (subtract line 16 from line 14). If $200 or more, fill out and file the declaration-voucher; if less, no declaration is required at this time	**17**	
18 If the first declaration-voucher you are required to file is due April 15, 1982, enter ¼ of line 17 here and on line 1 of your declaration-voucher(s)	**18**	
Note: If you are not required to file a voucher at this time, you may have to file by a later date. See Instruction D(1).		

Page 2

Reporting

The reporting procedures for withholding taxes are time-consuming. There are a number of forms that need to be prepared. The social security tax and the federal withholding tax are reported to the government on a quarterly basis. Each of the four calendar quarters (January 1 through March 31, April 1 through June 30, and so forth) are reported separately, and reports are due a month after the end of the quarter. The form on which these items need to be reported is referred to as Form 941. Proper reporting requires the employer to submit the amounts earned for the quarter being covered. Then the amounts of withholding for each of the employees and the total amount of social security are computed, and this total amount either has to have been already paid to the government (through bank depository) or must be paid at the time that the return is due.

The federal government requires that employers make deposits against their quarterly liability as frequently as weekly. State and local withholding taxes are

EXHIBIT 17-4, cont.

Form **1040-ES** Department of the Treasury Internal Revenue Service	**1982** Declaration-Voucher	

		OMB No. 1545-0087
A. Estimated tax $_____ Fiscal year filers enter year ending _____ (month and year) $	B. Overpayment from last year credited to estimated tax for this year $	Return this form with check or money order payable to the Internal Revenue Service Please do not send cash or staple your payment to this voucher.

1 Amount from line 18 on worksheet ▶	$	Your social security number	Spouse's number, if joint declaration
2 Amount of overpayment credit from last year (all or part) to be applied . . ▶			
3 Amount of this payment (subtract line 2 from line 1) . . . . ▶	$	First name and middle initial (of both spouses if joint declaration)	Last name
File this form even if line 3 is zero.			
Sign here ▶ _____ Your signature ▶ _____ Spouse's signature (if joint declaration)		Address (Number and street) City, State, and ZIP code	

Please type or print

For Paperwork Reduction Act Notice, see instructions on page 1.   E I. #52-1074467   ☆ U.S. GOVERNMENT PRINTING OFFICE : 1981—O-343-442   **Page 3**

generally reported on separate forms from federal taxes; however, they are also usually filed on a quarterly basis.

In addition to salary and a portion of social security expenses, an employer must also pay unemployment insurance, worker's compensation, and disability payments. The unemployment insurance contribution has a federal and a state component. The state component is usually the major dollar item and will vary from state to state. A typical state unemployment insurance contribution will be from 0.5 to 5.0 percent of the first $6000 of each employee's salary. The rate for each employer is set by the state and is dependent in part on the number of unemployment claims made against the employer (experience rate). The federal component is 3.4 percent of the first $6000 of wages and may be reduced by up to 2.7 percent of taxable wages for amounts paid to the state unemployment fund. Notice that the cutoff level for unemployment insurance is considerably lower than the cutoff level for social security contributions. Accordingly, the cost to the employer of unemployment is considerably less than the cost of the social security expense. The actual contributions required by each state differ. The purpose of the unemployment contribution is to provide a fund at the state level so that employees who are laid off from their jobs are eligible to receive dollar benefits during the period of time that they are no longer working. Unemployment at the state level is usually reported on a quarterly basis, and at the federal level it is summarized once a year on a Form 940. Payments may be required quarterly.

The second kind of payroll insurance expense is workers' compensation insurance. This compensates workers who are injured while on the job. A primary purpose for workers' compensation laws is to eliminate the employees' difficulties in proving negligence. Workers' compensation laws are either mandatory or voluntary. Where coverage is voluntary, the employer who opts out of coverage loses most or all of his or her defenses.

Employers covered by workers' compensation laws generally purchase insurance either from private carriers or from a state-operated fund. The cost will depend on the source of the coverage and on the nature of the occupation involved. Penalties for failure to comply with the workers' compensation requirement vary by state and may include fines, imprisonment, or both.

Disability insurance is a third type of insurance, found in California, Hawaii, New Jersey, New York, Puerto Rico, and Rhode Island. Disability fills the gap between workers' compensation and unemployment coverage. Its primary protection extends to workers injured while not on the job. (Disability also applies to pregnancy.) Disability rules allow the employer to charge part or all of the cost to the employee.

Employer ID Number

Every employer is required to obtain a federal identification number. This is usually a two-digit number with a hyphen followed by a seven-digit number. In order to obtain an employer's identification number, the employer must file Form SS-4 with the Internal Revenue Service. The form requires information concerning the name and address of the business, the number of employees expected, and the date when salaries will first be paid. This form should be filed as soon as the business commences so that the Internal Revenue Service can have time to put the business on the mailing list to receive the appropriate forms for reporting one's payroll tax liabilities. If a business does not receive the forms, it is not excused from its obligation to pay the tax or to file the information on time. The federal government will provide, upon request (or when the business files a form SS-4), a publication outlining the employer's obligation regarding payroll taxes (Circular E).

INCOME TAXATION OF A BUSINESS ENTERPRISE

Proprietorships

A proprietorship is not considered to be a separate tax-reporting entity. The income earned by a proprietorship is not reported by the proprietorship. A proprietor has to file an additional schedule with his or her tax return. This additional schedule is referred to as Schedule C and represents a statement of the proprietorship's income and expense. The expenses are subtracted from the income, and the net result, either a profit or a loss, is included in the proprietor's income for purposes of taxation.

A Schedule C requires information concerning a business enterprise's (proprietorship's) operations in terms of both revenues and expenses. All business receipts from whatever sources they are received are to be reported on that business's Schedule C. This is true whether the business is of a service nature, of a sales nature, or of a manufacturing and sales nature. The Schedule C also allows a proprietor to deduct from the receipts of the business all the expenses that are incurred in earning the income that is reported by the business. In examining Schedule C, one can see that many of the expenses that are to be reported are spelled out by captions on the form itself. These are not intended to be exclusive, and if a proprietorship incurs ordinary, necessary, and reasonable expenses in other categories, they should also be included on the Schedule C as part of the computation of the total net income or loss. Such expenses should be clearly labeled as to their nature, and all expenses, whether they go into the categories enumerated on the schedule or not, should be documentable by receipts, canceled checks, and so on.

Expenses   There are numerous expenses that a proprietor could incur as part of his or her business. We will not attempt to discuss all of these, however, but will mention several items that proprietors are likely to encounter, of which they should be aware. An element that creates much difficulty in computing income is the category of travel and entertainment deductions. It is not always immediately clear as to what travel expenses are deductible by a proprietor. This is because the tax law makes a distinction between deductible travel expenses and commutation expenses. An individual traveling from home to his or her main place of work and back is engaged in commutation. Commutation expenses are not deductible for employees or self-employed individuals. Once an individual has reached his or her first place of employment, if he or she travels to a second business location, this is a deductible travel expense. Thus, if a proprietor has a place of business and is required to travel from there to clients or to a second place of employment, the travel is deductible. The travel from his or her home to his or her place of business and from his or her place of business back to his or her home will not be deductible. If the proprietor travels directly from his or her home to his or her first client's place of business and from there to a second client's place of business, the travel cost from his or her home to his or her first client's place of business and from his or her last client's place of business back to his or her home is not deductible. The travel from his or her first client to his or her second to his or her third and so on is deductible.

In computing travel expenses, a taxpayer, if he or she is using his or her own automobile, may elect to deduct an amount computed by multiplying the number of miles driven on business by a government-established rate per mile. (In 1981 this rate generally was 20 cents per mile for the first 15,000 miles and 11 cents per mile thereafter.) As an alternative to this, the proprietor may compute the actual travel costs incurred and deduct this amount if it is greater. Actual travel costs would include the cost of gasoline, repairs, oil, and so on and would also include an allowance for depreciation based on the cost of the vehicle used.

Assets   A second area that causes some confusion is the treatment of an asset purchased for business purposes. If a proprietor purchases an item for use in business and if the item purchased has utility for more than one accounting period (i.e., more than one reporting year), then the full cost of the item may not be deducted as an expense in the year of payment but, in fact, must be treated as a capital asset and depreciated over its useful life. The specific number of years in question varies according to the nature of the asset and, in some cases, also according to the tax law in effect at the time that the asset was purchased. The deduction that is allowed for part of the cost of this asset is referred to as depreciation. There are a number of different ways of depreciating an asset, each of which produces a somewhat different result, and a proprietor should consult with his or her tax adviser to determine the method most appropriate for his or her use.

A second aspect of the problem of acquisition of a capital asset lies in the treatment of the financing cost of its acquisition. Where an asset is purchased and the purchase price is paid out over a period of years, the principal (amount of the loan), when it is repaid, does not represent a tax deduction. (The full cost of the asset may be depreciated.) However, the interest that is paid on the amount borrowed is a deductible expense. It is important when gathering one's tax information to identify the amount of interest paid on loans that were taken out for business purposes. There are different ways of computing interest amounts, and, if it is at all possible when one borrows money for purchasing an asset, one should find out from the lender the portion of each payment that represents interest. If the lender cannot give you this information, your tax consultant probably will be able to figure it out provided he or she knows the purchase price of the asset, the amount of each regular payment, the amount of the loan, the interest rate, and the number of payments being made.

Investment Tax Credit There is an additional tax benefit available to individuals who buy assets (new or used) for business purposes. (Business assets include automobiles used for trade or business.) In addition to being able to deduct the cost of the asset over the period it is being used, purchasers may take advantage of the investment tax credit. Investment credit is a dollar-for-dollar credit against the amount of income taxes owed. (It does not apply against the self-employment tax owed by a proprietor.) The investment credit is 10 percent of the asset's purchase price if the asset will be used by the proprietor in his or her business for five years or more. If the asset will be used for less than five years, the credit is 10 percent of two thirds of the purchase price.

Home Office Another item that creates questions for taxpayers is the availability of a deduction for use of a portion of one's home for business purposes. If a business is operated out of an individual's home without the use of any additional business space, a portion of the cost of maintaining one's residence is a cost of maintaining a business location and, therefore, is deductible. The cost of maintaining such a space would include not only a portion of heat, electric, and other utilities, but also a portion of insurance, maintenance, and other household expenses, as well as a deduction for depreciation on the portion of the property used for business purposes. The government has recently tightened rules for the deductibility of a ''home office'' and currently requires that before one can deduct expenses for business use for part of one's home, one must use that portion of the home exclusively and continuously for business purposes.

A proprietor may deduct business expenses related to use of his or her home only if that portion of the home is exclusively used for a regular business (1) as one's principal place of business or (2) as a place of business used by one's patients, clients, or customers in meeting or dealing with them in a normal course of one's trade or business or (3) in connection with one's trade or business if it is a separate structure not attached to one's home. Expenses applicable to space within one's home may also be deducted if it is the only fixed location of one's trade or business and used on a regular basis to store inventory held for use in one's trade or business of selling products retail or wholesale.

Records It is extremely important to be able to substantiate business expenses. As previously mentioned, businesses should pay expenses by check so that there is a record of the payment, and, wherever possible, bills or invoices should be obtained and kept as substantiation for the checks written. With respect to travel and entertainment, the substantiation is more difficult because one not only has to prove the expense involved, but also its relationship to the business. For this purpose, many people maintain a business diary. The diary becomes a useful document for proving that one has gone to certain places or entertained specific people and discussed certain aspects of business. When one is deducting travel expenses, it is recommended that the diary contain a notation of where the person has travelled, what the business reason is for traveling there, who was met, what was discussed, and how many miles were driven. It is even desirable to note the odometer reading at the time that one leaves one's place of work to go to the business meeting and when one returns. With respect to business meals, it is very important to note the parties with whom the business matter was discussed, the nature of the business matter being discussed, and, of course, the location and date of the meal.

The government requires that a particular expenditure be ordinary, necessary, and reasonable if it is to constitute a deductible expense. There is much litigation dealing with issues of whether something is ordinary or necessary, whether it is reasonable, and even whether it violates public policy. The cases dealing with these issues ultimately need to be examined on an individual basis. It is difficult in any given case to identify whether an expense would be acceptable within the guidelines set forth by the Internal Revenue Service. For example, an individual clearly needs an automobile to drive to and from work. Purchase of a small car would normally lead to an acceptable business deduction. There are, however, cases of people who purchase very expensive cars such as a Rolls-Royce and claim that the depreciation on such a vehicle should be included as a deductible business expense. The IRS often resists such claims. Another example lies in the area of traffic tickets. Many business persons have argued that it is essential in operating their business for them to violate certain laws. The IRS has consistently maintained that even if such violations are necessary in order to operate the business efficiently at an economic profit, allowing a deduction for any such fine would be contrary to public policy. It is best if you have specific problems in this area that you discuss them with your tax consultant so that you are aware of the limits of what is or is not deductible.

Proprietorship Where an individual maintains a proprietorship, an additional problem can result if the individual's spouse helps out in the business. If a spouse works for his or her own spouse and is paid, the spouse constitutes an employee of the proprietorship and imposes on the employer an obligation to pay some payroll taxes but not others. Before entering such an arrangement, an individual should check with his or her tax adviser to determine the applicable tax rules.

People who are engaged in a proprietorship that generates a profit are usually required to pay income and self-employment taxes on a quarterly basis. They do this by filing Form 1040 ES (see Exhibit 17–4). There are penalties assessed for failure to pay an appropriate amount of estimated taxes. There are also exceptions to the penalty provisions. One should consult with one's professional tax adviser to determine in any given case the most appropriate amount to be paid on quarterly estimates.

A proprietor is also subject to a self-employment tax on his or her income computed at the rate of 9.35 percent on the first $32,400 (1982 to 1984 rates); 9.9 percent in 1985; 10 percent in 1986 to 1989; 10.75 percent in 1990 and later years. This payment is a self-employed person's contribution to social security and entitles him or her to the same retirement, disability, and death benefits as an employee receives. Self-employment tax is also required to be paid on a quarterly basis and reported on 1040 ES.

Partnerships

A partnership, like a proprietorship, is not a tax-paying entity. Unlike a proprietorship, however, a partnership is an information-reporting entity. A partnership is required to prepare and file a federal income tax return every year—Form 1065. This form summarizes a partnership's income and expenses in many of the same categories that appear on a proprietor's Schedule C. The return ultimately computes the net income of the partnership and then allocates this net income among each of the partners. Each of the partners will receive a Schedule K-1, which will tell the partner the amount of income that he or she has earned from the partnership and also several additional categories of items that are relevant to the partner in preparing his or her individual tax return. The income earned by a partnership is reported by the individual partners on their personal income tax returns.

If the partnership is engaged in a business, the income from that business is subject to a self-employment tax when reported by each of the partners. If the partnership's operation is investment-oriented, then the profits are not subject to a self-employment tax.

A partner is not required to keep formal business records of the partnership's income and expense. These records are maintained at the partnership level, and all the support, verification, and documentation of income and expenses should be accumulated at the partnership level. A partner is also not subject to worker's compensation or disability coverages on his or her income.

Items of income and expense that are reported by the partnership are treated similarly to those reported by a proprietorship. Many of the same rules apply with respect to the nature of items that are deductible, the documentation required, and so on. If a partner is engaged in business and incurs expenses that are related to the operations of the partnership but not reimbursable by the partnership, these expenses may be deducted by the partner in his or her individual income tax return. In order to do this, the partner needs to file Form 2106 with his or her individual income tax return.

Corporations

A corporation is different from a partnership or a proprietorship in that it is a tax-paying entity. A corporation is considered a legally separate entity from both its management and its owners. (See Chapter 16.) As a separate legal entity, a corporation must report its revenues and expenses and may be subject to tax on the income it earned. The computation of revenues and expenses is basically the same for a corporation as was previously discussed for a partnership or a proprietorship.

In cases where a corporation pays income tax and distributes income to shareholders in the form of a dividend, there is "double taxation." The corporation pays tax at the following rates (for years beginning in 1983 and after): 15 percent on the first $25,000; 18 percent on the next $25,000; 30 percent on the next $25,000; 40 percent on the next $25,000; and 46 percent on the balance (everything over $100,000). When the income is distributed to the shareholders in the form of a dividend, they must report that income and pay a tax on it. The severest effect of double taxation is shown in the following example:

Corporate income before tax	$1.00
Tax (assumes the maximum rate of 46% on amounts over $100,000)	.46
Amount distributable to shareholder as dividend	$ .54
Tax on receipt by shareholder (assumes the maximum rate of 50%)	.27
Disposable income to shareholder (Excludes effects of state taxation at both corporate and shareholder levels)	$ .27

A corporation is responsible for paying social security, unemployment, workers' compensation, and disability on all salaries paid to all employees, including officers. A corporation, as the employer, is also responsible for withholding and paying federal and state income taxes. The officers who are in charge of payroll or who sign the payroll tax returns may be personally liable for penalties and tax deficiencies if taxes are not paid by the corporation. The penalties are the same as discussed in the payroll tax section of this chapter. Corporations are subject to the same record-keeping requirements as other business entities.

All states except Nevada, Texas, Washington, and Wyoming (as of May 1981) impose a corporate income tax. Some states impose a tax even in cases where the corporation suffers a loss. The tax is imposed for the privilege granted by the state of doing business within the state as a corporation (franchise tax). Some states impose both franchise and income taxes and require the corporation to pay the greater of the two. In the event that a corporation is no longer desired, it is necessary to go through an official termination procedure, or else it will continue to exist. If it continues to exist, the state, if we assume that it normally charges such a tax, will continue to be entitled to receive state income or franchise taxes or both.

Corporations may also be liable for the accumulated earnings tax. This tax is imposed on corporations "formed (or availed of) for the purpose of avoiding the income tax with respect to its shareholders . . . by permitting earnings and profits to accumulate instead of being . . . distributed" (I.R.C. § 532). The tax is imposed on excess accumulated earnings at the rate of 27.5 percent on the first $100,000 of excess accumulated income and 38.5 percent on all additional excess accumulated. *Excess accumulated income* is defined as accumulated earnings in excess of $250,000 or the "reasonable needs of the business," whichever is greater.

Advantages of Corporations An economic advantage of doing business in corporate form is the availability of liberal pension and profit-sharing provisions. Pensions established by corporations generally enable a corporation to set aside a greater percentage of earnings than those developed for the benefit of self-employed proprietors or partners or both. The ability of a corporation to set up a pension plan will depend primarily on its economic position. The advisability of setting up such a plan is almost always dependent upon the level of income of the employees and the corporation. This is a very sophisticated area of business planning, and it is recommended that you consult with a tax consultant before setting up a pension plan.

Another benefit, particularly for small corporations, is the availability of medical reimbursement plans. A corporation may elect to reimburse all employees for medical expenses not covered by insurance provisions. Such reimbursements will be received by the employee tax-free, but are deductible to the corporation.

Another possible economic advantage of doing business as a corporation is that the profit from the sale of corporate shares held by a shareholder for more than one year may be taxed at a lower rate than the profit from the sale of the assets of a proprietorship or partnership. Only 40 percent of the profits from the sale of stock held for more than one year will be included in the shareholder's income. On the sale of a proprietorship or partnership, all the profit on the sale of some of the assets will be included in the seller's income. The difference in the two tax treatments can be seen as follows:

	Sale of Shares	*Sale of Assets*
Profit on sale	$1.00	$1.00
Exclusion of 60%	.60	-0-
Income subject to tax	$ .40	$1.00
Tax (assume 50% rate)	$ .20	$ .50
Retained by owner (profit less tax)	$ .80	$ .50

Subchapter S The federal and some state governments have provided relief from double taxation of corporate profits. The relief is in the form of the tax option corporation (the Subchapter S corporation, sometimes referred to as a corporation taxed as a partnership). A Subchapter S corporation accumulates income and expense items and reports them on Form 1120S in much the same manner as an ordinary corporation. Each shareholder's share of the corporation's income is reported by that shareholder in much the same manner as a partner would report his or her share of the partnership income (Schedule K-1). Subchapter S corporations may have not more than twenty-five (25) shareholders and may have only one class of stock. All the shareholders must be individual persons, and the corporation must file an election signed by all members of the corporation. The election has to be filed any time during the year preceding the tax year for which it is to be effective or during the first 75 days of that tax year. The election is made on Form 2553.

Not all corporate businesses qualify to be Subchapter S corporations. A corporation engaged primarily in investment activities or in the ownership of real estate is not allowed to become a Subchapter S corporation. One of the requirements for a Subchapter S corporation is that it be engaged in the active conduct of a trade or business rather than mere investment. The use of a Subchapter S corporation in the appropriate circumstances enables a business person to obtain the advantages of limited liability that are offered by a corporate entity without the disadvantage of double taxation, which is a general obligation borne by corporations.

The Internal Revenue Code (§ 1244) provides a tax benefit to the shareholder who terminates or sells a corporate business at a loss. This benefit is available only if an election is made when the corporation is formed. Be sure you consider this when forming your corporation, and discuss it with your attorney and accountant before finalizing the corporation.

QUESTIONS

1   Mary Jones is married. Her mother, husband, three children from her former marriage, and two children from her present marriage live with her. Her social security number is 088–22–4693. Prepare a W-4 Form, the Employee's Withholding Allowance Certificate, for Mrs. Jones.

2   Referring to the information in question 1, assume in addition that Mary Jones anticipates losses from rental property in the amount of $2,000 and itemized deductions in the amount of $18,400. Prepare a new Form W-4.

3   Bill Smith is single, has one child, and is making $350 per week. Compute the amount of federal withholding tax that should be withheld from his salary each week.

4   You wish to form a business to operate a series of pushcarts on your campus. Prepare the appropriate application for an employer identification number (Form SS-4), supplying all of the particulars necessary (you will be operating five different pushcarts under the name of Katie's Fast Foods).

5   Listed below is information concerning a self-employed individual in the real estate business. Prepare a form Schedule C, Profit or Loss from Business or Profession, assuming that you are engaged in the business under your own name.

Gross commissions	$48,200
Payments to salespersons	15,800
Advertising	2,830
Dues	420
Office supplies	460
Telephone	2,400
Interest and bank charges	600
Gasoline for business car	1,690
Repairs for business car	260
New tires for business car (will last 3 years)	300
Depreciation on business car	600

6 Referring to the previous question, assume the self-employed person also has a salary of $15,000. Prepare a computation of social security self-employment tax, Schedule SE.

7 Referring to the following information prepare a 1065 U.S. Partnership Return for Mary and Joe doing business as M&J's Apartments.

Rental revenues	$12,715
Interest revenues	125
Advertising expenses	85
Interest on mortgages	5,820
Principal on mortgage	1,060
School taxes	980
Land taxes	540
Repairs	1,240
Utilities	1,680
Insurance	460
Depreciation on building	3,600
Depreciation on equipment	420

8 Assume you are an outside salesperson working for D&R Sales, Inc. You travel utilizing your own funds and vehicle. In 1983, you drove 22,000 miles of which 15,500 were job related. You incurred the following expenses: gasoline, $2,500; license, $25; oil, $250; parking and tolls, $325; repairs, $1,000; insurance, $1,200; interest on loan for purchase of automobile, $1,495; principal payments on automobile loan, $1,200. You purchased the automobile January 1, 1983 for $14,000 (assume the salvage value to be 0 and the useful life to be 4 years). Prepare a form Z106.

9 As part of your responsibility to your employer, you flew to several trade shows in Los Angeles, Chicago, and New York from your home office in Texas. You paid for the following expenses: airline tickets, $3,000; meals while away from home, $600; motels, $1,200; limousines and taxicabs to and from airports and business meetings, $300. Your employer reimbursed you $2,500 for all expenses during the year. This reimbursement was not included in your W-2. Prepare the Employee Business Expense Form, 2106, based on the above facts.

10 Jim Brady owns a drugstore. During the taxable year Brady purchased merchandise for $150,000. Brady's inventory at the beginning of the year was $22,500. His ending inventory was $72,300. Brady took merchandise from the store, which cost him $2,500 but which would have retailed for $3,400. Compute the cost of goods sold for the drugstore.

11 William Jones owns a house that he rents for $500 per month. During November it was not rented (the former tenant moved out at the end of October and a new tenant was not found until December 1). The expenses of maintaining the property are as follows: real estate taxes, $900; mortgage interest payments, $1,800; mortgage principal payments, $700; home owner's insurance, $150; utilities, $820; repairs, $200; and professional services (accounting, legal, and rental commissions), $500. The property was purchased on January 1, 1981 at a price of $32,000, $2,000 of which was for the land on which the building is situated. Assume the property has no residual value and may be depreciated on a straight-line basis over 15 years. Six months after the purchase of the property, Bill purchased new refrigerators, stoves, and dishwashers for the rental property at a cost of $1,500. Assume that this property may be depreciated over 3 years and that the salvage value is 0. Prepare the Schedule E for the year 1982 based on the above information.

12 Explain how the W-4 Form can be used to minimize federal income taxes withheld from a person's salary. Explain why it is desirable to minimize taxes withheld from a person's salary. Explain the potential danger involved in minimizing the taxes withheld from a person's salary.

13 You work for Carols Department Store as a manager. Your salary for the current calendar year is $37,000. Compute the amount of social security that has to be deducted from your paycheck for the year. Compute the total amount of social security that is deposited into your account for the current year.

14 The following is a payroll sheet from Jones' Diaper Service which you own. Your bookkeeper is out sick and Form 941 is due tomorrow. Prepare Form 941 for submission to the Internal Revenue Service.

			Amounts Deducted from Earnings						
		Gross Pay	Social Security	Federal W/H Tax	State W/H	DBL	Total Deductions	Net Pay	Check Number
Lisa Bergendorfer	Jan.	600	39.92	62.80	21.60	1.20	125.52	474.48	123
22 Prospect Drive	Feb.	750	49.90	78.50	27.00	1.50	156.90	593.10	137
Anywhere, U.S.A.	Mar.	600	39.92	62.80	21.60	1.20	125.52	474.48	151
123-45-6789									
	Total								
Andrew Smith	Jan.	480.00	31.92	39.20	14.80	1.20	87.12	392.88	124
17 Gilbert Road	Feb.	660.00	43.89	59.80	21.50	1.50	126.69	533.31	138
Anywhere, U.S.A.	Mar.	560.00	37.24	53.60	18.80	1.20	110.84	449.16	152
012-34-5678									
	Total								
Jason Johnson	Jan.	316.00	21.01	30.80	7.80	1.14	60.75	255.25	125
18–20 Page Lane	Feb.	300.00	19.94	22.40	6.40	1.34	50.08	249.92	139
Anywhere, U.S.A.	Mar.	192.00	12.76	9.84	3.50	1.02	27.12	164.88	153
901-23-4567									
	Total								
Katie Steinberg	Jan.	640.00	42.56	71.20	17.60	1.20	132.56	507.44	126
RD 31	Feb.	800.00	53.20	89.00	22.00	1.50	165.70	634.30	140
Elsewhere, U.S.A.	Mar.	640.00	42.56	71.20	17.60	1.20	132.56	507.44	154
890-12-3456									
	Total								

Glossary*

Abandon To relinquish completely.

Abandonment (1) The complete relinquishment of property or rights without reference to any purpose or person. (2) Failure to proceed in a law suit for an extended period of time. (3) Desertion of children. (4) Unjustified separation of one spouse from the other.

Abatement (1) Reduction or decrease. (2) The suppression or removal of a nuisance. (3) Proportional reduction of legacies when there are insufficient funds to pay them totally.

Abet To give aid, particularly in commission of a crime.

Abettor One who aids another in any way to commit a crime.

Abode A dwelling place. *Compare with* Domicil(e).

Abrogate To repeal or annul, e.g., to repeal a former rule or law.

Absolute Unconditional; totally unrestricted.

Abstract A summary. *Compare with* Transcript.

Abuse (1) To injure by improper use (v). (2) Improper use, e.g., of discretion or process (n).

Abut To border upon or touch.

Acceptance (1) Agreement to an offer; the basis for a contract. (2) Signed promise of drawee of bill of exchange to honor the bill as it has been presented. (3) The certification of a check.

Accessory A person connected with the commission of a crime but not present at the actual commission.

Accommodation A favor. An accommodation indorser signs a bill or note in order to lend his name to another. (This would be called accommodation paper.)

Accomplice One who voluntarily and knowingly aids in the commission of a crime.

Accord An agreement. In contracts, agreement to settle a claim.

Accord and satisfaction A fully executed accord.

Acquit To discharge from an accusation, usually criminal.

Acquittal Discharge from an accusation; a not guilty verdict.

Action A judicial proceeding.

Actionable Providing the basis for a judicial proceeding.

Actual Real; existing; not merely possible.

Ad litem *(Latin)* For the suit; during the suit; e.g., guardian ad litem.

Adhesion contract A one-sided contract presented by the stronger party and not bargained for by the weaker party.

Adjourn To postpone until a future session.

Adjudge To decide or render judgment.

Adjudicate To render judgment.

Administrative law The branch of law dealing with the operation of the various governmental agencies that administer specific branches of the law.

Administrator The person who is appointed by the court to be the personal representative of the estate of a dead person.

---

* This Glossary was adapted from R. Z. Volkell, *Quick Legal Terminology* (New York: Wiley, 1979). Used with permission.

Glossary*

Abandon To relinquish completely.

Abandonment (1) The complete relinquishment of property or rights without reference to any purpose or person. (2) Failure to proceed in a law suit for an extended period of time. (3) Desertion of children. (4) Unjustified separation of one spouse from the other.

Abatement (1) Reduction or decrease. (2) The suppression or removal of a nuisance. (3) Proportional reduction of legacies when there are insufficient funds to pay them totally.

Abet To give aid, particularly in commission of a crime.

Abettor One who aids another in any way to commit a crime.

Abode A dwelling place. *Compare with* Domicil(e).

Abrogate To repeal or annul, e.g., to repeal a former rule or law.

Absolute Unconditional; totally unrestricted.

Abstract A summary. *Compare with* Transcript.

Abuse (1) To injure by improper use (v). (2) Improper use, e.g., of discretion or process (n).

Abut To border upon or touch.

Acceptance (1) Agreement to an offer; the basis for a contract. (2) Signed promise of drawee of bill of exchange to honor the bill as it has been presented. (3) The certification of a check.

Accessory A person connected with the commission of a crime but not present at the actual commission.

Accommodation A favor. An accommodation indorser signs a bill or note in order to lend his name to another. (This would be called accommodation paper.)

Accomplice One who voluntarily and knowingly aids in the commission of a crime.

Accord An agreement. In contracts, agreement to settle a claim.

Accord and satisfaction A fully executed accord.

Acquit To discharge from an accusation, usually criminal.

Acquittal Discharge from an accusation; a not guilty verdict.

Action A judicial proceeding.

Actionable Providing the basis for a judicial proceeding.

Actual Real; existing; not merely possible.

Ad litem *(Latin)* For the suit; during the suit; e.g., guardian ad litem.

Adhesion contract A one-sided contract presented by the stronger party and not bargained for by the weaker party.

Adjourn To postpone until a future session.

Adjudge To decide or render judgment.

Adjudicate To render judgment.

Administrative law The branch of law dealing with the operation of the various governmental agencies that administer specific branches of the law.

Administrator The person who is appointed by the court to be the personal representative of the estate of a dead person.

---

* This Glossary was adapted from R. Z. Volkell, *Quick Legal Terminology* (New York: Wiley, 1979). Used with permission.

tions, criminal assault actually requires some physical injury.

Assent (1) Agreement (n). (2) To agree (v).

Assess To fix the value of some property, usually for purposes of taxation. To call for contributions from the various members of a group.

Assets Property of any kind whatsoever, e.g., money, stock, personal property.

Assign To transfer to another, e.g., to assign property to some interest therein.

Assignee A person to whom an assignment is made.

Assignment A transfer to another of property or rights.

Assignor A person who makes an assignment.

Assigns Assignees.

Assumption Taking over or taking upon oneself, e.g., assumption of a debt.

Assumption of risk Exposing oneself to danger of which one has prior knowledge. This may negate the liability of the one who has created the danger.

Assure To ensure; to make certain; to put beyond doubt.

Attach To bring property under custody of a court.

Attachment (1) The act of seizing property, through legal channels, in order to bring it under the custody of the court. (2) The creation of a security interest.

Attempt An inchoate crime; must include an overt act done with the intent to commit the crime. It is more than mere contemplation or planning.

Attest To affirm; to certify; to bear witness to.

Attestation clause The clause of a will in which witnesses certify that the will was properly executed.

Attractive nuisance A condition on property which is likely to attract small children but which is also dangerous to them. One who possesses property containing such a condition must take precautions to prevent injury to children.

Authority (1) Legal precedent. (2) The power of an agent to act for his principal.

Award (1) The decision of an arbitrator. (2) A judgment for payment of costs or damages.

Bad faith The opposite of good faith; involving deliberate and intentional action with some ulterior motive, be it will or self-interest.

Bail Money paid to secure the release of a prisoner from jail. Should the prisoner then fail to appear at trial, the money is forfeited.

Bailee A person to whom a bailment is made.

Bailiff A court official whose function is to help maintain order.

Bailment Entrustment of property by the owner to another person, usually for a specific purpose, e.g., storing an automobile in a garage.

Bailor A person who makes a bailment.

Bankruptcy The law under which an insolvent debtor may be discharged from his debts by bringing all his assets into court.

Bar (1) The railing that encloses the officers of the court. (2) All attorneys who are admitted to practice before a court.

Battery The intentional unlawful touching of one person by another person or by an object controlled or set in motion by the other person.

Bearer A person who holds a negotiable instrument that is payable to whoever holds it, usually payable to ''cash'' or ''bearer.''

Bench (1) The seat upon which judges sit. (2) The judges of a court collectively.

Beneficiary A person who receives a benefit as a result of a gift, a trust, a will, etc.

Bequeath To give personal property by will. *See also* Devise.

Bequest A gift by will of personal property, a legacy.

Bias Prejudice; preconception that makes it difficult or impossible to be fair.

Bigamy The crime of someone marrying a second time while already a party to a valid marriage.

Bilateral contract Contract in which both parties agree to do something (as opposed to unilateral contract).

Bill (1) A formal complaint in a lawsuit. (2) A law, as passed by a legislative body. (3) A negotiable instrument, e.g., a bank note.

Bill of particulars A written specification by the plaintiff of matters that have been set forth in the original pleading.

Bill of rights The first ten amendments of the U.S. Constitution.

Blackmail The crime of extortion of money by

threat, usually threat of exposure of some conduct of the victim.

Blue ribbon jury   A jury of specially qualified jurors.

Board of directors   The governing body of a private corporation.

Bona fide   *(Latin)* Acting in or with good faith.

Breach   A breaking or a violation of a law, contract, duty, or warranty.

Brief   A written statement of position prepared by each side in a lawsuit.

Burden of proof   The duty of proving to the court that one's assertions are in fact the truth by showing that the evidence favors them.

Burglary   At common law, the illegal entry, at night, of a dwelling with the intent to commit a felony once inside. Modern laws tend to eliminate one or more of the common law requirements.

Buyer   The party to whom property is transferred in a contract of sale.

By-laws   Rules for running a corporation or other business or society.

Calendar   In a court, the list of cases for trial.

Cancellation   Termination of a contract by agreement of the parties or because one side has breached the contract.

Canon   A rule or law.

Capacity   Legal competency, e.g., to act, to sue, to understand.

Capital   Assets used to make money. Total capital is the net worth of a corporation; stated capital is the total par value of the shares sold.

Capital crime   Crime that may be punished by death.

Carrier   A transporter of persons or property.

Cartel   A group of companies, usually in the same general business, associated together for some improper purpose, such as price fixing.

Case   A lawsuit. *See also* Trespass on the case.

Case law   The aggregate of reported cases (as opposed to statute law).

Cashier   An employee who is in charge of operating a cash register. In a bank, the cashier is an executive officer, often the chief executive officer, who is responsible for the bank's cash.

Causa mortis   *(Latin)* In contemplation of death. A gift causa mortis is a gift given in contemplation of death and takes effect only upon the death of the donor.

Cause of action   The right to start a lawsuit or the facts that give rise to such a right.

Caveat   *(Latin)* A warning to beware.

Caveat actor   *(Latin)* Let the actor or doer beware.

Caveat emptor   *(Latin)* Let the buyer beware.

Certificate   Formal written authentication of some fact or circumstance.

Certified check   A check that the bank accepts in advance, thereby guaranteeing that it is good.

Certiorari   *(Latin)* Voluntary review of a decision by a higher court; distinguished from an appeal, which is heard as a matter of right.

Chain of title   All successive changes in the ownership of a piece of real property.

Chambers   The private office of a judge, near but not actually part of the court, where some of the court's business is conducted.

Chancellor   Originally, the highest judicial officer in England. A judge of a chancery court.

Chancery   A court of equity jurisprudence. Today, American courts of law and equity have merged.

Charge   (1) To accuse (v). (2) The judge's instructions to the jury on matters of law (n).

Chattel mortgage   A mortgage on personal property.

Chattels   Personal property; movable property (not land).

Check   An order to a bank for payment of money to a named payee or bearer. A type of negotiable instrument.

Chose   *(French)* Literally, a thing; a cause of action.

Chose in action   A right to be paid, recoverable by bringing an action.

Circuit court   Court whose jurisdiction is wider than just one district. The name is derived from the fact that early judges ''rode circuit'' in order to serve their entire jurisdiction.

Circumstantial evidence   Indirect evidence; involves the use of the existence of one fact because it implies the truth of the conclusion desired to be proved.

Citation   (1) A summons or a writ commanding a person to appear in court. (2) A reference to existing legal authority in order to strengthen an argument or a position advanced.

Civil   Pertaining to the community.

Civil action A noncriminal court action, a lawsuit contested between two citizens to enforce a right or obtain redress for some wrong.

Civil law Roman law and its derivatives; law based on a code.

Civil rights The legal rights of individuals as guaranteed by the Constitution.

Class action An action brought by a small number of named plaintiffs on behalf of a larger group, all with similar causes of action.

Clean hands An equitable doctrine that prevents a person from seeking equitable relief unless he has acted properly with regard to the matter being adjudicated.

Clear and present danger The test of whether spoken words may be without the protection of the Constitution. Such words are unprotected only if they do create a clear and present danger of serious violence.

Clerk A person who keeps records for another. A clerk of the court is responsible for keeping the court's records.

Close corporation Corporation ownership that is limited to a few shareholders.

Code A published set of laws, usually arranged according to some numerical system of subdivisions.

Codicil A supplement, change, or addition to a will.

Coercion Compulsion of a person to do something against his or her will; may be accomplished by force or persuasion.

Collateral At or from the side; money or other property offered as security for a loan.

Collateral attack Indirect attack; an attack on a judgment by way of a proceeding which has a primary purpose other than attacking the judgment.

Collateral estoppel The doctrine that bars a court from making a determination as to facts that have already been determined by a competent court.

Color Semblance; appearance; e.g., color of law (not necessarily under actual authority of law).

Comity Courtesy; recognition by one state or nation of the laws of another.

Commerce All forms of trade and commercial intercourse.

Commerce clause Article I, Section 8, of the U.S. Constitution; it allows Congress to control all interstate and international trade.

Commercial paper Negotiable instruments.

Committee (1) A group selected to perform a particular duty. (2) The guardian of an incompetent person.

Common law Judge or court-made law that receives its binding force from custom, usage, and judicial decisions (as distinguished from legislation). It originated in early England and is constantly evolving.

Common law marriage A marriage that takes place without ceremony but solely because the parties live together as husband and wife for a certain amount of time.

Community property Property owned jointly by a husband and wife; in some states, all property acquired during the marriage is community property.

Comparative negligence Rule under which the negligence of plaintiff is compared to that of defendant to determine how much plaintiff is entitled to recover. *Compare with* Contributory negligence.

Competent Adequate, qualified.

Competent evidence Relevant, proper, and admissible.

Competent witness A witness who meets certain standards, such as age, intelligence, and ability to comprehend the importance of telling the truth.

Complaint In civil practice, a pleading setting out the cause of action; in criminal law, the formal charge.

Concur To agree, to act together.

Concurrent At the same time, e.g., two courts have concurrent jurisdiction when they each have jurisdiction to hear the same matter; two sentences of imprisonment are concurrent if they can be served at the same time instead of consecutively.

Condemnation (1) Exercise of the power of eminent domain; the taking of private property (with compensation to the owner) for public use. (2) The declaration that a building is unfit for use. (3) A finding of guilt.

Condition A provision in a contract that modifies rights or duties under the contract if a certain event takes place.

Condominium   Joint ownership of a multiple dwelling in such a way that each dweller has sole ownership of an individual apartment and all are joint owners of the common areas.

Confession   An admission of guilt of a crime.

Confidentiality   Requirement that the privacy of certain relationships (lawyer-client, doctor-patient, etc.) receive legal protection. For example, a lawyer may not repeat information obtained in confidence from a client.

Conflict of laws   The area of the law that governs when one nation or state will apply the laws of another.

Conjugal   Having to do with marriage.

Consanguinity   Blood relationship, kinship.

Consent   (1) Voluntary agreement (n). (2) To agree voluntarily (v).

Consideration   Inducement to a contract; the thing that is bargained for in a contract; that which is given by one party in exchange for the promise of the other party. Without consideration, there can be no valid contract.

Consignment   The turning over of goods to another for transportation or for sale. Title is retained by the consignor.

Consolidation   The trying of two or more different related cases as one case.

Conspiracy   A criminal offense consisting of the joining of two or more persons for the purpose of doing an unlawful act.

Constitution   General and basic set of laws and principles of government of a nation or state that may be either written or unwritten. The U.S. Constitution, adopted in 1787, is the supreme law of the land.

Constitutional   In agreement with or consistent with the Constitution.

Constitutional law   The study of the application and interpretation of the Constitution.

Constitutional right   A right guaranteed by the Constitution; cannot be tampered with by more legislation.

Construction   Determination of the meaning of words in a constitution, law, contract, etc., by considering the meanings of the words themselves and also all of the surrounding circumstances. It is more than just interpretation, which employs only consideration of the words themselves.

Constructive   Considered to be the case even though not actually so.

Constructive eviction   Eviction in effect; while the landlord has not actually evicted the tenant, the condition of the property has reached a state where it is no longer liveable, so that the tenant might as well have been evicted.

Constructive notice   Not actual notice. Where actual notice is not possible, such notice as the law deems sufficient, e.g., published in a newspaper.

Constructive trust   A trust established by law when the legal owner of property gained title improperly, and in the interests of fairness the legal owner is deemed to hold the property in trust for another.

Construe   To interpret.

Contemporaneous   At the same time.

Contempt   A manifestation of disrespect for a court or a legislature, including a deliberate refusal to obey an order of such a court or legislature.

Contingent   Possible but not absolutely certain to happen; depending on some other event, e.g., an attorney's contingent fee depends on the outcome of the case.

Continuance   An adjournment, i.e., of an action pending in court.

Contra   *(Latin)* Contrary to; against; in opposition to.

Contraband   Anything it is against the law to own or to transport, e.g., narcotics.

Contract   An agreement, supported by consideration and not contrary to any law, to do or not to do some act. A contract may be written or oral.

Contractor   A person who enters a contract.

Contributory negligence   Rule under which any negligence on the part of the plaintiff precludes recovering any damage from the defendant, even though the defendant was also negligent. *Compare with* Comparative negligence.

Conversion   (1) A wrongful act of ownership exercised over the property of another. (2) Changing one type of property to another; equitable conversion is the exchange of real property for personal property.

Conveyance A deed transferring title to real property.

Convict To find guilty.

Conviction An adjudication of guilt by a verdict or by a guilty plea.

Cooling time *(Cooling-off period)* Time to calm down after provocation; a waiting period prescribed by law before commencing a strike or a divorce action.

Cooperative A multiple dwelling owned by a corporation, which is in turn owned by the residents of the building.

Copyright The right of the author, artist, etc., to control publication of his work. Copyrights are regulated by federal law.

Correspondent The third party in a divorce action based on adultery.

Corporal punishment Physical punishment.

Corporation An artificial entity created by law strictly for business purposes and owned through purchase of corporate stock. It is liable only to the extent of the corporate assets, not the personal wealth of the owners.

Corpus *(Latin)* Literally, the body. An aggregate or mass, e.g., of men, laws, or articles.

Corpus delicti *(Latin)* Body of the crime; the actual item that was the subject of the crime; e.g., in a murder, the corpus delicti is the corpse.

Corpus juris *(Latin)* The body of the law.

Corroborate To support; to add credibility. Corroborating evidence supports that which has already been heard.

Costs The expenses of the successful party in a court action ordered to be paid by the losing party.

Counsel, counsellor A lawyer.

Count Each item of a complaint or indictment; each states a separate cause of action.

Counterclaim A claim by the defendant against the plaintiff in a civil suit.

Course The ordinary or usual way in which something moves.

Course of business The ordinary or usual running of the business.

Court (1) The governmental organ that dispenses justice. (2) The judge himself. (3) The place where the judge exercises his judicial function.

Court of appeals A court that hears appeals after a trial has been completed in a lower court. In most jurisdictions it is a middle-level court, but in some states, such as New York, it is the highest court.

Court of chancery An equity court, a court with the same jurisdiction as a chancellor. In America today, the courts have jurisdiction in both law and equity.

Court of claims A federal court that hears all claims against the United States.

Court of law A court administering the laws and statutes. In America today, the courts of law and equity have merged.

Court of probate A court with jurisdiction to probate wills, estates, etc.

Covenant Agreement contained in a deed which binds the buyer, the seller, or both. Some covenants are said to "run with the land" and bind all future purchasers (as opposed to only the party to the original covenant): e.g., covenant against encumbrances, which means that there are no outstanding interests against title to the land; or a covenant of quiet enjoyment, which assures buyer that seller will protect buyer from eviction by others claiming title.

Credible Worthy of belief.

Credit Money due to be received.

Creditor A person who is owed money by another (the debtor).

Crime An offense against the state; a violation of the penal law.

Criminal (1) Having to do with crime (adj). (2) A person who has committed a crime (n).

Criminal law Branch of the law dealing with crimes.

Criminal mischief Intentional or reckless damage to property.

Criminal trespass Unlawfully entering or remaining on property.

Cross-claim A claim by one co-defendant against another, related to the main suit.

Cross-examination The questioning of a witness for the opposition in order to test the truth of his statements.

Culpable Criminal; censurable; blamable.

Curtesy The common law right of a husband in the real property of his wife. (The wife's right in her husband's property is called dower.) Today, each spouse has the same rights to the property of the other.

Custody   Control; care; keeping.

Custom   A practice so well established that it takes on legal importance.

D.A.   District attorney.

D.B.A.   Doing business as, usually written d/b/a.

Damages   Money awarded by a court as compensation for an injury or wrong caused by another. They are classed as (1) actual or compensatory—as compensation for the actual injury, or (2) punitive (exemplary)—in excess of the actual damage, but intended as punishment.

Dangerous instrumentality   Something that is inherently dangerous, sometimes allowing for liability without actual fault on the part of the owner.

Dangerous weapon   A weapon capable of killing.

De facto   (*Latin*) In fact (even if not by law); e.g., de facto segregation existed even where no legal plan to segregate any longer existed; a business may be a de facto corporation even though it has failed to meet one of the small requirements of the law.

De jure   (*Latin*) By law; by right; valid in the eyes of the law.

De novo   (*Latin*) New; over again.

Deadly weapon   A weapon designed to cause death.

Death   The moment when life ends, the state of being dead. When a person is inexplicably absent for a certain period, usually 7 years, that person is presumed dead.

Debenture   A corporate bond, usually unsecured by any property.

Debit   Money owing; to be paid out.

Debt   Money that is owed according to some definite agreement.

Debtor   A person who owes something to another person.

Decedent   A person who has died; a deceased person.

Deceit   An intentional falsehood causing harm to another; a type of fraud.

Decision   The formal resolution by a judge of a lawsuit; the written report of that finding.

Declarant   A person who makes a statement (declaration) that may later be evidence.

Declaration   A statement in evidence made by someone who is not available as a witness. Some declarations are given more credence than others, e.g., a declaration against interest (a statement adverse to the interests of the declarant at the time the statement was made) and a dying declaration (statement made while in extremis, relevant to the wrongful cause of death, such as in a homicide) are both given extra credence.

Declaratory judgment   A judgment that answers a legal question without ordering that any action be taken or damages be enforced; it simply defines the rights of the parties. There must, however, be some actual dispute at issue.

Decree   A judgment in an equitable action.

Deductible   Something that may be used as a deduction for income tax purposes.

Deduction   Something that one is allowed to subtract from one's total income for tax purposes, e.g., charitable contributions. Deductions also exist in estate taxation.

Deed   A signed document stating the transfer of a piece of real property.

Defamation   Oral (slander) or written (libel) published statements injurious to the reputation of another. In order to be actionable, the statements must be false.

Defamatory   Bringing about defamation.

Default   An omission or failure to perform legal duty; failure to make a required payment or to appear or take a necessary step in a lawsuit.

Default judgment   A judgment entered against a defendant who is in default.

Defeasible   Subject to being defeated or annulled if some future event takes place.

Defect   An absence of some necessary part or legal requirement.

Defendant   The person against whom the suit is brought.

Defense   That which is brought forth by the defendant.

Defraud   To commit acts of fraud, to cheat.

Delivery   Transfer of possession or control of an item from one person to another.

Demand   A claim for performance of a legal obligation.

Demand note   Promissory note payable on demand (or at once).

Demise   To convey, to lease.

Demur   To interpose a demurrer.

Demurrer   A common law pleading which, assuming for the sake of argument that everything in the complaint is true, says that there still exists no basis for a recovery. In other words, a demurrer questions the legal sufficiency of the complaint.

Denial   In pleading, a refutation of the claims made by the opponent; a refusal or a withholding.

Dependent   A person who is supported by another.

Deponent   A person who makes a deposition.

Deposition   A written statement, given under oath, usually outside of court for use in court.

Depreciation   A drop in value. A certain amount of depreciation can sometimes be used as a tax deduction.

Descendant   A person who proceeds from the body of an ancestor, no matter how remote.

Descent   An inheritance from any ancestors.

Desertion   The abandonment of a post of duty or of a spouse or child.

Determination   A ruling of a court.

Detriment   Harm or loss.

Devise   Gift by will of real estate.

Dicta   *See* Dictum.

Dictim   *(Latin; plural: dicta)* A digression in the court's opinion, not necessary to explain the holding in the case at hand.

Digest   A collection of numerous books or materials in one volume for facility of reference.

Dilatory   Delaying, causing delay.

Diligence   Care and prudence.

Direct   Immediate; not remote.

Direct evidence   Proof of the fact in question without reference to other facts.

Direct examination   The first questioning of a witness by the party who called that witness.

Directed verdict   Jury verdict ordered by the judge, thus making it unnecessary for the jury to reach its own verdict.

Disability   A state of weakness or incapacity; lack of legal capacity.

Disbar   To revoke a lawyer's license to practice law.

Discharge   To release; to terminate.

Discharge in bankruptcy   To release a bankrupt from all debts, except those excluded for some reason.

Disclaimer   A refusal to accept responsibility, a renunciation.

Discontinuance   The cessation or termination of an action.

Discovery   The process by which the adverse parties in a lawsuit exchange information necessary for the trying of the suit.

Disinterested   Impartial; having no personal interest in the outcome.

Dismiss   To order a lawsuit ended or a motion denied.

Dismissal   An order ending a lawsuit without an actual trial, having the same effect as a judgment against the plaintiff. Sometimes a plaintiff may seek a voluntary dismissal without prejudice, meaning the suit can be brought again at a later date. If the dismissal is with prejudice, such a later suit is precluded.

Dissent   (1) To disagree (v). (2) The formal minority opinion of a judge who does not agree with the majority (n).

Dissolution   The breaking up, dissolving, splitting up into original component parts, or canceling of something, e.g., a corporation.

Distrain   To take the property of another and hold it until he performs some obligation.

Distress   The act or process of distraining.

Diversity of citizenship   One basis for federal jurisdiction, where the controversy is between citizens of different states.

Dividend   A gain, a share of some property, a payment by a corporation to shareholders.

Divorce   The ending of a marriage by order of the court. *Compare with* Annulment.

Docket   A list or record of cases of a particular court.

Document   Anything that records information.

Documentry evidence   Tangible evidence in the form of a document.

Doing business   A term that signifies that an out-of-state corporation has performed enough acts within the state to fall under the jurisdiction of the state for purposes of being sued and taxed.

Domicil(e)   *(Latin)* The place where a person makes his permanent home, to which he plans eventually to return. While a person may have several residences, he can have only one domicile at a given time.

Donee   The recipient of a gift.

Donor   The giver of a gift.

Double jeopardy   The trying of a person twice for the same offense. This is prohibited by the fifth amendment to the Constitution.

Doubt   Uncertainty. In order to render a verdict of guilty in a criminal case, the jury must be certain ''beyond a reasonable doubt.''

Dower   The common law right of a wife in the real property of her husband. *See also* Curtesy.

Draft   A negotiable instrument that contains a written order from one person (the drawer) to another (the drawee) to pay money to a third person (the payee); a bill of exchange.

Drawee   The party to whom a bill of exchange is advanced.

Drawer   The party who writes a bill of exchange.

Duces tecum   *(Latin)* Literally, bring with you. *See also* Subpoena duces tecum.

Due care   Sufficient care under the circumstances.

Due process of law   One of the most difficult concepts to define; the main idea is fairness. It always includes fair notice and a chance to be heard.

Duress   The wrongful compulsion of a person to do an act he would not otherwise have done. It may take the form of violence, restraint, threats, etc.

Duty   An obligation, legal or contractual; a tax on items imported into a country.

Dwelling house   A residence or abode.

Dying declaration   A statement by the victim of a homicide relating to the homicide, made while the victim is dying.

E.B.T.   Examination before trial; questioning of party to lawsuit by opposition as part of discovery procedure.

Earned income   Income obtained as a result of work or other efforts of the person to whom it is paid, rather than money merely paid to a person, such as dividends on stock. Simply, money earned from labor, not capital.

Easement   The right of one person to use the land of another for a specified purpose. An example would be a right-of-way across a neighbor's land in order to reach a road.

Ecclesiastical   Pertaining to religion or the church.

Effects   Personal property

Ejectment   A common law action to recover land.

Election   The act of choosing, be it in (1) political voting, (2) filing a tax return, or (3) choosing between inheriting under a will or taking a minimum prescribed legal inheritance.

Emancipation   The setting free or liberation of some person or persons from parental control or some form of bondage.

Embezzlement   The fraudulent taking of money that has been entrusted to the taker, who may be a trustee or an employee in a position to alter financial records.

Emigration   The leaving of one's country in order to move to another.

Eminent domain   The power of the government to take private property for public use by compensating the owner.

Employ   To hire or engage the services of another person.

Employee   A person who works for another (the employer) and who is under the control of the employer; a servant.

Employer   A person who hires another and directs him in his work; a master.

Employment   A job; the act of being employed or of employing.

Emptor   *(Latin)* A buyer.

Enact   To decree; to establish by law.

Encroach   To trespass, to accomplish encroachment.

Encroachment   An intrusion onto the property of another, e.g., a fence that extends onto a neighbor's property.

Encumber   To place land under an encumbrance.

Encumbrance   Any impediment that lessens the value of land (such as a mortgage).

Endorse   *See* Indorse.

Enjoin   To order or command, to forbid or issue an injunction.

Entail   To create an estate in tail, an estate that is limited in the way it can pass to future generations. *See* Fee tail.

Enter   To make an entry or a record. Entering judgment is the formal recording of the court's decision.

Entirety   The totality. The joint estate of a married couple is called estate by the entirety.

Entrapment   An inducement by police to entice a

person to commit a crime that he would not otherwise have committed. A person who has been so lured can use that fact in his defense.

Entry (1) Unlawful entering of a building in order to commit a crime therein. (2) The act of making a record or the record itself.

Equal protection of the laws A fourteenth amendment right which forbids denial to some people of protections that are accorded to others, the denial being based on race, color, creed, etc.

Equitable (1) Just; fair. (2) Emanating from a court of equity.

Equitable conversion The exchange of real property for personal property by a court of equity.

Equity A word with broad meanings, mostly centering around fairness and the court's power to do what is right in the situation; or to act even when no remedy exists at law. Courts of equity (also called courts of chancery) are now merged with courts of law; one court has both powers.

Error A mistake by a court made in trying a case. It may be a mistake of law or of fact, and it may or may not be serious enough to upset the judgment on appeal. If so, it is called reversible error; if not, a harmless error.

Escalator clause A contract clause, usually in a contract for sale or rental which allows the contract price to be raised if certain events take place, e.g., rising costs or raising the legal maximum.

Escheat The passing to the state of property that has no legal owner, e.g., on the death of a person with no heirs and no will.

Escrow The holding of some property or papers by a disinterested third party, delivery of the escrow items being contingent on some performance by the person to whom the items are eventually to be delivered.

Esquire A title formally applied to lawyers.

Estate (1) The interest of a person in a piece of real property measured by potential duration, e.g., for life; the property itself. (2) The total of all of a dead person's property (decedent's estate).

Estate at sufferance The interest of a tenant who remains on property after his right to be there has expired.

Estate at will A leasehold estate that can be terminated at the will of either party.

Estate for life *See* Life estate.

Estate for years An estate that ends after a specific amount of time.

Estop To bar or prevent; to stop.

Estoppel A bar that prevents a person from asserting something, even though it may be true. An estoppel usually arises as a result of some prior act, assertion, or promise by the person being estopped.

Et al. *(Latin)* An abbreviation for et alius, meaning "and another," or for et alii, meaning "and others."

Et seq. *(Latin)* An abbreviation for et sequitur, meaning "and as follows"; "and the following pages."

Eviction Dispossession, particularly of tenant by landlord.

Evidence Information presented in court through which the truth is to be determined. The rules of evidence determine which evidence is admissible and which is not.

Ex officio *(Latin)* By virtue of the power of the office.

Ex parte *(Latin)* By one side or party (without the presence of the other).

Ex post facto *(Latin)* After the act or fact. An ex post facto law, which is unconstitutional, makes an act a crime subject to punishment even though it was not considered criminal when it was committed.

Examination An inspection; questioning, especially under oath.

Exception (1) An exclusion. (2) A statement of objection to a judge's ruling during trial to be decided at a later time.

Exchange (1) To trade or swap (v). (2) A forum for trading or swapping (n).

Excise tax A tax on the sale or use of any item or on any activity.

Exclusionary rule The rule that prevents illegally obtained evidence from being admitted in a criminal case.

Exclusive Sole and undivided; not allowing any others.

Exculpatory Relieving of guilt or responsibility.

Execute (1) To complete; to make valid; to carry out. (2) To put to death by order of law.

Executor The person chosen by a person making a

will to carry out the will by following the instructions therein for distribution of the estate.

Executory Still to be executed or performed to some extent.

Exempt Free from some obligation (such as military service).

Exemption (1) Freedom from some obligation. (2) A specific amount of money, prescribed by law, to be subtracted from income in computing tax. Each family member receives an exemption.

Exhibit Anything offered as evidence at a trial.

Exoneration A release from a burden or absolution from a charge of criminal conduct.

Expert witness A person who is so knowledgeable on a subject that he is allowed to testify as to his conclusions. An ordinary witness is allowed to testify only to facts.

Expiration An ending due to passage of time.

Express Explicit; clear. For example, express authority is established when one person tells another that he has authority to act on his behalf.

Expropriate To condemn, or to take private property for public use.

Expulsion The driving out of someone or something.

Expunge To obliterate; to erase; to wipe out.

Extension A lengthening, either physical (an extension to a house) or chronological (extension of a lease or a time to reply to a motion).

Extenuating circumstances Facts that tend to excuse misconduct and are taken into account in determining punishment.

Extinguishment Termination, e.g., of a right or a property interest.

Extort To compel by illegal threats.

Extortion Compulsion by force or threats, usually to pay some money.

Extradition The transfer of a person accused of a crime to the place where he is accused from some other state or nation.

Eyewitness A person who is able to testify as to what he has actually seen or heard.

F.O.B. *See* Free on board.

F.T.C. Federal Trade Commission.

Facsimile An exact copy of something.

Fact Something that is real and true, which exists or has happened.

Factor A person who buys and sells goods for others on a commission basis. One who finances accounts receivable, usually for a percentage of the sales.

Fair Equitable, reasonable, and proper.

Fair consideration A reasonable equivalent, more than just nominal.

Fair hearing A hearing held in accordance with certain fundamental rules of justice and fair play.

Fair market value The actual value; the price that would be arrived at by an equally anxious buyer and seller.

Fair trial A trial held in accordance with the law in an impartial atmosphere.

Fair value The present actual value.

False Untrue, particularly unintentionally.

False arrest The unlawful restraint of one person by another.

False entry An entry in the financial accounts of a bank which is intentionally made incorrectly with the intention of defrauding the bank.

False imprisonment Unlawful restraint of one person by another.

False pretenses A misrepresentation used to defraud another.

Falsehood A willful lie designed to deceive another.

Family A word whose meaning varies depending on the context in which it is used; usually describing a group of persons who are related to each other or who live together as a unit.

Fault A wrongful act, omission, or breach; a failure to do what is necessary; negligence.

Fear The apprehension or anxiety caused by actual or supposed danger.

Feasible Possible; capable of happening.

Feasor A doer; one who does.

Federal Joined and having a common central government. In American law, federal government and laws are national as opposed to their state and local equivalents.

Federal question A case or lawsuit that involves the U.S. Constitution or federal laws.

Fee (1) A charge for services. (2) An estate (real property) without restrictions or alienation even after the death of the estate builder, when the estate passes to his heirs.

Fee simple   The most extensive estate in real property, capable of enduring forever. Also called fee simple absolute. *See also* Fee.

Fee tail   Same as fee simple except after death it can only be passed on to "heirs of the body" (children) of the owner.

Fellow servant   One who serves the same master or employer.

Fellow servant rule   A common law rule which at one time held the employer not liable for injuries caused by one employee to another.

Felon   A person who commits a felony.

Felonious   Done with intent to commit a felony; malicious; malignant.

Felony   A very serious crime, e.g., murder, robbery.

Felony murder rule   Any homicide committed during the commission of a felony is considered murder.

Feticide   The destruction of a fetus.

Fiction   A manufactured situation in which something possibly false is assumed to be true in order to advance the cause of justice.

Fictitious payee   A made-up (false) person to whom a negotiable instrument is made out with no intention that he shall ever actually be paid.

Fiduciary   (1) A person who holds money or something of value in trust for another. (2) A situation in which one person is trusted to act for another.

Filiation   The relation of parent and child.

Finding   A decision as to a question of fact. Also called finding of fact.

Fine   A sum of money paid as punishment by a person who has been found guilty of an offense.

Fiscal year   A 12-month accounting period. The federal fiscal year runs from July 1 to June 30.

Fixture   An article that is physically attached to land and is therefore considered a part of it and cannot be removed.

Force   (1) Physical power. (2) Wrongful violence.

Forced sale   A sale to pay off a judgment of court.

Forcible entry   (1) Entry by breaking doors or windows. (2) Entry against the will of the owner.

Foreclosure   The total shutting out of the mortgagor by the mortgagee; it involves taking of the property and ending of all rights of the mortgagor. Foreclosure is generally a result of nonpayment of the mortgage.

Foreign   Of another state or nation.

Forensic   Having to do with the courts.

Foreseeable   Capable of being anticipated.

Forfeit   To lose, often as a consequence of an offense or a failure to perform some necessary act.

Forge   To fabricate a document by imitation with intent to commit fraud.

Forgery   The crime of falsely making or altering a document with intent to defraud.

Form   (1) A model of a common legal paper. (2) The technical aspects of procedure (as opposed to the "substance" of a proceeding).

Fortuitous   Chance; unforeseen; accidental

Forum   A court.

Foundation   A basis; a support. A foundation must sometimes be laid before evidence can be admitted.

Franchise   A right that exists as a matter of law (such as the right to vote).

Fraud   Deceit or trickery used to deceive another.

Fraudulent   Done with intent to defraud.

Free   Without legal constraints.

Free on board   (*F.O.B.*) Loaded for shipment at no cost to buyer.

Freehold   An estate in real property either in fee or for life.

Frivolous   So inadequate as to be totally without merit.

Full faith and credit   Total recognition. The Constitution requires that each state give full faith and credit to the judgments of its sister states.

Fungible   Things that are identical and can therefore be substituted for each other, e.g., dollar bills.

Future interests   An existing right to use property at some time in the future.

Garnish   To notify; to warn; to summon.

Garnishee   The person holding the property that is the subject of a garnishment.

Garnishment   A process by which a creditor can collect a debt from a third party (the garnishee) who is holding the money or property of the debtor.

Gift A voluntary transfer of property without consideration or payment by the person receiving the gift.

Gift causa mortis A gift given in contemplation of death which takes effect on the death of the donor.

Good faith Fairness; honesty.

Goodwill The reputation of a business and the expectation that customers will continue to patronize it; the difference between the actual value of the business and the value of its physical assets.

Grand jury A jury that decides whether or not an accused is to be indicted.

Grant (1) To give (v). (2) The transfer of real property (n).

Grantee One who receives a grant.

Grantor One who grants.

Gratuitous Without consideration; as a gift.

Gross Great; flagrant; total.

Gross income Total money taken in before deduction of expenses.

Guaranty (1) A promise to perform the obligation of another should the other fail to perform. (2) A merchant's warranty that goods are of a certain quality.

Guardian A person who has custody and control of another who is not capable of taking care of himself, such as a minor or incompetent.

Guilty (1) Not innocent, convicted of a crime (adj). (2) The plea of a person who admits that the charge against him is true (n).

Habeas corpus (Latin) A writ which demands that a prisoner who is illegally held be brought into court so that the legality of the imprisonment may be determined.

Habendum (Latin) A clause in a deed that describes the extent of the estate being transferred.

Habitual By habit; customary.

Half-brother, half-sister Persons who have one parent in common.

Harassment A minor offense, including cursing, jostling, etc., with intent to bother another.

Harbor To shelter or give refuge to a person, particularly a person who is being sought by the police.

Hazard Danger or risk.

Hazardous Subject to hazard.

Hearing (1) A formal proceeding in which issues are tried. (2) A proceeding before an administrative agency.

Hearsay Evidence in the form of a written or oral statement by a person who is not available to testify at the actual trial and cannot, therefore, be cross-examined. It is offered as proof of what is asserted in the statement itself. Hearsay evidence is generally not admissible, although there exist many exceptions to this rule. The exceptions usually involve some set of facts that tends to make the evidence more believable, such as the fact that the statement in question was against the speaker's own interest at the time that it was made.

Heir One who inherits property; one who inherits real property from an intestate.

Heir apparent One who would inherit real property from another should the other die intestate.

Heirs Those who would inherit an estate in the case of an intestacy.

Heirs and assigns Words used in the habendum clause to denote the passing of a fee simple.

Held Decided (by a court).

Hereditary Capable of being inherited.

Hire To employ a person; to rent the use of something.

Hold (1) To decide. (2) To own something.

Holder A person in possession of a negotiable instrument.

Holder in due course A holder who pays fair value for a negotiable instrument and has no reason to believe there is anything wrong with it. A person can be a holder in due course even if there is a defect in the instrument.

Holograph A handwritten will, entirely in the handwriting of the person making the will.

Home A dwelling place.

Homestead A home, including the actual house and surrounding property. Some states protect the homestead from creditors.

Homicide The culpable killing of a human being (it may or may not be a criminal act, depending on the circumstances).

Honor To accept and pay, e.g., when a check is presented.

Honorarium A gift or payment.

Hostile witness A witness called by one party to a suit who so favors the other side that he can be cross-examined as if he or she were the other side's witness.

Housebreaking Breaking into and entering a dwelling with the intent to commit a crime once inside. (If done at night, it is considered burglary.)

Household People who live together as a family.

Hung jury A jury that is unable to agree on a verdict.

Hypothesis A supposition, theory, or assumption.

Hypothetical question A question (which in court can only be asked of an expert witness) that assumes a set of facts and asks for an answer or an opinion based on the assumed facts.

I.C.C. Interstate Commerce Commission.

I.R.S. Internal Revenue Service.

Identity Sameness.

Ignorance Lack of knowledge.

Illegal Against the law; unlawful.

Illegality The state of being unlawful or illegal.

Illegitimate Against the law; born to unmarried parents.

Illicit Illegal; unlawful.

Illusory Deceiving, e.g., an illusory promise is one in which the person making the promise is not actually bound to perform but can do so at his option.

Immediate Present; not far away.

Immigration Entry into a country by foreigners who intend to establish residence there.

Imminent About to happen; impending. Imminent danger of death may justify a killing in self-defense.

Immunity Exception contrary to the general rule, either from a duty or a penalty. Immunity from prosecution may be granted to certain witnesses.

Impair To obstruct or make worse.

Impanel To make a list of prospective jurors or to select the actual jury for a trial.

Impartial Disinterested; not prejudiced.

Impeach To accuse or discredit.

Impeachment The discrediting of a person or of a witness; a trial to determine if a public officer should be removed from office for misconduct.

Impediment A disability, obstruction, disqualification, or bar, e.g., to a marriage or to entrance into a contract.

Implead To bring a new party into a lawsuit.

Implied Understood, although not specifically stated.

Impossibility That which is not possible. If a contract is impossible, it is not enforceable.

Impound To hold in legal custody.

Imprisonment The holding of a person; the exercise of restraint on personal liberty.

Improvement A change for the better; an addition to real property that makes it more valuable.

Imputed Charged to a person whether or not actually done by or known by that person (knowledge, negligence, income, and notice can all be imputed to a person in certain circumstances).

In loco parentis *(Latin)* In the place of a parent.

In personam *(Latin)* A suit brought to enforce rights against an individual. *See also* In rem.

In re *(Latin)* In the matter of.

In rem *(Latin)* A suit brought to enforce rights as to a particular piece of property. The rights thus established are valid against all persons. *See also* In personam.

In terrorem *(Latin)* Literally, in threat; a clause in a will that revokes a gift to any person who contests the will for any reason.

In toto *(Latin)* Completely.

Inadmissible Things that cannot be allowed as evidence.

Incapacity Legal or physical inability to do something.

Incarceration. Imprisonment.

Incest Sexual intercourse between people who are close blood relatives (too close to marry legally).

Inchoate Unfinished; incipient; incomplete.

Income Monetary gain, especially from work and capital investments.

Income tax A tax based on income.

Incompetency Lack of some ability or legal right to perform some act; mental or physical incapacity. Incompetent evidence is evidence that is inadmissible.

Incorporate To create a corporation.

Incriminate To demonstrate or to make it appear that someone is guilty of a crime.

Incumber *See* Encumber.

Indebtedness The state of being in debt.

Indefeasible Not able to be avoided or defeated.

Indemnify To secure against loss or to reimburse for past loss.

Indemnity A contract to secure another against a possible future loss.

Independent contractor One who does work for another not as an employee, subject to the orders of the other, but under contract to be performed according to his own methods.

Indictment A formal charge of the commission of a crime made by a grand jury after it hears testimony about the crime.

Indigent Poor, needy.

Indorse To write one's name on the back of a negotiable instrument (such as a check).

Indorsement Signing a negotiable instrument on the back to authorize transfer to another person.

Inducement Something that convinces a person to perform an act, enter into a deal, or sign a contract.

Infancy A person who has not yet reached the age of majority, usually 18 years.

Inference A deduction from known facts.

Information (1) A written accusation of a crime, a complaint. (2) A formal written accusation preferred by a prosecutor. (3) Acquired knowledge.

Information and belief A qualifying statement, usually found in an affidavit, indicating that what follows is believed by the affiant to be true but is not necessarily offered as a fact.

Infra *(Latin)* Below.

Infraction A violation of a law, usually a minor law.

Infringement An encroachment; a violation of some right (such as copyright or patent).

Inherent Intrinsic; inseparable from the thing itself.

Inherently dangerous An item or situation that is dangerous by its very nature.

Inherit To take or receive property as a result of an intestacy.

Inheritance (1) Property that is inherited (n). (2) The taking of property as a result of an intestacy or by descent. Also sometimes used to describe taking by will (v).

Injunction The order of a court that a person either perform an act or refrain from some course of conduct.

Injury The violation of some legal right of a person. Sometimes used to describe the resultant damage to the person.

Innocent Not guilty, having done no wrong.

Inquest A coroner's investigation into the cause of a death.

Insanity The condition of having an unsound or deranged mind to the extent that one is unable to cope with ordinary situations. As a defense in a criminal action, it means that the defendant is incapable of having the intent to commit the crime or that he cannot distinguish right from wrong.

Insolvency The state of having insufficient assets to pay one's debts.

Inspection Careful examination.

Instant Present; this one; current.

Insubordination Refusal to obey orders or instructions.

Insurable interest A person's real interest in the item or person to be insured. Without a real financial interest, there can be no valid insurance contract—it would merely be a wager.

Insurance A contract under which one party agrees to indemnify the other against loss or liability resulting from some event (such as death, automobile accident, or a fire).

Intangible assets *(Intangibles)* Incorporeal items; things with value but no physical substance; rights such as debts, owed to persons or bank accounts.

Intent Determination to achieve a particular end by a particular means.

Inter *(Latin)* Between

Inter alia *(Latin)* Among other things.

Inter vivos *(Latin)* Between the living; an inter vivos gift is a gift made between living people (as opposed to a gift by will).

Interest Any right in something; compensation paid by debtors to creditors for the use of money belonging to the latter.

Interim *(Latin)* Temporary, in the meantime.

Interlocutory A judgment by a court in a matter related to or part of the main case; an intermediate decision, but not the decision of the case itself.

Interloper Someone who enters or interferes where he has no right to be.

Interpleader A procedure under which a person

holding money that may belong to one of several other parties may force all of the parties into court in order to determine who is entitled to the money.

Interpretation The act of determining what is meant by a set of written words.

Interrogatories Questions, usually written, asked of a witness, generally during the discovery procedure.

Interstate Between two or more states.

Intervention The voluntary appearance of a new party in a lawsuit, with the permission of the court.

Intestacy The status of one who has died without having left a will.

Intestate Without having made a will.

Intra *(Latin)* Within.

Intrastate Within the state.

Inure To take effect.

Invalid Inadequate; having no effect; null and void.

Involuntary Unintentional.

Ipso facto *(Latin)* By the fact itself.

Irregularity A failure to follow proper procedure.

Issue (1) To send forth (v). (2) The descendants of a person (children, grandchildren) (n). (3) An item of contention (n).

J.D. Juris Doctor, the basic law degree.

J.P. *See* Justice of the peace.

Jeopardy Danger; the risk of being punished when one is on trial in a criminal case.

John Doe A fictitious name used in hypothetical situations or when a party's real name is not known.

Joinder Joining together. Parties can be joined (e.g., two parties can unite as plaintiffs in a case); causes of action can be joined if a party has two or more separate causes against the same defendant and wishes to try them together.

Joint United; combined.

Joint and several Both together and separately. If liability is joint and several, money can be collected from the group or any individual member.

Joint enterprise The engagement in some activity by two or more persons with a common interest or goal. Persons acting together with equal control toward the same purpose are said to be engaged in joint enterprise, and the negligence of one may be imputed to the other.

Joint venture A short-term joint enterprise in business.

Judge A public official who presides over a court of justice.

Judgment The final determination by a court in a proceeding before it.

Judgment-proof A person against whom a judgment for money is useless because the person is unable to pay or is somehow protected from paying.

Judicial Having to do with justice or with a judge.

Judicial notice The recognition by a judge that certain commonly known and indisputable facts are true even though they have not been presented as evidence.

Judicial review (1) The power of the courts to declare acts of the legislature unconstitutional. (2) The actual process of using that power.

Judiciary The branch of government that interprets the law and administers justice through a system of courts.

Jurisdiction The right of a court to exercise its power over a particular person or type of case.

Jurisdictional Necessary for jurisdiction. In some courts a minimum jurisdictional amount (of money) must be at stake before a case will be heard.

Jurisprudence The study of the law.

Jurist An expert in the law.

Juror A member of a jury.

Jury A group of laypersons who are selected to hear the facts and render an impartial verdict as to what is the truth. A grand jury determines whether the evidence justifies an indictment in a criminal case; a petit jury determines issues of fact in a trial.

Just Fair; legal.

Justice (1) The fair treatment under the law sought to be achieved by the courts. (2) A judge of a superior court.

Justice of the peace A minor local judge.

Justification A valid reason for doing something that would otherwise be illegal.

K.B. King's Bench, an English common law court.

Kidnapping Movement or imprisonment of a person against that person's will. Under early common law, the person had to be moved across county lines.

Kin Blood relatives.

Laches An equitable doctrine that prevents a person from winning a claim if he has delayed too long in pursuing it.

Landlord A person who leases land to another.

Lapse (1) Forfeiture of some right or privilege caused by a failure to perform a necessary act within a time limit. (2) The failure of a gift by will, causing the subject of the gift to go back into the residual estate. One common cause of failure is the death of the intended recipient occurring before the death of the testator.

Larceny Stealing, wrongfully taking. Grand larceny involves stealing more than a certain amount set by law; petit larceny less than that amount.

Last clear chance The principle that a negligent plaintiff may recover for his injuries despite his negligence if the defendant could have avoided the damage after recognizing the danger (i.e., if the defendant had the ''last clear chance'' to avoid the accident).

Latent Hidden; concealed.

Law (1) The entire set of rules which a government promulgates to regulate the behavior of the population. (2) Any individual statute enacted by the legislature.

Lawful Legal.

Lawyer A person licensed to practice law; an attorney.

Layman A nonmember of the profession.

Leading case An important case deciding a particular point of law and looked upon by courts and counsel as a guide in future cases.

Leading question A question that suggests to the witness what answer the questioner wants.

Lease A contract for the rental of real property, creating a landlord-tenant relationship.

Leasehold The estate of a person who occupies real property by lease.

Ledger An account book.

Legacy A gift by will of personal property.

Legal According to law.

Legal age The age of majority, usually 18, at

which a person becomes able to make a contract.

Legatee A person who receives a gift by will.

Legislate To enact a law.

Legislation (1) The process of enacting laws. (2) The laws enacted by a legislative body.

Legislative Referring to the branch of government that enacts laws; having to do with making laws.

Lessee A person who rents property from another; a tenant.

Lessor A person who rents property to another; a landlord.

Letters testamentary The notice of official appointment of an executor by the court.

Levy (1) To assess or collect (as a tax) (v). (2) A seizure (n).

Liability Legal responsibility.

Liable Responsible.

Libel A written defamation; a false statement in writing which causes some injury. If a statement is libelous per se, one need not prove any damage; if libelous per quod, the injurious effect of the statement must be proved.

Liberty Freedom; absence of restraint.

License (1) A privilege to engage in a particular activity. (2) Unrestrained activity.

Licensee (1) A person who has a license. (2) A person who enters the property of another with permission, but to accomplish his own purposes rather than at the invitation of the owner.

Lien A claim against property as a result of some legal obligation of the owner; e.g., a mechanic may have a lien on property he has repaired.

Lien creditor A person who has a lien on property as a result of a debt that is owed to him.

Life estate An interest in property that lasts until the death of the holder of the life estate or some other person.

Life tenant The holder of a life estate.

Limit (1) To restrain (v). (2) A restraint (n).

Limitation A restriction.

Limited Restricted.

Limited liability The liability of owners of a corporation. They are liable only to the extent of their investments in the corporation, not their personal wealth.

Liquidate   To pay a debt.

Liquidated   Paid; fixed. Liquidated damages are a sum determined in advance by parties to a contract as the damages that will have to be paid in the event of a breach.

Liquidation   (1) The settlement of a debt. (2) The winding up of a company.

Lis pendens   *(Latin)* A pending suit.

Litigant   A person engaged in a lawsuit.

Litigate   To carry on a lawsuit.

Litigation   A lawsuit.

Local   Relating to a particular place.

Local action   An action that can be brought only in one jurisdiction, the place where it arose.

Long-arm statute   A law that extends the jurisdiction of a state's courts in certain cases to people outside of the state.

Loss   Damage.

Lot   (1) A piece of land. (2) A collected group of items.

Magistrate   A minor judge or justice of the peace.

Major   A person who has reached the age, usually 18, where he is allowed to make contracts (the age of majority).

Majority   Legal age.

Malfeasance   Wrongdoing.

Malice   Ill will.

Malicious   Motivated by malice, e.g., malicious injury is prompted by ill will toward the person injured; malicious mischief is willful destruction of property; malicious prosecution is brought without just cause but only to harass the defendant.

Malpractice   Incompetence or misconduct by a professional, usually a doctor or a lawyer.

Mandamus   *(Latin)* Literally, we command. An order of a court that directs some government official to do something.

Mandate   A command issued by a court.

Mandatory   Obligatory; imperative.

Manifest   Obvious; evident.

Manslaughter   Unlawful homicide, either voluntarily or involuntarily, but without malice.

Marital   Having to do with marriage.

Market   A place set aside for buying and selling.

Market price   *See* Fair market value.

Marketable   Salable.

Marketable title   Good, clear title to land.

Marshal   A federal court officer whose duties, like those of a sheriff, include serving process, etc.

Master   (1) A special court official. (2) An employer.

Material   Germane; important: e.g., a material fact is crucial to a case.

Material witness   A key witness in a criminal case, whose testimony is so important that he may be incarcerated until the trial.

Matrimonial   Pertaining to marriage.

Matrimony   Marriage.

Mechanic   A skilled workman.

Mechanic's lien   A workman's claim against the property he has worked on—he may hold onto the property until he has been paid.

Mediation   Settlement of disputes by arbitration or intervention of a third party who seeks to reconcile the disputing parties.

Meeting of minds   Agreement by the parties to a contract as to the purpose and terms of the contract.

Memorandum   (1) A brief submitted to argue a point of law. (2) An informal writing.

Menacing   A statutory offense much like common law assault, in which the victim is placed in fear of physical harm.

Mens rea   *(Latin)* Guilty mind; wrongful intent.

Mental anguish   Grief; mental suffering

Mercantile   Commercial; having to do with business.

Merchant   A retailer.

Merchantable   Of salable quality, suitable for the purpose for which it was purchased.

Merger   Joining of two or more separate things, e.g., corporations.

Merits   The substantive issues of a case (as opposed to procedural issues).

Minor   An infant under the age of contractual capacity (usually 18).

Minority   The status of an infant (a child under the age of 18).

Miranda rule   The rule that a prisoner must receive certain warnings before he can be questioned by the police (e.g., he has the right to remain silent and to have a lawyer present).

Miscegenation   Intermarriage between persons of different races.

Misdemeanor A crime of less gravity than a felony.

Misfeasance Wrongdoing.

Misrepresentation A false statement.

Mistake An error or an unintentional act.

Mistrial A trial that ends as a nullity due to some error that occurs during its course. The jury must be dismissed and a new jury selected.

Mitigate To lessen in degree or severity, e.g., a mitigating circumstance may lower the punishment for a crime.

M'naghten rule A test to determine whether a person can be held responsible for a criminal act. The determining factor is whether the person was able to distinguish right from wrong at the time of the act.

Modus *(Latin)* Method.

Modus operandi *(Latin)* Method of operation. Abbreviated M.O.

Moot Abstract; hypothetical; academic.

Moot court A make-believe court in which students practice arguing cases.

Moral turpitude Vile and immoral behavior; depravity.

Mortgage A contract under which real estate (or personal property in the case of a chattel mortgage) is used as security for a loan.

Mortgagee The lender in a mortgage contract.

Mortgagor The borrower in a mortgage contract.

Mortis causa *(Latin)* Because of death.

Motion An application to a judge for a ruling on some point in a case.

Movant A person who makes a motion.

Move To make a motion.

Moving papers Papers filed in support of a motion.

Murder An unlawful homicide, committed with malice aforethought or deliberate intent and no justification. *See also* Felony murder rule.

Mutual Common to both parties; the same for both parties.

Mutuality Reciprocating; the state of being mutual.

Neglect Failure to perform some legal obligation.

Negligence The failure to exercise proper care or due diligence.

Negligent Careless; exhibiting negligence.

Negotiable instrument A written and signed instrument (document), absolutely promising to pay to order or to bearer a specific sum of money at a specific time or on demand.

Negotiate (1) To transfer a negotiable instrument. (2) To reach a compromise or an agreement; to make a deal.

Next of kin A person's closest blood relatives.

Nolo contendere *(Latin)* Literally, I will not contend; equivalent to a plea of guilty.

Nonfeasance Failure to meet some obligation.

Nonsuit A judgment against plaintiff because he has failed to take some necessary action.

Not guilty Innocent. The plea of a person who does not admit guilt when accused of a crime.

Notary public Public official who is able to certify documents and administer oaths.

Note A promise (in writing) to pay a specific sum of money at a specific time.

Notice Information; knowledge. Actual notice is actual knowledge; constructive notice means the person should have known, and the knowledge is charged to him.

Novation The substitution of a new contract for an old one.

Noxious Harmful.

Nuisance Something that causes harm or inconvenience to another.

Null Void; having no effect.

Nullity Something that is null.

Nuncupative will An oral will.

Nuptial Having to do with marriage.

Oath Formal promise to tell the truth or to perform some act.

Object To protest or raise an objection.

Objection A statement of protest or opposition to some statement or action by the other side in a lawsuit on the grounds that it is in some way improper.

Obligation A duty that arises out of a contract, promise, or debt.

Obligee A person to whom an obligation is owed.

Obligor A person who incurs an obligation.

Obscene Offensive, such as being lewd or indecent.

Obstruct To impede or hinder.

Obstructing justice The crime of interfering with justice, e.g., by hiding evidence or keeping a witness from reaching court.

Occupancy Possession of real property.

Occupant   Person in possession of real property.

Occupation   (1) Possession of real property. (2) One's profession.

Offense   A violation of the criminal law.

Offer   (1) A presentation or proposal of terms for a contract or deal. (2) A presentation of possible evidence.

Officer of the court   A general term for persons responsible to the court, including judges, clerks, other official employees, and attorneys.

Officers   The persons who fill the offices created by the by-laws of a corporation (president, secretary, etc.).

Official   (1) Pertaining to an office, formal (adj). (2) A person who occupies an authoritative position (n).

Opening statement   A statement that the opposing lawyers may make, on the record, at the start of the trial. In it they outline what they plan to demonstrate with the evidence they will present.

Opinion   The court's statement which announces and explains the court's decision.

Option   An agreement in which, in exchange for some consideration, one person agrees to sell something to another at a specified price if the second party wishes to buy within a certain time period.

Oral   Spoken.

Order   A command; a written demand for payment of money to a third person.

Ordinance   A law enacted by a municipality.

Overdraft   A check written for a larger amount of money than is in the account upon which it is drawn.

Overrule   To deny; to declare an earlier ruling or precedent no longer valid and replace it with a different decision.

Overt   Open; public.

Ownership   The rights of an owner to possess and control property.

Par value   Face value

Paralegal   A person who is not a lawyer but has some legal training and works assisting lawyers.

Parcel   A piece of real estate.

Pardon   Forgiveness granted by the sovereign or highest executive (president or governor) ex-

empting a person from punishment for a crime.

Parol   Oral; verbal.

Parol evidence   Oral evidence; evidence not in writing. The parol evidence rule prevents the consideration of oral evidence to modify a written contract.

Parole   Early release from a prison sentence provided that the convict abides by certain conditions placed upon him at the time of his release.

Particulars   Items of an account; details of a claim.

Partition   Division of property belonging to co-owners into smaller pieces to be owned by each individually.

Partner   A member of a partnership.

Partnership   An association of two or more competent persons to be co-owners of a business for a profit.

Party   A person who is directly involved in a transaction or a lawsuit.

Passive   Inactive.

Passive negligence   Negligence resulting from a failure to act.

Patent   (1) Evident, obvious (adj). (2) The exclusive right, guaranteed by the government of an inventor, to produce and sell an invention (n). (3) A government grant of land (n).

Paternity   The state of fatherhood.

Pay   To discharge a debt.

Payee   A person who is designated on a negotiable instrument as the person to whom payment is to be made; a person to whom payment is made.

Payment   The discharge of a debt or obligation by the transfer of money or the equivalent.

Payor   A person who makes payment or is designated on a negotiable instrument as the person by whom payment is to be made.

Pecuniary   Having to do with money.

Peers   Equals.

Penal   Punishable; having to do with punishment.

Penal law   The law relating to crimes and their punishments.

Penalty   A punishment brought about by operation of law.

Pendens   (*Latin*) Pending.

Pendent jurisdiction   The doctrine that allows federal courts to hear nonfederal questions when they are related to federal questions properly before the court.

Pending Begun but not yet finished.

People The state.

Per *(Latin)* By; through; by means of.

Per annum *(Latin)* By the year.

Per capita *(Latin)* By the head.

Per cent *(Latin)* By the hundred.

Per diem *(Latin)* By the day.

Per se *(Latin)* By itself.

Per stripes *(Latin)* Literally, by roots. Giving equally to each branch of the family rather than to each person, as in per capita.

Peremptory Absolute; conclusive.

Perfect To complete; to make complete, to execute.

Perfected Completed; executed.

Performance Complete fulfillment of a duty (such as a contractual obligation).

Perjury Willful lying under oath.

Perpetrator A person who actually commits a crime.

Perpetuity A limitation on the use of property for a period longer than a life in being, plus 21 years. Such a limitation will not be enforced. (This is known as the rule against perpetuities.)

Person An individual human being (a natural person) or a corporation (an artificial person).

Personal property Movable property as opposed to real property.

Personalty Personal property.

Petition A formal written request or application.

Petitioner One who presents a petition.

Plaintiff A person who brings a suit or complaint against another.

Plea The answer of a defendant to a criminal charge.

Plea bargaining The process by which a defendant is given an opportunity to plead guilty to a lesser offense than the one with which he is charged, instead of going to trial.

Plead To make a plea or file a pleading.

Pleading A formal written statement of position submitted by each party to a case.

Pledge The bailment (handing over) of personal property as security for a debt.

Plurality The greatest number of votes received by any candidate (even if not a majority or more than half of the total).

Police Governmental law enforcement agency.

Police power Generally, the power of the government to regulate the activities of the populace.

Political Having to do with the administration of government.

Polling the jury Asking each member of the jury to state his agreement with the verdict in a case.

Polygamy The illegal practice of having more than one spouse at a time.

Possess To occupy or control property; to have in one's physical control.

Possession Occupancy and control of property.

Post *(Latin)* After.

Post-mortem *(Latin)* After death.

Posthumous Occurring after death.

Power The right or ability to take some action.

Power of attorney A written instrument authorizing another to act as agent or attorney for the writer.

Practice (1) Custom or habit; procedure. (2) The engagement of a person in a profession.

Precedent (1) An earlier judicial decision that has authoritative effect on a case to be decided. (2) Something that has already taken place.

Prefer (1) To prosecute. (2) To favor.

Preference The payment of one creditor before another.

Prejudice (1) A preconceived opinion; bias. (2) Detriment.

Prejudicial error Error that was detrimental enough to affect the result of a case.

Premeditation Forethought; planning.

Preponderance of evidence The greater weight of the evidence; the set of evidence that is more convincing.

Prerogative A privilege.

Prescription To obtain title to property by adverse possession. *See also* Adverse possession.

Presentment The presenting of a bill to the drawee for acceptance.

Presumption A rule that orders that a certain inference be drawn if a certain fact is ascertained.

Pretermitted heir A child or other legal heir left out of a will.

Prima facie *(Latin)* On its face.

Prima facie case A case in which enough evidence is presented to prove what is alleged unless the other side puts forth evidence to disprove it.

Primogeniture   The system under which all real estate passes automatically on the death of the owner to his eldest son.

Principal   (1) Primary (adj). (2) A person who is responsible for the acts done for his benefit by others appointed by him (his agents) (n). (3) A person who is directly involved in a crime (n). (4) The body of a loan, which must be paid back together with interest that accrues (n). (5) In suretyship, the original debtor (n).

Principle   A general or fundamental truth.

Prior   Previous; earlier.

Priority   Precedence.

Privacy   The basic right to be left alone.

Private   Belonging to an individual or individuals.

Privilege   A right that is not held by the public at large, but only by an individual or a group of individuals.

Privity   (1) A direct financial relationship between the parties to a contract or a deal. (2) An identity of interest between people.

Privy   (1) A person who is in privity with another (n). (2) Private (adj).

Pro   *(Latin)* For.

Pro rata   *(Latin)* Proportionately.

Pro se   *(Latin)* For himself.

Probable cause   Reasonable cause under the circumstances.

Probate   The process of judging whether or not a will is valid.

Probation   A period of being under observation for a length of time instead of being incarcerated after being convicted of a crime.

Probative   Tending to prove something.

Procedure   The rules of carrying on an action in court.

Proceeding   A court case.

Proceeds   Money or other valuable property received in exchange for something.

Process   (1) The legal means of securing a defendant's appearance in court; a summons. (2) A method of doing something. *See also* Due process of law.

Profits   Gains.

Prohibit   To forbid.

Promise   To bind oneself to do something.

Promisee   A person to whom a promise is made.

Promissor   A person who makes a promise.

Promissory note   A written promise to pay a specific amount of money at a specific time.

Promoter   A person involved in forming a corporation.

Proof   The conclusive establishment of a fact by means of some evidence.

Proper   Suitable; appropriate.

Property   Anything that is capable of being owned, either personal (movable) property or real (land) property.

Proponent   A person who offers or proffers something.

Proprietary   Relating to ownership.

Prorate   To divide on a pro rata basis; to distribute proportionately.

Prosecute   To proceed against in court.

Prosecution   A criminal proceeding.

Prosecutor   A government official who prosecutes criminal cases.

Prospectus   A description of property or corporate stock that is for sale.

Provisional   Temporary.

Proviso   A condition or restriction or a clause that imposes one.

Proximate   Immediate; direct.

Proximate cause   The cause that actually leads to an injury; the one event without which the injury could not have taken place.

Proxy   A written authorization to one person to act for another.

Public   Pertaining to the state or nation as opposed to individuals.

Publication   Making known to the public, either orally or in writing.

Publish   To make known to the public.

Punishment   A penalty brought about by operation of law.

Punitive   Having to do with punishment.

Purchase   To buy.

Purport   To appear on the surface.

Pursuant   Consequential; in accordance with.

Quantum meruit   *(Latin)* What it is worth; what has been earned.

Quash   Suppress or vacate; annul.

Quasi   *(Latin)* As if; similar to.

Quasi in rem   An action in which the rights of the parties are determined with regard to some particular property.

Query   Question.

Quid pro quo *(Latin)* Literally, what for what, or something for something. The consideration underlying a contract.

Quiet enjoyment Legal, quiet, and peaceful possession of real property.

Quit To leave or vacate.

Quitclaim A deed giving up any claim of right that one might have regarding some property.

Quorum The number of members (usually a majority) of a body needed for the body to vote or conduct business.

Rape The crime of a person unlawfully forcing another person to engage in sexual intercourse. *See also* Statutory rape.

Ratification Approval, acceptance, confirmation of, or giving effect to an act already performed.

Re *(Latin)* Concerning; relating to; in the matter of.

Real evidence Physical evidence or other evidence that can be sensed directly by the jury without relying on testimony.

Real property Land and other immovable property (such as buildings).

Realty Real property.

Reasonable Sensible; proper; usual.

Rebut To deny; to refute; to contradict.

Rebuttable Arguable; disputable.

Receipt Written acknowledgment that something, usually money, has been received.

Receiver The person who acts as custodian for property in receivership.

Receivership The placing of property into the hands of a court-appointed custodian (receiver) to ensure that it is managed properly.

Reciprocal Mutual.

Reciprocity Mutuality.

Reckless Extremely careless.

Reckless endangerment The offense of behaving in such a reckless manner as to place another in danger of serious injury.

Record (1) To make an official notation; to enter in writing (v). (2) A written account of some proceeding (n).

Recorder An official in charge of public records.

Recording act A statute that regulates the recording of certain documents, usually deeds and other instruments involving real estate.

Recoupment Holding back something from another party as a setoff for what the other party owes you; recovering lost money.

Recovery The amount that the plaintiff is awarded on winning a lawsuit.

Redeem To recover or buy back.

Redeemable Subject to redemption.

Redemption A recovery or buying back of property.

Referee A person appointed by a court to try certain issues.

Referee in bankruptcy A federal judge who hears bankruptcy cases.

Register (1) An official record (n). (2) To record (v).

Registrar A person who keeps records in a register.

Regular Lawful; proper.

Regulate To control or place restrictions but not prohibit.

Release Abandonment of some claim against another.

Relevancy Logical nexus between evidence and what is to be demonstrated by the evidence.

Relevant Relating to the issue at hand in such a way as to be helpful in determining the truth about the issue.

Relief The remedy granted by a court, be it money, damages, injunction, etc.

Remainder An interest in property that takes effect only on the expiration of the interest previously in effect (e.g., ''estate to A for life, remainder to B'' means that B's interest takes effect when A dies).

Remainderman A person who is entitled to a remainder.

Remand To return or send back. A higher court may remand a case to the lower court from which it came for a new trial or further proceedings.

Remedial Corrective, relating to a remedy.

Remedy What is done to compensate for an injury or to enforce some right.

Remit To send; to pay.

Removal The transfer or movement, either of a person from one place to another, or of a case from one court to another.

Render To yield or deliver.

Rent (1) The compensation paid for the use of real estate (n). (2) To let real property (v).

Repeal To end the effect of one law through the passing of another.

Replevin *(French)* An action to recover property unlawfully taken.

Reply An additional pleading by a plaintiff in response to defendant's answer. Not all cases call for a reply.

Report An official record of a proceeding.

Reporter A person who is charged with recording the proceedings of a court.

Represent (1) To assert. (2) To act for.

Representation (1) An assertion of fact (whether or not it is true). (2) Acting for another, e.g., as a lawyer acting for a client.

Representative One who acts for another.

Reprieve A temporary postponement of the carrying out of a sentence.

Republication A reinstatement of a will which had been revoked but not destroyed at some earlier time.

Repudiate To reject; to deny.

Repudiation Rejection; refusal to accept as valid.

Res *(Latin)* The thing.

Res ipsa loquitur *(Latin)* Literally, the thing itself speaks. When a person had control immediately before an accident of the thing that caused the accident, the person is presumed responsible. The person thus held responsible may, of course, offer evidence to the contrary.

Res judicata *(Latin)* Literally, the thing already adjudicated or decided. Once a question is decided between two litigants, they cannot bring another suit to determine the same question.

Rescind To bring about a rescission.

Rescission Annulment of a contract either by agreement or judicial order.

Residence The place where a person lives.

Residuary That which is left over.

Residuary estate The part of the estate that is left over when specific gifts have been paid.

Respondeat superior *(Latin)* Literally, the master answers. The doctrine that establishes an employer's liability for acts of his employees done in furtherance of their employment.

Respondent (1) The person who answers an appeal. (2) The winner in a lower court against whom an appeal is taken; the appellee.

Restitution The paying back or restoration to a person who has been deprived of what was rightfully his.

Restraining order An injunction.

Restraint of trade Illegal interference with normal competition.

Retainer Preliminary fee given to a lawyer at the time he is officially engaged.

Retract To take back, e.g., to retract an offer.

Retraction The withdrawal of an earlier statement.

Retroactive Relating to what has already taken place.

Retrospective Retroactive; looking backward.

Revenue Income; profit.

Reversal The setting aside of what has been done and, usually, substitution of the opposite.

Reverse To set aside; e.g., an appellate court can reverse the decision of a lower court.

Reversion A future interest in real property held by a person who transfers the property to another. It takes effect at the end of the other party's estate.

Revert To return to.

Review A reconsideration of a case at the appellate level.

Revocation A taking back; nullification; cancellation.

Revoke To nullify or cancel.

Right (1) Proper; legal; correct (adj). (2) Something to which a person is entitled, be it a thing or a privilege (n).

Riot A tumultuous breach of the peace by three or more people.

Riparian Having to do with the bank of a river.

Robbery Taking of property from another against his will by force or threat of force.

Rule (1) To decide an issue (v). (2) A regulation (n).

Ruling A decision on a question during a trial.

Running with the land An agreement that binds any owner of the land, present or future.

S.C. Supreme Court.

S.E.C. Securities and Exchange Commission.

Said Previously mentioned.

Salable Capable of being sold.

Sale A transfer of ownership of property in return for payment or a contract to pay.

Salvage The property recovered from the remains of an accident or disaster.

Sanction   (1) Approval. (2) A penalty imposed by law.

Satisfaction   Final discharge of an obligation.

Scienter   *(Latin)* Knowledge, especially guilty knowledge.

Seal   An official symbol on a document signifying authenticity.

Sealed   Authenticated by a seal.

Sealed verdict   A verdict reached by jury after court is adjourned. It is sealed in an envelope and read at the next session.

Search   An examination or investigation involving an intrusion into the privacy of the subject.

Search and seizure   The discovery and confiscation by law enforcement officials of property belonging to a suspected criminal.

Search warrant   A written authorization from a judge or magistrate allowing the police, upon a showing of probable cause, to search a designated area for specific evidence of a crime.

Secure   To guarantee payment with some collateral or security.

Secured creditor   A creditor in a transaction where the debt is guaranteed with some security.

Secured transaction   An obligation secured by a property interest.

Securities   Instruments, such as stocks or bonds, sold publicly by a company.

Security   Property in which a debtor gives a creditor some interest in order to guarantee payment of the debt.

Seizure   The forcible taking of a person or thing. *See also* Search and seizure.

Self-defense   The use of force to protect oneself or others from harm.

Seller   The party who transfers property in a contract of sale.

Sentence   The judgment of a criminal court as to what punishment shall be inflicted upon a convicted defendant.

Sequester   (1) The seizing of property by a court to guarantee obedience of the court's decree (n). (2) To isolate a jury during its deliberations to prevent contact with outside influences (v).

Servant   An employee.

Service   The delivery or other communication of notice of a lawsuit or other legal papers to the opposing party.

Setoff   A claim by a defendant against the plaintiff based on an unrelated basis but which would, if proven, reduce the amount plaintiff can recover from defendant.

Settle   (1) To reach an agreement about disposition of a pending suit or other claim of one person against another. (2) To establish a trust.

Settlor   A person who establishes a trust.

Several   More than two; separate and distinct.

Sewer service   The throwing away of a paper that was to have been served on a party and then claiming that it was, in fact, properly delivered.

Shareholder   *See* Stockholder.

Sheriff   A public official who serves as a peace officer and is responsible for serving process in various civil and criminal actions.

Show cause order   An order by a court to a party before it to offer reasons why the court should not take action that an opposing party has requested.

Sign   To affix one's signature.

Signature   A person's name, on any instrument or document, affixed by himself, with the intent to authorize the instrument or document.

Site   A specific place used or intended to be used for a specific purpose.

Situs   *(Latin)* Location.

Slander   Oral defamation; words spoken falsely with intention to injure another.

Slander per se   Slander in and of itself, actionable even without a showing of damage to plaintiff (e.g., false statement that a person has committed a crime of moral turpitude or has a loathsome disease).

Small claims court   A court that has jurisdiction over claims that do not exceed a certain sum (usually $500 to $1,000), providing a brief, simple, and inexpensive proceeding, and where a person can sue without engaging an attorney.

Sodomy   Deviate intercourse; any unnatural sex act.

Solicit   To entreat, ask for, or entice.

Solvency   The state of being solvent.

Solvent   Able to pay one's debts as they come due.

Special appearance   Appearing in court solely to argue that the court has no jurisdiction over one's person.

Specific performance   The compelling (by a court) of a party to a contract to do what the contract requires.

Speedy trial   A trial free from excessive delays, a right of every accused.

Standing to sue   Capacity to bring an action because one's interest in the outcome is direct.

Stare decisis   *(Latin)* Literally, the decision should stand. The doctrine that gives authority to prior decisions of a court and makes courts reluctant to reverse their prior decisions.

Statement   A declaration or allegation.

Status   Condition or position.

Status quo   *(Latin)* The existing state of things.

Statute   A law enacted by the legislature.

Statute of limitations   A law setting forth the respective periods of time within which various actions may be brought.

Statutory rape   Intercourse with a person below a certain age, regardless of whether or not there is consent.

Stay   (1) To stop or postpone (v). (2) A postponement (n).

Stipend   A periodic payment; a salary.

Stipulate   To agree; to concede.

Stipulation   An agreement made by the attorneys on opposite sides regarding some matter in a lawsuit.

Stock   (1) Certificates of ownership in a corporation. (2) Goods held for sale by a merchant.

Stockholder   A person who owns shares of corporate stock.

Strict   Precise; exact.

Strict construction   Very literal or narrow reading of a statute.

Strict liability   Absolute responsibility for damage, even in the absence of a showing of negligence.

Strike   (1) A work stoppage by employees involved in a dispute with the employer (n). (2) To expunge; remove (v).

Subject matter jurisdiction   The power of the court to hear a particular type of case.

Subpoena   A court order that a person appear in court.

Subpoena duces tecum   A subpoena ordering a person not only to appear but also to bring some evidence with him.

Subrogation   The substitution of one person for another in a claim against a third party. The person who is substituted is entitled to all the rights of the original party.

Subscribe   To sign at the end of a document.

Substantial   Material; real; significant; valuable.

Substantive   The part of the law that regulates rights (as opposed to procedural law, which regulates enforcement).

Succession   The transfer of property to legal heirs when a person dies intestate.

Sue   To institute a lawsuit.

Suit   A legal action; a lawsuit.

Summary   Short; immediate; abbreviated; concise.

Summary judgment   A judgment rendered when the evidence offered by defendant is patently insufficient to controvert plaintiff's case.

Summation   Concluding argument of a lawyer after the last testimony and before the judge charges the jury.

Summons   The writ that informs a defendant of the existence of the case. A summons, when it is properly served, commences a proceeding.

Superior   Higher.

Supersede   To set aside and replace.

Supervene   To intervene or interpose.

Supplemental   Additional; added to make the original complete.

Suppress   (1) To prohibit or restrain. (2) To keep out of evidence.

Surety   A person who enters a contract of suretyship.

Suretyship   An arrangement under which one party agrees to guaranty the payment of the debt of another.

Surrogate   (1) A judge in charge of probate of wills. (2) One who acts in place of another.

Sustain   To uphold; to grant.

Swear   To administer an oath.

Sworn   Under oath; verified.

Tangible   Real; tactile; subject to physical possession and being touched.

Tax   A forced contribution to the government, based on some reasonable system of apportionment of the burden.

Taxable income   That part of the income (after deduction and exemptions, etc.) upon which the income tax is computed.

Temporary restraining order   A temporary injunction; an order of a court that is issued to curb some activity until a full hearing can be held.

Tenancy   The estate, or occupancy, of a tenant.

Tenant   One who occupies real property owned by another, under some understanding with the owner.

Tender   Offer of payment coupled with the intention and the ability to deliver.

Test case   A suit brought for the specific purpose of litigating a particular point in order to determine the law establishing a particular right.

Testacy   The state of dying leaving a valid will.

Testament   A will.

Testamentary   Having to do with a will.

Testate   A person who dies leaving a will.

Testator   A person who makes a will.

Testify   To give evidence under oath.

Testimony   The evidence given by a witness in a case.

Third party   A person not a party to the original transaction (contract, lawsuit, etc.) but who might be connected indirectly or brought in in some way.

Third party beneficiary   The beneficiary of a contract made by two other parties.

Time is of the essence   A condition in a contract that makes it a material breach to fail to perform within the time specified.

Title   Estate in fee; absolute ownership of real property.

Toll   (1) To suspend or put off the running of a statute of limitation (v). (2) A fee for use of a public road or bridge (n).

Tort   A wrong or injury inflicted on another as a result of a breach of an existing legal duty.

Tortfeasor   One who commits a tort.

Tortious   Wrongful.

Totten trust   A trust consisting of a bank account deposited by one person in his own name in trust for another. It is generally revocable at the will of the depositor, but passes to the beneficiary at his death.

Tract   A parcel of land; a piece of real estate.

Trade   (1) Commerce. (2) A profession or business.

Trademark   A unique emblem that distinguishes the goods of a particular business; it is eligible for protection under federal law.

Transaction   The doing of some business; a dealing or the occurrence of some event between two parties.

Transcript   A copy; a complete record of a case taken from the court reporter's notes.

Transient   (1) Temporary (adj). (2) A person whose stay is temporary (n).

Treason   Attempting to overthrow the government or helping others to do so.

Treaty   A formal written agreement between nations.

Treble damages   Triple damages; awarded in certain suits to discourage certain classes of wrongs.

Trespass   A wrongful entry onto property; any wrongdoing. *See also* Criminal trespass.

Trespass on the case   Common law action for injury resulting from anything but physical force, e.g., negligence, nonfeasance.

Trespasser   A person who commits trespass.

Trial   (1) A test. (2) A judicial proceeding.

Tribunal   A court.

Trover   Common law action for recovering wrongfully taken or retained property.

Trust   A fiduciary relationship in which one party, the trustee, manages, holds, or controls some assets for the benefit of another, the beneficiary.

Trustee   A person who holds property in trust for another.

U.C.C.   *See* Uniform Commercial Code.

Ultra   *(Latin)* Beyond; in excess of.

Ultra vires   *(Latin)* An act or contract that lies beyond the powers granted in the charter of a corporation.

Unconscionable   Morally objectionable.

Unconscionable agreement or bargain   An agreement or bargain made where one side has such a tremendous bargaining advantage and forces the other side to agree to such onerous term or terms that courts will not enforce the agreement or bargain.

Unconstitutional   Contrary to the constitution.

Underwrite   To insure.

Undue   Unnecessary; inappropriate; more than needed.

Unequivocal   Clear; certain.

Uniform Commercial Code   A comprehensive code regulating most aspects of commercial transactions. The U.C.C. has been adopted, at least partially, by almost every state.

Unilateral   One-sided.

Union   (1) A labor union; an association of workers

for the purpose of collective bargaining. (2) Any merger or joining.

Union shop A place of employment where workers are required to become union members.

United States Code The codification of federal statutes.

Unjust Not rightful and proper.

Unjust enrichment Improper or unfair gain, the fruits of which are required to be returned to the rightful owner.

Unlawful Illegal; contrary to law.

Unlawful imprisonment The restraining of a person against his will.

Usage A usual course of conduct in a specific business.

Usurious Having to do with usury.

Usury The charging of illegally high interest rates on the loan of money.

Vacant Unoccupied.

Vacate (1) To set aside, annul. (2) To make vacant.

Vagrancy The state of being a vagrant.

Vagrant A person who moves about idly from place to place with no job or other source of income.

Vagueness Uncertainty; lack of precision.

Valid Legal; effective; operative.

Value Worth.

Variance (1) An exception from the effect of a zoning regulation. (2) A difference between the pleading in a case and the proof offered.

Vendee Buyer.

Vendor Seller.

Venue The locale where a case is to be tried. Where several courts may have jurisdiction, venue may be set at the most convenient for the parties. If venue is not properly set originally, it may be changed later.

Verdict The decision of a jury.

Verification A sworn statement that facts alleged in a document are true.

Verify To substantiate or conform; to make a verification.

Versus (*Latin*) Against.

Vest To take effect.

Vested In effect; no longer subject to conditions.

Violation A minor infraction, usually punishable only by a fine.

Void Not valid; having no effect; null.

Voidable Capable of being voided or declared void.

Voir dire (*French*) Literally, to speak the truth. An examination of prospective jurors by the parties to see whether or not they are qualified.

Voluntary Of one's own free will.

Wages Salary, pay, or compensation for labor.

Waive To relinquish or disclaim.

Waiver The intentional relinquishment of a right or privilege.

Wanton Reckless; foolhardy.

Ward A person under care of an appointed guardian.

Warrant (1) To promise (v). (2) A form of process, e.g., arrest warrant. *See also* Search warrant (n).

Warrantor One who makes a warranty.

Warranty (1) A guarantee or promise that an allegation is true. (2) A promise by a vendor to indemnify against defects in what is being sold.

Waste Loss of assets through abuse of property by one who is lawfully in possession of it.

Wilful Voluntary; intentional; deliberate.

Will An instrument in which a person outlines the way in which his property is to be distributed after his death. It must be executed according to certain statutory formalities.

Witness (1) To observe (v). (2) A person who has observed a transaction; a person who testifies as to what he has observed (n).

Writ A process; an order of a judge either authorizing or requiring that something be done.

Wrong An infringement on a legal right.

Wrongful Unlawful; injurious; inequitable.

Zoning Division of a municipality into areas, or zones, with specific restrictions on the use of property within each zone. Serves to separate commercial property from residential.

Table of Cases

INDEX